Canadian
Women's Issues

Volume I
Strong Voices

Canadian Women's Issues

Volume I
Strong Voices

Ruth Roach Pierson, Marjorie Griffin Cohen,
Paula Bourne, and Philinda Masters

James Lorimer & Company, Publishers
Toronto, 1993

James Lorimer & Company Ltd. acknowledges with thanks the support of the Canada Council, the Ontario Arts Council and the Ontario Publishing Centre in the development of writing and publishing in Canada.

Canadian Cataloguing in Publication Data
  Main entry under title:

Canadian women's issues

Includes bibliographical references and index.
ISBN 1-55028-414-2 (bound) ISBN 1-55028-415-0 (pbk.)

1. Feminism - Canada. 2. Women - Canada - Social conditions. 3. Women - Canada - Attitudes.
I. Pierson, Ruth Roach, 1938-

HQ1453.C36 1993   305.42'0971   C93-093812-7

James Lorimer & Company Ltd., Publishers
35 Britain Street
Toronto, Ontario M5A 1R7

Printed and bound in Canada

This book is dedicated to all of the women in Canada who made
the women's movement possible. The royalties from this book
will be donated to various women's groups.

Contents

Preface

During the period covered by this book, 1967 to 1993, our world has changed considerably and sometimes in dramatic ways. For example, in 1967 there was no hint that the Soviet Union would disappear as a political entity and the possibilities for the abolition of apartheid in South Africa remained remote. Likewise, the inferior position which women held in the world was a fact which appeared to be universal, although the actual conditions and extent of women's inequality did differ over time and space. This book is about women in English Canada and the issues they struggled with in order to change the trajectory of women's subordination. It begins with 1967, which is somewhat arbitrary since women were certainly active collectively as feminists before this period. But we start with 1967 because this was when women's issues began to be recognized publicly and when women were beginning to be perceived as a political force with the potential to change the existing power dynamics.

Mostly this book is about women: how they identified their issues, how they acted on them, and the resistance and successes they experienced. Trying to deal with the tremendous diversity of women's experiences in this vast nation has been a challenge and we, the authors, quickly realized that we could not provide a comprehensive history of all that has occurred over this period. What we have tried to do, rather, is to focus on some of the major issues and how these were experienced by different women in different places. This book, which was originally perceived as one volume, has expanded to become two. This volume will cover the women's movement in English Canada, the politics of the body, the politics of difference, social policy and social services, women and the justice system, and women, culture, and communications. The second volume will deal with the domestic sphere, education and training, employment, economic issues, and global issues. Volume II will also carry the bibliography for both volumes.

We have chosen to proceed in each chapter not only by providing an analysis of what has happened, but also by including historical documents of the women's movement so that women's diversity could be represented through their own voices. Throughout the process of working on this project, we have been acutely aware of the limitations that we bring to it, simply because of who we are. While we have all been active in one way or another in the women's movement, we are unmistakably privileged and mainstream: we have not experienced racial oppression, the extraordinary disadvantages of being poor or disabled, nor the very different set of problems encountered by women who live in rural or remote places. While we have tried to correct for our class- , race- , location- , and language-bound perspectives in the selection of documents and in the composition of our texts, we know we have in no way fully overcome our many limitations. We hope, nonetheless, that our book will contribute to the immensely complex history of feminist activism in English Canada since 1967 and that it will spark debate and inspire other studies.

One of the enormous pleasures in working on this project has been the heightened sense we have of women's strengths — hence our title, *Strong Voices*. In searching through the documents in the archives of women's groups, we could not ignore the unmistakable evidence of the extraordinary dedication and effort of individual women who are often invisible to us because of their work within groups. Our world has changed and it has been because of the vision, tenacity, and sheer determination that these women exhibited. While many of the issues women struggled with initially are taken for granted today, we hope that a reflection on how much work was involved in bringing about change will give some glory to the women who worked to make our issues visible.

M.G.C.

Acknowledgements

A study of this sort is inevitably a collective enterprise. We are therefore indebted to a great many people. Heading that list are all those who gave us permission to reprint, in whole or in part, their views and voices in the documents included in this volume and all those who allowed themselves to be interviewed. We are also grateful to the following archives for their generosity in sharing their resources with us: the Canadian Women's Movement Archives; the Centre for Newfoundland Studies, Memorial University of Newfoundland; the Archives of the National Action Committee on the Status of Women; the Vancouver Status of Women Archives; the Victoria Status of Women Action Group Archives; the Women's Educational Resources Centre, Ontario Institute for Studies in Education; and the Archives of the Montreal Women's Centre.

We would also like to thank a number of people who did documentary research for us and who worked on the production: Sandra Awang, Brenda Beagan, Marg Brennan, Peggy Bristow, Michael Dempster, Frieda Forman, Diane Hallman, Anne Hart, Joss Maclennan, Marg Malone, Guida Mann, Martha Muzychka, Deidré Rowe, Sherene Kazack, Georgia Sitara, Pat Staton, and Lucy Tantalo. Special thanks are owed to Nathlyn Jones, Jill Given-King and Ruth Nieboer.

We are grateful for funding we received from: an Ontario Ministry of Education Transfer Grant to the Ontario Institute for Studies in Education, a Secretary of State Canadian Studies Program Grant, a Canadian Employment Work Study Grant, and Social Sciences and Humanities Research Council of Canada Small Scale Grants.

In the final stages of preparation of this volume, we have received invaluable assistance from our freelance editor, researcher, and indexer, Beth McAuley, and our Lorimer editor, Diane Young. We also thank copy editor, Dianne Broad, and Lorimer publishing assistant, Melinda Tate, for their work on the manuscript.

Chapter 1

The Canadian Women's Movement

Marjorie Griffin Cohen

The ideas and practices of feminism are not static, but have evolved and changed over time, so that even when people become comfortable with some feminist ideas, the ideas themselves seem to shift and once again something unfamiliar, difficult and disruptive is demanded. Feminism has always pushed boundaries and changed what exists and is familiar. This is why it is constantly subject to criticism. Nevertheless, feminism has been successful in Canada in influencing public opinion so that much that was unacceptable and appeared revolutionary, or perhaps was even scorned as trivial in the early periods of the movement, has become recognized as legitimate and reasonable.[1]

In Canada the women's movement is now an established political force and in all the major political debates in this country, a feminist perspective is aired. Usually the feminist position is provocative and out of step with current wisdom. The national referendum in 1992 on changes to the Constitution is a dramatic example of one issue where the organized feminist movement through the National Action Committee on the Status of Women (NAC) adopted a principled and risky stance in the face of extraordinary opposition. This opposition was staggering: all the parties in Parliament, the governments of all the provinces including Quebec, the trade union movement, the Assembly of First Nations and organizations speaking for business interests supported the Charlottetown Accord. NAC foresaw that the Accord would have negative effects on women.[2] It had many reasons for not wanting this version of the Constitution to pass, but the critical consideration was whether standing firmly on this made any sense at all since for the first time in Canada's history, there appeared to be unanimity on an issue that had long divided it. When NAC first announced its opposition to the Charlottetown Accord, it was done with the expectation that the Accord would pass. But over the ensuing weeks it became apparent that the political elites of the country underestimated the mood of the people. I am not suggesting that the Accord was defeated because everyone agreed with NAC's position. Many voted against it for reactionary reasons: because they felt Quebec was getting too much or because they did not believe native people should ever have autonomy. But many people voted against the Accord because they supported NAC's position that the proposed Constitutional changes would fundamentally alter ways in which the country worked — ways that would threaten social programs and equality rights.[3] On this issue, the women's movement was the leader in establishing a different voice. But it did not endear itself to many of its allies in the trade union movement, the NDP and the native community.[4]

As with all issues the women's movement has encountered, this one generated a great deal of debate within the feminist community over objectives and tactics. This chapter will show that the question of how to achieve effective change has been a constant source of tension within the women's movement. Many of the ideas about what is wrong, and therefore what needs to be the focus of action, derive from different political philosophies that are encompassed within feminism.[5] Other differences arise because the experiences of women are not homogeneous and what can appear to be the most pressing issue for one group of women can be inconsequential for another. Also, because women's circumstances differ substantially, what can be considered a successful outcome of an action or objective for some women can be detrimental to the objectives of others. None of the issues of class, race, ethnicity, age, different physical abilities, sexual orientation, language, culture and location have been resolved within the women's movement in Canada, or anywhere else for that matter. Yet the strength of the movement and its dynamic character arises from the diversity within it.

In the early periods of the revival of feminist activism, there was a great deal of emphasis on the shared experiences of women and the common nature of women's oppression. Men, their organizations and the way they had constructed society were the problem, not other women. Perhaps the enormous hostility to feminism, because of its threats to male power and privilege, perpetuated this myopic tendency to insist on the "sisterhood" of women as a basis for unity among us.[6] Certainly women needed to be united on some level to achieve change, yet many women in a variety of situations experienced other women as their oppressors. The ways in which women were also part of a hierarchy of power could not be ignored if the movement was to expand to reflect the diversity of the needs of all women. The process of moving from ignoring to accommodating diversity has been part of the history of the recent manifestations of the women's movement. But accommodation itself is not sufficient — there is a growing recognition that understanding domination in all its forms and how these systems of domination are related will be crucial to the further development of the women's movement.

In the following chapters we will attempt to understand how the women's movement in Canada organized, how its understanding of problems developed and changed, and how various types of actions were tried, abandoned, or retried. In writing about the women's movement, most of us do so from a particular experience with it. Even women who have been active over a long period can only truly know a small corner of what has become a very large movement. Therefore any interpretation can be only partial, even when we attempt to understand more fully by reading the documents of groups other than those we know well. This statement is true of any political movement at any stage in history. There is also a problem with the written records themselves. As someone who was involved in writing documents that are now part of our history, I am acutely aware of the political process of writing on a specific issue at a specific time. Often much of what was part of our analysis was not written. Other times, arguments were put forward that concealed deeper realities. The reasons for this reflected the politics of the time.

Sometimes we wrote to accommodate the diversity of opinion within our own groups. At other times we presented arguments that could be "heard" by people who were unfamiliar with the long trajectory of feminist thought and debate. Sometimes we wanted to be outrageous, to be provocative and to gain attention. The cautionary note to raise is that evidence of motives, philosophy and reasoning of a particular group cannot be fully understood by pointing to a single document. For many feminists, their immediate work was more absorbing than writing about it. Consequently, incidents and experiences were invariably more complex than what was recorded.

The Feminist Surge

Feminism gained strength and began to be recognized as a movement during the 1960s. It had been a significant social movement with political force in the early part of this century when women organized to win the right to vote in federal elections and to gain equality rights. But its effectiveness as a movement with widespread support appeared to dwindle in the ensuing years. Yet even during these periods of relative feminist obscurity, women acted to bring about change. As we begin to uncover our history, we recognize that feminists have continually persisted in pursuing social change and were sometimes successful in advancing women's causes. After the Person's Case in 1929,[7] the sensational issues that gained national attention subsided, but women succeeded in articulating a feminist view in other less dramatic areas. The legislative changes, such as women winning the vote in Quebec in 1941, their inclusion in unemployment insurance, the recognition of equality issues for women workers during World War II and the equal pay laws of the 1950s all occurred not because men spontaneously recognized women's needs, but because women worked to see that these things happened. A feminist voice persisted throughout this century in the works of women writers, and within farm organizations, trade unions, religious institutions, service groups, professional organizations and political parties.[8]

Remembering or rediscovering the work of these feminists gives a better sense of the latent force of ideas that persisted over a thirty- or forty-year period. This process of rediscovery is significant because often the explanations for the re-emergence of active feminism in the 1960s in Canada rely too heavily on the influence of forces outside this country as the catalyst for the new feminist movement. The burgeoning of feminist ideas in the U.S. is associated with the civil rights movement, the opposition to the Vietnam War and the discontent of the American housewife.[9] The growth of American feminism and its influence in Canada through books like Betty Friedan's *The Feminine Mystique* and the activism of American women who came to Canada with draft-dodging men were undoubtedly influential — ideas permeate national boundaries and tend to germinate in fertile ground. But these ideas were already here. Writing of the sixties generation north of the forty-ninth parallel, Myrna Kostash traces the origins of Canadian grassroots feminism to Canada's own anti-war, student power, countercultural, and Québec nationalist movements.[10] Doris Anderson, editor of *Chatelaine* throughout the 1960s, tells of how, when Betty Friedan submitted chapters of *The Feminine Mystique* for publication in *Chatelaine,* Anderson rejected them. She was sympathetic to their message and thought they were well written, but because articles on similar topics had been common features in the magazine, Anderson did not think they added anything to arguments that had been put forth even more strongly by Canadian writers. While Anderson recalls this with a sense of irony over a lost opportunity, there is also the recognition that feminism in Canada was not dormant, but was gathering steam here just as it was elsewhere.

The Royal Commission on the Status of Women

The most significant single event in establishing a sense of a women's movement in Canada was the Royal Commission on the Status of Women (RCSW), which issued its report in September 1970. Establishing a royal commission is far from a revolutionary or threatening act, but rather is a convenient Canadian way of dealing with troublesome issues. It is common for governments to set up a royal commission so that immediate action on annoying problems can be avoided by legislators. Despite general public scepticism over the effectiveness of royal commissions to bring about change, some women who had been active in women's organizations felt that this would be the best way to examine the conditions of Canadian women and to publicly highlight discrimination and injustice. It is hard to know where the idea for a RCSW originated, but it was pursued by Laura Sabia, president of the Canadian

Federation of University Women, after meeting with women from thirty-two organizations to discuss women's issues and change in May 1966.[11] From this meeting, the Committee for Equality of Women in Canada was formed and this committee, together with a newly formed group in Quebec, the Fédération des femmes du Québec (FFQ), did the necessary work to get the government to appoint the Commission in February 1967. Much work was needed for this to occur but probably most significant was having feminists in Quebec supporting the call for a royal commission. As Monique Begin[12] has pointed out, the call for the Commission came from English Canada, but a "royal commission demanded by English-speaking women only was politically impossible."[13] A royal commission was not a priority of the FFQ mainly because its members felt that more studies were "a waste of time ... we knew what had to be done." Nonetheless, the FFQ did lend its support to the call so that it would have a greater chance of success.[14]

When Prime Minister Lester Pearson, at one stage appeared to have rejected the whole project, Laura Sabia threatened to bring two million women to Parliament Hill to encourage the government to establish the Commission.[15] Apparently the militant tone of her statement, coupled with the threat of violence ("If we have to use violence, damn it, we will") caused Sabia a great deal of anguish after it appeared on the front page of *The Globe and Mail* and she had to explain to the groups she represented that the quotations were taken out of context. As she later recounted, these words were her immediate reaction after a reporter told her that the government was turning down the idea of a royal commission: "I wouldn't have been able to get three women to march on Ottawa! We were always trying to be nice to the women to keep them with us. It was pacify, pacify, pacify!"[16] In the folklore of the women's movement, it was this spectre of two million women on Parliament Hill that forced the government to reconsider. But others interpreted Sabia's threat as damaging to the cause and saw the work of women close to the government, specifically the pressure of Judy LaMarsh, a Liberal cabinet minister, as more significant in establishing the commission. The effectiveness of any specific action, in this case as in others in the women's movement, will be continuously debated because of the different perceptions women have about what brings change. Getting the government to appoint the royal commission has been variously attributed to militant threats, powerful women working behind the scenes, the example of President Kennedy's Roundtable on Women, reasoned argument, the strength of women's solidarity and media support. Probably all of these actions contributed to a climate that made the government respond to women's demands.

There is no doubt that many women collectively and individually focused on the Commission and its work for the three years it operated. In addition to establishing a research program, the Commission held public meetings throughout the country, many of which were televised, and received 480 briefs from individuals and organizations.[17] The process of hearing women's own articulation of the problems they encountered and what needed to be done undoubtedly affected the Commissioners. When the Commission began, only one Commissioner, Elsie Gregory MacGill, was an avowed feminist, but through on-the-job training "... quite rapidly the remaining four women sitting on the commission (Florence Bird, Lola M. Lange, Jeanne Lapointe, and Doris Ogilve) became feminists in their own right."[18] The issue, though, was what kind of feminism the Commission represented. For many women, such as Solveig Ryall who prepared a brief for the Commission, the guidelines for submissions were exceedingly narrow. Ryall felt that what was needed was not more investigations into things that had long been identified as problems but "radical change in the structure and institutions of Canadian society. Nothing less will do."[19] The 167 recommendations of the Commission spoke squarely to many of the demands women had been making for some time, but the process was frequently faulted for the failure "to understand the root causes of our oppression," and how this oppression resulted from "an economic system based on the exploitation of many by a few powerful owners and a social system dependent on racial, national and sexual chauvinism."[20]

While other women saw the Commission's work as a necessary step towards women's emancipation, the one issue on which there was almost unanimity, was that the Commission's work would not be sufficient to effect change. Throughout Canada, its recommendations were the impetus for women to organize to see that the momentum generated by the Report was not lost and that the government acted on women's behalf.[21] This certainly was the stated objective for the creation of NAC, which was formed out of the Strategy for Change Convention in 1972.[22] The groups that organized initially to see that the recommendations were put into effect usually extended their mandate and tactics over time, as other approaches and issues became more important. It is unlikely that anyone thought that achieving the objectives of the recommendations of the Commission would be sufficient to meet women's objectives. But for many women and groups, the lobbying action, which the RCSW seemed to demand, was a liberal approach that ignored or diluted the possibilities for radical change.

Various Forms of Organizing: Internal Processes

From the beginning, women became part of the "movement" in a variety of ways. While an organizational connection was the most obvious manifestation of belonging, many women never joined formal organizations, but felt an affinity with other women and worked to further the goals of feminism through personal actions in their homes and workplaces, and through friendships with other women. There were an infinite number of ways in which a feminist consciousness was awakened, but the phenomenon of the "Click!" was something many of us recognized as the time when we had a sudden insight because of a particular incident. For Diana Douglas of Vancouver, the moment occurred when she insisted in court that she was neither a "Miss" nor a "Mrs." The judge said, "You mean you are a nonentity."[23] For me, this insight occurred at a discussion at a dinner party in the late 1960s. The discussion was about *The Feminine Mystique,* which I hadn't read yet, and one of the men asked the women if we were feminists. One woman, who was amusing and quick-witted, replied, "Oh, no, I know my place!" The irony was marvelous, we all laughed, and I suddenly knew my place — I was a feminist.

Trying to get a sense of the ways in which women organized to meet common objectives, whatever they were, is difficult to achieve by pursuing the usual historical approach to the development of a movement. Merely focusing on the chronological presentation of events tends to miss much of the dynamic of the surge of feminism throughout the past twenty-five years. There was no single trajectory women pursued over time, but the different circumstances women encountered meant that they organized in ways that were appropriate to various objectives, locations, cultures and the numbers of women involved.

Often women's groups formed because a few women got together and just talked — something women have undoubtedly done from the beginning of time. But this became political and feminist when the objective was to understand the ways in which a woman's personal, individual experiences had relevance for other women. The process of talking about the personal became a distinct form of feminist-organizing through consciousness-raising (CR) groups. Usually consciousness-raising involved a group of eight or ten women who met regularly to discuss their own experiences of being female. The descriptions of how CR groups worked were remarkably similar throughout the country, and invariably focused on the significance of trust and confidentiality among the women; the importance of continuing with the same groups of women and not admitting new members; the necessity of having no leaders; and the willingness to suspend judgement and to let each woman speak freely about her own experiences.[24] The main objective was to raise consciousness so that each could "... begin to recognize that our private humiliations are universal and part of a larger pattern."[25]

The objectives of CR could be limited and presented the danger of not moving beyond the process of telling stories. The storytelling could get too comfortable, as many of us have witnessed at meetings where it is impossible to move beyond recounting experiences, meetings where attention is riveted on the woman who has dared to tell the most horrific and intimate details of her life to the group. The stories are important, but are never enough. It is essential that the understanding that comes from women's own experiences, the sense of solidarity that women reach through identifying common problems and the discovery that the "personal" has political significance leads to some recognition that collective action is possible to change women's circumstances. An article from the *Northern Woman* indicates that those involved in CR knew they had to be careful not to become a closed group where "the sense of a larger feminist community is lost. And it must be remembered that our ideas can only be tested and expanded through action. CR is a method of communication and through it, women have discovered their common oppression, but the discovery of our oppression is only an initial stage in ending our oppression. It is not a solution."[26] Some women were sceptical of CR because it was "just talk," while others were concerned about its exclusivity. In hindsight it is easy to see how working only with friends or people in similar circumstances would be unlikely to raise consciousness about the various forms of women's oppression, depending on race, ethnicity, age or any other distinction.[27] But CR was one method of meeting the immediate needs of some women through friendship, intimate discussion and trying to understand the larger dynamic of sexual politics.

Frequently CR groups lead to other forms of action, as was the case with those who ultimately formed the women's centre in Montreal: there was a split between "people who wanted to go into action, and ... people who preferred to stay in the group and keep on discussing the things that we were discussing."[28] In other cases, a strong sense developed that a more comprehensive analysis of women needed to occur so that feminism could grow and become more effective. This was attempted through study groups, which were usually formed by women with socialist backgrounds who wanted to develop a political theory of feminism with the hope that a clear analysis would lead to more effective action. The aims of these groups were specific and clearly were not designed for mass participation, rather, as is indicated by a Toronto "political rap group," there was care to "exclude women who have allegiance to male-dominated political groups committed, on principle, to destroying [the] movement."[29] Since this was a group designed to show that "feminism and socialism are not in contradiction," this exclusion clearly refers to socialists who had characterized women's liberation as a dilution of the aims of socialism itself.

The issue of who could be included or excluded in any group was a problem. The exclusion of men was not usually contested because this was considered essential for women to find their own voice and not to have their movement co-opted by a male approach, no matter how sympathetic and encouraging.[30] Similarly, as in the case of the DisAbled Women's Network (DAWN), fostering a group identity was important for women who found that a "positive sense of self is hard to sustain within male-dominated organizations, or organizations dominated by non-disabled feminists," and specific organizations to meet specific needs were essential.[31] But frequently women who did not have the same political philosophy were excluded from the organizing of mass events, as was the case with the Abortion Caravan.[32] The tension was clearly present between those who believed in the purity of their own political approach, and those who were perceived as corrupting it.

In writing about the women's movement, there is a tendency to dwell on the difficulties women experienced among themselves in the process of building the movement, particularly as one reads the documents that speak of what women struggled with as they tried to form organizations and initiate action. Different allegiances to organizing methods was often the spark that produced friction and caused divisions within a group. In hindsight, the ways in which these fractious issues are recounted is often amusing, particularly if the most contentious issues have been reconciled over time. A case in point is the split that occurred in the Newfoundland Status of Women Council (NSWC) when it initiated a women's centre.[33] The women's centre operated as a collective with consensus decision-making, while the Council operated in a more traditionally structured way. Tension was clearly evident when at one point the women from the collective "taped a sign over a back window of the Water Street NSWC that read 'Workers of the World Unite'."[34] NSWC members saw this as a provocative action, entirely idealistic and inappropriate. The ultimate break occurred when the NSWC wanted to hang curtains in the centre, an act that was viewed as aggressively bourgeois by the collective.[35] Obviously something more was going on than an inability to tolerate differences in style. Real political differences existed, and these affected what were perceived as the most pertinent issues and the most authentically feminist ways of pursuing change. Splits occurred even within groups with common political ideologies, as is clear from the various socialist feminist groups that developed from the Women's Liberation Movement in Toronto in the late 1960s and early 1970s.[36]

In many groups, a great deal of energy was expended to ensure that the traditional forms of organizing (where votes are taken, someone chairs the meeting and officers are elected) were avoided so that no one's voice would be lost and a hierarchy within the organization was not established. Women's centres and service-oriented groups tended to operate as collectives where decision-making occurred on a consensus basis,[37] a process that frequently became identified as authentically feminist.[38] This process, which involved direct participation in all decision-making, was less likely to be followed as groups combined and formed larger organizations. Documents showing how to establish a women's group varied considerably in their advice about the method of organization to pursue. Some documents, like the early advice from the Vancouver Women's Caucus, counsel against beginning with a constitution or even a detailed program of aims,[39] while others like the National Association of Women and the Law specifically state "first, you should draw up a constitution, or governing document," then elect a chair, and suggest using Roberts' or Bourinot's *Rules of Order* as guidelines for running a meeting.[40]

Undoubtedly many groups operated successfully as collectives with consensus decision-making and found ways to maintain accountability and effective leadership,[41] while others that began with the notion of "collective leadership," found it unworkable, for many reasons. In one case, as the group grew, it discovered that attempting consensus resulted in a "thoroughly unhealthy decision-making process," particularly as more forceful women dominated the discussion and decision-making, and felt that "a simple vote at the end would give every woman, whether or not she had contributed to the discussion, an equal voice in the final decision, and a chance to take a political stand."[42] Other groups tried to invoke rules about how often each person could speak, but there was also the recognition that "women who are confident to speak are often put down for taking power, while women who don't speak are in fact exercising power by not risking their options for group discussion and letting others take leadership roles for them."[43] Some groups struggled bravely without a clear structure and accountability but, as occurred in the case of various chapters of DAWN, they ultimately found that reorganizing with a specific structure and defined leadership prevented one or two individuals from being burdened with most of the work without recognition and adequate resources.[44]

Over time there has probably been a recognition that there is not just one "feminist process." Rather, various different types of organizations are compatible with feminist objectives and some are more appropriate for specific circumstances than others. This recognition does not mean the problem of organizing has not continued to plague feminism, particularly as groups with different modes of operating come together in one organization, as they do in NAC. Trying to find a way to organize that would satisfy all groups involved wasn't just an academic or trivial exercise. There was a real need to explore methods that did not duplicate the oppressive structures that women had long worked under, yet also to find a way to simultaneously be effective, to respond quickly when necessary, and to adapt and change as circumstances warranted. At NAC, the issue of feminist process became a crisis at the 1988 Annual General Meeting (AGM). The organization had grown dramatically, expanding from 360 groups in 1986 to 570 by 1988, yet its structure and resources could not accommodate the demands for involvement in decision-making by its various members. The formal process of the AGM, which operated under Roberts' *Rules of Order,* was particularly frustrating for women who wanted more discussion but so too was the inability of the organization to find effective ways of having women throughout the country directly participate in NAC.[45] Obviously the organization needed to change if it was not going to alienate the very women who were its members, but this was not a simple choice between two methods of organizing, since a method that could work for a small group of individuals clearly would not work in an organization of close to 600 member groups. Likewise, a traditionally structured organization would not meet the needs for a different kind of participation. Fortunately, the differences in NAC did not fragment the organization, but instead propelled the various groups within it to work together, through countless meetings and discussions, to bring about change. While a formal structure with elected officers and regional representatives remains, the process of decentralizing committee work has begun to involve many more individual women in NAC's political work. But this process certainly is not yet complete and the organization is acutely aware of the distance-manywomen feel from NAC's activities because its membership is of groups and not of individual women.

Defining and Meeting Needs

From the beginning of the movement women worked at meeting specific needs in different ways. At the local level, the discriminatory circumstances that women encountered daily needed to be addressed and groups organized to see that these needs were met. In some respects trying to deal with desperate needs fit into the traditional public service role that women had always performed. But feminists organized with a specifically feminist consciousness: when services were provided, these services were not charity, but women working together to solve common problems. Service organizations were a specific type that were designed to deal with problems women faced when they were raped or encountered violence; needed medical help or abortions; encountered discrimination in their jobs or just needed help finding a job; required day-care, language training, or legal help; or just needed to communicate with other women. Women's centres sprang up all over Canada, and while they took different characters in cities and towns, and in remote and rural areas, their common objective was to respond to needs in their communities. Everywhere women's centres were organized they achieved this, at least initially, under difficult conditions, frequently operating in cold, inadequate buildings and with either volunteer or underpaid help. In some places, women's centres expanded over time to become very large organizations with extensive staff, providing a range of services, such as in Montreal.[46] Here the women's centre not only provides emergency services, counselling and information, but also runs an extensive educational program with courses for immigrant women, assertiveness training, information sessions on tenants' and domestic workers' rights, language classes, as well as income tax clinics and courses in arts and crafts.[47] The more typical centre, such as the East Prince Women's Centre in P.E.I., offers space for women to "drop in," and hold meetings, and focuses on providing information and referral services.[48] In other places, particularly poorer and less populated sections of the country, the obstacles for sustaining women's centres were too great. Although amazonian efforts were exerted in an attempt to help them succeed, they failed, either because of community hostility or because they simply were never able to generate the money they needed to operate. But even

LOOT member Rosemary Barnes at the Gala Opening of the Lesbian Centre in Toronto, 12 March 1977.

in cities, the hazards of maintaining a women's centre were great, as is apparent in Edmonton, where the women's centre that began in the early 1970s, closed in 1975 and reopened in 1982.[49] In other cases, as with LOOT (Lesbian Organization of Toronto), the problems of maintaining a centre with only volunteer help and little money seemed to undermine the energies of other types of political action.[50]

Meeting needs was frequently identified as the work done at the local level where the day-to-day issues women faced could be addressed in practical ways. The term "grassroots" is often used to describe these groups and to distinguish them from the more state-oriented approach to achieving liberation, which is sometimes labelled "institutionalized feminism."[51] Trying to label groups or to identify their philosophy, based on types of activities, is a common way of distinguishing between groups. For example, dealing with legislative change and focusing on the actions of government is often characterized as the objective of liberal, institutionalized feminism, while community-based organizations operating as collectives, with consensus decision-making, and "reaching out to women on the street" are associated with radical and socialist feminism. But the exceptions and overlaps are too common for these distinctions to work well. Often community-based organizations were neither radical nor socialist and did not want to be associated with the radical overtones of "Women's Lib."[52] Other groups, such as the Thunder Bay Anishinabequek chapter of the Ontario Native Women's Association (ONWA), elected officers and in addition to providing services for native women and their families, also recognized the need to deal with government and legislation. This was certainly a "grassroots" organization, counting as its members 175 of the 250 native women in Thunder Bay.[53] Also, despite the characterization of work toward legislative change as "liberal," many socialist groups also worked to change the law, particularly as it dealt with labour and human rights issues.[54]

Through the process of providing services, groups often found themselves pushed toward political action that focused on changing legislation, such as in the process of organizing abortion clinics. The tension between providing services and doing the necessary work to change the most oppressive features of state practices was a problem — not because women did not want to do both, but because limited resources often forced them to choose between one approach or another. As groups in northern British Columbia in the mid-1980s recognized, there was also the problem of "biting the hand that ..." since almost all service-oriented groups were supported by some form of government.[55] The issue of money was a complex one with which groups continuously struggled. Service-oriented groups quite rightly expected that funding for their activities should come from government sources, whether federal, provincial, or municipal, but government funding has been fraught with difficulties.

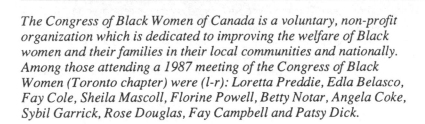

David Maylor Courtesy: SHARE

The Congress of Black Women of Canada is a voluntary, non-profit organization which is dedicated to improving the welfare of Black women and their families in their local communities and nationally. Among those attending a 1987 meeting of the Congress of Black Women (Toronto chapter) were (l-r): Loretta Preddie, Edla Belasco, Fay Cole, Sheila Mascoll, Florine Powell, Betty Notar, Angela Coke, Sybil Garrick, Rose Douglas, Fay Campbell and Patsy Dick.

The issues on which women focused varied considerably. Some groups dealt with whatever issue was at hand, while others focused specifically on one issue such as abortion rights or day-care. In the early stages of the movement there was considerable controversy about which was the proper approach, with some groups, such as the Saskatoon Women's Liberation group, arguing that single-issue campaigns diluted efforts to bring about liberation and obscured both the ways in which issues were connected as well as the systemic character of women's oppression.[56] There was also the fear that success in any one area would lead women who had worked on that issue to feel that their work was done, which many people believed had occurred after women won the vote earlier in the century. The experience, however, did not bear out this fear, particularly as both multi-issue organizations and single-issue ones existed side by side, and finding solutions to any problem was either elusive or proceeded at a snail's pace. The reality was that it was usually the single-issue groups that did the primary research, analysis and planned the action on specific issues — an occurrence that was particularly valuable because it was then the people who were closest to the issue and who had the most experience with it who would take the lead. Multi-issue organizations were important for bringing women in various parts of the movement together, and through them groups were able to support each other's work. In this way, for example, groups other than abortion rights groups were able to support the abortion campaign, and child care groups, teachers, nurses and farmers support NAC's campaigns against free trade.

Meeting women's needs took very different forms throughout the country. While some themes were voiced almost everywhere and seemed to have universal support among women's groups (e.g., the need to eradicate violence and provide adequate child care) others were distinct because of issues of race, class and other circumstances that made women's day-to-day experiences special. In a meeting with two provincial cabinet ministers in March 1986, native women's groups in Labrador highlighted their most pressing concerns, most of which dealt with the desperate conditions of their communities. The Davis Inlet Innu Women's Group needed a bathhouse because there were no water or sewage facilities in individual homes; the Sheshatshit Innu Women's group requested a full-time interpreter at the Melvill Hospital and wanted access to specific health services, such as an eye specialist; the Postville Women's Group was concerned about teenage pregnancy; and the Hopedale Women's Group protested the community's application for a liquor licence. These requests were interspersed among other, more familiar, demands to women in the south: day-care, a refuge centre for battered women and children, and family planning services.[57]

The survival of native culture and way of life has been paramount in native women's organizations, and related to this has been an emphasis on promoting arts and crafts as integral to native women's political action. This focus on culture was at the heart of native women's politics because the contempt with which native culture has been held by white society has had dire consequences which, among other things, has deprived native peoples of their own children and all but eradicated a way of life which was economically viable. At the Northwest Territories Native Women's Association's founding convention in 1976 in Yellowknife, promoting native culture and fostering arts and crafts was integrally related to dealing with specific issues such as alcohol abuse and the whole problem of non-native care and adoption of native children.[58] The frustration of native women with bureaucracy and the Indian Act has been a consistent theme in their organizing. The sit-in at the Department of Indian Affairs in B.C. in 1981 is only one, albeit a dramatic example, of the kinds of actions that native women have taken in their struggle with government.[59] The issue of cultural identity was often the motivating force for many other women, as was apparent from the account of the beginnings of the National Congress of Black Women.

This group, which was originally organized by "professional or business women, or [women] involved in education, the arts, etc."[60] over time expanded its activities to deal more directly with the racial discrimination that black women faced.[61]

The power of cultural issues to bring women together was often sparked by controversy about specific cultural events. The presentation of an ancient Greek play, *Lysistrata,* in Prince George in 1972 created considerable debate, since the play dealt with female sexuality and women's ability to use it as power. Women began meeting to discuss the play's subject and out of this grew the beginnings of a women's centre.[62]

It is unlikely that any groups originally organized with a full understanding of the various facets of their own oppression, something that developed as women worked together, associated with women who were not in similar circumstances and tried to effect change. One of the major initial tasks was to understand the extent of oppression, something that was not always easy to uncover, at least in a documented way, and a great deal of energy was spent on research on current conditions.[63] For example, when the International Coalition to End Domestics' Exploitation (INTERCEDE) began organizing in 1979, its focus was both on action and on publicizing the racist nature of government policy toward domestic workers from other countries. Organizers documented not only how many women had been denied landed status in Canada, but also the miserable wages and working conditions that these women experienced.[64]

Acquiring knowledge, keeping records and sharing information has been a critical part of feminist organizing. Resource centres, which provided all kinds of material on women that was not available in traditional libraries, were formed as part of women's centres and in universities, schools and some workplaces. Some of these developed into significant libraries, such as the Women's Education Resource Centre at the Ontario Institute for Studies in Education in Toronto, and the Canadian Women's Movement Archives, established by a collective in Toronto. Many, usually because of poor funding, relied mainly on donated or free material. In the 1960s and 1970s there was very little feminist material and distribution was a challenge, particularly because women's bookstores, if they existed at all, were in large cities. The problem of providing material for rural women was addressed by Judith Quinlan and Ellen Woodsworth, through "Cora," the Women's Liberation Bookmobile, which distributed material to women outside urban centres in the mid-70s.[65] Even for women in cities obtaining material on women was difficult, but for women in rural areas, it appeared almost impossible. In northern Ontario, a lesbian archives was established to serve women in rural areas. While it was intended it to be accessible to all women, the archives' keepers favoured rural lesbians up until its closure in 1986.

Members of the Canadian Women's Movement Archives collective, hard at work. The archives are housed in the University of Ottawa's Morisset Library, Special Collections.

CORA, the Women's Liberation Bookmobile, distributed material to rural women in the seventies.

Feminism for rural women took distinct forms and many of the issues that women in urban areas identified as primary were not those that most affected these women's lives. The main issues for farm women were the problems associated with specific federal government policy to make farming more competitive.[66] The resulting decline in farm income increased pressure on farm families to take off-farm jobs and for farm women, this effort to maintain the family farm through work for wages usually involved travelling long distances for part-time jobs that paid low wages.[67] While women in urban areas were well-acquainted with the problem of low pay and a double or triple day of work, the distinct economic problems of agricultural communities were certainly foreign to urban women. Some of the problems for rural women were parallel to those of women in the city, but were exacerbated by the isolation of farm communities. So while women in both rural and urban areas had a need for child care, these took distinct forms in rural areas where population density was low and the possibilities for getting child care were remote. But other issues that were seen as crucial to a feminist perspective were not always supported by women living in small communities. For example, while a strong stand on the repeal of the abortion law was a critical issue for feminism, many groups, such as those in smaller communities in Newfoundland and Labrador, did not take a public stand on this issue.[68] For women in areas where feminism was not widely supported, community pressures were undoubtedly greater and made supporting the abortion campaign difficult. For other women, such as Myrt Lenton, a Manitoba farmer, feminism is itself, "An image that is foreign to rural women. They cannot afford it."[69] Feminism, to her, meant a "point of view with demands for more rights for just women," something that seemed like treachery in a time when the united efforts of the farm family were essential when faced with an attack on their way of life. This problem of supporting and showing solidarity with men who are also part of an oppressed group is not unique to farm families, and has been an issue for women in native groups, and others who have a way of life that is distinct and has been threatened by the dominant culture. For many, feminism's identity with white, urban, middle-class women meant that espousing a feminist viewpoint merely supported a perspective that was anathema to their own way of life. The task of women in these groups, as they saw it, was not to adopt the perspectives of urban or white women, but to articulate the ways in which they, as women, had been relegated to inferior positions within their own communities. But their issues were certainly larger than merely dealing with inequalities in their own communities: they also needed to address the structure of domination that affected their communities. Organizations like the National Farmers' Union were forced by the feminists within it to become more responsive to women's issues and to focus their struggles with government not only on what policy meant for male farmers, but also on how this could have a specific and different impact on farm women. As these groups have had more contact with other feminists, they have had an effect on the movement in general. As subsequent chapters will show, as a result of broadening the perspective on what constitutes discrimination and inequality, every facet of life has become a subject of women's attention. While early in the recent history of the feminist movement there was a distinct tendency to deal with things that were identifiable as "women's issues," over time we recognized that there was no issue that did not pertain to women.[70]

Dealing with the State

Women's groups that were seeking changes on specific issues invariably encountered "the state," a term that embraces all forms of government power. As alluded to above, there was often the perception that any group looking to the government for remedies for women's oppression had a benign view of the state and was optimistic about enlisting state help in eradicating discrimination. In the early periods of the movement this characterization was probably not far off the mark because there is a sense, in reviewing documents, that there was a belief that if government could at least provide conditions for "equal opportunity," women would then be on an equal footing with men:[71] related to this was the idea that the logic of equality could be attractive to government, if properly phrased. Working with these assumptions led to specific types of actions that smacked of pandering to power. The whole concept of "lobbying" conjures up images of insiders (well-clothed, expensively shod people with good haircuts) meeting over drinks to cajole politicians into supporting their cause. This approach assumes that there is some common interest over which the politicians and lobbyists can agree, but that it is up to the lobbyists to show, through reasoned argument and subtle threats, how any change in current policy will be in the politician's interest. Not surprisingly, this approach repelled many women who did not want to rely on feminist elites to bargain for them with government and who felt that the strategy of reasoned argument would not take the movement in the revolutionary directions it needed to go.[72]

Over time, even groups like NAC, which initially could have been characterized as having a "belief in the welfare state, a belief in the efficacy of state action in general to remedy injustices,"[73] became more cynical about any government as an ally when they saw the ways in which women's demands were treated. Experience showed that male, political, and corporate power and privilege would not be given up easily and even the meagre scraps of concessions that were thrown women's way could be perverted by a state that wanted to appear responsive for political reasons, but also wanted to ensure that traditional power was not threatened in any serious way. I am not implying that attempts to change laws through lobbying and inside connections was not a useful approach in some instances, particularly when a political party in power experienced pressures from inside it to respond to women. Many groups spent a great deal of time and effort in countless consultations to inform government of their issues and to indicate to politicians that there was weight behind their demands in the form of an organized body of women who were voters and who had the power to command media and public attention.[74] Reasoned arguments presented through formal briefs to government committees, "consultations" with ministers and talks with people who drafted legislation could work in cases like getting equal pay for work of equal value in the Federal Human Rights Act in 1977[75] and changes to specific legislation, such as that dealing with divorce reform or sexual assault.[76]

But there were limits to this approach. Reasoned arguments definitely did not work when women's interests were pitted against the major interests of the state and its primary supporters — in these cases lobbying became confrontation.[77] This was particularly evident after the Progressive Conservatives came to power federally in 1984 and began gutting social programs, instituting a program of privatization and free trade, and defining women's groups as "special interests" representing enemies of the state.[78] With a hostile government, one would imagine that lobbying, or at least meeting with government officials and presenting briefs to parliamentary committees, would end, but it did not and for very good reason. Women learned that as organizations became stronger and more visible publicly, the presentation of briefs could often be an effective and inexpensive way of giving publicity to specific issues. This was certainly my experience in NAC when dealing with issues like free trade, privatization and the federal budgets. I had no illusions that my wisdom and logic would bring about a sudden Tory conversion to my point of view or that the Tories would reverse their draconian policies. Rather, each presentation was invariably a confrontation, which the media often found interesting. By making our issues public and having them reported in the media, we were able to provide information and rally support in a way that would have been simply too expensive to achieve through other means. While the tactic of presenting briefs and meeting politicians might sound like lobbying, it was lobbying with a difference.[79]

The state has attempted to contain feminism from the moment it appeared to have the potential for becoming a significant political force. At the Strategy for Change Convention in 1972, for example, women supporting government initiatives argued that efforts would be best expended in seeing that a strong body was established to deal with women's issues within government, rather than working on an independent national women's organization. This idea was rejected by most women at the convention and the result was the beginnings of NAC. However, confusion about just which groups were government agencies and which were independent has persisted, mainly because as the government instituted its own organizations to deal with women's issues, their names, like Status of Women Canada, and the Canadian Advisory Council on the Status of Women, were remarkably similar to that of the National Action Committee on the Status of Women. By co-opting names, the government has added to this confusion. NAC, however, goes to considerable lengths to make sure that it is recognized as an independent group.[80] The bodies established by government and staffed with government appointees often provided important support for feminist initiatives, but since they were not accountable to the women's movement itself, they often acted in ways that received a great deal of criticism from the movement. Undoubtedly in the Secretary of State's programs for women there were dedicated feminists who did much to advance women's issues within government and to help women's groups obtain necessary funding. The Canadian Advisory Council on the Status of Women, as an advisory group to government, often was able to provide significant research on specific issues that was indispensable to women's lobbying.

Despite the often supporting role of these organizations in developing feminist objectives, they were ultimately accountable to governments, not the movement — something that was problematic. In one instance, some members of the Advisory Council, in response to needs of the feminist movement, tried to organize a constitutional conference, an act that conflicted with what the government of the day wanted. Doris Anderson, as the Council president, ultimately resigned her position because the minister she reported to, Lloyd Axworthy, cancelled the conference to avoid embarrassment to the government.[81] Anderson's resignation was decidedly embarrassing for the government as the Council's work after this event was increasingly treated with scepticism by the women's movement. This scepticism turned to outright hostility over a report on *Immigrant Women in Canada: A Policy Perspective,* which was published in 1988. Women's groups were appalled at the implications of the report, which seemed to prove, among other things, that immigrant women had more advantageous positions in the labour force than Canadian-born women. For immigrant women, this report certainly did not reflect their experience.[82]

There is no doubt that a strong independent feminist movement has existed in Canada, but state influence in the movement has been considerable, particularly because many groups receive at least part of their funding from government, something that was always recognized as having the potential of influencing not only the programs, but also the very existence of groups.[83] Whether or not to accept government funding could be contentious within groups, as is evident from the discussions among women at the Saskatoon Women's Centre in 1974 when they received a Secretary of State grant.[84] There was no doubt that women's groups needed money that could not be generated through the usual sources. Many women felt that the government should support women's initiatives, since women paid taxes and yet so little funding went to support services for women — something that women were trying to provide for themselves. Even groups with avowedly political aims argued that government funding should be provided because women's voices needed to be heard throughout the country and this representation could not be achieved without proper funding. But accepting money was fraught with danger: the government could at any time withdraw funding and for groups that had been built on government funding and relied on it, this could mean the end of their existence. Other groups recognized that they spent more time and energy applying for government grants and tailoring their proposals and programs to fit grant requirements, than doing the real work they wanted to do.[85] Some groups with overtly political objectives, like the Ontario Committee on the Status of Women, steadfastly refused to accept government funding, although they were frequently encouraged to do so by the Secretary of State. Other groups like NAC depended heavily on government funding, with about half of its total budget coming from government sources. But as Lynn McDonald argues, having a group that is highly critical of government submit its plans for action to the government annually for approval for funding creates a situation that is "truly preposterous."[86] There is no indication that NAC, at least in recent years, has tailored its actions to fit a government agenda. That it has not done so in itself has been provocative and funding cuts have not just been threatened, but have actually occurred as the women's movement has increasingly irritated government. Not only has NAC's funding been seriously reduced, but so too has that of women's centres and other groups.[87]

Political Parties

Part of the solution to dealing with the state seemed obvious — get more women involved in formal politics. With women as roughly half the voters of the nation, this seemed like a possible strategy for change, at least at the level of state politics. From the early 1970s, women's groups across the country were established to encourage women to run for office and to raise money so that they could succeed. For example, in Newfoundland a "Women in Public Life Group," was established in 1972,[88] in British Columbia in 1975 the North Shore Women's Centre held a workshop on "How to Get Elected,"[89] in Toronto in 1972 Women for Political Action was formed and in the mid-1980s, The Committee for '94 was formed.[90] These were usually non-partisan groups whose primary aim was to get more women elected in all of the parties.

But the problem was that few women had the same resources as men and often the women who ran for office were not supportive of feminist objectives. Party politics were not very responsive to women generally; from 1968 to the 1980 election the proportion of major party candidates who were women increased from four to only eight per cent, and in the 1980 election campaign women were only six per cent of those who won.[91] But the 1984 election was different: 23 per cent of the NDP's candidates, 16 per cent of the Liberal's and 8 per cent of the Progressive Conservative's were women, double the number of women who ran in the previous election. Although after the votes were counted, women still only comprised 10 per cent of the membership of the House of Commons. What made the 1984 election different was that for the first time women's issues became election issues. In fact, an entire debate between the prime ministerial candidates focused on women. The spectacle of three men, who at best had only a nodding acquaintance with women's issues before this debate, being heavily briefed by the women in their party in order to debate each other on how women would be best treated by their own party, was an historic first that feminists thoroughly enjoyed.[92] The debate had been orchestrated and organized by NAC in order to raise women's issues in the election. By and large, the responses of the men were unremarkable, as they each tried to show how they would advance women's issues if elected, but the closing question by one of the women questioners was memorable. Kay Sigurjonsson asked: "Why should we trust you now?" This electrified the crowd of women who throughout the evening had been strictly controlled because this was a televised event and any gasps, exclamations or other signs of disapproval from the audience were considered inappropriate for the CBC. The question startled the candidates, and each tried to outdo the other in assuring us that they were honest and trustworthy, but Sigurjonsson's point was made.

As I write this, Kim Campbell has just become Prime Minister and over the past two elections federally, and especially provincially as the NDP has won elections in three provinces, more women have been

*The Feminist Party of Canada was established in the late seventies.
Although short lived, the party demonstrated feminists' commitment to
politics that mattered for women.*

successful in winning elections and holding cabinet positions.[93] In many
cases women have run as feminists and have pursued feminist objectives
when in office, but this appeared so unlikely in the late 1970s, that the
Feminist Party of Canada was established. Its purpose was to elect
women who were avowed feminists and part of a party that defined itself
as feminist. The party was formed not only because of the long-standing
difficulties of getting women elected, but also because of the recognition
that usually when women were elected through the major parties, they

tended to lose their feminist will and voice through the process of loyalty to party discipline.[94] The Feminist Party did not succeed and never ran any candidates, but it was important for focusing on the problem of what women could do once elected and if committed to feminist principles.

The first woman elected to the federal parliament was Agnes MacPhail in 1921, soon after women won the right to vote. But women's political representation has proceeded at a snail's pace. Over a 70-year period, women even now only comprise 13 per cent of the members of the House of Commons and at this rate, it will take another 45 years before women have parity with men in this body. The major problem appears to be the difficulty in getting women nominated in ridings where they have a chance of winning, because it seems that once women are nominated, voters do not discriminate much at the polls.[95] As feminists have become more powerful within parties in recent years, there has been more attention to seeing that women are nominated in ridings where they can win, but this alone will not solve the problem women have in taking office. The ways in which political campaigns are run, the traditional ways in which politics are conducted and the great need for money to win are all major difficulties for many women, particularly those with young children.

Although Kim Campbell is Canada's first female prime minister, she is not the first woman to head a political party in this country. In 1975 Rosemary Brown, a politician from Vancouver, ran for the federal leadership of the NDP.[96] Her campaign was distinctly feminist, and although she did not win her bid for leadership, she paved the way for Alexa McDonough to become the NDP leader in Nova Scotia in 1980 and Audrey McLaughlin, in 1989, to become the first woman to head a major federal party in Canada.[97] In the early stages of the feminist movement, we frequently talked about "firsts" for women, something which in most areas of life is no longer news, but in political life there are many "firsts" that are still occurring, which indicates just how far women still have to go to achieve anything like parity in the political system. In Vancouver Central, Kim Campbell's riding, for the first time in any election for a prime minister, three women are contesting the election.[98] But for women in the women's movement, the crucial issue is not simply having more women run and win; rather, it is ensuring that feminist ideas and principles are pursued once women obtain office. While women politicians often perceive themselves as feminists, as does Kim Campbell, to many this feminism does more to advance the interests of the individual politician than it does to advance the cause of all women. If women in the movement seem less than enthusiastic about Kim Campbell being elected prime minister, it is not because women fail to support each other in critical times. Rather, it is because she espouses and has been party to all the measures of Brian Mulroney's government that have made women's lives harder.

Nadine Chan Courtesy: NAC

Judy Rebick and Sunera Thobani in Saskatoon, Saskatchewan, days before NAC's Annual General Meeting in May 1993.

Conclusion

Feminism has not merely existed in Canada, it has thrived, developed and changed over the years considered in this book. Subsequent chapters will show how women have analysed and acted on specific issues and through this, some sense of the energy, joy and fun that women have experienced in the process may come through. In groups I have joined, having fun while doing serious political work was important. I learned this from Lorna Marsden when we were active in the Ontario Committee on the Status of Women and while after all of these years I do not remember her exact words, her sense was that if you could not have fun while advancing feminism, it would be grim work indeed. Some of the joy of feminism was evident at demonstrations and rallies. For instance, in the 1970s in various parts of Canada, feminists revived the celebration of International Women's Day (IWD) on March 8. From then until the present, IWD celebrations are used to raise awareness of all kinds of issues from abortion rights to racism, but at the same time are occasions for fun and celebration.[99] Feminists deal with serious things, so often our public face does not convey the pleasure women have experienced as we have worked together and played together, and in the process changed our world.

Throughout this period, the women's movement has received constant criticism, both from within and from outside the movement. At various times the movement has been pronounced irrelevant, anachronistic, unrealistic, or even dead: a few years ago a favourite journalistic buzz-word was "post-feminism," and now we are familiar with the concept of the feminist "backlash." At times the backlash has been considerable: in the late 1980s REAL (Real Equal and Active for Life) Women appeared to be a serious challenge to feminist initiatives. While the media encouraged REAL Women's attack on feminism, support for this group did not gather momentum. The appeal of the group to many women in the home was real and this had the effect on the feminist movement of making its policy positions on homemaking more public. But particularly dangerous were the homophobic stands and anti-abortion activities of REAL Women.[100]

It is not surprising that feminism has been the target of criticism. Much of what feminism has attacked has dealt with the heart of relations between men and women as well as with the most powerful institutions in society. But also, not enough has changed quickly enough and sometimes feminism is faulted for this lack of progress: we either did not focus on the right issues, or we used the wrong tactics. As Judy Rebick, former president of NAC, says, "If you move, you're a target,"[101] and feminism certainly has moved. What has been remarkable about the women's movement has been its willingness not only to take chances, but also to change and respond to women's voices that had not been heard in the past. Women have not always listened to each other, but we have recognized this and realized that strength can be developed from a variety of perspectives. Sunera Thobani, NAC president, points out that while feminism has made gains over the past 20 years, these have benefited only a minority of women: "It is only when the concerns of the women who face the harshest levels of discrimination are addressed that the women's movement will remain true to its principles of empowerment and equality of all women."[102] The women's movement still has much work to do, both within its own organizations and in the wider world, but there is much about which we can be proud.

NOTES

1. Feminism's acceptance among women has grown over the years. According to a *Weekend* magazine poll in 1979, 42 per cent of Canadian women called themselves "feminists," and a *Chatelaine* poll in 1986 indicated this figure had grown to 47 per cent. A general poll in 1987 found that about three-quarters of Canadians felt the feminist movement has had a positive effect on Canadian society. (Naomi Black, "The Canadian Women's Movement: The Second Wave," in *Changing Patterns: Women in Canada*, ed. by Sandra Burt, Lorraine Code, Lindsay Dorney, second ed. (Toronto: McClelland & Stewart, 1993) 151.

2. These issues will be elaborated on in Chapter 5.

3. Judy Rebick, "Why to Vote No in the Referendum," *Globe and Mail*, 17 September 1992.

4. Many native women's groups urged NAC to take this position because they felt their equality rights were threatened by the Charlottetown Accord. Also, analyses after the

referendum indicate that a majority of people in Quebec and natives voted against the Accord.

5. Much has been written about the distinctions between liberal, radical and socialist feminism. See, for example, Alison Jaggar, *Feminist Politics and Human Nature* (New Jersey: Rowman and Allanheld, 1983). See Jill Vickers, "The Intellectual Origins of the Women's Movements in Canada," for a discussion of the ideological perspectives on English Canadian feminism and Micheline Dumont, "The Origins of the Women's Movement in Quebec," for the intellectual origins of the women's movement in Quebec. Both articles appear in *Challenging Times: The Women's Movement in Canada and the United States,* ed. by Constance Backhouse and David H. Flaherty (Montreal & Kingston: McGill-Queen's, 1992), 39-71.

6. For a discussion of the strengths and problems with the concept of "sisterhood," see Nancy Adamson, Linda Briskin and Margaret McPhail, *Feminists Organizing for Change* (Toronto: Oxford University Press, 1988).

7. For a discussion of the Person's Case, see Catherine L. Cleverdon, *The Woman Suffrage Movement in Canada* (Toronto: University of Toronto Press, 1950) 141-155, and Beverley Baines, "Law, Gender, Equality," in Burt, Code, Dorney, op. cit., 253-258.

8. For information on feminism throughout this period, see Alison Prentice et al., *Canadian Women: A History* (Toronto: Harcourt, Brace, Jovanovich, 1986).

9. See for example, Sara M. Evans, "The Women's Movement in the United States in the 1960s," in Backhouse and Flaherty, op. cit., 61-71.

10. Myrna Adamson, *Long Way From Home: The Story of the Sixties Generation in Canada* (Toronto: James Lorimer and Company, Publishers, 1980).

11. Cerise Morris, "Determination and Thoroughness: The Movement for a Royal Commission on the Status of Women in Canada," *Atlantis,* 5, no. 2 (Spring 1980), 1-21.

12. Monique Begin was secretary and director of research for the Royal Commission on the Status of Women and later was elected to Parliament and served in Pierre Trudeau's cabinet as minister of national revenue and then as minister of national health and welfare.

13. Monique Begin, "The Royal Commission on the Status of Women in Canada: Twenty Years Later," in Backhouse and Flaherty, op. cit., 23.

14. Interview with Monique Begin by Cerise Morris, February 1978, in Morris, op. cit.

15. "Women's March may back call for Rights Probe,", *Globe and Mail,* 6 January 1967, reprinted in document section.

16. Interview with Laura Sabia by Cerise Morris, August 1978, Morris, op. cit.

17. Florence Bird, "Brief notes on the machinery involved in setting up and carrying out the work of the Royal Commission on the Status of Women in Canada," Canadian Women's Movement Archives (CWMA), File: RCSW 1966-70, reprinted in document section.

18. Monique Begin, "The Royal Commission on the Status of Women in Canada: Twenty Years Later," op. cit, 28.

19. Solveig Ryall, "Brief to the Royal Commission on the Status of Women in Canada," March 1968, CWMA, File: RCSW 1966-70.

20. "Pie in the Sky," *The Pedestal* 3, no. 1 (January 1971), 8, reprinted in document section.

21. See, for example, an early 1970s pamphlet from the Ontario Committee on the Status of Women that explains that it was formed "... to press actively for the implementation of the recommendations of the report of the Royal Commission on the Status of Women. The Committee is composed of women from a cross-section of occupations and associations and is affiliated with the National Action Committee on the Status of Women," CWMA.

22. There was a clear relationship between NAC and the earlier groups that worked to institute the Royal Commission. The Committee for Equality of Women in Canada (CEW) later became the Ad Hoc Committee on the Status of Women, after the Commission issued its report in the 1970s. This committee convened the Strategy for Change Convention in Toronto in 1972 and out of this convention NAC was formed.

23. "Click," *Status of Women News,* 2, no. 2 (September 1975), 28. Reprinted in document section.

24. Ann Crocker, "Consciousness Raising: What it is and what it isn't," *Equal Times,* Fredericton, October 1975, reprinted in document section.

25. "Consciousness Raising Meetings — What Goes On," *Northern Woman,* 2, no. 3 (Fall 1975), CWMA.

26. Ibid.

27. For a further discussion of this see Adamson, Briskin and McPhail, op. cit., 208ff.

28. Interview with Mona Forrest by Ruth Pierson, Montreal, 11 March 1991, reproduced in document section.

29. "How to Start a Political Rap Group," *The Other Woman* 2, no. 4, reprinted in document section.

30. Males were usually permitted to attend public events, but this could be contentious. One year some organizers of the International Women's Day March in Toronto attempted to make men march at the end of the parade, but ultimately this did not occur. Some demonstrations, such as Take Back the Night marches, specifically exclude men.

31. Joanne Doucette, "The DisAbled Women's Network: A Fragile Success," in *Women and Social Change: Feminist Activism in Canada,* edited by Jeri Dawn Wine and Janice L. Ristock (Toronto: James Lorimer, 1991), 225.

32. "How We Differ," *The Pedestal,* 2, no. 5 (June 1970), 8-9, reprinted in document section.

33. Shirley Goundry, "A History of the Newfoundland Status of Women Council," Newfoundland Status of Women Council from April 1972-January 1975, reprinted in document section.

34. Sharon Gray Pope and Jane Burnham, "Change Within and Without: The Modern Women's Movement in Newfoundland and Labrador," unpublished paper, ca. 1991.

35. Ibid. Jane Burnham interview with Sally Davis, October 1991.

36. Letter from Val Perkins, Corresponding Secretary of the New Feminists, to Dawn Haites, Women's Liberation Movement, Toronto, January 27, 1971, CWMA, File: The New Feminists, reprinted in document section.

37. For one example of how consensus could be reached see Women's Self-help Network, *Working Collectively* (Campbell River, B.C.: Ptarmigan Press, 1984), reprinted in document section.

38. Jill Vickers, "Bending the Iron Law of Oligarchy: Debates on the Feminization of Organization and Political Process in the English Canadian Women's Movement, 1970-1988," in Wine and Ristock, op. cit., 83.

39. Vancouver Women's Caucus, "On Starting a Women's Liberation Group: some suggestions based on how we did it, ca. 1970, WERC File: Women's Liberation Movement, reproduced in document section.

40. National Association of Women and the Law, "Getting Started: Organizing a Women's Group and Your Responsibilities as a Director," no date. CWMA, File: National Association of Women and the Law, reprinted in document section.

41. See, for example, Joan Holmes and Joan Riggs with assistance from the Collective, "Feminist Organizations Part II: Conflict and Change," *Breaking the Silence* 3, no. 1 (Fall 1984).

42. "How We Differ," *The Pedestal,* op. cit. For an early discussion of how power can be exercised in structureless groups see Jo Freeman, "The Tyranny of Structurelessness," in *Radical Feminism,* ed. by Anne Koedt, et al. (New York: Quadrangle, 1973).

43. "How to Start a Political Rap Group," *The Other Woman,* op. cit. This article is not dated, but it must have been a long time ago because they also had rules that "only one person smokes at a time."!!

44. Doucette, op. cit., excerpt reprinted in document section.

45. For discussions of different perceptions of this crisis of feminist process, see Vickers, "Bending the Iron Law of Oligarchy," and Lorraine Greaves, "Reorganizing the National Action Committee on the Status of Women 1986-1988," in Wine and Ristock, op. cit.

46. For a discussion of the Women's Centre of Montreal's beginnings, see Mona Forrest interview, op. cit.

47. "This Fall at the Women's Centre of Montreal," *Communiqu'ELLES* 15, no. 5 (September 1988), reproduced in document section.

48. "Welcome to The East Prince Women's Centre," Summerside, P.E.I., pamphlet ca. 1987, CWMA File: East Prince Women's Centre, reproduced in document section.

49. "Edmonton Every Woman's Place Society," 1982 flyer, CWMA File: Every Woman's Education Centre, Edmonton.

50. "Loot," 1978 flyer, CWMA File: LOOT General History. *See also* Becki L. Ross, "The House That Jill Built: Reconstructing the Lesbian Organization of Toronto, 1976-1980," Ph.D. thesis, University of Toronto, 1992; revised for publication as *The House that Jill Built: Lesbian Nation in Formation* (Toronto: University of Toronto Press, forthcoming).

51. Adamson, Briskin, and McPhail, op. cit., 12.

52. Noreen Lavoir, "What's in a Name," *Northern Women* 11 (July 1974), reprinted in document section.

53. "Regional Reports: Thunder Bay Anishinabequek," *The Northern Woman* 2, no. 3 (Fall 1975), reprinted in document section.

54. See Perkins letter, op. cit.

55. "Service or Political Action?" *Aspen* 4, no. 4 (Summer 1982), reprinted in document section.

56. "Editorial," *Saskatoon Women's Liberation Newsletter,* April 1974, CWMA, reprinted in document section.

57. Pope and Burnham, op. cit., 37.

58. Barbara Mackenzie, *History of the Native Women's Association of the N.W.T. and Resource Manual* (Yellowknife: NWA/NWT, 1984), 7-8, CWMA File: Native Women's Association of the Northwest Territories, reprinted in document section.

59. See communique from F.J. Walchli, Regional Director General of the B.C. Region of the Department of Indian Affairs, July 20, 1981; and memo from the Union of B.C. Indian Chiefs to the National Indian Brotherhood, July 21, 1981, CWMA File: native women, both reprinted in document section.

60. Lotta Dempsey, "First congress of black women coming in April," *Toronto Star,* (no specific date — probably March 1973), CWMA File: National Congress of Black Women.

61. "Our Possibilities Are Endless," *The Womanist* 1, no. 3 (February/March 1989), 9, reprinted in document section.

62. H.E. Norman and A. Micco, *A History of the Women's Movement in Prince George* (Prince George: Women's Resource Centre, 1985), CWMA File: Prince George Women's Resource Centre.

63. Uncovering women's history was often as important as doing research on present conditions for many groups, particularly for those whose culture and history has been made invisible because of the racism and homophobia of the dominant white culture.

64. Judith Ramirez, "Domestic Workers Organize," *Canadian Woman Studies* 4, no. 2 (Winter 1982), 89-91, excerpts reprinted in document section.

65. "The Adventures of Cora, the Bookmobile," by ellen, typed by judy, revised by boo, Fall 1974, CWMA File: Case study, excerpts reprinted in document section.

66. For a brief analysis of the impact of government policy on farmers since 1984, see Nettie Wiebe, "What happened in agriculture in the last ten years?" *The Womanist* 3, no. 2 (Fall 1992), 15.

67. "Farming No Picnic," *The Manitoba Women's Newspaper* 2, no. 1 (April-May 1981), 7, reprinted in document section.

68. Pope and Burnham, op. cit., 51.

69. Myrt Lenton, "Rural Ramblings," letter to the editor of *The Manitoba Women's Newspaper* 2, no. 1 (April-May 1981), 11, reprinted in document section.

70. Darlene Henderson and Jacie Skelton, "Every act a 'political' act," *The Manitoba Women's Newspaper* 2, no. 1 (April-May 1981), 10.

71. See, for example, Gail C.A. Cook, ed. *Opportunities for Choice: A Goal for Women in Canada* (Ottawa, 1976).

72. For a discussion of the ways in which concepts of equality have been challenged in male-dominated courts by feminist lawyers, see Sherene Razak, *Canadian Feminism and the Law* (Toronto: Second Story, 1991).

73. Vickers, "The Intellectual Origins of the Women's Movement," op. cit., 40.

74. For an example of the kinds of issues discussed with ministers, see Dr. Christina Lee, "Consultation Meeting with the Federal Ministers, Ottawa, June 1-3, 1985," *British Columbia Task Force on Immigrant Women Newsletter* (Summer 1985), reprinted in document section. This consultation was instrumental in the formation of the Action Committee on Immigrant and Visible Minority Women, which evolved into the National Organization of Immigrant and Visible Minority Women of Canada. Information provided by Christina Lee, 30 July 1993.

75. Lorna Marsden, "The Role of the National Action Committee on the Status of Women in Facilitating Equal Pay Policy in Canada," in *Equal Employment Policy for Women: Strategies for Implementation in the United States, Canada, and Western Europe,* edited by Ronnie Steinberg Ratner (Philadelphia 1980)

76. For a discussion of the relationship between feminism and the state, see Sue Findlay, "Feminist Struggles with the Canadian State: 1966-1988," *RFR/DRF* 17, no. 3 (September 1988), 5-9.

77. See, for example, the excerpts from transcripts of a meeting with Pierre Elliot Trudeau during the election campaign of February 1980, reprinted in document section. A more detailed account is available in a piece compiled by the author and Laurell Ritchie, "Trudeau on Women," *The Canadian Forum,* (March 1981).

78. This is in reference to Kim Campbell's remark during a leadership debate where she identified those who were against free trade and deficit reduction as Canada's enemies.

79. For further discussion of this form of lobbying, see the report I wrote as Chair of NAC's Employment and Economy Committee, "Employment Committee Report to the Committee on Organizational Review," (November 7, 1988), NAC archives.
80. See, for example, NAC's 1987 information pamphlet which explains how it differs from the Canadian Advisory Council on the Status of Women and Status of Women Canada, reprinted in document section.
81. Marjorie Cohen, "The Need for Independent Feminism," editorial, *The Canadian Forum* (March 1981), excerpts reprinted in document section.
82. "Canadian Advisory Council on the Status of Women: Contradictions and Conflicts," *RFR/DRF* 17, no. 3 (September 1988), 90, reprinted in document section.
83. For an analysis of state funding in relation to immigrant community groups, see Roxana Ng, *The Politics of Community Services: Immigrant Women, Class and State* (Toronto: Garamond, 1988).
84. "Grant Granted!!!!," *Saskatoon Women's Liberation Newsletter,* November 1974, CWMA, reprinted in document section.
85. See, for example, Cindy Player, "Governmment Funding of Battered Women's Shelters — Feminist Victory or Co-optation?" *Breaking the Silence* 1, no. 5 (Summer 1983), 4, reprinted in document section.
86. Lynn McDonald, "The state of federal funding," *The Womanist* 2, no. 2 (Fall 1990), 37, reprinted in document section.
87. For examples of how this has affected women's centres, see the editorial, *The Northern Women's Journal* 10, no. 1 (August 1986), and Mona Forrest, "The loss of the women's centres," *The Womanist* 2, no. 2 (Fall 1990).
88. Pope and Burnham, op. cit., 55.
89. Cathy Stewart, "Report on the "How to Get Elected" Workshop," *Kinesis* (January 1974), 14.
90. Sylvia B. Bashevkin, *Toeing the Lines: Women and Party Politics in English Canada,* 2nd ed. (Toronto: Oxford, 1993).
91. Lynda Erickson, "Canada," *Gender and Party Politics,* edited by Joni Lovenduski and Pippa Norris (London: Sage, 1993), forthcoming. For an analysis of women in the party system see also Bashevkin, op. cit.
92. "Debate historic benchmark for women," *The Citizen,* (n.d. 1984), CWMA, reprinted in document section.
93. For a discussion of changes in women's representation in the Canadian political system, see Janine Brodie and Celia Chandler, "Women and the Electoral Process in Canada," in *Women in Canadian Politics: Toward Equality in Representation* 6, *Royal Commission on Electoral Reform and Party Financing,* ed. Kathy Megyery (Toronto: Dundurn, 1991).
94. "The Beginnings of the Feminist Party of Canada, *Newsletter* (February-April 1979), and "Feminist Party of Canada — Parti Feminist du Canada Principles," *Newsletter* (March 1980), reprinted in document section.
95. Erickson, op. cit.
96. Rosemary Brown, "Running a Feminist Campaign," *Branching Out* (November 1977), 16-18, excerpts reprinted in document section.
97. Therese Casgrin had been elected leader of the CCF, the forerunner to the NDP.
98. In addition to Kim Campbell, Betty Baxter is running for the NDP and Heddy Fry is running for the Liberal Party.
99. "Bread and Roses," the song that has become the anthem of the women's movement.
100. REAL Women, "Laws Protecting Homosexuals or "Sexual Orientation" Legislation," pamphlet, n.d., CWMA File: REAL Women of Canada.
101. Judy Rebick, "Women leading the way: in the country and in the women's movement," *The Womanist* (Spring 1992), reprinted in document section.
102. Sunera Thobani, "Feminism's new colors (sic)," *Vancouver Sun,* 26 May 1993.

Documents: Chapter 1

The Royal Commission on the Status of Women

"Women's March May Back Call for Rights Probe"
January 1967[1]

Two million Canadian women may be asked to march on Ottawa if the federal Government fails to announce by the end of the month a Royal Commission on Women's Rights.

Mrs. Michael Sabia of St. Catharines, head of the Committee for the Equality of Women said yesterday her organization, representing 2,000,000 women in 33 groups across Canada, has given an ultimatum to the Government: establish a royal commission or face the consequences.

This month, in a meeting scheduled for the University Women's Club in Toronto, the committee will decide what action it will take if the Royal Commission isn't announced by then. Mrs. Sabia said yesterday the committee is likely to suggest to the 33 organizations that they plan marches on Ottawa.

"We're tired of being nice about trying to get an official inquiry into women's rights in Canada," Mrs. Sabia said. "If we don't get a royal commission by the end of this month, we'll use every tactic we can, and if we have to use violence, damn it, we will."

Brief Notes on the Machinery Involved in Setting Up and Carrying Out the Work of the Royal Commission on the Status of Women in Canada
Ottawa, nd[2]

The Royal Commission on the Status of Women in Canada was appointed by the federal government in 1967. It reported in 1970 at which time the work of the commission was over and other continuing organizations and agencies took over the job of implementing the 167 recommendations contained in the report.

7 members: 2 men, 5 women. They were chosen because they were responsible, informed people accustomed to reading research material and making decisions.

They did not represent the government, any political party, or any organization. This was essential in order for them to have an objective point of view.

1. *Globe and Mail* 5 January 1967.
2. Barry Craig, Florence Bird, C.C., Chairman of the Royal Commission on the Status of Women in Canada. Canadian Women's Movement Archives (hereafter CWMA) File: RCSW, 1966-70.

For the chairman it was a full-time job. She was the chief executive responsible for building up and supervising the Secretariat as well as all the other things required of a chairman.

The other six commissioners worked part-time since they all had jobs. Three of them were professors, one was a judge of a Family Court, one was the wife of a rancher and the mother of three children, one was an engineer.

We were paid travelling expenses and a per diem salary by the federal government for the time spent at meetings and for the time that was needed for reading and for the analyzing of documents.

It is a tradition of Royal Commissions that once the commissioners are appointed there is no interference or influence by governments or by anyone else. We decided what needed to be done and we did it.

A Royal Commission has great powers under the Inquiries Act — legislation that has been in the statute books for a long time. We had the right to bring witnesses before us and to be provided with any documents or material we considered relevant to our inquiry.

Our work was confidential. Our conclusions and recommendations could not be made public until the printed report was presented to the Prime Minister ...

The first job of the chairman was to organize a Secretariat of qualified people in a number of disciplines. That was necessary because of the wide scope of our mandate: we had been instructed to inquire, report and make recommendations as to what steps the federal government should take to give women equal opportunities in every aspect of Canadian Society — a monumental undertaking.

That meant that we needed people to conduct research in sociology, criminal law, family law, labour laws and practices, taxation, education, political participation and economics ...

What did we do?

1. Asked for briefs — publicity — speeches — Radio/T.V. folders in supermarkets. Press Releases.
2. Gave people 10 months to prepare. The preparation of briefs had great educational value. It made women study — discuss and think about the things they needed and wanted. It was a consciousness-raising exercise for women.
3. While briefs were being prepared the commissioners studied existing research material so as to avoid duplication of effort.
4. After that we set up a research program.
   a) we commissioned 40 studies which were made for the most part by academics, by university professors, 11 of them published;
   b) Secretariat prepared background papers;
   c) We asked advice of consultants in various disciplines;
   d) Interviews;
   e) Seminars;

f) Statistics from Women's Bureau — Bureau of Statistics, Government departments;

g) 480 briefs studied by commissions and analyzed by Secretariat. Each Commissioner prepared her own questions.

Public Hearings

9 weeks — 14 cities — Every province and Territory of this huge country that stretches 4000 miles from sea to sea. The chairman and one other Commissioner went into the Arctic in order to interview women. We held hearings morning, noon and evening. The atmosphere was informal. The participants sat at the table with us. Participants read digests of their briefs and then answered questions. After the presentations at each session we opened the meetings to the people on the floor so that people who had not written to us could speak to us.

The hearing turned out to be an inspiring example of participatory democracy. We reached the grass roots and heard from women of all kinds who told us what they needed and wanted. We heard from individuals organizations — men and women — women's national and local organizations — unions — provincial governments — churches — lawyers — sole support mothers — poor people — universities — students, practically every level of society.

We were the first Commission to allow TV as well as radio into the conference room. We were well covered by the media. The chairman held a press conference in every city ...

After that came the difficult matter of writing the report and deciding what should go into it. The recommendations were the most difficult part of all. We found we had to agree on specific criteria on which to base them. In fact it was essential to have a philosophy about the sort of society we wanted.

After considerable debate we agreed on the following principles.

–*"Everyone is entitled to the rights and freedoms proclaimed in the universal Declaration of Human Rights"*,

–*"The full use of human resources is in the national interest,"* consequently we recommended continuing education, retraining, etc.

–*"There should be equality of opportunity to share the responsibilities to society as well as its privileges and prerogatives,"* consequently, for example, we recommended that women be held responsible for their husbands and children as men are now held responsible for their wives and children. We were convinced that if women are to have equal opportunities they must regard themselves as adults.

–*"Women should be free to choose whether or not to take employment outside their homes,"* consequently, for example, we recommended that family allowances, paid to the mother, should be substantially increased. Fair employment practises for women's equal pay, equal training, equal opportunities for promotion.

–*"The care of children is a responsibility to be shared by the mother, the father and society,"* we stressed, for example, the psychological importance of the father, the need for Day Care Centres.

–*"Society has a responsibility for women because of pregnancy and child-birth, and special treatment related to maternity will always be necessary,"* consequently, for example, we recommended maternity leave with pay — Day Care Centres — contraception or information.

–*"In certain areas women will for an interim period require special treatment to overcome the adverse effects of discriminatory practices"*, education — training — encouragement ...

"Pie in the Sky"
Vancouver, January 1971[3]

"Paid vacations for housewives!" So the Vancouver Sun announced the release of the report of the $3 million, 3 year old royal commission on the status of women. Many of us read with some surprise the recommendations of the commission: maternity leave with pay, free abortion on demand, a national day-care program, equal job and promotion opportunity, pensions and paid vacations for housewives, guaranteed annual income for all one parent families, an end to sex-typing in the classroom, liberalization of divorce laws, etc., etc ...

For two days the papers gloated over the promised liberation of women. Those of us who have been fighting so hard for many of these very demands could hardly help but be impressed.

And yet an actual reading of the report gives less reason for optimism. It is hardly surprising that the demands in many ways echo our own ... The only surprising thing about the recommendations is that it should have taken three years to document our obvious needs.

In fact, given three years and three million dollars (of tax dollars collected from 2.3 million underpaid working women), the recommendations of the Royal Commission are remarkably short-sighted. While the commissioners were shocked into recognizing that women are oppressed, they failed somehow to understand the root causes of our oppression. For example, they recommend equal job opportunities and lament the ineffectiveness of the existing legislation which is supposed to guarantee women's right to equal pay for equal work. They argue that women should be admitted to the boards of directors of the major corporations, federal boards, task forces, the Senate. It is hard to believe that they can be so naive. When the recommendations of the Commission were made public, the response of business to the recommended provisions for working women was made quite plain by the president of

3. *The Pedestal* 3, no. 1 (January 1971), 8.

the Employers' Council of B.C. He promised that the companies would simply stop hiring women. This is no empty threat, as B.C. women laid off in the forest industry after fighting for equal pay can testify.

The federal government itself has been notoriously lax in its hiring and wage policies vis-a-vis women. The question to be asked is why a government closely inter-linked with business and industry would effect laws which will cut off a cheap pool of labour? Why equal pay? Why equal job opportunity? Big business is concerned about profit, not human equality. As women we are oppressed by the kind of society we live in — an economic system based on the exploitation of many by a few powerful owners and a social system dependent on racial, national and sexual chauvinism. A few token women or even a significant minority of women sitting in corporation board rooms will not and cannot liberate women whose exploitation is the key to profits in quite a few industries.

The discussion of the recommendation for a national day-care program also suffers from a similar misunderstanding of the sources of women's oppression. Most women need to be liberated from their almost total and overwhelming responsibility for the socialization of their children ... The care of children has been a haphazard individualized affair for so long that social responsibility for child care will require a lot of thinking, talking and experimenting. Most public institutions are neither flexible nor democratic.

The media coverage of the Commission's report has given a lot of basic demands a wide hearing. As these demands gain wider and wider support it is important to investigate and make clear those basic changes which will be necessary to make the liberation of women a real possibility. We should not be fooled into thinking we have won any major victory in the mere publication of the recommendations of the Commission. We have already seen how limited even legislative reforms can be with the B.C. Human Rights Act (see "Equal rights", Pedestal, November 1970), the abortion laws and the Ontario Equal Opportunity Act ... Given the usual plight of the recommendations of Royal Commissions, there is reason for a certain cynicism about the likely destiny of this report. Traditionally these studies seem to serve to fire the enthusiasm of groups on the move and to keep them quiescent during the following years when the promised changes are supposed to be imminent. All too often, despite the intentions of the liberals who serve on them, these studies end up as mere political ploys to win votes ...

The liberation of women will take more than a few legislative reforms. Our oppression is basic to the smooth functioning of our society as presently organized. Only an organized and determined women's movement can understand what's necessary and desirable and make it possible. We may gain a few minor improvements in our general condition through the efforts of the Commission, but for the most part it's likely to turn out to be just pie in the sky to assure the ladies that if they'll just be patient they'll all be free by and by.

Various Forms of Organizing: Internal Processes

"Click"
September 1975[4]

Diana Douglas reports the following:

> Scene: Vancouver Small Claims Court, me in witness box after being sworn in by honourable judge.
> Judge: Your name please.
> Me: Diana Douglas
> Judge: Miss or Mrs.?
> Me: Ms.
> Judge: Pardon!
> Me: Ms ... M ... S ...
> Judge: What does that mean?
> Me: It means that I feel that it is not relevant whether I am married or not.
> Judge: Ummm ... you mean you are a nonentity ...

"Consciousness Raising — What It Is and What It Isn't"
Fredericton, N.B., October 1975[5]

... What is consciousness raising? You've probably heard the term and perhaps not been quite sure what it meant. But it definitely conjured up all those old media portrayals of what seemed to be very angry women burning bras, or perhaps some amateur approach to encounter therapy. The truth is, CR is much less shocking in appearance but much more important to your life as a woman than either of these images would indicate.

CR groups or rap groups consist of several women who meet on a regular basis to talk about their feelings and problems as women. These meetings have been referred to as 'bitch sessions', and although they do serve as a release valve for rage and frustration they should also help to provide you with a framework for the analysis and solution of at least some of your difficulties.

Trust and Commitment

Who is in a CR group? First of all, it should be small ... certainly no more than 10, probably ideally about 8 women. The element of trust and confidence is absolutely essential. What is said in CR, is never repeated outside CR. Trust and confidentiality can be acquired. Groups initially

4. *Status of Women News* 2, no. 2, (September 1975), 28.
5. Anne Crocker, *Equal Times* (October 1975).

can be composed of total strangers if you can agree on the basic ground rules of confidentiality and commitment. It goes without saying that men have no place in your CR group. Once a group feels it has established itself, it should not admit new members. More important, all members should attend all meetings as far as is possible in order to maintain continuity and trust ...

Where? Anywhere you can be assured of privacy. Usually in your homes if other members of your family will co-operate by making themselves scarce. A husband or boyfriend hovering between den and kitchen will make the women uncomfortable and mitigate against ease and honesty.

When? Depending on convenience, probably once a week. Perhaps more often in the beginning, perhaps less often as the group becomes really sure of itself. Special raps to help a member going through some crisis are often desirable.

No Leaders

How? There are no leaders. Everyone participates on an equal basis. To get things started, one woman may take the lead by asking a question, or bringing up a particular problem, but no one directs. This demands a great deal of co-operation and sensitivity. There is no one to call the meeting to order if you interrupt a sister. And that is a cardinal rule — never interrupt, except to clarify a point you've missed, and then only rarely ...

After each woman has spoken, uninterrupted, there is room for discussion. But another woman's experiences are never challenged and she is never judged ...

Why CR groups? ... In a CR group you will discover that your fears, anxieties, problems and crises are the legacy of all women — that your experience, as individual as it may be, is simply adding another facet to the total female experience. A CR group provides women with the opportunity of being taken seriously and of offering support to other women. Your joys and sorrows to a certain extent become those of your sisters, while you learn from theirs. In a rap group you will become more aware of the political position of women, the power relationships that control your life, and you learn of practical ways to shift the balance of power ...

Topics for Starters

What do you talk about? Anything and everything that affects you as women. It is probably a good idea to set down various topics and work on them one at a time — giving everyone a chance to speak personally and then opening the floor to discussion. Short autobiographies of each member as women are often good for openers — it's a subject each women knows well and it covers a lot of ground. Some other topics: Who do you live with and how do you like it? This will probably cover everything from sex, privacy, kids and parents to housekeeping hang-ups. What do you usually confide in a woman or a man? Why? Do you feel like a grown-up? How do you feel about sex? What makes you achieve orgasm? How do you feel about lesbians? Who manages the money and why? What was your earliest childhood awareness of being a 'girl'? How do you get along with other women?

Consciousness raising groups are not T-groups or encounter groups or clumsy attempts at home grown group therapy except in the most literal sense that knowing yourself and what makes you who you are can only be healthy. They are women sharing with and helping each other — to become stronger in and of themselves. You can start one in your college dorm, in your basement rec room or in the church hall, if you've a mind to. All you need is several women who want to discover what is means to be a woman and to grow as people by growing as women. Women must be important to themselves.

Mona Forrest Interview
Montreal, March 1991[6]

Q: Please say something about the beginnings and the development of the women's centre.

A: It started in 1973. Actually, we'd been a group of women from the downtown area who had been working on this in 1972, ... and we had been working together on a feminist section of the local community paper. It has since gone defunct, but there were a lot of them at that time which were called underground papers. A lot of draft-dodgers were working on them. And women who were in a consciousness-raising group at the time, myself included, got kind of fed up that this underground paper wasn't reflecting any-thing at all about what women's realities were and what was going on in terms of the women's movement ...

As usual, many consciousness-raising groups at the time were split up into two parts: people who wanted to go into action, and there were people who preferred to stay in the group and keep on discussing the things that we were discussing. So the "actionists" took off, and we planned and executed a very fine raid on the newspaper offices one night. We went over there all set, you know, to make some demands that we get some space in the paper, that we have autonomy to write our own stuff. They were getting advertisers that we felt were putting themselves in there because they were looking for female clients, whether it was hairdressers or whatever else. And we felt that the advertising revenue from that should at least support a page of something that would give us what we were looking for and we assumed other women were looking for. When we got there, we stormed in and there was this one guy all by himself who was very happy to see anybody who

6. Mona Forrest, Interview by Ruth Roach Pierson, March 11, 1991.

wants to come in the door and help him by contributing enormous free labour in putting out this newspaper ... . We ended up with eight pages with editorial autonomy right in the middle of the paper. Like an insert, called *Feminist Communication Collective*, that we edited and wrote and took photos for and put together ourselves. And, in fact, we were the most cohesive gang on this paper, and we ended up helping put out the rest of it. All of us — or many of us were working day jobs besides and spending every night of the week and weekends at the *Logos* offices — which was the name of the paper, it was called *Logos* ...

Q: This was in 1972, and you were still associated with this other publication, with *Logos*?

A: All we were was a group who were putting out women's feminist stuff in *Logos*. That's all we were ... We thought that if we put out only a women's newspaper, we would have more revenue, we would have staff to take care of phone answering and stuff, we would get the money for it ourselves — nobody was making a fortune off this, but any revenue from ads went to keep paying for putting out *Logos*. As I said, nobody was making money on it, but we thought that we could make money on a women's paper and have more ways of coping with a deluge of requests for information we were having ... So we planned four or five community meetings downtown, in what was called the St. Louis Telegraph ... What we thought we wanted to find out was what needs for information women had, and what they would want out of a woman's paper. What came out of the meetings is that's not what they wanted at all; they wanted a place where they could go and find out — from somebody they could trust and rely on — what they needed to know to take charge of their own problems. That's what we found out.

So we dropped the idea of the paper and we started working, developing a project to open a women's information referral centre. At the same time, when we were going around to find out what grants were available. That was the time of the PIL in French — LIP groups, Local Initiative Projects ... we were sitting in some government office trying to find out some things and the woman asked us what we were doing. We said we were gathering information, we're putting out this piece in the newspaper. We told her all our problems that we were having, so many calls for information we didn't know what we were going to do. She said, "well what you need is a *grant*". So this woman explained this grant form and gave us a grant form; ... We used the grant form to apply for a place and we went to see our member of parliament who supported us from day one ...

Anyway, we applied for a grant, we got a grant, and we opened the doors of the Women's Information Referral Centre at the end of January 1973. So that's how it started, but the irony of it all is that in the end, after a couple of years [in an empty building in downtown Montréal], I don't think it was more than two or three years later, Jackie Menthorn, who was a volunteer at the women's centre said, "what we need is a newsletter". So what happened is we started a newsletter which grew so big it became the magazine which is *Communiqu'elles*, right now, which became also a publishing house and publishes books, and became an autonomous organization that is fulfilling that need that always was there anyway. So we ended up being a publishing house anyhow in the end. So that's the story ...

"How To Start a Political Rap Group"
Toronto, nd[7]

Feminists are talking about the need for a more detailed analysis of women and more positive strategies. The women's movement has grown in numbers but not correspondingly in power, as we tend to be isolated in small service-oriented collectives. Small groups were emphasized originally to avoid repressive bureaucratic structures and are valuable to a broad-based movement; however, we have not used them to understand the political implications of our practice. We are still setting up in contradiction the personal and the political, concentrating our energies on a personal level rather than integrating the two.

As a response to this problem, many women are setting up groups designed to discuss the political theory of feminism and to develop a more comprehensive analysis of women in Canada. And other women are trying to deal with these things in their working collectives. We feel that both these routes are important, and they must happen simultaneously.

How then can a political study group be formed? This paper is written from the experience of one such group, and taking into consideration that of others we know about.

We started with twelve women who knew each other through common work and friendship, from a variety of backgrounds and political realms. The thing we have in common is that we want to build an independent women's movement, and accept that feminism and socialism are not in contradiction. This group thus has to exclude women who have allegiance to male-dominated political groups committed, on principle, to destroying such a movement.

When we first met, we set rules that we felt would be necessary for the group to survive. We were strict about attendance and meeting times, as we felt we would otherwise treat this group as we did others — coming late to meetings, missing meetings without notice or good reason (we are tired a lot). We chose to meet once a week in the informal space of each others' homes. We also ruled that no one could speak more than

7. *The Other Woman* 2, no. 4, nd.

twice until everyone had spoken. This way we felt that those who speak a lot would talk less, those who are reluctant to speak would be forced to present opinions. In fact, this was one of our biggest problems, and we began to understand how women who are confident to speak are often put down for taking power, while women who don't speak are in fact exercising power by not risking their opinions for group discussion and letting others take leadership roles for them. This problem is still not resolved.

After a few weeks, we decided to close the group to newcomers so that we would not be disrupted by having to explain every week what had happened and so that we could build some confidence with each other. We encouraged women who wanted to join us to start their own groups and took it upon ourselves to do the phoning etc. necessary for forming a second group. Since then two other groups have started.

At first the discussions were very unfocussed. Eventually we set up a program where each woman would present a completed paper or set of ideas on a subject for group discussion. The group would read papers or books she recommended as a background for this discussion ...

We discovered that we actually had little idea of each other's background, and were making assumptions that were not necessarily true. We started having one woman give her life history each week, then bi-weekly as these were often several hours long and nothing else could be discussed. We feel that this is an invaluable part of such a group, to give some idea of what we could expect from each other, what each of us could contribute, and to break down distrust.

Some other rules that were agreed upon were: only one person smokes at a time, every part of our lives and political practice is to be open to discussion and criticism, meetings have a fairly specific ending time. People leaving the group discuss their reasons with us. Four women have left since we started, all because they felt too overworked and had other things to do with their time that they considered of higher priority.

Topics were raised by members of the group with a personal interest in dealing with these problems. We have discussed The Women's Movement in Toronto, Anti-Feminism, Music and Revolutionary Culture, Liberalism, Spiritualism, Our Work Situations, Criticism and Self-Criticism, all with varying success. ...

Suggestions To Anyone Wanting to Start a Group

1. Start with women you already know and trust at some level.
2. Start with women who are committed to a women's movement and are not part of an organized male left group.
3. Try to organize one within your own working collective.
4. Be tough on each other at the beginning—impose some sort of discipline around attendance, ongoing commitment, etc.

5. Deal with structural problems as soon as they arise. Deal with them politically.
6. Try to keep written copies of presentations, etc.
7. Be flexible enough to change the rules as necessary.
8. Avoid parliamentary procedure — it's dynamite. Invent your own rules!
9. Let other women know what you're doing and help other groups get started.

"How We Differ"
Vancouver, June 1970[8]

The Abortion Caravan was the first nation-wide action taken by Women's Liberation groups in Canada and marked a great step forward in the development of our struggle for human dignity. For those women directly involved, it was an action that was at once physically gruelling, emotionally exhausting, and politically educational. It is difficult to describe the enormous inspiration which sprung out of almost every one of the public meetings and rallies held across the country — the strength which came from the knowledge that so many Canadian women, from all sorts of backgrounds, identified with that action and with the women's liberation movement as a whole.

This is the context in which we must examine the problems which we in the Caravan faced as a group — problems which centred mainly around decision-making within the group, and political differences over how to build a mass movement. In many ways, it was inevitable that these political differences came up in the caravan, as they are questions facing a number of women's liberation groups across the country, including Vancouver Women's Caucus. Also, it is not surprising that we did not settle our differences within the two-week period of the caravan. We can, however, critically examine these questions now and hopefully learn in the process ...

In any political group, there will inevitably be some form of leadership, and some method by which decisions are made. Within the caravan, we attempted to create a collective leadership, that is, to draw everyone into the decision-making process and to get direction for our actions from the group as a whole. Our attempts, however, did fail to some extent. Some people expressed frustration when decisions which were thought to have been made were not carried out, or when actions were taken then without the group's consent. The 'To Vote or Not to Vote' debate often came up, but throughout almost the entire period, we took no votes, and worked strictly on a consensus basis. In other words, we talked issues through until people seemed to agree. This method of decision-making has a dynamic of its own: often there would be varying opinions the next day as to just what the 'consensus' had been; sometimes people would stop raising opposition simply because they were

8. Mary Trew, *The Pedestal* 2, no. 5 (June 1970), 1, 8-9.

too tired to continue; the most articulate, forceful women tended to do most of the talking and thus dominate the decision-making; and finally, silence was taken to be support for, or understanding of, the 'consensus'. All these factors add up to a thoroughly unhealthy decision-making process — one which, in such a large group, is extremely undemocratic and unable to meet the task of providing a basis for discussion that is rounded and conclusive, so that everyone in the group knows what the decision is, why it is the best decision, and how it is to be carried out. Only through this kind of full discussion, can we arm and educate ourselves, and particularly new women, to explain and defend the policies of women's liberation. A simple vote at the end would give every woman, whether or not she had contributed to the discussion, an equal voice in the final decision, and a chance to take a political stand.

These organizational problems are important, and we should continually fight to establish democracy within our ranks, but they *are* questions which tend to flow from political differences, and within the caravan, differences over how to build a mass movement for women's liberation.

To take this up we must go into the question of excluding [some] women from the movement. This operates, seemingly, on two levels. The first consists of excluding women from the group, or from actions the group carries. An example of this occurred in Toronto during the caravan. There, a broad steering committee had been set up with a number of groups participating — The Women's Liberation Movement, the New Feminists, the NDP Women's Caucus and the Young Socialists. The latter three groups were, in effect, excluded from decision-making meetings by the Toronto Women's Liberation group with the acquiescence of some of the women on the caravan. The caravan as a whole was never consulted about that decision; it was never fully debated. Some women on the caravan did, in fact, oppose the exclusion — but it was not dealt with and when raised, those who supported it treated even the limited discussion as a diversion from the task of organizing for Ottawa.

We should see this not as a diversion, but as a very important question which could well have undermined our numbers, and therefore, our effectiveness in Ottawa. Had these three groups as a result withdrawn from the abortion action, we would have mobilized considerably fewer women, drawn fewer into the struggle that was destined to radicalize every woman involved.

Those who supported the exclusion put forth the argument that including groups with which the leadership of the WLM has 'political disagreements' will somehow dilute or weaken our actions. These differences have to be demystified and spelled out more clearly. Why are we excluding anyone who is willing to fight for free abortions on demand? We've got a lot against us — a whole organized state as a matter of fact, and a lot of people who believe in anything that state peddles, including the abortion laws as they now exist. We want to mobilize every woman, every group of women, who opposes the abortion law, who wants to see it repealed. Only in this way can we have the kind of impact that we need. And what an opportunity to have large numbers of women in direct contact with women's liberation — we can move out and bring them directly into the movement.

We should ask ourselves who will enter this movement if only so-called Marxists are included? Certainly not the majority of Canadian working women, and probably not even a small segment of them. How strong will our movement be if only revolutionaries are included? Perhaps only a small number from the universities. This is not the way to mobilize the women of Canada for women's liberation ...

We should now turn to the second type of exclusion, the more prevalent type, which amounts to exclusion within the group — that is, the attempt to exclude women who weren't 'pure' in their politics from in fact playing any kind of leadership role, to exclude them from major decision-making, to isolate them from the group by a sort of witch-hunting in reverse ... This sort of action will only alienate women, and unless they are remarkably strong, drive them from a movement that is as much theirs as anyone's.

We can't dupe women — we can't say they are part of the group and then turn around and exclude them whenever they think or say something which the present leadership doesn't endorse. These women *are* the movement for women's liberation! If they are not following the present leadership now offered, then let's assess that leadership. We can't contain the movement, purify it, keep it under our hats, within our own halls. It's bigger than that, more powerful, more angry. Let's really join with these women, go out to all of them, prove, test our leadership in action, in motion ...

A democratic, effective movement knows how to make its mistakes valuable as well as its victories — we have a chance now to draw on both types of experiences from the caravan. Only by seriously discussing where we succeeded and where we failed, can we learn those essential lessons, so we may then move forward with the effectiveness and strength we need.

Women's Centre
Newfoundland, 1972–1975[9]

... The Interim Committee was from the beginning interested in having a centre where any woman in the community would be welcome, where they could be involved in the women's movement without feeling they had to join an organization and be involved with meetings, fund raising, and all the other necessary things in order to function as an organization. Talks with Bonnie Kreps helped to firm these plans considerably and

9. Shirley Goundry, "A History of the Newfoundland Status of Women Council from April 1972-January 1975" (St. John's, Newfoundland: np, 1975). Document in personal possession of Ruth Roach Pierson.

during the summer of 1972 members of NSWC met with several women who had participated in consciousness raising groups who were also planning to set up a women's centre. Out of this, a committee was formed to submit an application for funding. The Secretary of State's office granted $3,000 which was received in February 1973. The NSWC turned this money over to a women's collective to administer the Centre autonomously. In March THE WOMAN'S PLACE opened at 203 Water Street. NSWC kept their records there, held their meetings, helped to staff and thus became part of the collective which operated the centre. At this time the collective and NSWC published a joint newsletter. There was considerable co-operation on events such as the local feminist symposium and the celebration of International Women's Day (IWD) and each group of women supported each other in many ways. There was a difference in philosophy and I can only describe this difference as I saw it. The NSWC accepted the responsibility to try to speed up the implementation of the recommendations of the RCSW but also generally to improve the status of women. This was done deliberately because the women involved at that time did not want to become totally involved in legislation, but wanted to remain conscious of the fact that to change attitudes and to analyze ways to achieve goals was equally important if women's relative status was to change. It was believed that as this male-dominated society had been in existence for at least two thousand years, it was not going to change through legislative reform only. A social revolution is what the women's movement is and that means individual women determining their society. However, the NSWC found it necessary to have some sort of structure with designated women responsible for certain specific actions, on a continuing basis and on an ad hoc basis. The collective worked on a consensus basis and seemed to emphasize working with individual women through CR groups and generally appeared to be more radical. Briefly, I would say they saw the present society as oppressing women and they wanted women to get themselves out from under this oppression rather than to try to remove the oppressive elements in society. In December 1973, it was necessary for the collective to vacate 203 Water Street because of construction in the area and at that time NSWC re-assessed its position and each group decided they would be freer to operate in their own particular way in separate centres. NSWC was interested to note that Jane Taylor of the Secretary of State's office who visited all women's centres across Canada stressed the need for such centres, and noted that many groups had split into two or more groups and thought this was an indication of strength in the movement as a whole and was good. I personally know that the association with the women's collective group was interesting and inspiring, perhaps because of the individual women involved or perhaps because of their experimentation with a different method of operation.

Letter from Val Perkins, Corresponding Secretary, New Feminists, to Dawn Haites, Women's Liberation Movement Toronto, January 1971[10]

Dear Sister:

In your recent letter you requested information about the New Feminist organization for your study of the history of the feminist movement in Canada. You were enquiring about how, why, when and where we got started, how we are organized and what we are currently doing.

Some of your members will recall that the New Feminists organization was started by a few women in the Toronto Women's Liberation Movement who decided to break away and form their own group because of a difference in their way of thinking. The philosophy of the Women's Liberation Movement was basically Marxist (until society changes women can't change — ie. a revolution is necessary). The splinter group who formed the New Feminists were feminists essentially, rather than being primarily concerned with politics. In short, Women's Liberation said the revolution came first: New Feminists said feminism came first. We believe that the attitude of society that women are inferior to men is basic, that as long as women are considered inferior we will never really make it, no matter what kind of political system the country may have.

The first meeting of the New Feminists was held early in April, 1969, and there were about seven people present. For the first few months we were busy organizing and we met in various people's homes. We have tried to avoid having leaders or a highly structured organization: just what was necessary to carry on, with the minimum of red tape ... Currently, we have a very flexible type of operation, with new members forming cells, or older members returning to cells again if they feel the need to do so. People interested in a particular project may contact other members and work along with them on whatever it is they want to do.

About the end of May 1970 a group broke away from the New Feminists and formed the Toronto Women's Caucus. Our main difference here was that the New Feminists wanted to remain fairly small, working in cells, with a small core group. Although we were interested in doing some 'actions' we felt some analysis was still necessary, especially for new members. The splinter group was interested in a mass-movement, action-oriented type of organization.

The New Feminists had just barely started to organize their own group when they decided to do their very first 'action' on May 1, 1969, in front of the Maclean-Hunter Building, to protest the *cover* story in Canada's National Magazine about the book by Lionel Tiger. This article was entitled "The Natural Inferiority of Women" and was really bad ...

Since the first demonstration we have done many things on our own or in cooperation with other organizations. These things include: appear-

10. Val Perkins, Corresponding Secretary, New Feminists, letter, Toronto, 27 January 1971. CWMA File: The New Feminists.

ances on many TV and radio programs, especially TV — a demonstration at noon Nov. 27, 1969, at City Hall on behalf of an Equal Pay program in support of the nursing aides at Greenacres Home for the Aged — Demonstrations at beauty contests — participation in the Abortion Cavalcade that went to Ottawa in May 1970 — cooperation in preparing the brief presented to Premier Robarts to have the word 'sex' included in the Ontario Human Rights Code. Currently a few of our members have had some success in trying to break the custom of 'men only' at the noon luncheon in two of Toronto's better known hotels. Various members of New Feminists have also actively supported day-care centre proposals. There are probably some things that I have missed, but these are the things that come to my mind at the moment.

.... .

Yours sincerely
Val Perkins
Corresponding Secretary

Collective Decisions
North Vancouver Island, 1984[11]

Why Operate Collectively?
Working collectively is difficult for people used to managing in a hierarchical individualistic society. Those of us working collectively do so because we are looking for respectful and kind ways of working together. Learning co-operation and sharing is difficult when our experience is individualistic and competitive.

Collectivity offers us more control over our lives, helps us learn to respect others' ideas and contributions and allows us to share tasks, rewards and mistakes. It's a joyous and trying process that will be improved and refined as we learn more about collectivity.

After electing to work collectively there are some decisions to be made regarding how you will operate.

Structure for Making Decisions
How is the collective going to make decisions?
Most collectives use consensus as the structure for making decisions.

Consensus requires that all members participate equally in the reaching of a decision.

Procedure for Consensus Decision Making
The issue is presented by either the facilitator or a group member.

11. Women's Self-help Network, *Working Collectively* (Campbell River, BC: Ptarmigan Press, 1984), 2-5.

The members connected with the issue explain it and begin discussion.

Agreement may be reached at this point and a decision made. If, however, there are differing viewpoints, consensus is not reached.

A round may then be initiated.

In a round each person comments on the issue.

A round is not interrupted.

Each member has her say without others commenting on it. Questions are asked only for clarification (if something wasn't understood or clear).

A round may be timed. Each member receives equal time (2 or 5 minutes). Equalizing time helps to equalize participation.

When the round ends the facilitator summarizes what was said and clarifies the current status of the issue.

Another round may be needed if consensus is not reached. On the other hand, individual differences may have merged after hearing other group members' viewpoints. The facilitator may then ask if there is agreement on the issue. If the total group is in agreement the decision is recorded.

A decision is reached when all agree.

Starting a Women's Liberation Group
Vancouver, ca. 1970[12]

In the past few months women from various parts of North America have been writing to us, asking how to set up a Women's Liberation group in their area. Although we are always glad to get these requests since they show how rapidly our movement is growing, specific advice is difficult to give because our situations are often extremely different from one another. What we are trying to do in this paper however, is to tell you what we did, and to draw some broad generalizations which we hope will be useful to newly forming women's liberation groups.

A group of women beginning to become conscious of their oppression will want to talk about it, and this perhaps is how most groups begin. This group of women doesn't have to be very large; even 3 or 4 women might want to get together to talk about women's liberation — why you are interested in the topic, what you think of women's liberation groups that exist, how you could involve more women in your group. You might also want to read and discuss specific articles or ideas in various women's liberation journals or newspapers.

But talking of course isn't enough to build a strong women's liberation group. Action is important too. It helps to get people familiar with our ideas, and begins to challenge the system that has kept us down for so long. A group undertaking a particular action — such as picketing, presenting briefs to public committees etc. — should agree on the gen-

12. Vancouver Women's Caucus, "On Starting a Women's Liberation Group: some suggestions based on how we did it," ca. 1970. Women's Education Resources Centre (hereafter WERC) file: Women's Liberation Movement.

eral aims of this action (what you want to achieve, who you want to reach), but it is probably unrealistic to expect that you will agree on everything. A group however shouldn't feel that it must work out a constitution or a detailed program of aims before it can carry out any actions since we have found that through actions we are continually learning new things, and revising old ideas, and for this reason wouldn't want to bind ourselves to an old analysis before we begin.

In the formative period of Women's Caucus in Vancouver, we undertook a variety of actions and projects which were generally directed toward getting publicity and letting the public know what we thought about various issues. These kinds of actions also gave us practical experience in writing and speaking which many of us never had before. One example of this kind of action was entering a protest candidate into a beauty contest. Also, around the issue of abortion we held demonstrations, confronted the prime minister when he was in town, and organized a "caravan" to Ottawa. In Edmonton, Women's Liberation picketed the city newspaper for classifying help-wanted ads according to sex. Many groups hold widely advertised classes on women's liberation. These, of course, are only some of the possibilities for good actions to help get the group off the ground ...

As the group grows larger it may want to subdivide into various "workshops" according to specific interests members of the group may have, such as daycare, abortion, theatre, etc. Or the group can also subdivide according to work situations — eg. working women, high-school and/or university students, women on welfare, housewives, etc. We found that subdividing into workshops allowed individual women to concentrate on the aspect of women's liberation that most concerned or interested them, and that this system allowed more women to participate in discussion and decision-making. This system does not diffuse the group's strength since the group as a whole can decide what its priorities will be in the coming period ...

We feel it is very important that as women's liberationists we continually criticize and evaluate our own actions and that we discuss and clarify short and long term goals — what these goals are and how we can achieve them. We must work towards developing an analysis of society and how we as women, and we as part of the women's liberation movement, fit into this analysis. There are all kinds of political and not so political groups around that are eager to foist their ready-made analysis upon us, but we have to beware of swallowing these answers whole. In our society we are led to believe that there is Some One with all the answers. But of course that is not true. It's those answers that we as women are in the process of working out together and it must in part arise from an honest evaluation of our own political experiences and our own life experiences ...

Getting Started: Organizing a Women's Group and Your Responsibilities as a Director
Ottawa, 1986[13]

How to Organize

1   First, you should draw up a constitution, or governing document. Consider what the purpose of your organization is, and how you wish to provide for the day-to-day operation of the group if that is necessary. Make provision for the internal workings of the group, how executive members will be elected, how often meetings will be held and how the decision-making process will be carried out.

2   Call a meeting. To attract supporters, you could advertise throughout your community with flyers, place notices in community centres and other women's centres or groups, or call your local radio station and inquire about free public announcements. Word of mouth can also be successful.

3   At the first meeting have a copy of the constitution for all present. You may wish to appoint a Chairperson to conduct the initial meeting. You will also need someone to take complete and legible minutes of the discussions that take place, including the date, time and place of the meeting and the names, addresses and telephone numbers of all who attend.

4   While you may not wish to be too formal, it will be helpful to review Roberts' *Rules of Order* or Bourinot's *Rules of Order*. They provide simple guidelines for conducting a meeting. Most meetings will run smoothly if all members are considerate of the others present. If the group is a large one, a list of meeting procedures covering issues like time limits for individual discussions on a topic or how to introduce an item for debate may be helpful.

5   After the meeting is called to order, the constitution should be discussed. All proposed changes should be noted and voted on. The results of the vote should be recorded. When there are no more changes to discuss, the constitution as a whole should be adopted by a vote of all those present.

6   Executive members should then be elected according to the procedure set out in the constitution. At the very least you will need a chairperson and a secretary/treasurer. You may wish to expand your executive committee to include a vice-chairperson and individuals in charge of "special issues" like fundraising or social gatherings if your group is a large one.

---

13. National Association of Women and the Law, Pamphlet, Ottawa, 1986. CWMA file: National Association of Women and the Law.

7   Depending on the nature of your group, you may wish to consider
      incorporation.
8   Now you're ready to go ahead and discuss the policies and activi-
      ties in which your organization is going to engage ...

Directors Have Responsibilities

Executive committee members or "directors" of non-profit organizations
have a responsibility to their members and to the public at large. They
have an obligation (duty) to conduct the activities of the group in accordance with the law. They must also accept the blame if things are not
done in accordance with the law. In other words, they are liable for
damages suffered by other individuals, or for losses sustained by the
organization if it is not incorporated.

When someone accepts the position of a director or executive committee member, she commits herself to acting in good faith, and in the
best interests of the organization. She must take care to avoid any
conflicts of interest which may arise between her personal activities and
those goals or objects of the organization. She cannot act for personal
gain or profit in her capacity as a director, but must always act on behalf
of the organization itself.

A director is responsible to see that the internal operation of the
organization runs smoothly. This would include bookkeeping and controlling the finances of the organization; taking and distributing minutes
or meetings to other members; setting the agenda and organizing meetings; ensuring that the goals (policies) are being met through the organization's activities; maintaining effective communication with other
directors and members of the organization; notices to members of meetings, resolutions or special activities.

Directors' Liabilities

In addition to the responsibilities that a director owes to her organization,
she is also exposed to liabilities. She may be held personally responsible
for damages or losses to the organization, or others, if the organization
is not incorporated.

A director is not, however, responsible for mere errors of judgment.
In the absence of fraud, negligence or acting for personal gain in a
conflict of interest situation, a director will not be held personally liable.
The director is held to a standard of loyalty and good faith in her dealings
with, and on behalf of, the organization.

In order to avoid personal liability, a director should fully and frankly
discuss problems and issues with other directors and members and,
where possible, seek approval and ratification of actions or expenditures
prior to undertaking them.

"The DisAbled Women's Network: A Fragile Success" Toronto, 1991[14]

Implementing the Goals

Feminist Structure and Process

Originally DAWN was to operate as a collective. Rather than a hierarchical organization with formal positions, DAWN was envisioned as a network of equals. In order to function, however, networks require constant communication among members. Communication after the Ottawa meeting soon broke down. In retrospect, an observation from that founding meeting appears ominous: "It is remarkable that often networks fail because members neglect the most basic, elementary factor in the life of a network: feeding information into the system" (Pelletier 1985, 39).

Meanwhile, several local groups discovered that the collective approach did not work for them. At DAWN Toronto and DAWN Montréal, for example, one or two women found themselves doing all of the work of the organization without formal recognition and often in isolation. Members expected a lot, but the degree of personal involvement was low in many groups. This led to frustration and burnout among those active.

It also led to a phenomenon known as "the tyranny of structurelessness" (Freeman 1973). Freeman argues that there is no such thing as a structureless group working for social change. All such groups have leaders, even when leaders are not formally recognized. She argues that hidden leadership is more manipulative and less democratic than formal, visible leadership. She urges groups to adopt formal structures to make leaders accountable, and she called for the distribution of authority.

During DAWN's first year, however, there was effectively no formal leadership. Instead, power was concentrated in the hands of those who did the most work, and those workers were acutely uncomfortable with both the workload and the power. The situation was in opposition to the original intent of empowering other disabled women and sharing responsibilities. DAWN Toronto addressed the problem by electing a board of directors in the fall, 1986, and adopting a constitution and by-laws. DAWN Montréal did the same. DAWN BC and DAWN Ontario bypassed the problem by holding elections at their initial meetings. At the second national meeting in Winnipeg, DAWN Canada, the national network, elected a board of directors.

Coming Together

Meetings are obviously necessary to address both organizational issues, formulate goals, boost morale, etc. Whether at the local level (in monthly

14. Joanne Doucette, in *Women and Social Change: Feminist Activism in Canada*, eds. Jeri Dawn Wine and Janice L. Ristock (Toronto: James Lorimer, 1991), 226-227.

meetings) or at the provincial and national levels (in semi-annual or annual meetings), meetings are essential. More than anything else, they foster a sense of group pride and identity. They are fundamental for consciousness-raising and empowerment. As remarked after the 1986 DAWN BC conference: "The conference was very powerful. It was the first time that disabled women had a chance to talk with other women about ... intimate topics ... Several of the women who participated spoke of the importance of having their experiences and feelings validated."(Pollock & Meister 1986)

Another wrote after the 1987 DAWN BC conference:
"What happens to a disabled woman attending her first conference of DAWN ... ? For me, it was culture shock. Instead of being the only special needs person in my household and immediate neighbourhood, I was just one of many. That at first was scary, but within hours it became liberating as I began to feel the bonds of unity and the stocks of shared interest. Now I am a part rather than apart." (Brooks 1987, 4)

Meetings and the ability to meet are often taken for granted, yet meetings are significant achievements to be celebrated. Socially, physically and economically isolated, disabled women have to work hard just to meet. They must consider the logistics of transportation, attendant care, sign language interpretation and other special needs, as well as services such as child care. In a large, sparsely populated country, with a harsh and extreme climate, transportation and communications are particularly expensive and difficult ...

Defining and Meeting Needs

"This Fall at the Women's Centre of Montréal"
September 1988[15]
The Women's Centre of Montréal, now in its 15th successful year, is a unique multi-service centre.

Services
— Information, referral, emergency services, legal information service, counselling; (514) 842-4780, 842-4781
  — Services for Immigrant Women and Their Families: 842-0814
  — Option'Elle (vocational counselling service): 842-6652
  — Volunteer Service: 842-4780, 842-4781

Courses & Workshops
Tea and Tai Chi: Tai chi is a Chinese martial arts technique based on a series of slow, continuous movements. After class, enjoy a cup of aromatic Chinese tea. Shower facilities available. $45/15 classes.

15. *Communiqu'ELLES* 15, no. 5. September 1988.

Women and Health: Re-evaluate your diet, exercise and life-style. Explore the medicalization of women's health issues. $40/15 hours.
Women and Aging: The "golden years" ... or are they? $40/15 hours.
Savings and Investments: Manage your budget. Information on life insurance, wills, RRSPs investing, income tax, more! $40/15 hours ...
Assertiveness Training: $40/15 hours ...
French as a Second Language: 90 hours. Given in two 3-hour weekly sessions. $30 ($5/landed immigrants, those with refugee status, women with low incomes).

Professional Courses
Fund Raising for Women's Centres, with Mona Forrest. Identify your needs, appropriate sources of funding, how to approach potential funders, etc. Limited of 10 participants. $100/8 hours ...

Services for Immigrant Women and their Families
Workshops
Orientation Sessions for newly arrived immigrants: Practical, legal, social, health, community and immigration information.
Budgeting: Consultations, consumer protection information courses. By appointment.
Clay Modelling: Make vases, ashtrays, etc ...
Employment Orientation: Job search techniques and resources. Day and time to be announced.

Information Sessions
Tenants' Rights and Information
Domestic Workers' Rights
Immigration Laws and Problems
Day Care
How to Attain Canadian Citizenship: Preparatory course.

Activities
Montréal Tours: A fun way to learn about Québec culture. *Open House at the Women's Centre of Montréal*: Cultural theme days ...

Meetings
Oasis: The place for immigrant and Québec women to meet, exchange ideas, see films, play cards, etc.
Conversational Spanish: For those with a basic knowledge of Spanish who wish to improve their skills.

Clinics
Income Tax: Held annually for immigrant women on welfare or unemployment insurance, those on low incomes and seniors ...

Welcome to The East Prince Women's Centre
Summerside, PEI, ca 1987[16]

The East Prince Women's Information Centre was set up in 1984 by a group of Summerside women. It is the only women's organization in the East Prince area whose main purpose is to support change in the status of women and encourage women's full and equal participation in the economic, social, political, and legal spheres of daily life of the community.

The achievement of this goal is approached through the following objectives:

1   By providing a meeting place and drop-in centre for all women at our space at 240 Water Street.
2   By serving as an information and referral source to community resources.
3   By supporting women whose lifestyles are changing because of relocations, return to work, change in marital status.
4   By offering volunteer opportunities in new areas in order for women to develop work skills, fulfil personal goals, and meet other like-minded women.
5   By contacting elected representatives to inform them of changing needs and concerns of women ...

Aside from its informal atmosphere and convenient location, the centre offers women an impressive selection of books, periodicals and brochures about a multitude of issues — mental health, reproductive health, parenting, legal and financial matters to name a few. All materials may be borrowed and there is always someone available to recommend additional sources of information or advice ...

People often ask what we do at the centre. It is such a difficult question to answer because everyday is so different. Individual women's needs determine our direction and daily activities. Most enquiries and problems stem from discrimination against women in the larger sense. A lack of money and/or knowledge means limited access to society's services. For instance, you can have all kinds of legislation designed to protect women and ensure their equality, but without information about those laws and without the money for legal help, most women are denied the benefits. Because of this recurring theme, *we held numerous public sessions on legal topics* in the fall of '85. Unfortunately, just as we were becoming a little confident, a new federal divorce law came into effect in Sept. 86. So we organized another lecture series on separation, divorce and custody.

16. Summerside, PEI, pamphlet ca 1987. CWMA File: East Prince Edward Island Women's Centre.

Edmonton Every Woman's Place Society
Edmonton, 1982[17]

Edmonton has been without a women's centre since 1975. A women's centre had been established in Edmonton in the early seventies, but funding and staffing problems caused it to close. The need for a centre has continued and Edmonton Every Woman's Place Society was formed in June of 1981 to meet this need.

The purpose of the women's centre is to provide a friendly and comfortable space for women to meet and exchange information. All women in Edmonton are welcome to come alone or with their children. Part of the function of the centre is to provide a meeting space for women who are isolated in their homes or who are lonely and wish to meet other women.

The centre also has available both office and meeting space for women's organizations. We facilitate a number of educational and recreational events such as workshops, lectures, films and socials ... We also encourage professionals and those receiving professional training to offer their services to women either free of charge or at reduced prices.

A library of resource materials on issues of interest to women is being established. Presently we have over 300 books, subscriptions to a dozen or so magazines, and numerous brochures and pamphlets from other women's organizations. We are very excited to be able to offer this service to the women of Edmonton.

Every Woman's Place is open seven days a week and is staffed by volunteers who are trained to provide simple support and referral services ...

We are financially self-supporting and at present have a membership of over 150 women. We have raised monies through monthly pledges and through memberships. As we enlist more members, this source of revenue will increase. Also, the Society has sponsored several successful fund raising events, and will continue to raise money in this manner ...

On Monday, May 21, Participate in a Lesbian Dialogue. The Topic: Loot, The Community, and 342 Jarvis St.
Toronto, 1978[18]

Following the 1976 Lesbian Conference in Ottawa, a group of 50 women met in Toronto to discuss the state of the Toronto lesbian community. A number of needs were identified, the most pressing of which seemed to be better communication, a place to meet, and a base for political action. At this point, a small group of women joined to form a task force to accomplish these goals. Luck was on our side, and we were soon able to join two other Toronto feminist Organizations, the Three of Cups coffeehouse and The Other Woman newspaper, to rent a house at 342

---

17. Every Women's Education Centre (Edmonton) 1982. Flyer, CWMA.
18. "Loot," 1978 flyer, CWMA, file: Loot.

Jarvis St. The Lesbian Organization of Toronto (LOOT) was born during the winter of 1977.

In the last two and a half years, LOOT has sponsored a variety of activities, and the house on Jarvis Street has been a busy place. Various collectives have organized a phone-line, a weekly drop-in, a newsletter, a library, Sunday brunches, New Year's dances, open houses, and various political actions. The Three of Cups and The Other Woman have passed on into herstory, but since then 342 Jarvis St. has been used at different times by Sappho Sound, Women Against Violence Against Women, and Superbia Press.

Two years ago our dream was to have a house and an umbrella organization to sponsor a variety of women's activities. For sometime, this dream has been a reality. At this point, the dream isn't very exciting, and as the dream passes, energy and enthusiasm are drying up at the house on Jarvis Street. At $300 per month ($425 with utilities) the house itself is still a remarkable bargain. However, LOOT, one tenant, and Superbia Press are the only contributors to our rent, and the house is often empty. The task force, which has the crucial job of seeing that the rent money is in the bank, is seriously short of women, and many of the lesbians who are in collectives are uncertain about the future of their activities. We need some new women's energy and some new visions about where to go from here.

Has LOOT as an umbrella organization outlived its usefulness? Should LOOT break down into smaller, independent collectives with varying political outlooks? If LOOT continues, how can we alter our structure or our image to attract women with strong political beliefs without alienating the apolitical amongst us? Can we create a rejuvenating vision, a vision that will make lesbians want to raise money to help see it fulfilled? 342 Jarvis Street was intended for the use of the entire lesbian community. Are we making the best use of the house? Has 342 Jarvis become too closely identified with LOOT? At the Monday workshop we want to explore these and other questions. We want to find out what the lesbian community of 1979 needs, and how 342 Jarvis Street can most effectively accommodate those needs. Come to the meeting on Monday at 11: 30 (after the morning plenary) to talk about the future of the Lesbian Organization of Toronto, and 342 Jarvis Street.

"What's in a Name"
Thunder Bay, Ontario, July 1974[19]

I am concerned about the image of the Northern Women's Centre ... "Women's Lib"?

Although we have received some publicity in three of the smaller local papers most people encountered either haven't heard of us or ask what exactly we do there.

---

19. Noreen Lavoie, *Northern Woman Journal* 2, no. 3 (July 1974).

Women's Centres ... there are at least twenty-four across Canada now, are trying to meet a multitude of needs re women and it is difficult to sum it all up in a few words. Those of us active in the Northern Women's Centre are "trying to provide help and encouragement to women dealing with the many needs and problems peculiar to them and to assist their efforts to improve the status of women in the whole community".

There are many terms bandied about when people refer to women's groups and the label "Women's Libber" is a put down process that turns liberationist into libber just as it once turned suffragist into suffragette.

"Women's Liberation" is frequently used as a catch-all expression to describe the entire current women's movement. But more accurately it is a branch of the movement that had its origins in the student activism of the early 1960's. These women, mainly Radical Feminists, have thus far been primarily concerned with analyzing the origins, nature and extent of women's subservient role in society.

"Women's Rights" refers to the branch of the women's movement primarily active in bringing about legislative, economic, and educational reforms to eradicate sex discrimination in society. The most famous of them in Canada were the women's groups involved in the Royal Commission on the Status of Women and more recently the Advisory Council on the Status of Women and the Ontario Advisory Council on the Status of Women. In the U.S. the best known is the National Organization for Women (NOW) founded by Betty Friedan who wrote *The Feminine Mystique.*

Women's Movement describes the entire spectrum of women's groups and activities and herein lies the Northern Women's Centre. The "Women's Movement" is not an organization you join ... become a member and pay dues, rather it is a state of mind ... a new awareness ... an education ... a personal growth and many more things to different women. Women in the movement are concerned about minorities and injustices done to them and as women living in a male power structure our influence in decision making is negligible, making us part of an oppressed minority class.

As I said, I am concerned about the image of the N.W.C. Is the label "Women's Lib" (we don't like it either) preventing many women from participating? I hope not. There is a place in the centre for all women and we need those of you who find their home, family or occupation does not take all their time and energy. When you are next downtown Thunder Bay South come and see the Centre. Take the stairs to the right and up one flight. The coffee pot is always on ...

Thunder Bay Anishinabequek
Fall 1975[20]

The Thunder Bay Anishinabequek, our local chapter of the *Ontario Native Women's Association* (O.N.W.A.) was formed October 11, 1972. It is not incorporated but is investigating the possibility. It is one of the 37 locals in Ontario — quite a compliment for a new provincial organization. Our local Anishinabequek has a membership of 175 out of approximately 250 Native Women in Thunder Bay. We are pleased to outline the various projects and activities of our local over the past three years. We are proud of our organization which is a self-help group composed of volunteers in the executive and in the membership. Our most recent election occurred at Our Native Women's Festival (to be described later). The new executive consists of: Mrs. Priscilla Simard, President; Ms. Anna Spuzak, Vice-President; Ms. Christine Rochette, Secretary; and Ms. Beverly Sabourin, Treasurer.

Our aims and objectives are simple and viable as we try and incorporate them into all proposed projects and activities. These are as follows:

> a)To enlist and organize the energies and efforts of all members and associate members in promoting the aims of the O.N.W.A. and in particular the aims and objectives of the local chapter.
> b)Take advantage of government programs that will improve and will advance the ambitions of the organization.
> c)Visitation programs in homes, hospitals, jails, etc.
> d)Interpret the problems of Native people to agencies, etc.
> e)Promote job placement
> f)Social care for Native children in local homes.
> g)Education
> h)Develop awareness of government legislation
> i) Promoting the use of Native language in homes, schools, etc.
> j)Setting up information in bus depots, etc. for Native people.

We sponsored an Indian Awareness Workshop, March 2, 1974 at the Indian Friendship Centre for the benefit of the foreign students at Lakehead University. Here Native people from the community met with students and discussed various topics, such as adjustment to city life, culture, employment, education, etc. and shared life experiences. Special attractions included Indian dancing and an Indian Food Banquet. It was very interesting and very beneficial to all involved. Our local does several fund raising projects. These included coffee houses, penny auctions, bingos (held at the Indian Friendship Centre), hockey pools, bake sales, bazaars, etc. Various members of our club perform speaking engagements, seminars, and workshops upon request from various agen-

20. "Regional Reports: Thunder Bay Anishinabequek," *The Northern Woman Journal* 2, no. 3 (Fall 1975).

cies, institutions, clubs, etc. Our local Anishinabequek has sponsored several social activities for the community, ranging from the annual Christmas Banquet and Dance (at the Friendship Centre) the annual Native Children's Christmas party and various others. We organized a Fashion Show for the General Assembly of O.N.W.A. We also pride ourselves in having helped draw up various recommendations made by O.N.W.A. on behalf of all Native Women's Groups and presented to various relevant Cabinet Ministers. We pride ourselves in cooperating with other Native and Non-Native organizations and in promoting harmony and unity amongst ourselves, our brothers.

Mothers on Budgets

On June 16th, our group hosted a luncheon for two single parent groups: Budgeting Mothers and Single Parents. The groups were from Nipigon and Geraldton, with a couple of members from Red Rock. They came down by Grey Goose on the morning bus and went back that evening. The Ministry took care of their transportation to and from the bus depot. There were 10 women here. We spent the afternoon talking about what MOB was, and our current activities. They were quite interested to hear of our experiences.

MOB has a pilot project going called 'Freedom Week'. We received a grant for special camping from the Cambrian Presbytery of $1,000. The United Church is renting their camp at East Loon to us from July 18-25th. What makes this camp unique is that it's set up for mothers only—those on FBA and Welfare, and working, single parents. Word just came back today from the city that they would contribute $50 per mother toward babysitting fees. The balance needed would have come from the funds we have for the camp, after the food is bought. A student, Marilyn Bates, was hired through the Secretary of State program to coordinate the camp and set up activities and crafts. This camp is now closed to further applicants. Hopefully this can be done again next year.

'Sanity House' is an idea where single parents, mothers or fathers, can leave their child or children for a period of from 1 to 3 days while they have time to recuperate and gain strength to handle their children and themselves again. Right now a survey is being put together to show the need for this facility. NIP is working on this with us. It's been a lot of work already and the end is still not in sight. However, I'll let the readers know via the Northern Woman of any future action.

"Service or Political Action?"
Prince George, B.C., Summer 1982[21]

When a woman's group forms it must make basic decisions about the direction it will take. That direction essentially lies in a service orientation or in political action. Are they mutually exclusive?

---

21. *Aspen* 4, no. 4 (Summer 1982), 7, 9. CWMA.

Political action involves attempts made to bring about changes in legislation and its application involving women. Lobbying to get amendments to the current rape laws serves as an example. Political action also includes those moves to affect a change in social values. Making the public aware of pornography and its objectification of women is an obvious example. The women's group which chooses a service orientation focuses more on meeting the needs of women that are presently not being met by social institutions. In Quesnel, for example, at the Women's Centre, members may get a break from their children while attending an exercise class or discussion with other women.

A group which chooses the service route often ends up narrowing its feminist objectives. The reality of providing a drop-in centre, counselling services or a resource library is such that the majority of members' energy is taken up doing just that. What little time is left over is usually spent chasing after government funding in order to be able to continue providing a specific service for women.

A women's centre can of course offer more than just one service. In Terrace for example, a congenial drop-in atmosphere is combined with a resource library and regular consciousness raising lectures or workshops. Obviously the objectives of such a centre include more than just the services themselves. In a recent interview with *Aspen,* Terrace Women's Centre Co-Ordinator, Francis Birdsell, talked about appealing to a broad base, of interesting the 'woman on the street' in status of women issues. The existence of a non-threatening centre, which provides, in this case, community support services, is seen as one avenue to attain that goal.

Choosing to provide services for women does not preclude political involvement. The Rape Crisis collectives in both Terrace and Prince George are examples of groups who, while meeting the immediate needs of women who have been raped, are also very active in politicizing the general public on the whole issue of rape as the ultimate extension of a chauvinist society.

However, doing both is difficult. In the first place, there is the issue of time and energy as well as the need to 'keep your nose clean' in order to get future funding. There's that old saying about biting the hand that ... Also, those women who make use of the service provided by a group are often not in any personal position to be politically active. A battered wife seeking refuge at the Prince Rupert Transition House is unlikely to be found out on the streets in a demonstration against failing family assault law enforcement ... at least not in the immediate future.

In Prince George, the current women's group, WERA (Women's Equal Rights Association) at its inception consciously chose to go the political action route. This decision was one that was made by a group of women already informed in feminist issues and experienced in some political action.

During interviews with several WERA members it became clear that this decision was based on the belief that society should be providing services for women and that local feminist energy would be best spent trying to bring about legislative or social change for women. Political action can also be a rallying point around which to involve people, on a single issue, who might previously have never been associated with the women's movement.

As the providing of a service does not preclude political action so the reverse is also true. In fact meeting some immediate needs of women often enhances future political work. In Prince George, for example, *Aspen* is currently involved in the weekly Family Planning Clinics provided by the Health Unit. The contacts made and reputation earned through this community service will hopefully add credibility to future, more controversial political activity.

"Editorial": Saskatoon Women's Liberation Newsletter April 1974[22]

The goal of women's Liberation is to end the oppression of women. Women are oppressed by male chauvinism and by capitalism. Women are the most exploited sector of the work force.

All our efforts must be directed to end this oppression rather than simply cope with it.

The Women's Movement is in danger of being co-opted unless it adopts an *overall perspective* which directs women's consciousness of their oppression towards a strategy to end that oppression. The "single issue campaign" such as child-care, abortion law-repeal and self-help is susceptible to co-optation by government. Isolated demands can become diluted government programs that do not alter the status and role of women. For example, day-care is being made more accessible to poor women but the Saskatchewan government still maintains that women's place is in the home caring for children.

We are formulating an editorial policy and the following is what we have come up with so far. We invite criticisms and additions:

1 We must continue and encourage a theoretical discussion of historical reasons for what we are today.
2 We see women's oppression as an integral part of this society but confronting masculine and feminine roles cannot be done in *isolation*. In other words, we steer clear of taking a fragmented view of our oppression and attempts to change it in isolation from the rest of society. Society functions as a whole; therefore, parts cannot fundamentally change — the whole society must change.

---

22. *Saskatoon Women's Liberation Newsletter* (April 1974). CWMA File: Saskatoon Women's Liberation Newsletters.

3   We seek to destroy power relationships, not usurp power. This leads us to work towards a socialistic society where women and men have control of (not power over) the means of production. The present goal of industry is to create profit, not to meet the needs of people. Women in positions of power can be as oppressive as men. Therefore, all our actions must encompass a striving towards this goal.

4   It is necessary that women work together and concentrate their energies in developing an analysis and strategy that will destroy sexism. *Present socialist analysis does not ensure this.* Only as women together can we create the base, make accessible the information, direct our energy and develop the skills necessary to break down their oppression.

June Bantjes
Nadia Greschuck
Christiane Richards

History of the Native Women's Association of the NWT And Resource Manual Yellowknife, 1984[23]

1970's
... In the 1970's there were women's groups in the NWT who represented women in general. There were also male-dominated native organizations which separately represented the Inuit, Dene and Métis political interests. However, there was no unified group of native women in the NWT to represent their own grassroots interests and priorities. The moccasin telegraph was really the only existing communications network.

At this same time, southern native women's groups were starting to organize around issues such as discrimination under the Indian Act. Individual native women in the NWT attended some southern native women's conferences and started promoting their own regional concerns. At that time these concerns included the political issues of the proposed Mackenzie Valley Pipeline and land claims and the immediate social and economic issues affecting Northern women and their communities directly.

Numerous submissions by Dene, Métis and Inuit women were also made to the Mackenzie Valley Pipeline Inquiry headed by Mr. Justice Thomas Berger. They emphasized the vital importance to the North of its women and children and their concerns about the human element of development and the problems of an educational system that encourages confusion about people's values, aims and identities.

23. Barbara Mackenzie, (Yellowknife: NWA/NWT, 1984), 7-8. CWMA file: Native Women's Association of the Northwest Territories.

The Native Women's Association of Canada was incorporated in 1974 to promote the interests of all Canadian native women regardless of status. Bertha Clark Jones, from Fort McMurray, Alberta, was the first NWAC President and later worked for the NWA/NWT for a period in 1979.

Events such as International Women's Year in 1975 gave encouragement to Northern native women to get together to voice their particular concerns. An Inuit Women's Conference was held in Pangnirtung in the summer of 1975. Some women from the Delta attended.

Also, some NWT communities started to organize their own local native women's groups. Esther Lazore, Adeline Landry and Margaret Vandel started a group in Fort Providence with about 15 local women to work on various community projects including arts and crafts.

Native Women's Association of the NWT Founding Conference
In 1976 the idea of an all-native women's conference was conceived for the native women of the Mackenzie Valley and Western Arctic, spearheaded by a planning committee including Bertha Allen (Inuvik), Albertine Rodh (Fort Simpson), Eliza Lawrence (Fort Resolution/Yellowknife) and Alizette Potfighter (Detah).

Right from the beginning they decided that all Northern native women, regardless of status — Métis, Dene or Inuit — would be welcome to participate.

Funding was provided by the Department of Indian & Inuit Affairs and Doreen Mullins of that Department helped with the planning for the initial meeting. At the second planning meeting of the interim committee, Gina Blondin was hired to co-ordinate the first native women's conference to be held in the summer of 1977.

Albertine Rodh felt that getting involved with the native women's assembly was great. "The reason was there; the time was right. The most important thing the native women wanted to do was to prove they could accomplish something and we've done that—there's a lot of hidden talent out there."

The historic meeting took place July 19–21, 1977, at Akaitcho Hall in Yellowknife and delegates attended from 29 different communities in the Mackenzie Valley and Western Arctic. The theme was "Community Action".

The Founding Conference opened with prayers by Elizabeth Yakelaya from Fort Norman. Bertha Allen, later elected as First President of the NWA/NWT, chaired the meeting. She encouraged all the women who attended to discuss and identify specific issues that concerned them and then begin to act constructively in their own communities to solve them. Unity was the key to effective action, she stressed.

Mary Ann Lavallee, a native woman from the Cowessess Reserve in Saskatchewan, was the keynote speaker. Mrs. Lavallee told the delegates that they represent the soul of the North and that it was up to them to educate their children in their own culture and languages. Her main message was that women are the key to the survival of the native people and in order for them to continue they must first love their people, love their ways and live them instead of just talking.

The first executive of the Native Women's Association was formed at this founding conference:

- Bertha Allen, President;
- Rosa Brunt, Vice-President;
- Esther Lazore, Secretary-Treasurer
- Alizette Potfighter (Tatsiechele), Secretary.

From day one arts and crafts was of major concern to the women. Other concerns were alcohol abuse, foster care and adoption of native children, nutrition, health and education. These were the issues around which the Native Women's Association was formed.

Communique from J.F. Walchli, Department of Indian Affairs British Columbia, 1981[24]

The following is a message from
F J Walchli
Regional Director General
BC Region

At 9:15AM today (July 20, 1981) the Regional office of the Department of Indian Affairs at 700 West Georgia Street Van. was partially occupied by 30–40 Indian people mostly women who stated that they did not represent chiefs or councils or any political association, but that they had a number of concerns. They refused to discuss those concerns with me.

This occupancy has caused an interruption in services and has therefore required me to close down the regional office until further notice.

District offices will stay open and provide services as usual. Should it be necessary for regional staff to meet with band councils, we will attempt to do so at the district or reserve level.

We will notify you as soon as this problem has been resolved. Thank you for your understanding and consideration.

Memo to the National Indian Brotherhood from the Union of BC Indian Chiefs British Columbia, 1981[25]

July 21, 1981
To: National Indian Brotherhood
From: Union of BC Indian Chiefs for the Aboriginal women of

24. J.F. Walchli, Regional Director General, BC Region, Department of Indian Affairs, 20 July 1981. CWMA file: native women.
25. Memo to the National Indian Brotherhood from the Union of BC Indian Chiefs, July 21, 1981, CWMA File: native women.

BC who are occupying the BC Regional Office of Indian Affairs

Please release the following to the news media and wire services including foreign press reps who are in Ottawa to cover the summit conference being held in Monte Bello.

This organization was set up by a group of women without any organizations backing it. It was done through frustration. [We are] just plain fed up with the way we are treated by the Department of Indian Affairs, Councils and Indian organizations. The money is going everywhere but to the community level people. The pittance that Indian organizations do get they are fighting over.

The stand we are making as 'concerned aboriginal women' is born from frustrations suffered at the hands of the Department of Indian Affairs and different organizations. The band level people have so many different organizations working on their behalf that the situations at the band level are worsening. The poverty that people are experiencing at the band level is caused by the controls set up by government policies. These policies are not given in the interests of people but in the interests of government bureaucrats. The cut-backs imposed by government on the Department of Indian Affairs is felt hardest by the band members at the community level. We have no security such as the other worker groups have in that we cannot strike to bring our standard of living up to par with the rest of the country. The workers at the community level are at the mercy of the people who are doling out the money. Our resources are not being used to make life better for community people as a whole but help develop corporations of rich individuals.

Fred Walchli: We won't talk to him because we don't trust him, because of the way he has handled other situations dealing with Indians.

A) Bands are continuously waiting for funding for band operations. This caused a lot of frustration being suffered by the community people and workers at the community level.

B) Whenever Indian people want decision making authority the Department of Indian Affairs steps in and forms an organization of its own — like the Regional Forum and the way this forum is set up is contradictory to what we envision as Indian Government for our individual nations.

Demands:

1 We demand the resignation of Fred Walchli because of the political manner in which he disperses funds to the Indian people. We therefore demand a meeting with the Minister of Indian Affairs.

2   We demand an independent inquiry into activities of the Dept. of Indian Affairs in the BC region.

"Our Possibilities Are Endless"
February/March 1989[26]

The Congress of Black Women of Canada in planning its biennial conference for May 5-7, 1989, has chosen as the conference motto, "Our Possibilities are Endless."

As black women we need to alternately whisper and shout these words so that we can reaffirm our inherent strength and capabilities.

As we contemplate not only February's Black Heritage Celebrations but also the significance of International Women's Day and the ongoing struggle in Canadian society we realize more than ever the need to strive for the reality of endless possibilities.

In recent months we have seen not only the issues of intense racism which have characterized much of the police work in Canada, but also ongoing realities of the inequalities within the government, service delivery systems, the systematic approach to discrimination in the provision of social services, the involuntary joblessness of our sisters, the barriers to employment retraining and education, as also the lack of employment equity in the workplace.

While we know that we cannot expect to eliminate all the problems which are associated with our struggle and our survival we do realize that we have an obligation to actively align ourselves to facilitate the development of concrete actions which will enable us to provide leadership and face the ongoing challenges which confront us in our daily lives.

As we go forward in the struggle for justice and equality for our work, the Congress salutes all of our sisters in their celebration of Black Heritage Month and International Women's Day.

We invite you all to join us in combatting the injustices which affect all our lives and the lives of our families. With united analyzing, planning and affirming of our abilities, together we will be able to bring about meaningful change, especially if we as women truly believe that our possibilities are endless.

"Domestic Workers Organize!"
Winter 1982[27]

"Landed status now!" they chanted in the bitter cold of last November. Domestic workers from the Caribbean, the Philippines, and Great Britain were in the streets together, along with their many supporters. They were demonstrating in front of the immigration office at 480 University Ave-

---

26. Conference announcement by the Congress of Black Women of Canada in *The Womanist* 1, no. 3 (February/March 1989), 9.
27. Judith Ramirez, *Canadian Women's Studies* 4 no. 2 (Winter, 1982), 89-91.

nue in Toronto, an act that was the culmination of many months of organizing.

"We scrub the floors, we cook the meals, we raise the children — why aren't we good enough to stay?" asked Eulene Boyce, a West Indian domestic worker. "We are here ... united in our stand ... calling for an end to the system of indentured servitude which, since 1973, has denied over 60,000 domestic workers the right to landed status in Canada," said spokesperson for the International Coalition to End Domestics' Exploitation (INTERCEDE).

In March, 1980, Immigration Minister Lloyd Axworthy promised changes in Canada's immigration policy at the First National Conference on Immigrant Women. At the same conference, delegates unanimously passed a resolution calling for the abolition of the temporary-work-permit system.

Since 1973 the system of temporary "employment visas" had tied domestic workers to one specific employer. They not only could not change sector of work — that is, from domestic work to factory work — they could not even change from one domestic job to another without government permission. They were, quite simply, a captive labour force. As if that weren't enough, domestic workers were forbidden by law to change their status from temporary workers to permanent residents in Canada, despite the fact that it was virtually impossible for domestic workers to *enter* Canada as landed immigrants.

The pay for domestic labour is extremely low and the working conditions are completely unregulated. For example, the Montréal Household Workers' Association estimated in 1979 that the average pay was fifty dollars per week, plus room and board, for a fifty- to sixty-hour work week! As a result, domestic work in Canada has been the preserve of third-world women. The majority come from the economically depressed Caribbean countries and, more recently, from the Philippine Islands. The average stay was restricted to three years, after which the majority of domestic workers were ordered to leave the country.

In January, 1979, the Advisory Council on the Status of Women published Sheila Arnopoulos's *Problems of Immigrant Women in the Canadian Labour Force*. A hard-hitting section on domestic workers documented the exploitation inherent in the temporary-work-permit system. Later that year the Committee to Advance the Status of Housework held a public forum in Toronto titled: "A View from the Kitchen: Immigrant Women Speak Out on the Value of Housework." Sheila Arnopoulos was one of the keynote panelists, as was Jamaican feminist Joan French. The workshop on domestic workers that followed led to the formation of INTERCEDE.

It grew quickly from a handful of groups to a coalition of fifty-strong, including the United Church of Canada's Division of Mission in Canada and the World Conference on Religion and Peace. INTERCEDE's chief objective was to become a strong and effective lobby for legislative change. To that end, it prepared a lengthy brief for the Task Force on Immigration Practices and Procedures, appointed by Immigration Minister Lloyd Axworthy in September, 1980.

In June, 1981, INTERCEDE led a twenty-five-member delegation from Toronto, Ottawa, Montréal and Vancouver to meet with Mr. Axworthy and outline the brief's recommendations. Chief among these was that domestic workers on temporary work permits be allowed to apply for permanent residence in Canada.

Shortly after, the minister announced changes in immigration policy that granted domestic workers with experience and formal training (such as diplomas in house-keeping and childcare) the right to apply for landed status. There was immediate outcry from third-world domestic workers and their allies. In a nationwide letter-writing campaign to Mr. Axworthy, INTERCEDE protested:

> ... recent changes you have made restrict landing only to those women who have had the opportunity to take formal childcare or housekeeping training and who come from countries able to offer them stable work experience as nannies and housekeepers. The result will be that a 'select few' from the UK and northern Europe are granted landed status, while the thousands of domestic workers from the Caribbean and the Philippines won't have a chance. This kind of racist immigration policy is intolerable.

The Filipino domestic workers organized an Ad Hoc Committee for Landed Status and, with the support of the International Association of Filipino Patriots, held the first demonstration of domestic workers on record. In front of a high-class Toronto restaurant where the Liberal Party was holding a fund-raising dinner, they cornered Lloyd Axworthy and handed him thousands of signed protest letters. They reminded him of his promise to ease the plight of domestic workers and of the fact that his recent changes only made things worse ... On November 26, Immigration Minister Lloyd Axworthy announced the long-awaited changes in Canada's immigration policy, changes that finally granted temporary workers the right to apply for landed status. Domestic workers who have been working in Canada for at least two years can now apply for permanent residence when their work permits are due for renewal. They undergo an initial assessment to determine their "potential for self-sufficiency," which takes into account such factors as education, skills, family and community ties in Canada, and "personal suitability ..."

Immediately following Mr. Axworthy's announcement INTERCEDE held several community meetings, attended by as many as 250 domestic workers, where possible guidelines for implementing the policy were thrashed out. While most domestic workers were happy that they could finally apply for landed status here, the very notion of having to prove "self-sufficiency" to the Canadian government was offensive to many. "I supported five children *before* I came here, and I've supported five children since I came here, and they want to know if I can manage on my own?" said Mary Dabreo from St. Vincent.

The fate of older domestic workers who had little formal education at home and who have been out of school for decades was a special concern in drafting recommended guidelines. INTERCEDE argued strongly that short-term, community-based courses be recognized as valid for "upgrading" purposes. Any woman who has come to Canada to perform a service in great demand — that is, housework — should not have to acquire a second trade, *unless she wishes to*, in order to qualify for permanent status. The value of her skills in performing housework and in meeting a need in the Canadian economy should contribute toward a positive assessment under the new policy.

The provinces have a critical role to play if this policy is to give domestic workers a *bona fide* chance at gaining landed status. Minimum-wage legislation must protect domestic workers by giving them an adequate rate so that those who choose this work can earn a living wage and be self-sufficient. Otherwise the new policy will become a cruel joke that puts foreign domestic workers in a Catch-22 position. They will have to prove "self-sufficiency" to the federal immigration Commission, but they will be unable to do so because provincial labour laws are so weak that a "self-sufficient" wage for domestic work is a contradiction in terms. In Ontario the legally required rate for domestic workers is only three dollars per hour with a potential work week of 132 hours! It is third-world domestics who will be penalized for the fact that Canadian society holds housework in such low esteem. As one domestic worker put it, "they want it done, but they don't want to pay for it."

The Adventures of Cora, the Bookmobile
Ontario, Fall 1974[28]

by ellen, typed by judy, revised by boo

Once upon a time.

A huge long bus painted fire engine red with Women's Liberation Bookmobile firmly printed in foot high letters across the side, barrels into a small town (could be your town if you want it).

She (Cora) drives up and down the main street far outdoing the local mufferless convertibles, the farmers in their pick-up trucks and even the local businessmen in their 74 Impalas. On the back of the bus is a large yellow 'Women Working' sign, and beside that a 'Wages for Housework' sign.

A woman in Stouffville saw the sign 'Wages for Housework'. She said, "If I believed that, I'd be on strike right now." Her husband took her arm and hurried her away.

We try to park in the most conspicuous spot in town. Then we haggle with the town clerk or local police chief for permission to park. Sometimes we park in the middle of a farmer's market, or in front of a

28. Ellen Woodsworth. CWMA File: Case study.

rummage sale, supermarket parking lots, University campuses, libraries, empty lots, or on the main street.

Then comes the work of setting up the bus. This consists of putting up 'OPEN' signs, setting up an outdoor display rack (until we ran over it in Huntsville), with a selection of pamphlets, picking up books that have bounced on the floor while driving, sweeping and dusting, and then going out for breakfast.

We take a flyer about the bus to all the stores, laundromats, newspapers, TV and radio stations, and public places. We try to find out about any sympathetic individuals or groups and contact them.

Then comes the wait. Sometimes this can be anywhere from a few minutes to a few hours. Ideally we would like to continue leafleting all day, drawing people off the streets and into the bus ...

In some towns we were able to help women find each other. Everywhere we went women were quietly starting to change things. Through working on local papers, and slipping in pro-women's liberation articles, through working in libraries and ordering women's books, through working in YWCA and women's organizations, and calling discussions on women's liberation, or through slowly changing their own lives, and talking about it with their friends.

The Women's Movement is alive and well in rural Ontario.

How did we get started?
We have had the idea for two years. Judith and Ellen started saving money in September, 1973. The bus was bought in the spring of 1974, after a winter of hard work, advance publicity, and fund-raising. We painted Cora (named after E. Cora Hind — pioneer suffragist, grain expert, Taoist and journalist), put in shelves, display racks, and a children's corner. On the first of May Cora was on the road (at 35 miles per hour — with a tailwind). We received an OFY grant at the end of June, and four more women joined us — Wanda, Marcia, Scamp and Boo. The bookmobile has been going steadily since May, and will continue year-round, except during the cold winter months.

Where have we been?
We have been to Waterloo, Kitchener, Cambridge, Sarnia, Hamilton, York, Aurora, Stouffville, Stratford, Barrie, Orillia, Huntsville, Gravenhurst, Go Home Lake, Parry Sound, Midland, Oshawa, Peterborough, Belleville, Kingston, Mississauga, Midland, Owen Sound, Walkerton, Clinton, Wingham, St. Mary's, London, Scarborough, Ottawa. We stayed at least two days in each town.

Why are we doing this?
To disseminate and make people aware of existing material, available only in wealthy centres. To help women in isolated situations find each other, to facilitate communication between different groups, to learn

how city and rural women can support each other, to help break down media mystification of what Women's Liberation really is, to encourage Canadian women to write, to encourage schools, libraries and community centres to teach and display more women-oriented and women-supportive materials, to create more dialogue about existing problems, and old and new solutions, and to try to activate action and support groups in every small town ...

What do we carry?

We carry material on: Wages for housework, daycare, birth control and abortion, herstory, autobiographies, novels and poetry, feminist analysis, lesbianism, legal rights, working women, non-sexist children's books, third-world women, stickers, posters, T-shirts. We have a large supply of free materials (send us anything you have that we could distribute). We try to stress Canadian material. We want to print our own articles and reprint Canadian women's articles over the winter for distribution in the spring of 1975 ...

We also carry local material from Women's Centres across Ontario, and anything free that we can get our hands on.

"Farming No Picnic"
Manitoba, 1981[29]

It is a harsh reality, but the family farm in Manitoba has been replaced by the large corporate farm and the break-up of the traditional rural community is the result.

Those most adversely affected are rural women who are now being forced into wage labour in the processing plants. Here women fill the low skilled, labour-intensive jobs, while men dominate supervisory and skilled positions.

Out in the field the situation is no better. Although men and women receive equal pay for equal work, women have few opportunities to advance into better paying skilled and supervisory positions. Most farmworkers are native indians. In the Portage la Prairie area, for instance, about 75 per cent of the workers are natives and 60 per cent of these are women. However in the native Manitoba Farm Workers' Association (MFWA) there are no women on the executive, according to representatives of the MFWA and the Portage Farm Labour Project.

This is the result of the transformation of the family farm into agribusiness over the past three decades. The process has forced farm people into low wage, farm related industry and created a substantial increase in rural unemployment. This damage to the health of rural Manitoba is permanent.

Between 1966 and 1975 almost 500,000, or 25 per cent of Canadians on farms left after being caught in the squeeze between low income and fast rising costs. Farmers found that more and more land was needed to

29. Gene Jamieson, *The Manitoba Women's Newspaper* 2, no. 1 (April - May 1981), 7-8.

keep up with farm costs. For those few farmers with easy access to investment capital (usually from food processing companies interested in vertical integration of their businesses) the going was easy as other farmers had to sell or else face bankruptcy. But most farmers who bought out their neighbours did so by throwing themselves deeply into debt. As if this was not problem enough, the drive by individual family operators to increase farm size resulted in more work than the family could handle.

According to a 1975 National Farmers Union (NFU) report this over-extension by family farms caused farmers to abandon some of the older farm practices which, although time consuming, helped preserve the land's productivity. It also meant that rural unemployment increased because the number of jobs lost with the decline of the family farm has dramatically outstripped the number created by the food processing industry.

The concentration of farm land into fewer and fewer hands has struck a blow to the rural social fabric, particularly the position of women. As the farm work increased, more and more of the burden falls on the farm wife. She, as recent legal cases have shown, has limited legal access to the farmstead she has worked to create. The salaried farm wife has little access to daycare facilities and other supports working women require
...

While family farms in Manitoba have been dealt a fatal blow over the past three decades, women members of those families have come out with an even shorter end of the proverbial stick.

"Rural Ramblings"
Manitoba, 1981[30]

Dear MWN

Delighted to be part of the Rural Women's Conference sponsored by the Manitoba Women's newspaper.

Yes, we rural women agree, that if, the paper is to be a Manitoba paper, rural input is a must.

However, one pitfall I foresee in it being accepted by rural women is the reference to it being a feminist paper.

Why you ask?

Because feminist is an image that is foreign to rural women. They cannot afford it.

Much of the rural community is created by the family farm. And a family farm in order to survive must rely on family input. That is, all members must contribute at the level of their ability. Mum must pitch in and drive the tractor, grain truck, whatever. Dad in turn must help with the dishes, meal preparation or child care, Junior pitches in wherever she is able.

30. Myrt Lenton, Letter to the Editor, *The Manitoba Women's Newspaper* 2, no. 1 (April-May 1981), 11.

Family labour is one of the remaining survival tools left to the family farm. Without it many would have succumbed long ago.

For rural women to take a stand as a feminist on a rural issue would make her feel like a traitor to those she struggles with, namely other family members and community members. Issues must be attacked like her work as a combined effort.

Currently the most pertinent farm issues are of an economic nature. There is much instability in farm economics; especially as it relates to the family farm. All family farm members are fighting to maintain their existence ...

... Now if the MWN could be used as a medium for rural women to present the rural condition, I then believe rural women would submit material and feel part of it. But if it is to project only a feminist view point with demands for more rights for just women, then I do not see it as a medium that rural women will utilize.

I believe that when we label issues as female issues we become part of what we fight. Isn't equality what the women's movement is all about? How can segregation create equality?

One more thing, we women are schooled in being assertive. I agree with that but how assertive can one be with the weatherman? This spring he is the threatening, and controlling, force that has all us rural people in a flap.

See what I mean? Rural problems are very complex. To surmount them we need all our combined strengths

We can't afford any type of segregation and thus we cannot indulge in the term feminist.

Myrt Lenton
Miami

"Consultation Meeting with the Federal Ministers"
Ottawa, June 1-3, 1985[31]

Thirty-seven women representing more than 40 immigrant and visible minority women's groups from across Canada met with four federal Cabinet ministers: Jack Murta of Multiculturalism, Flora MacDonald of Employment and Immigration, Walter McLean of Secretary of State and Jake Epp of Health and Welfare.

The main purpose of this consultation meeting was to present concerns of immigrant and visible minority women and to make recommendations in the formulation of policies regarding immigrant and visible minority women. The principles behind the issues addressed were: self-help, partnership and accountability, integration not ghettoization and concern for the most disadvantaged.

The following recommendations were made to the Cabinet minsters:

31. Dr. Christina Lee, *British Columbia Task Force on Immigrant Women Newsletter* (Summer 1985).

A) *Equal opportunity for access to language programs*

  i) language training for those in the labour market and destined for the labour market by funding of pilot projects of language training in the workplace
  ii) language training prior to employment by providing access to official full-time language training programs
  iii) funding of community based special language training projects for the most disadvantaged immigrant women: the illiterate and the women at home.

B) *Equal opportunity for access to skill training and employment*

  i) special funding for skills courses and on-the-job training
  ii) affirmative action programs should take into account immigrant and visible minority women by establishing a monitoring and enforcing agency and by exerting pressure on the provincial government and the private sector
  iii) recognition of training and degrees from other countries by working with provincial educational institutions, and professional and trade associations to establish equivalency of courses offered in other countries.

Other recommendations included labour standards for domestic workers, financial assistance for entrepreneurial, small business initiatives, and access to social programs and benefits, language and skills training for refugee women.

C) *Improvement of the status of immigrant and visible minority women through government programs*

This advocates the integration of immigrant women's concerns across the federal government, particularly the Secretary of State — Women's Program, the Status of Women, the Canadian Advisory Council on the Status of Women. These divisions should take into account the concerns and issues of immigrant and visible minority women in their policy considerations, and reallocate funds to promote the social and economic status of immigrant and visible minority women.

D) *Health and Welfare* issues included the emphasis of preventive approach by hiring bilingual, bicultural service providers, by funding for volunteer training, by funding for culturally sensitive health-related materials and the translation of such materials into different languages. Also recommended were the need for core and stable funding for community-based programs, the representation of immigrant and visible minority women in the National Council of Health and Welfare, and pensions for elderly immigrant women ...

National Action Committee on the Status of Women — Meeting with the Right Hon. Pierre Trudeau, Leader of the Liberal Party, during the Election Campaign Toronto, February 1980[32]

Date: February 12, 1980
Location: Royal York Hotel, Toronto
Delegation: Lynn McDonald, Wendy Lawrence,
        Kay Macpherson, Laurell Ritchie, Betsy Carr,
        Margot Trevelyan, Marjorie Cohen,
        Pauline Harper (Indian Rights for Indian Women),
        Ann Hill
Observer: Irma Melville
Liberal Party: Pierre Elliot Trudeau, Lorna Marsden,
        Ursula Appolloni, Aideen Nicholson,
        Senator Florence Bird, Martin O'Connell,
        Jim Fleming

MacDonald:

I think we're going to have to move on though. Pauline Harper, Indian Rights for Indian Women.

Harper:

I guess you know the history of Indian Rights for Indian Women. We've been in existence for a few years and have done a lot of work to change the Act: lobbying Ministers, lobbying Government and also to talk to our chiefs and councillors in regards to retroactivity. Last July we met with NIB and they had agreed fully that they would accept retroactivity, but the only thing is the compensation. And, we met with the Tory Government and they said they would change the Act immediately. And that was supposed to come about before their downfall. And then after that we met with the National Committee for Indian Rights for Indian Women on the Sunday and we talked about what we were going to do and what was our strategy. And what we have so far done is, come up with the retroactivity on the reserves. But the only thing we're really concerned about is, is the Government prepared to pay for the resources to pay for the amounts of people who are going to be reinstated? What kind of resources is the Government prepared to pay? Are they prepared to pay that price? And that is the kind of commitment I have been ordered to ask you from the National Committee ... if you are the Government.

Trudeau:

What kind of resources are you asking for?

32. Transcript of Meeting, February 1980. In possession of Marjorie Griffin Cohen.

Harper:

Well, we know when they're going to be reinstated on the reserves, they're going to create social problems. We're prepared to work with that ... In our surveys we have found out that in a seven year span, there are about 3,000 women that were enfranchised ... The fact is that I know the reserves. The band councils are really concerned about how they are going to provide this. There's hardly any land space and there's no money on the reserves, hardly any on some of them. Of course, some of them, like on our reserve, they have oil rights ... Look, ... I'm asking you, is the Government prepared to ...

Trudeau:

Well, there's two questions, not only the legal question. Let me remind you that in 1969 our Government offered to the Indians in Canada to abolish the Indian Act completely. Not only that particular clause, but the whole works. And it's the Indian people themselves, their leaders, who said "no, don't do that."

Harper:

But that has changed, Sir.

Trudeau:

... The next phase was for Indian women to sort of say "Just abolish, not the whole Act, but that one particular clause." And every time I would meet the National Indian Brotherhood of heads of bands, they would say "Well, we're working towards it but we're not ready for it." Now, if they *are* ready for it, then I can give the unequivocal commitment that we'll take that clause out of the Act. There's not magic there. I mean, it's easy, if the Indian people want it. But now, this is a new demand. First time I heard of it. You want money too. I just can't give that commitment. I don't know how one increases the size of the reserves, to make room for a massive entry of white men now who will be living on the reserves and who will be receiving benefits that until now only have been given to Indian people. How will you prevent the return to the reserves of, if you do it retroactively, of people who are happy to get a free ride? I can see, if you're looking at the future, how we could cooperate with the problems created. We have no idea of what it would mean ...

Harper:

Well, we have stated in our resolutions that it's going to be quarter blood line, and the first generation, those people are going to be reinstated. So that would mean that these white men aren't going to be coming in.

Trudeau:

But do you want *more* people to go back into the reserves?

Harper:

No. That is not the issue you know. It's women ... . like in my case. I was born on a reserve and I lost my status when I married my husband, who was a Métis, who was an unregistered Indian. And from there I lost all my rights. I couldn't go back and live on the reserve. But before that, we had three children. Two of my children were his and are registered, and the rest of my children are not. What I'm saying is I would like to tell the world, or at least Canada, that I am a native person, that I do have status as a native woman. And I would like to retain that right to be a native person. And for my children too, to get those rights back. So they could go there (if they want) to live ... I don't want to go live on the reserve myself. I live here in Toronto and I have my job to do, but other women too, do not want to go back to the reserve. But, the fact is that we want to be treated as equals, as status persons, and be entitled to those benefits. We want to strike that discriminatory clause where it states that if I marry a non-registered Indian, then I have no status at all. Whereas, if a native man marries a non-registered Indian, she is automatically entitled to all the benefits.

Trudeau:

And still live on the reserve?

Harper:

They can live on the reserve. They can go to university and I couldn't go to university because of that. And meanwhile there are non-native women who are on the reserves, who are entitled to all those benefits and all those birthrights that we have.

Trudeau:

Well, I can see the giving of the birthrights and so on ... I just don't see how a government can sort of increase the size of the reserves, particularly when they're surrounded by privately-held lands, and I quite honestly can't see why the Government would be pouring more money into the reserves so that your children would be given an incentive to go and live on the reserve and get free services that my children can't get.

Harper:

There's a lot of land in Canada.

Trudeau:

There's a lot of land, I agree.

Harper:

Why can't we not only increase the reserves but give us other lands for those people who want to go back, for those people who do not have any space on the reserve?

Trudeau:

Well, you mean the Caughnawaga Indians would be given some land up near James Bay or something? And they'd live there?

Harper:

Well, if the women who were reinstated, if they wanted that for their children, that could be so.

Trudeau:

I don't see anything preventing a woman who married a white man on the island on Montréal from moving back to Caughnawaga except that there's not enough place as you say, and if there's not enough place, would they want to go and live somewhere in James Bay? If they do, there's homesteading provisions that they can make. Why would they want to go and live on a reserve? In terms of rights, if that's what the Indian people want — I think I'd feel sorry about it — but I'm sure it could be done. In terms of calling, you know, yourself an Indian and so on. But in terms of being able to move from one society back to the other and claim benefits retroactively, which would mean new land and more money, maybe you ...

O'Connell:

Yes. I think it's difficult. As far as the rights go, yes, I think it's long overdue and surely the delay has been related to the petitions by Indians time after time not to move too quickly till they see the whole Act in perspective. Well, I think it can't wait any longer. So I believe that. Now, if a person therefore regains Indian status, they do have rights on the reserve, ... well, they certainly then share the revenues presumably. They are entitled to whatever the band has and developed and so I should think that would include the right to live there and it would then be up to the band to accommodate them. I personally don't think there's very much shortage of land on the reserves. And if people ended up in apartment buildings, there would be at least a right to be there. Now most of the reserves I've been on have a lot of land that's not used. Some of them are putting up commercial establishments and industries and so on. So I don't see a big difficulty if that gives those persons the right of access. Now, does it give, would it automatically give, say the white husband the right to go back and live there. Now, so far as the claims on the Canadian people and through Government ... .

Trudeau:

What would happen if he stopped paying taxes because he lived there?

O'Connell:

Well, I think these are the great complications.

Harper:

Yeah, they are ...

O'Connell:

There's the question of taxation on the reserves, the income taxes, and so on. I think that should all be worked through subsequent to the granting of the right, the establishment of the clear fight. I just find it impossible to calculate in my mind all the ramifications down through the property chain, the income chain and the housing implications.

Trudeau:

That's the difficulty in the negotiations we've had with the Indians. They don't want a settlement once and for all. Aboriginal rights and treaty rights and everything else. They sort of want to have a settlement in the past and then continue and being different and building up a claim for another settlement in the future. You know, if there were a once and for all way of solving that and saying: "Okay, all those who've intermarried, in the way you say, up till now, we will solve their problem and here's the money settlement and the land settlement, and so on." But I have not yet met the Indian negotiators who would say: "Well, that settles it and our children won't continue to ask special exemptions and special status." And so on and so on.

McDonald:

May I just ask for clarification? Apart from questions of any additional resources, leaving that aside, what is your position on the reinstatement of women who've already lost their status?

Trudeau:

Well, I think in fact our position has been demonstrated as a couple, three of our women Ministers who have been acting almost illegally and you would know that. I mean they've refused to sign orders disenfranchising women. So, in a sense, all through the last part of our government, I guess from 1974 on, all those orders are stacked up and I suppose some Indian men could take an injunction against our Government and our Ministers for not having done their duty. What do you do when women Ministers want to break the law in order to help other women?

Macpherson:

Get more women into the House I should think.

Trudeau:

No, because more women in the House wouldn't solve the ...

Hill:

Clarify the law so it's unnecessary to be "illegal" to help women.

Trudeau:

But you don't get the point. You don't get the point. We are prepared to change the law. It's the women/men who run it and who have not been prepared to do it ... The *Indian* men who have not been prepared to do it.

McDonald:

Should Indian men have the right to say these Indian women shouldn't have these rights?

Trudeau:

Well, think of that. I mean, do you want the government to impose its will on the collectivity of aboriginal Canadians and say this is the way your culture should work: We white people in parliament are a majority and we will tell you how your society should operate?

Macpherson:

Isn't that precisely what happened in 1867?

McDonald:

That's what the Indian Act is.

Trudeau:

Hmmmm. Wrong. The Indian Act is that because the Indian men wanted it that way and they still want it that way today ...

McDonald:

But the Indian Act applies to all of them.

Cohen:

What would reinstatement of rights mean if a woman could not go back to live on the reserve?

Trudeau:

Well, we're prepared, as Martin says, to see them go back on the reserve. It might mean building some highrises so that they can all be accommodated. We have no objection to that. It's the amount of money.

Macpherson:

Let's hope they would object to the highrises ...

McDonald:

I'm still not clear on the position of changing the Indian Act ...

Trudeau:

... . We will not do it if it means disrupting the Indian society and having the men and the women fight together and having them fight with the government. You have to get the people themselves, when you're dealing with a cultural minority like this, to evolve in a way that ... Well, I'm sure the women are evolving towards, and if that is right that the National Indian Brotherhood now is taking a different line and preparing to see this section abolished, as I answered earlier, we are prepared to abolish it. But then if there's a hooker that we've also got to give more land and more money, I just say I wouldn't, as Leader of the Opposition, undertake to do that until I knew more precisely what it meant.

Trevelyan:

It seems to me that the cards are getting a little bit stacked here.

Trudeau:

> I know. And I really feel for you. Because I'm just throwing out all the traditional difficulties. And if I were on your side, I suppose I'd feel frustrated.

Trevelyan:

> When are you going to be on our side?

Trudeau:

> No ... no ... I mean if I were sitting there saying "Well, how do we change the laws", I'd be frustrated because many of you can't find good easy ways to change the laws ... as in the Indian case, as in the pensions to housewives, and so on. And it's, I'm sorry about it, I wish I could say we've got answers, we've been hiding them until now, but here they are ... they're crystal-clear and we'll legislate them.

Trevelyan:

> What I'm referring to is the fact that both in terms of unemployment insurance and people going back to Indian reserves, it seems to me that you're basing policy and legislation on people, as you say, who want to get a "free ride". You know, as though the majority of people on unemployment insurance go to Jamaica, as though there's Anglo-saxon men wandering around in this country who can't wait to get on to Indian reserves to live high off the hog. And that obviously is a distortion of the facts and you're implying that those are the reasons on which your policies are based. Now, also in terms of when we talked about equal pay for work of equal value. You said the problem was we'd have to fight with the men who traditionally wanted to keep this traditional wage structure between jobs. In the case of native rights, the problem is that the men have always wanted this. And it seems that on all these issues, what the women want doesn't seem to be a strong enough influence in influencing Liberal policy.

Trudeau:

> Now, I'm sorry. I guess I shouldn't be giving you these answers because I'm afraid you know them all. What I will say, if you wish, is that we will do our best to make the changes that you are asking for. And I think maybe in the time we have, it's my role to point out the difficulties, you know. And we would like to see greater equality amongst Canadians of all origins and sexes. We would like to see our Human Rights Commission more effective. But we'll do what we can ...

NAC Information
May 1988[33]

The National Action Committee on the Status of Women (NAC) is the largest women's organization in Canada representing over 500 non-gov-

---

33. NAC pamphlet, May 1988.

ernmental women's groups whose combined membership totals three to four million Canadian women.

NAC was formed in 1972, two years after the Royal Commission on the Status of Women presented its report to the House of Commons. As a result of the commission's report, and the need to lobby for the implementation of its recommendations, the first national women's conference called "Strategies for Change" was held in Toronto. The major outcome of the conference was the formation of NAC, created to carry on the work of the commission, to ensure government action on the report's recommendations, to monitor government performance and to unite women's groups from every region of Canada.

In the 15 years since NAC began, the organization has grown to represent groups in every region of Canada. Each group contributes to NAC in a variety of ways by exchanging information, distributing NAC materials, discussing issues of concern to NAC and sending representatives to the NAC annual meeting.

NAC publishes Feminist Action and the Action Bulletin to inform readers about NAC's activities and keep groups and individuals up-to-date on developments in women's issues. NAC also presents and publishes research papers and briefs on government policy. These publications are provided on request.

What are NAC's Objectives?

According to the NAC constitution, the objective of the organization are to initiate and work for improvements to the status of women by:

1.　actions designed to change legislation, attitudes, customs and practices;
2.　evaluating and advocating changes to benefit women, including measures proposed by the Royal Commission on the Status of Women and those adopted by NAC;
3.　encouraging the formation of, and communication and co-operation among, organizations interested in improving the status of women in Canada;
4.　exchanging information with member organizations and other interested persons or groups, and providing information to the public about the status of women and the recommended changes for improvement.

Who are NAC's Members?

A group of 10 or more individuals can become a voting member of NAC providing it shows one of its primary purposes to be advancement of the status of women. Member groups must subscribe to the objectives and purposes of NAC. Government departments and agencies are not eligible to become members.

NAC's 500 member groups range from community-based women's action and service delivery groups to provincial and national federations, to women's groups in churches, unions and political parties. Some groups focus on single issues such as pay equity or violence against women. Other groups work on behalf of a particular constituency — native women, disabled women, or visible minority and immigrant women's groups. Women of both official languages are represented, as well as women of all political persuasions.

How to Participate in NAC

A group can apply to join NAC by filling out a membership application form and sending it, along with the appropriate annual fee to the NAC membership committee. The annual fee is based on a sliding scale according to the size of the group's membership.

An individual may associate with NAC as a "Friend of NAC". Individuals do not receive voting privileges, but are welcome to participate in the annual meeting and in the work of the policy committees.

What is the Structure of NAC?

NAC is run by a 25 member volunteer executive elected each year at the annual general meeting. This executive meets seven or eight times a year. Thirteen of the 25 members are regional representatives elected by the groups within their region. The other 12 executive members, including seven table officers and five members at large, are elected by all delegates present at the annual general meeting ...

How Does NAC Differ from the Canadian Advisory Council on the Status of Women and Status of Women Canada?

NAC is Canada's largest voluntary feminist non-governmental lobby organization.

The Canadian Advisory Council on the Status of Women (CACSW) is a paragovernmental organization which reports to Parliament through the Minister Responsible for the Status of Women. Council members are government-appointed. The CACSW advises the federal government and informs the public through its research and communications programs.

Status of Women Canada is the federal government department of the Minister Responsible for the Status of Women ...

Where Does NAC Get its Money?

Over half of NAC's annual budget is provided by the Women's Program of the Secretary of State. The remainder is raised from annual membership fees, Friends of NAC fees, subscriptions, the sale of publications and direct mail fundraising drives.

Does NAC Support a Political Party?
No, NAC is a non-partisan organization. NAC does not endorse any political party nor does it support individual candidates.

"The Need for Independent Feminism"
March 1981[34]

... When it established the Advisory Council on the Status of Women, the government placed itself in a position to influence what was said about its actions towards women. And, by and large, it has been successful. Because it appoints its own supporters to the Council the government can count on rather soft criticism. The press has co-operated by relying solely on the Advisory Council's opinion whenever a feminist voice was called for.

What the government did not bargain for was Doris Anderson's rather un-Canadian political defiance. Under Anderson's leadership the Council has gained credibility with the feminist movement; she worked with feminists throughout the country and tried to learn from them. As a feminist first, she took up their fight. But for the majority of council members party loyalty proved stronger than loyalty to women when the Council decided to cancel a scheduled women's meeting on the constitution. This action was rationalized by appeals to "playing the political game;" that is, if we don't embarrass the government, perhaps it will be grateful and throw a crumb to the ladies. This contorted logic is perfectly illustrated by Council member Florence Ievers' explanation of why she was voting to cancel the conference: "I say that it's about time we start being nice to them. So if this conference is going to be an embarrassment let's play it their way and cancel it."

Lloyd Axworthy's blatant manipulation of the Council is despicable but it is not surprising. After all, the Council is the government's creation, and every member is there because the government thinks she should be there. The real lesson to be learned from this episode is that feminist watch-dog activities cannot be left to government, and if the feminist movement in Canada is to have an impact in the future it must not be tied or obligated to the government in any way.

Right now the major national feminist organization in Canada, the National Action Committee on the Status of women (NAC), receives a major portion of its funding from federal Government sources. That the government understands the implications of this is demonstrated by remarks made by Jim Fleming during NAC's meeting with Trudeau (see "Trudeau on women" in this issue). He said: "You may be frustrated by the lack of an acceleration in activity taken but there is some. Your very being is as a result of federal funding."

Feminists do not deliberately allow themselves to be controlled by government, but the line between cooperation and co-optation is a thin

34. Marjorie Cohen, Editorial, *Canadian Forum* (March 1981).

one and it can be a hair's breadth when an organization's whole existence depends on not making the government too mad. This becomes a subtle muzzle on activity. Few issues are dramatic enough for an organization to risk attempting to become totally independent overnight. Many things are not said and all issues are subconsciously weighed to determine whether or not they will invite a cut-off of government funds. More direct government pressure is felt through the conditions of the grants (none are condition-free) and through government review of how monies are spent. It would be foolish for any organization to believe that it could remain above manipulation under these circumstances. But rather than slowly extricating itself from this unfortunate position, NAC is relying increasingly on the government for money. This is dangerous. The women of Canada have everything to lose if their major feminist organization stays in the pocket of the government.

NAC has been essential to the development of a feminist voice in Canadian politics. This voice will remain loud and strong only if NAC maintains its credibility with the women of Canada through being independent.

"Canadian Advisory Council on the Status of Women: Contradictions and Conflicts" September 1988[35]

In the ... article which appeared in the *Toronto Star* on December 18, 1987, Lois Sweet examines the controversy over the recently released *Integration and Participation: Women's Work in the Home and in the Labour Force* in order to question the capacity of the Canadian Advisory Council on the Status of Women (CACSW) to produce independent research. As Sweet also referred to political interference in a document on free trade, she might have reminded her readers about Lloyd Axworthy's interference in Council plans to consult Canadian women on amendments to the Constitution in 1981 — an interference that sparked the resignation of Council president Doris Anderson and the mobilizing of hundreds of women in Ottawa that eventually led to the entrenchment of women's rights in the Charter of Rights.

If she were to write the article today, she would have to refer to the protests that erupted throughout the community of immigrant and visible minority women upon the release of the Council's report on "Immigrant Women in Canada: A Policy Perspective" in February 1988. Expressing their outrage at the failure of the Council to consult with them *before* the release of the document, representatives of this community outlined various ways in which it distorted the realities of the lives of the women for whom it purported to speak. In particular, they charged the Council with its failure to address "racism and systemic discrimination ... as a fundamental barrier that immigrant women face in integrating in society at all levels, whether in school, or employment" (from a statement at the

35. Sue Findlay, *RFR/DRF* 17, no. 3 (September 1988), 90.

Press Conference held in February 9, 1988). In the report, the authors vaguely noted that the larger issues were beyond the scope of the document. This would appear to be yet another indication that the Council cannot tackle some of the fundamental inequalities that shape their lives.

Why not? Is it really a case of political interference? Is it self-censoring in a conservative political climate: What's going on?

The Council is not an independent body. It never has been. It was established by the government in 1973; it reports to the Minister Responsible for the Status of Women; its budget is approved by the Treasury Board, and its staff is appointed by the Public Service Commission. More importantly, its membership is appointed by Order-in-Council in consultation with elected members of the government and the only objective criteria that is used is consideration for regional representation. Although it is true that the creation of a council was recommended by the Royal Commission on the Status of Women in 1970, and subsequently endorsed by feminists across Canada, it was not established in any way that would guarantee or facilitate accountability to the "women's movement," or even to Parliament as the Commission had recommended. While its mandate to advise the public on issues affecting the status of women in Canada justified the development and distribution of research documents that have been useful to feminists over the years, it did not alter the more fundamental fact of its accountability to the government. It is inevitable therefore that feminists with expectations that the Council could always act in their interests — that it was independent — would have complaints about it ...

"Grant Granted!!!!"
November 1974[36]

The acceptance of government grants is fraught with pitfalls. On the negative side, a salaried co-ordinator could result in the loss of volunteer help. The job of running the Centre is an immense one, requiring a lot of support. Volunteers tend to drift away when there is someone else being paid to do the work. Difficulties also arise when one woman is in charge of the Centre, when one woman knows what's happening. Should she leave, a void is created that no one else can fill. The information, the contacts, the proceedings, have all been resting with one individual. Should she leave, everyone else is at sea, and things fall apart.

Another problem with short-term funding arises when the money is gone. There is a danger of being in a position of having no funds, thus no co-ordinator, and projects begun under new-found wealth must cease.

Preceding all of these difficulties are the problems created by deciding how the money is to be allocated. Such decisions are potentially destructive and divisive. Priorities must be established, goals and philosophies must be determined.

36. Saskatoon Women's Liberation Newsletter (November 1974). CWMA.

Another possible danger of a large financial input is that of forced growth. It is essential to consider carefully where the money is to be spent, and to ensure that when the funds are depleted it does not mean the end of projects and programs begun under relative financial stability.

On the positive side, the Women's Centre is in need of money. Our financial resources are in a sad state and questions of paying the rent and utilities are pre-eminent. Should refusal of the grant mean a shutdown of operations we must consider the issue even more carefully.

Another utilitarian aspect of the issue is that of setting a precedent for receiving government funding. However "political" a motive this may be, it is a valid one. In addition, the possibility is there to prove our worth to the government and the general public. The women's movement has never been respectable, and perhaps as the word is normally used we do not wish to be, but these funds would make possible innovative and relevant programs and enable us to reach more women than we do at present.

Another consideration is our right as women to receive these funds, even the necessity of government support for women's issues and concerns. Women's groups should be funded. Our work deserves such financial support.

The issues are complex and we could use your ideas and your help. Come to the general meeting December 7 at the Zodiac Centre to make your feelings known.

"Government Funding of Battered Women's Shelters — Feminist Victory or Co-optation?" Ontario, Summer 1983[37]

The annual meeting of the Ontario Association of Interval and Transition Houses was held June 9-11 this year at McMaster University in Hamilton. The general mood at the conference was optimistic. Women seemed to feel that, in spite of many struggles ahead, we are making significant progress. It was, indeed, time to look at how far we've come and to give ourselves some well-deserved credit.

A 1982 survey indicated that there are 37 operating transition houses in Ontario. In addition, there were 12 groups actively working towards opening a house in the near future. Currently operating houses make available 524 beds for women and children in crisis. We have come a long way since 1977, when there were only 123 transition house beds available in the province.

The subsequent announcement by Frank Drea, Minister of Community and Social Services that over the next two years, 12 transition houses will be opened in Northern Ontario at a cost of $1.7 million, was warmly received by many women.

Isn't this what we've all been fighting for? Abused women's lack of access to shelter, particularly in remote areas, has been decried repeat-

37. Cindy Player, *Breaking the Silence* 1, no. 5 (Summer 1983), 4.

edly by concerned feminists. We have also been protesting inadequate funding for transition houses for at least a decade.

So why has this news, and the conference in general, left me feeling vaguely uneasy? Perhaps, in part, because I realize that very few transition houses are (or can afford to be) explicitly political. This was brought home to me in a number of ways at the conference. I was amazed that so few houses function as collectives. I was surprised that I was challenged on the lack of male involvement in Ottawa Interval House by other transition-house workers. I was angered by the fact that our energy is still being spent in gathering statistics to establish our credibility. Why are we still trying to demonstrate to the government that there is a need for transition houses? I wonder whether this is a deliberate strategy designed to leave us with less time for political action. Women who are underpaid and over-worked pose less of a threat to the patriarchy.

Undoubtedly, it is wonderful that more women living in abusive situations will have the alternative of supportive shelter. That is no small achievement. But I have been saddened by the sense that many of us are losing touch with our feminist roots. And I fear that more government funding may move us further in this direction. It seems that along with growth, expansion, and more adequate funding, come externally-imposed rules and regulations and a watering-down of our politics. Our greater numbers are a stronger threat to the existing order and necessitate stricter control on their part ...

There are no easy answers. We desperately need funding in order to provide necessary support and shelter for women and children. But far too often, the strings attached to that funding run counter to our feminist philosophy. At times it seems that all we can do is try not to compromise too much. At this point, if we want to survive, we do have to compromise. But it is important to remember what we are working towards — the end of violence against women and children. And I think it may be important to also recognize that at some point we may have to do it on our own. The time may come when we have the strength and/or are forced to say no to government money and all its constraints and scrape by in whatever way we can. But I hope it will be in our own feminist way.

"The State of Federal Funding"
Fall 1990[38]

The federal government's cuts in the Secretary of State's Women's Program put a new urgency into the question of how the Canadian women's movement should be funded. The organized women's movement here, unlike that in any other country, is financed largely by government, overwhelmingly by the Secretary of State Women's Program. With the latest budget cuts some organizations, especially

38. Lynn McDonald, *The Womanist* 2, no. 2 (Fall 1990), 37.

women's centres, will close down completely, while others will have to reduce services. The National Action Committee on the Status of Women, the umbrella organization comprising 600 plus women's groups, had been cut the previous year and advised of future decreases. These have already resulted in reductions in staff, office space, executive and committee meetings, publications and lobbying.

To address the funding issue we have first to distinguish between organizations that exist to provide a service-women's centres, sexual assault crisis centres, shelters for battered women, job counselling and various innovative programs — and those whose chief purpose, like NAC's, is lobbying. Some organizations, of course, do both. The National Association of Women and the Law, for example, lobbies governments and provides services to law students. Sexual assault crisis centres lobby on criminal justice and enforcement practices as well as provide direct services to victims.

Bearing this complication in mind, let me make the argument that lobbying organizations should not be funded by government for their normal operations. Service organizations should be. If the lobbying organizations, especially NAC, were independent or more independent in their financing they could fight more vigorously and effectively for the service organizations. The Canadian women's movement as a whole might obtain more money from the government if its lobbying organizations asked for less. For the women of Canada this means that a voluntary investment in lobbying organizations, by membership dues and donations, could be rewarded with better funding for all the services women need ...

The opponents of independent funding for groups like NAC have many arguments in their pockets. They argue that "Women are poor", and indeed most poor people are women and women earn, on average, less than men. Yet millions of Canadian women earn enough to pay dues of $25 or $50 per year, some even $100 per year. Women favouring ongoing dependency on government argue an entitlement to the money on the basis of the worthiness of the services provided. Here lobbying is redefined as a service to legislators, which, in fact, it usually is. Still, the cold, hard fact remains that grants are being reduced and they always come with strings attached. They have always diverted organizational time from real work ...

This is not to object to any form of public funding of voluntary organizations, women's or other. Tax credits even a better system of tax deductions, could work, assuming the permitted aims and objectives included lobbying. The government could go even further to provide for a system of allocating a certain sum of money to voluntary organizations through the tax system ... . Organizations, presumably including environmental, cultural and other worthy causes, would make their pitch to the public at income tax time. Organizations would survive and flourish on the basis of their popular support, without any ability of government to censor. There are no guarantees here either, of course, for a government could suspend the whole system or de-register an organization. However, an enormous degree of independence would be attained, and for that reason it's unlikely to be legislated by any government.

The current situation is truly preposterous: a department of the federal government, the Secretary of State Women's Program, asks its major lobbyist, NAC, what lobbying it plans to do next year and then decides how much to pay it for this service! Nowhere else in the world does this happen. The National Organization of Women in the United States receives not a dime in government funding. Nor do the women's organizations of Europe, north or south, large or small ...

"Debate Historic Benchmark for Women"
Toronto, 1984[39]

There were no knock-out punches landed by any of the leaders Wednesday night — few were even thrown — and it's doubtful the debate changed the course of the election.

But as a formal acknowledgement that so-called "women's issues" were now hot stuff politically, the evening was clearly historic.

"It is a large step forward in political terms for the women of Canada," said Chaviva Hosek, president of the National Action Committee on the Status of Women, the sponsor. "I have never seen political leaders so well briefed on women's issues."

The numbers showing how important these issues are to men and women voters have been in the pollsters' data banks for some time. But that three federal party leaders would appear on one stage for two hours, debating these issues in both languages in a live broadcast, is a new benchmark.

From now on, it is going to be hard for politicians to ignore the blatant discrimination women face in the market-place or the abuse they endure from pornographers, rapists or wife beaters.

For Ed Broadbent, it was familiar territory because his New Democratic Party has been long out front of the other two party leaders in putting together policies that address these issues.

Unlike Turner and Mulroney, Broadbent didn't find it necessary to closet himself for many hours with specialists on women's issues to prepare.

He acted as an effective foil throughout the evening, challenging Brian Mulroney and John Turner whenever they lapsed into generalities.

When Turner waffled on the question of day care, offering the familiar excuse of federal politicians that it is an area of provincial jurisdiction, Broadbent scoffed. That was exactly what the Liberals had said 20 years ago about medicare, he said.

---

39. John Ferguson, *The Citizen*, 1984. CWMA file: NDP Federal.

Adequate child care in state-run facilities should be as fundamental a right as health care and the federal government should spend $300 million immediately to get such a system underway, Broadbent said.

When Turner countered that such a system would cost $600 million and a federal-provincial agreement would have to be worked out, Broadbent said he should go ahead anyway and offer the money to provinces ready to take action.

When Mulroney said women didn't have equal access to credit from the banks, Broadbent asked whether he would make banks lend a set proportion of their funds to companies run by women.

Mulroney ducked the question.

But as Turner reminded everyone in his closing remarks, Broadbent won't become PM. That makes panelist Kaye Sigurjonsson's final question the most important of the evening.

She pointed out that so far there has been too much talk and only a little action.

"Why should we trust you now?" she asked.

Turner gave his stock reply about his commitment to women's equality and cited the record number of women candidates running for the Liberals in this election. Mulroney said he would appear before them again to be judged after he had a chance to act.

Both clearly will be held to account, either as prime minister or as opposition leader.

"They sounded sincere to me," said Hosek. "We'll see after Sept. 4 if they are sincere."

Fifty-two per cent of the electorate will be watching.

"The Beginnings of the Feminist Party of Canada"
Toronto, February–April 22, 1979[40]

The original Hart House meeting held on Sunday, February 11, 1979 was called for the purpose of founding a women's political party. When we gathered together, there was a division amongst us as to whether this would be the most effective direction to pursue. Clearly, we were dissatisfied with the present situation in government but we could not agree on the most effective approach: should it be that of a political party or that of a feminist caucus. A troublesome question was raised: How could we expect women, with only their gender in common, to take a unified action and overcome the years and allegiances of ideological differences? We looked to a volunteer interim committee to explore both the philosophical practical alternatives. These women here before you made up that committee.

.... At our first meeting on Sunday March 4 we discussed the major issue facing us: how to increase women's participation in the political system. Again we were divided as to the best approach; some of us were committed to the formation of a party, others were convinced that this

40. *Feminist Party of Canada Newsletter* (February–April 22, 1979).

would be unworkable. We were at an impasse. Then in an attempt to get a wider perspective, we recounted the records of women already in politics, those women who had achieved positions of power. From this cursory analysis, we discovered that most female politicians, regardless of background or party affiliation, reduced their connections with women's organizations to a minimum, when they obtained office ... . This, then, is the problem: no matter how many women are elected, from the evidence we have thus far, they do not, on the whole, address themselves to those issues of concern to women that have been continually neglected by everyone else. Collectively, women work to elect qualified candidates but at the moment of victory these women shake off political debts and walk on alone.

At this point, some of us who had been resistant to the formation of a feminist political party, realized that a feminist caucus is rendered ineffectual for this very reason; it has no reliable voice to depend on. And it was at this point that the interim committee resolved its indecision. We recognized the necessity of a women's political party; for only then, when the potential candidate has a context within the party and is shielded by the party structure, would she be able to maintain feminist beliefs while in office. When we saw that a feminist party was the only method that could truly be representative of women's needs and desires for change, the choice was clear. We now ask you to join with us in the realization of this vision. Once the commitment was made, we were, and are, and will continue to be, faced with the formidable task of turning vision into policy and policy into strategy ...

This, then, is the vital question: If there were a women's political party, would you support it? We have only germinated the idea, now we must all help to realize it; for this we need support, dedication, imagination and not least of all, commitment to our goal. And so we present to you our statement and afterwards we welcome a discussion.

April 1979.
Feminist Party of Canada, Interim Committee ...

"Running a Feminist Campaign" November/December 1977[41]

... The approach I took when I ran for the NDP leadership in 1975 illustrates the qualities that feminism can bring to politics. I was asked to consider running by a search committee that wanted a feminist socialist woman to make a serious bid for the leadership of the party. After many open and frank discussions with my constituency executive, the constituency membership, my running mate, women across the country and many others, I decided to "throw my hat in the ring".

We established five ground rules for conducting a campaign. The campaign was not going to be a star oriented personality campaign. I was going to stay in until the very end and not play the role of "stalking

41. Rosemary Brown, *Branching Out* (November/December 1977), 17-18.

horse" for everyone. There would be no deals. The campaign was to be run on the issues of feminism and socialism, and all decisions were going to be arrived at collectively.

Through the months, my campaign did emerge as different from the others. My campaign committees across the country were made up largely but not exclusively of feminist women. Decision making was decentralized with each provincial committee making its own decisions about how to conduct the campaign within its borders. The emphasis was on education through discussion of issues, not on a slick, well-packaged campaign. We used volunteer labour to prepare and distribute gestetnered policy statements. Children played an active role, from working the gestetner, stuffing envelopes, stapling material, to staffing the information booth at both provincial and federal conventions.

The campaign was intended to be a learning experience for women. They prepared policy statements, designed the final leaflet and organized the fundraising ...

More than anything, we concentrated on ensuring that the "Brown" campaign was well organized, that the policy statements were well researched, that we were serious and that as many women as possible benefited from the campaign.

We soon came to realize that because we were outspoken in our demands for socialism with feminism and because of our continued open exchange of ideas, we were contributing in a very real and meaningful way to the examination of issues and to a change of direction in the party. As a result of this we found ourselves dominating discussion and strategy on the convention floor. We concluded that, although we may have started out as amateurs and naive idealists, we were emerging as mature exponents of a new kind of politics, both personal and collective. We had proven that the creative and co-operative use of power would give birth to new political forms ...

For me, feminist politics embodies and encompasses socialist politics and vice versa. The achievement of either one without the other is impossible. In addition to my responsibility to all the constituents of my electoral district, I have made the decisions to represent and work on behalf of all women and I have been prepared to take the consequences of such a decision. I am convinced that until we have more women in politics — openly, flagrantly and unashamedly committed to the struggle for the liberation of women and determined to change traditional power politics to make it more responsive to the dispossessed of this earth — we as women are doomed to many more years of oppression and exploitation.

Together

"Women Leading the Way: In the Country and in the Women's Movement"
Spring 1992[42]

I think the key to being a feminist leader is accountability. To me, feminist leadership is about furthering the interests of the collective, of women in general. Leadership in a collective doesn't mean that everyone plays the same role but rather that leaders speak for the collective and not for themselves.

Accountability means several things to me. It means providing individual feedback to women leaders, and it means developing structures for democratic decision making that support both the interests of the group and the spokesperson. It is important that we learn to direct our leaders, and to be critical of them in constructive and not destructive ways ...

"If you move, you're a target" is a mantra that I have repeated for years. This applies to groups as well as individuals. Women who provide leadership in whatever way — arguing for new ideas and policy, fighting against racism in the women's movement, speaking publicly for an organization — are putting themselves out on a limb. No matter how we collectivize our positions, those who speak them, or those who push for them most effectively will be identified with them as individuals. No matter how strong their organizational base, they risk, as individuals, public disapproval and criticism in order to further the struggle for feminism. Women who put themselves in these positions need critical support ...

Representation has always been a demand of, and an issue within, the women's movement. It is very difficult for any one woman to adequately 'represent' the voices of the diversity of the movement in this country. Our movement is fiercely democratic and is very hard on its leaders. As a result, a lot of very talented women have burned out on the women's movement. At the same time as we are working towards more representative groups, events and organizations, I think we need to understand and use leadership more strategically. We need to understand the extra stress and responsibility leadership creates for individual women, the responsibility of providing them with feedback and support, and the strategic moments when we need to mobilize the strengths of our leaders and spokeswomen to make our points heard loud and clear.

Sharing leadership skills is also an important part of feminist leadership. Rather than competing for leadership as men have done historically, women should be promoting others with talent and ability and training them in the necessary skills. The women's movement has not

---

42. Judy Rebick, *The Womanist* (Spring 1992), 6.

devoted very many resources to training leaders. Experienced women should be encouraging younger women and sharing their skills ...

Newsletter of the Metro Toronto NDP Women's Committee Toronto, 1974[43]

Bread and Roses

By popular demand we are printing the words to the song "Bread and Roses." This song came out of a 1911 textile-workers strike. The workers were striking against the long hours for children in the factories. The bosses finally agreed to allow the children to work a maximum of 40 hours (instead of 54), but simultaneously cut the workers' hours and pay so that most did not make enough to live on. They went out again and one of the bosses was heard to say "What do these women want, roses?" The next day strike banners read "We Want Bread *and Roses.*" Only the second line in the second verse has been changed. To learn the tune, come to a meeting; we are very fond of singing it.

> As we come marching, marching, in the beauty of the day,
> A million darkened kitchens, a thousand mill-lots grey,
> Are touched with all the radiance that a sudden sun discloses,
> For the people hear us singing, Bread and Roses, Bread and Roses.
> As we come marching, marching, we battle too for men,
> When they get themselves together, we will work with them again,
> Our lives shall not be sweated from birth until life closes,
> Hearts starve as well as bodies, give us Bread but give us Roses.
> As we come marching, marching unnumbered women dead,
> Go crying through our singing, their ancient cry for bread,
> Small art and love and beauty, their drudging spirits knew,
> Yes, it is bread we fight for, but we fight for roses too.
> As we come marching, marching, we bring the greater days,
> The rising of the women, means the rising of the race,
> No more the drudge and idler, ten that toil share one reposes,
> But a sharing of life's glories, Bread and Roses, Bread and Roses.

43. NDP Women's Committee, Toronto.

Chapter 2

The Politics of the Body

Ruth Roach Pierson

In 1970, in an address to the Abortion Caravan Rally in Toronto, Doris Powers spoke out against the double bind imposed on many poor women when a hospital "therapeutic" abortion committee issued the ultimatum: be sterilized or we won't grant you an abortion. If the woman agreed to the sterilization, Powers argued, "she ... lost all power to make any future decisions over her own body."[1]

Gaining control over our own bodies has been a central concern of the Canadian women's movement since its revival in the late 1960s. For centuries dominant Western culture has accepted René Descartes' proposition "I think, therefore I am" as axiomatic proof of one's existence. Women in the second half of the twentieth century have challenged the disembodiment implied by the airy Cartesian[2] stance as sexist and racist. Proof of our embodiment, women have asserted, confronts us at every turn. But so does proof of our lack of control over that embodiment, and that is what women have sought to change. On a wide range of fronts women have struggled to assert or regain control over our bodies, seeking to wrest control away from the state, the medical establishment, institutionalized religion, pharmaceutical companies, advertisers, pornographers, institutionalized censorship, the violence of men.

Reproductive Rights

Control over our bodies' reproductive capacities has been at or near the centre of this struggle from early on. Prior to 1969, women in Canada could not legally obtain information on, or prescriptions for, artificial birth control, as both were outlawed by the Criminal Code. Then, in 1969, in response to years of pressure from such organizations as the Planned Parenthood Federation of Canada, the liberal government of Prime Minister Pierre Elliott Trudeau legalized the public distribution of birth control information and the advertisement and sale of contraceptives.

While at first jubilant over the decriminalization of artificial contraception, women soon had reason to be concerned with the side effects of many under-tested birth control drugs and devices. For instance, intra-uterine devices (IUDs) could become embedded in the lining of the womb, causing painful inflammation and excessive bleeding. Some brands of the birth control pill were found to cause weight gain, headaches and worse.[3] Later, decades after it had revolutionized birth control, "the Pill" was linked, in instances of long-time use, to cardiovascular problems in women who smoke. In April 1985, *The New England Journal of Medicine* published two reports linking IUD use, particularly use of the Dalkon shield, to infertility.[4] In all these cases, the disabled and dispossessed were the most vulnerable. For instance, even when the controversial, needle-administered drug Depo Provera was banned from birth control use in Canada because of its known health hazards, it was being given to Canadian women with mental and physical infirmities as well as to women in the so-called Third World.[5] Depo Provera has never been "licensed for use as birth control in Canada, although doctors can prescribe it." As recently as 1992, women throughout the Northwest Territories were being offered Depo as a birth control method.[6] Many women came to decry and combat a pharmaceutical industry more interested in profits than in the ill effects of their products on women's health.[7] Why, women have asked, have these companies pushed prescription contraceptives, like the Pill, at the expense of less dangerous options, like the diaphragm? Why, if a sterilization procedure is needed as a birth control measure, has the medical establishment preferred performing the complicated tubal ligation on women over the much simpler vasectomy on men?

From the very start, many regarded the 1969 liberalization of the law governing birth control as an incomplete victory, because it left abortion in the Criminal Code. As spelled out in "Abortion: A Woman's Right," only under certain conditions and in exceptional cases could a woman with an unwanted pregnancy have a legal abortion. Moreover, it could be performed only in an accredited hospital. Furthermore, the determination of what constituted a justifiable condition or legitimate case was beyond her control: the decision was made by a "therapeutic abortion committee," consisting of not fewer than three members, each of whom had to be a "qualified medical practitioner," appointed by the board of the accredited hospital.[8] Moreover, in many parts of Canada, the nearest hospital lacked the "therapeutic abortion committee" empowered by law to make the determination.

One of the first large-scale national actions of the new women's liberation movement was the spring 1970 Abortion Caravan from Vancouver to Ottawa to demand the decriminalization of abortion. Organizers understood the fundamental, underlying proposition of the Caravan to be: "It is the right of all women to have control over their own bodies." In the 1970s, invaluable assistance was given to the movement to de-

The Pedestal

The Abortion Cavalcade left Vancouver on 27 April 1970 and travelled cross-country in support of free abortion on demand.

criminalize abortion by the Montreal physician Dr. Henry Morgentaler.[9] A survivor of a Nazi concentration camp, Dr. Morgentaler was deeply affected by the plight of women in desperate need of ending a pregnancy. To provide relief to such desperate women, he began performing abortions in a clinic in defiance of the existing law. In 1973, he was brought to trial, charged with performing an illegal abortion. When the Quebec jury brought in a verdict of not guilty, the Quebec Ministry of Justice launched an appeal and, in an unanimous decision, the Quebec Court of Appeal in 1974 reversed the acquittal and "found Dr. Morgentaler guilty as originally charged." The Supreme Court of Canada's hearing of the case in 1975, International Women's Year, resulted in a six to three decision upholding Dr. Morgentaler's conviction and eighteen-month sentence. While he was serving his jail sentence, the Quebec Ministry of Justice began laying further charges against Dr. Morgentaler for performing abortions. But in the first of these trials, the jury once again acquitted the doctor and this time, when appealed, the Quebec Court of Appeal, on January 19, 1976, unanimously upheld the acquittal. Later that year, the Attorney General of Quebec declared safe, medical abortions in free-standing clinics legal in the province.

A large organization, originally called the Canadian Association for Repeal of the Abortion Law, was formed in 1974 to support Dr. Morgentaler's challenge of the 1969 abortion law. Later changing its name to Canadian Abortion Rights Action League/Association Canadienne pour le Droit a l'Avortement, with provincial and local chapters across Canada, CARAL/ACDA has spearheaded the campaign for decriminalized abortion. According to its constitution, CARAL/ACDA's purpose

Mary Lyons Courtesy: *Broadside*

Fire set by an arsonist bent on destroying the Morgentaler Clinic upstairs gutted the Toronto Women's Bookstore in the summer of 1983.

has been to "ensure that no woman in Canada is denied access to safe, legal abortion" and to gain recognition of "the right to safe, legal abortion as a fundamental human right." Together with other groups, such as the Coalition québècoise pour le droit à l'avortement libre et gratuit and the Ontario Coalition for Abortion Clinics (OCAC), CARAL/ACDA has kept the issue before the public with press releases and protest marches, such as the National Day of Action on Abortion of October 14, 1980, which was observed with demonstrations and candlelight vigils in cities and towns across Canada. And they have kept up pressure on government with postcard- and letter-writing campaigns. Organization newsletters and telephone "trees" have been effectively used to assemble masses of women at short notice to protect abortion clinics from anti-abortion attacks. In Halifax, the formation of the Abortion Information and Referral Service (AIRS) in 1980 "was prompted by the refusal of the Victoria General Hospital to perform an approved abortion on a Cape Breton woman when her husband, from whom she was separated, threatened to sue the hospital."[10] Feminists have also supported Morgentaler's free-standing abortion clinics because the technique they use—vacuum suction—is in fact safer than the standard "D & C" (dilation and curettage), a more invasive procedure, preferred by many hospitals.

Childbirth

But abortion has certainly not been the only reproductive rights issue of importance to women. The right not to prevent but to give birth has been the issue for many women who do not enjoy the privilege of a regular good income,[11] and of membership in the white, able-bodied, heterosexual mainstream. For example, women with disabilities[12] and lesbians have had to fight for the right to have or to adopt a baby. Race, poverty, disability and/or unmarried status can render women vulnerable to involuntary sterilization. Such women are concerned with gaining protection against being "sterilized without informed consent"[13] as much as with gaining access to safe legal abortions. In general, in the area of reproductive rights, to be seen by the authorities as deviant from the norm is to be disadvantaged, as in the case of the unmarried Native woman who gave birth to the first baby born in 1992 in a Saskatchewan hospital but saw the publicity and baby product prizes for that honour go to a white, married mother of a baby born a few seconds later.

Women from many walks of life and vantage points have struggled to regain control over childbirth. Parts of the women's movement developed a scathing critique of what came to be regarded as the excessive intrusion of the male-dominated medical establishment and of medical technology into the "natural" process of birthing. Singled out as examples of this unnecessary medicalization were the extremely high rates of Caesarean deliveries, induced labours, and episiotomies.[14] These operations were being performed, it was charged, more for the convenience of the male practitioner than for the health of either the mother or the child. A movement for the return to "natural" childbirth spread. Pregnant women took classes in techniques of breathing and pushing to facilitate delivery without anaesthetics. Less widespread, but not unrelated, has been the movement to restore the practice of birthing at home, rather than in hospital. Some hospitals have responded by offering "birthing centres," where partners or "birth coaches" can attend women during labour. At the same time, midwives (largely female) have had an ongoing struggle to regain official recognition and to wrest the right to minister to women in childbirth from the exclusive control of obstetricians (largely male).[15]

While women were struggling to retake control of birthing in various ways in Canada's urbanized South, women in the North were losing control. According to two analysts of this development, "[t]he medicalization of child birth in the North is one dimension of the extension of southern power into northern Canada and the relationship between illness and colonialism."[16] With the introduction of medical personnel and practices from the South beginning in the 1950s and accelerating in each subsequent decade, birth, once a social, cultural and spiritual act among the Inuit, was turned into "a medical act." Increasingly, pregnant Inuit women, who had once given birth within the circle of their families and communities, have been evacuated to hospitals in towns and settlements further south. There they are delivered in an isolated and impersonal environment. Often, "women are transported to southern hospitals for periods ranging from two weeks to two months prior to delivery." Separated from husbands, children and other family members and friends, they suffer "loneliness, boredom, anxiety, [and] fear." It is known that high levels of anxiety and stress are associated with difficulties in childbirth, but, as Betty Anne Daviss-Putt has written, "[p]erhaps the greatest personal risk posed by evacuation is the woman's loss of control over her own experience."[17]

New Reproductive Technologies

At the same time, by the second half of the 1980s, advances that women in the South were making with the demedicalization of birthing in some areas were matched by a growing loss of control in others resulting from the proliferation of "new reproductive technologies" (NRTs). Ostensibly designed to help women, and to a lesser degree men, overcome the "problem" of infertility, this "revolution in reproduction" was occurring in the absence both of carefully conducted research into the physical consequences of widespread use, and informed public debate about the moral implications. There is no question that women who want to get pregnant and find they cannot suffer an excruciating sense of loss of control over their bodies.[18] Rather than women's gaining increased control over their fertility, it appeared that fertile and infertile women's bodies were being subjected to drugs and procedures that were insufficiently tested and hence putting women at risk. Rather than taking measures to prevent chlamydia, one of the leading causes of infertility in women, the medical establishment was developing invasive NRTs to "give" fertility to women rendered infertile.[19] Techniques like in vitro fertilization have extremely low success rates but women participating in the so-called "life" programs were seldom informed of the eighty or ninety per cent likelihood of failure.[20] Sounding the alarm, feminists pointed out that, on the contrary, women desperate to have children were being exploited as guinea pigs and exposed, at high financial cost as well as high physical risk, to potentially dangerous medications and dubious surgical procedures.[21]

Moreover, in the context of proliferating reproductive technologies, such as ultrasound testing and fetal monitoring, there is a growing tendency for the judicial and medical systems to treat the pregnant woman as a potential adversary of her own fetus. Changes in the language of ordinary discourse reflect this major shift. A scant twenty years ago, it was the woman's experience of pregnancy that was central. "In the history of pregnancy," according to medical historian Barbara Duden, "women were pregnant and at some point they were pregnant with child—after quickening, in the second part of pregnancy."[22] Now the expectant mother is a woman carrying a fetus and increasingly regarded as separate, indeed somehow disembodied, from the developments taking place within her own womb. In turn, Duden argues, "the content of the womb," made visible through fetal images, has achieved the status of "a public fetus,"[23] a subject for judicial or medical intervention independent of the woman's will. In the alarming *Baby R* case, the British Columbia Family and Child Services Act was used to apprehend the soon-to-be-born child of a Vancouver welfare mother in order to force her to undergo a Caesarean section deemed necessary by the doctor. On September 3, 1987, in a hearing that treated the mother "as little more than a baby container," a British Columbia family court judge ruled both the apprehension of the fetus and the coerced Caesarean entirely proper. He also awarded permanent custody of the woman's baby boy to the Ministry of Social Services and Housing.[24]

To respond responsibly to the bewildering possibilities opened up by the NRTs, the Canadian Coalition for a Royal Commission on New Reproductive Technologies was formed in 1987, largely at the instigation of the sociologist and feminist activist Margrit Eichler.[25] Appointed in 1989, the Commission has been plagued by undemocratic procedures and by unprecedented interference on the part of the federal government into the functioning of a royal commission. A group of disaffected commissioners became convinced that regard for the vast social and moral implications of the new technologies was losing out to a medical management approach. By 1991-92, the commission was coming under attack from the very women's groups that had lobbied so hard for its creation. Calling in February 1992 for a boycott of the Commission, the

National Action Committee on the Status of Women (NAC) charged that the Commission's research had been biased in favour of doctors and pharmaceutical companies who stand to gain from the marketing of the new reproductive technologies.[26] In March 1993, the NAC New Reproductive Technologies Committee and the DisAbled Women's Network of Canada (DAWN) agreed to form a national network to respond to the Report of the Royal Commission and to present their positions "on both new reproductive and genetic technologies, as well as to raise awareness within the women's movement of the detrimental consequences of these technologies on women's reproductive rights."[27] Meanwhile, as this book goes to press, one of the first studies released by the Royal Commission on New Reproductive Technologies reports that some Canadian fertility programs have been so careless as to expose women "to the possibility of infection with the AIDS virus."[28] "This is hardly news," exclaims Gwynne Basen, co-chairwoman of the NAC reproductive technologies committee. "The experimental nature of these technologies and the low success rates were two major reasons for demanding the creation of the commission in the first instance, and that was in 1987."[29]

Sexualities

Gaining control over our sexuality has also been at the centre of women's endeavours to take charge of our own bodies. As Barbara Herringer said in 1988, "Ten years ago ... I discovered my body for the first time, by making love with another woman ..."[30] Among the first targets of late 1960s/early 1970s feminist criticism were those heterosexual practices predicated on the assumption of the priority of a male sexual urge and a male right to sexual pleasure. The radical feminist slogan "the personal is political" took on powerful new meanings as women insisted that sexual relations between men and women be seen as political, power relations. Kate Millett's widely read *Sexual Politics* (1970)[31] contributed importantly to the politicization of heterosexuality by providing a scathing exposure of the extent to which the celebration of male sexual power and privilege was enshrined in white male western literature. One of her targets was Sigmund Freud, whose popularized psychological theories were widely disseminated throughout North America.[32] And one of the specific doctrines of Freud that Millett critiqued was the myth of penis envy. If at all present among girls or women, such envy was directed, she argued, not at the male body part itself but rather at the power that that body part symbolized. Another of Freud's doctrines singled out for attack in early second-wave feminist criticism was the overriding importance he assigned to vaginal orgasm. According to Freud, women did not attain sexual maturity until they transferred the site of their genital pleasure from the clitoris to the vagina. In medical and psychiatric circles, the woman incapable of a vaginal orgasm was labelled frigid. An early 1970s article by the New York radical feminist Anne Koedt contested the Freudian view. Entitled

"The Myth of the Vaginal Orgasm,"[33] the article circulated with telegraphic speed through 1970s white North American feminist circles. Not only was vaginal orgasm a myth, Koedt maintained, but a myth propagated in the face of the counterfactual evidence that the vagina contains very few nerve endings while the clitoris is physiologically the female homologue to the male penis. Clearly the purpose of the myth, Koedt argued, was to hoodwink women into subordinating their own sexual pleasure to that of men.

It was a short step from such revelations to the proposition that men were not needed for women's bodily sexual pleasure. Indeed the radical feminist scrutiny of male-dominated heterosexuality helped open the door to the legitimation of lesbian sexuality. At the same time, women-only organizing at the grassroots level brought women together for long periods of time in emotionally charged atmospheres that encouraged woman-to-woman intimacies and increased the possibilities for women's discovery and exploration of same-sex sexual pleasure. In urban centres across Canada, the upsurge in feminist activity became closely intertwined with the struggle to cast off the negative labels and liabilities trammelling lesbian existence. The right to free and open expression of one's lesbian sexual identity was everywhere curtailed by threat of job loss and social opprobrium.[34] If non-vaginally orgasmic married women got a bad rap from the medical and psychiatric establishment, lesbians got worse. The preference for same-sex sexual relations was stigmatized as a sign not merely of immaturity but of deep-seated mental and physical pathology. At the root of this negative labelling, lesbian feminists came to theorize, lay fear of the threat to the societal norm of male-dominated heterosexuality posed by women who dispensed with men as sexual partners altogether.

One of the most visible accomplishments of late twentieth-century feminism has been the forging of positive lesbian identities.[35] But that has not been accomplished without sometimes heartbreaking struggle within feminism itself, as we will see in the next chapter. As has been the case with other feminist struggles, so too in this struggle, a new vocabulary was coined consisting of words and phrases like "homophobic" and "woman-identified." Some heterosexual feminists, sharing the homophobia of the dominant culture, initially feared that the credibility of feminism would be undermined (or feared that the stigma attaching to lesbianism would rub off on feminism) if lesbian demands were articulated and if publicly "out" lesbians were allowed to be spokeswomen for the movement. Written to counter such fears and to argue that feminism required lesbianism was the "Radicalesbian" position paper of 1970 "The Woman-Identified Woman," which enjoyed wide circulation in Canada throughout the decade. Defining lesbianism less by sex than by commitment to women, this famous paper identified "the primacy of women," that is, the putting of women first in one's consciousness, as "the heart of women's liberation."[36] But, coined in the same period, the lesbian feminist slogan "feminism is the theory, lesbianism the practice" continued to be understood, and to be intended, as referring to sexual relations. In whichever sense, this "recasting of lesbianism as a political imperative, ... the logical outcome of one's feminism,"[37] is present in the 1985 *Broadside* editorial that speaks of lesbianism as "Feminism's Psychic Imperative," and of lesbian women as "the clergy of the movement," the driving force "toward total female autonomy."[38]

Under the influence of an ideology that named men as the oppressors of women and in a period when one's sexuality was seen as forming the core of one's identity, it appeared logical to some feminists at various times that having nothing to do with men sexually (or otherwise) might be an important step toward gaining control not only over one's body but also over one's self. In some feminist circles, having heterosexual sex was regarded as "sleeping with the enemy."[39] But for other feminists, for instance, married women with children, and/or women with strong loyalties to the men in their ethnically or racially oppressed communities, lesbian sexuality or lesbian separatism was not a desired nor, even when appealing, a realistic option. Another famous and widely circulated article, this time by the poet Adrienne Rich,[40] provided a conceptual framework in which the gulf between heterosexual and lesbian feminists might be bridged. Using the key concept of "compulsory heterosexuality," Rich argued that heterosexual relations were not "natural" but rather compelled by pervasive social, cultural and institutional enforcement, and she asked heterosexual women to reflect on the privilege of the arrangement they had "chosen." At the same time, using the key concept of "the lesbian continuum," she argued a variation on the "Woman-Identified Woman" theme, namely that heterosexual women were not separated by an unbridgeable chasm from women in same-sex sexual relationships but rather existed on a "lesbian continuum" so long as they acted from a woman-centred perspective in their dealings with the world. Some heterosexual feminists welcomed "the lesbian continuum" as a way of validating their passionate friendships with other women; but some lesbian feminists rejected the concept for minimizing the real social consequences of "coming out" as a lesbian in the conventional sexual sense.

By 1985, as is clear from the "Personal Responses and Reports from the Women's Sexuality Conference," held in Toronto in October of that year, there were feminists who wanted to get beyond the lesbian versus heterosexual divide and to welcome women of all sexual preferences, celibate and bisexual women included, to the pursuit of an enhanced understanding of women's sexuality through co-operative discussion and study. A new consensus seemed to be emerging that a women's sexuality, whether lesbian, heterosexual, celibate or bisexual, would not, as Susan G. Cole put it in her keynote address, eroticize violence or dominance and subordination. It would, in contrast, "eroticize equality."[41] In June of that same year, seventeen women with disabilities came together in Ottawa for the founding meeting of the DisAbled Women's Network of Canada (DAWN). The total denial of their sexuality, their sexual needs and desires, ranked as one of their key concerns.[42]

Images of Women

The espousal of eroticized equality grew out of the early radical feminist analysis of institutionalized, male-dominant heterosexuality as central to women's oppression. Instances of this institutionalization could be found everywhere in the media in the sexual objectification of women. The reduction of women to sex objects, that is, to mindless bodies designed to be sexually alluring, sexually available and sexually subordinate to men, was seen as an assault on women's claim to full humanity. Here the struggle of women for control over our bodies became the struggle to gain control over the representation of women's bodies in the media and in cultural events more generally. One category of event that feminists opposed as degrading to women was the "beauty contest." Parading young women in bathing-suits and judging them on their breast, waist and hip measurements, beauty pageants were denounced as "sexploitative" of women. For instance, in February 1970, two hundred women students from universities across Ontario and some male supporters picketed the Miss Canadian University Pageant. The protestors carried signs reading "Women are not commodities," "Women are not for sale," and "Women's liberation is human liberation."[43] In January 1992, spokeswomen for the National Action Committee on the Status of Women hailed the decisions, taken by the events' sponsors, to cancel the forty-five-year-old Miss Canada pageant and the fifty-five-year-old Miss Toronto beauty contest as "a reflection of the fact [that] the women's movement has had a powerful effect on the culture."[44]

Also celebrating this victory were spokeswomen for MediaWatch. Formed in 1981 initially as a subcommittee of the National Action Committee on the Status of Women, the mainly Vancouver-based group has monitored the popular media for offensive representations of women for more than a decade. But as early as the 1970s, feminists were protesting sexist advertising, as is clear in the *Windsor Woman* account of an action taken against an offending tire advertisement in 1972.[45] Similar grassroots actions were organized in towns and cities across Canada. In 1974, for instance, feminists in St. John's, Newfoundland, denounced Harry Summers' autobody shop for its billboard advertisement featuring a more-than-life-size figure of a scantily clad, exaggeratedly curvaceous woman.[46] Since the 1980s, in its nationwide monitoring of television and radio, newspapers, magazines and advertising, MediaWatch has racked up a series of successes in persuading media to rectify, or drop altogether, sexist images of and derogatory references to women.[47] One of its earlier interventions led to the censuring of a radio station by the Canadian Radio-television and Telecommunications Commission (CRTC) for a remark that, according to Me-diaWatch, "constituted incitement to hatred and violence against women."[48]

Along with objectifying women, beauty pageants were assailed for setting an "unrealistic" standard of female beauty. As such they were an easily targetable culprit within a culture awash in images of women embodying standards of beauty to which very few women in the real world could conform, even when they belonged to the same race as the pictured "beauty." Other culprits have been the fashion and cosmetics industries and the medium of the fashion magazine. If anything, the heavily made-up faces and tall, willowy slim bodies of the high fashion models on the covers of magazines displayed in drugstores and super-markets, doctors' offices and beauty parlours represent an ideal of fe-male beauty even more remote than that of the beauty contestant. Self-image was identified as a key concern by the seventeen women with disabilities who gathered in Ottawa for the founding meeting of DAWN in June 1985. And, as Jillian Ridington has claimed,

> Images that foster feelings of insecurity in able-bodied women can be devastating to a woman who is in a wheel chair, a woman whose disability requires her to repeatedly insert needles in her legs, a woman whose body or brain reacts in ways she can neither antici-pate nor control.[49]

Poet Maxine Tynes, a descendant of Nova Scotian Black Loyalists, writes vividly of her alienation from the racist and sexist norms of beauty paraded across the pages of glossy fashion magazines and of her defiant assertion of her own full-bodied self.[50] In an imperialist and racist world, bodies are as indelibly raced as they are gendered. For women of all races, to aspire to the unlined, blemish-free face and pencil-thin, cel-lulite-free body of the fashion model is a recipe for despair. But because of the pressures on women in western, industrialized culture to be the object of the male gaze and to be judged on the basis of appearance, women, especially young women, feel compelled to try to live up to these impossible standards. The diagnosable eating disorders of anorexia nervosa and bulimia are but the extreme end of a continuum of concern with eating food and losing weight that stretches from mild fascination to near obsession.[51] And a majority of North American women find themselves somewhere on that continuum at some time in their lives.[52]

Violence Against Women

Women's efforts to combat the objectification of women gathered steam from the growing awareness that the depiction of women as mere things, to be toyed with or discarded at the whim of men, contributed to men's violence against women. The prevalence of rape was and remains a phenomenon of major concern to women. Many North American women came to believe Susan Brownmiller's analysis that the wide-spread occurrence of rape benefits men, whether or not they are rapists, for it functions as a form of terror that keeps women subordinate.[53] Women identified a host of causes for the commonplaceness of rape, including society's trivialization of rape in jokes. But one of the chief causes was seen to be the impunity with which rape could be committed. The earliest feminist research on rape revealed that most commonly the rapist was someone the woman knew. Spousal rape was condoned by institutionalized religion and the laws of the state. In Canada, it was only in 1983 that the spousal rape exemption was removed from the Criminal Code.[54] Recently, feminist studies are uncovering how common the occurrence of "date rape" is and how unsafe for women many college campuses are.[55] Early Canadian analysts of rape revealed the extent to which rape law was concerned not with the violation of the person of the woman but with the violation of a property right held by a husband or a father to a particular woman's sexuality.[56] The woman herself was regarded as merely holding her sexual/reproductive property in trust. If she played fast and loose with that trust, by taking rides in cars with strange men or drinking and dancing with men in bars, she lowered her property value and exposed herself to the likelihood that the law enforcement and judicial systems would not take a charge of rape laid by her seriously. The sex/gender, race and class systems intermingle in such a way that a woman's sexual property value is steadily decreased the further she is by race or class from the white, propertied norm. At the same time, the credibility of the man accused of rape increases in direct relation to his proximity to membership in the dominant race and class. The violent sexism present in rape can escalate into murder, as happened in the 1971 brutal rape and murder of Helen Betty Osborne, a young Native woman student in The Pas, Manitoba, by a group of white, "joy-riding" male youths whose guilt was kept a white community secret for nearly twenty years. In this case racism clearly contributed to the violence of the crime and to its cover-up.[57]

Before women's successful lobbying for the "rape shield" provision, in rape litigation, a woman's past sexual history was more on trial than the defendant's. This "revictimization" of the raped woman and the difficulty of securing convictions accounted in large measure for the massive under-reporting of incidents of rape. Arguing that the crime was more violent than sexual in nature, women seeking to reform rape law initially pressured to have the term "rape" replaced with sexual assault. Later, women legal reformers recognized the importance of retaining the notion that rape is a sexual crime, not merely a crime of assault. For, even though the rapist is less driven by uncontrolled sexual urges than by uncontrolled violent contempt for women, the woman victim experiences the rape as an attack on the very core of her sexual being.

Putting the problem of woman battering on the public agenda has been another proud achievement of second-wave feminism. Convincing federal, provincial and municipal governments that woman battering is both a serious and a pervasive problem has taken some doing. Linda MacLeod's 1980 report *Wife Battering in Canada: The Vicious Circle*, commissioned by the Canadian Advisory Council on the Status of Women (CACSW), publicized the results of the first attempt to collect information on wife battering from across Canada and to calculate its incidence nationwide.[58] The Report's estimate that one out of every ten Canadian women was a victim of battering by her male partner was shocking news, as was also the Report's claim that battering was no respecter of race, class, religion, or ethnicity. Yet, on May 12, 1982, when Margaret Mitchell stood in the House of Commons to ask what the federal government was going to do in response to the Report on Wife Battering tabled by the Standing Committee on Health, Welfare and Social Affairs the day before,[59] laughter rippled through the august, male-dominated assembly.[60] Outraged by "this public display of levity" on the part of Canada's male political leaders toward a life-threatening issue for one out of ten Canadian women, women's groups across Canada demanded that action be taken. They demanded that more government monies be put toward public education on this issue and that more money be allocated "to services to help battered women and their children." Medical personnel had to be educated to recognize the "injuries and other symptoms" that "appear with some regularity" in women who have been battered and to ask the right questions.[61] In her June 1987 study for CACSW on *Preventing Wife Battering in Canada*, Linda MacLeod could report positively that "[t]he number of transition houses providing shelters for battered women more than tripled from 85 shelters in 1982, to 264 shelters in 1987."[62] But this number is far from adequate to accommodate those in need (for example, one transition house in Toronto reported that, in 1985, "they turned away ten women for every one they sheltered")[63] and, since 1987, federal budget cuts to women's organizations have threatened the survival of battered women's shelters as well as rape crisis centres.

Meanwhile there is growing awareness of the deep-seated and complex nature of the problem. For instance, many rejoiced when Ontario became the first province to adopt, in November 1982, a policy of encouraging police to lay charges in wife-battering cases, thus removing the onus of initiating criminal proceedings from the battered woman. But, for practical, economic reasons, a poor woman may not want her male partner jailed and therefore out of a job. Moreover, given the indisputable evidence of racism within the law enforcement and criminal justice systems, many women belonging to racially or ethnically oppressed minorities "have come to mistrust the police" and the courts and to fear their intervention in domestic conflicts.[64] Furthermore, a woman from a racially or ethnically oppressed group who brings a charge of battering or sexual harassment or assault against a man from her own community knows she runs the risk both of reinforcing racist stereotypes

Catherine Maunsell Courtesy: *Broadside*

Take Back the Night Marches have been organized by feminists in cities across Canada since the late 1970s, as part of a country-wide campaign to end violence against women.

in the larger society and of appearing as a traitor to her race in the eyes of her own community.[65] Clearly there is no one simple solution to the problem.

But indisputably the battering of women is part of the larger issue of violence against women that is, as Sunera Thobani, founding member of the South Asian Women's Action Network (SAWAN), has noted, "a reflection of the subordinate position of women in society."[66] An ignorant but common response to woman battering has been to ask why the woman doesn't leave. What this question ignores is the mountain of obstacles put in the way of the woman's leaving, as laid out in Linda MacLeod's 1980 report excerpted below. Chief among these obstacles are the societal attitudes that condone violence against women. The response also ignores the criminality of the batterer's actions and the question of why he is not made to stop and to be the one to leave. Moreover, recent data reveal the gruesome reality that many women who leave abusive relationships do not escape the abuse but rather are hunted down like prey and killed in cold blood by their former lovers, partners and spouses. In 1977, branches of the international Women Against Violence Against Women (WAVAW) were founded in Canada.[67] Now, it has become an annual tradition for women to hold a "Take Back the Night" march the third Friday in September through the streets of their towns and cities, protesting against the multiple kinds of violence perpetrated against women and children throughout the world and demanding that the spaces we inhabit, both public and private, be made safe for all children and women.[68]

The feminist movement, in all its diversity, can take credit for creating a public discourse that has raised society's consciousness of men's violence against women as a societal problem. Moreover, feminists who are not members of the white, middle-class, able-bodied majority have raised the consciousness of those who are, with respect to the special threats of violence that less privileged women face. For instance, feminists committed to the struggle against racism in our society are increasing awareness of how the colour of a woman's skin, or the economic insecurity of immigrant status,[69] or the political precariousness of refugee status can expose women to violence in stark ways. In 1989, the Women's Coalition Against Racism & Police Violence circulated a petition to protest the police shooting in Toronto of Sophia Cook as she was sitting with her seatbelt buckled in a car. The shooting, by white police of a black woman, left her paralysed from the waist down.[70] Likewise, lesbian-feminist analyses draw attention to the heightened risk of harassment directed against women who publicly defy heterosexual norms.[71] Similarly, feminists organized in older women's networks and disabled women's networks are sounding an alarm as to the increased vulnerability that age and disability can bring. According to Jill Ridington, "A woman in a wheel chair or a woman using a cane is seen as fair game by some men."[72]

Feminists' insistence on bringing issues of sexuality and violence out of the closet into the light of day also gave courage to victims of child sexual abuse to break their silence, particularly victims of father-daughter incest.[73] Coming forward to tell one's story and the amassing of these stories became one of the main mechanisms by which the "reality" of the victims' experiences acquired credibility.[74] But in cases of incest as well as of other forms of physical and sexual abuse, women as well as men can be found among the perpetrators.[75] According to a 1987 study by the DisAbled Women's Network of Ontario, "the most dangerous place for a disabled girl or woman to be was in her own home," assailed by her own mother and/or father or female caregiver.[76] But the issue of the violence women commit against other women is only beginning to be discussed in the women's movement.[77]

Pornography

The focus of the women's movement has been on the issue of men's violence against women. While in the early years, feminists seemed to agree that a connection existed between that violence and the sex objectification of women, when the focus shifted from the objectifying images of women in the general culture to pornographic images that not only objectified women but also showed them shackled and beaten or worse, the so-called pornography debate ensued.[78] Particularly frightening to some feminists was the notion of relying on the state, in the form of laws and their enforcement by the civil or criminal justice system, to suppress sexually explicit literature and images depicting the degradation and victimization of women and children. While those in favour of such state-administered regulation believed in the efficacy of guidelines to distinguish between the pornographic and the erotic, others were less sanguine and feared the power of the state would be turned, in the first instance, against lesbian and gay erotica. Even calling for adherence to a program of "eroticizing equality" seemed to some to smack too much of prescription. Fantasy can't be policed, it was argued. That was the "pleasure" side of the debate. Those on the "danger" side, particularly victims of child sexual abuse, rape and/or woman battering, found the idea of giving utterly free rein to fantasy a frightening notion and were unconvinced by the argument that no concrete evidence exists to prove a connection between women-degrading pornography and violence against women. Certainly the authors of the 1986 report on "Pornography in the Northwest Territories" saw a connection between the increased availability of pornographic videos and sexual assault on women.[79] And certainly the Vancouver Status of Women read the contempt for women as persons and the disgust for women's bodies "freely expressed" in the pages of *The Red Rag*, the newspaper of the University of British Columbia's School of Engineering, as helping to create an environment in which violence against women is condoned.[80]

Apparently, the Justices of the Supreme Court of Canada were persuaded of that view when, on February 27, 1992, they unanimously ruled that the obscenity provisions (Section 163) of the Criminal Code may well justifiably limit freedom of speech and freedom of expression in the case of the depiction of "sex coupled with violence" or "exploitative sex that degrades or dehumanizes a person" and in cases of "explicit sexual material employing children in its production." Taken into consideration in arriving at their decision in the *Butler* case was the notion of the harm certain kinds of pornography can have on women. "If true equality between male and female persons is to be achieved, we cannot ignore the threat to equality resulting from exposure to audiences of certain types of violent and degrading material," declared the ruling, written by Mr. Justice John Sopinka. "Materials portraying women as a class as objects of sexual exploitation and abuse have a negative impact on the individual's sense of self-worth and acceptance."[81] Founded to advance women's sex equality claims in courts of law under the Charter of Rights and Freedoms, the feminist Women's Legal Education and Action Fund (LEAF) was allowed by the Supreme Court to present arguments in the obscenity case. LEAF undoubtedly helped weigh the balance in favour of the Court's definition of "obscenity as an offense against equality."[82] Not all feminists are pleased with the Court's ruling in the *Butler* case, however. Anti-censorship feminist Thelma McCormack, for instance, argues that "the enemy of gender equality is the stereotype of the idealized traditional woman, not the one-dimensional lust-driven nymphomaniac of pornography." "Censorship," she maintains, "infantilizes women and contributes to [our] dependency."[83]

The event that finally brought official condemnation of the rampant sexism that for years had gone unpunished in the newspapers and "frolics" of Canada's Schools of Engineering was the murder by Marc Lépine, on December 6, 1989, of fourteen young women at the Engineering School of the University of Montreal, the École polytechnique.[84] Deeply shocking because it was a mass murder and because it occurred in the "hallowed" halls and classrooms of academe, the event also finally brought the murderous violence of men against women to national attention. Many in the media initially depicted Lépine as "a madman," as he had predicted they would, and his gunning down of fourteen young women as an aberration, a "senseless slaying." But as Jane Pepino, chairwoman of METRAC (the Metro Toronto Action Committee on Violence Against Women and Children), pointedly asked on December 7, 1989, "If we say this man was crazy, does that mean every wife batterer is insane, or anyone who assaults a woman physically or sexually is insane?"[85] Whether the gunman was "mad" or "deeply troubled," spokeswomen for women insisted that we look at the context for his choosing women as the targets of his rage. His actions, these women have argued, cannot be understood apart from the widespread societal devaluing of women. Nor can they be separated from the special resentment reserved for "uppity," "pushy" women who enter fields once monopolized by men. Nor can his explicit anti-feminism be isolated from the widespread media disparagement of "strident," unreasonably demanding feminists.[86] A failed applicant to the École polytechnique and resentful of the women students who had, in his eyes, usurped the place that was rightfully his, the murderer Lépine reportedly yelled, before firing his first volley, "You're women, you're going to be engineers. You're all a bunch of feminists. I hate feminists."[87] The statement he left behind, though deemed a "suicide" letter by *The Globe and Mail*,[88] would be more accurately described as a "femicide" letter.[89] In 1991, in response to the lobbying efforts of women's groups, the Canadian federal government designated December 6 as a National Day of Remembrance and Action on Violence Against Women.[90]

Prostitution

Prostitutes have been among the most vulnerable to violence and harassment against women in our society. Mainstream feminism has come to recognize that the violence and harassment to which prostitutes are exposed are of a piece with other anti-woman attitudes and practices.[91] As the Calgary Status of Women Action Committee's Brief to the NAC Special Committee on Pornography and Prostitution argued in 1984, the double standard of sexual morality, which punishes women's active sexuality but not men's, works to divide women into the "false" categories of good and bad women. In fact, prostitutes are no different from other women, including wives, who "trade their sexual services for a pay off." Moreover, the laws to control prostitutes are part and parcel of a larger system to regulate and control female sexuality. A major reason prostitution should be decriminalized, the Calgary Status of Women claimed, is that the "illegality of prostitution traps women in the life" and increases their vulnerability to violence.[92] In 1983, prostitutes in Canada formed the Canadian Organization for the Rights of Prostitutes (CORP). Their founding premise, as asserted in Point 1 of the Toronto Chapter's position paper, is that "Prostitution is a human rights' issue, involving the right to choose, the right to govern one's own body and the right to security of person."[93] In 1986, prostitutes went to the NAC Annual General Meeting (AGM) to seek the support of the largest women's organization in Canada. After much heated discussion, the AGM passed a resolution expressing ongoing opposition to *Bill C-49* and support for prostitutes' rights.[94] In the words of Lorraine Greaves, chair of the NAC Prostitution Committee, the resolution signalled "the beginning of a new dialogue" and symbolized "our solidarity with our prostitute members." She saw the resolution as based "on a long tradition of listening to and honouring individual women's experience."[95] Opinion among representatives of NAC member groups, however, remained sharply divided. Nonetheless, the NAC Prostitution Committee could report to the 1987 AGM that it was moving in the direction of lessening "the distance between 'prostitutes' and 'feminists'."[96]

Women's Health/Self-Help Groups

The founding of CORP exemplifies the distinction the women's movement has drawn between being victimized and being a victim.[97] As this chapter illustrates, women have indeed identified many ways in which women's bodies are victimized, by the medical and pharmaceutical establishments, by the laws and agencies of the state, by the media, by men's violence. Women, however, have not resigned ourselves to victim status but rather have become active agents and organized ourselves to take defensive and proactive action against the victimization. Exemplifying the self-help organizational ingenuity and dedication of second-wave feminists, rape crisis centres sprang up in urban centres across Canada in the 1970s. With the formation of the Canadian Association of Rape/Assault Centres in 1979, centre workers from across Canada were able to compare notes and work out common strategies. Shelters for battered women and their children provide another major example of women organizing to help women. So that we could feel confident and able to defend ourselves on the streets and in our homes, Canadian women invented Wen-Do, the art of women's self-defence, fashioned from the moves of the Asian martial arts. Women have formed women's sports and athletic associations to promote women's bodily strength and health in defiance of the cultural celebration of women's physical weakness and of the cultural stereotype of unmuscled female bodies.

There is no clearer example of this determination to overcome victimization than the Women's Self-Help Groups and Health Clinics, such as those created in Saskatoon, Saskatchewan, and in Fredericton, New Brunswick.[98] Using materials, such as the *Birth Control Handbook* of 1968 and 1969[99] and the widely distributed *Our Bodies/Our Selves: A Course By and For Women*,[100] women have learned about how our bodies function and, through that self-knowledge, have gained self-confidence and a positive attitude towards our bodies and our bodily needs. But if white women, born or long resident in Canada, could be intimidated by health workers, how much more intimidating, the Regina Immigrant Women's Centre realized in 1991, must immigrant women find a medical establishment that does not speak the immigrant's language or possess any knowledge of the culture from which she came.[101] And as government, the science of medicine and the mainstream media remain male-dominated and male-centred, women continue to have to struggle against inadequate attention to and inadequate funding for research on health issues of importance to women. In the case of the little researched, almost taboo subject of menopause, women have taken the initiative to dispel myths and make useful information available.[102] AIDS in women is another case in point. "Currently in Canada women and youth constitute the fastest growing groups of HIV-positive people," *Healthsharing* reported in its Spring/Summer 1992 issue. But because of the male orientation given to treatment and education strategies, women's needs are going unmet.[103] Breast cancer provides an even more alarming example. "We are facing an epidemic," the Winter/Spring 1992 issue of *Healthsharing* proclaimed. "One in 10 of us will be diagnosed with breast cancer at some point in our lifetime."[104] In 1992 women with breast cancer and breast cancer survivors organized Breast Cancer Action-Write Now to ensure that the House of Commons Sub-Committee on the Status of Women examining breast cancer issues would receive input from women directly affected.[105] The activism paid off. The Sub-Committee's Report recommended that more of the Canadian research dollar be allocated to breast cancer research and that review committees, established to assess current curriculum on breast cancer in university medical schools, "should include in their membership, and work in close consultation with, local breast cancer survivor, support and activist groups ..."[106]

Gaining control over our bodies through learning about what is conducive to our bodies' well-being remains a central concern of the Canadian women's movement. To counter the under-representation of women's health issues in mainstream medical journals and to provide a forum for sharing information crucial to women's health, the feminist journal *Healthsharing* was created in 1979. In 1992/93, *Healthsharing* played a key role in the successful organizing of the Canadian Women's Health Network.[107] According to Amy Gottlieb, a former managing editor of *Healthsharing*, the Network will provide a self-help health model for women across Canada, on both an individual and a collective basis. For individual women, the Network will increase opportunities to access health information and information on feminist health activism that is not readily available anywhere else. Collectively, the Network will provide a tool for the kind of political organizing so necessary for combatting the difficulties women face in the existing health care system.[108]

NOTES

1. See "Statement to Abortion Caravan Rally by Doris Powers of the Just Society Movement," excerpted below.
2. Of or relating to René Descartes (1596-1650), a French thinker of the beginning of the so-called Enlightenment.
3. See Ruth Dworin, "My Horror Story," *The Other Woman* 4, no. 1 (December-January 1976), 12-13, reprinted below.
4. Jane Covernton, "Thinking Through Infertility," *Healthsharing* 11, no. 1 (December 1989), 29-33, provides a moving account of experiencing IUD-induced infertility as a "scary" "loss of control."
5. See letter by Mary E. Billy to Mr. Jake Epp, Minister of Health & Welfare, 15 December 1985; Michelle, "One Woman's Story: A Disabled Woman Speaks Out on Depo Provera," *Interaction* no. 2 (September 1986); and the "Fact Sheet on Reproductive Rights," produced by DAWN Toronto, ca. 1988, all reprinted below.
6. Lynn Brooks, "Northern Women's Health at Risk: Depo Provera in the NWT," *The Womanist* 3, no. 1 (Spring 1992), 34.
7. A recent example is Dow Corning's decades-long self-serving disregard and denial of the scientific evidence linking silicone gel breast implants to cancer and other medical problems. Associated Press and Canadian Press, "Breast implants spurred complaints for decades," *Globe and Mail*, 11 February 1992, A15. See also Linda Wilson, "The Dangers of Meme Breast Implants," *The Womanist* 3, no. 1 (Spring 1992), 28.
8. See Alice Van Wart, "Abortion: A Woman's Right," *Equal Times*, November 1975, 3, reprinted below.
9. For a concise account of the Morgentaler trials in the 1970s, see Paula Bourne, *Women in Canadian Society* (Toronto: Ontario Institute for Studies in Education, 1976), 44-52.
10. "Abortion," *Wimmin's Words* (Halifax, Nova Scotia), January 1983, 1.
11. See Eunice Lavell, "Women Study Class: Gleanings of a White Poor Woman," *The Womanist* 3, no. 1 (Spring 1992), 38, passage on "Reproductive Freedom," reprinted in documents section of Chapter 3.
12. See the "Fact Sheet on Reproductive Rights," produced by the DisAbled Women's Network [DAWN] of Toronto, ca. 1988, reprinted below.
13. See "Fact Sheet on Reproductive Rights," produced by DAWN Toronto, ca. 1988, reprinted below.
14. An episiotomy is a surgical incision, made to the tissue between the vagina and the anus, to widen the birth canal just prior to birth to prevent the vagina from tearing. "Among women giving birth to their first baby in a Canadian hospital, 70-90 per cent will have an episiotomy." Marion Lokhorst, "Episiotomy Study," *Healthsharing* 10, no. 3 (June 1989), 7. According to a Montréal research study headed by Dr. Michael Klein, episiotomies are "usually unnecessary and may do more harm than good." "The most alarming finding of the study was that an episiotomy may promote severe tearing in some women rather than prevent it." Paul Taylor, Medical Reporter, "Childbirth procedure questioned," *Globe and Mail*, 7 July 1992, A1, A8.
15. Shelley Romalis, *Childbirth: Alternatives to Medical Control* (Austin: The University of Texas Press, 1982), reviewed by Andrée Lévèsque, *Ontario History* 75, no. 1 (March 1983), 104-105.
16. John O'Neil and Patricia A. Kaufert, "The Politics of Obstetric Care: The Inuit Experience," in W. Penn Handwerker, ed., *Births and Power: Social Change and the Politics of Reproduction* (Westview Press, 1990).

17. Betty Anne Daviss-Putt, "Rights of Passage in the North: From Evacuation to the Birth of a Culture," in Mary Crnkovich, ed., *"Gossip": A Spoken History of Women in the North* (Ottawa: Canadian Arctic Resources Committee, 1990).

18. For a powerfully moving account in poetic form of this sense of deprivation, see Betsy Struthers, "Baby Blues," in *Running out of Time* (Toronto: Wolsak and Wynn, 1993), 11-15.

19. Planned Parenthood Alberta, "Infertility: Prevention Instead of Intervention," *The Womanist* 2, no. 3 (Winter 1991), 39.

20. Linda S. Williams, "Behind the Headlines: The Physical and Emotional Costs of In Vitro Fertilization," *Healthsharing* 10, no. 3 (June 1989), 20-25. See also Christine Overall, ed., *The Future of Human Reproduction* (Toronto: The Women's Press, 1989).

21. Rona Achilles, "Desperately Seeking Babies: New Technologies of Hope and Despair," in Katherine Arnup, Andrée Lévèsque, and Ruth Roach Pierson, eds., *Delivering Motherhood: Maternal Ideologies and Practices in the 19th and 20th Centuries* (London and New York: Routledge, 1990), 284-312. See also Gwynne Basen (director), Mary Armstrong and Nicole Hubert (producers), *On the Eighth Day: Perfecting Mother Nature*, Part 1 *Making Babies*, 50 min. 45 sec., Part 2 *Making Perfect Babies*, 50 min. 49 sec., National Film Board of Canada, a Studio D production (1992).

22. Barbara Duden, "History Beneath the Skin," *CBC IDEAS Transcripts*, 7-8 October 1991, 7.

23. Ibid., 15.

24. Maggie Thompson, "Whose Womb Is It Anyway?", *Healthsharing* 9, no. 2 (March 1988), 14-17. For LEAF's subsequent intervention in the appeal of this case to the Supreme Court of British Columbia, in which LEAF made "the connection between the apprehension of a foetus and infringements upon a pregnant woman's liberty and security of her person," see Sherene Razack, *Canadian Feminism and the Law: The Women's Legal Education and Action Fund and the Pursuit of Equality* (Toronto: Second Story Press, 1991), 120-122.

25. See Canadian Coalition for a Royal Commission on New Reproductive Technologies, "New Reproductive Technologies in Canada: Some Facts and Issues," March 1988, reprinted below.

26. The National Action Committee on the Status of Women, *The New Reproductive Technologies: A Technological Handmaid's Tale*, a brief presented to the Royal Commission on New Reproductive Technologies, October 1990. See also Heidi Walsh, "Tight lips sink ships," *Kinesis*, February 1992, 12-13.

27. "National NRT Network Formed," *ACTION NOW!: Monthly Newsletter from the National Action Committee on the Status of Women* 3, no. 5 (May 1993), 2.

28. Rod Mickleburgh, "Fertility programs attacked in study: 'Very alarming' AIDS risk cited," *Globe and Mail*, 28 April 1993, A1.

29. Gwynne Basen, "Experiments on Women and Children," *Globe and Mail*, 21 May 1993, A27, reproduced below.

30. Barbara Herringer, "For the Sounds of our Bodies," in The Telling It Book Collective: Sky Lee, Lee Maracle, Daphne Marlatt, Betsy Warland, eds., *Telling It: Women and Language Across Cultures—the transformation of a conference* [the TELLING IT conference held in Vancouver in November 1988] (Vancouver: Press Gang Publishers, 1990), 99-102, excerpts from Herringer's text reproduced below.

31. (Garden City, New York: Doubleday & Company, Inc., 1970).

32. Freud's popularized theories had already been severely critiqued for their male-centredness in Betty Friedan's still earlier *The Feminine Mystique* (1963), a book that many urban, white middle-class North American women felt spoke to their discontents.

33. Anne Koedt, "The Myth of the Vaginal Orgasm," *Notes From The Second Year: WOMEN'S LIBERATION—Major Writings of the Radical Feminists* (New York: Radical Feminism, 1970), 37-41.

34. Madiha Didi Khayatt, *Lesbian Teachers: An Invisible Presence* (Albany, NY: State University of New York Press, 1992).

35. See Sharon Dale Stone, ed., *Lesbians in Canada* (Toronto: Between The Lines, 1990). See also Aelyn Weissman and Lynne Fernie (directors), Margaret Pettigrew (producer), *Forbidden Love: The Unashamed Stories of Lesbian Lives*, 84 min. 37 sec., National Film Board of Canada, a Studio D production (1992).

36. Alice Echols, *Daring to be Bad: Radical Feminism in America 1967-1975* (Minneapolis: University of Minnesota Press, 1989), 215-217.

37. Ibid., 238-9.

38. Editorial, *Broadside* 6, no. 10 (August/September 1985), 2, reprinted below.

39. See Joan Holmes, "Heterosexual and Feminist: A Contradiction?," *Breaking the Silence* 4, no. 2 (December 1985), 23-24, reprinted below.

40. Adrienne Rich, "Compulsory Heterosexuality and Lesbian Existence," *Signs: Journal of Women in Culture and Society* 5, no. 4 (Summer 1980), 631-60, reprinted in Adrienne Rich, *Blood, Bread, and Poetry: Selected Prose 1979-1985* (New York: W.W. Norton, 1986), pp. 23-68, with a new Afterword, 68-75.

41. Lynne Tyler, "Coming Together: Personal Responses and Reports from the Women's Sexuality Conference," *Breaking the Silence* 4, no. 2 (December 1985), 20-22, reprinted below.

42. Jillian Ridington, "Who Do We Think We Are?: Self-Image and Women with Disabilities," Position Paper #1 prepared for DAWN Canada (February 1989), 1. See Debbie McGee (director), Nicole Hubert (producer), *Toward Intimacy*, 61 min. 28 sec., National Film Board of Canada, a Studio D production (1992).

43. Robert Noreault, "Women's Lib. Protests Beauty Pageant," *THE ONTARION*, 6 February 1970, 2.

44. Andrew Duffy, "End of an era: Two pageants axed," *Toronto Star*, 4 January 1992, A3; Alanna Mitchell, "Sponsor cancels Miss Canada Pageant," *Globe and Mail*, 4 January 1992, A1-A2.

45. "Boobs Sell Tubes," *Windsor Woman* 1, no. 6 (August 1972), 3, reprinted below.

46. *Newfoundland Status of Women Council Newsletter* 1, no. 7 (October 1974), 9; "Signs Offend Women's Council," *St. John's Evening Telegram*, 13 December 1974, 10; letter to the Newfoundland Status of Women from Harry Summers & Sons Ltd., 17 December 1974; letter to Mr. Harry Summers from the Newfoundland Status of Women Council Committee, 20 December 1974, reprinted in the *Newfoundland Status of Women Newsletter* 2, no. 1 (January 1975), 11. Copies at the Centre for Newfoundland Studies, Queen Elizabeth II Library, Memorial University of Newfoundland.

47. See "MEDIAWATCH: SOME SUCCESS STORIES," 1986, excerpted below.

48. J.G. Patenaude, Secretary General, CRTC, "Concerning a Complaint Against CKVU Television, Vancouver, British Columbia by MediaWatch," 1983, reprinted below.

49. Jillian Ridington, "Who Do We Think We Are? Self-Image and Women with Disabilities," Position Paper #1 prepared for DAWN Canada, (February 1989), 36. See also Diane Driedger and April D'Aubin, "Women with Disabilities Challenge the Body Beautiful," *Healthsharing* 12, no. 4 (Winter/Spring 1992), 35-38.

50. Maxine Tynes, "Being," in *Woman Talking Woman* (Lawrencetown Beach, Nova Scotia: Pottersfield Press, 1990), 30, reprinted below.

51. Sheila Nopper and Joyce Harley, "How society's obsession with thinness is consuming women," *Herizons: Women's News and Feminist Views* 4, no. 7 (October/November 1986), 24-27, 29, 42; Donna Ciliska and Carla Rice, "Body Image/Body Politics," *Healthsharing* 10, no. 3 (June 1989), 13-17.

52. Éva Székely, *Never Too Thin* (Toronto: The Women's Press, 1988); Katherine Gilday (director), *The Famine Within* (1990), colour, 1/2 inch VHS, 120 min., Toronto Kandor Productions, distributed by McNabb and Connolly, Toronto, Ontario.

53. Susan Brownmiller, *Against Our Will: Men, Women and Rape* (New York: Simon and Schuster, 1975).

54. Canada, *Criminal Code* (R.S.C. 1991), c. 125. Section 278; Rita Gunn and Candice Minch, *Sexual Assaults: The Dilemma of Disclosure, The Question of Conviction* (Winnipeg: University of Manitoba Press, 1988), 117.

55. Helen Lenskyj, "An Analysis of Violence Against Women: A Manual for Educators and Administrators," in *Educational Campaign to Combat Date and Acquaintance Rape on College and University Campuses* (Toronto: The OISE Centre for Women's Studies in Education, 1992). See also the video *The Chilly Climate for Women in Colleges and Universities*, 30 min, distributed by the Employment Equity Office, University of Western Ontario (1991).

56. Lorenne M.G. Clark and Debra J. Lewis, *Rape: The Price of Coercive Sexuality* (Toronto: The Women's Press, 1977).

57. Lisa Priest, *Conspiracy of Silence* (Toronto: McClelland & Stewart, 1990); and Francis Mankiewicz (director), Suzette Couture (writer), and Gail Carr (producer), "Conspiracy of Silence," CBC docudrama, 1-2 December 1991.

58. Linda MacLeod, *Wife Battering in Canada: The Vicious Circle* (Ottawa: The Canadian Advisory Council on the Status of Women, 1980), summary of its findings reprinted below.

59. Canada, House of Commons Standing Committee on Health, Welfare and Social Affairs, Marcel Roy, M.P., Chairman, *Report on Violence in the Family: Wife Battering* (Ottawa: Queen's Printer for Canada, May 1982).

60. Canada, House of Commons, *Debates*, 12 May 1982, 17334.

61. See "Health Care Services and Battered Women," prepared by Debra J. Lewis for Battered Women's Support Services, Vancouver, B.C., 1983. Copy at Vancouver Status of Women files.

62. Linda MacLeod, *Battered But Not Beaten ... Preventing Wife Battering in Canada* (Ottawa: Canadian Advisory Council on the Status of Women, June 1987), 3.

63. Ibid., 7.

64. Sunera Thobani, "South Asian women: Whose point of view?" *Kinesis*, February 1992, 11.

65. See, *inter alia*, Toni Morrison, ed., *Race-ing Justice, En-Gendering Power: Essays on Anita Hill, Clarence Thomas and the Construction of Social Reality* (NY: Pantheon Books, 1992).

66. Thobani, "South Asian women: Whose point of view?"

67. See "WAVAW Demands," Toronto, November 1977, reprinted below.

68. The first Take Back the Night march was held in Germany in 1978. Ravida Din, "Take Back the Night," *The Womanist*, December 1988/January 1989, 5.

69. Michelle Andrene Lurch, "Where Does the Torturer Live?," *Healthsharing* 12, no. 3 (Fall 1991), 9-12.

70. See "Petition to End Police Violence," *Diva: A Quarterly Journal of South Asian Women* 2, Issue 2 (January 1990), 6, reprinted below. See also Wei Feng, "Police Violence & Racism: Part 1," *Diva* 3, Issue 1 (October 1991), 52-56.

71. See "Lesbian Harassment" and "Lesbian Witch Hunt," reprinted as documents in Chapter 3.

72. Jillian Ridington, "Who Do We Think We Are?: Self Image and Women with Disabilities," Position Paper #1 prepared for DAWN Canada (February 1989), 25.

73. Anne Pierre, "Into A Wood," *Healthsharing* 10, no. 3 (June 1989), 10-12, excerpted below.

74. See, *inter alia*, Alicia Dowling, "A Personal Account," *Broadside* 2, no. 7 (May 1981), 11; Sylvia Fraser, *My Father's House: A Memoir of Incest and of Healing* (Toronto: Doubleday, 1987); and Beverley Shaffer (director), *To a Safer Place: One Woman's Account of Her Life as a Survivor of Childhood Incest*, produced by Studio D, National Film Board of Canada, 1989.

75. Heidi Vanderbilt, "Incest: A Chilling Report," *Lear's*, February 1992, 49-77.

76. See "DAWN TORONTO FACT SHEET ON VIOLENCE," ca. 1988, reprinted below.

77. Kerry Lobel, ed., *Naming the Violence: Speaking Out About Lesbian Battering* (Seattle: Seal Press, 1986); Carol LeMasters, "Contradictions: Mother/Daughter Incest," *Sojourner: The Women's Forum* 15, no. 3 (November 1989), 10-11; and "Listen to the Battered Lesbians!," *Sojourner* 16, no. 12 (August 1991), 4-6.

78. For different positions in this debate, see Varda Burstyn, ed., *Women Against Censorship* (Vancouver & Toronto: Douglas & McIntyre, 1985); Laurie Bell, ed., *Good Girls/Bad Girls: Sex Trade Workers & Feminists Face to Face* (Toronto: The Women's Press, 1987); and Susan G. Cole, *Pornography and the Sex Crisis* (Toronto: An Amanita Publication, 1989). See also Bonnie Sherr Klein (director), *Not A Love Story: A Film About Pornography*, colour, 70 min. (Studio D, National Film Board of Canada, 1981).

79. See N.W.T. Advisory Council on the Status of Women, "Pornography in the Northwest Territories," August 1986, reprinted below.

80. See "Women Troubles?," *The Red Rag*, February 1982, 3, and Letter by Nadine Allen, Vancouver Status of Women, to the Editor of *The Vancouver Sun*, 5 March 1982, both reprinted below.

81. Jeff Sallot, "Ruling paves way for child-pornography bill, minister says/Supreme Court finds obscenity law's limits on rights justifiable for the protection of society/Law on pornography upheld by Supreme Court," *Globe and Mail*, 28 February 1992, A1-A2.

82. Michael S. Serrill, "Smut That Harms Women: In a landmark ruling, Canada's Supreme Court defines obscenity as an offense against equality," *Time*, 9 March 1992, 48.

83. Thelma McCormack, "If Pornography Is the Theory, Is Inequality the Practice?", paper presented at "Refusing Censorship: Feminists and Activists Fight Back," a public forum on issues of censorship, the Glenn Gould Auditorium of the CBC, Toronto, 7-8 November 1992.

84. Louise Malette and Marie Chalouh, eds., *The Montreal Massacre*, trans. by Marlene Wildeman (Charlottetown, P.E.I.: Gynergy Books, 1991). For an excellent mystery novel that touches on these events, see Nora Kelly, *My Sister's Keeper* (Toronto: HarperCollins Publishers Ltd., 1992).

85. Frances Kelly and Bill Taylor, "'Never Again' Should be Vow Women Plead," *Toronto Star*, 8 December 1989, A30.

86. Ruth Roach Pierson, "Violence Against Women: Strategies for Change," *Canadian Woman Studies/les cahiers de la femme* 11, no. 4 (Summer/Été 1991), 10-12.
87. Ibid.
88. "Last Words from a Woman Hater," reprinted in *The Globe and Mail*, 27 November 1990, A21, reprinted below.
89. We would like to thank Dianne Hallman for this insight.
90. Canada, Status of Women, *Perspectives* 4, no. 4 (Fall/Winter 1991), 5.
91. See, for example, the feature-length documentary on street prostitution in Canada, Janis Cole and Holly Dale (directors and producers), *Hookers On Davie*, colour, 83 min., 1984, distributed by Canadian Film-Makers Distribution Centre (Toronto).
92. Calgary Status of Women Action Committee, "Summary of Recommendations on Prostitution," 9 January 1984, reprinted below.
93. Peggy Miller, "A Position Paper by the Canadian Organization for the Rights of Prostitutes (Toronto Chapter)," a submission to the Fraser Commission, January 1984, reprinted below.
94. Bill C-49, which became law as Section 195.1 of the Criminal Code in January 1986, prohibited all "communicating for the purposes of prostitution" and thus legitimated massive arrests of prostitutes in police "street-sweeps." The legislation also established unreasonable bail conditions.
95. Lorraine Greaves, "Forum on Prostitution," *Feminist Action: News from the National Action Committee on the Status of Women* 2, no. 1 (December 1986), 7.
96. Report of the Prostitution Committee, *1987 Annual Report of the National Action Committee on the Status of Women*, 15.
97. See, *inter alia*, Helene Moussa, *Storm & Sanctuary: The Journey of Ethiopian and Eritrean Women Refugees* (Toronto: Artemis Enterprises, 1993).
98. See documents reprinted below under SELF-HELP GROUPS AND HEALTH CLINICS.
99. *Birth Control Handbook*, rev. ed. (Montréal: Students' Society of McGill University, 1969).
100. *Our Bodies/Our Selves: A Course By and For Women* (Boston: Boston Women's Health Course Collective and New England Free Press, 1970).
101. Susan Dusel, "The Regina Immigrant Women's Centre: Primary Health Care Project," *Healthsharing* 12, no. 3 (Fall 1991), 32-33, reprinted from *Network of Saskatchewan Women* (Winter 1991), excerpted below.
102. See, for example, Miryam Gerson and Rosemary Byrne-Hunter, *A Book About Menopause* (Montréal: Montreal Health Press, 1988). See also the Winter 1990 issue of *Healthsharing*.
103. Beth Easton, "Women & AIDS," *Healthsharing* 13, no. 1 (Spring/Summer 1992), 12-13. See also Lisa McCaskell, "We Are Not Immune: Women and AIDS," *Healthsharing* 9, no. 4 (September 1988), 12-17; and Lorraine Munro, "Women and Aids," *The Womanist* 3, no. 2 (Fall 1992), 22.
104. Hazelle Palmer, "One in 10," *Healthsharing* 12, no. 4 (Winter/Spring 1992), 3.
105. Pam Bristol, "The Politics of Breast Cancer," *Healthsharing* 12, no. 4 (Winter/Spring 1992), 9-13.
106. See Barbara Greene, Chair, Sub-Committee on the Status of Women, *Breast Cancer: Unanswered Questions*, Report of the Standing Committee on Health and Welfare, Social Affairs, Seniors and the Status of Women (Ottawa: House of Commons, June 1992), ix-xiv.
107. Anne Fraser, "A Dream Comes True," *Healthsharing* 13, no. 1 (Spring/Summer 1992), 3.
108. Telephone interview with Amy Gottlieb, Toronto, 12 May 1993.

Documents: Chapter 2

Abortion

"Parliament Forced to Listen"
Vancouver/Ottawa, June 1970[1]

After travelling for 11 days across Canada, picking up women from all across the country, we finally arrived in Ottawa. Meeting with our sisters in a shopping centre we proceeded to cavalcade through the town. The response we got was overwhelming. People lined up outside their houses and on the streets, giving us V's, fists and waves and shouting encouragement for our venture.

Next day at 1:30, after an open rally outside parliament, we held an open meeting in the Railway Room of the Parliament Buildings to present a brief to [Prime Minister Pierre Elliot] Trudeau, [and cabinet ministers John] Munro and [John] Turner. None of the government officials [was] there. Trudeau was on the eve of his mid-Pacific tour, Munro was at a World Health Conference in Geneva (where, however, he was met by 50 Austrian women reminding him of the health of women in Canada) and Turner was out playing tennis. The only MPs who were there were Grace McInnis, David Lewis and Lorne Nystrom (all NDPers) plus the Conservative butterfly Gerald Baldwin complete in mustard jacket and flashy tie.

Judy D'Arcy of Toronto Women's Liberation read a brief and Grace McInnis addressed the house. The best she could say was that she was "solidly behind" us but that she did not believe abortion would be removed from the Criminal Code unless we got petitions from all across Canada and presented them to the government. This, she said, would take two years. Women jumped up to their feet and immediate cries of "That's too late" and "We can't wait" greeted this last luke-warm proposal.

Doris Powers capped off the afternoon, speaking of her experience as a welfare mother, who upon seeking an abortion was generously [offered] a sterilization. "We the poor of Canada are dirt shoved under the rug of a vicious economy ..." and "I am not a young woman. I'm not one of the women who sang on the way up here, because I don't have a goddamned thing to sing about." This was the high point of the afternoon and after some more talking and more speeches we decided to march to Trudeau's house in order to present him with the coffin![2]

1. Gwen Hauser, *The Pedestal* 2, no. 5 (June 1970), 8-9.
2. The coffin symbolized all women who had died from backstreet abortions.

Trudeau, of course, was not there and after pushing past the pigs at the gate and being stopped by the ones around the house, we decided to wait on the lawn and tried to get a government official from the house. None appeared (except for a gum-chewing, pink-cheeked Gordon Gibson, oozing with grease and phoney concern). So after about an hour of arguing with the pigs and various exchanges back and forth, we decided to take the coffin to the House of Commons. This we did, with a heavy police escort, and placed the tools of a hack abortionist on top of the coffin.

On Monday, we went into the last phase of our action—direct confrontation of the government in parliament. Thirty-six of us got into the galleries, and chaining ourselves to the chairs proceeded to disrupt parliament. At first we were not taken seriously, but, as more and more women got up to speak, and the guards were unable to stop us, the MPs became increasingly disturbed. Shouting cries of "Whores!" "Sluts!" and other goodies from a male chauvinist repertoire, some of them rushed up into the galleries and the speaker was finally forced to adjourn parliament.

Outside a support demonstration was going on and when our sisters came out of parliament smiling and walking arm-in-arm we knew that the action had been successful and the first in-road on parliament was made.

However, we believe that despite [McInnis's] prediction — two years of red tape without any action — our action in Ottawa was successful. Although the government officials weren't there, the women of Canada have finally been heard — at least by the people of the country — and the first declaration of war has been made with the first exposure of Parliament. The form that this declaration of war will take is actions in hospitals all across Canada to force the officials to be responsible to the women they supposedly serve. We will not be stopped by red tape or other measures of diversion. All power to the people! Women-power to the women-people!

"Statement to Abortion Caravan Rally"
Toronto, May 1970[3]

... As you can see, I am pregnant. Under our new LIBERALIZED abortion laws, I applied for a therapeutic abortion at a Toronto hospital. I was interviewed by two psychiatrists, and one medical doctor. The questions I was asked were unrelated to my feelings about this child, the welfare of this child, or indeed the reality of the life this child will face. For instance, I was asked *how* I got pregnant (My method was terribly unoriginal — it's thousands of years old). Social or economic factors are not considered — only the mother's physical and mental health.

---

3. Doris Powers, a Just Society Movement flyer, Toronto. Canadian Women's Movement Archives (hereafter CWMA) file: Just Society Movement.

These doctors are hopelessly ignorant of the pressures and strains involved in maintaining a family on an income lower than the poverty level, and how that affects a mother mentally and the relationships within that family.

When I was refused the abortion, the doctor asked if I would obtain an illegal abortion. I replied that many women did. He then said, "Well, take your rosary and get the Hell out of here."

One of the questions low-income women are asked when applying for abortions is, "Will you agree to sterilization?" When this question is posed to a woman who feels trapped by an unwanted pregnancy, she is unable to make a rational decision. This places the woman who is poor in a double-bind, for if she agrees to what is essentially a demand, she has lost all power to make any future decisions over her own body. Let me make myself clear — had I agreed to sterilization, I may have been granted an abortion. We are *not* against sterilization — but it must be available to women on demand — not as a prerequisite to abortion, and *not* enforced on a certain *class* of people. The sale and advertisement of contraceptive devices was a criminal offense until recently. Contraceptives are *not* widely or freely available to all women.

We have people who oppose birth control, but never question the quality of life ...

"Abortion Caravan Demands"
Ottawa, 1970[4]
WE DEMAND:

I.   REPEAL That in this session of Parliament the government sponsor a bill removing all mention of abortion from the Criminal Code.

PARDON That all persons charged under sections 209, 237 and 238 of the Criminal Code be pardoned by the Minister of Justice.

II.   That the government provide access to FREE AND SAFE BIRTH CONTROL for all women.

III. The construction of women's community-controlled clinics to

- provide free birth control,
- abortion on demand, and
- pre-natal and post-natal care;

4. CWMA file: CARAL.

- to be financed 50% by Federal funds and 50% by Provincial funds to come from taxing corporate profits specifically for this purpose.

"The Great Chain Debate"
Ottawa, 1970[5]

It's one-thirty in the morning. We're all sitting huddled together in the middle of the main room of the old abandoned school which is our headquarters, trying to plan strategy for tomorrow, the day we declare war on the Canadian government. Or rather, for today.

We are all nervous, strained, exhausted. The police have been circling the school all night and only an hour ago three plain-clothesmen entered and began searching through our sleeping-bags and gear. They tried to pass themselves off as Board of Education officials, but luckily, one of the Ottawa Women's Lib members knew who was on the board, and these men were definitely not from it. Only one of the cops would show his I.D.; the others refused.

We speak quietly, for fear our voices can be heard outside through the windows. I am more afraid than I have ever been, and I am angry that I am afraid, that I am letting myself be hassled.

Discussion has been tense and confused since they searched us. Should we go on with our plans, or do nothing? Should we risk being arrested? Is it worth it? But we must act. Some of the women have travelled 3,000 miles for this campaign, and we just can't give up now.

We break up into our city groups. We want to make some kind of speech in the galleries, but we know there is a good chance of being whisked out before we finish what we're saying. The women who have worked in our birth control centre think we should chain ourselves to the seats in the galleries. How can we smuggle chains in? Won't we be hauled out just as fast? How do we handle security? And what about arrests?

The technical problems of the chains really bother the rest of us. We are undecided. It's getting late and we can't make up our minds. Finally, Sarah speaks up. "It's not enough to shout some phrases from the galleries that nobody's going to understand, because you've been dragged out before you can finish. We can't go in the House after all this and be hauled out after five minutes. What will we say to those women who count on us when we go back? We went into the House and said something but got dragged out before we finished?"

"Well, yeah," says Meg, "but the risks will be greater if we use chains. Is it worth it? Won't we be dragged out anyway?"

"Look," says Sarah intensely. "I've been doing abortion referrals for three years, and I've seen how those women are fucked around, how they're really in chains. Chaining ourselves is the symbol of what their lives are, and of what our lives as women are. The only way we can

5. Kathryn Keate, *Toronto Women's Liberation Newsletter*, 22 June 1970, 6-7. Copy at CWMA.

ensure that we get heard is by chaining ourselves to the seats in the public galleries—that's what democracy is in this shitty society."

She looks at us, desperate, her face strained and pale in the harsh shadows cast by the lone lightbulb in the room. She continues, voice breaking.

"I just can't go back, not after all I've seen. We can't fail, those women, they're depending on us." She starts to cry. Several hands reach out to comfort her.

We look at each other. Shall we do it, or not? There's a long, uncomfortable silence.

Meg speaks for us all. "It seems to me," she says with an embarrassed smile, "the more we listen, well, chains it is."

Then Doris Power, a woman on welfare, a member of the Just Society, and in her eighth month of a pregnancy she wanted terminated six months ago, speaks. "I want chains," she says, "What Sarah says is right. I can see for some of you it's hard to make a choice, because it makes a real difference to your lives if you go to jail or not. For me, there isn't any difference. I'm in chains wherever I am, jail or out. I'm screwed no matter what I do. So, I'll leave you to make your decision yourselves, because I know how hard it is to make a decision when you have a choice."

That settles it. Chains it is for us.

When we get back to the main room, we find that it is chains for everybody.

"Abortion: A Woman's Right"
Fredericton, New Brunswick, November 1975[6]

One of the most heated and continuing debates in Canada centres on the issues of legal abortion on demand. As an issue concerned with a woman's body it seems absurd that abortion is controlled by the legal system and that today abortion is still illegal in North America, most of Europe, and parts of Asia.

In Canada, as in some states, abortion is permitted in cases where the continuation of pregnancy means a risk to the woman's life or health. Yet, there are 100,000 illegal abortions in Canada each year and at least 20,000 admissions to hospitals for post-abortive complications ...

Canadian Law

The Canadian Abortion Law denies most women the right to make the final decision. Bill C-150 states that an abortion can be legally performed if a "therapeutic abortion committee" of an accredited or approved hospital agrees that the continuation of the pregnancy would be likely to endanger a woman's life or health, or if she were physically or mentally ill, or in certain exceptional cases such as rape and incest. A

6. Alice Van Wart, *Equal Times* November 1975, 3, 8. Copy at CWMA.

"therapeutic abortion committee" is defined as "a committee of not less than three members, each of whom is a qualified medical practitioner, appointed by the board of that hospital for the purpose of considering and determining questions relating to terminations of pregnancy within the hospital." Hospitals, however, are not obligated to set up abortion committees, and women in rural areas and in predominately Roman Catholic areas find that they have to travel to larger city centres even to have their cases reviewed. Like any bureaucratic procedure the process of reviewing an abortion case takes time. To have a case reviewed by a committee it must have the certification of one or two doctors, a gynae-cologist or a general practitioner and a gynaecologist. A general practi-tioner cannot make the referral without the approval of the gynaecologist. In turn the abortion committee (which cannot include the doctors making the recommendation) must pass a majority vote for the case to be approved. Obviously this whole procedure takes time, usually a month, which in the case of an abortion can mean the difference between a relatively simple operation and one that involves the risk of more complications.

Abortions in Fredericton

The Victoria Public Hospital in Fredericton has an Abortion Committee Board made up of five doctors. One of the board members, Dr. D. H. King, admitted the doctors' hands were tied behind their backs, but that most straining for abortions was done in the office. Dr. King said that Canadian doctors, in general, support the Canadian Medical Policy on Abortion (CMA) which was determined and outlined at the Halifax meeting of the General Council in 1971. In brief the CMA position states that therapeutic abortion by qualified medical practitioners should be permitted, to protect the life or health of the pregnant woman; that there is justification on non-medical social grounds for the deliberate termi-nation of pregnancy; that the decision to conduct the therapeutic abortion should be made by the patient and her physician; and that therapeutic abortion should be conducted in accredited or approved hospitals only. The CMA policy is more comprehensive than Bill C-150. It includes socio-economic factors as conditions for terminating a pregnancy and brings the decision down to a more personal level.

Referred Elsewhere

What happens, then, to a woman who finds herself pregnant, wants an abortion for whatever reason, yet is either turned away from the doctor's office, or has her case refused by an Abortion Committee? One thing a woman may be advised is to see someone at a Family Planning Clinic. In Fredericton there is The Family Planning Association, a part of the Planned Parenthood Federation of Canada. Its policy on abortion follows that of the CMA. Although the association is basically a counselling organization concerned with sex education and birth control, it will give advice on abortion. As Sue Lewis of Fredericton's branch said, "We will do counselling and refer patients to certain certified and medically approved clinics in New York, Boston, and Maine. These clinics usually have links with hospitals in cases where a salient [saline?] abortion may be needed." Ms. Lewis pointed out that it is extremely important for a woman to have counselling before she goes off to have the abortion. Once a woman receives counselling and has made up her mind to have an abortion, the Association will refer her to a clinic. Once she has made her appointment a woman can fly to New York one day and back the next. The whole procedure takes only a short time but it is expensive considering the cost of airfares and the costs of abortions (usual price is $185.00 but can vary within clinics and according to methods used). Ms. Lewis also said that "There seemed to be a need for a clinic that was closer to home, and one has been established at Bangor, Maine." "It is important to remember," she said, "that doctors at these clinics reserve final judgement on the abortion."

Butcher Abortionists

Unfortunately, many women who become pregnant without desiring to and who cannot afford a legal abortion will resort to any means to terminate their unwanted condition as quickly as possible. They may attempt to induce their own abortion, using such drastic measures as passing a sharp object such as a knitting needle or a coat hanger through the vagina and into the uterus. Needless to say these kind[s] of measures can result in infection, shock, or death. Women who can pay for an abortion rarely resort to such methods, but out of fear and desperation will go to semi-skilled or butcher abortionists who will induce labour through various undesirable means. Many women end up in hospitals bleeding profusely, where the abortion is finished, cleaned up, and the woman's life saved. These cases will usually appear on the hospital records as "miscarriages" which means there are no legal implications for the woman. Women who go to unqualified abortionists put their lives in serious danger, a fact attested to by one woman interviewed (name withheld), who, at the age of 20 found her way from Fredericton into an abortionist's office in Montréal:

> The man was recommended by another woman I know who had gone through the same experience. He had lost his licence for some reason but he was supposed to be reliable and quite good. So my friends got the money together, $300.00 and the plane fare up and back. It was all arranged for me and I was supposed to be up and back over one night, so my parents wouldn't find out. I was just finishing university then and living at home. Anyway the whole thing was disastrous. I guess I was just unlucky because when I got to his place, which was actually a room at the back of the house, he seemed a bit drunk. I had another person with me but she wasn't allowed in the room. Anyway, he gave me a couple of

drinks and then made [me] take two pills. I was pretty hazy at that point but he seemed nice enough. He was certainly sympathetic. I don't remember a lot of it except I was sick, and one horrible moment when it looked as if he was exposing himself. I don't know if he did or didn't but it didn't really make much difference at that point. He performed the abortion all right, but there were a few problems. I was still intact, which means that technically I was still a virgin. I was also carrying twins and it was just about three months. To top if off I had a tilted uterus, so he got a lot more than he bargained for. So did I, when I got back complications developed which seems to have made me sterile. My parents never did find out though. They thought I was at a friends. Now I'm married and trying to adopt a child ...

Morgentaler 'Competent'

The price of that abortion cannot be measured in monetary terms. The virtues of qualified abortionists and certified clinics are unlimited and absolutely essential in the case of abortion. Another woman interviewed had quite a different experience two years ago. Finding herself pregnant she went to Montréal to the clinic of Dr. Morgentaler:

There was a good feeling about the place, well, as good as can be expected under those kind of circumstances. Basically it was because the women there knew they were in competent hands and it was all going to be over soon with the minimum of hassle. There was just a tremendous feeling of relief being there. It was very efficient, very quick, and everyone was very nice. There were women there of all ages. There were no complications, just relief to be rid of the incredible problem.

One Way or Other

A woman who wants an abortion will have one, one way or the other, whether the law or the medical profession agree with her or not. Until women have the right to decide the fate of their own bodies, and until there are legal abortions available on demand for women of the western world there will be illegal abortions and death due to incompetency. There is certainly no question that abortion is a serious matter, and a woman considering abortion must take other aspects into consideration including risk to her own health, and personal feelings and beliefs as well as the initial reason before making her decision on abortion. She should be aware of all aspects including alternative solutions. But once a woman has decided on abortion her decision should be respected. Yet is there any real chance of independent and rational choice for a woman when there are laws affecting her own body, laws concerning contraception and abortion (written by men) which deny all freedom of choice in a matter that ultimately concerns only herself.

The Reproductive Rights of the Disabled

"DAWN Toronto Fact Sheet on Reproductive Rights"
DisAbled Women's Network
Toronto, ca. 1988[7]

DAWN TORONTO
FACT SHEET ON REPRODUCTIVE RIGHTS

Reproductive rights is an important civil rights battle being fought by disabled feminists, both individually and collectively. This includes the right to have a baby, the right to adopt children, the right not to have children and to have access to abortion clinics, the right not to be sterilized without informed consent, the right to know about birth control and its side effects, and the right to access the health care system.

*Because of the shortage of housing in the community for persons with all types of disabilities, many women are forced to make an institution their home. Sexuality in institutions is most often denied and repressed.

Sterilization is the preferred form of birth control practised by institutional staff over teaching women how to use other forms of birth control. In the past they have been sterilized without their consent to spare the institution the embarrassment of pregnancy or the mess of cleaning up menstrual blood.

Women with disabilities in institutions are not encouraged or assisted in getting pap smears.

*In recent years, institutional staff and members of the medical profession have administered Depo Provera (a form of birth control given by needle) to women with both mental and physical disabilities, without informing them of the side-effects of this medication. Up until this year Depo Provera had not been approved for use as a contraceptive in Canada because of concerns around the possible link between this drug and cancer as well as other dangerous long-term side effects.

Through a loophole in our legislation, however, Depo Provera has been given to women with disabilities for many years in Canada.

A study conducted by Donald Zarfas of the University of Western Ontario indicates that the death rate among disabled women who have taken Depo Provera is significantly higher than normal.

In an Ontario study done on 533 women with intellectual impairments who were injected with Depo, [it was found that] twenty-one women [had] died. There was also a noted increase in the frequency and severity of epileptic seizures. Fifty-nine of the women experienced visual impairments with an additional thirty-one totally losing their sight. Other disabling effects associated with the use of this drug included depression,

---

7. CWMA file: DAWN.

loss of hair, limb pain, and diabetes. (Jani Sarra, "The Case Against Depo-Provera," *Healthsharing*, 1982).

*Basic sex education and information [are] not provided to disabled women and girls. Birth control counselling centres are often physically inaccessible and the materials in these centres are not produced in a useable form for women with visual disabilities. Technical Devices for the Deaf (T.D.D's) to allow deaf and hard of hearing women to communicate with these centres are not provided. As of yet, generic services have not met the information needs of women with disabilities.

*Women with disabilities must have access to reproductive health practices such as pap smears and breast examinations. Doctors should be encouraged to buy examining tables that may be raised or lowered to accommodate the disabled woman.

*Disabled women need to know how the medication they are taking will affect their fetus during pregnancy and how different types of birth control can interact with their physical condition and the medications they may be taking.

Contraception

"My Horror Story"
Toronto, Ontario, January, 1976[8]

Most articles you read about birth control are full of statistics: the Pill is 99% effective, 15% of women got infections from Dalkan Shields, 4% of women have side effects from the Pill, etc. But these statistics don't mean too much to me, because every woman I've ever talked to who's used birth control has some sort of horror story to tell. Here's mine.

I guess it all started when I was 16 [and still living in the USA]. I wanted to fuck men, but I didn't want to get pregnant. So I got myself down to my local clinic, lied about my age, sat for 3 hours in a filthy waiting room. After a cursory examination (no medical history taken) and a moral lecture on the evils of premarital sex, I was issued a three month's supply of pills. Because I experienced some spotting, when I returned to the clinic I was given another, stronger kind of pill — this time two year's worth.

By the time my supply ran out, I was living in another city. I went to another equally filthy clinic, where I was told that the pills I had been taking had been removed from the market because they were too dangerous. No one had the time to answer my questions as to why they were too dangerous, I was just handed another two-year supply of another brand of pill and sent on my merry way.

8. Ruth Dworin, *The Other Woman* 4, no. 1 (December-January, 1976), 12-13.

Several months later, I missed a pill one night and, as I was accustomed to doing, simply took two the next day. About 36 hours later I began to bleed very heavily, although I'd had my period only a week before. I let it go for a couple of day's but I was in so much pain and bleeding so much that I began to worry. (I was going through a large box of Tampax *and* one of Kotex daily, running to change every hour or more often.) So I went to the local emergency, where an intern informed me that my hormone dosage was too low, and I should triple my pill intake until it stopped. This I did, but the bleeding only increased.

A week later, when the bleeding hadn't stopped, I heard that there was a woman doctor at another hospital, so I went to see her. I explained that I felt I had been misdiagnosed. After an angry lecture about the sanctity of the medical profession and my morals, she jammed her cold speculum into me as hard as she could, looked at my cervix, and handed me a package of "sequentials". After telling me to take them only in the morning, and not less than 3 hours before or after eating, she slammed the door in my face. When I opened her door to ask "why", she said, "Because if you don't, you'll get very sick", and pushed me out of her office. I walked away from the hospital crying, and threw the pills away.

I ended up in bed, exhausted and bleeding for a month before I had enough sense to stop taking the pills and not start again until my period finally stopped. I realize now that all those hormones were causing my uterus to work extra hard to build up a lining, while at the same time I was losing it as fast as it grew.

After about 2 1/2 more years of the Pill [and then living in Canada], I decided perhaps it was time for my body to take a rest. I consulted several (male) doctors, all of whom said, "No, keep taking the pill. Don't want any little ones running around, do you?" But by now, my trust in the medical profession had diminished considerably and I decided to stop taking birth control pills for two months anyhow. I was living communally at the time, and after the first month, my housemates started saying to me. "Gee Ruth, you've been so much easier to live with lately. What's happened?" With some shock, I realized that when I stopped the pill, a 5 year long depression had lifted, and I was much less insecure and much less tense. I had grown up assuming that that was what my personality was like, that I was a really fucked-up person. But it was mostly chemical.

I spent the next few months alternating between feeling rotten on the pill, and being terrified of getting pregnant off the pill. So I decided it was time for an I.U.D.

At the time, the Copper-7 had just come on the market and was touted as the greatest thing since abstinence: 99% effective, no adjustment period, no risk of infection. Well, now we know better, but at the time ...

Anyhow, I had one inserted, most painfully. About 2 weeks after the insertion, the pain had not subsided, but was in fact getting more intense, and I was running a low fever. I called the doctor who had done the insertion, but she was on holiday, so one of her associates saw me. He put me up on his table, felt around for a minute or two, and said, "I think it's all in your head. Take these." and handed me a prescription for Darvon. Luckily, my regular doctor returned the next week. She listened to my story and got me an appointment that afternoon with a gynaecologist. By this time, my ovary was so badly infected that it was 4 times its normal size, and I was put to bed for 3 months and on antibiotics for four.

A month after I got off the medication and returned to work, a routine examination indicated that my infection had returned, along with a mysterious lump in my breast. I went to a surgeon for a breast examination. She informed me that I had not one lump, but 40 to 50 small ones. My condition is called fibrous cystatic disease, and, she informed me, it's a very common side effect of the birth control pill. "They don't tell you about that when they prescribe the pill, do they?" I asked. "No." "They don't tell you about the depressions, either?" I again asked. She answered, "No, when I took the pill, I got so depressed I had to stop after 3 months."

I wish this story had a happy ending, but it doesn't. My pelvic infection returns whenever I dance, ski, go for a long bicycle ride, or sleep less than 8 hours a night. At this point, I'd like to have a baby, I've even found a doctor who could get me artificial insemination. But, apparently, I'm sterile. One fallopian tube was blocked a year ago, the other one probably is by now. The infection is chronic and incurable.

One good thing's come out of it all though. Through trial and error, I've found an excellent doctor. She listens to what I have to say, takes me seriously, and is completely competent in her diagnoses and referrals. If any woman who reads this needs a good doctor, write to me care of *The Other Woman* and I'll give you her name.

Depo Provera
Squamish, BC, 15 December 1985[9]

Mr. Jake Epp
Minister of Health & Welfare
Parliament Buildings
Ottawa, Ontario

Dear Mr. Epp,

I am very concerned about the possibility of your department's approval of the drug *DEPO PROVERA* as a contraceptive for women in Canada. Your director, Dr. Ian Henderson has been quoted as saying "... it is

9. Mary E. Billy, Letter to Mr. Jake Epp, 15 December 1985. Vancouver Status of Women files.

now culturally acceptable to say that menstruation is a nuisance and that they (women) will be able to take a drug that eliminates menstruation and that women will need to be educated that to stop menstruation is a natural side effect of this drug and that it is not unhealthy for their genitals to be in a dormant state. Their genitals will be just like they were when they were 9 or 10 years old."

What kind of monster have you let loose in the department of Health and Welfare that a person in such a responsible position could be considering such archaic and insane ideas in regard to the women of this country? Certainly menstruation is a nuisance, but so is regular bowel movement, however no one is considering stopping that. Saying a side effect of such magnitude is "natural" is like saying a side effect which rendered men impotent for life was "natural" and should not be of any great concern to them. Menstruation is a natural cleansing function of any healthy woman and is usually only stopped by very unnatural means such as a hysterectomy. When will those who seek expedient solutions to big problems ever learn that the body like the earth is built on systems and that to cripple any part of a system whether physiological or environmental is to threaten the whole thing. To use a word like "natural side effect" in regards to a drug that is known to cause cancer of the breast and uterus, [and to] increase diabetes and severe mental depression, is like saying the poisoning of the Great Lakes is a "natural" side-effect of industry.

It may be in the best interest of mental hospitals not to have to bother with the "nuisance of menstruation," but it certainly is not in the best interest of the patients so drastically affected, and may even add to their original problem. As for the rest of us, the natural plan is for cessation of menses in middle age, not through a chemical injected to render women infertile. Don't get me wrong, I am all for safe methods of birth control, and for a choice of easy and safe methods of abortion, but DEPO PROVERA is none of these things. The only ones to benefit from its use are those who are making it and selling it and they have never been known to have the best interests of women at heart. The only precautions taken are those that decrease their risk of lawsuits. Doesn't the fact [that] it has been used up until now in Third World countries and in mental hospitals tell you that you can sell anything to anybody where someone in authority is making decisions for those who are illiterate or otherwise unable to make informed decisions for themselves?

To suggest [that] anyone would want their genitalia or any other part of their bodies as they were at 9 or 10 years old, says more about Mr. Henderson than I care to think about.

I urge you to take a long hard look at this inhuman *unnatural* drug and listen to how the people who will be most affected by it think about it before you allow its use here or abroad on the female population. All these side effects will one day come home to roost and the cost to "health and welfare" will be more like a holocaust than anything else. We are not expendable, us women. You need us to help build this country and you need us healthy.

Yours sincerely,

Mary E. Billy

Canadian Coalition on Depo Provera Press Conference Vancouver, 10 September 1986[10]

Welcome

The Vancouver Women's Health Collective, one of the founding members of the Canadian Coalition on Depo Provera, has convened this press conference hoping to draw public attention to the issue of Depo Provera. Depo Provera is an injectable hormone that is currently being considered by the Health Protection Branch of Health and Welfare Canada for approval as a contraceptive in this country.

The Canadian Coalition on Depo Provera is made up of about 75 organizations addressing women's health and service provision, development education and international aid, consumer and health education, needs of immigrant, native and teenaged women and individuals with physical and mental disabilities. The Coalition was formed in November 1985 when it first became known that the federal government might allow Upjohn Company Canada, manufacturer of Depo Provera, to promote and sell the drug as a contraceptive. Depo Provera was very much in the news at that time as members of the Coalition met with reporters and media representatives in an attempt to educate the public about the hazards associated with this controversial drug and the implications of its being made available in Canada for contraceptive use.

Depo Provera, often called simply Depo, is the trade name for the injectable form of medroxyprogesterone acetate, a synthetic progesterone-like hormone. It prevents both ovulation and menstrual bleeding by disrupting a woman's normal hormone pattern. Depending on the dosage, a single shot will prevent pregnancy for three to eight months. Although it is currently used in over 80 countries and has been given to approximately 10 million women for birth control, the drug is the subject of world-wide controversy. Short-term side effects include weight loss or gain, depression, dizziness, loss of hair, limb pain, abdominal discomfort, vaginal discharge, darkening spots of the facial skin and reduced interest in sex. Problems which have been linked to long-term use include cancer of the uterus, breast cancer, drastically increased incidence of diabetes, severe mental depression, and, after stopping the injections, irregular or excessive bleeding, and temporary or permanent infertility. Its long-term use is also linked to birth defects and it is transmitted to nursing infants through breast milk in dosages proportionately equal to that of the mother. The effects of Depo on babies is not known.

On December 18, 1985, members of the Canadian Coalition on Depo Provera met with Jake Epp, Minister of Health and Welfare Canada, to request, among other things, public hearings to assess the safety of Depo Provera before any decision was made to approve the drug for use as a contraceptive. Mr. Epp at the time assured the Coalition that full investigation would take place before Depo would be approved for unrestricted use.

In February, 1986, the Coalition received invitations to attend closed-door, invitation-only meetings to be held in six cities across Canada to discuss the issue of fertility control. Was this the federal government's idea of a public inquiry into Depo Provera? Was this its way of placating us, of deflecting public attention away from its unwillingness to hold public hearings?

Clearly, the meetings are not, and were never intended to be public. Only those invited will speak. Notice of the sessions was so short that many organizations that would have taken part were unable to [do so]. No financial assistance was made available for groups to attend, thereby excluding groups geographically distant from the six cities chosen for consultations. Press are not invited to attend (although word has it they will not be turned away if they show up.)

Our request to include medical *and* consumer representatives on any review panel has been ignored by government officials. An expert panel comprised solely of medical doctors cannot, regardless of the best of intentions, encompass the many dimensions of contraceptive methodology, planning and service provision ...

We are gravely concerned that Depo Provera might be approved on the basis of findings at those closed hearings. Once Depo is approved, we can expect it to be widely advertised and promoted by the manufacturer. Although it is not a new drug, it will be newly available as birth control and we can expect that many doctors will delight in having a "new" and convenient method of contraception to offer to the many women who are disillusioned with, can't or don't want to (in the interests of their health) use existing methods. Consequently the drug will be used on large populations of otherwise healthy women.

Because of its injectable mode of delivery, Depo Provera is very susceptible to abuse. The drug requires almost no cooperation from the woman using it. We are concerned that women will not be adequately informed about the drug before getting an injection.

Already certain groups are being targeted for Depo use: women who "aren't sufficiently motivated to take the Pill every day, cannot or WILL NOT use the Pill or the IUD, who are illiterate, unreliable or irresponsible." ("Depo Provera: A Review," *Scottish Medical Journal* 23, July 1975, p.3) Who decides whether or not a woman fits in one of these categories? The implications are frightening!!...

"One Woman's Story: A Disabled Woman Speaks Out on Depo Provera"
Calgary, Alberta, September, 1986[11]

A testimony given to [a member] of the DisAbled Women's Network (DAWN). The woman's name has been changed to protect her identity.

Michelle: I took Depo shots every 3 months for ten years. Doctors should've known that people who are always sitting down, like me, in wheelchairs should never take that kind of drug. It causes bad circulatory problems. I gained weight like crazy. I was 90 pounds then. I stopped Depo when I could no longer get my clothes done up.

It caused irregular bleeding, but, really problems with the whole area, my reproductive system. It changes cervical cells. My lining to my uterus got very thick. It inhibits mucous and makes intercourse very, very difficult and painful.

I have very serious gynaecological problems now. I keep telling them that I think my problems are related to Depo. They don't seem to hear me. Maybe they are afraid of what I'm saying. I have been in severe pain for over a year now. They think it may be a fibroid or cysts, or something like that.

Legalizing Depo, I say, forget it! Just don't. It's a dangerous drug.

New Reproductive Technologies

"New Reproductive Technologies in Canada: Some Facts and Issues"
Toronto, March 1988[12]

Only a decade ago, the world was stunned by the birth of Louise Brown, the first "test-tube baby", conceived through in vitro fertilization. In the decade since her birth, reproductive technology has moved with astonishing speed. In Canada and the U.S., there are now almost 200 in vitro clinics. In some clinics, embryos are frozen and stored for future use, other embryos are transplanted, while still other embryos are used solely as research material. Eggs have been flushed from one woman, to be re-implanted in the womb of a second woman. Pre-conception contracts for the conception of children (so-called surrogate mothers) are being used by couples to have a child. A child conceived through a variety of artificial reproductive technologies can have as many as five different "parents": the sperm donor, the egg donor, the gestational mother and the parents who rear the child. Fetal diagnostic techniques such as amniocentesis and chorionic villi sampling can determine some genetic characteristics and abnormalities and are asking genetic parents

---

11. *Interaction* no. 2 (September 1986), 1. NAC files.
12. Margrit Eichler, Canadian Coalition for a Royal Commission on New Reproductive Technologies, March 1988, 1-3.

to make decisions they have never had to make before. Sometime this year, scientists will begin the first human trials involving gene therapy.

What we are seeing is nothing less than a revolution in reproduction. But do we, as a society, want this revolution to continue without limits?

Below, we discuss a few of the techniques and arrangements currently in use in Canada:

Sex-Selection: Refers to either (a) the identification of the sex of an already existing embryo or (b) the choice of the sex of an embryo before fertilization.

Facts: The first sex-selection clinic in Canada opened in Toronto in the Fall of 1987. It is run on a private franchise basis.

Questions & Issues: Given that there is an international preference for boys as only or first children, widespread adoption of such practises is likely to lead to a distortion of the sex ratio. With an 80% sex-selection success rate, what are the long term consequences for the 20% of the "wrong sex"?

Prenatal Diagnostic Techniques: Include a variety of procedures such as amniocentesis, ultrasound, and chorionic villi sampling, used to determine some genetic characteristics, abnormalities, as well as the sex of the fetus.

Facts: Although these techniques were developed for problem pregnancies, their routine administration to all pregnant women is now becoming the norm. They carry the risk of harm to the woman and the fetus.

Questions & Issues: Is the woman patient informed about the risks? What eugenic principles underlie the decisions made? Who makes the decisions?

Superovulation: A woman is given a regimen of fertility drugs and hormones (in Canada, often Clomid) to stimulate her ovaries to increase her production of eggs.

Facts: Known adverse effects of Clomid include: disturbances of the intestines and bladder, eye and liver problems, and enlargement of the ovaries among other things. Long-term effects on women and resulting children are unknown. This drug is similar in structure to DES, a drug used earlier on pregnant women and found to be carcinogenic in the women and their children. One Canadian woman describes her experience as follows: "The other day, ... the nurse ... gave me two pills, told me to take them in the bathroom. But she didn't tell me what they were. We're not animals, we want to know what they're giving us." Toronto East General Hospital has announced that, in the Spring of 1988, it will start an egg donation programme which will use such drugs on the donor women.

Questions & Issues: To what degree are patients informed? Follow-up of previously treated women and their offspring is imperative but not presently required. Who owns the ova that are produced but not transferred into the woman from whom they were taken? How will donor and recipient women be informed of the risks they incur?

In Vitro Fertilization (IVF): The technique involves the joining of eggs and sperm outside the female body. The eggs are surgically removed from the woman's body, placed in a laboratory dish, fertilized, and reintroduced into a woman — either the one from whom the eggs were originally taken or another woman, who is then not genetically related to the child.

Facts: Canada now has 12 IVF clinics. This is a highly experimental technique involving many risks. The success rate is around 10%, i.e., about 90% of the women undergoing this "treatment" will NOT end up with a child. It includes superovulation (see above). The long-term effects on women and their offspring are unknown. Canada does not currently regulate these techniques.

Questions & Issues: Before proceeding further, should the effects on women and their offspring not be studied — including the effects on the approximately 90% of women who do NOT end up with a child? How many women are physiologically and psychologically damaged in the process? What are the immediate and delayed effects on offspring?

Preconception Contracts for the Production of Children (So-Called Surrogate Motherhood): This involves contracts between a woman and a client who orders a child from a woman. The latter consents to be impregnated, carry the child, and hand it over to the client upon birth, usually for money. Contracts are often arranged by agents (such as lawyers or surrogate companies) who receive high fees for making the arrangements.

Facts: Such arrangements are now occurring in Canada, as well as taking place across the Canada /U.S. border. However, contracts are currently not enforceable in Canada. The Ontario Law Reform Commission (1985) has recommended that contracts be legally recognized, scrutinized and enforced. This would include taking the child by force of the state from the contractual mother who has changed her mind. The New Jersey Supreme Court has identified the practise as "the sale of a child." Contracts may also regulate the lifestyle of the pregnant woman, to ensure a better quality product.

Questions & Issues: Does Canada wish to legally permit the selling of children? In adoption procedures, the natural mother can change her mind and keep the child. Under the recommendations of the Ontario Law Reform Commission, the mother would NOT have such right. If appropriate behaviours for pregnant women are identified in a legally binding manner, how will we protect the pregnant woman's autonomy?

Most of the techniques described above have been developed in cattle. They are being transferred to women without adequate primate research and without appropriate public debate or scrutiny. In the process, the nature of human life and childbirth are being redefined. Parental and family relationships are being transformed. Yet we are largely ignorant about the various causes of infertility, at least some of which are preventable. Canada as a nation needs to face up to the issues and develop a national response to them. If policy responses are left to the provinces, this will result in reproductive tourism — people will obtain in another province what they cannot get in their own. A federal Royal Commission on New Reproductive Technologies would involve the nation in coping with this reality ...

"Experiments on Women and Children"
Montreal, May 21, 1993[13]

Infertility/ It is time to 'end the masquerade' of the reproductive technologies as medical treatment, says a critic of the royal commission on the subject. After 25 years, their failure rate remains dramatic.

Let the buyer beware! That was the best Patricia Baird and her Royal Commission on the New Reproductive Technologies could say to women last month in releasing their survey of Canadian infertility clinics.

As research, the report is an embarrassment, providing no useful data about the practices of fertility programs in this country. Dr. Baird announced that Canadian centres do a very poor job of record-keeping, and that there is a wide variation in the standards of practice, putting women and the babies they may have at risk. This is hardly news. The experimental nature of these technologies and the low success rates were two major reasons for demanding the creation of the commission in the first instance, and that was in 1987. Now, after four years and $25-million, the best Dr. Baird can do is to tell women they need to ask a lot of questions.

This performance raises some troubling concerns about the commission and its responsibility to the Canadian public. The commission spoke of possible HIV infection from artificial insemination, but it would not name the doctors who may be responsible.

And what of other unethical practices disclosed in the report? Almost half the centres with artificial-insemination programs have no limits on the number of inseminations they will perform from a single donor. A recent newspaper account reports that one student sold sperm to a Montreal clinic 200 times in two years. Since each ejaculation is divided into many separate inseminations, he may well be the biological father of hundreds of babies.

The commission repeatedly asked Canadians to wait for its report, but the risks associated with reproductive technologies already have been well documented.

In 1990, the World Health Organization report stated that "there has not been adequate research on the short-term and long-term risks associated with IVF [in vitro fertilization]." It described the limited effec-

---

13. Gwynne Basen, *Globe and Mail*, 21 May 1993, A27.

tiveness of IVF — fewer than 10 live births per 100 treatment cycles — and noted the serious health risks to women taking ovulation-stimulation drugs, a standard part of infertility treatments. It documented a perinatal mortality rate of IVF babies of four times that of the general population.

An Australian report published in 1987 by the director of the National Perinatal Statistics Unit noted that some kinds of congenital malformations occurred more frequently than expected in Australian IVF pregnancies. Data from France gathered between 1989 and 1991 show that the spontaneous abortion rate of IVF pregnancies is double, the multiple birth rate is 22 times as high, and the cesarean birth rate seven times higher than in normal conception.

There was never any reason to assume that Canadian findings would be significantly different. Why didn't the royal commission warn us about these risks years ago, at the beginning of its mandate?

Most of this information was presented to the commission by groups such as the National Action Committee on the Status of Women, the Vancouver Reproductive Technologies Committee and DES Action during public hearings almost three years ago. Patricia Baird has now seen fit to grant legitimacy to some of these health dangers. Why has it taken her so long?

The commission has sat back and allowed the media to make a circus event out of these serious concerns, as the "heartless feminists" were pitted against the "long-suffering infertile."

Dr. Baird claims to be alarmed by the findings of the survey but continues to do nothing, leaving the onus on the couples in the clinics to "ask questions." But it is the commission that needs to ask the questions: Why are doctors not following guidelines set up by their own societies? Why are they refusing to report their success rates to their own professional organizations? Why are they not providing adequate information to their patients on both the known and potential risks of these technologies?

The commissioners have focused public attention on the scandal of HIV infection and delinquent doctors who don't follow the rules. They claim that regulation will solve these problems.

But it is time to end the masquerade of the reproductive technologies as medical treatment. After 25 years, the failure rate remains dramatic, and there have been no evaluations of the long-term effectiveness or effects of these procedures. Let's recognize them for what they really are: experiments on women and children.

At the same time as these techniques multiply, society continues to create infertility as a by-product of sexually transmitted disease, environmental pollution, work-place hazards and our social and political structures.

More than a year and a half ago, four of the original commissioners were fired by the Prime Minister's Office after they claimed in court that the commission was not respecting the terms of the act under which it was created. The commission's shoddy research program and its refusal to divulge information was criticized by women's, legal and academic groups that called for it to be disbanded.

This latest episode is only the most recent in the history of irresponsiblity of this commission. It does not have the credibility and the trust needed to investigate the risks associated with reproductive technologies, or organize a regulatory body. The Canadian public must not be hoodwinked into thinking that the federal government is safeguarding the health of women and children or the future of human procreation ...

Lesbian Conception
Vancouver, May 1985[14]

Self Insemination

1. Establish when you ovulate as accurately as possible using a basal thermometer or the mucous method for at least three months. Most women ovulate on the twelfth to fourteenth day after the first day of the last period but each woman is different. Detailed information about how to [recognize] when you are fertile is available at the Vancouver Women's Health Collective.

2. Choose your donor and let him know the dates you plan to inseminate. For fertilization to take place, insemination usually must occur [some] time between one day prior to ovulation and up to one day after ovulation. Sperm lives one to three days in the female genital tract. The egg lives up to 24 hours. There are lots of factors involved in choosing a donor, but in terms of fertility, men with the lowest overall fertility are heavy red meat eaters, take no vitamins, drink a lot, or smoke more than a pack of cigarettes a day. Also, many prescription drugs can adversely affect sperm count and sometimes cause genetic damage without visibly altering the semen analysis. For best results, the donor should abstain from orgasm for two days before the insemination. As well, he should abstain from alcohol, cigarettes, hot tubs and hot baths for at least 72 hours prior to ejaculation.

3. One way to inseminate is to arrange for the donor to ejaculate into a container of suitable size to draw up the semen with a syringe or turkey baster. Sperm is sensitive to light, heat and air, so it should be kept in a clean glass jar with a lid on, in a brown paper bag, and stored or transported at room temperature.

4. Use a clean syringe (without a needle) or turkey baster to draw up the semen from the container, insert the syringe into the vagina like a tampon and press the plunger. Lie with your hips raised on some cushions for about 20 minutes. The usual quantity of semen

14. *Angles* 2, no. 5 (May 1985), 12-13. Copy at CWMA.

ejaculated averages 3.5 millilitres so don't expect a large amount of fluid.

5. Optional: properly insert your own fitted diaphragm that you've practised putting in to keep the sperm close to the cervix and not dripping out.

6. Other methods: if your donor can be available in the same building he can ejaculate into a condom. You can then insert the condom into your vagina. Or you can put the sperm into a diaphragm and insert the diaphragm, if you can do this without spilling the sperm. Or you can insert a tube into the diaphragm and inject the sperm into the tube, with the edge of the tube going into the diaphragm. You probably have to lie at a steep angle to do this.

7. Two inseminations per cycle are standard. You may do more than that but it takes a few days to build up a maximum sperm count. You should inseminate at 24 to 48 hour intervals for four to five days during ovulation. The time between ejaculation and insemination should not be longer than an hour.

Sexualities

"Feminism's Psychic Imperative"
Toronto, 1985[15]

Two conferences held recently in Toronto, the International Gay Association and another on gay history entitled Sex and the State, left many lesbian feminists feeling conflicted.

Where does a lesbian feminist fit in the political universe? Some activists (albeit homophobic) in the women's movement, wanting to make feminism seem as accessible and non-threatening as possible, feel that lesbians should keep a safe, low profile. Elsewhere on the political matrix, within gay liberation, many lesbians believe the goals of feminism are so diluted, especially in the area of sexuality, that feminism cannot engage lesbian activists in a serious struggle.

At various conference workshops, lesbians complained of the failure of feminism to cope with lesbian experience. Even if the Yankee chauvinism — many of the participants being American — did get in the way of hearing some of the speakers, the discussions *were* an important contribution to a dialogue that is already ongoing in our own communities.

Still, many lesbians felt that feminism had been unfairly maligned and they regretted that so many feminists kept silent while our politics came under such a strong attack. But this frustration assumes that difficult questions can be resolved within the time frame of a conference. As it is, the women who wanted to discuss butch/femme lesbian dynamics

15. Editorial, *Broadside* 6, no. 10 (August/September 1985), 2.

moved the discussion within an atmosphere of openness and appreciated the absence of judgement. The women who wanted to reclaim prostitution as a dissident sexuality brought up issues of commercial sex that feminism has to address. And regarding the often-mentioned controversy over the Toronto's Women's Bookstore's refusal to sell materials called erotica by some and pornography by others, this is no longer an abstract issue, but part of our community experience, a community of both lesbian and non-lesbian women.

We mention all of this with the conviction that these issues should matter to non-lesbian feminists. In a future issue of *Broadside* we will be carrying a feature on the relationship between feminism and lesbianism. The article, we hope, will address some of the concerns raised by some of our readers who cannot understand why we carry any lesbian content at all. But feminism, whose psychic imperative is lesbianism, cannot afford to minimize the role of lesbian feminist activists. Neither can gay liberation, which went through a powerful political renaissance precisely because the gay movement was expressing a feminist critique of gender and a strong opposition to sex-role stereotyping.

In the meantime, *Broadside* recognizes why it is that lesbian feminists cannot call either political place home, and how difficult it is for lesbians to resolve all of the contradictions. Some believe that a feminist vision that does not embrace men is doomed, and that such a point of view should be emphasized. Others agree, but want to be plain practical, to declare with pride that if you intend to join the women's movement, get ready for some close contact with lesbian women, the clergy of the movement, feminism's basic drive and force toward total female autonomy.

"Coming Together: Personal Responses and Reports From the Women's Sexuality Conference"
Toronto, 4–6 October 1985[16]

The feminist sexuality conference was for me a curious combination of challenging political concepts and freeing but sometimes painful personal revelations, many of which are still tumbling out as I continue to think about my experiences at the conference. Although I found there was often a gulf between the intellectual and the emotional levels of the conference, they came together very well in its most satisfying moments, and have been increasingly knitting together in the time since.

On the personal, emotional level, I was deeply touched by many of the sessions I went to, and by many of the informal chats in corridors and over meals that discussed points raised in the formal sessions. This may be partly due to the nature of the topic, sexuality being a rather intense and personal issue, but I also think it had a lot to do with the open way in which the speakers and workshop leaders addressed us.

16. Lynne Tyler, *Breaking the Silence* 4, no. 2 (December 1985), 20–22.

Several sessions brought me face-to-face with questions in my own life about intimacy: emotional, physical, sexual, and — is there a word to describe intimacy at such a profound level that the only concept I can think of is "soul"? ("How corny," says my jaded public persona, and yet ...) With these questions came all the attendant terrifying risks and dizzying ecstasy. It raised issues of passion, power and surrender.

Intimacy in both friendship and sexuality (I am beginning to see that the two overlap much more than I ever thought) involves trust, comfort, caring, love, curiosity, vulnerability, a willingness to learn about myself and be led into parts of myself I didn't know were there, and risk.

A strong and positive intimacy is essentially a relationship between equals: two people who are equally powerful, equally trusting, although often in different ways. But there is sometimes a momentary imbalance of power — it passes back and forth between the two. There are times when I let go of the world and myself, and virtually float free with no idea of where I will end up emotionally and psychologically, simply trusting the other person completely. I call this "jumping off the cliff," and it is not something I do frequently. It's bloody terrifying. And incredibly rewarding. I get the impression that this will always be terrifying, and that if it is not, I am not really letting go, I am only risking partially and the rewards in the relationship will somehow be diminished.

How do we learn to take these risks? What are the steps along the way — are there skills in developing intimacy? How do we choose when to risk? There are certainly situations and relationships in which we would lose more than we would gain, where the balance of power is too unequal.

These personal issues of power, surrender, and equality were reflected in the political questions that were raised at the conference. Susan G. Cole, for example, talked about the need to "eroticize equality" in the context of a wide range of legitimate sexual choices, to replace the pornographic images and limiting choices that society now presents to women.

I agree with her, but for me "eroticizing equality" is still an intellectual concept, an ephemeral but "politically correct" objective. How do we make it a visceral, passionate experience?

Working to create and validate a range of sexual choices is somewhat easier for me to see concretely. Learning from other women about their experiences of intimacy, sharing mine, discussing how much and in what ways each of these was a loving and empowering experience — these are all possibilities I can envisage.

Tied in with this are points that Connie Clement raised, including work that needs to be done to present heterosexuality, lesbianism, bisexuality and celibacy as equally valid options. Clement pointed out the transition from a time not so long ago when lesbians were invisible and silenced in the women's movement, to the present situation, when heterosexuality has become virtually untenable as a political philosophy. Sexual preference seems to be moving into sexual persuasion and eventually coercion.

As part of this, she reinforced how the evolution of a clear and positive lesbian sexual identity has been a powerful and creative force, and suggested that it might be equally beneficial for heterosexual and bisexual women to undertake similar work, and to create their own definition of their sexuality within a feminist context.

Clement also raised the idea of "waffling groups," or support groups for women who are changing or reconsidering their sexual preference. This makes a lot of sense to me — surely inherent in the concept of choice is the option to change your mind periodically ...

"Heterosexual and Feminist: A Contradiction?"
The Women's Sexuality Conference, Toronto, October 4-6, 1985[17]

I want to respond to some of the comments that panellist Mercedes Steedman made about heterosexual women. Much of what Steedman said did not speak to me or my experience, and some of it I found downright offensive. I reacted most strongly to two of her assertions: "we (heterosexual women) fuck the enemy" and "we (heterosexual women) love men's power." I'll deal with them separately.

First, I really dislike the use of the word "fuck" to name consensual sexual activity. That word does more than describe or name intercourse; it connotes that it is dirty, brutish and violent.

When women talk about sexuality in those terms, we support and legitimize popular male-culture images of sexuality — images that trivialize intimacy, deny tender emotions and obscure the loving nature of sex. The use of that language reminds me of the distinction Connie Clement made between bad-touch and good-touch. "Fuck" is bad-touch language.

In her keynote address, Susan Cole challenged us to put the love back into sex. I suggest that we begin by putting love back into our language. When we are talking about loving relationships, we should use loving language; and not reduce every sexual feeling or action to a "fuck."

Connie Clement asked us, "Where is the love in sexuality?" To illustrate her concern she related the story of a young woman who, pressured to be sexually active, "fucked" but never kissed. The girl explained that "kissing was too intimate." When this young woman was growing up, the male-culture model of casual, promiscuous sex was packaged and promoted as "liberating" women. Connie spoke about the sad and bitter consequences for women, if we understand our sexuality in terms defined and delineated by this popular male model.

---

17. Joan Holmes, *Breaking the Silence* 4, no. 2 (December 1985), 23-24.

Many heterosexual women have succeeded in developing good, loving relationships with men. To describe them as "fucking" their mates ("the enemy") grossly misrepresents a significant part of their lives.

It is too simplistic to identify men as "the enemy." The same ideology and material conditions that create and uphold male dominance also promote inequality based on class, ethnicity and race. This complex social hierarchy causes divisions between classes and races that many women feel more acutely than the divisions between themselves and their men.

The attitude that men are the enemy negates the reality of many women. It denies the possibility that they can work towards a better existence for women if they form significant relationships with men. The most devastating consequence for heterosexual women is that this attitude prohibits us from feeling we have a legitimate forum for discussing our particular needs, frustrations and accomplishments. We fear we cannot expect to get support from other feminist women if we consort with "the enemy."

This attitude suggest that female separatism is the only legitimate choice of feminists, a stance which alienates many women from feminism and the women's movement.

The second point that I would like to address is that "we (heterosexual women) love men's power." It is true that we have all been socialized to admire male power and ways of expressing power. Perhaps this patriarchal unconscious is responsible for us "falling in love" with powerful macho types.

To assert that heterosexual women love men's power, however, suggests that we have not been able to overcome the values instilled in us by this patriarchal world. It denies that, in reality, many women have consciously purged themselves of the admiration of male power, and replaced it with respect for female-centred values, such as sensitivity, nurturing and tenderness.

In fact, many women do not love, but fear, expressions of male power and privilege. Consequently, they are attracted to men who have little power or are sensitive to gender inequality and actively seek an egalitarian balance with women.

Furthermore, to say that we love men's power suggests that strong and powerful women do not exist, or that we do not recognize women's capabilities as being worthy of admiration and emulation ...

"For the Sounds of Our Bodies"
Vancouver, November 1988[18]

... I'm an ex-nun. Ten years ago though, I discovered my body for the first time, by making love with another woman and, believe me, that

---

18. Barbara Herringer, in The Telling It Book Collective: Sky Lee, Lee Maracle, Daphne Marlatt, Betsy Warland, eds., *Telling It: Women and Language Across Cultures—the transformation of a conference* (Vancouver: Press Gang Publishers, 1990), 99-102.

really changed the landscape and my mother tongue, especially when I began calling myself by one of the world's most feared words, which is "lesbian."

I remember times then, which are unfortunately infrequent these days, when I would write all night long in an attempt to name or tell or locate who I was with that change. And I kept coming back to the old father language, the God language I had grown up with, and I couldn't find it. Writing as a lesbian is making what other people call the "forbidden," visible. It's exploding the language that I grew up with — transforming it too, into mother tongue. Mother tongue is a familiar place to a lot of us, but it's a very dangerous place when we really start speaking it out there in the world.

One of the things that angered me most, and still does actually, is that when I began to uncover the layers of what it meant for me to call myself a lesbian ten years ago (and believe me I struggled over that word too, having grown up Catholic) was what it meant in the eyes of society. Not just that vague old society out there, but my mother, my brothers, my friends. It didn't matter what I had done in the past, what jobs I had held, what things I had done — all of a sudden I was who I slept with. And I found that hard.

When I first started to uncover myself in that way, I was dismissed because of my body and I think that's a measure of the threat that we face. We are with and for women; consequently, as lesbian women, we lose our children, lose our jobs, lose our housing, and lose our lives. We're not allowed to participate in communal ritual or religion. We're asked to leave convents and, along with our gay brothers, we are not allowed to minister in most churches. When lesbians speak of our lives others flinch and get kind of "creepy" or else they get angry. Why do you have to call yourself a lesbian writer? Why do you have to call yourself a lesbian social worker, or a lesbian anything: why do you have to say anything at all? Well, that's my core.

... I am a Lesbian poet and any poetry I write is Lesbian poetry. I write from that care, that place that's mine, so that I'm not invisible. There are risks with that and some of us stay hidden. Some of us stay hidden by ourselves or along with our lover; we pass, you wouldn't recognize us. We write about anything but ourselves, the way a lot of women poets do and have done in the past; write in the male voice without even thinking about it, assuming "he," because he is universal — "she" doesn't exist. We're all human, they say, well yeah, OK, we are, but we're also beings with differences that need to be acknowledged and that really cry out to be celebrated.

Believe it or not, all lesbians are not the same. We are of varying classes, races, ethnic backgrounds and ... "sizes," and ages. Some of us are mothers or aunties or spinsters or celibate, some of us are sexual, monogamous: call them A and call them B, we're not the same. Not all lesbians are feminists, not all lesbians like women, not all lesbians call themselves lesbians. There is one thing we share though, in all this, and that's an oppression. That oppression — from family, from our friends, from the church, from the state, from the legal profession, from the educational system, from other women, from the women's community — is homophobia. And although it's slowly changing, we're also invisible in the cultural mainstream and our work is all too frequently greeted with silence. Often we must publish our own work, establish our own journals, newsletters, galleries, and networks. But we are telling it and our work and the work of other women here today is challenging that dominant culture ...

Images of Women

"Boobs Sell Tubes"
Windsor, Ontario 1972[19]

"Look at her boobs."

"She's a doll."

"Go on home. You're just jealous that you're not up there."

Last month, we picketed Uniroyal Tires for displaying Miss Uniroyal, a 25-foot, bikini-clad statue. We were a small group but we felt that our message got through. We are sick of being used to sell products that have nothing to do with being a woman. Exploitation of this kind in advertising makes our lot more difficult. It makes us out as sex objects and gimmicks. If a product doesn't speak enough for itself, the advertisers just drape a woman over it. *Then* people pay attention.

Most women who passed by were encouraging. They understood why we were there. Several truck drivers responded with "Right on!"

But sadder comments came from some male passers-by. They thought it was a big joke. Sometimes we answered back to their coos and cat calls. "Why don't you get up there with a jock strap if you think it's so great?" But it was a waste of time to try to explain that women were something more than a set of measurements. They missed the whole issue of objectification.

Because our ranks were so small, we decided not to contact the media. It turned out though that a woman newspaper reporter just happened to be in the area, as well as a TV crew. The coverage was excellent. When the media takes us seriously, they are a great ally in raising awareness of women's issues. This time the media enhanced and reinforced our message.

During the week, many men and women phoned the manager of the service station to complain about such sexist advertising. He said that women should be honoured to get this kind of attention. He also mentioned that several of his female customers liked Miss Uniroyal. Because

19. *Windsor Woman* 1, no. 6 (August 1972), 3.

the phone conversations were so hopeless, we felt that we had to speak more publicly. But even after the demonstration, a contest was started to guess the weight and measurements of the statue. Uniroyal must be going into the cattle business.

Many women have expressed interest in taking more actions of this nature. We have started a phone list at the office so that quick contacts can be made. We will continue to speak out against advertising's sex-ploitation of women.

"MediaWatch: Some Success Stories"
Vancouver, ca. 1986[20]

CASE # 3
DATE:	May 1984
AD/CONTENT:	Ad – Bronztan
SOURCE:	Canadian Living Magazine
MEDIUM:	Print
OBJECTION:	Visual: nearly nude woman shown from waist to calf dressed in leopard skin bikini
	Script: It'll save your hide
RESPONSE:	- concern from AAB[21]
	- Bronztan stated ad will not reappear

CASE # 4
DATE:	May 1984
AD/CONTENT:	Ad – Secrett Jewellers
SOURCE:	Globe and Mail
MEDIUM:	Print
OBJECTION:	Script: "Ring her neck with gold"
RESPONSE:	- apology from Secrett Jewellers printed in Globe & Mail
	- ad only ran one day because of complaints

CASE # 22
DATE:	October 1985
AD/CONTENT:	Content – Hallowe'en Promo
SOURCE:	Switchback
MEDIUM:	Television (CBC)
OBJECTION:	Visual: - head of a woman mannequin was punched and smothered
RESPONSE:	- apology from associate producer, and will look at other promos differently

CASE # 23
DATE: October 1985
AD/CONTENT: Ad – Comp U Car
SOURCE: TV Guide
MEDIUM: Print
OBJECTION: Visual: - woman in a bathing suit is draped over
                     a car
                     Script: "Call me — Free N' Easy"
RESPONSE: - ad was pulled by TV Guide Group

"Being"
Dartmouth, Nova Scotia, 1990[22]

Being real and whole and bodyful;
turning pages,
greeting women who are flat and
glossy, magazine-slim and
dressed to kill budgets and men's eyes;
breasts of a perfect no-size
with hips to match;
hands that spread wings and
fly in colours like birds,
and feet that perch and point
in heels and leather, or
perfect pink and brown barefoot footprints
in some Caribbean sand.

Being real and whole and bodyful;
with big hips and breast and belly,
filling rooms and other eyes
with this image
which does not slip across a glossy page
full of staples and designer fantasy.

"Anorexia Nervosa"
Thunder Bay, June 1979[23]

... Seven years ago, I was diagnosed as having anorexia nervosa. Looking at my 79 pound body one didn't have to be too perceptive to gather
that something was wrong. My weight loss began long before it was
labelled. At first it was gradual. Soon though I was frantic with not eating
at the same time thinking of food constantly — the food that I would
not let myself put in my mouth. I stopped menstruating, I took laxatives,
I forced myself to vomit by sticking my finger down my throat if I ate
a bit more than I allotted myself. I weighed myself daily and would not

22. Maxine Tynes, *Woman Talking Woman* (N.S.: Pottersfield Press, 1990), 30.
23. Wendy Stevens, *The Northern Woman* 5, no. 3 (June 1979), 12-13. Copy at CWMA.

allow myself to eat that day if I weighed one ounce over what I had weighed the day before. I never allowed myself any rest. I woke up at five in the morning to exercise and ran laps around the block after meals. I became so thin that it hurt to lie down. I lost all interest in being sexual and remained celibate for the 14 months that I was at my thinnest.

Anorexia is a condition which, like compulsive eating, is directly related to the expectations placed on women in this society concerning our identity and role. Anorexia nervosa causes us to examine the way in which women are able to gain some sense of self-respect in their lives. Women are disproportionately concerned with pleasing others; we rely heavily upon others to validate our sense of self-worth and frequently devote our lives to fulfilling the feminine role rather than viewing ourselves as individual persons.

The triggers which lead a woman to become addicted to not eating in much the same way a compulsive eater is addicted to food are not fully known. Frequently, anorexia comes at a time when a woman's internal desires and needs clash with the external expectations of family and culture. Society's unattainable and superficial standards for women's appearance and behaviour create a pressure cooker effect in young women. Developing breasts and hips is horrifying to most young women who have been taught that being a boy is equivalent to being effective. The rigid control of eating habits is a desperate attempt to gain self-control of one's body and be self-directed.

Although undocumented, most young women experience some sort of crisis at the realization that the development of a female figure puts an end to most possibilities. Some women run away from home, others react by going for all the trappings of femininity, thereby trying to prove that they can still be effective at something (even if it is at only being a woman).

At the same time that anorexia is seen as a struggle for independence, it is also a plea to remain dependent. For an adult woman, independence only means trading in one form of dependence for another, and frequently the retreat into an androgynous, child-like state is far more satisfying than the mind-boggling messages handed women on the subject of being "one's own person." There is a parallel to anorexia nervosa in the way that some women turn to marriage. Many believe that marriage is a way of gaining independence from their family as well as social integration when, in fact, it usually provides another dependency.

All of this is very painful to write. I have never put most of this down on paper before; it is embarrassing, and ugly and more than I would like to admit, self-hating. When confronted about my self-imposed starvation by the gynaecologist to whom I [had] gone concerning [my] non-existent menses, I, like most anorexics, denied everything. When he accused me of trying to kill myself, I got angry because I know that wasn't it at all. My weight had been dropping for two years, my first two years of college. Although I had always known that I wanted to be a writer, I was in college studying pre-med hoping that this achievement might finally prove me worthy of some recognition from my father. I wanted more than anything in the world to have my father's praise and therefore his caring, but I also wanted my own life and all the possibilities that lay ahead. It was too confusing. I had spent most of my growing years trying hard to please an all too unpleasant man.

I also knew all the things that I did not want from adult womanhood and I knew very little about what the repercussions of rejecting them were. The only sense of power I had ever felt in my life up until that point, had been the power of my sexuality. The power of denying or rewarding men with my body. I knew the falseness of this power and wanted no part of it anymore. As my body grew more childlike, I withdrew in a world filled with food. I would run my fingers over my naked body feeling for the familiar bones which meant I was safe from the world that I felt I wanted no part of. I had positively no idea of how thin I was — my hair stopped growing and became brittle, I was constipated and burped constantly during my waking hours from the anxious paces I put myself through. Once, while waiting in a line in a drug store, the tightness in my body caused my throat to close in on me and as my face turned blue, the Pharmacist ran to my aid. Yet I could confide my situation to no one.

While women in the women's movement can find confirmation in the impossibility of women's role by talking to one another, anorexics struggle in increasing isolation.

I was lucky to have been referred to a woman therapist who after hearing my story affirmed that I was reacting to a very real predicament. She helped me deal with the discrepancies I felt between who I felt I had to be as a woman and who I wanted to be. I gathered the strength to go home and visit my father (whom I hadn't seen in a year and a half) to tell him that I was not going to be a doctor.

None of this is clear-cut or simple. The anorexic's isolation and individual sense of craziness are as bad as the physiological effects themselves. Yet I know that anorexia is, like many other female manifestations, a desperate reaction to the predicament of womanhood.

Violence Against Women

Interesting Facts ...
Montréal, 1981[24]
did you know that:

-       1 in every 17 Canadian women is raped at some point in her life;
        1 in every 5 women is sexually assaulted.

24. Canadian Advisory Council on the Status of Women, Fact Sheet #3, *Communiqu'ELLES* 7, no. 5 (June 1981), 19-20.

- A woman is raped every 29 minutes in Canada — a woman is sexually assaulted every 6 minutes.
- In 1979 alone, there were 3,388 rapes reported to police in Canada; studies show that only 1 in every 8 rapes is reported to police.
- Since 1969 reported rapes have increased by 125%.
- Rape victims have ranged in age from 6 months to 90 years.
- 1 out of every 3 rapes occurs after the rapist forcibly seizes the victim without warning or breaks into her home.
- 49% of all sexual assaults and 18% of rapes occur in broad daylight.
- Not all attackers are strangers; only 30% of rape victims and 33% of sexual assault victims are attacked by total strangers.
- 1 out of every 6 rape victims is assaulted by a friend.
- An attacker may seem perfectly "normal"; nearly half of all rapists are married or living common-law at the time of the assault. One quarter of all rapes occur after assailants make initial contact with the victim, like requesting information or posing as servicemen.
- One thing is certain, victims suffer in many ways;
- 62% of rape victims are physically injured in the attack, 9% are beaten severely, 12% are threatened with a weapon, 70% experience verbal threats.
- In 1 out of every 12 reported rapes the victim becomes pregnant as a result of the assault.
- Our legal system is very selective; out of every 10 rapes reported or known to the police, only 7 are investigated further and only 3 ever result in the arrest of suspects ...
- A man who rapes stands a 94% chance of not being arrested.
- Rape of a woman by her husband is not a criminal offence in Canada (1980).
- Help can come from Rape Crisis Centres, organizations operated by women which provide direct services to rape victims (emotional support, counselling, accompanying the victim to hospital or to court as well as providing educational services to the public).
- Yet such services may not even exist in your area; there are only 35 Rape Crisis Centres in all of Canada (August 1980).
- 67% of the Canadian population lives in an area without the service of a Rape Crisis Centre (August 1980) ...
- Two-thirds of all divorce applications are filed by women; more than one-quarter of these divorces are requested on grounds including physical cruelty (1979).
- 8 out of 10 of the women seeking shelter in a Canadian transition house had been beaten while they were pregnant.

- Often the police don't even want to get involved — for example, in Vancouver 45% of the callers requesting police presence during husband-wife disputes were given only phone advice (1975).
- Domestic disputes are dangerous for police officers. 15% of Canadian police killed between 1961 and 1973 died while investigating such disputes.
- But the dangers to women are even greater ... 58% of women murdered compared to 24% of men murdered are killed by family members ...
- Until 1968, being a battered wife was not valid ground for divorce in Canada.

"Women Challenge CKVU"
Vancouver, BC, June 1983[25]

Media Watch is beginning the process of filing a complaint with the Human Rights Branch against CKVU television. The charge follows Doug Collins's May 12th [1983] editorial on CKVU's Vancouver Show, in which he criticized Media Watch, saying, among other things, that "if there is ever another conventional war it is my hope that Media Watch and its army of snoops will be found in the front line where they can be raped by the Russians."

Collins began the editorial by objecting to the recent funding Media Watch received from the Secretary of State but peppered the statement with what can only be seen as vitriolic and misogynist words: "The usual hot-eyed feminists who would look good sitting at the foot of the guillotine with their knitting just like Madame Lafarge." ... "... there's discrimination afoot here since there is no minister responsible for men. That could be because there are so many lesbians loose in the world ..." ... "They won't be happy until there is not a bosom in the country worth looking at ..."

On May 17th, Media Watch's lawyer wrote CKVU, stating that the station had violated Section 281.2 of the Criminal Code, which deals with hate propaganda, specifically public incitement of hatred. The letter demanded a public apology from Collins on his weekly editorial, [one] where he would summarize the May 12th editorial, give accurate information as to the real role of Media Watch, and then apologize and retract the May 12th statement.

Media Watch received a letter from CKVU president Peter Viner the next day in which no mention was made of the request for an apology. Instead, Viner talked about freedom of speech and the necessity of hearing both sides of a question. He invited Media Watch to appear on the show to present their position, and referred all further communication to his lawyers.

25. Emma Kivisild, *Kinesis*, June 1983, 4.

According to Media Watch's Maureen MacDonald, CKVU's lawyers recommended to the station that a public apology take place according to terms negotiated by both parties. Apparently, CKVU has informed their lawyers they are choosing not to follow that recommendation.

"MediaWatch Demonstrators Form Protest at CKVU Studios" Vancouver, BC, June 1983[26]

When it comes to media watching, it seems supporters of Media Watch don't like being watched by part of the media.

About 150 protesters taking part in a street demonstration Thursday outside the studios of CKVU television refused to cooperate with a crew from the station trying to videotape the event.

Supporters of the Ottawa-funded group had gathered to protest comments made by broadcaster Doug Collins on a Vancouver Show.

But the supporters of Media Watch — a group concerned about the portrayal of women in the media — refused to air their grievances on Thursday's show or be interviewed by show host Laurier Lapierre. And at one point a demonstrator dumped water from an umbrella down Lapierre's neck.

Demonstrators obstructed the view of cameramen, chanted when Lapierre tried to speak and moved away when he tried to use them as a backdrop for a televised monologue ...

Protest organizer Megan Ellis defended her group's refusal to appear on the Vancouver Show or cooperate with Lapierre, saying: "Debate has to take place in an atmosphere where there is some baseline of respect."

She said the station has effectively sanctioned Collins' remarks by refusing to apologize.

Lapierre refused to defend Collins' remarks, calling them "unprintable hatred — the same kind The Sun prints three times a week."

He said he would arrange to have Collins removed from the Vancouver Show when columnist Les Bewley is removed from the pages of The Sun.

Station executives issued a statement saying that while free speech may cause pain, it is vital to democracy.

CKVU vice-president Barry Duggan said people are free to express any opinion within the forum of the Vancouver Show, including advocacy of violence against women and minority groups.

Collins said later the protesters lacked a sense of humour. He said his remarks were intended to be fun.

"The studio audience laughed like hell," he said.

"The people in Media Watch are a bunch of damn fools ... Soon we're going to be living in a society where everybody is watching everybody else and reporting on them just like they did in Nazi Germany."

26. *The Vancouver Sun*, 17 June 1983.

Concerning a Complaint Against CKVU Television, Vancouver, British Columbia, by Media Watch Ottawa, 1983[27]

... In the Commission's view, CKVU has failed, in the circumstances of this case, to discharge its responsibility to provide programming of acceptable standard to the community it is licensed to serve and has breached the duty it owes to it by refusing to accept responsibility for a program broadcast. The Commission stresses that this complaint is not based on an allegation of lack of balance in programming which can be cured by offering the offended party an opportunity to present a differing view. The Commission agrees with the complainant that the issue of whether or not women should be raped is not debatable ...

The Commission issues this statement as a form of censure against CKVU and for the information of all broadcasters at a time when the broadcasting industry has committed itself to a program of self-regulation combined with public accountability with regard to the problems associated with the portrayal of women in the broadcast media discussed in the report of the Task Force on Sex-Role Stereotyping in the Broadcasting Media entitled *Images of Women*. The Commission will follow closely the manner in which CKVU or any other broadcaster handles any issue of a similar nature in the future and reminds all licensees that the standard of their programming and their acceptance of responsibility for the programs they broadcast are among the matters for consideration by the Commission at renewal in determining whether a licensee should continue to be licensed.

J. G. Patenaude
Secretary General
CRTC

Women Against Violence Against Women [WAVAW] Toronto, November 1977[28]

WAVAW DEMANDS

1. *We insist* on freedom of movement for all women, in any part of the city or country, at any time. *We insist* on our right to remain unmolested physically and verbally wherever we are and whoever we are. *We insist* on our right to defend ourselves and each other by any means available.
2. *We insist* on action which focuses on taking the profit out of violence and hate propaganda wherever it occurs and NOT harassment of working women who have few enough choices as it is.

27. Canadian Radio-television and Telecommunications Commission, "CRTC Public Notice 1983-187," 17 August 1983, 7-8.
28. CWMA file.

We insist that the current hypocritical 'cleanup Yonge Street' campaign be stopped. *We insist* that police, who now 'serve and protect' business interests which profit from violence and hate, stop harassing lesbians and prostitutes. *We insist* on full civil rights for all women, especially lesbians and visible minorities.

3. *We insist* on the decriminalization of prostitution.

4. *We* insist that rape is a crime based on hate and not on sex. It is an act of violence against the whole person of the woman intended to intimidate and to confirm men's power over all women. *We insist* that the law and the courts treat it as an assault and not a 'sexual' crime.

5. *We insist* that police and court respond to wife and child beating as they would (or should) to any assault. *We insist* that women cease to be coerced to remain in or return to intolerable home situations. *We insist* that all women but especially poor, native and immigrant women, have the means to escape and a place to escape to. *We insist* on adequate support for Nellie's Hostel for Women, Rape Crisis Centres and other places necessary for our safety and survival. *We insist* that these remain under the control and direction of [the] women who staff them and [the] women they serve.

6. *We insist* on the elimination of female job ghettos and the growing wage gap between men and women. *We insist* on full economic self-sufficiency of women.

7. *We insist* on the right of any woman to bear and raise children in dignity and freedom from economic want. *We insist* on adequate support for single mothers and welfare women, and on day care for all children who need it and want it. *We insist that children not be separated from their mothers because of their mothers' lesbianism.*

8. *We insist* that abortion be taken out of the Criminal Code. *We insist* on the provision of women-run clinics where good healthcare, birth control information, and safe abortions will be available free to all women. *We insist* that the need for back-street abortions be removed.

9. *We insist* on dignified treatment of women in prisons and all so-called correctional institutions. *We insist* on feminist training and good pay for female staff and on non-sexist counselling for all women.

10. *We insist* on the right of women to express themselves sexually and not be harassed or discriminated against for lesbian sexual orientation. *We insist* that lesbians be covered by the Human Rights Code.

11. *We insist* that forced sterilization of immigrant and native women be stopped.

12. *We insist* on an end to violence against women in mental health institutions and the offices of private psychotherapists. Such vio-

lence takes the form of sexist counselling, the abuse of shock treatment, extensive drug therapy and psychosurgery. We insist on provision of adequate feminist therapy and referral services.

THESE DEMANDS ARE MADE AND OUR CAMPAIGN CONDUCTED ON BEHALF OF ALL WOMEN

"Wife Battering in Canada: The Vicious Circle — A Summary"
Ottawa, January 1980[29]

One in ten married women in Canada — or approximately 500,000 women — it is estimated, are battered by their husbands every year. (This estimate is based on Canadian and American studies which have estimated incidence of wife battering, as well as more concrete evidence gleaned from police records of family dispute cases, records from transition houses for battered wives and hostels which accept women who have been battered, and statistics on divorces filed on grounds of physical cruelty.) And yet wife battering is not considered a major social problem, no widespread national or provincial programs have been designed to reduce its incidence, and the help that is available to women who have been battered touches only the tip of the problem. Public concern for women who are battered is not aroused, because wife battering is generally considered to be a private family dispute. Public consensus merges in the attitude that wife battering is a personal problem, and that if women didn't deserve or like the violence, they would leave their abusive husbands.

The evidence presented in the report *Wife Battering in Canada: the Vicious Circle* challenges these popular beliefs ...

Most of the facts for this report were gathered through in-depth interviews with workers in 73 transition houses for battered women across Canada, through the statistics these houses collected in 1978 on the women who came to them to temporarily escape their batterings and perhaps start a new life, and through first- and second-hand reports of the experiences of women who have been battered. The picture that emerges is very different from the picture which forms the popular view of wife battering.

Wife battering is rarely a one-time occurrence — one-third of the women surveyed were beaten weekly or daily. Wife battering occurs at all socio-economic levels, in rural areas as well as large urban centres. It frequently results in serious injury, miscarriage, permanent disability, even death ...

Wife battering is more than a number of isolated incidents of physical violence by a man against his wife. It has an added, crucial dimension.

---

29. Canadian Advisory Council on the Status of Women (Ottawa: January 1980), 1-4. Copy at the Vancouver Status of Women.

Wife battering includes the unspoken licence society gives the husband to use violence against his wife without fear of retribution. He may never take this licence, but he possesses it nonetheless. Women who are battered and look for help learn very quickly that violence by a husband against his wife is an integral part, not just of certain family interactions, but of the dominant, accepted model of the family, and that violence in the family is indirectly supported by our laws, by practices and policies of the police, by the doctors, lawyers, social workers and the psychiatrists to whom battered women may go for help.

If a woman who has been battered phones the police, she frequently finds that they are hesitant to interfere in family disputes; [and] that even if they do intervene, they rarely take the batterer out of the home or offer the woman and her children any long-term protection. Most women find that their legal options are not explained to them early, that court dates are pushed back interminably, and that through all the legal delays they still must live in the same house with their attackers. Women discover to their confusion that their legal rights stop at the doorstep of the matrimonial home, and that wives do not have the same rights as other citizens [have] to call on the law for assistance and to expect true potential for action when they feel that the law is their only or best possible recourse.

If a woman who has been battered goes to a doctor for help she will often be referred to a psychiatrist or given a prescription for tranquillizers to deal better with family stress. Marriage counselling is usually ineffective because few husbands who batter their wives recognize that there is anything wrong with their behaviour. Even friends and family often place the blame on the wife and implore her to try harder to make her marriage work. So, women stay with husbands who beat them, not because they enjoy being beaten or are psychologically weak ... they stay because they have nowhere else to go.

Wife battering is not one problem — it is many tangled problems. Wife battering is undeniably a health problem; many women have been permanently disabled from attacks by their husbands, others have endured a brutal death. Wife battering is also a legal problem. The law supports wife battering through archaic ordinances and ineffective procedures. It is a civil rights problem: married women who are battered find that they have fewer rights than other citizens because the protection of the law stops at their doorstep. In addition, wife battering is an economic problem. Because the work of women in the home is given no financial recognition and the work of women outside the home is usually poorly paid, many women who are beaten do not have the option to leave, especially if they have children to support.

Finally, wife battering is an educational problem. The majority of women who are battered don't even realize there are other women who share their experiences. And what about the children in homes where the wife is battered? They learn from first-hand experience that violence is acceptable behaviour. They see outsiders take their father's side; they often join the majority and turn against their mother. They learn to accept women as appropriate victims of violence within the family.

Petition to End Police Violence
Toronto, Ontario, January, 1990[30]

To: The Solicitor General, Steven Offer & The Premier, David Peterson

In the last fifteen months we have witnessed the shooting of three Black people by Metro police officers, two of them killed and the most recent, Sophia Cook, now lies in a hospital paralysed from the waist down. She was unarmed, sitting with her seatbelt buckled, when she was shot by Constable Cameron Durham.

While the Black community has been most visibly affected by police violence in the past year, this is just part of the pattern of racist and police violence in Toronto and across the country against **Native peoples, Blacks, other People of Colour, Women, Gays and Lesbians and Working peoples.** The recently proposed reforms made by the Solicitor General in no way meet the demands for an independent civilian investigative body called for by the Black and other communities affected by police violence.

We demand that the Province of Ontario set a precedent for its counterparts across the country by immediately establishing an independent civilian investigative body with broad representation, selected by and from the communities affected by racist and other forms of police violence. This body must have the power to investigate, to demand that charges be laid, and to recommend that disciplinary actions be taken against the officers involved.

Please return petitions to the Women's Coalition Against Racism & Police Violence.

Petitions may be mailed to: PO Box 248, Station "P", Toronto, Ontario, M5S 2S6

"Into a Wood"
Summer, 1989[31]

> *There was a man who was no good*
> *Took a girl into a wood ...*
> *Bye bye blackbird ...*

My father was singing in his husky Irish tenor as he drove. I shifted uncomfortably in the back seat of the family two-tone Chevrolet. Those

---

30. *Diva: A Quarterly Journal of South Asian Women* 2, Issue 2 (January 1990), 6.
31. Anne Pierre, *Healthsharing* 10, no. 3 (Summer 1989), 10-12.

were the only words to the song that he seemed to know. It trailed off, unfinished in its dark intent. He repeated the tune in a low whistle.

Bye bye blackbird ...

I am nine years old. Nine years old, in the bathroom, experimenting with Daddy's razor. I marvel as it cuts a small clearing on the tiny blonde forest of hairs on my forearm. Then on my shin. Just a little patch. It looks clean and smooth. Then I turn the razor to the soft longer hairs that have recently and disturbingly appeared under my arms. Just a little patch. My experiment is finished. I hoist myself up onto the sink to put the razor back in its place on the top shelf.

Later that morning my father summoned me sternly into the bathroom. The illicit razor was in his hand. Caught. Didn't I put it back in the right place? Did I break it? I try to gauge my wrongdoing by the measure of his anger. He locked the bathroom door.

"Did you use my razor?" he demanded. His dark eye-brows knitted closer together. There was no room to step away in the close confines of the bathroom. I backed into the toilet and then stumbled awkwardly over the weigh scale.

Maybe I didn't tighten the handle properly. Is he going to hit me?

"I, I did use it. I'm sorry." I stammered. "I won't do it again."

"Where did you use it?" he menaced. I squinted and ducked against the anticipated blow.

"Show me what you did," he demanded. No blow.

I stretched out a forearm weakly indicating the little denuded patch.

"Where else?"

"My leg."

"Show me."

"Where else?"

"Here." I was crying quietly, caught in my guilt and trespass.

He lifted my arm and brushed a forefinger along the remaining tuft of hairs. His eyes grew distant as he ran his fingers over the bud of my left nipple.

"That's nice," he purred. His eyes blinked now at regular intervals. Blink ... blink ... blink ... blink ... like the blind eye of a lighthouse. He seemed different.

He touched the pink nipples again.

I came to the slow conclusion that he was not going to hit me.

"Did you use my razor anywhere else?"

"No," I said. "No, I didn't."

"What about down here?" he suggested reaching down my pants.

"No, I didn't, I didn't," I pleaded, trying to scoop his hands away.

"Let me see, let me see ...," he said in a low soft insistent voice that I had never heard before.

"But I didn't use it there ..."

I don't know how long I stood half naked in goose-bumps in the bathroom watching his eyes blink as his hands moved over me. My relief at not being hit was clouded by shame and confusion.

blink ... blink ... blink ...

Sitting in the back seat of the Chev, my father was at the wheel.

Was a man who was no good ...

I looked at Mom's impassive face.

Took a girl into a wood ...

I watched my brothers fight over the comics.

Bye bye blackbird ...

I looked out the window and wondered what happened to her there.

I was the girl in the story *Into a Wood*. Unfortunately, the story did not stop there. The abuse continued, and intensified for three years. This is a difficult story to write, but I think that it is important for readers who have not experienced child sexual abuse to understand how destructive it can be. It is important for those who have experienced it, to examine their experience as adults and to be compassionate and caring enough with themselves to heal the wounds of childhood.

Child sexual abuse is a very common experience. A number of scholarly works have shown that one in three girls and one in four boys have experienced highly invasive sexual assault before the age of sixteen. Much child sexual abuse takes place in the family. Most often the perpetrator is a man; usually the father or stepfather. It is a problem that transcends social class and race. It is a problem.

The time has come to speak of family secrets. Children who are experiencing child sexual abuse are frequently too intimidated to be able to speak. Adult perpetrators, especially those within the family, have all the authority, power and privilege. As the story illustrates, they know how to exact the compliance of a child.

"It was a long time ago. Why don't you just forget it?" For too long the sentiments behind these words have underscored our whole approach to the issue of assistance to incest survivors.

Child sexual abuse has consequences for those who experience it. It is not unlike the impact of rape or other sexual assault. Response and recovery is personal and may vary greatly from one person to another. It may affect how we view ourselves and how we relate to others.

Let us return to the young girl in the story. When my father initiated a sexual relationship, I lost him as a father. I could not trust him to undertake my best interests. If I was nice to him, I could not trust that he wouldn't understand it as a sexual invitation.

I had a close relationship with my mother as a child. I had been afraid to tell her what Dad was doing. At first I was only afraid of his anger. Later, as I came to understand that what he did with me he also did with her, I was afraid of her anger. I was 10 years old. I needed my mom. I kept silent.

At 12, I was maturing. I started to menstruate. My father was moving closer and closer to intercourse. I was finally so afraid of being raped, that I told my mother about it.

I was believed. This is unusual. In most instances when children disclose sexual abuse to their mother, they are not believed. I believe this is because the mother does not have the emotional support to deal with a problem of this dimension nor the economic means to leave her husband. The mother is asked, in effect, to choose between the child and the husband. In the absence of support, she may not have the strength or conviction to act. The child is silenced. And in the silent aftermath the betrayal spreads. Father, mother, brothers, sisters, family, neighbours, community, church are all too often careful to distance themselves from the ugly truth.

Incest survivors are well versed in betrayal. When a parent, someone whom a child must trust for basic survival, is prepared to exploit a child's defenceless trust, for their own gratification, a child may grow up not trusting anyone. There may be a delayed reaction.

Despite my mother's initial supportive reaction, later she decided to mend her marriage with my abuser and suggested I leave. It was years later that I noticed I was constantly looking for a home, and always walking away. I realized that I was not out of the woods.

I have decided to look at how my early family experiences have affected my life. It was painful to confront the feelings of anger, shame, powerlessness and humiliation that I experienced as a child. But neither do I wish to act out that destructive legacy in my adulthood.

At 25, I was afraid to go home. Afraid because my father resumed a sexual interest. On my infrequent visits he would attempt to corner me in the basement and run his hand up my blouse. An adult by any measure, and I was still afraid to go home. Later that year, a stranger in a bus ran his hand up my thigh. To my shame, I did nothing. It was too hard to put it together. I went to a therapist to discuss it.

Incest has an impact. The statistics are compelling. Boys who are abused may become perpetrators when they grow up. Girls grow up and find themselves in relationships that mirror their abuse as children. But this need not be the case. If we as a country, as a culture, can look at child abuse honestly, speak honestly and act, these tragedies of childhood need not cripple their victims nor be perpetuated in succeeding generations.

Cowichan Rape/Assault Centre: Quarterly Newsletter Duncan, BC, September 1982[32]

... September 17th was the annual Take Back the Night march. About forty women came out for a march that lasted about an hour and included stops at the sites of the rape and murder of one woman and the gang

32. Vancouver Status of Women files.

rape of a second woman. This was our first march in Duncan and we considered it a successful one. Certainly next year's will be even larger and more impressive.

... Newspaper coverage of that event was disappointing: the reporter wasn't proficient at night time photography, so no picture or story appeared in the paper, but we did march by CKAY radio and were interviewed there ...

Currently we are running two self-defence courses out of the community centre; one for women and one for teens. These classes are very well attended, and we have had good feedback from people in town on their effectiveness.

A group of C.R.A.C. workers will be attending this year's B.C. Federation of Women's Conference November 11-14. The Canadian Association of Rape Assault Centre's (C.A.S.A.C.) annual convention was to be held in B.C. this fall, but it was cancelled due to lack of funds ...

Our next training session for C.R.A.C. workers will begin in November. There are now forty-two women who are involved in some aspect of work at the Centre and we welcome new women to take the training course and choose an area of work at the Centre.

The 24-hour crisis line is working well. The R.C.M.P., Human Resources and local doctors are referring women to us. We do crisis and ongoing counselling for all women who've been assaulted. Our phone number is conveniently 748-RAPE (7273).

Please feel free to contact us for more information. We welcome every opportunity to do speaking engagements and to talk to interested people about our work ...

Sincerely, Barbara Park
Cowichan Rape/Assault Centre

"Dawn Toronto Fact Sheet on Violence"
Toronto, ca. 1988[33]

Women with disabilities are speaking out against violence and making it an important agenda item. In at least two provinces in Canada they have initiated specialized self-defence courses. But dialogue, discussion — and action — must be increased if we wish to attack the roots of violence against disabled women and to assist them in freeing themselves from situations of this kind.

In a survey of women with disabilities carried out by DAWN Ontario and funded by Community and Social Services in 1987, it was discovered that 67% of those surveyed had been physically or sexually assaulted as children compared to 66% of non-disabled women who reported that they had not been abused. Almost half of those had been sexually assaulted compared to 34% for non-disabled women.

---

33. DisAbled Women's Network (DAWN). CWMA file.

Thirty-three percent of the disabled women reported they had been battered during their adult years, mostly by husbands, while only twenty-two percent of non-disabled women reported similar abuse.

Thirty-one percent of disabled women reported being sexually assaulted as adults compared to twenty-three percent of the non-disabled women.

The DAWN study found that the most dangerous place for a disabled girl or woman to be, was in her own home: "Her most common assailant was her own mother or/and father. Female caregivers were the next most likely assailants. Many disabled women reported that adults in numerous roles (teachers, attendants, older brothers, etc.) had beaten them ... It might be speculated that the victim was perceived as an ideal target both because of her disability (with weakness, inability to flee, inability to communicate and tell, etc.) and her femaleness (smaller stature, socialized passivity, etc.)." These statistics are born out by the Seattle Rape Relief Development Disabilities Project of 1984 which found 90% of the children, adolescents and adults who had been referred to them had been exploited by relatives or individuals the woman knew.

Despite the high rate of assault and sexual assault of women and girls with disabilities only 20% of all adult rape cases [involving disabled women] are reported to social service agencies or the police. This is not surprising when one considers the lack of credibility disabled women have when they take such cases to court. Women with psychiatric disabilities and developmental disabilities, as well as women who have difficulty communicating and [who] must use alternative devices such as bliss boards, are almost never believed in court cases concerning assault.

This situation is further complicated by the public's perception that the woman with the disability should be "grateful" for the attention since she probably wouldn't have sex any other way, or by the disbelief that violence or sexual assault against her could ever happen at all.

Well-meaning professionals reinforce these attitudes when they encourage women with disabilities to stay in abusive relationships because they suggest that she can't expect anything better.

In the short term, an assault on a woman with a disability can trigger severe physical reactions — a woman with cerebral palsy may develop even more unclear speech, staggering gait or spasms than is normal for her; a woman with diabetes may go into insulin shock; a woman with epilepsy may have a seizure.

In the long term, it may be more difficult for the woman to get over what has happened because of her dependency on others and the isolation created by the disability.

Assertiveness training courses and self-defence courses have proven to be helpful in street-proofing women with disabilities. While there is no guarantee that women who take these courses will not be attacked, persons who take such courses have been found to recover more quickly from assault.

Disabled victims of assault have a difficult time escaping from their assailants because they are often financially dependant on these individuals and the physical means of fleeing assault — such as accessible transportation — is not available to them on short notice or after midnight. Once they get out of an abusive situation, however, they are faced with the further obstacle of finding very few women's shelters available to them because of the physical inaccessibility of the buildings that house these facilities. Few shelters have T.D.D.'s for deaf women or attendant care for women who need this kind of assistance. A woman with quadriplegia can expect to find herself referred to a hospital or institution in such a situation.

Women with disabilities who have children and try to free themselves from an abusive relationship run the additional risk of losing custody of their children.

"Last Words from a Woman Hater"
Montréal, December 6, 1989[34]

Text of suicide letter by Marc Lépine who killed 14 women in Montréal last December, sent to La Presse columnist Francine Pelletier and distributed by Canadian Press:

Forgive the mistakes, I only had 15 minutes to write it.

See also Annex.

Please note that if I am committing suicide today ... it is not for economic reasons (for I have waited until I exhausted all my financial means, even refusing jobs) but for political reasons. For I have decided to send Ad Patres (to the fathers, or death) the feminists who have always ruined my life. It has been seven years that life does not bring me any joy and being totally blase, I have decided to put an end to those viragos.

I had already tried in my youth to enlist in the Forces as an officer cadet, which would have allowed me to enter the arsenal and precede (Québec gunman Denis) Lortie in a rampage. They refused me because asocial. So I waited until this day to execute all my projects. In between, I continued my studies in a haphazard way for they never really interested me, knowing in advance my fate. Which did not prevent me from obtaining very good marks despite not handing in my theory works and the lack of studying before exams.

Even if the Mad Killer epithet will be attributed to me by the media, I consider myself a rational erudite (person) that only the arrival of the Grim Reaper has forced to take extreme acts. For why persevere to exist if it is only to please the government. Being rather backward-looking by nature (except for science), the feminists always have a talent to enrage me. They want to keep the advantages of women (e.g. cheaper insurance,

34. Marc Lépine, *Globe and Mail*, 27 November 1990, A21.

extended maternity leave preceded by a preventive retreat) while trying to grab those of the men.

Thus, it is an obvious truth that if the Olympic games removed the Men Women distinction, there would be Women only in the graceful events. So the feminists are not fighting to remove that barrier. They are so opportunistic they neglect to profit from the knowledge accumulated by men through the ages. They always try to misrepresent them every time they can. Thus, the other day, I heard they were honouring the Canadian men and women who fought at the frontline during the world wars. How can you explain then that women were not authorized to go to the frontline??? Will we hear of Caesar's female legions and female galley slaves who of course took up 50 percent of the ranks of history, though they never existed. A real Causus Belli.

Sorry for this too brief letter.

Marc Lépine

The letter is followed by a "hit list" of the names of 19 women, with an added note:

Nearly died today. The lack of time (because I started too late) has allowed those radical feminists to survive.

Alea Jacta Est (the die is cast).

Pornography

Excerpt from the Red Rag (UBC Engineers' Newspaper) Vancouver, BC, February, 1982[35]

Women Troubles?

Are you one of those super-cool, good looking, virile, humorous, but sensually sensitive modern man [sic] of the eighties? You've had so much sex that you're building up scar tissue on your penis? Everywhere you go, you meet some girl who wants to sleep with you. But now you're starting to get pussy whipped. You haven't slept for five nights now. You show up at work and you fall asleep. You can't stay awake at important meetings. All your projects are late, and you're [sic] reputation as a professional is going down the tubes. You have four girls in love with you, you have a paternity suit, and have been named as an adulterer in six divorce cases.

Well, the only way to get women and all those problems out of your life is to be the world's lousiest lover. But you've forgotten how, since the fine art of lovemaking has become second nature. Well, say no more.

35. UBC Engineers, "Women Troubles?" *The Red Rag* (February 1982), 3. Vancouver Status of Women files. In reponse to the request for permission to reprint this article, Dean Olund, the president of EUS, wrote, "I don't care if you print it, just attach a date (i.e., 1982). The engineers of today are much more aware of social values and by and large do not share the views of our predecessors; to perpetuate the stereotype would be unfortunate."

We at the Red Rag have prepared the following list to help you in becoming the world's shittiest lover. Follow these thirteen suggestions and watch your girl problems go away:

1) Always fuck on her side of the bed so she gets to sleep in the wet spot. If she complains, buy her a rubber nightgown.

2) Never wash. If she doesn't like the smell, tell her it's really body aromas that turn people on. You know, sex pheromones and stuff like that.

3) Screw your women with a cigarette hanging out of your mouth. Tell her that it adds an element of danger to fucking and that nicotine increases the blood pressure in your dink.

4) Get thoroughly drunk before screwing. Tell her that it helps you keep it up longer and to build to a greater climax. Then puke all over her.

5) Since most women like to be reassured about their looks, tell your girl that you don't mind her stretch marks one bit, and that even though some men would be turned off by her shrivelled up prune breasts and baggy looking pussy, you can still get it up for her even though she's that bad.

6) Never change your bed sheets. Tell her how proud you are of all those cum stains and your collections of soiled panties.

7) While most men whisper "Wow, you drive me wild" in their lover's ear, you should just fart. Tell her that farting is a big turn on and shows how uninhibited you are in bed, and that it's proof you're not just another shallow guy trying to make an impression.

8) Since open and frank dialogue is so important in lovemaking, tell her about the time you had V.D. Ask if she's had it, and if she says she hasn't, ask her why not.

9) Since a lot of men treat women as nothing more than sex objects, let her know she's different by asking her to come over and clean your apartment and do your laundry. Tell her that its all part of developing a meaningful relationship which isn't based entirely on sex.

10) Tell her that the importance of foreplay is just a myth created by Alex Comfort to sell books. Then tell her to take off her clothes and go lay in your bed while you go take a shit.

11) Agree with her on the importance of oral sex, but that a girl doesn't know what a real blow-job is when she's been sucking on the withered and sanitized dinks that most men have these days. As you peel back your foreskin, tell her how nicely dried pussy juice, fresh pee, stale pee, and jock sweat combine to create such a wondrous taste.

12) Don't use those lovely nouns "sweetheart" or "my dear" or "my love" or "beautiful woman." Just call her "Bitch" or "Cunt" or "Whore." Then later on call her a "Hole" and a "Slut."

13) And finally, don't let her achieve orgasm, ever. Always make sure that you cum first and cum quickly. Then roll over and fall asleep, and snore as bloody loud as you can.

If you use these techniques, we guarantee that never again will you have girl problems. Then you can get to the important things in your life, like your car, watching football and going fishing.

Letter to the Editor Re the UBC Engineers
5 March 1982[36]

Editor
The Vancouver Sun
2250 Granville Street
Vancouver, B.C.

Dear Sir or Madam:

Why is it that after more than ten years of public and private pressure to curtail the illegal activities of the UBC engineering students, they are still able to break the law with impunity?

The Red Rag, their pornographic, sexist and racist publication, which clearly contravenes the obscenity provisions of the Criminal Code and possibly the hate literature sections as well, and their Lady Godiva Ride, which contravenes the public nudity section of the Code, are repeated year after year with flagrant disregard for the law.

As a member of one of the six women's organizations which were involved in laying a Human Rights complaint against the UBC administration and the engineering students two years ago, I have finally recognized the source of their immunity from prosecution.

It is because their behaviour is condoned by the male-dominated educational, professional, legal and government establishment which runs British Columbia.

It is condoned first of all by UBC president Dr. Douglas Kenny who has failed to provide leadership on this issue. His lawyer told the Human Rights Branch in February of 1981 that the university "is not prepared to interfere with the free expression of opinion, whether in print or otherwise, in the academic community."

It is condoned by the UBC Senate, which refused on March 19, 1980, to approve a statement in support of efforts "to bring an immediate end to such activities."

It is condoned by the RCMP, which turns a blind eye to persistent law-breaking by the engineers.

It is condoned by the Professional Engineers Association of B.C. (most of whose members are UBC graduates), which has consistently refused to take a public stand against the excesses of the students.

It is condoned by universities minister Pat McGeer, education minister Brian Smith, and attorney general Allan Williams, all of whom have never spoken out on this issue.

36. Nadine Allen, Letter to the Editor, 5 March 1982. Vancouver Status of Women files

It is condoned by the leading business associations of B.C., all of which feel compelled to speak out on every social issue of the day, but have completely ignored this one.

The only person in authority who has made a concerted effort to end the engineers' illegal activities, Dr. Martin Wedepohl, Dean of Applied Science, has received almost no support from the university administration or the professional engineers.

When Dr. Wedepohl announced in the spring of 1980, following the Human Rights complaint that he was going to boycott the annual engineers' ball, President Kenny made a point of attending.

When Dr. Wedepohl asked the council of Professional Engineers for their support, he was told that controlling the students was his problem, not that of the professionals in the field.

It is clear that as long as the key opinion makers in engineering, educational and government circles condone through their silence the racism, sexism and pornography practised by the engineers, it will never end.

Surely one of them will muster up enough courage to speak out before another ten years goes by.

Nadine Allen
Vancouver Status of Women

"Hard Core Horror"
Toronto, 1983[37]

A few years ago, while researching for "Drying Up The Streets," a CBC TV drama about organized crime's exploitation of children, my producer suggested to me I could not adequately write about pornography if I had never looked at any. I agreed, and my researcher and I went to Project P in Toronto; "P" for Pornography, a joint exercise by the RCMP, the OPP and the Toronto City Police.

I walked into Project P, your typical soft-bellied liberal, conditioned to a negative knee-jerk stance against censorship, feeling that what a person chose to do in the privacy of her bedroom was none of my business. I walked out sick to my stomach, paranoid, frightened, and angry. And quite incoherent! I had no language, I had no analysis, and I could find no support at all ...

Project P was a collection of material that had been seized and presented as evidence in court, material, I was told, that had *not* been deemed sufficient proof to stop the importation or sale of the magazines, material which had, in effect, *lost* in court.

Those who defend dissemination of such material talk of "art" and of "freedom of expression."

Art: A *photo roman* of a very blonde, very buxom, very scantily and suggestively clad young woman driving a huge chrome-boat which

37. Anne Cameron, *Broadside* 4, no. 4 (February 1983), 5.

breaks down and leaves her stranded on the side of the road. Along comes the older farm pickup truck, driven by the handsome, dark haired, white skinned lifeguard type who offers her a ride to a phone. No more is she in the pickup than she is fondling him. Of course, the erection rips his pants and the pickup careens down the road as she fondles, strokes, sucks and slobbers all over him. Not to the phone, not to the gas station, no, to his farm. Sexual acrobatics all over the farm house, all graphically close-up in black and white, of course, including the part where he can take no more and races in desperation from the house and the insatiable female inside. She, of course amuses herself by trying to fuck the doorknob. He returns, bringing an enormous pink boar with black blotches on its hide. She sexually conquers even the boar. The *photo roman* ends with a close-up of her performing oral sex on the hog. Art, huh?

I saw magazines in which dark-skinned children who ought to have been in elementary school were exploring each other's genitals. I saw children with no external sign of puberty at all sexually involved with adult men. I saw children with only the first external signs of puberty exhibiting the track marks on their inner elbows and thighs, the track marks that are the sign of the addict. I saw children debauched and with eyes that looked like peepholes into the inner rim of hell, posed for the camera.

I saw women photographed in every conceivable position, undergoing and enduring the most god-awful assortment of treatment. And many of these women also had track marks.

Freedom of choice, huh? Art? Sensuality? Eroticism?

Now, for the really erotic, let's look at this memory, the one I call the chapter from the do-it-yourself-instruction-handbook. And this was *not* a series of cartoon or drawings. This, again, was *photo roman*. Photographs of real people doing real things to each other. I don't care if it was scripted or not, I don't care if these were "models" who got "paid" for their "work." It was documentary, and it was geared to be instructional.

The man, ordinary looking, that kind of face you forget even while you're still looking at it, goes to the animal shelter. Gets two bitch dogs. Takes them to his basement. Then takes one of them to a vet, vet gives dog a shot and an arrow drawn on the picture zeroes in on the injecting syringe and [the] word "hormones" is printed above the arrow. Takes that bitch back to the basement, gets the other, goes to a different vet, same thing, injection of hormones. Back to the basement, now we have half a dozen bitches, injected with hormones. Buddyboy is doing some home repair on the basement, insulating, and covering the walls and windows. Then buddyboy is in a car watching young girls going to school. Then we're in an alley, and buddyboy has grabbed a girl, is shoving her into his car, tape over her mouth. Then we're in the basement, the girl is tied face down to a table, and buddyboy is smearing the secretions from the back end of the hormone injected bitches on the bare genitals of the girl. Then in comes buddyboy with an enormous male dog. An enormous, slobbering, leaping, bounding male dog in stud. A male dog in stud in a basement that reeks of bitch-in-heat, and a little girl smeared with secretions, and what's this, chairs, lots and lots of chairs, and men sitting, with bottles and cans of beer, laughing, and a table with a little box full of money and buddyboy is providing the entertainment and the little girl is being sexually explored by a god damned dog.

Everything you need to know to set it up right in your own neighbourhood. Be the first on your block to ...

Erotic, huh?

Then how about the picture and article explaining how to hold, position and sexually penetrate a four year old girl. The dark-skinned man looks to be Pakistani or Hindu, the agonized baby also appeared East Indian, that enormous erection is real, and so is the blood pouring from that child. Freedom of choice? Who gives a fat rat's ass for *her* freedom, *her* choice? That baby could not have lived long after that article was researched, photographed and set in motion.

That's when I lost my morning coffee into the wastebasket at Project P. That's when I started to cry. And that's when I knew that my broad-minded liberal opposition to censorship was really a very stupid and uninformed way of supporting the exploitation and slaughter of my own sisters. That's when I realized that, for me, there was a very clearly defined choice to be made: find a way to stop the profiteering in the blood of babies, or support the freaks doing it. I have never more clearly understood the "if you aren't against it, you're for it" choice ...

Summary of Recommendations on Pornography
Calgary, Alberta, January 1984[38]

Pornography

- women feel cynical about the intentions of government, the system does not work to our benefit
- images women see everywhere have a drastic effect on their sexuality — feel dirty, alone, repulsed by women's/our sexuality as depicted in pornography and sexist ads
- we are missing the concept that our bodies are for our own pleasure and control
- boys and men learn definitions of masculinity from pornography; it teaches that a whole range of violent, exploitive and coercive behaviours are okay

---

38. Calgary Status of Women Action Committee, "Brief to the Special Committee on Pornography and Prostitution: Summary of Recommendations," 9 January 1984, 1-2.

- we see connections between men controlling our bodies through such avenues as abortion laws, economics — ie poor child care, making only 59% of what men do, cutbacks in social programs for women, midwifery restrictions, etc.
- pornography is not the only problem facing women, it is only the depiction of the misogyny in society and is tied to a whole range of social problems concerning women
- results of several studies by Neil Malamuth at the U of Manitoba confirming the link between exposure to violent pornography and violent behaviour towards women by men
- pornography teaches lies about women — women enjoy being raped, if we say no we really mean yes, women are responsible for initiating incest and enjoy it, women like pain, etc.
- pornography is a 600 million dollar business per year in Canada, it is far more widespread than men would like us to believe
- child abuse, sexual assault and incest are condoned in pornography; one in four girls and one in ten boys will be victims of incest or sexual assault by age eighteen
- being raped keeps women silent; being battered keeps women silent; being sentenced to jail instead of being given counselling and reassurance and developing social programs to deal with victims of violence, keeps all women from reaching out for help
- we need freedom to be sexually self-determining and be accorded respect as human beings

we recommend
- increased funding for women's programs, at least $1 per year per woman, not the few cents we get now
- male cooperation for our goals, commitment to struggle with us, not against us
- explicit sex must be taken out of obscenity laws, it is used far more as a tool against women's self expression and attempts to produce erotica than against porn
- hate literature laws must be amended to be workable and to include women
- we need better sex education, so that we have the concept that our bodies are to be enjoyed and respected
- we need to fight incest and child abuse and to treat men who buy sex from children as the child abusers that they are
- we need governments who will quit spouting liberal rhetoric about their concern for violence against women, while passing laws which further restrict our freedom and do nothing to protect us; we demand change!

"Pornography in the Northwest Territories"
Northwest Territories, 1986[39]

Pornography is one of the "entertainments" substituted in the place of traditional culture. While it can be argued that no culture is free from abusive individuals, western culture is one, among many cultures, which *needs* all its members to assume an aggressive personal stance in order to survive. Aggressive male impersonality is the 'holy of holies' in western culture. This is *the* standard of behaviour which men, and now women, are raised to emulate. So pornography is useful in both eroding aboriginal culture *and* teaching the behaviour that is necessary for the 'personal gain' ethic to survive. This corrosive effect is taking its toll on northern people. The following are a variety of the concerns expressed by northerners:

Due to video movies, there is a wrong image ... as to how they [women] should be treated.

Children have wide access to video movies because there is no age restriction in most communities.

Hard core video films and magazines which depict incest and violence are being obtained.

Children or young people are tempted to try acting what they have seen in video movies.

Sexual assault on women has increased since the video movies have been readily available.

Women do not feel confident in themselves when they feel they are visualized as the women seen in pornographic materials.

One video distributer in the Northwest Territories is open 24 hours a day; the children watch video movies all night long and are often sent to get video movies.

Our community has a scrambler so we are able to regulate our viewing. There have been shows we felt should not have been shown; they aired on Cinemax.

There is strict control of video rental movies in one other community; however, one can walk into a bookstore and the magazines are readily available and accessible to children. They [band members] feel bands should have control of what goes into their community.

Anybody can rent video movies and we feel sexual assault is increasing in the north as a result.

Blue movies are shown during prime time and also children under 12 years of age are watching pornographic movies.

The movie rating should be made known to the children and adults so that they know what to watch and what not to watch.

Anybody has access to video movies — restricted or otherwise. There is no control as to what people watch. Cinemax does show x-rated movies during prime time. There have been instances where hard core

39. N.W.T. Advisory Council on the Status of Women, August 1986, 6-9.

materials were ordered, then taped, then were rented out. Why are pornographic materials available when the intention is to exploit women?

Due to ongoing changes in store management we women have formed a group to regulate pornographic magazines in the stores.

Education is needed to make people aware of the implications of pornography.

How can we get rid of HBO and Cinemax?

Some people have gone to the RCMP — however they can't do anything about it.

In the north there is a unique challenge to create a quality of life sensitive to individual and collective rights. Television, movies, and magazines as 'entertainment' formats erode the emphasis on participatory or collective entertainment. Individuals are put in a passive position and then fed information/entertainment which, in many instances besides pornography, encourages sexism, racism and a weakening of the cultural fabric. All this creates tremendous confusion and discouragement in young people and adults. When these media are used for pornography they add insult to injury. Not only then is the medium for entertainment destructive, but the messages of violence and inhumanity overwhelm people with hopelessness, confusion and anger.

Prostitution

Summary of Recommendations on Prostitution
Calgary, Alberta, January, 1984[40]

Prostitution

- we do not recognize the right of males to make laws about and for us without our consent

- we do not believe the government has the best interests of women at heart— the evidence is all around us
- we feel that the new laws will further victimize women who see no viable economic alternatives to them outside of prostitution
- men express their revulsion for uncontrolled female sexuality through repressive laws, while justifying them with 'moral' reasons; we do not need to be protected from other women, only from men
- sexual double standard used to create good and bad women, to divide us, to isolate us

40. Calgary Status of Women Action Committee, "Brief to the Special Committee on Pornography and Prostitution: Summary of Recommendations," 9 January 1984, 2.

- when 'scoring' is how boys see sex, women become sexual objects of conquest
- there is an apartheid system in our country between two classes of women
- illegality of prostitution traps women in the life, makes them vulnerable to violence, pimps and police
- prostitution laws control the behaviour of all women, not just prostitutes
- most women trade their sexual services for a pay off, wives and hookers just make a different deal
- the majority of prostitutes were victims [of] sexual assault or incest leading many to see their only worth as sexual
- we need economic alternatives for young offenders and incest victims besides prostitution
- at the same time the government expresses concern about juvenile prostitution, it cuts off social assistance for young women under eighteen
- legalization of prostitution will only make governments and police the pimps, further reducing women's control over their bodies
- decriminalization is the only option that will open up alternatives for women, that will be acceptable to us, along with widespread programs to promote social change to promote equality for women and an end to male control of our bodies and our lives and the sexual double standard

Position Paper by the Canadian Organization for the Rights of Prostitutes (TORONTO CHAPTER)
Toronto, n.d.[41]

CORP asserts that:

1. Prostitution is a human rights issue, involving the right to choose, the right to govern one's own body and the right to security of person;
2. "Prostitution" is treated totally out of social context resulting in the systemic abuse and victimization of the prostitute;
3. Women must win the right to say "yes" before they can establish the right to say "no";
4. The tyranny of both legalization and criminalization is unacceptable by any civilized standard. Decriminalization must be seen as the only desirable objective ...

---

41. Canadian Organization for the Rights of Prostitutes (CORP), "Position Paper," Toronto, n.d.

Speech to the Police Commission by the Canadian Organization for the Rights of Prostitutes (CORP) Toronto, November, 1987[42]

My name is Valerie Scott. I'm a ratepayer who lives in an area where street soliciting occurs. I'm also a spokesperson for the Canadian Organization for the Rights of Prostitutes (CORP). I'm here once again to advocate the decriminalization of prostitution. We said in 1985 that the proposed communicating law, like the soliciting law before it, wouldn't work. You guys said it would. And it hasn't. Your hands were untied and you still weren't able to do anything to stop street soliciting. Now we think your hands should be tied up again; and maybe your wrists should be slapped too. But more on that later.

Criminalization of street prostitution hasn't worked for two reasons. Firstly, the courts and the Canadian public don't think that prostitution is serious enough to warrant the penalties necessary to significantly decrease it, that is life (or death) sentences. We're not trying to be cute here. The needs for money and sex are very powerful and a fine or short jail term will not deter them ...

The second reason criminalizing street prostitution won't work is that you can't drive the business off the streets unless it's allowed to move somewhere else. In fact, as you guys readily admit, it was the closing of the body rub parlours in the 70s that caused the influx of prostitutes onto the streets in the first place. When given the choice most prostitutes worked indoors. That choice was taken away ...

If you were really interested in doing what was best for the public, you wouldn't be arresting prostitutes at all. Instead you'd be explaining that enforcing prostitution laws requires too many police resources that would be better spent on high priority crimes such as rape, assault, murder, child abuse and robbery. But that would mean giving up what you really want: control of prostitution.

You guys like controlling prostitution because it's a lot safer than going after real, and potentially dangerous criminals. There are a lot worse ways for an officer to spend his shift. You also like controlling prostitution because it is one of the only offenses for which nearly 100 percent of reported cases result in arrest. The inclusion of this high percentage in the overall arrest rate gives a false account of overall police protection. In other words, it makes you look like you're doing a hell of a lot better job than you actually are ...

Obviously you guys will say whatever is necessary to convince the public that you should be allowed to control prostitution, even if it's a lie. Well it's high time the public knew the truth. And it's high time the press started reporting it. Police control of prostitution is an absolute waste of money; all it does is give you guys a cushy job, at the expense

42. Canadian Organization for the Rights of Prostitutes, "Speech to the Police Commission," 5 November 1987."

of prostitutes' and human rights. We're made to suffer. And for what? A law that doesn't work. If people want less street soliciting then stop expecting the cops to help you. They can't. The only way to affect street soliciting is to let prostitutes work indoors, like any other business people, and without police interference. Decriminalize prostitution.

Thank you.

Self-Help Groups and Health Clinics

"A Self-Help Clinic for Women"
Saskatoon, 1974[43]

During the summer of 1973, ten women in Saskatoon worked on the women's self-help clinic, a project that developed out of the women's liberation movement. It was funded by an Opportunities for Youth grant. The objectives of our project, as conceived in early 1972, were to:

- Increase women's knowledge of their bodies, emphasizing the reproductive and sexual organs.
- Develop a sensitivity and a positive attitude to their bodies and their needs as women.
- Develop optimal health potential, enabling women to prevent or adequately deal with health problems.
- Develop an understanding of quality health care so that women expect and demand such care.
- Equip women to participate in decisions regarding their health care.
- Conduct a survey into the particular needs of women and their perceptions of the care received from health workers.

Several factors pointed to the need for the clinic project. For over three years, the women's movement in Saskatoon has run the birth control and abortion information centre. The centre, staffed by volunteers, gives women information on birth control and abortion, and provides referral to helpful doctors and other workers. Feedback to this centre, along with our own experiences, led us to conclude that many doctors are insensitive to the needs of women and that women lack information about their bodies.

As women feel intimidated by health workers, they are reluctant to ask questions that might be regarded as stupid. This is a real fear in the light of the negative attitude of many doctors and nurses toward patients who ask questions.

We were particularly concerned about the number of women who use inadequate methods of birth control; those who wait until the second

---

43. Audrey Hall, *The Canadian Nurse* (May 1974), 33-36. Copy at WERC.

trimester of pregnancy before seeking an abortion; and those with recurrent vaginal infections and cystitis, who know nothing about how to prevent these conditions and who ask in vain for assistance from health workers. The technique of vaginal self-examination was of special interest to us ...

The clinic project was set up in two parts — education and research. The educational section had two teaching teams each consisting of two women. Each team prepared material and class plans and organized its own classes.

The research section compiled a twenty-page questionnaire that covered general gynaecological matters, menstrual problems, vaginal infections, abortion, pregnancy, and menopause. It also set up a filing system for the women's centre in Saskatoon and published a leaflet on the project for promotional purposes ...

Our philosophy and approach to the educational part of the project have been greatly influenced by our experience in the women's movement. We have not wanted to set ourselves up as experts nor to propose theoretical norms to which women should compare themselves. Problems of women have received little study until recently, and we believe it is impossible to state what is normal for women, as all the norms have been defined primarily by men in the context of a patriarchal society.

We have aimed to establish a situation in which each woman can consider her own experience as valid and in which she can try to communicate her feelings about her experience in an atmosphere of trust and empathy. This situation should enable information and feelings to interact.

Classes are held in discussion-type groups, with a maximum of ten to twelve people. A maximum of eight would be ideal, as larger groups have proved unsatisfactory. To promote a comfortable atmosphere, meetings take place in the homes of the group leaders.

Teaching aids are simple: posters and diagrams of the internal and external genital and reproductive organs, and, for the classes on contraception, samples of contraceptives are available for members to look at and handle. Copies of the Montréal collectives' handbooks on birth control and venereal disease and the Canadian Cancer Society's pamphlet on breast self-examination are given to participants. We buy copies of *Our Bodies, Ourselves*, in bulk, and offer them to participants at cost price ...

By December 1973, six months after classes had started, more than 130 women had participated in the course. Approximately 70 percent were middle-class and well educated, and 30 percent were working-class, with less formal education. We also ran a short series for girls in an institution for socially deviant adolescents. Our basic information and approach could be adapted to meet the needs of people from different backgrounds.

Verbal feedback from participants has been positive. Many women say how much better they feel when they realize that the problems that they believed were peculiarly their own are experienced by many women. They also say they are more confident when they consult health workers and when they cope with common problems, such as vaginitis and cystitis. Many women have also reevaluated their method of contraception. Those who were not satisfied with [either] the Pill or an IUD are pleased to discover that effective alternatives, such as the diaphragm, are available ...

"Women Seek Better Health Care"
Fredericton, New Brunswick, June 1975[44]

A women's health collective has recently formed in Fredericton. Interest in this area was confirmed at a workshop on Women in Health at the "New Directions for New Brunswick Women Conference," held at Memramcook and at a later workshop at the Women's Centre. The immediate concern was breast cancer, but it soon became apparent that there was a need for change in almost all aspects of women's health care.

The Fredericton Women's Centre has thus embarked on a study of the quality of women's health care in New Brunswick. The study aims to determine what rapport women here have with their doctors, and what the attitudes of the medical profession are to women's health problems. Nine areas of concern common to most women were established and used as a guideline for change. Examples are the "paternalistic" attitude on the part of members of the medical profession; lack of explanation by medical personnel regarding problems diagnosed and treatments prescribed; and lack of evidence that New Brunswick health professionals want to or are able to change the current system of health care. The study, therefore, hopes to give women a voice in determining their own health care and aims to find out where there is a breakdown of adequate health services and what can be done about it.

One way in which this is being accomplished is through neighbourhood meetings. A woman familiar with the centre and its projects is asked to invite women in her neighbourhood to a meeting in her home. At these meetings films on cancer in women, dealing especially with breast self-examination and Pap tests will be shown. There will be discussion of different health problems encountered by women, and the women will be asked to fill out questionnaires. The questionnaires merely try to determine each woman's attitude to her own health and what information and co-operation is being provided by her physician.

One of these neighbourhood meetings was held recently in the home of Ms Pat Darling in Silverwood. Three women from the Centre were there and met with eleven women from the Silverwood community. In

44. Andrea Fullerton, *Equal Times* (June 1975).

the discussion following the films, the women gave their opinions on what they considered the negative attitude of most doctors concerning the traditional approach [to] the "neurotic woman". Some other topics covered were the "Keep Women Alive" registry organized by Dr. M.T. Richards and the possibility of a clinic for women. Questionnaires were filled out. The response from these women was very positive, evidently there is a need for women to be able to discuss their concerns regarding their own health ...

"The Regina Immigrant Women's Centre: Primary Health Care Project"
Saskatchewan, 1991[45]

When Pas Alejandria, a native of the Philippines, discovered she needed surgery to remove an ovarian cyst, she was afraid to tell her supervisor at work. "Because it was a woman's disease I thought it was related to sex, and it wasn't something I could talk about to other people," she says.

In the Filipino culture, women don't talk openly about serious problems to people they don't know personally. As a result, Alejandria ended up in trouble at work because she had not given her supervisor enough notice of her need to take sick leave.

Dealing with the medical system can be a frustrating and frightening experience for anyone. But for immigrants who have to cope with cultural differences from language barriers to conflicting social customs the experience is even more confusing and stressful.

Alejandria was taken aback by the barrage of seemingly personal questions she was asked by any number of medical personnel. "Did my mother or father ever have this health problem or that disease? I was afraid to answer. It seemed so unusual and I had never even heard of some of these diseases." In the Philippines, people don't have much contact with doctors because they don't seek out medical treatment unless they're extremely ill, says Alejandria.

Immigrant women and their families face innumerable obstacles as they attempt to maintain their health in Canada. Often they have left behind the healers and community supports that helped them deal with health concerns in their own countries.

Some of the health problems immigrant women have are directly related to the fact that they are in a different, strange environment. Isolation is a common problem, but it is usually not addressed until it becomes a full-blown crisis, according to Erika Cancino, coordinator of the Regina Immigrant Women's Centre. "Then the doctor will call it mental illness and prescribe pills."

"We need to make immigrant women more aware of the health services available in the community. We have to help them overcome

45. Susan Dusel, *Healthsharing* 12, no. 3 (Fall 1991), 32-33.

cultural difficulties," says Cancino. "Many immigrant women do not even want a doctor to see them nude," she adds.

To help overcome these barriers to good health, the Regina Immigrant Women's Centre has launched a primary Health Care project. The goals are to help immigrant women work together to learn about healthy ways of living in their new communities; to learn about common diseases and treatments; to explore existing health services and to work out ways of relieving stress.

Popular education techniques, which include role playing and other forms of non-verbal communication and focus on action-oriented problem solving, are an integral part of the project. Project participants are encouraged to act out their problems with other members of a drama group. "Our problems become a lot less stressful when we can laugh at them," says Cathy Ellis, the group leader and coordinator of the health care project.

Because many of the participants have a limited knowledge of English, Ellis has developed materials with a visual focus as opposed to materials with a language orientation.

Ellis, a registered nurse with a background in midwifery, has 10 years experience in the health care field in Central America and Mexico. She leads informal sessions and brings in guest speakers to talk about a wide range of issues. Classes are offered once a week during the day and in the evening to accommodate everyone's schedule. A popular theatre group has been formed to help participants work on problems and solutions in a creative and enjoyable atmosphere.

"The classes and the drama group are designed to give immigrant women a support system, a group of friends to help them look at the issues in their lives that affect their health," says Ellis.

The project emphasizes primary and preventive health care. One of the first educational sessions dealt with home health issues, including how to set up a first aid kit and what to do in an emergency. The session also looked at how to deal with the harsh Saskatchewan climate. Immigrants may not know how to winterize their home, how to avoid frostbite or where to get economical winter clothing.

Mental health is also a theme highlighted in the program. "Many immigrant women face an overwhelming amount of stress," says Ellis. There are immigrant women, for example, who are well-educated, qualified professionals in their own countries who cannot pass language requirements or whose credentials are not recognized in Canada. "When you don't deal with that stress positively, you're going to get sick," says Ellis.

The program looks at ways of coping with stress, such as yoga and tai chi, dealing with alcohol and drug abuse, as well as the pitfalls of cigarette smoking.

Reproductive issues, from how conception takes place to birthing and breast feeding, are discussed as part of the health care project. The focus is on child-birth customs in Canada and includes visits to the hospitals. There are discussions on prenatal and postnatal care, family planning and menopause.

Raising children in a new culture can be a confusing experience. One of the sessions considers cultural differences in child rearing, as well as practical answers to questions about accessing day care, getting the necessary vaccinations and common Canadian childhood diseases.

Chapter 3

The Mainstream Women's Movement and the Politics of Difference[1]

Ruth Roach Pierson

One of the most difficult issues with which the white, mainstream women's movement has been faced is the issue of difference: not in the sense of the difference of one individual woman from another but rather in the sense of the difference of one social group of women from another. These groupings are social and not merely arbitrary, as membership in the group determines individual access to social power and status. The social differences that can divide women are many. They include social categories such as race, class, ethnicity, age, sexual preference, and physical and mental ability. The difference that matters is the difference in levels of social power and social acceptance.

Focusing as it often has on the general disempowerment and oppression of women, the dominant women's movement has been slow to come to terms fully with the implications of the fact that some women, by virtue, for instance, of class and race and able-bodiedness, are more privileged and have more power than others. This chapter attempts to address this difficult issue of difference, and to provide glimpses into the history of how this issue has been played out in the politics of Canadian second-wave feminism.

The Discovery of Women and Gender as Social Categories

In the first heady days of the "rebirth of feminism" in the late 1960s and through much of the 1970s, the lightning bolt of revelation was the "discovery" of women's oppression, both historically and in contemporary society. The overwhelming majority of those who experienced this conversion to feminism and became the spokeswomen for the movement were white, middle class, able bodied and college educated. And most resided in towns and cities. And most, at least initially, identified themselves as heterosexual. As the women's movement developed, both at local community and at provincial and federal levels, the struggle in those early days was to have the category "women" taken seriously as a crucial category of social analysis. Feminists had to work hard to demonstrate that discrimination on the basis of sex actually occurred. It was an uphill struggle to gain acceptance for the proposition that women's subordination is immoral.

To convince others of these feminist arguments, new vocabularies were developed and increasingly complex analytic schemes were elaborated to reveal and explain women's place in society. There was a veritable revolution in language, as neologisms were created and existing words were reclaimed and/or invested with new meanings. One of the potent new terms was "sexism," coined to articulate the systemic and pervasive nature of sex discrimination and of beliefs in male superiority and female inferiority. The terms "patriarchy" and "patriarchal" pre-existed feminism's so-called second wave but now were charged with new significance, referring to a system that established not just the rule of the fathers but the dominance and privilege of men, whether fathers, husbands, lovers, brothers, co-workers, or classmates. Another old word that was exhumed, dusted off and pressed into more frequent use was "misogyny," the Greek-derived term for hatred of, and contempt for, women. And in resistance to the notion that biology determines all the existing, conventional and traditional arrangements governing the relations between men and women, a distinction was drawn between "sex," in the sense of the biologically given, and "gender."[2] The latter was then used to stand for all of the "sex differences" that are social and cultural in origin as well as for the myriad means by which these now-called "gender differences" are socially and culturally inculcated, regulated, enforced and reinforced. Examples of these means include: social structures, such as the patriarchally organized family; social practices, like dressing little girls in pink clothes and little boys in blue; institutions, such as those of education, of religion, and of federal, provincial and municipal government; bodies of thought, like medicine, law and theology; the organization of the labour market, as in the hierarchical and vertical segregation of workers by sex; and popular and "high" culture. The term "gender" was thus turned into a conceptual tool to expose the extent to which gender permeated every aspect of social life. At the same time, the use of "gender" rather than "sex" was meant to convey that the "gendered" character of society was man- and woman-made, not dictated by biology.

Women as a Unitary Category/Gender as a Single Variable

"Sisterhood is powerful" was the rallying cry. While early second-wave feminism was quick to point to the discrepancy between dominant cultural constructions of the ideal "woman" and real historical women, the movement still placed emphasis on the common bonds uniting women — "the bonds of sisterhood." Thus, in much, if not all, of this outpouring of writing and speaking and thinking, the category "women" went undifferentiated. And once "gender" was taken up as a conceptual tool to distinguish the socially constructed from the biologically determined, gender was often employed as the primary, if not the only, variable. Gender was thus often treated as operating separately and independently from other variables, such as race, sexuality, ethnicity and class. For those of us whose race, class, sexuality, age and able-bodiedness positioned us close to the dominant norm, only "gender" was immediately experienced as problematic. The difference that mattered was the difference between women and men. Therefore, gender difference and gender inequality were the focus of our concern. And we thought that one could isolate gender from other dimensions of our social location, as if we had no class or race membership. Such thinking produced the kind of encounter Dionne Brand, a Black Caribbean-Canadian, has recorded as a part of her experience:

> I remember a white woman asking me how do you decide which to be — Black or woman — and when. As if she didn't have to decide which to be, white or woman, and when. As if there were a moment that I wasn't a woman and a moment that I wasn't Black, as if there were a moment that she wasn't white. She asks me this because she only sees my skin, my race and not my sex. She asks me this because she sees her sex and takes her race as normal.[3]

"Gender," when thought of in this way, operated to obscure other systems of oppression and to silence women whose oppression was not exclusively a matter of gender, but rather of race or class or disability.

Women as Victims/Women as Nurturers

One identifiable component of the psychic structure of mainstream feminism has been a victimization mentality. This has contributed to privileged feminists' inability to acknowledge our role in the oppression of other women. In a culture that has historically discouraged the voices of women and either denied women's subordination or justified it as part of the natural order, even white, college-educated feminists have felt compelled to stress women's wrongs[4] in order to be heard. That is, in order to persuade governments and educators, union bosses and social service agencies to take appropriate action to end women's subordination, we have had to harp on a whole series of gender inequities, such as women's low pay, women's overwork, and the sexual harassment and battering of women, before these were taken up as serious social issues. Given this emphasis on victimization, however, it has been difficult for women who are privileged by race and class to see ourselves, the victimized by gender, as victimizers of others. The stress on gender oppression, in other words, has translated into a slowness to see and support struggles against other patterns of domination. From the perspective of privileged women who have felt victimized by gender discrimination, women as oppressors of other women has seemed a contradiction in terms. Women, as victims, occupy a position of innocence.

Closely paralleling the woman as victim construction has been a strand of feminist thought that extrapolates from women's nurturing role as mothers to posit as a general characteristic of women a caring, non-violent and life-affirming approach to the world. This identification of women as inherently associated with the creation and preservation of life has provided a rich spring from which both the feminist-pacifist and the eco-feminist movements have drawn. But this identification also draws on a long-established construction in western, racist, imperialist culture of the white, middle- to upper-class woman as lady bountiful, as a do-gooder who, in her innocence and virtue, can do no wrong. Later I will discuss how oppressive this construction has been, and continues to be, to non-white, non-middle- to upper-class women. My point here is how the construction of white women as dispensers of charity who are by nature opposed to violence and death has precluded the possibility of seeing these same women as oppressors of other women. It has seemed impossible that peaceably inclined, nurturing women could victimize other women. "Yet," as Maxine McKenzie, a feminist woman of colour, wrote in 1987, "if the theorists of the movement did not make eradicating their own prejudices a priority, then they were themselves being the oppressors of women."[5]

The Colonization Metaphor

One vivid example of white, middle-class women's universalizing from our point of view, and thus doing violence to the experiences of other women, was our frequent use in the early stages of second- wave feminism of the metaphor of colonization.[6] White, western feminists of the late 1960s and early 1970s drew an analogy between women's oppression and the oppression of peoples colonized by western, imperialist states. We spoke of women's colonization and women's colonial mentality.[7] The metaphor of colonization graphically captures certain operations and effects of unequal power relations, such as marginalization and appropriation and, most especially, internalization by the oppressed of self-damaging norms.[8] But because we used the language of colonization uncritically, that is, because we did not distinguish between and among different kinds of colonization, we white western feminists participated in the continuing colonization by the western world of women among "Third World" peoples. In particular, by finding facile analogies between their oppression and ours, we white western feminists have been guilty of diminishing more horrific forms of oppression. At the same time, our use of the term "colonization" in a general, undifferentiated sense contributed to the marginalization and silencing of women belonging to those social groups colonized within our own country, i.e., poor, aboriginal, disabled, Black, Asian and others. Above all, universalizing from the point of view of white, able-bodied, heterosexual and middle-class women has masked our participation in other women's oppression.

The Systemic Nature of Structures of Dominance

As effectively as the intellectual and psychic dynamics discussed above have operated to obscure, and to feed the denial of, the racism or homophobia or class oppression or discrimination against the differently abled in the women's movement, they are not the fundamental cause. Rather, the racism, heterosexism, ableism, and classism of the mainstream women's movement are rooted in those institutions, economic practices and cultural expressions that structure the dominance in society at large of whites, heterosexuals, the able-bodied, and the middle to upper classes. And these structures are as socially pervasive as those of gender. From the point of view of racially oppressed women, it must seem a terrible irony that a feminism that coined "sexism" on analogy with racism failed to see the racism in its own midst. As Maxine McKenzie remarked in 1987, "Although the radical women who were the pioneers of the movement had a history and a familiarity with the civil rights movement, they did not see a necessity to incorporate either their knowledge or experience of race oppression into their rhetoric."[9] This "not seeing," a metaphor that itself is based in the social dominance of those with sight, is an attitude of dominance. Those who enjoy a position of dominance (and have no self-criticism) do not have to fear the consequences of what they say or do and are immune to feelings of shame for what they say and do. Occupying an unself-critical position as dominant, one does not feel any compulsion to adjust anything in one's world view to accommodate "the other." Rather, one relaxes into one's class privilege, one's whiteness, one's heterosexuality, one's able-bodied good health and assumes that everyone else also sees the world from one's own point of view. As Elizabeth Spelman has written, "in feminist theory it is a *refusal* to take differences among women seriously that lies at the heart of feminism's implicit politics of domination."[10]

That there is no such thing as "women as women" has been a hard lesson for mainstream feminism to learn. The claim that we can or should take up women's issues in isolation from issues of race or class is usually made from a class- or race-dominant position that, as Dionne Brand's words quoted earlier so vividly illustrate, suppresses the "dif-

After much struggle, anti-racism became a major theme of International Women's Day rallies and marches, like this one in Toronto in March 1986.

ference" of the dominant position and instead universalizes it as "normal." To quote from feminist philosopher Spelman again:

> no woman is subject to any form of oppression simply because she is a woman; which forms of oppression she is subject to depend on what "kind" of woman she is. In a world in which a woman might be subject to racism, classism, homophobia, anti-Semitism, if she is not so subject it is because of her race, class, religion, sexual orientation. So it can never be the case that the treatment of a woman has only to do with her gender and nothing to do with her class or race. That she is subject only to sexism tells us a lot about her race and class identity...[11]

Furthermore, those who want feminism to focus only on sexism fail to see that forms of sexist oppression are shaped by racism, classism, ableism, ageism, heterosexism. Rape is indisputably a form of sexist oppression, but even the experience of rape is not reducible to gender.[12] For instance, the treatment of a rape victim by law enforcement agents and the judicial system has historically differed according to the woman's race, class, age, sexuality.[13] White, middle-class women are situated very differently in relation to rape from less privileged women, particularly women of colour, as a result of the historic cleavage of women into ladies and loose women, and the long-time projection in North American racist culture of the image of sexual looseness onto non-white women, to say nothing of the history of lynching on this continent of Black men on the trumped-up charge of having raped a white woman.[14] At the same time, the non-white race and/or tenuous immigrant status of a woman can make her extremely vulnerable to rape. Consider the traumatic experience of Hyacinth, who, within a month of having been brought from St. Lucia on a temporary employment visa to work in Canada as a domestic, was raped repeatedly by her employer for the next seven months.[15] And consider her failure to report this horrific experience to immigration authorities for fear of losing her work visa and therewith her ability to stay in Canada and earn money for her family.

Documentary Cases

Many of the documents included in this chapter have been written by women who have experienced the women's movement as practising the kind of exclusionary thinking discussed above. Accounts detailing experiences of exclusion abound in the publications of the women's movement. The power dimensions of difference are rarely far from the surface.

Lesbians

For instance, to present a united face to the world and to avoid being "divisive," women have not infrequently been asked to suppress difference. Time and again this was the experience of lesbians in feminist groups not explicitly committed to gay liberation. As a lesbian anonymously wrote in 1972 for *The Other Woman*'s first issue, in a women's liberation group in Toronto, the gay women were told that "making the gay-straight distinction was being divisive, cutting ourselves off from other women, 'alienating the new women'."[16] In response, lesbians mounted one of the earliest challenges to the assumed homogeneity of the women's movement. In May 1973, a Saskatoon women's liberation group held a "lesbian rap" in order to openly discuss lesbian difference. In one of the responses to the rap selected for printing in the *Saskatoon Women's Liberation Newsletter*, a self-identified lesbian commented that "Power politics are in force in the movement here and elsewhere." She was especially disturbed by those at the rap who had implied that "being lesbian is not ... political — not a valid issue to organize around," like "abortion, day care, women's studies, women's unions, etc." In closing, she asked rhetorically if her not being able to sign her own name to her account of the rap, "because of very real legal implications," was "not political?"[17] According to another of the responses to the rap printed in the *Saskatoon Women's Liberation Newsletter*, some women present manifested a strong resistance to "talking about how lesbians, in particular, are oppressed by straight women in the movement." An uneasiness

Nina K. Herman

OWN on the March, International Women's Day, 1990. The Older Women's Network (OWN) is an organization with a feminist outlook that focuses on issues affecting older women.

with the whole subject of lesbian difference was evident in one respondent's relief at finding out that she was not "a latent lesbian" and in another's rush to return to the familiar terrain of similarities between and among women and to the concept of women "as women."[18]

Older Women

Older women have also felt excluded. "I discovered the Women's Movement in 1972, and life has never been the same since," recalled Jane Taylor in 1986, by then a member of a group of older feminist women in Ottawa. In 1979 she and her "sister Crones" had come together to support one another in the face of "the negative image our society has of older women," a need they felt was not being sufficiently met by the mainstream movement. Nonetheless, as women of the mainstream in other respects, they could still remember the early days of second-wave feminism as a time when they "experienced an exhilarating explosion: the resurgence of a new, clear feminist voice."[19] As the once-young participants in early second-wave, grassroots feminism themselves have grown older, the issues of women and ageing and societal sexism, such as the high incidence of poverty and depression among older women, have begun to appear somewhat more frequently on the mainstream feminist agenda.[20]

The Quebec/Anglophone Divide

A colonization that Anglophone women in Canada have not always acknowledged is that of Francophone women by the dominant English-speaking majority, and this has been the case within the women's movement as elsewhere. A lack of sensitivity to Quebec feeling stemming from this colonization largely explains the estrangement of Québécoises from Anglophone women in the National Action Committee on the Status of Women (NAC) at the time of the 1980-81 constitutional crisis occasioned by the Liberal government's "patriation" of the constitution. To respond to the crisis and to prepare for the Women and the Constitution Conference planned by the Canadian Advisory Council on the Status of Women, NAC struck a subcommittee, on which the Fédération des Femmes du Québec (FFQ) had representation, to address the issue of women and constitutional change. Anglophone women's concern soon focused, as discussed in Chapter 5, on the inadequacy of the equality guarantees with respect to women in the proposed Charter of Rights and Freedoms to be entrenched in the "patriated" constitution. At the same time, a split developed between federalist Quebec feminists who were in favour of entrenchment and Quebec feminists who were opposed for fear that Quebec would lose self-determination. Many Québécoise feminists were incensed at the ways in which some Anglophone feminists assumed that, without the protection of the sex equality provisions of the federal Charter of Rights and Freedoms, women in Quebec would be worse off than women in the rest of Canada. Unfortunately, a resolution passed at a NAC mini-conference on the constitution held in Toronto in October 1980 was misrepresented to the press and to the NAC executive as unequivocally in support of entrenchment in principle. Moreover, a resolution stating such support was subsequently adopted by the NAC subcommittee on the constitution and by the NAC executive. This caused a great deal of bad feeling, contributing to the decision taken by both the FFQ (representing 100,000 women) and l'Association féminine d'éducation et de l'action sociale au Québec (l'AFEAS) (representing 35,000 women) to resign from NAC in the course of 1981.[21] Quebec member groups did not return to NAC for years. With those who had done so by the time of the second major constitutional crisis, occasioned this time by the Meech Lake Accord, NAC succeeded in hammering out a position acceptable to both Québécoise and Anglophone member groups.[21]

Disabled Women

Women with disabilities are another social group who have experienced exclusion from the dominant women's movement. Although "[m]ore than one million, or 12 to 18 percent of Canadian women are disabled," women with disabilities in Canada have felt left out of the movement's very definition of what it means to be a woman. When a group of

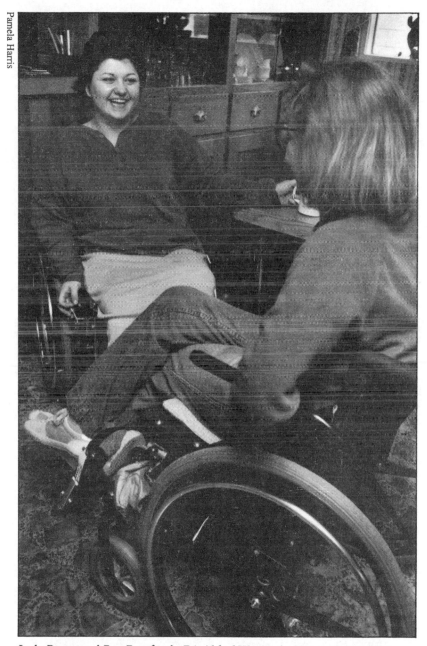

Pamela Harris

Judy Ryan and Pat Danforth, DisAbled Women's Network (DAWN).
Regina, Saskatchewan, 1986.

disabled women founded the DisAbled Women's Network (DAWN) in 1985, "the first national organization of disabled women in Canada," they identified six issues as "priorities of concern to disabled women." Heading the list was "accessibility to the women's movement and women's services."[23] To assess the accessibility in just one part of the country, the Consulting Committee on the Status of Women with Disabilities, a local Winnipeg group that antedated but is now affiliated with DAWN, carried out a survey in 1986 of "women's organizations in Winnipeg and found that when the needs of hearing, visually, and mobility impaired women were taken into consideration, not one was accessible."[24] It is this degree of inaccessibility that led DAWN Toronto to declare in its "Fact Sheet on Accessibility to the Women's Movement and Women's Services" that women with disabilities have not been considered women — either by the women's movement or by the providers of mainstream women's services.[25] It was this lack of accessibility that prompted DAWN Toronto to draft in 1986 an open letter to the women's movement that accused most feminist events of posting, in effect, a big sign saying "DISABLED WOMEN NEED NOT APPLY."[26]

Feminist filmmaker Bonnie Klein acquired full awareness of feminism's inhospitableness to women with disabilities only after she became disabled, at age 46, from a brain-stem stroke. Almost two years post-stroke, she was invited to participate in a foreign festival of Canadian women's films, organized by other Canadian women filmmakers. "The women who had organized the festival," Klein was dismayed to find out,

> had promised to "accommodate" me, but they make no provision for my needs. I am expected to fit in and keep up. They schedule my films late at night when I am too tired; they do not include me in panel discussions or press conferences; they arrange social events in inaccessible places.[27]

Klein writes of her stroke as having given her "a telescope on aging." The lesson that she has learned from her own experience and would like to impart to the feminist movement as a whole is that we are all on "the continuum from 'ability' to 'disability'."[28]

The Exclusion of Women by Race

Many non-white women also speak of having experienced exclusion from feminism's very category of "woman." The title of Maxine McKenzie's article "You Mean, I Still Ain't?" echoes the question asked in 1851 by Sojourner Truth at a women's suffrage meeting in Akron, Ohio. When white female and male members of the audience questioned her right to speak, the Black ex-slave woman, who supported the women's suffrage movement at the same time as she worked for the abolition of slavery and helped countless slaves escape along the under-ground railroad to freedom in the northern states and Canada, strode to the podium and demanded to know "a'n't I a woman?" She, who had borne thirteen children and nursed them and seen almost all of them sold into slavery while she had borne the lash and a burden of hard labour in the fields equal to that borne by Black slave men, returned again and again to the repeating refrain: "And a'n't I a woman?"[29] That that question still resonated with a Black woman's experience of the women's movement in Canada in 1987 is a measure of the extent to which white feminists "continue to see their reality as the norm and everything else as a deviation."[30]

Socialist Feminism and the Category of Class

But, some will maintain, the criticism that mainstream feminism has not been open to, and representative of, all women is unjustified. One can point to many examples of how the movement has not focused exclu-sively on "gender" issues identified as the concerns of white, able-bodied, middle-class women. For instance, while in disagreement as to whether there was a single system of domination (capitalist) or a dual system (capitalist and patriarchal), socialist feminists clearly addressed class as well as gender oppression.[31] The infusion of socialist feminist perspectives into mainstream feminism has meant giving attention to the concerns of working-class women. And insofar as socialist feminist voices have made themselves heard in mainstream feminist organiza-tions, support has been forthcoming for women involved in class strug-gles, such as in the Dare strike of 1972 in Kitchener[32] and the Fleck strike of 1978 in Centralia, Ontario.[33] Yet Eunice Lavell, a white, poor woman, mother of three children, and graduate student completing a master's degree in educational psychology at the University of Mani-toba, writes in 1992 that, in her experience, "feminists are just as likely to accept and perpetuate the negative and disempowering stereotypes of poor people as non-feminists."[34] Socialist feminism can also be credited with adding "race" to the feminist litany of "race, class and gender" as interlocking categories of oppression. Nonetheless, as a 1983 conversa-tion among Himani Bannerji, Dionne Brand, Prabha Khosla and Makeda Silvera, excerpted below, suggests, even socialist feminists who are white could be experienced by socialist feminists of colour as insensitive to issues of race.[35]

Native Women

When charged with insensitivity to issues of race, defenders of the record of mainstream feminism might ask, but what about the movement's support for Native women? Take, for instance, mainstream feminism's support for the struggle by Native women to end the sex discrimination encoded in the Indian Act of 1869. According to the Act, Indian status was determined patrilineally, that is, by a person's relationship, through birth or through marriage, to "'...a male person who is a direct descendant in the male line of a male person...'" According to section 12(1)(b) of the Act, whenever a woman who enjoyed Indian Status by birth "married a non-status man, even a non-status Native or Métis man, she lost her original status and was never able to regain it even if she was divorced or widowed." The loss of status entailed loss of the woman's membership in the band and "her property, inheritance, burial, medical, educational and voting rights" on the Band's Reserve. At the same time, whenever a non-status woman married a status man, "'Indian status' was conferred upon her."[36]

The first woman to speak out publicly against the sex discriminatory provisions of the Indian Act was Mary Two-Axe Early. After the death of her non-status husband, she moved back in the 1950s to the Mohawk reserve in Quebec where she had been born. Local Mohawk government granted her a right of residence in keeping, according to Shirley Bear, with the matrilineality of traditional Mohawk culture. But section 12(1)(b) of the Indian Act blocked her access to federal government-administered financial assistance and would have denied her the right of being buried in her ancestral lands. In 1968, "Mohawk wives of non-status husbands organized under Early's leadership a group called Indian Rights for Indian Women."[37] In the late 1960s and early 1970s, other Native women joined the struggle. Two women, Jeanette Lavell and Yvonne Bédard, who were deprived of band membership by Band Councils in Ontario because of their marriage to non-status men, had their cases argued up through the courts, only to have the Supreme Court of Canada rule, in 1973, in a five-to-four decision, "that the Indian Act was *exempt* from the Canadian Bill of Rights."[38] In 1977, Maliseet women of the Tobique reserve in New Brunswick, such as Caroline Ennis, came up with the strategy of taking the issue of the sex discriminatory clauses of the Indian Act to the Human Rights Committee of the United Nations.[39] In 1981 it ruled in favour of Sandra Lovelace, whose case (she had been denied a right of residence on the reserve of her birth) had served as exemplary of the general plight of Native women in Canada who had been stripped of Indian status. Though embarrassed by the U.N. ruling, the Canadian government still took four more years, that is, until 1985, before passing Bill C-31, which eliminated sex discrimination from the Indian Act and gave the right of reinstatement to band membership to "all women who had lost their status through 12(1)(b) and subsequently, [to] all the first generation children," but not to grandchildren.[40] Meanwhile, in the context of the federal government's failure to honour its undertakings to ease the increased burden on bands with inadequate resources, the passage of Bill C-31 has brought new problems to many reserves by creating overcrowding and exacerbating conditions of poverty, unemployment and inadequate educational facilities.

Throughout this long struggle initiated and waged by Native women, they sought and received support from mainstream feminist organizations. For instance, Mary Two-Axe Early attended the founding meeting of NAC in 1972, where she made an appeal for support of the native women's struggle and received a pledge that such support would indeed be one of NAC's priorities.[41] Mary Two-Axe Early became a member of the Board of Directors of the Canadian Research Institute for the Advancement of Women (CRIAW) at the time of its founding in 1976, and effectively used that position to gain further support among non-Native women of privilege for opposition to section 12(1)(b).[42] White women's groups, such as the Ad Hoc Committee for Women's Rights in Ottawa, were leafleting against the Lavell/Bédard Supreme Court decision in the mid-1970s.[43] In the early 1980s Caroline Ennis became a member of the executive of NAC, reinforcing NAC's long-term support of the Native women's campaign, personified in the unstinting efforts of Madeleine Parent, co-chair for years of the NAC Committee in Support of Native Women. And Shirley Bear's appointment to the New Brunswick Advisory Council on the Status of Women put her in a position to mobilize provincial support for eliminating the sex inequalities of the Indian Act.[44]

Innu Women

White women's response to the call for help from Innu women to save Nitassinan, their homeland, from military destruction is another example of mainstream feminist organizations hearing the cry for help against injustice uttered by the heavily disadvantaged. For centuries, the Native peoples of Canada have suffered genocide, both cultural and actual, in the form of forced assimilation at the hands of "well-meaning" and not so well-meaning agents of government, business, and Christian churches. Protected until more recently by their isolation, the Innu of Labrador have only become, in the last forty years, the target of genocidal practices. First, more than ten large hydroelectric projects undertaken by the provincial governments of Quebec and Newfoundland/Labrador flooded vast tracks of the hunting and fishing lands of the Innu and the sites of Innu camps, including their burial grounds. The Innu were persuaded to abandon their traditional nomadic existence with the promise of houses and Canadian social benefits if they took up residence in settlements. Year-round life in settlements, however, involving as it has the abandonment of their traditional way of life, has had a devastating impact on the Innu. Colonization has robbed them of their sense of identity and self-worth.[45]

In the 1980s, the situation of the Innu worsened as Canada's military presence in Nitassinan escalated. The Canadian government stepped up its efforts to attract a North Atlantic Treaty Organization (NATO) base to Goose Bay and turn the Quebec-Labrador peninsula into a testing ground, complete with bombing ranges for the training of NATO pilots

An Innu woman protests outside a Goose Bay police station in 1989 in support of Innu Indians arrested on charges of public mischief for demonstrating against low-flying NATO test flights.

of low-flying jets. Bombing practice nearby and low-flying jets overhead have had a horrific effect on Innu of all ages, but particularly on children and pregnant women. The military manoeuvres have also taken their toll on the animals hunted by the Innu.

Innu women began to take a prominent role in the struggle of their people to regain their homeland and to protest against its militarization. In 1989, the NAC subcommittee on peace invited a group of Innu women to attend NAC's annual general meeting in Ottawa in May. On the second day of the conference, three Innu women presented a workshop on the Innu struggle against annihilation. They mentioned in particular the sexual exploitation suffered by Innu women, such as the increase in rape and in the birth of babies, called "souvenir babies," fathered by British, American and West German military personnel. The workshop was well attended and word of its powerful impact spread. The next day, the three Innu women were asked to lay their concerns before the six hundred women assembled in the final plenary session of the NAC conference. The delegates unanimously passed a resolution requesting the Canadian government to demilitarize the Innu homeland immediately. They also took up a collection to help the Innu pay some of the legal costs of their struggle.

Feminism Identified as White

The support by mainstream feminist organizations of Native women against the Indian Act and Innu women against the militarization of their homeland would seem to contradict my earlier account of white feminism's exclusionary ways of thinking and acting. In light of these and other cases of mainstream feminism's coming to the aid of marginalized women, white feminists have sometimes reacted defensively when "their" movement is charged with racism. How, the defensive ask, for example, could Mary Pitawanakwat feel "shut out by feminism," when she has served, *inter alia*, as a board member on the Saskatchewan Action Committee on the Status of Women, and as a member of NAC's Committee in Support of Aboriginal Women, of the Saskatchewan Battered Women's Advocacy Network, and of the University of Regina Women's Centre Collective?[46] Why, in her description of herself "as a middle-class Caribbean woman of Indian descent," does Fawzia Ahmad say she "left out the word 'feminist' since, in this society, it refers to white feminism"?[47]

For one thing, some issues have been less disruptive than others to white feminists' sense of self and understanding of our place in the world. It could be argued that white feminism's support for the Innu is compatible with long-established feminist-pacifist and anti-militarist work. Similarly, support for the struggle of Native women to regain their status under the Indian Act was assimilable to characteristic aspects of the mode of operation and world view of mainstream feminism. The campaign was largely in the language of rights discourse and involved challenging sex discrimination and sex inequality in law and judicial judgements leading to legal, constitutional change. Moreover, while the federal government was one of the major players on the side of wrong, the Native women's loss of status could also be seen as a matter of inequality between Native women and Native men. And it is more comfortable for women in the dominant group to see inequality between the men and women in a subordinate group than it is to acknowledge the inequality between, say, white women and Native women.[48] For years, women of colour have been telling white feminists that a focus on sex discrimination is too narrow.[49] Not only does it not encourage examination of how women in a position of dominance participate in the oppression of others, it belies the experience of women of many racial and ethnic minorities that racism is at the core of their oppression.[50] It is the systemic racism in society and the racism in our own ranks that women who experience racist oppression have wanted put on the feminist agenda.

Cultural Appropriation and the Question of Voice

Being made invisible in and being silenced by androcentric, patriarchal culture are what white women have raised our voices in objection to since the late 1960s. What so-called "minority" women and women of colour have been trying to tell us is that we have often silenced them and made them invisible in the women's movement. Women situated differently from the white, middle-class majority have found it necessary to found their own organizations to deal with their own concerns and to found their own journals and other cultural media in order to create their own voice. For instance, inspired by bell hooks' saying in Toronto in 1985 "that black women should voice their own experiences, not let others speak for them," five women, two born in Canada, two in Trinidad and one in England, founded the theatre collective Ebony Voices in 1987.[51] At about the same time, *Tiger Lily: The Magazine for Women of Colour* was founded, evolving later into *Tiger Lily: Journal by Women of Colour*. In 1989, the founding of *Waterlily* created for a time a forum for a feminist voice in Newfoundland and Labrador. Indeed, Canada, already regionally diverse, was becoming increasingly multi-racial and multicultural during the very period of the growth and flourishing of the mainstream women's movement. But because of its initial reluctance or inability to accommodate Canadian society's incredible diversity, an array of diverse women's organizations have been founded across the country. The founding of the group Indian Rights for Indian Women in 1968, as already mentioned, actually antedates the founding of most of the organizations usually credited with building Canada's second wave of feminism. Women's groups have sprung up out of almost every ethnic, racial, cultural and religious community. Local groups join together in provincial and national organizations, and national organizations prompt the founding of local groups. For instance, the National

Congress of Black Women of Canada, established in 1973, now has provincial congresses, such as the Congress of Black Women of Nova Scotia, founded in 1987, with local chapters, by 1988, in Halifax, Dartmouth, North Preston, Cherrybrook, Sackville, Beechville, Hammonds Plains and the former Africville community. "To develop other local chapters in the province" has been one of the Nova Scotia Congress' objectives, together with providing "opportunities for Black women to meet openly to discuss issues which affect us, our families and our communities" and "ways and means for bringing Black women in Nova Scotia and Canada to be one voice for achieving human rights and liberties for Black women in Canada."[52] In March 1992, the first national conference of Chinese Canadian women in 150 years of Chinese-Canadian history was held in Toronto. "'We should not be relegated to the ethnic fringes,'" Susan Eng, Chairwoman of the Toronto Police Services Board, told the more than 100 delegates, "'...we have to make sure our concerns are heard not only at conferences but at our day jobs where we must speak out against harassment and discrimination in the workplace.'"[53]

Not only have marginalized women felt silenced. They have felt robbed when their culture and experience have been appropriated by writers and artists not of their community. We white Euro-Canadians have been steeped in an imperialist culture that regarded it as right and proper to steal the artifacts of ancient Africa, China, Egypt and Greece and display them in our museums in the English- and French-speaking western world. But slowly we are being made increasingly aware of the harm that results from the pillaging of the cultures of others. The issue of cultural appropriation, with its question of who should rightfully speak about and/or for whom, has also been a source of conflict within mainstream feminist circles.[54] As we will see in the chapter on feminist communications, the Women's Press in Toronto divided into two separate presses in the late 1980s largely over differing points of view on this issue. In cultural production, the politics of difference are once again very much a matter of the politics of domination. In the case of writing, both fiction and non-fiction,[55] and of other forms of cultural representation, what members of subordinate groups object to is a member of the dominant group's assuming she or he has the right to speak for or represent whomever she or he wants. This speaking for, this representing, is experienced as particularly harmful and hence objectionable when it is done arrogantly and ignorantly, without adequate consultation and without establishing channels of accountability. Given the dominant group's greater access to, if not control of, the means of communication, that is, publishing houses, newspapers, academic journals and popular magazines, television, movies and the theatre, it is all too easy for a member of the dominant group simply to "rip off" the story, the song, the dance, the image of the subordinate group, incorporate it within her or his work and market it as her or his own. Worse still, the dominant group member's account might well involve painful misrepresentations, misunderstandings and distortions of the subordinate group's experience.

Some women writers, however, using the stories from cultures other than their own have tried to proceed responsibly. Take, for example, the retelling by white writer Anne Cameron of North Pacific Native women's tales in her widely read *Daughters of Copper Woman*.[56] Cameron was married for seventeen years to a Métis man; her adopted daughter is status Haida, and the rest of her children, Métis. Cameron's accountability to her sources further ameliorates her cultural imperialism. The elderly Native women whose stories she retold "vetted every word she wrote." Moreover, she has turned over all royalties from the sale of the book to Native projects, including the preparation of an anthology of Native women's writings by the Native women's collective Ts'eku. Nonetheless, there are Native women who are uneasy with Cameron's cultural appropriation.[57] According to Cameron, the old Native women asked her to put the stories down on paper and she has "no regrets." She listens now, however, to younger Native women, Lee Maracle among them, who have asked her "to take a step or two to one side. Not down. To one side." And Cameron pledges she will try to do what they have asked.[58]

Similarly, Marie Wadden, a white Newfoundlander and author of *Nitassinan: The Innu Struggle to Reclaim Their Homeland*, has subjected herself to considerable soul-searching for having written and published the book rather than an Innu person.[59] Personally acquainted with members of an Innu family and through them with the struggle of the Innu, Wadden, a trained journalist, became convinced that the Canadian public was not getting the whole story of the Innu struggle from the Canadian media. Short news clips could not provide the necessary historical context. She sought and secured the support of the Innu community of Sheshatshit for a comprehensive study, took three years off from her salaried work to research and write, applied for a small grant to defray some of the expenses she incurred and spent every waking moment for many months living with the Innu in their struggle. Never does she presume to know without evidence what the Innu were thinking or feeling. Rather, wherever possible, she reproduces their own words as recorded in transcripts from trials, speeches, conversations and interviews, or in journals kept by Innu while in jail. Her Innu friends and informants read the book before it was published and she has promised to turn over to the Innu any royalties the sale of the book generates once the advance she received to cover costs has been recouped. Nonetheless, Wadden still has misgivings. A part of her wonders whether she should instead have facilitated the publication of, say, the Innu prison journals. She recognizes, however, that an account of the Innu struggle might never have been published had she not done what she did. In response to the Canada Council's recent proposal not to fund works involving

David Maylor Courtesy: SHARE

*Attending the inaugural meeting of the National Organization of
Immigrant and Visible Minority Women were (l-r): Nela Rio, Dorothy
Ellis, Betty Lee, Leti La Rosa, Marge Nainaar, Patsy George, and
Carmencita Hernandez.*

"appropriation of voice,"[60] Wadden has recommended that the Council
commit itself to providing funds for overcoming the obstacles often
standing in the way of the subordinate group's coming to voice —
obstacles such as having to write in a second language or needing the
services of translators. Given the overcrowding in their homes, and the
life and death political struggles in which their communities are involved, would-be aboriginal writers, Wadden suggests, would require
the provision of solitude and relative peace of mind[61] — what Virginia
Woolf once called, when thinking of middle-class women aspiring to
write, "a room of one's own."[62]

Language, Labels and the Complexities of Coming to Voice

The gendered natures of the English and French languages have posed
difficulties for white Anglophone and Francophone women seeking our
"authentic" voices. But these difficulties pale alongside the inadequacies
of language to accommodate the complexities of racial and ethnic differences. Terms, such as "women of colour," developed in order to

facilitate coalitions among different groups of "non-white" women, can and do also function to lump all "non-white" women together in one category and thereby obscure important differences in history, experience and social location. Similarly, the label "visible minorities," also coined, but this time by government, to cover a wide range of "non-white" groups, highlights the degree to which skin colour is taken as synonymous with racial identity at the same time as the term mocks the "invisibility" to which members of "visible" minorities are consigned by mainstream institutions and culture.[63] And, applying as it does to whites who have come to Canada from middle-class Anglophone or Francophone backgrounds as well as to "non-whites" from poor, so-called "Third World" countries, the term "immigrant" can mask, as it did in a Canadian Advisory Council on the Status of Women report on Immigrant Women in Canada, "the racial and economic inequities which women who are not white or English speaking face."[64] In the mid-1980s, the specificity of the National Immigrant Women's Organization (NIWO), which developed earlier in the decade from a conference funded by the federal government, was further diluted by state intervention. In 1985, NIWO applied to the Secretary of State for funds for another conference at the same time that a just forming visible minority women's group also applied for funds for a founding national conference. In the end, the Secretary of State gave funds to NIWO on the condition that a certain proportion of the delegates would be visible minority women chosen from the group just getting under way. The ensuing conference, held in Winnipeg in 1986, gave rise to The National Organization of Immigrant and Visible Minority Women. The positive potential for overcoming divisions to form a unified front and the negative potential for obliterating real, lived differences offered by organizing under the new, combined rubric were heatedly debated at the conference. But delegates felt that the message they had received from the federal government left them with little choice: there will be funds for only one, not two groups, they were told; so join together in one organization, or else.[65]

In a 1990 conversation entitled "Sisters in the Movement," excerpted below, Ravida Din points to the limitations of identity politics and poignantly expresses the difficulty of trying to capture one's identity in language labels when one is a complex mix of races and cultures. "I've only recently been able to call myself Asian," she confesses to her friend.

> In the past, I never thought the word included me. I've been reading and seeing anthologies on Black women, Latin American women, Arab women, etc., and in each I find a part of myself. But, as a woman born in Nairobi, raised in a Muslim family, and having lived in Canada for over ten years,...[66]

It was at the "End of the United Nations Decade for Women" Conference held in Nairobi, Kenya, in the summer of 1985 that Ravida Din had, for the first time in her feminist life, the empowering experience of finding herself in a majority and being able to name the racism that she had felt for years in the company of white feminists.[67]

The Right to Speak for "Canadian" Women

In the debates over "voice," members of the privileged, white majority have often denounced as "censorship" — as a curtailment of "our" freedom of speech — requests that we refrain from speaking for and representing the racially oppressed, immigrants, the disabled, or the poor. Under the circumstances, it is ironic that after Sunera Thobani's uncontested nomination to the presidency of NAC in April 1993,[68] she was attacked as not having the right, as an immigrant woman of colour, to head the nation's largest women's organization. While these racist attacks were led by Tory MP John MacDougall, who stood up in the House of Commons and called Thobani an "illegal immigrant,"[69] white women were also to be found among those who challenged her election. One, writing to the *Toronto Star* and identifying herself as a "white and fifth-generation" Canadian, questioned Thobani's ability to represent the needs of "women whose forebears built this country."[70] Another, writing from New Glasgow, Nova Scotia, and identifying herself as "a feminist," accused Thobani of "creating divisiveness within the ranks" by speaking "of the doors that remain closed to women of color" and by challenging women "'who live [with]in the four walls of their relative privilege'."[71]

The Backlash Against Feminism and Anti-Racism

Thobani herself identified these attacks "as part of the backlash against feminists, particularly feminists of color who challenge white domination."[72] White feminism has not been innocent of this backlash against anti-racism. In 1989, Glenda Simms wrote that "attempts at discussing racism within the white women's movement have been *incoherent, condescending and patronizing*."[73] Feminists of colour, who have dared to challenge white feminists on their racism, have not infrequently been met with hurt, anger, denial and countercharges. This defensive reaction is fed, in part, by the two problematic components of white feminism discussed above: the victim mentality and the construction of white womanhood, particularly privileged, white womanhood, as a source in society of goodness and benevolence. But the defensiveness is also very much a result of the deep entrenchment in society of systems of power and privilege along axes of race, class, gender, sexuality, and mental and physical ability. Given their systemic natures, racism, classism, sexism, homophobia and discrimination against the disabled are not necessarily overt. As Carolann Wright points out, racism is "not just about burning crosses."[74]

A dramatic case in point involves one of Canada's icons of social commitment, June Callwood, co-founder of Nellie's, a Toronto hostel for abused women, and the founder of Jessie's Centre for Teenagers in Toronto and of Casey House, the Toronto AIDS hospice named after her son who was killed in a motorcycle accident in 1982, at age twenty. In 1989, after an event at Roy Thomson Hall when Toronto was hosting that year's International PEN Congress, Callwood, then incoming President of PEN Canada, walked up to two women passing out leaflets challenging the Canadian organization's racial composition and told them to "fuck off."[75] Then, at a Nellie's board meeting in December 1991, staff member Joan Johnson read out a painful statement complaining of the racism she and other women of colour felt needed to be addressed in the running of the hostel. According to published accounts, including the most sympathetic, Callwood reacted with anger, hurt, denial and countercharges, reminding Johnson that she herself had previously been a Nellie's client. Johnson responded: "'Do I have to be grateful all my life?'" In May 1992, June Callwood resigned from the board of directors of Nellie's.[76] Michele Landsberg's column in the *Toronto Star* pointed out that the clientele at Nellie's has changed over the years, with more than half now "immigrant, refugee and minority women." She pleaded with white feminists to draw a lesson from Nellie's and begin the painful process of "dismantling [our] hidden patterns of discrimination" and learning to share power, authority and ownership.[77] With the exception of Landsberg's column and an article co-authored by Carolann Wright, also in the *Toronto Star*, the women of colour who have been hurt and angered by the fracas at Nellie's have had little or no access to the mainstream media. "What a tragedy," Landsberg wrote, "if the media whip up a backlash which then short-circuits the necessary changes."

Many powerful voices in Canada's mainstream media, however, leapt to Callwood's defence, among them Pierre Berton and Peter Gzowski, and articles appeared in the mainstream media, some more than a year and a half after the events, bearing titles like "White Woman's Burden"[78] and presenting June Callwood as the "Battered Woman,"[79] or "the Mother Teresa of Ontario [who] has been victimized."[80] What the publishers of *The Womanist* have called "the June Callwood phenomenon" has all the markings of "the politics of gratitude" in white women/women of colour relations that stem from our shared historic legacy of colonialism, imperialism and racism.[81] Moreover, a white woman like Callwood, who has suffered her own personal tragedy, "can never be challenged without a hue and cry. Their good works," Carolann Wright argues, "are like an immunization against criticism or challenge on their racism."[82] Already in 1989 Glenda Simms wrote of the "Miss Ann" persona who resides in the psyches of both white women and women of colour: "She sits in the 'big house'. She is both mistress and victim. She embodies all our contradictions."[83] She is a construction that women on both sides of the colour line need to dislodge from our psyches.

Positive New Directions

"Feminism has fallen into the trap of using difference to divide," charged Maxine McKenzie in 1987.[84] And many would say in 1993 that not nearly enough has changed. The basic condition laid down by McKenzie — "Without a personal investment in acquiring as much knowledge of Women of Colour as Women of Colour have of white women, white feminists cannot address issues of concern to all women" — has still to be met. But one can point to positive developments. In an effort to make their annual "Take Back the Night" events accessible to Jewish women, Women Against Violence Against Women (WAVAW) in several On- tario cities moved their march from Friday to Thursday night in 1988, since Friday is the beginning of the Jewish Sabbath.[85] Another sign of positive change is the putting of the issue of racism on the agenda of International Women's Day (IWD) festivities across the country, as in Mayann Francis' address on racism in Nova Scotia, delivered at the IWD celebrations in Halifax on March 9, 1991.[86] Another is the decision of the Canadian Research Institute for the Advancement of Women (CRIAW) to devote its 16th annual conference, held in Toronto in November 1992, to the subject of "Making the Links: Anti-racism and Feminism." While some participants felt that there were problems with continuing racism on the CRIAW Board and on the part of some white participants at the conference,[87] others felt empowered by the coming together of

> an unprecedented number of anti-racist and feminist activists from across the country and around the world. For the first time, more than three quarters of the delegates at a national meeting of a mainstream women's organization were women of colour and Aboriginal women.[88]

And, finally, there is the growing responsiveness of Canada's largest feminist organization, NAC, to the interests and needs of the differently situated. Over the 20 years of its existence, NAC has become increas- ingly inclusive, representing now among its member organizations an impressive range of different perspectives. Under Judy Rebick's presi- dency, NAC made a decided effort to shift its balance of power in the direction of the traditional outsiders — immigrant women, visible mi- norities, aboriginal women. And the assumption of the NAC presidency by Sunera Thobani signals a further advance in NAC's commitment to the politics of inclusion. Vancouver-based feminist historian Frances Wasserlein hails Thobani's election as strengthening NAC's regional representation — she is the first woman from British Columbia to head the national women's organization. Dionne Brand hails Thobani's presidency as "'a watershed for women of colour...'" At the same time, Cenen Bagen, from the Committee for Domestic Workers and Caregivers, wants it clearly understood that Thobani earned the position from her years of service to feminism, as a NAC executive board member for the past two years and before that as a founding member of the South Asian Women's Action Network (SAWAN). "It wasn't as if white women handed it to her," Bagen stresses. Brand agrees. For her, Thobani's presidency "ultimately comes as a result of the work women of colour have done in the women's movement in Canada, in terms of race."[89]

But a challenge still faces white feminists privileged by race, class, sexual orientation and able-bodiedness to confront our prejudices with respect to difference and to end our colonizing practices *vis-à-vis* the different among us, in ways barbara findlay discusses.[90] As Thobani has stated:

> Today, feminism stands at a critical juncture. Either the women's movement will forge ahead under the leadership of the women most marginalized in society, and make its commitment to the politics of inclusion and diversity real.
>
> Or it will be contained within the status quo, as the women who have benefited from the struggles of the past help shut the doors on the majority of women who still continue to be excluded and silenced.[91]

NOTES

1. The title has been suggested by Iris Marion Young, *Justice and the Politics of Difference* (Princeton, NJ: Princeton University Press, 1990).
2. For one of the earliest statements of the distinction, see Ann Oakley, *Sex, Gender & Society* (New York, Hagerstown, San Francisco, London: Harper Colophon Books, 1972).
3. Dionne Brand, "Bread Out of Stone," in Libby Scheier, Sarah Sheard & Eleanor Wachtel, eds., *Language in Her Eye: Writing and Gender* (Toronto: Coach House Press, 1990), 46.
4. In the sense of the wrongs done to women, as in the 19th-century phrase "Women's Rights and Women's Wrongs." See Juliet Mitchell and Ann Oakley, eds., *The Rights and Wrongs of Women* (Harmondsworth, England: Penguin Books, 1976).
5. Maxine McKenzie, "You Mean, I Still Ain't?," *Breaking the Silence* 5, no. 3 (March 1987), 62, excerpted below.
6. White, second-wave feminists' use of the metaphor of colonization parallels in some respects white, first-wave feminists' use of the metaphor of slavery to convey the status of (white) women. See Vron Ware, *Beyond the Pale: White Women, Racism and History* (London, New York: Verso, 1992), 102-109.
7. Of many possible examples, perhaps the most influential was Kate Millett, *Sexual Politics* (Garden City, NY: Doubleday, 1970), 43, 55-57, 354, 356.
8. For a working definition of colonization, I have turned to Chandra Mohanty, according to whom, "However sophisticated or problematical its use as an explanatory construct, colonization almost invariably implies a relation of structural domination, and a suppression — often violent — of the heterogeneity of the subject(s) in question." Chandra Talpade Mohanty, "Under Western Eyes: Feminist Scholarship and Colonial Discourses," in Chandra Talpade Mohanty, Ann Russo and Lourdes Torres, eds., *Third World Women*

and the Politics of Feminism (Bloomington and Indianapolis: Indiana University Press, 1991), 52.

9. McKenzie, "You Mean, I Still Ain't?," 8, excerpted below.

10. Elizabeth V. Spelman, *Inessential Woman: Problems of Exclusion in Feminist Thought* (Boston: Beacon Press, 1988), 11.

11. Spelman, *Inessential Woman*, 52-53.

12. See the section on "Race and the Limits of Sisterhood," in "We Appear Silent to People Who Are Deaf to What We Say," *Women of Colour,* special issue of *Fireweed: A Feminist Quarterly,* Issue 16 (Spring 1983), excerpted below.

13. Think, for example, of the cover-up of the brutal rape and murder of Native woman Helen Betty Osborne in The Pas, Manitoba, in 1971. Suzette Couture (writer), Gail Carr (producer), and Francis Mankiewicz (director), *Conspiracy of Silence,* CBC television docu-drama, 1-2 December 1991.

14. See, for example, the discussion of rape in Himani Bannerji, Dionne Brand, Prabha Kosla, and Makeda Silvera, "We Appear Silent to People Who Are Deaf to What We Say," *Women of Colour,* special issue of *Fireweed: A Feminist Quarterly,* Issue 16 (Spring 1983), excerpted below.

15. Makeda Silvera, *Silenced* (Toronto: Williams Wallace Publishers Inc., 1983), 61-70, excerpted below. A second edition of this book has been published, with a new Introduction by the author. Makeda Silvera, *Silenced* (Toronto: Sister Vision/Black Women and Women of Colour Press, 1989).

16. "Women's Liberation AND Lesbians," *The Other Woman* 1, no. 1 (May-June 1972), excerpted below.

17. "In closing I would like to discredit the 'lesbianism is not political' theory with the fact that I am at present unable to sign my own name to this article because of very real legal implications. Is that not political?" "LESBIAN RAP," *Saskatoon Women's Liberation Newsletter,* July 1973, p. 6, excerpted below.

18. "LESBIAN RAP," *Saskatoon Women's Liberation Newsletter,* July 1973, pp. 5-6, excerpted below.

19. Jane Taylor, "On Being Older and Wiser," *Breaking the Silence* 4, nos. 3/4 (June 1986), 8-9, excerpted below.

20. See, for example, Ella Haley and Ann Hauprich, "Elderly and Able?," *Healthsharing* 9, no. 1 (December 1987), 24-28. See also Ellen M. Gee and Meredith Kimball, *Women and Aging* (Toronto and Vancouver: Butterworths, 1987).

21. Minutes of NAC Executive Committee, 14 June 1980, 2, 3; NAC Memo (December 1980), 9; letter from Lynn McDonald, Past President, to Jean Wood, President, 3 July 1981; Lynn McDonald, "The Charter of Rights and the Subjection of Women," *Canadian Forum,* (June/July 1981), 17-18. Copies in NAC files. See also Lynn McDonald, "The Supreme Court of Canada and the Equality Guarantee in the Charter," *Socialist Studies,* no. 2 (1984), 45-65.

22. This was achieved by taking a position in opposition to the Accord that accommodated both women who wanted a stronger federal system and Québécoises who wanted a stronger Quebec. Conversation with Lynn McDonald, 2 July 1993.

23. The remaining five were: "2. prevention of violence against disabled women; 3. affirmative action; 4. assertiveness, awareness and self-image; 5. sexuality rights; 6. parenting and child care." Joanne Doucette, "The DisAbled Women's Network: A Fragile Success," in Jeri Dawn Wine and Janice L. Ristock, eds., *Women and Social Change: Feminist Activism in Canada* (Toronto: James Lorimer & Company, Publishers, 1991), 225.

24. Doucette, "The DisAbled Women's Network," 221, 223, 231.

25. "Women with disabilities have been considered sexless in the past (disabled but not a woman) and therefore they have been excluded from the women's movement and mainstream women's services." DAWN Toronto, "Fact Sheet on Accessibility to the Women's Movement and Women's Services" (Toronto: DAWN Toronto, with the financial assistance of Secretary of State, 1986).

26. Both the Canadian Research Institute for the Advancement of Women as well as the National Action Committee on the Status of Women made available their organizational newsletters and mailing lists for wide distribution of the DisAbled Women's Network open letter to the women's movement, excerpted below.

27. Bonnie Sherr Klein, "'We Are Who You Are': Feminism and Disability," *Ms.* 3, no. 3 (November/December 1992), 72, excerpted below.

28. Ibid., 74.

29. Frances D. Gage, "Reminiscences of Sojourner Truth," Document 7 (I: 115-17): Akron Convention, Akron, Ohio, May 28-29, 1851, in Mari Jo and Paul Buhle, eds., *The Concise History of Woman Suffrage: Selections from the Classic Work of Stanton,*

Anthony, Gage, and Harper (Urbana/Chicago/London: University of Illinois Press, 1978), 103-105.

30. McKenzie, "You Mean, I Still Ain't?," excerpted below.

31. See Lydia Sargent, ed., *Women and Revolution: A Discussion of the Unhappy Marriage of Marxism and Feminism* (Boston: South End Press, 1981).

32. See the Chapter on "Economic Issues" in Volume Two.

33. Ellen Tolmie, "Fleck: Profile of a Strike," *This Magazine* 12, no. 4 (October 1978), 22-29.

34. Eunice Lavell, "Women study class: Gleanings of a white poor woman," *The Womanist* 3, no. 1 (Spring 1992), 38-39, excerpted below.

35. "We Appear Silent to People Who Are Deaf to What We Say," *Women of Colour,* special issue of *Fireweed: A Feminist Quarterly,* Issue 16 (Spring 1983), excerpted below.

36. Shirley Bear with the Tobique Women's Group, "'You Can't Change the Indian Act?,'" in Wine and Ristock, eds., *Women and Social Change,* 1991.

37. Alison Prentice, Paula Bourne, Gail Cuthbert Brandt, Beth Light, Wendy Mitchinson, Naomi Black, *Canadian Women: A History* (Toronto: Harcourt Brace Jovanovich, 1988), 397.

38. Bear, "'You Can't Change the Indian Act?,'" 205.

39. See *Enough is Enough: Aboriginal Women Speak Out,* as told to Janet Silman (Toronto: Women's Press, 1987).

40. Bear, "'You Can't Change the Indian Act?,'" 215. See below, "Super Personal News: Reinstatement as Status and Band Member."

41. Telephone conversation with Madeleine Parent, 1 September 1993.

42. See text of letter suggested by Mary Two-Axe Early, November 1977, reprinted below.

43. See below.

44. Bear, "'You Can't Change the Indian Act?,'" 214. See the pamphlet of the Native Women's Committee of NAC, prepared for distribution in New Brunswick in the early 1980s by Caroline Ennis of Fredericton and Shirley Bear of Big Cove, reprinted below.

45. The suicide rate for native people in Labrador is five times higher than the national rate among Canadians and twice as high as that of other native people in Canada. Most often the victims are between the ages of fifteen and twenty-four. Marie Wadden, *Nitassinan: The Innu Struggle to Reclaim Their Homeland* (Vancouver/Toronto: Douglas & McIntyre, 1991), 79.

46. "As an Aboriginal woman I've been banging on the door to feminism for years but I'm never let in. I'm not welcomed in the feminist movement. I don't feel I or my beliefs as an aboriginal woman are respected by the feminist movement." Quoted by Mary Rose Cowan in "When Will Justice Be Done?," *Herizons* 7, no. 2 (Summer 1993), 22.

47. Fawzia Ahmad, "...a sense of oneness," *Kinesis* (December 1992/January 1993), 16.

48. In Dianne Hallman's review of the feminist scholarly journals *Atlantis, RFR/DRF* and *Canadian Woman Studies* from their inception to 1990, she found almost nothing written on Native self-government, Native land claims, the effects of northern development and lack of environmental protection on aboriginal peoples, or Native control of education.

49. For instance, Glenda Simms wrote in 1989: "The problem with this issue [racism] lies...in [white women's] inability to move their analysis from the exclusive focus on gender as the base for the construction of feminist theory." Glenda Simms, "Racism and Sexism," *The Womanist* 1, no. 3 (February/March 1989), 21.

50. See, for example, Verona Reid, "My Experiences as a Black Woman in Canada," *The Womanist* 1, no. 1 (September 1988), 12-13. See also Brendalyn Ambrose, "The day I tasted Police Justice," *The Womanist* 1, no. 3 (February/March 1989), 9, excerpted below.

51. See Lynn McGuigan, "Creating a voice for Black women," *The Womanist* 1, no. 3 (February/March 1989), 35.

52. Linda Carvery, "Congress has ambitious goals for Black women," *Pandora* 4, no. 1 (September 1988), 27.

53. Susan Campbell, "Delegates urged to raise voices against race, sex discrimination: Chinese Canadian women hold first national conference," *Globe and Mail,* 23 March 1992, A5.

54. See, for example, Ngaire Genge (with a lot of help), "Who is telling my story?," *The Womanist* 3, no. 1 (Spring 1992), 18.

55. For how this question relates to the writing of Canadian women's history, see Ruth Roach Pierson, "Experience, Difference, Dominance and Voice in the Writing of Canadian Women's History," in Karen Offen, Ruth Roach Pierson, and Jane Rendall, eds., *Writing Women's History: International Perspectives* (London: Macmillan; Bloomington and Urbana: Indiana University Press, 1991), 79-106.

56. (Vancouver: Press Gang Publishers, 1981).

57. Christine St. Peter, "'Woman's Truth' and the Native Tradition: Anne Cameron's *Daughters of Copper Woman*," *Feminist Studies* 15, no. 3 (Fall 1989), 499-523.

58. Anne Cameron, "The Operative Principle Is Trust," in Libby Scheier, Sarah Sheard and Eleanor Wachtel, eds., *Language In Her Eye: Views on Writing and Gender by Canadian Women Writing in English* (Toronto: Coach House Press, 1990), 69.

59. Long-distance telephone conversation between Ruth Roach Pierson and Marie Wadden, 22 March 1992.

60. Stephen Godfrey, "Canada Council asks whose voice is it anyway?," *Globe and Mail*, 21 March 1992, C1-C2.

61. Letter by Marie Wadden to the editors of *The Globe and Mail*, March 1992, reprinted below. *The Globe and Mail* chose not to publish Wadden's letter. Instead *The Globe and Mail* did publish an "op ed" by the Toronto writer and journalist Erna Paris that ridiculed the Canada Council position on "cultural appropriation." Erna Paris, "A letter to the thought police," *Globe and Mail*, 31 March 1992, A16.

62. Virginia Woolf, *A Room of One's Own* (London: The Hogarth Press, 1929).

63. Glenda P. Simms, "What is a 'Visible Minority?,'" *The Womanist* 2, no. 1 (Fall 1989), 39.

64. "New Wave of Progaganda — Immigrant Women Get The Shaft," *Our Lives* 2, no. 4 (Spring 1988), 3.

65. Conversation with a former employee of the Department of Secretary of State, Vancouver, B.C., April, 1992. See also Linda Carty and Dionne Brand, "'Visible Minority' Women — A Creation of the Canadian State," *RFR/DRF* 17, no. 3 (December 1988), 39-42.

66. "Sisters in the Movement," in *Asian Canadian Women: Awakening Thunder*, special issue of *Fireweed: A Feminist Quarterly*, Issue 30 (1990), 36, excerpted below.

67. "Arriving in Nairobi... WOW! Not only was it my birthplace but here were 13,000 women and two-thirds were women of colour. Nairobi was a coming home for me in more ways than one. Many white women have said feminism or the women's movement is 'coming home.' I was amongst women who thought and felt just like I did. There were finally names for all those feelings of being 'other,' of being 'separate' and most of those feelings had to do with acknowledging the fact that racism existed in the women's movement." Ibid., 37.

68. Geoffrey York, "Rebick's departure from NAC marks shift in balance of power," *Globe and Mail*, 21 April 1993, A1.

69. At the time of this attack, landed-immigrant status for Thobani has been approved pending medical clearance. Deborah Wilson, "Heir to NAC stung by attack," *Globe and Mail*, 10 May 1993, A1.

70. Letter to the Editor by Michele Moffett, Willowdale, Ontario, *Toronto Star*, 11 June 1993, A26.

71. Letter to the Editor by Cheryl Campbell, New Glasgow, N.S., *Toronto Star*, 11 June 1993, A26.

72. Sunera Thobani, "Feminism's new colors," *The Vancouver Sun*, 26 May 1993, excerpted below. Also appeared as "Making a commitment to inclusion," in *The Ottawa Citizen*, 3 June 1993, A13, and as "Why I am a feminist" in *The Toronto Star*, 3 June 1993, A21.

73. Glenda Simms, "Racism and Sexism," *The Womanist* 1, no. 3 (February/March 1989), 21.

74. Carolann Wright, "It's not just about burning crosses," *The Womanist* 4, no. 1 (Spring 1993), 21, excerpted below.

75. The two women were M. Nourbese Philip and Sheelagh Conway. See M. Nourbese Philip, "Disturbing the Peace" and "Letter: September, 1990 — Am I a Nigger? Incident at Congress," in M. Nourbese Philip, *Frontiers: Selected Essays and Writings on Racism and Culture 1984-1992* (Stratford, Ontario: The Mercury Press, 1992), 134-154. *See also* Michele Landsberg, "Callwood furor masks real racism struggle at Nellie's," *Toronto Star*, 18 July 1992, K1, K7.

76. Adele Freedman, "White Woman's Burden," *Saturday Night* 108, no. 3 (April 1993), 40-44, 74-84; Elaine Dewar, "Wrongful Dismissal," *Toronto Life* (March 1993), 32-45; Catherine Douglas, "Checking In: June Callwood talks about her feelings, her faults, and the failing of feminist groups struggling with issues of racism," *Quota Magazine: Toronto's Free Lesbian Monthly* (April 1993), 6.

77. Landsberg, "Callwood furor masks real racism struggle at Nellie's."

78. Title of Adele Freedman article in *Saturday Night* (April 1993).

79. Under a photo of June Callwood on the cover of the March 1993 *Toronto Life* carrying the article by Elaine Dewar.

80. Nazneen Sadiq, "A beige person sees red over Callwood," op-ed, *Globe and Mail*, 3 June 1992, A18.

81. Joan Riggs, ed., "The June Callwood phenomenon," *The Womanist* 4, no. 1 (Spring 1993), 20, reprinted below.

82. Wright, "It's not just about burning crosses."

83. Glenda Simms, "Racism and Sexism," *The Womanist* 1, no. 3 (February/March 1989), 21.

84. McKenzie, "You Mean, I Still Ain't?," 62.

85. Ravida Din, "Take Back the Night," *The Womanist* (December 1988/January 1989), 5.

86. "Racism alive and well in Nova Scotia," *Pandora* 6, no. 3 (June 1991), 3, excerpted below.

87. Cassandra Fernandes and Fatima Jaffer, "So, what did you think?," *Kinesis* (December 1992/January 1993), 15.

88. Fatima Jaffer, "Making the links: Anti-racism and feminism," *Kinesis* (December 1992/January 1993), 13.

89. Anjula Gogia, "NAC gets new head," *Kinesis* (May 1993), 3.

90. barbara findlay, "Racism: Learning to change," *The Womanist* 3, no. 1 (Spring 1992), 20, excerpted below. For an expanded version, see barbara findlay, *With All of Who We Are: A Discussion of Oppression and Dominance* (Vancouver: Lazara Press, 1991). For a discussion of the distinction between the terms "different" and "other," see Rhea Tregebov, "Some Notes on the Story of Esther," in Libby Scheier, Sarah Sheard and Eleanor Wachtel, eds., *Language in Her Eye: Writing and Gender*, 269.

91. Thobani, "Making a commitment to inclusion," excerpted below.

Documents: Chapter 3

Lesbian Women

"Women's Liberation AND Lesbians "
Toronto, May – June 1972[1]

I am writing out of my experience as a gay woman in a left oriented women's liberation group in Toronto. There is no independent gay women's movement here, and I think the existence of one would help overcome some of the problems of integrating lesbianism into the women's movement. When I came into the group, some women had come out within the movement, and many women liked to say that gay women were integrated into it. A lesbian collective existed in name only, and women's liberation continued to skirt the gay issue.

One of the first things I worked on was a series of educationals on sexuality, where I had hoped we could break down into small groups and discuss people's feelings around sex, both gay and straight. This never happened, probably because people were afraid to get to that level, and when lesbianism went unmentioned, gay women felt they had to push within the large mixed groups [for] the gay thing [to] be dealt with and a place made for it by everyone.

One of the first things we were told is that making the gay-straight distinction was being divisive, cutting ourselves off from other women, "alienating the new women." On a personal level, some women often say sexual distinctions are irrelevant to them, "people are just people." I am dubious of people who say this on any occasion, for I feel that sexuality is a basic part of our lives, and our relationships in a sexist society are mainly defined in sexual or sexually-related power terms. But I am particularly dubious of women who say this in women's liberation meetings discussing sexuality. Why would there be a need for a women's liberation movement at all if it were so easy to transcend the sexism conditioned in all of us and to relate to "people as people." I feel that women who say this are telling me that my sexuality is irrelevant to straight women or is somehow not a factor in the meeting situation. Telling women who are gay that the distinction between them and heterosexual women is artificial or unimportant is the same as the male left telling us that the distinction between male and female is unimportant within some broader politics.

---

1. *The Other Woman* 1, no. 1 (May-June 1972), 1-3. Copy at Canadian Women's Movement Archives (hereafter CWMA).

Some women said they couldn't talk about lesbianism because they weren't gay, and were content to have sexuality discussed only from the male-female viewpoint. It is not only gay women's responsibility to make space for discussion of gay sexuality, something that we have been coerced all our lives into hiding as dirty and evil. I resent being put in the position of being a token lesbian, a strange species who must always be defining to other women why I am gay, while no heterosexual women are put in the position of having to define why they are straight.

Many women, when forced to discuss lesbianism, skirt the issue by talking about holding hands with women in public, how women in Europe hold hands while in North America we don't, etc. Though these kinds of discussions are well and good, they are not really about sexuality or sexual feelings. Discussions of sex between men and women are never done in these terms.

I realize many of these attitudes come from fear and ignorance about gay women that is socially conditioned, and when I was adolescent I knew many of the same fears and disgust and fascinations with lesbianism. I did not feel oppressed by women who honestly expressed these feelings, women who said they did not know anything about lesbianism and wanted to know, a woman who said she was afraid of having to deal with sexuality among women because they had always been a refuge for her from the exploitation she had experienced with men. I feel that we have a lot to share with each other on this level, but on the level sexuality is usually discussed, we seem to be in a familiar circle of oppression ...

... the lack of support for gay liberation and the lack of identification with gay oppression, even among women who are gay themselves, in women's liberation. While everyone is always crying out that we must relate to the perennially absent working class women and Third World women, lesbians are the scum of the earth. Many women have too much Marxist analysis to come to an exclusively gay meeting, a gay bar or party. Safe within the middle-class subculture of women's liberation, they feel superior to the self-destructive trips many gay women went through coming out before there was any support for being gay, to the underground that gay people were forced into in order to survive, to the role playing and the dating language, and all the messy products of sexual oppression ...

"Lesbian Rap"
Saskatoon, 1973[2]

There was a need in the Saskatoon movement to communicate with each other about lesbianism. The rap was held on May 22, 1973. The following articles are responses to that rap ...

I was invited to attend a rap on lesbianism. How did I feel? Nervous? Yes, a little. Afraid? A little of that, too. People and situations in life

2. *Saskatoon Women's Liberation Newsletter* (July 1973), 5-6. Copy at CWMA.

that I don't understand are always frightening to some degree. Excited? Yes, definitely! What a chance it offered to air some of the whispered and joked-about taboos and, maybe, learn some truths at last. Would I find that I was a latent lesbian? Well, that was a chance I'd have to take.

The rap "happened." Result: I discovered that lesbians are, after all, people with the same range of feelings that all humans experience. Like any human in our imperfect society, they want to be accepted and respected, but, as is common when one's life style varies from the norm, they find such consideration badly lacking.

I was grateful for that rap. I know, now, that never again will I be able to be silent when I hear slurs against lesbians. I must defend their rights as well as my own.

No, I don't think I'm a latent lesbian but I'm not afraid anymore, either ...

My reason for attending the political rap was to help bring the issue of lesbianism out into the open, and to discuss the fears that people have towards lesbianism. In so doing it was hoped that the rift that has been occurring between lesbians and straight women in other centres might be avoided.

The problems seem to occur firstly, because lesbianism is not seen as a political issue, merely a personal problem, and secondly, because women in the movement do not seem willing to deal with their own lesbianism.

On the first question the women at the political rap, for the most part, seemed sympathetic but I felt a strong reluctance to discuss 'personal' issues, and communication in the group was difficult and painful. I also felt that the issue of lesbianism was side-stepped by getting into arguments like "who is more oppressed" instead of talking about how lesbians, in particular, are oppressed by straight women in the movement.

Secondly, the women's movement in Saskatoon is in the position of having a small number of lesbian feminists and ideally would not be threatened by such a small number. This only seems to be true when these lesbian feminists act like proper feminists and do not become preoccupied with the lesbian issue. When this occurs, lesbians are accused of 'laying trips', of pushing a 'correct political stance' on people. Thus, the problem of being a token lesbian, for whether or not you believe a certain line or agree with everything every lesbian and lesbian feminist has ever said — you are held responsible.

My feelings about this particular political rap, then, is one of frustration. I don't see the point of having lesbianism accepted in the women's movement only to have it tucked away in some appropriately labelled administrative box. If it is necessary, then, to recognize our differences, it should be done with the same understanding and appreciation as the recognition of our similarities ...

Several things happened at this rap that have become typical of lesbian-straight discussions. To avoid talking about lesbianism specifically, straight women introduce celibacy, masturbation, heterosexuality, monogamy, etc. These are all important topics for discussion — at another time. The rap was [not] set up to discuss that, let alone all the other subjects. There is a tendency to discuss individuals rather than the lesbian lifestyle. Because of the unusual situation in which B. and myself were the only two public lesbians — the movement's token "gay women" — there was a tendency to analyze our relationship and lesbianism per se. We were seen to represent *all* lesbians, whether singles or couples. I do not set one straight women's relationship with her man up as representative of *all* straight relationships. I feel that this was very unfair and "unsisterly." In short, the whole rap was extremely painful for me.

Power politics are in force in the movement here and elsewhere. Here, there are only a few lesbian-feminists, so the "problem" can be largely ignored. Elsewhere, lesbian-feminists are in the majority and the tables have (understandably) been turned. Straight women are leaving the movement due to *their* inability to deal with the lesbian women.

One of the most common attacks against lesbians is the personal-political thing. Being lesbian is not supposedly political — not a valid issue to organize around. I find it interesting that it is politically sound to organize around abortion, day care, women's studies, women's unions, etc., but not lesbianism. Who says there is no value system in the movement?

Several women asked important questions which did not receive answers and many more women were unable to ask theirs. I recognize that much smaller groups are a more fruitful way of discussing other than business matters and hope that this will occur in the future. I want to express appreciation to the one woman who did seek me out to learn more.

In closing I would like to discredit the "lesbianism is not political" theory with the fact that I am at present unable to sign my own name to this article because of very real legal implications. Is that not political?...

I came away with the distinct feeling that not only Lesbian women in the movement, but most other women, feel that they do not conform to the traditional Women's Liberation image. The problem of stereotypes applies to us all. It made me realize the importance of de-mystifying the "liberated women" so that we can all feel we have a right to be in the movement. The image of the "men-are-bastards-bra-burning-toughies" was never a reality, yet women in the movement are consistently being labelled with it so that women outside the movement have difficulty seeing beyond that.

The most important realization I had at the meeting was that other women don't join the movement because of this, although they are sympathetic to its aims because they feel they won't fit in. Here's one woman in a monogamous, wedding-ringed relationship with a man who almost dropped out of the movement because I felt I didn't fit in; who has dropped back into it feeling that I have as much right as any other woman to be there. I vote we forget our individual labels of polygamous, monogamous, lesbian, celibate, etc. and get on with supporting each other as *women*.

Lesbian Harassment
Vancouver, 1979[3]

This is a story of increasing police interference and brutality. This is a story that concerns all lesbians, all feminists and all BCFW [British Columbia Federation of Women] members.

At the last Rights of Lesbians Subcommittee meeting, it was brought to our attention that a Vancouver store, the California Gift company, had a sexist window display:

— a woman sitting on a toilet, her knees elevated, toilet paper tucked in her bodice, a book strategically placed at the base of the toilet was entitled: "How To Play With Your Pussy."

— next to this was a mannequin of a young boy wearing small briefs. A sign (key-ring) hanging from his finger read: "Under 21."

On behalf of the Rights of Lesbians Subcommittee, I wrote a letter protesting this offensive display.

We had anticipated one of two things:

— The California Gift Co. owners would immediately recognize the error of their ways, being gay brothers and all, and change the display while apologizing profusely.

— They would disagree with us and do nothing.

We were unprepared for what *did* happen.

The following day, a local TV station called me, *at work* (interesting how quickly that connection was made) to ask for my comment on a "series of actions against the California Gift Co." Apparently, during the past three nights, the store's window had been stickered and spray-painted. No group had claimed responsibility for the actions.

I responded with a general rap on sexist advertising and the objectification of women and said that although I did not know who had stickered and painted, the Rights of Lesbians Subcommittee could certainly understand *why* women would be that angry.

The same day, I was visited, at home, by the Vancouver City Police. The purpose of the visit was to investigate a complaint of destruction of property by the California Gift Co. Listening with shock and amazement, I pointed out that while the Rights of Lesbians Subcommittee would assume full responsibility for our letter, we were in no way connected with the actions. The police replied saying that he knew that those "This Exploits and Degrades Women" stickers were BCFW stickers (not true),

---

3. Yvette Perreault for the B.C. Federation of Women-Lesbian Rights Subcommittee, Vancouver, BC (1979), 1-4. Copy at CWMA.

and that these types of actions were typical BCFW ones (also not true).
He wanted information on:
— who had defaced this private property?
— what were we planning to do next? (After all, this had to be
  nipped in the bud before windows were smashed!)
— And, if I wouldn't tell him anything, would I give the women
  connected with this, the message to stop: "Better that you tell
  these women to stop before this gets worse and we have to kick
  down a few doors and bash in a few heads."
The visit ended. I thought they only talked like that in the movies.

My reactions varied from anger to fright (I know that other women
have experienced far worse) to the realization that I was/am not anonymous anymore. This means that you too, sisters, are not anonymous
anymore.

As a feminist, I have written dozens of "appalled and disgusted"
letters. This is the first time I have done so on behalf of a *Lesbian*
Feminist organization. The reasons for and implications of the police
harassment at this time because of this letter are clear:

Lesbianism is an easily identifiable symbol of *Rebellion*.

The authorities understand the threat of women taking power over
our lives and they connect, in fact they *equate Lesbian* with *Feminist*
with *Radical*. They may not always be right, but police don't have to be
right to threaten and harass you!

I'm hoping this reinforces what you already know in your guts. There
is a war on: this is a backlash/swing to the right. As lesbians, as feminists
and as women, we have good reason to fear and to be angry and to
struggle even harder. Many of us have been lulled into a false sense of
security. Being a lesbian in the women's community in Vancouver is
relatively safe. It's easy and seductive to assume that because it's okay
here, it's getting better, or at least safer, for everyone, everywhere. So,
why not relax a bit, lower our defenses, quit talking about it so much
... lose that keen, raw sense of awareness (some call it paranoia), and
that's alright ... IF WE NEVER INTEND TO WIN.

"Lesbian Witch Hunt"
Charlottetown, August 1985[4]

... In August 1985, the Charlottetown Rape Crisis Centre organized a
conference for the Atlantic provinces' rape crisis centres, transition
houses and women's centres. The objective of the conference was to
share information and develop skills. At the opening of the conference,
women were asked to speak about how and why we work in the women's
movement. It was made clear that the discussion was confidential and
many of us spoke candidly about our lives. Some of us spoke of our

---

4. Tamarac, *Breaking the Silence* 5, no. 1 (September 1986), 18-19. Copy at CWMA.

lives as lesbians. Many of us spoke of our experiences as survivors of incest, rape and other forms of brutality by men.

One woman, who did contract work for Pictou County Women's Centre, left the conference early, stating that it was not what she had expected. Breaking confidentiality, she went to local church organizations and, with the support of a local minister, launched an attack on the Pictou County Women's Centre and all other centres which hire lesbians and receive government funding. The information from the conference was twisted and distorted and the discussion of our lives was summarized as negative, man-hating sentiment.

Lesbians and radical feminists bore the brunt of this attack. As is often the case at women's centres, there are lesbians working at the Pictou County Women's Centre. Their credibility as workers, the Centre's ability to serve the women's community and their funding was called into question. The reputation of other women's groups attending the conference came under attack, as they were viewed as being pro-lesbian. As an invited speaker, I was publicly identified as a lesbian. Articles I had written on incest from a radical feminist perspective were taken to my employer as evidence to fire me.

The witch hunt was quickly taken up by REAL Women, who published inaccurate information about the conference in its newsletter entitled *Reality*. It stated that lesbian organizations are the primary recipients of government money and cannot be tolerated. It called for a letter-writing campaign demanding that the Secretary of State investigate all groups receiving money and stop funding organizations that support and/or hire lesbians.

REAL Women is concerned with the preservation of "the family." It is against abortion and no-fault divorce. It does not support equal pay for work of equal value, affirmative action and Section 28 of the Charter of Rights which guarantees equality. It is against daycare, sex education in the schools and lesbianism ...

As lesbians, we are alarmed that any degree of intolerance to our lifestyle be accepted. We have only to look to recent history to know that prejudice can escalate to genocide. The REAL Women intolerance of different lifestyles, their demands upon the government to impose economic sanctions and their circulation of hate literature parallel a frightening history ...

Older Women

"On Being Older and Wiser"
Ottawa, 1986[5]

Back in '79, fully aware of the negative image our society has of older women, three women decided that a space or group was needed where older women could begin to counteract that message and define themselves from their own experience. So the "Positive Ageing Group" began.

For the first few years we met on the first Monday evening of every month at a restaurant just to enjoy being with other older like-minded women. We tried many places and finally settled on a Chinese restaurant, because it was the only one that had round tables — a non-hierarchical seating arrangement. There were only a few of us at first, usually four or five. But after a while word got around and we began to grow. As our numbers increased we began to experience difficulty when everyone wanted to talk and to hear. We experimented with various forms of structure, hoping to contain our vibrant enthusiasm within a manageable form, but none of them lasted very long.

In the end the Crones had to clone. By this time we were calling ourselves The Crones — with thanks for Mary Daly for her positive redefinition of the word. When we could no longer squeeze another woman around the biggest table in the restaurant, we split into two or three smaller groups. The option was left open for anyone to attend the once-a-month restaurant dinners, which continue to this day.

Who are we then, we Crones? "Feisty, feminist women over fifty." A slightly facetious description, but it holds a kernel of truth. In our gab-group, we have settled down to a minimum of three and a maximum of eight members. Most of us are battle-scarred veterans of the institution of marriage. Some of us are divorced, one of us has never married and some are still married. But all of us recognize the oppression of women and the desperate need to do something about it. We were all young girls in the thirties and forties, one of those recurring periods in history when awareness of feminism was at a very low ebb.

When we were teen-agers, soldiers of war were held up to us as heroes. The war ended, and we were led to believe that if we married a hero, raised a large family and did everything a proper wife was supposed to do, we would live happily ever after. We were all taught that proper ladies were nice. Oh, how we struggle with niceness! Now we have learnt to be quite nasty when necessary, especially when women are maligned, ignored or attacked.

At the beginning of our lives feminists were not audible. In mid-life we experienced an exhilarating explosion: the resurgence of a new, clear

5. Jane Taylor, *Breaking the Silence,* nos. 3/4 (Spring/Summer 1986), 8-9.

feminist voice. We have experienced life before and since feminism. The group gives us space to struggle; to struggle without criticism because we all acknowledge the common pressures we were subjected to as young women. We understand only too well the wear and tear on the psyche that comes from scrutinizing our lives, past and present, in the light of a feminist perspective.

Our support group offers safe space — a space to be ourselves, where we can talk and be heard. A space where we can be as we truly are — mature, wise, funny, loving and courageous women. Which doesn't mean that at times we are not outrageous, stubborn, noisy and even impossible ...

We have done many things together. We have spent a weekend in the country where one of us was introduced to skinny-dipping. We have protested outside the courtroom on Nicholas Street [Ottawa], demonstrating our outrage at a legal system that condones, covertly and overtly, violence against women.

We have marched in International Women's Day parades. At last year's march we were asked to lead the parade and carry the banners ...

Most of all though, we talk, And talk and talk and talk. We talk about all those things not considered suitable subjects for polite conversation. We talk a lot about death and dying. How we would wish to die, when we would wish to die, the abysmal situation of those who are now dying, what we can or would do to change things so that control of our last moments is returned to us.

As women our position in society is minimal at best; as older women we are well-nigh invisible. So we spend some of our time affirming ourselves as we are ...

Differently Abled Women

An Open Letter from the DisAbled Women's Network, DAWN Toronto, to the Women's Movement
Toronto, 1986[6]

Who would think of putting out a flyer saying:

Important feminist event featuring Ms. Daring Daisy, well known author Nov. 30, 8:00 PM, Everywoman's Hall. Admission *Free* Childcare. *Disabled women need not apply.*

Of course not!

Yet often, even usually, that's what the publicity for feminist events says to disabled women ... and you, the group responsible, may not know it, want it, or expect it. Your intentions may be, probably are (we hope) good. But we all know what road is paved with good intentions.

6. DisAbled Women's Network (DAWN), Toronto, 1986. CWMA file: DAWN.

Your problem is usually that you just plain don't know what accessibility is. Our problem is that we can't get in to even tell you.

Accessible means different things to different people. *What follows is the bare minimum for accessibility for most disabled women. And remember disabled women are 18 per cent of all women.*

For a woman who uses a wheelchair, accessibility means no steps (a good ramp and/or level entrance), an adapted washroom (with grab bars, a sink that her chair will fit under, room to get the chair in the cubicle and make a transfer sideways from the chair onto the toilet), and a place to sit, preferably with her friends.

For deaf and hearing impaired women, access means sign language interpreters. It means an office with a Telecommunications Device for the Deaf (TDD) or a meeting with a loop amplification device ...

For blind and visually impaired women, accessibility means having printed matter (books, brochures, agendas, etc.) on cassette tape, in large print, or, sometimes in Braille. It means that her Seeing Eye Dog is welcome and that you don't pet or feed that dog (it's working) without the owner's express permission. It means you offer to guide a blind woman to her seat. *You don't grab her by the arm and drag her there.* That's not help; it's assault.

For developmentally disabled women, your attitude and language are the key to accessibility. When was the last time you jokingly referred to someone as "an idiot, imbecile, space cadet"? While we're on the subject, how do you think severely mobility impaired women feel about "basket case"? Or deaf women about "dumb"? Or psychiatric survivors about feminists who call other women "crazy, nuts, looney tooners, or really out of it"? Another cliche to watch is, "Confined to a wheelchair". You don't usually think of yourself as confined to your car even though you are incapable of travelling 50 miles an hour unaided. Of course not, you drive your car. And we *use* our wheelchairs (and crutches, canes, walkers, etc.).

For most invisibly disabled women, those whose disability you can't see, access is often a matter of attitude and flexibility. For a woman with epilepsy, it means no strobe lights or flash bulbs. For a woman with diabetes, it means nutrition breaks. We thought non-disabled women liked to eat too, but we have been to all day feminist events where no lunch break was planned. (Is this the planning of a workaholic?)

For women with environmental illnesses, access means *Smoke Free* meetings and events. Yes, Virginia, smoking is an equality issue. If Mary dropped out of your planning committee, it may mean that Mary had an asthma attack after that last meeting from your cigarette. Nice.

For some women accessibility means an attendant to help her with her basic needs. You will need to supply trained attendants or she may want to bring her own attendant. If she does, the attendant should be admitted to the event free of charge ...

Even when events are accessible, you may not see disabled women out. This is often because of [inadequate public] transportation ...

So disabled women may need a ride. Someone, somewhere, somewhen, please. PLEASE give DAWN our own wheelchair van. If there's a goddess out there ...

Last, but never least, accessibility means publicity. Organizers in the women's movement rarely seem to think of publicizing events in the newspapers or on the phone lines of the disabled movement. If you want us at your event, or in your group, advertise where we read.

And when you advertise events, every event should have information about accessibility. If the event is not accessible to disabled women, it should say so ...

At this point, maybe your heads are shaking and your finance committee is yelling, *"It's Not Cost Effective"*. (Perhaps the rest of you are simply saying. "It's too expensive").

Being disabled has never been cost effective and it never will be ...

So forgive us if we retch when we hear the same argument from feminist groups who have not put accessibility at the top of their agenda. And don't tell us that we're unreasonable, bitter, twisted and even strident when you shut us out and can't cope with our rage.

We must never, never, never shut any women out. All women are equal. All belong in the women's movement. Or it's all a *Big Lie*. You need to deal with your problem of excluding us. We won't go away. We are your sisters. And we are organizing around the world! Soon the spectacle of disabled women picketing inaccessible women's events will become a reality. Every minority has a point when collectively we say *Enough* is *Enough*. We are no exception. *We are your sisters.*

"We Are Who You Are: Feminism and Disability" November/December 1992[7]

... About two a half years poststroke, I have an experience that begins to clarify my thinking about feminism. We spend the winter in Beersheba, Israel, where Michael is working to help me escape Montréal's ice and snow. A woman from the local chapter of the Israel Women's Network phones: as a visiting feminist, would I speak on any "women's issue" of my choosing at their next meeting: Again my first reaction is negative: "I am no longer engaged with women's issues; I have been so self-obsessed with my stroke that's all I could possibly talk about." Her response is quick: "That's exactly what we want to hear about, but were too shy to ask!"

I have forgotten how wonderful it is to share intimately with a group of women! I read bits from my journal, and my story prompts theirs. One woman says, "My relationship with my husband is fine as long as I'm healthy, capable, and available sexually, but I don't know what

7. Bonnie Sherr Klein, *Ms.* 3, no. 3 (November/December 1992), 72-74.

would happen if I were incapacitated." She hadn't read the United Nations statistic that disabled women are twice as likely to get divorced or separated as disabled men. We realize that we rarely talk about illness, disability, and dying, though we will all confront these realities.

Every issue is a woman's issue; relationships, dependence, and autonomy are as much a part of feminism as day care and violence. I have undersold feminism. I slowly recognize that the way I am living my stroke has everything to do with myself as a feminist — as well as with implications for feminism itself.

"Coming Out" Disabled

I feel comfortable and stimulated in this group of Isreali women; they are middle-class, middle-aged, married Jewish women like me. But no one else there is disabled. I am "other." I desperately need company.

I had first heard of DAWN (the DisAbled Women's Network, Canada) years earlier when it approached Studio D to make our screenings more accessible. We appreciated being sensitized, favoured wheelchair-accessible venues, and enjoyed the aesthetics of sign language interpretation with our movies. But sometimes DAWN's demands seemed "excessive"; our meagre resources were already exhausted by items on our agenda that seemed to affect *most* women. But in retrospect, I know that as a not-yet-disabled woman I was afraid of disability.

As soon as I return to Canada, I dig DAWN's phone number out of a feminist newsletter. I realize that its agenda is identical to mine (and feminism's): dependence and autonomy, image and self-esteem; powerlessness, isolation, violence, and vulnerability; equality and access; sexuality. Three years after my stroke, I go to my first DAWN meeting at the local YWCA.

I feel apologetic, illegitimate, because I was not born disabled, and am not as severely disabled as many other people. I feel guilty about my privileges of class, profession (including my disability pension), and family. I am a newcomer to the disability movement; I have not paid my dues. (Doesn't this litany sound "just like a woman"?)

Our talk keeps moving between the personal and the political, because disability – like gender, race, age, and sexuality – is a social as well as biological construct. The DAWN members, typical of disabled women, are mostly unemployed, poor, and living alone. It is like the early days of consciousness-raising in the women's movement: sharing painful (and funny) experiences, "clicks!" of recognition; swapping tips for coping with social service bureaucracies and choosing the least uncomfortable tampons for prolonged sitting. It is exhilarating to cry and laugh with other women again.

Here I am not other, because everyone is other. It is the sisterhood of disability. The stroke has connected me with women who were not part of my world before — working-class women with little education, women with intellectual and psychiatric disabilities, women with physical "abnormalities" from whom I would have averted my eyes in polite embarrassment. All women like me ...

Happily, the timing of my personal journey is synchronous with the women's movement. The Canadian Research Institute for the Advancement of Women (CRIAW) announces the theme for its 1990 national conference: "The More We Get Together ... " on women and disability. I decide to go, alone, to Prince Edward Island. Thanks to the joint efforts of CRIAW and DAWN, this historic event is not only totally accessible but empowering - for both the women with disabilities and those without. Every woman with disability is paired with a "sister" who gives us whatever assistance we need - and who learns firsthand about disability.

It is a coming-out experience for many of us. For me, it is the first time I identify myself publicly as a woman with disability, and revel in the company of so many others. Because women with disabilities are often isolated, for many this is their first conference. They learn from the experience of longtime feminists.

Many of the so-called nondisabled women come out as well. Kay Macpherson, 79, and Muriel Duckworth, 83, are well-known Canadian peace activists and feminists. But we have never considered them "disabled." Now for the first time, Kay talks about what it means to be losing her sight. She talks loudly because her close friend Muriel has learned to be assertive about her increasing deafness. Muriel and Kay describe their support networks of friends who look after each other by sharing meals, and house keys in case of falls. Our stories lead us to discover the continuum from "ability" to "disability." My stroke has given me a telescope on aging. We are all disabled under the skin — each of us has vulnerabilities, visible or not, and they are part of us. We are interdependent. Feminism is strongest when it includes its "weakest."

I leave CRIAW with a new sense of purpose and continuity. No longer illegitimate among either feminists or people with disabilities, I feel I have a particular contribution to make: perhaps I can help to bridge the gap between our two cultures. After all, my life's work has been about telling each other our stories ...

Bonnie Sherr Klein's films include "Not a Love Story:" and "Speaking Our Peace" (National Film Board of Canada).

Classism

"Income Makes All the Difference"
Ottawa, 1986[8]

Question: What is a low-income woman's definition of feminism?
    Answer: A young university-educated woman with a career.

8. Dorothy O'Connell, *Breaking the Silence* 4, nos. 3/4 (Spring/Summer 1986), 12-13.

According to this definition, low-income women are excluded from feminism. Is the definition true? By and large, I would say it is fairly accurate. Most feminists *are* young university-educated women.

Low-income women do not think much about being feminists, any more than they would think about being Americans, or anything else which is theoretically possible but unlikely to happen. In this article, a few of the reasons why are explored ...

Nobody is suggesting to young low-income women that any interesting roles but motherhood are open to them; not the schools, because such women are not considered career material; not their parents, because they were brought up in the same way and think that women's careers (as teachers, hairdressers or nurses) should only last until marriage, or be pursued only if the extra income is necessary ...

With this kind of conditioning, it is not surprising that low-income women feel that feminism has little to do with them ...

In order to involve low-income women in feminism, it is necessary to convince them that they will in some way benefit ...

Feminism seems to threaten the importance of women's role in the family, and it is the only role low-income women have. Jobs are just something to do until marriage, or afterwards, for extra money. Friends are okay, but there is still a lot of competitive feeling among women, so a firm basis of support does not always exist. Feminism does not seem even a safe thing to consider, and talk of equal pay for work of equal value often meets with disapproval, since the father of the family must reign supreme or the whole foundation is threatened.

When a marriage breaks down and the family is not supportive, sometimes a low-income woman will start to consider feminism. Let us consider such a young woman. She is now trying to raise a family on her own, she needs employment, she needs support. Will feminism help her to find those things?...

Suppose that at this point she picks up a feminist publication, looking for people who share her state of mind. She is finally ready to take a stand about women and equality. What does she read? Is it about women like herself, with their backs to the wall, facing poverty and discrimination? Or does she read something which, in the first place, is in such academic terms that she has trouble understanding what it's about? If she manages to get past the academic jargon and the buzz words of the cognoscenti, does it have anything at all to do with her? Nine times out of ten the answer is no.

Furthermore, the women she meets who are feminists are apt not to be fighting for Canadian women who live in poverty, but for women in some other part of the world — like Africa, Nicaragua, El Salvador, whichever is in this year. If she tries to talk about Canadian poverty, she may well get a lecture on real poverty, and how lucky we are that Canadians, except maybe Native people, do not have to worry about it. When she tries to say that she does not have enough food in the house and may not be able to pay next month's rent, these feminists are liable to look the other way, or tell her how poor they are too, with not a penny extra.

If they have a meeting on, say, whether or not the Child Tax Credit should be paid to women once a year or quarterly, they may infuriate her with long philosophical debates which do not, in her opinion, reflect the reality or the urgency of many women's need for money. In despair, she may decide that she was right in the first place — feminists have nothing to do with her.

"Women Study Class: Gleanings of a White Poor Woman" Spring 1992[9]

I too "begin from a position of love of women" and believe that "inclusiveness is a foundation of an effective women's movement" (*Womanist*, Summer 1991). My own definition of love is broad and includes constructive criticism and loving confrontations. In this paper, I want to share my understanding of the relevance of social class for feminists. This view is based on my own analysis, which grows out of my experience, I describe my process in gaining this understanding as gleaning: gathering together bits of knowledge into an organized whole. I share with you those little subversive gems of knowledge.

I identify myself as both a poor woman and a feminist, a joint identity which is not always comfortable to maintain. The majority of poor women I know don't identify themselves as feminist. But more to the point, most of the self-identified feminists I know are unaware of the relevance of social class. In my experience, feminists are just as likely to accept and perpetuate the negative and disempowering stereotypes of poor people as non-feminists.

Feminism in its basic sense - an understanding of women's situation in patriarchy, and in its radical sense - a deeply felt respect for women and yearning for the Female, has been one of the most empowering experiences of my life.

I write to give voice to the often-unheard perspective of a feminist poor woman and to promote an understanding that the women's movement can never be a dynamic force for all women unless it accepts the views of poor women, validates our experiences, and includes our analysis. Many poor women have a very different perspective from that of other-class women. We have our own experience of being woman. Our own view of what has to change, and how.

Capitalist society is by definition classist. Many feminists fail to recognize their own deeply embedded classist assumptions, while others understand issues of social class only theoretically, basing their analysis on the works of Karl Marx. You don't have to read Marx to learn about

9. Eunice Lavell, *The Womanist* 3, no. 1 (Spring 1992), 38-39.

social class, classism and poor women. You need only listen to poor women.

Some key areas in which poor women's experience differs from those of non-poor women are:

Reproductive Freedom

For many feminists, reproductive freedom is about having the freedom to choose not to become pregnant, not to continue a pregnancy, not to mother a child. This springs from the fact that for centuries, non-poor white women in this country have been struggling to have access to birth control information and to abortions. Denial of freedom for these women has taken the form of forced reproduction. But this is not poor women's history.

Poor women have been the subjects of campaigns to "keep the unfit from reproducing", programs which were often endorsed by the upper-class white women now revered as First Wave feminists.

Poor women have been victims of involuntary abortion and sterilization. Our babies have been stolen from us and adopted by "nice (non-poor) couples." Native women in particular have lost their children to adoption, residential schools, and white foster homes. Denial of freedom for poor women has been denial of our right to have children.

- My paternal aunt Beatrice, at the age of fifteen, was sexually abused by two adult men and contracted venereal disease. She was "Treated" with confinement to a Home for Delinquent Girls, and a hysterectomy.
- My paternal aunt Eileen, at the age of seventeen, was given an involuntary abortion by a doctor-friend of her abusive employer. She died of a hemorrhage.
- My maternal aunt Madilla, at the age of twenty, became "hysterical" while being "disciplined" by her abusive husband and was admitted to a mental hospital. She "miscarried" and was then given a hysterectomy because of her husband's agreement with the hospital to "limit family size."

These incidents are not confined to the past. Many of the poor women I know who are against abortion are against it because of their own, or a family member's experience of being forced to have an abortion or sterilization. It is the very young poor women in this country as well as poor women of Third World countries who even now are guinea pigs for untested and dangerous fertility control drugs. In addition, many poor women on welfare have had abortions and "tubals" because of the threat of withdrawal of funds. ("Why should we pay just because you can't keep your legs together", one woman was told by her social worker.)

Work-for-Pay

One of the most visible accomplishments of the women's movement has been its effort to make room in the paid work force and get better pay for women. Unfortunately, for some feminists this one area of effort is often seen as the focus for the women's movement. For me this emphasis is problematic. The majority of poor women haven't a hope of a "career" which is personally satisfying, financially rewarding or even pleasant. Mostly, we get jobs. And our jobs give us no prestige or power, very little pay and often are very bad for our health. Yet feminist theory continues to assume that all women want to work-for-pay because of the "personal satisfaction" we get from our "careers".

I am not saying that pay level is unimportant to us. Obviously, for those of us who live in poverty, every extra dollar is of vital importance. I am saying that an exclusive careers-for-women focus does not truly serve poor women.

Poor women can only be served by radically changing the system. As long as you accept the capitalist system, you perpetuate the oppression of poor people, because poor people are what makes capitalism work. And a large proportion of poor people will always be women.

Finally, I want to point out the relationship between the particular institutions that we as feminists choose to criticize and our own beliefs and values. If feminists want to question all institutions which oppress women, they must begin by looking long and hard at the institution of paid work. To me there is a glaring inconsistency in the willingness of many feminists to unquestioningly endorse women's greater participation in the paid work force, but to approach every aspect of our participation in families with suspicion. I am not saying women should not work for pay. I am saying we need to examine the whole system. Paid work is an essential component of a system which oppresses poor women more than it does non-poor women.

These are some of the main areas in which poor women often have differing experiences, and thus very different perspectives, from women of other classes. The longer these differences remain unaddressed, the more divisive they become. Non-poor feminists become more convinced of the universality of their perspective, while poor women continue to assume they don't qualify to be feminists. Not only does this rob the women's movement of the rich contribution of poor women, but it also makes poor women vulnerable to the propaganda of anti-feminists and right-wing "fundamentalists".

Think of this as an invitation. For non-poor women, it is an invitation to challenge yourself to recognize the classism you have been taught all your life.

Sisters, listen to the voices of poor women and learn from them. Poor women, this is your invitation to know that your experience as a poor woman is essential to yourself as a feminist. Remember feminism must ring true to your life. Liberation begins with learning to honour those aspects of yourself which you have been taught to value the least.

I believe the women's movement hovers at the moment of decision. Will we strive for inclusiveness, challenge ourselves to listen to all women, flower out in diverse directions? Or do we go the linear, hierarchical, ultimately destructive route of the machines before us? It is our choice.

Immigrant Women and Women of Colour and Racism

Immigrant Women's Action Group
Toronto, early 1970s[10]

At the recent "Women in the Work Force" conference held at Toronto's Humber College, a workshop was held on "special problems of immigrant women." The discussion was led by Evelyn Murialdo, of the Centre for Spanish Speaking Peoples; Judith McCallum, of the Woman's Community Employment Service; and myself, representing Centro Donne. All three of us are immigrants to Canada and our work is among the South American, West Indian, and southern Mediterranean immigrant communities.

With the twenty-five participants we touched on a wide range of problems endemic to the situation of the immigrant woman — from the low-paying job ghettos reserved for her, to discrimination surrounding language study and retraining courses at Manpower, to social isolation within the immigrant communities, to the vast amounts of housework and the oppressive controls involved in the immigrant family.

Not surprisingly, what emerged clearly from our discussion was that the immigrant woman is even more trapped in the traditional role of wife and mother than her native-born sister. And [moreover] because of this fact she is at an even greater disadvantage when she looks for a second job outside the home. We focused on the extraordinary length of her cumulative work day — something which effectively prevents her from "taking advantage" of the "available opportunities" such as night school English courses, or organizing on the job for higher wages. *Time* seems to be the central problem; no matter what we discussed we came up against the fact that immigrant women are overworked and unable to make time for themselves.

This emphasis caused some consternation among those who had come to the workshop from trade unions which professed to be interested in "helping immigrants." They couldn't understand why we weren't tackling the problem in terms of "advancement on the job" and accepting the unions as the friends, so to speak, of the immigrant woman. But we were dealing with those who have always been ignored by the unions — women and immigrants — and who have no reason to think that any new found interest on the part of the unions is anything other than suspect. And this was only confirmed when the conference ended by

10. Judy Ramirez, flyer, Toronto, (n.d.). CWMA file: Immigrant Women's Centre.

passing a resolution advanced by the trade union women (who were in the vast majority) to develop ties only with women in "bona-fide bargaining units," explicitly bypassing the "unorganized"!

Since the conference, several women from the workshop have been meeting to discuss the need for a fresh start in assessing the specific condition of immigrant women and arriving at an overall strategy from that. Those of us working within our communities and looking for political direction in our organizing are not satisfied with the available options; we want to open up the whole question of immigrant women in relation to work, unions, time, money, the family, etc. We know we have to start from the ground up to analyze our own condition from our own point of view and organize on that basis alone.

We are holding our first public meeting on Tue., August 19 at 8 pm at Centro Donne 368A College St., Toronto. Topic: "Does the wm's [women's] movement have anything to offer immigrant wm who want to organize?" Wm only.

"Hyacinth's Story"
Toronto, 1983[11]

"I couldn't believe my luck"

After a while I use to work as a waitress in a hotel back home [in St. Lucia]. That is where I met the couple who sponsored me up here. I meet them and we talk with each other and they ask me how I would like to come up and work for them. I jump at the chance. Boy, is like my dream come true, I couldn't believe my luck. A couple months later they send my ticket with a letter saying when I come up they would take it out of my pay. This was in 1980 and I was twenty-four years old. I didn't stay with them long, only for eight months.

The first week I walked into the house the man start to bother me and want sex. I was frighten like a mouse, I didn't really expect that. When I got the job, I was suppose to look after their two little children, a girl and a boy, do the housework, wash and cook. I had my own room in the basement. It was nice, I had a T.V. and my own little bathroom in the basement. The man was a doctor, and his wife didn't really do anything. She use to leave the house in the day time but I don't know where she goes.

"He said if I had sex with him he would raise my pay"

I remember the first time I think something was funny was one night I was sleeping and I feel someone in my clothing, feeling up my private parts. This happen after I was here for a month. I jumped up because I was frighten and when I look it was him, the man I was working for. I nearly scream out, but he hold my mouth and tell me to be quiet. He

11. As told to and transcribed by Makeda Silvera in Makeda Silvera, *Silenced: Talks with working class West Indian Women about their lives and struggles as Domestic Workers in Canada* (Toronto: Williams-Wallace Publishers Inc., 1983), 64-66.

smell of alcohol and I don't know where his wife was, but it was late at night. He ask me if I wasn't attracted to him, and I just look at him, I was really afraid to answer.

I remember he kept pushing his finger down in my private parts and blowing hard. It really hurt and when I told him so, he ask me if I didn't give birth to one baby already.

He tried to push me down on the bed but I wouldn't let him, and he had his hand over my mouth so I couldn't scream.

He ask me if I was going to shout, I shake my head and say no, so he let go of my mouth. I remember him telling me that if I had sex with him he would raise my pay. I tell him that I couldn't do that because he was married and his wife was upstairs. I didn't know if she was but I just say that. He laugh and ask me what Black girls know about marriage. He said some really dirty things to me. I didn't know that man had so much filth in him, and a doctor and all.

Is like it was the end of the world for me. I was so frightened ... he was blowing so hard, so I could smell the alcohol strong on him. Before I know it he tear off my night clothes and he was with me right there in the bed. The more I fight the more he seem to enjoy it, so after a while I just lie down quiet and let him finish. After he finish he jump off me, spit on the floor and tell me if I tell his wife or anybody he would see that they send me back to St. Lucia or that I go to jail. I was really frightened. I really believe that I could get locked up. For what I don't know. It happen again seven or eight other times. I was just scared to say anything to anybody, further I didn't know where to turn to. I didn't know anybody here.

I didn't know where his wife was when he came to my room at nights. If she knew about it she didn't give any indication of it. Sometimes she use to stare at me, but she didn't say anything. I continue to do my work in the house — the cooking, the ironing and the cleaning — and looking after the children. There was times when I really felt ashamed, like a nobody, but I couldn't tell anybody, because there was nobody to tell about it.

Many nights I just cry, because even when I write home to my grandmother and my little boy, I had to write like everything was fine.

"I was scared to tell Immigration"

As time goes by and I take the children to the park, I start to notice that there was another West Indian girl who always was in the park with children. So one day I says good morning to her and we start to talk. I got to know that she just lived around the corner from me and that she was in the same line of work. We start to talk, and I get to like her and she like me, and of course we talk about the people we work for. One day I tell her what was going on with me at the house and she tell me that I could go to Immigration to complain and that I could look for another job. I was scared, because I thought that maybe they would deport me.

She promise to come down with me, and she did, but she didn't come in with me. She wait close outside at a restaurant for me. I go in and tell my story. I think I tell it six different times to six different officers. They wanted to know everything. I felt so cheap talking to them, they wanted to hear every little detail of what *really* happen with me and the doctor. That was the Friday, and they said I was to get back in touch with them the Monday morning. I don't know what happen, but when I go home the evening is like all hell break loose. I never know that Immigration work so fast. When I go in I get one big cussing from his wife. She call me ungrateful-jealous-slut-black-bitch. I can't even remember some of the words. She said, "If you and Don had a problem why didn't you come to me? Why Immigration, we could have worked it out." Then she started shouting again and calling me black bitch. I just run to my room and scream down the place. I was scared. Before I know it his wife just come into my room, open the door without knocking and started slapping me up, telling me that is me bring sex argument to her husband, and that we "nigger girls" are good for nothing else, and asking me if I like it when her husband have sex with me. I was crying the whole time, because I wasn't use to this treatment. Then she tell me I had to leave her house. So I pack up my little things and went and stay with my friend.

When I go down to Immigration the Monday morning they told me that I could go and look another job, but that I shouldn't waste any time fooling around. The man that I talk to never even ask me if I felt sick with what happened, or if I went to see a doctor, not one word about what happened to me ...

"We Appear Silent to People Who Are Deaf to What We Say" Toronto, 1983[12]

Race and the Limits of Sisterhood

Makeda: I'm really sick of some of these white feminists when they talk about rape. It's always from *their* perspective — being knocked down somewhere in a dark alley or a park and being raped. They never mention other kinds of rape, other abuse that women of colour and immigrant women experience, like men hassling you on the bus or train at night, calling you names, the day to day social rape ... A couple of nights ago I was waiting for the train and this drunk guy, big redneck, came up and started shouting, "Bitch! Bitch!" There was me and two other guys waiting for a train and he's shouting out "Bitch! Bitch!" I'm really frightened because this guy is really big and I'm wondering what would happen if he came up and attacked me physically. What was I

12. Himani Bannerji, Dionne Brand, Prabha Khosla, and Makeda Silvera (conversation), *Women of Colour*, special issue of *Fireweed: A Feminist Quarterly*, Issue 16, (Spring 1983), 8-12, 14-15.

going to do? This white woman walks up on the platform and he starts up again. We kind of look at each other in solidarity and I feel less scared because at least there is another woman. But then, this drunk started calling out, "Nigger! Nigger!" and looking directly at me. That woman, she just looked right through me and there wasn't that kind of connection, that solidarity, anymore. It was really frightening. I didn't know what to do. I was angry, I was filled with rage, I wanted to attack the man, I wanted to cry, and suddenly I felt really embarrassed. I didn't know why.

Dionne: I know how it is, I know that feeling.

Himani: So, while the whole thing was about women, when he was calling you "bitch," she was ready to relate to you. But as soon as your race came into focus, she too went over to the other side and didn't identify with you any more. So, in some sense, the women's movement in Canada is mainstream and does not seek to identify with women of colour.

Dionne: It doesn't address other issues that concern women of colour.

Himani: There is also the whole question of the book *Still Ain't Satisfied! Canadian Feminism Today* (Women's Press, 1982). It claims to anthologize the experiences of women in the movement for the last ten years in Canada, but actually leaves women of colour and immigrant women under-represented ... We are made invisible in the mainstream. And there is talk about "coming from the woman's perspective, coming from the woman's standpoint." It seems to me very empty, this standpoint, because I do not know who this woman is that they are talking about. It never comes down to a specific group of women. They talk about women as an empty category. They will not talk about women as class, about a particular type of woman, about woman as race, so it leaves you very empty at the end ...

Class and the Limits of Sisterhood

Himani: Vast numbers of immigrant women work outside of the home all the time. Even in terms of house work, they do this in other people's houses as domestic workers.

Dionne: If one were to identify [the problems of] immigrant women, black women, women of colour [as having to do with] domestic work in the home, it would perhaps represent 25 per cent. The other 75 per cent would be ...

Prabha: ... struggles of living within this society ...

Makeda: What about women of colour, immigrant women in factories and the difficulty of organising unions there? Nothing. It's like our experiences are not valued. Our experiences in organising and becoming part of unions are varied, particularly because of our being immigrants, where the fear of deportation is ever present — and the other immigrant women in factories, whose first language is not English.

Himani: They are always saying ... that immigrant women are silent. I don't think that immigrant women are silent. You appear silent to people who are deaf to what you say.

Prabha: They have their own idea of what we should be saying and until we say those things they pretend to be deaf.

Himani: So, if you don't fit into that, then as far as they're concerned, you're not saying anything. And they have a particular way of deciding what they'll count as "saying" and that "saying" is not how we speak.

Dionne: As a matter of fact, I think they like us like that — not "saying." They like us to join with them and struggle with them — but just as a symbol. We don't even have to say anything. It's worth it to them if we are completely illiterate or at least appear that way. You don't have to say anything as long as they can get a few women of colour and immigrant women out to a demonstration. That's wonderful, because symbolically we've always meant some kind of radical idea.

Himani: But, also, we've legitimised what they are doing by going there. But, I think the other question about even illiterate people is not that they don't say things, it's *how* they say it. There is only one way of "saying" that counts. In that sense, they are forcing all the most middle class, the most male bourgeois ways of speaking and doing things on us. And if you don't do things that way, then you're not doing it, you're not "saying" it right. What I challenge is this whole notion of the silence of people.

Prabha: It's also because a lot of the women in the women's movement are fairly well-educated and have a university education, so they have writing skills. Because we don't write, they cannot read our articles, and they figure that we don't have experience, or that we don't exist as coloured women who are actively organised.

Makeda: I would even challenge that. There are many of us who write, they just don't want to read it; they don't want to publish it. Reading and publishing our work would definitely force white women to look at themselves, at racism and at what has been laid on us for years. The latest issue has been how patriarchal our culture is and how male-identified women of colour and immigrant women are. We are labelled male-identified every time we talk about struggling with Third World men to end racism and imperialism. This view of the world and the relationship of peoples in the world is certainly not compatible with mine.

Dionne: Any immigrant woman/woman of colour analyzing her situation in the world has to analyze it beyond the point of being a woman, because there are other people who are in the same condition and some of them are men. We cannot analyze the world as though men of colour are not oppressed too, because that way of analyzing the world gives us no way out of it ...

Rape and the Myth of the Black Savage

Dionne: What is also interesting is the issue of rape ... Rape has always been used in America and here against Black men, and it's very, very tricky for us. Of course, we feel the same way about rape as white women do, but I'm always suspicious when I hear of a Black man raping a white woman.

Prabha: Do you remember that happening last summer here in Toronto? There was this composite picture in the newspaper of this Black guy — dreadlocks. Then three months down the road the picture changed. He was white — he just had curly hair. He had gone to a salon before the rape.

Dionne: But the picture was white, for godsake! They said first of all that it was a Black man, a Rasta who had raped the woman in High Park. Then the picture changed and they said he was a mulatto. Then it started to change (laughter). Soon he was octoroon, quadroon, and he was white six months later.

Makeda: During that period, whenever I was around white women and the rape came up I felt really isolated. I felt that I couldn't discuss the rape and the rapist with them because this man was supposed to be Black and I'm Black. This man was supposed to be a Rastafarian and I am a Rastafarian. Somehow, I felt they had stopped seeing me as a woman; I was now Black and Rastafarian — devoid of sex. For them, the central issue seemed to be his Blackness. I felt that to partake in that racist discussion would be saying something against my race. He simply wasn't a man who raped a woman. He was Black and she was white. He was not a man, he was not a person who had committed a crime, just Black, Black, and that made me really uncomfortable. I feel connected to this person because he's Black and because we live in a racist society and I'm reminded of that every day, every hour of my life.

Himani: In fact, what they were doing was replaying the whole myth ...

Makeda: ... a Black, a savage, a wild Black. He may have been a Black man, but that is irrelevant. We knew as soon as that came out that it would reinforce the myth.

Dionne: Not only that, but he would then be responsible for all the rapes, before and after. This depravity, this person violating white womanhood — the whole business all over again.

Makeda: When they had that demonstration to protest the rape, you didn't know whether the women who were demonstrating were out there protesting because it was a Black savage. I remember I really wanted to go, but I was hesitant. I wondered whether half of the people who had gone went to demonstrate against this Black that they wanted to find and kill. This might not have been foremost in their minds, but I can't help thinking that it might have been at the back ...

"You Mean, I Still Ain't?"
Ottawa, 1987[13]

Before any discussion of racism takes place there are some truths which must be spoken. North America is a sexist, racist and classist society. The Feminist Movement was an ideological reaction to one of these oppressions. The motivating stimulus behind the women's movement of the late 1960s was to end the oppression of women by men. Although the radical women who were the pioneers of the movement had a history and a familiarity with the civil rights movement, they did not see a necessity to incorporate either their knowledge or experience of race oppression into their rhetoric. What feminism purports to change is the unequal balance of power between men and women. Knowing that their doctrine was incubated in a racist environment, feminists chose to address only the issue of sex oppression, the implied decision being that other oppressions were irrelevant to a discussion of the oppression of women. Feminism and its theories are by definition racist.

Even within the safety of the sisterhood, women of colour were being ignored and discriminated against. There existed, even among women, an unequal balance of power. Betty Friedan, in that bible of feminism, *The Feminine Mystique*, blatantly ignored the reality of non-white and working-class women.

In the late 1970s radical feminist theorists did begin to pay lip service to the existence of race privilege within the movement. It was then admitted that all women do not share a common lot, that all women do not experience oppression in the way that the privileged white theorists did. Granted, this society does favour men over women. It also favours white over black, brown and yellow, middle and upper classes over the working class. White middle-class feminists, who developed original feminist discourse, started to say out loud that racism existed ... out there, that they were privileged because they were white. They were, needless to say, very reluctant to say that they as white women were racist. Yet, if the theorists of the movement did not make eradicating their own prejudices a priority, then they were themselves being the oppressors of women.

Unlike the patriarchal culture from which it sprang, feminism attempted to analyze the differences among women. In eager pursuit of a unified feminism, theorists incorporated theories about racism and privilege into the rhetoric of the movement. Yet there is, on the part of these same women, either a reluctance or an inability to find a way to use this analysis to help bridge the gaps between the races. Feminist analysis of the issue of race has become instead the foundation of battle lines. There is now a feminism of women and a feminism of Women of Colour. We are not women struggling against oppression together. I see no rationale in delving into the nature of differences unless it is to be of some benefit

13. Maxine McKenzie, *Breaking the Silence* 5, no. 3 (March 1987), 8-9.

to the common cause. Feminism has fallen into the trap of using difference to divide. There has been no attempt to synthesize the knowledge of the sexual oppression of all women and the racial oppression of Women of Colour into a true analysis of the oppression of women. What should have resulted from all this debate was a new feminist definition of womanhood, a definition that included the realities of all women. Instead, white feminists continue to see their reality as the norm and everything else as a deviation. As a result, feminists encourage the emerging pattern of separatism within the movement.

I still recall with extreme discomfort a recent encounter with a group of white feminists representing a local organization. The discussion centred around a criticism by women of the community who felt that a poster chosen to represent the organization perpetuated racist and classist stereotypes. Throughout the meeting I had the distinct impression that the Women of Colour attending the discussion were actually there to prove that the criticisms were not just the hysterical ravings of emotional women. Nevertheless our objections were duly noted. I began to feel optimistic. My optimism was, however, short-lived. Toward the end of the meeting one of the white women explained that [al]though she recognized that the poster did reinforce racist stereotypes of Women of Colour, she was still reluctant to remove the offensive poster from circulation. Why? Because this poster was the only way the organization could get its message to women. My question here is, what message? And to which women? By implication the pain and discomfort of Women of Colour who are oppressed by their sisters should not be a deterrent to the real goal of reaching real women (read white women). Also implied by this blatant insult is that it is white women for whom they will be supplying their services.

This is racism. As well, it is an effective way to prevent women from working together. If in every utterance of the word "woman" you do not envision a kaleidoscope of colours and take into account the gamut of realities and lifestyles that are the true lives of women then you do not speak of or for women.

In defining this world as feminists, we must redefine our uses of differences. Differences should not divide. We must unlearn this habit. The fear of difference, the perception of difference as deviation and therefore as undesirable is the baggage of the patriarchy. Feminism runs a lesser risk of perpetuating oppressive behaviour if the knowledge of race difference is used as a measuring stick. What keeps the feminist movement from embracing Women of Colour is still fear that differences are incompatible. Each woman who defines herself as feminist must accept that, in fact, the working definition of womanhood is incomplete. Differences of realities and experience due to differences of race and class make for a different definition of woman, not for many types of womanhood.

Combating racism requires that you have more than a merely superficial comprehension of race, colour, and [the] history of and the culture of Women of Colour. Without a personal investment in acquiring as much knowledge of Women of Colour as Women of Colour have of white women, white feminists cannot address issues of concern to all women. This is the unifying potential of an analysis of racism. Sometime soon, we as feminists may truly address the oppression of all women ...

"The Day I Tasted Police Justice"
1989[14]

I am a Black woman who arrived in Canada within the last ten years. For a while I used to think that those people in Canada who treated me with indifference were only those with false perceptions and lack of tolerance for anyone who looks different. I also held the mistaken notion that police officers did not fall into this category. Much to my dismay, I found out differently when I sought justice from a police officer a few years ago.

I am prompted to write this story as a result of all the attention the media has given to the rights of the police and how the community in Toronto has stood up for the police. Blacks are the minority in this society and practically helpless. The police force is predominantly white, armed with their guns and the force of the law behind them. Does such a powerful majority need protection from its weak minority: That is the question to be answered ...

The shooting incidents have brought the problems to public attention, but there have been frustrations building up over a number of years between police and blacks. Many people have related to me their own heartbreaking experiences with the police.

It was two days after I was discharged from hospital after delivering twins, and I needed a few items so desperately that I dragged myself from home to look for a nearby corner store ... I picked up a few small items that amounted to just under five dollars. Finding a five dollar bill in my wallet, I placed it on the counter and watched as the cashier picked up the money. He was an elderly gentleman who appeared to be the store owner. Soon afterwards, he turned to me and asked me for my money. I told him I put my money on the counter and I saw him pick it up. He replied that the money belonged to a young boy who stood in line ahead of me. I argued that I saw him pick up the five dollar bill I had put down. He replied that the boy gave him two five dollar bills, and the one he picked up was the boy's. I insisted that he had my money, and I was not leaving unless he gave me the goods, as I was not responsible for this misunderstanding.

While we argued about the matter, a teenage girl rushed from the back of the store and declared that the five dollar bill belonged to the young boy, and I was trying to steal the boy's money. She then picked up the phone and called the boy's home and told the person on the phone

14. Brendalyn Ambrose, *The Womanist* 1, no. 3 (February/March 1989), 9.

the boy would be late getting home because "there is a lady here who is trying to steal his money."

When she said those words, I told her, "What did you just say, you called me a thief, and I have always lived with respect, integrity and honesty wherever I go, so as you are infringing on my integrity, I insist that you call the police." As I was adamant, she called the police.

When the policeman entered the store and asked what the matter was, the teenaged girl spoke up first. She related the entire incident from beginning to end and explained that I was trying to take the boy's money.

"You explained everything from beginning to end, where were you when it happened?" (She had been at the back of the store the whole time). No sooner had I opened my mouth than the policeman ordered me to go outside and wait there. I did as I was told. I waited outside for almost an hour, eager to tell him my side of the story.

When the policeman came out of the store, he refused to allow me to say one word. All he said was "I have listened to the story from all three people (the elderly man, the young boy and the teenaged girl - all white). They all said the same thing, so it is three people's words against you; therefore I do not want to hear anything from you. I believe their story."

He then ordered me not to go back into the store and told me if I did he would arrest me and beat me up. He also made other verbal threats. I told him he was dishonest himself for the way he handled the situation and reminded him that if I had really been trying to take the money, I would not have been the one to insist the police be called in. He said he would hear nothing from me, and I could have neither the goods nor the money back. I told him I would report him to the Chief of Police and he remarked that it would not make any difference. I went home sick and stunned as I asked myself, "Where can I turn for protection in Canada?"

The reason for the problem with the police is lack of proper education, the way blacks are presented in the media, and the way adults, bureaucrats, teachers, etc., have been socialized to view blacks. It is society's duty now to re-evaluate their thinking and do some soul-searching. This is not the time to form COPS. Those who administer the school boards must look at the curriculum and the relevance given to blacks of prominence in Canadian society. And what about the role of the Church? Is it simply to stand by and say nothing?...

The United Nations Declaration of Human Rights has guaranteed all people the following rights under Article Seven of its charter:

> All are equal before the law and are entitled without discrimination to equal protection against discrimination in violation of this Declaration and against any incitement to such discrimination.

In addition to the Charter of Human Rights, our own Canadian Charter gives all Canadian similar assurances in Section 15 (1) which states:

> Every individual is equal before and under the law and has the
> right to equal benefit of the law without discrimination based on
> race, national or ethnic origin, colour, religion, sex, age or mental
> or physical disability.

When such rights have been suppressed or obstructed, as the police did
to me, and have been doing to many other blacks, it is proper for black
groups to speak out and seek justice.

Section 25 (1) of the Canadian Charter also states:

> Anyone whose rights or freedoms, as guaranteed by the Charter,
> have been infringed or denied may apply to a court of competent
> jurisdiction to obtain such remedy as the court considers appropri-
> ate and just in the circumstance.

I consider myself entitled to all such rights, just like white Canadians. I
am guaranteed police justice, not police harassment. Why should society
expect me or any other black to accept anything less?

Racism Alive and Well in Nova Scotia
Halifax, Nova Scotia
March 8, 1991[15]

... I want to read to you a letter to God written several months ago. It
is a letter of confession. It is the story of a child and of her transformation
into a woman of colour, proud to be what she is and who she is. I read
this letter to you in hope that you will have an idea of what oppression,
omission, patriarchy and discrimination can do to a woman of colour
who grew up in Nova Scotia.

Dear God:

I used to hate You because You made me black. I asked You to make
me white. I wanted to have thin lips and long silky straight hair. I told
You my hips were too big and You did nothing to help me. You see
God, I was not pretty because I was black. I was so afraid. Sometimes
I even asked You to let me die.

I told You I wanted a white mother. Remember when she came to
see me when I was in grade school? It was raining outside, and I did not
have a hat. She left home to make sure that I would not get wet. I did
not want anyone to see her because she was black. I was angry she came,
and I was angry with You for letting her come. Didn't You know that
being black would cause me to be insecure, sad and angry? Why did
You do this to me? Little white kids called me "nigger." White girls did
not want to hold my hand because they believed that my blackness would
dirty them. I remember standing at the front of the line in grade school
and the teacher telling me to stand at the back of the line. She put two
little white girls up front. One had blonde hair. Her name was Paula.
The other one had brown hair. Her name was Donna. When I was in

15. Mayann Francis, address given on International Women's Day, Halifax, NS, 9 March 1991.
Reprinted in *Pandora* 6, no. 3 (June 1991), 3.

grade six a white boy told me he did not like my girlfriend because her face was black. I was confused because my face was also black. I ran home, looked into the mirror and saw me, still black. Why did he say that to me? Why did You try to fool me?

In all my school books I did not see anyone who looked like me. All the pictures were of little white kids, white mothers and fathers. All my teachers were white. That's why I knew that black was different and ugly.

When I was sixteen I worked in a store for Christmas holidays. I packed bags at the cash register. That was nice. One afternoon a man said "hey, nigger." I cried when I got home. I was so hurt. It was supposed to be Christmas. Did I do something wrong? Maybe I was supposed to keep my head down and not look at anyone. That's it, maybe I can hide my black skin. What do You think, God?

We often went to the movies in our area where most blacks lived. The area was called the "subway." Whenever we went into "town," people always stared at us. I hated that. I had fun sitting on the steps with my black friends. I did not need to go into town. Some white boys came around, but people said they did not mean black women any good. White girls came around. They wanted the black guys. The white girls' parents were upset. They did not want their daughters with black guys.

I remember going to college. It was my first year. There were very few blacks; maybe two, maybe three. I did not like that experience. My grades were fine. It was just that I wanted to be white. I thought if I used plenty of make-up I could pretend. It did not work.

After my first year was over, I moved away to study x-ray technology. I do not remember my training too well. I was the only black in my class. It was lonely but I did have fun. When I finished x-ray school, I tried to find an apartment. I had trouble because I was black. This damn skin — look at all the problems. What was I to do? Going shopping was not any fun. Someone was always watching. They thought I was going to steal. They did not know that my father was a respected school-teacher and I would never steal. They thought all blacks were thieves.

I needed something in my life. I went to university. I met my husband. We moved from Nova Scotia to the United States. Later we divorced. Times were hard. I moved to New York, armed with my Bachelor's degree and determination. I could not find a job. I decided to volunteer my time as an x-ray technologist. A doctor felt sorry for me and found me two part-time jobs working in ghetto clinics. I was grateful. I x-rayed all types of people. They were nice to me.

After working there I earned a paralegal certificate. After many attempts, I found a job on Wall Street as a corporate paralegal. You know, God, if I were not black I would have found a job much sooner than I did. I did well as a paralegal, both on Wall Street and in mid-town. I had to show them that black people are capable.

I suppose You know that I earned my Master's degree while living in New York. As time went on, I somehow was getting used to my blackness. I began to like myself. There were so many other blacks all working as doctors, lawyers, judges, actors and actresses, nurses, oh, so many. All beautiful people. I joined black women's groups. I went to dances and saw beautiful black faces. I had long hair, short hair, braids, red hair, blonde hair, blue eyes, anything I wanted. You can do that in New York. I had fun. You do know that I always prayed to You. I did not stop. I felt that I needed your Presence. You helped me through good times and bad times.

Now You brought me back to Nova Scotia. Did You send me to the United States to find myself? Did You believe that I would not have grown if I stayed in Nova Scotia? When I came home, I went to look for an apartment. God, my blackness still was a problem. Guess what? It did not make me hate myself. You see, I can now face racism. Isn't it sad? God, Nova Scotia still has some problems.

Dear God, I now pray to You and ask that You make peace in the world. I ask that You create a world where the colour of a person's skin is unimportant ... a world where there is no drug abuse, no battered women, no sexism, no racism; oh God, I know You can do this ... You made me love me ... so I know you can make everyone love everyone.

Oh yes, dear God, I am not afraid of my blackness. I don't hate You any more. I love You. It took me 16 years to find myself. God, can You forgive me, please, and thanks. I will write soon.

Sincerely,

Tera.

P.S. I do not hate anyone. I am no longer angry. Hatred and anger are negative forces. We all need love and acceptance.

Native Women and Northern Women

Native Indian Women and Section 12(1)(b)
Fredericton and Big Cove,
New Brunswick, ca. 1980[16]

What is 12(1)(b)?

12(1)(b) is that clause within the Indian Act which strips a Native Indian woman of rights normally enjoyed by any other registered Indian. The Indian Act is Federal law which governs all aspects of Indian Life.

12(1) (b) states:

"The following persons are not entitled to be registered, namely ...

... (b) a woman who marries a person who is not an Indian."

16. Caroline Ennis, Shirley Bear and Beth Sherwood, pamphlet, Native Women's Committee of NAC, printed by Mount St. Vincent University, n.d. Copy at Women's Educational Resources Centre, OISE (hereafter WERC).

Who is Affected?
Any Native Indian Woman who marries any non-Indian, or any Indian outside of her Band, or an Indian outside of Canada. Her children are also affected the same way.

Indian men are not affected; they can marry anyone they choose without penalty. In fact, when an Indian man marries a non-Indian woman, he automatically confers upon this non-Indian woman all the rights of a registered Indian under the Indian Act.

How Does This Affect the Native Indian Woman?
The Native Indian Woman is affected by:

1. the loss of her nationality
2. the loss of her right to reside where she was born
3. the loss of close family ties
4. the loss of her culture and religion
5. the loss of her right to family property and inheritance
6. the loss of her voting rights
7. the loss of health services
8. the loss of educational rights
9. the loss of her right to be buried on Indian land.

How and When Did This Come About?
In 1869, the Government of Canada tried to settle the Indian problem once and for all, by forcing the Indian to disappear into Canadian society. The Indian Act was to be the instrument used by the government to destroy the Indian people by cutting off the woman. The woman embodies the culture and language of any nation, and once she is gone, the Nation has no chance to survive.

What Can We Do?

1. You can support this campaign morally and financially.
2. Write and circulate petitions.
3. Ask your local politicians what their stand is on Native Indian Women's issues.
4. Write letters to M.L.A.s and Federal M.P.s in support of this campaign.
5. Urge your church or organization to address the government to abolish the discriminatory law concerning Native Indian women.

Where Do I Send Donations?
　　Native Women's Committee
　　c/o National Action Committee on the Status of Women

Native Women Are Divided
Vancouver, BC 31 July 1975[17]

In B.C. there are several native women's groups with numerous chapters throughout the province. The only feminist Indian women's organization is the Ad Hoc Committee on Indian Rights for Indian Women. It was set up three years ago to advise native women about their rights under the Indian Act.

"The native women are divided," says Ms. Phyllis Lavallee, Assistant Executive Director R.S.W. for the Vancouver Indian Centre. "We can't seem to get together because some are status Indians and others are not."

The native woman who marries a non-Indian man loses her right to live on a reserve and her children's band inheritance rights. She loses her birthrights as an Indian.

"When I got married, the Department of Indian Affairs handed me a piece of paper to sign," says Ms. Cantryn, Executive Director of VIC. "In those days you did what they said. There was no explanation. We didn't find out what it meant until it was too late."

"Today, I would simply refuse to sign the paper," she says, "We know we will not be recognized by the government but it hurts to be banished by your own people. You can't help who you fall in love with."

Currently the women's movement is quite concerned with marital property laws. Ms. Carol Nessman, a VIC counsellor is matter-of-fact about it. "When you are poor, there is no property to divide up and you can't afford a divorce. We just separate and live common-law with someone else."

What is the basic problem for native women, whether they live on or off the reserve, whether they are status or non-status Indians? "Everything," says Ms. Vivian Ignace, a VIC aid. "Keeping the family together, furnishing your home, nutrition. It's all a problem if you don't have enough money."

Family responsibility usually falls on the native woman. This is not so much because of any motherhood role as that many of them are single parents. "Mothers help one another," says Ms. Cantryn. "We take care of each other's children. You'll never find an orphan among us."

These days, some of the young native women with ambition and some advantages eventually become nurses, teachers or social workers. But the majority drop out of school by grade 10 and end up on welfare or "on the streets."

Contrast this to a past in which many coastal tribes in B.C. had a matriarchal tradition. The women owned the wealth of each band as well as its culture. The women were the "nobility."

17. Karen Richardson, Ad Hoc Committee on Indian Rights for Indian Women, West Vancouver, B.C., Western Canadian Women's News Press Release, Vancouver, B.C., 31 July 1975. Copy at the Vancouver Status of Women.

"Some young women are more eager to become chiefs than the young men," says Ms. Nessman. "Today, the men are figureheads but the women do all the politicking." (Out of 188 Indian Chiefs in B.C., 10 are women.)

What is the major barrier between white and native women? "Many of us have no mobility," says Ms. Ignace. "Even if we could get around we are demoralized because we can't dress as well as white women."

Another problem is the way white women view them. "The Indian woman is shy in public, soft-spoken. People think we are backward because we don't speak up, but we are vocal amongst our own friends," she says.

There is a theory that native women's rights will follow from the settlement of Indian land claims. Until then, many of the B.C. bands are refusing government financial assistance. Some of the hardest hit will be the single parent women.

Indian Women's Rights
November, 1977[18]

At the recent annual meeting of the Canadian Research Institute for the Advancement of Women, Mary Two-Axe Early announced that Indian women who have lost their status under the Indian Act (because they married non-Indian Men) are now being evicted from reserves.

She asked that people who are concerned about this situation write to appropriate members of the government, particularly to the Prime Minister, expressing their support for the cause of Indian women.

Text suggested by Mary Two-Axe Early for a letter to be sent to the Prime Minister, Minister of Justice, Minister of Indian Affairs
> that the Indian Act 12.1b be immediately amended to give Indian women equality and that eviction of Indian women from the reserve be stopped at once pending the completion of the revision of the Indian Act.

Super Personal News: Reinstatement as Status and Band Member
Kamloops, B.C. 1986[19]

WEY EK (hello)

I share with you super personal news! As of March 3, 1986 I have been reinstated as Status [with] Band membership to Kamloops Indian Band. Although in my heart, mind and soul I have always been a native Woman. Believe me the pride and dignity is overwhelming. I strongly encourage all of you wonderful Native women to apply for reinstatement.

18. Flyer in WERC file: Women's groups 1977-78.
19. *B.C. Native Women's Society Newsletter* (Kamloops, B.C.), January-February 1986. Copy at the Vancouver Status of Women.

As your first Vice-President the last few months have been extremely busy. I am pleased to announce that I am now field worker/researcher for Implementation for Bill C-31. I also maintain to represent you on the National level. As of November, 1985, I was appointed on the Constitution Working Group of Native Women's Association of Canada.

If you have any questions or concerns about reinstatement on Bill C-31, please feel free to contact me or Sharon at our office. We would be more than happy to do a workshop in your area at your convenience. In order to speed the process of application for reinstatement, be sure to apply to Vital Statistics for your and your children's long form birth certificate. These documents can be obtained in your local court house or at government agencies in your area. Unfortunately there is a $10.00 fee for this service but it is a very small amount to pay, considering the benefits you will gain. Baptismal certificates are also considered evidence, if a birth certificate cannot be proven.

I encourage all Indian Women concerned about the future generations to lobby your bands, Native organizations and have impact on developing band membership codes. And please don't forget to support B.C. Native Women's society in your membership drives, the more members the greater our voice is. I leave you with my kind thoughts and extend good health, good luck and much happiness.

COOK'S JUM
Jo-Anne Gottfriedson
P.S. note my legal name change.

Cultural Appropriation and the Question of Voice

The Question of Cultural Appropriation
St. John's, Newfoundland,
March, 1992[20]

Editors
Globe and Mail
Toronto
Regarding Stephen Godfrey's article "Canada Council asks whose voice is it anyway?"

I am a writer who grappled with many of the issues raised in this article and as a consequence have some suggestions for agencies like the Canada Council.

My book *Nitassinan: The Innu Struggle to Reclaim Their Homeland* is the non-fiction account of an extraordinary time in the history of another culture. I never considered writing from the Innu point of view, and wherever possible used transcripts from interviews conducted with

---

20. Marie Wadden, Letter to the Editor, *Globe and Mail*, not published. Copy in private possession of Ruth Roach Pierson.

Innu people. My original grant application to the Canada Council contained a letter of support from Daniel Ashini, then band council chief at Sheshatshit. Yet on several occasions individuals in the community confronted me, suspicious that I was trying to make money off their suffering. I knew this was not a widespread point of view and was reassured when the community flew more than a dozen representatives to St. John's for the official book launch. The community was gracious and thanked me for this written document, yet I am still not entirely comfortable with my role. Deep down I know that I was able to tell their story because I was born with privileges most of them don't enjoy. Someone from Sheshatshit could have written this book, but that won't happen until the Canada Council and other funding agencies mount an affirmative action program that will remove the obstacles which prevent indigenous people from becoming writers.

Let's face it. Writing is a luxury of rich societies, and indigenous societies in Canada are far from wealthy. The art of writing is still a luxury most indigenous people cannot afford. In Labrador, Innu homes lack plumbing; individuals face a daily battle to provide for their large families on welfare, the disease of alcoholism plagues many, and the time and space required to write are simply not available. There's a serious shortage of housing in native communities. In Sheshatshit single people live with extended families, there are no apartments or houses for rent. That means solitude is rare, and you need solitude to write. (Innu women kept journals while in prison for occupying the runways of CFB Goose Bay, but there's got to be an easier way!) Granting agencies like the Canada Council would have to provide money for office space so the native writer could work in the community but away from his or her busy household. A salary would also have to be provided. The grants I received from the Canada Council and Secretary of State were not enough to live on while I was researching and writing my book. Fortunately I had savings to draw from — another luxury few Innu enjoy since most of them have always lived on the edge of poverty.

The daily preoccupation of the educated elite in native communities is to procure their peoples' legal rights. They are in the best position to write, but they don't have time. Instead they puzzle over the legal and political impediments to land claims talks, or take direct action to oppose damaging environmental projects. These are considered life and death issues for native cultures. Who has the peace of mind to write under these circumstances?

Most Innu over the age of 40 do not speak, let alone write, English or French. Theirs is an oral culture. The language is only now being written, yet the people, through word of mouth, have safeguarded tales as ancient as the mammoth. If indigenous communities want written records of these legends, the elders should be encouraged to record their tales electronically so they might eventually be transcribed. If there are stories people like the Innu want the outside world to hear, funding for translation must be provided. Will the Canada Council, and the Canadian publishing industry provide the editorial assistance needed to help people write in a second language? Most publishers will turn a book down if it looks like it needs too much work.

I have no doubt that if given the right support, people like the Innu will write as well as any in our society. In fact, they must write, for they have important stories to tell. In the meantime there is a role for people like myself, but I try not to delude myself into thinking I am doing them any favours. My life has been greatly enriched as a result of my contact with the Innu, and the process of writing this book has helped assuage some of my guilt, for I know my privileges have been bought at the expense of their lands and way of life.

The Complexities of Coming to Voice

"Sisters in the Movement"
Toronto, 1990[21]

We have worked with the women's movement for over six years. For the most part this has meant challenging white feminists to be accountable for their racism. We continue our involvement with the hopes of forging links between women of colour and white feminists. Our commitment lies with building a movement with and for women of colour. "Nothing short of a revolution" (Cherie Moraga and Gloria Anzaldua, introduction to This Bridge Called My Back*).*

Identifying as Feminists

Mutriba: I've always been a feminist ... however, I never sought it out.

Ravida: I never "looked" for feminism either, I fell into it. I was in my second year of university and Women's Studies classes were just being introduced. The student newspaper started a "Women's Page" ... we were both involved immediately ... there was no questioning it. Later, I became involved with the Calgary Status of Women Action Committee (SWAC) ... it was such a natural progression. I saw SWAC as a forum to continue writing on and for women. I was never conscious of joining "the women's movement."

M: My work at SWAC was mostly done in isolation. I used to go in during the days and read, file, catalogue books, etc ... There were always meetings and CR groups going on. I didn't know what they involved and the thought of talking with more than one woman terrified me because I was so shy. As well, I didn't think I had anything to say.

R: I remember when we first articulated that we were feminists. I was seventeen and you were eighteen years old. Both of us were working

21. Mutriba Din and Ravida Din, *Awakening Thunder: Asian Canadian Women*, special issue of *Fireweed: A Feminist Quarterly*, Issue 30 (1990), 35-39.

with SWAC, the "Women's Page," taking Women's Studies courses and therefore reading the "classics" (de Beauvoir, Greer, Friedan) ... I asked you if you were a feminist and you very matter-of-factly said, "Yes, of course I am." I mumbled and fumbled thinking, "Well — if you are, so am I."

Identifying as Women of Colour ... As Asians

M: Again ... the terms colour, immigrant, Asian were not part of my vocabulary. I've never identified as Asian because it always meant you were Chinese, Japanese, etc. I prefer to identify as a woman of colour.

R: Yet, we did refer to the Muslim population, which included us, as Asian.

M: Yes, it was a term the British used to identify anyone who wasn't Black and, of course, white ...

R: I've only recently been able to call myself Asian. In the past, I never thought the word included me. I've been reading and seeing anthologies on Black women, Latin American women, Arab women, etc., and in each I find a part of myself. But, as a woman born in Nairobi, raised in a Muslim family, and having lived in Canada for over ten years, I still have to glean information from these anthologies. When I saw the notice for this issue, I thought perhaps I'll read chapters and who knows, maybe the whole book, and I'll say, "Yes, this is me ..."

M: It's difficult finding that niche, one that speaks to us in totality. In fact, its been an annoyance for me to have to define or identify myself as anything other than a woman of colour. But I also know that I am immediately drawn to anything that mentions Asian or Muslim.

R: It would be interesting to examine how we are constantly changing and adding to the ways in which we self-define. I use woman of colour, lesbian of colour, feminist, Asian, all interchangeably, always depending on the context.

M: I first called myself a woman of colour after you returned from Nairobi.[22] You specifically used the term woman of colour and it felt absolutely right and it felt good. I felt for the first time a sense of pride in my colour.

R: I went to Nairobi as a youth delegate ... I had never thought I'd get marks for being a woman of colour. Nairobi was a turning point for me. The Canadian delegation itself was about forty percent women of colour. Things started "clicking" even before arriving in Nairobi. In an orientation meeting in Toronto, the women of colour came together, separate from the white women. We talked about our lives, our work and what it meant for us individually and as a group to be going to Nairobi. We were aghast at the questions white women asked. For example, "How do you say sisterhood in Swahili?", or, "How do I know

22. The End of the United Nations Decade for Women Conference, held in Nairobi, Kenya, 1985.

when a Kenyan man is coming on to me?" ... Arriving in Nairobi ...
WOW! Not only was it my birthplace but here were 13,000 women and
two-thirds were women of colour. Nairobi was a coming home for me
in more ways than one. Many white women have said feminism or the
women's movement is "coming home." I was amongst women who
thought and felt just like I did. There were finally names for all those
feelings of being "other," of being "separate" and most of those feelings
had to do with acknowledging the fact that racism existed in the
women's movement.

M: We knew racism outside of the women's movement and it went
as far as slurs and being called "Paki."

R: Before Nairobi, it didn't make sense to talk about racism in the
context of the women's movement just as it didn't make sense to identify
as anything other than woman. Nairobi was very empowering ... I was
in a community of women who listened and understood me and suddenly
so much was spilling out of me ... I never realized I had been so silent.

M: It was exciting to call myself a woman of colour ... finally
something that's positive.

R: Yes. We've grown up hating our colour because everyone else
did. In the Muslim community as well, the lighter your skin colour, the
more "attractive" you are thought to be.

M: That desire to be white ... it brings with it powerlessness.

R: Of course ... wanting something we could never have.

M: How did you feel as a woman of colour in Nairobi as compared
to Canada?

R: Nairobi was probably the ideal setting ... we were so many, the
majority. It was also ideal because we came together in a political setting
and so many of us were women of colour living in "white" countries.
The biggest difference ... I never felt silenced.

M: So true ... I often still feel silenced and I can hear some white
women saying, "You've been involved in the women's movement for a
long time, you always speak up" ... but when they are being racist, I
find myself going through that whole process of building strength, taking
a few deep breaths ... and I often don't end up challenging a racist
remark.

R: I find myself reacting the same way many times. Whether I
challenge or ignore a racist remark, I'm left feeling sickened. What
thought process do you go through?

M: It's the same thing ... I don't want to create conflict or I don't
want to do the educating ... *and* ... It's the SHOCK! It's not about
offending anyone ... it stuns me, the ignorance. I think, "Don't these
women know me?"

R: So we remain silent and that leaves us feeling, once again, powerless, and I often feel defeated.

M: That's where the support from the women of colour group is so
important for me ... that we don't internalize this.

R: It's becoming increasingly difficult for me to work with the women's movement ... it comes back to what you said ... "I thought they knew me." It's a movement that doesn't understand us ... what's worse is that it now knows all the appropriate rhetoric and uses it!

M: What angers me is that white women often think they are fooling us by using the rhetoric ... and we continue to be polite. Perhaps I'm generalizing and should say, I continue to be polite."

R: I think it's safe to assume that a lot of us continue to be polite because we don't want to spend any more energy on educating white women. For some of us, we have no alternatives. With all its problems, it's still a community of women that I need to live and work with. In an anthology by Pacific/Asian lesbians, one woman writes, "I find myself the only lesbian in a group of Asians, and the only Asian in a group of lesbians." I understand that feeling, and so my search for community continues.

M: I continue to work in the women's movement because the goal for me, still, is to have an all-inclusive women's movement. I don't want to leave the movement; I want to change it. Each woman has to decide for herself how much she can give and maybe one day both or one of us will renounce feminism entirely ... maybe never ... Right now, there are white women I can work with. I also think there are many white women who don't realize that one of the goals of the Women of Colour Collective is to work towards an all-inclusive feminism. We have not "left" the women's movement.

R: It is vital for me to work with women of colour because it's the "safest" space for me. Just recently I went to a workshop on lesbian feminism. In a room of thirty I was the only lesbian of colour. I felt silenced and remember thinking I don't want to identify as a lesbian — there's no community for me.

M: That's a problem ... even in the Women of Colour Collective, we are all middle-class, heterosexual women of colour.

R: Is it a problem?

M: For me, yes it is. My vision is of an all-inclusive women's movement. That has to begin with our collective.

R: That heterosexual, middle-class collective is still "safer" for me than the all white lesbian group. It's a constant trading off — homophobia or racism. I've always believed there are no hierarchies of oppression but I have to say at this point in my life I have more energy to deal with the homophobia from my sisters of colour than with racism. I can deal with the anger and fear that arises from hearing homophobic comments but when I hear racist remarks from women/lesbians, the feeling of pain and powerlessness is incomparable.

M: White people don't acknowledge or recognize how sensitive we are to racism ... the hurt.

R: I have to constantly remind white women that there are no degrees ... racism is racism is racism.

The Politics of Reaction or the Politics of Inclusion

"The June Callwood Phenomenon"
Spring 1993[23]

In the March issue of *Toronto Life* magazine, an article by Elaine Dewar entitled "Wrongful Dismissal" had as its intent, to explain why June Callwood had left Nellie's, a women's shelter in Toronto.

The story put forward a wide range of theories and assumptions which concluded that "angry anti-racists drove June Callwood from Nellie's, ... because she couldn't share her white skinned privilege."

Elaine Dewar attempts to link June Callwood's resignation to a take-over by black women of not only Nellie's but other services and political positions in Toronto.

As part of her article Ms Dewar names many individuals and organizations including the Coalition of Women of Colour Working in Women's and Community Services, the Communist party, the Canadian Research Institute for the Advancement of Women, Clarissa Chandler (a US facilitator), and Carolann Wright, an employee of Women's Help in Women's Hands and a member of the Coalition.

The article focuses at some length on Carolann, her personal and professional life, and anybody she has been associated with throughout her life. Sweeping assumptions and unsubstantiated allegations are made throughout the article.

Elaine Dewar's article is consistent with the media's response to the Nellie's story, which has been to feel sympathy for June Callwood and outrage at those ungrateful black women who challenged her. As Peter Gzowski, host of *CBC's Morningside*, put it, he felt women's groups should be working on issues such as breast cancer, which he sees as "an issue that presumably would embrace all women in the way that perhaps the issue of racism would not."

The publishers of *The Womanist* do not believe that the mainstream media have dealt fairly with the story at Nellie's.

The question of why a group of women — some white, some women of colour — could not agree on what problems they were having and how to resolve them remains to be answered. On one point, we do agree with Elaine Dewar: it does relate to power, politics and money. It relates to the power to be able to access the media and tell your story. Ask yourself, whose story have you heard? June Callwood has had a forum in the *Toronto Star*, *Saturday Night*, *Toronto Life*, *CBC Morningside* and many other media. Have you heard from the 20 women that Elaine Dewar has named in the article. Why not?

It is about an emerging politic — the politics of gratitude where women are expected to be eternally thankful to women who came before

23. Joan Riggs, ed. *The Womanist no. 1 (Spring 1993)*, 20.

and manifest that through not questioning, not challenging, not inviting change in these women and society. The politics of gratitude is about power — about who gets to define the world, decide what needs to change and when.

The response to a staff member's request at the Board of Nellie's to discuss race, procedures and values was met by June Callwood as, "Are you the same Joan Johnson all these women helped?" Joan responded by saying, in effect, "you want me on my knees forever."

What was June Callwood expecting when they helped Joan Johnson? Blind loyalty from a Joan Johnson that they constructed as the black immigrant woman victim that they helped?

Why was the discussion of race and values construed as "White women being pushed out of the movement"? Don't white women, even the ones that helped start some of our organizations, need to change?

Finally, this issue is about money and about who do we trust to have control over the money in women's organizations.

Why is it that, when Women of Colour begin to join a Board in significant number, maybe even as the majority, suddenly there are questions about financial management? Why are Women of Colour assumed to be less competent, less skilled? Why is it that their perspective is "skewing" the financial priorities of the organization while white women's perspective on money is "neutral"? Are critics like Elaine Dewar trying to suggest that all the previous boards of white women didn't have their own agenda? And that it wasn't influenced by race?

We at *The Womanist* believe there is much more to be said on this question. The article that follows is an important contribution from someone who has been involved in it for many years. We plan to continue the discussion in future issues.

"It's Not Just About Burning Crosses"
Spring 1993[24]

I received a call from a white woman who said she had just read the *Toronto Life* article ...

Her second question, "didn't I feel I owed women like June Callwood some loyalty (in other words why wasn't I grateful), because it was June Callwood and women like her that marched the halls of Parliament in the name of women's equality?" I was struck by the anger in her statement. She actually believed that I, a seventh generation African Canadian, could owe anything to anyone other than the Africans that came before me. In particular my African mothers.

I pointed out to her that during the time that June Callwood and those like her were marching the halls of Parliament, my mother and grandmother were ensuring my very survival, by cleaning the homes and raising the children of those who were marching the halls. Our very

24. Carolann Wright, *The Womanist* 4, no. 1 (Spring 1993) 21.

survival in Canada depended on their ability to fight racism as a community of African people.

The comment "shouldn't I be grateful" was symptomatic of what is at the heart of the Nellie's issue. It's at the heart of issues in many organizations, either mainstream or community based, the politics of gratefulness. It is why people like June Callwood can never be challenged without a hue and cry. Their good works are like an immunization against criticism or challenge on their racism. It is a dangerous precedent when we immediately exonerate people based on their good works of the past, and the good works they may do in the future, and not on how they are conducting themselves in the everyday interactions with Black people and People of Colour.

What is even more racist is that the white media have decided, as in the case of Nellie's, when we "have gone too far" as Black people. They decided to redefine racism so that it is more palatable for Canadians. When Black people speak of racism in Canada, when we demonstrate, when we rally, when we protest, we are coming from the immediate, everyday realities of our lives.

Racism is talked about by whites in Canada as an American phenomenon, something that they as white liberals could never be guilty of; Canadians are not as crude as Americans, who in the sixties hosed down people in the street, set dogs on demonstrators and lynched Black men and raped Black women. Canadians don't do that, therefore we aren't racist ...

The news coverage of Nellie's only ... points out [the] ability [as a white person] to rewrite and rename reality. It seems a bit ironic that the very person who was named in Nellie-gate as being inappropriate as a board member because of racist actions and statements — June Callwood, has now used her media power to exploit the pain of Black women and Women of Colour.

No truer horror is experienced than the one of meeting the face of the halo-laden victim on the cover of a magazine looking beleaguered and worn out from the daily task of fighting off Women of Colour. We are still expected to explain ourselves regarding this issue, not because of the issue of racism but because of who was accused, which brings us to a very dangerous place in the fight against inequity.

What has received no coverage at all is the fact that Women of Colour have been emotional wrecks as a result of this issue; it has prevented the employment of some, and for those who remain employed in mainstream organizations it have made them almost apologetic about bring forth issues of racism. Many have been accused of making this "Nellie's Issue": if they do raise the issue of racism. It is important to note that the only reason that Nellie's received the coverage that it did was because of June Callwood's connection with the media and her need to exonerate herself before the news of her resignation reached the public.

These issues are being grappled with by organizations all over the country without the sensational media coverage ...

I cannot allow white society to tell me how to feel my experiences and how to direct them. A continuation of this would only betray my ancestors and negate my mother's struggle and how she taught me to thrive. It would also keep the needed change from happening. My intention is be consistent in the struggle in support of Black women and Women of Colour and to continue to challenge and make change whenever and wherever necessary.

"Racism: Learning to Change"
Spring 1992[25]

Racism. What does it mean for white feminists? I am looking forward to the day when, in a feminist meeting, someone can say, "Do you think that comment was racist?" and have a discussion which is not charged with anger or judgement.

Just as I was socialized by sexism as I was growing up to believe women were inferior, weak, unreliable, hysterical — you know the list — and just as I was socialized as a lesbian to believe I was (pick one) criminal/evil/crazy, I also learned that as a white person, as an able-bodied, christian-raised anglophone, I was the norm. Ordinary. Unremarkable. Normal.

Socialization into normalcy is just as powerful, and just as pervasive, as the training I got as a woman, and as a lesbian.

I went to my first unlearning racism workshop, given by Gloria Yamato, a black woman from Seattle, in 1987. The experience was very much like one I had when I read my first feminist book, around 1970. Suddenly whole aspects of the world made immediate, and different, sense to me.

Of course I had absorbed the racism of the society, along with its sexism, and homophobia, and so on. Of course racism had twisted, contorted, confused my thinking in the same ways that sexism and homophobia had done. And of course I would need to work systematically to re-learn the world again. That "of course" experience was very liberating for me. But the scrutiny of myself in the world as a white person was both painful, and shameful. And the work of looking at internalized dominance is very difficult.

First of all, nobody talks about internalized dominance precisely because the dominant place is regarded as the normal, ordinary, unproblematic, unexceptional place. The dominant place is the place from which all other people are viewed different. We think "difference" is some quality that lives in other people. And we forget to think about who is doing the thinking.

28. barbara findlay, *The Womanist* 3, no. 1 (Spring 1992), 20-21.

What is normal? Normal-cy is the absence of the abnormal. For example, you wouldn't hear co-workers confiding to each other, "did you know, she's heterosexual," of "Charmaine knew her first husband, and he says her family was Christian." But you might hear someone say, "did you know she's a lesbian?" or, "Charmaine knew her first husband, and he says her family was Jewish."

In referring to people, we speak of the way in which they are not part of the norm. So you have white men who write being called "writers"; white women who write being called "women writers," and black women who write being called "black women writers."

The stylistic convention is that unless someone is noted for being different then she/he is Norm-al. Think about characters in novels, where the writer must give the reader all the relevant details about her characters. It is very very rare for a character to be described as "white"; if she/he is not though, the fact of their colour is remarked upon.

Marilyn Frye, a white writer, says, "it was breathtaking to discover that in the culture in which I was born and reared, the word 'woman' means white woman, just as we discovered before that the word 'man' means male man."

Since 1987, I have been part of Alliance of Women Against Racism Etc (AWARE). "Etc." because racism operates along with, and not separate from, other forms of oppression: sexism, anti-semitism, heterosexism, classism, ablebodiedism, ... etc. It is an alliance group of women of colour and white women. We facilitate unlearning racism workshops in teams consisting of a woman of colour and a white woman. We talk about racism, internalized racism, internalized dominance, and how people of colour and white people can work as allies.

As I began to work on racism I paid attention to my own reactions.

I noticed that I did not look people of colour in the eye. I had few people of colour as friends. I read mostly books by white women. I was ignorant of the struggles, the history, the leadership, the issues of (for example) Japanese Canadian people, or disabled people.

Because I was afraid of being called racist, I noticed that I tended to treat people of colour with an exaggerated deference. I found that I wanted to "help," so I would do things like finish the ends of sentences begun by a woman of colour. I was eager to display my bona fide intentions but terrified that I would get it wrong. I felt awkward: I didn't want to be pushy, but I didn't want to seem uncaring or distant.

I knew that my reactions were not just "personal" but were embedded in the racism of the society.

What I noticed about myself and other white people is how much intense shame, guilt and denial there is in talking, writing, and admitting to ways I have learned racism. I did not grow up thinking about myself as racist. I have a deeply embedded Presbyterian antipathy towards Bad People who are racist. Racist people like the Ku Klux Klan.

So although it was liberating intellectually to distinguish between myself and racist training and misinformation I have been taught, at a gut level I was/am still terrified that someone — especially a person of colour — will call me racist, or anti-Semitic, etc. As I thought about the force of my fear, I realized how powerful social denial was operating. It goes: Racists are Bad. I am good. Ergo I am not racist. Flip that over, it goes: If you say what I did was racist, you are saying I am a Bad Person. This makes it very difficult for me to hear that what I did or said was racist.

In fact, we are all good people. We could no more have avoided the racism of this society than we could its sexism. As Antoinette Zanda put it, "It is not our fault we are racist. But it is our responsibility to work on it".

I am struck by how powerful the fear of mistakes, and the sense that we are Bad People, are among white people. This is no accident. This is a very powerfully structured, and socially sanctioned way of preserving the status quo. It is a massive social denial. It is like the denial of wife battering, sexual harassment, child sexual abuse. Only this time, as white women, we participate in the denial.

Think about language. Take my favourite example "women and visible minorities". Think about that phrase – a very common phrase that is usually used to refer to some common experience of oppression. Watch closely. Where in that phrase are women of colour? Are they among the "women," in which case the phrase means "women, and men of colour and other visible minorities"? Or are women of colour among the "visible minorities," in which case the phrase really means "white women and people of colour and other visible minorities"?

And what is a "visible minority"? Is that really a code for people of colour? If not, does it include, for example, people with disabilities? (In which case all over again you have the problem of figuring out where women with disabilities fit). And where are Jewish people? Notice too the phrase is "visible minorities." Insofar as the term is used to refer to people of colour, it is simply inaccurate as a description of the world, where people of colour are a majority. And it subtly imports the idea of legitimized powerlessness. In a democratic system, after all, that's what a minority is.

Or take the phrase "outreach." Outreach is a favourite activity of white feminist organizations. When you do "outreach," where is the centre?

Or take the phrase "You are different from us." Compare it to "We are different from you." Notice the shift in who is not different.

White feminists are very aware of how many women there are in a room, compared to how many men. But we do not notice the numbers of white people compared to the number of people of colour.

Lesbians — but not heterosexual women — look immediately for lesbians in the room. We notice when we are targeted. When we are not, we literally do not notice.

Education. We were educated in a system that lied to us by omitting completely both the facts about, and perspective of, people who are not white men. As a feminist I have been aware of sexist bias for a long time. I automatically look for sexism and correct for it. Yet, I found it very hard to accept that the whole of my education was systematically wrong, mistaken, inaccurate and unreliable.

Canadian society is profoundly racist, just as it is profoundly sexist. Fighting racism means changing laws, instituting affirmative action programs, redistributing the resources of society — including the resources which we, as white feminists, have. But just as we fought sexism in the bedroom as well as in the courts and the legislature, we have to recognize racism at home, where we are. We have to change the ethos of silence about racism. To do that we have to look at how we have been silenced about racism, and break that silence.

If we are to work toward the liberation of all, we have to look both at the ways we are oppressed and the ways we participate in oppression.

Just as we treated the personal as political in doing a feminist analysis of the world, we must treat the personal as political in naming and dealing with our internalized dominance.

Just as we had to work on emotional, intellectual, and political levels in exposing and working against sexism, we will have to do the same to work against our own internalized dominance. In doing that work, we must be gentle with each other as white people. And we must work in alliance with people of colour.

"Making a Commitment to Inclusion"
Ottawa, 1993[26]

I am a feminist because feminism refuses to submit to the brutalization of women, whether it is the "casual" brutality of national politics (as one reporter pointed out), or the not so "casual" brutality of poverty, unemployment, racism and violence.

It is because feminists have a vision, know the world can be different, know that the political process can be different, that I am part of this movement committed to equality.

Today feminism stands at a critical juncture. Either the women's movement will forge ahead under the leadership of the women most marginalized in society, and make its commitment to the politics of inclusion and diversity real.

Or it will be contained within the status quo, as the women who have benefited from the struggles of the past help shut the doors on the

26. Sunera Thobani, *The Ottawa Citizen*, 3 June 1993, A13. Also appeared as "Feminism's New Colors" in *The Vancouver Sun*, 26 May 1993, and as "Why I am a Feminist" in *The Toronto Star*, 3 June 1993, A21.

majority of women who still continue to be excluded and silenced. Women have made some gains in the last 20 years but, by and large, these gains have been of benefit to a minority. It is only when the concerns of women who face the harshest discrimination are addressed that the movement will remain true to its principles of empowerment and equality of all women.

Women of colour have been active inside and outside NAC for decades, demanding to be heard. As NAC faced an attack initiated in Parliament by a Tory MP over my incoming presidency, we understood this to be one form of retaliation for the increased visibility and effectiveness of the organization. As protests were heard, almost entirely from outside the women's movement, about the audacity of an immigrant woman of colour daring to run for the presidency, we also understood this as part of the backlash against feminists, particularly feminists of colour who challenge white domination.

NAC remains committed to the central role we have played in building bridges at the local and national level over the past few years, bringing together organizations of aboriginal women, working women, women of colour, immigrant women, women with disabilities, lesbian women, domestic workers and poor women.

As racism and homophobia increase in society, it is inside the women's movement that we are building unity. As violence against women remains at epidemic levels, NAC member groups have developed our own campaign, including a policy document with recommendations based on the experiences of 20 years of front-line work. As the poverty and unemployment of women increase, NAC remains committed to the struggle for jobs, for pay equity and employment equity, and for ensuring that domestic workers have the same rights as any other group of workers.

As social programs come under increasing attack by the federal government, NAC continues to work within coalitions to stop the erosion of existing programs, to ensure universal access and the implementation of much-needed programs, such as a national daycare. With anti-immigrant sentiments increasing as conditions worsen, the women's movement refuses to be divided ...

The present government has adopted policies which have had a disastrous effect on working women. In the face of the attacks which NAC and other progressive advocacy groups experience, we know it is in our refusal to be pitted against each other that our collective voices will grow stronger ...

When I first attended a NAC annual general meeting, I was the only woman of colour of 33 delegates from BC. This year, a full third of the delegates to the BC regional conference were women of colour. We have learned that, if the women's movement is to have relevance for the lives of women who seek equality, then NAC has to remain committed to opening the doors to women who have had all other doors in society shut in their faces. And, it is these women who understand our society better than those who live in the four walls of their relative privilege.

We are holding the doors open in NAC, and in doing so, we know we can only go from strength to strength.

Chapter 4

Social Policy and Social Services

Marjorie Griffin Cohen

Social policy in Canada has developed based on certain ideas about what is "normal" about life in this country. The male is considered the human archetype and most social institutions are constructed around the male experience as the norm. Whenever women have been considered in some aspects of policy, such as when special allowances have been given in the past to mothers, this was more a recognition of women's deviance from the male norm, than it was a recognition that social policy, social institutions and social services should be constructed in such a way that a wide variety of different experiences can be accommodated.

This chapter will focus on women's attempts to change the state's approach, at the local, provincial and national levels, to social policy and meeting the needs of women.

Social Policy

Investigative social reporting that documented the condition of women was an important initial project of feminism in the late 1960s and the early 1970s. These reports were often referred to as the "horror stories" of feminism. There were several reasons for focusing on women's conditions and the social policies that reinforced their subordination. One was to make visible that which had been kept invisible by social convention: it told the stories people did not want to hear — those that made them uncomfortable. Another was to try to understand what it was about social and economic policy that fostered and promoted unjust and unequal conditions for women. But the main point was to bring about change: women believed that if an injustice was talked about and recognized by enough people, social policy could change and the injustice itself could be eliminated.

So while feminism tried to analyse the structures of contemporary life (the economics and the sexual politics) to uncover the origins of women's oppression and the institutions that perpetuated it, feminism also had a more concrete project. That was to concentrate on the day-to-day experiences of women and how they could be improved: more women seemed to be facing poverty and more children seemed to be without decent care. As women lived longer, they needed financial security in old age, and as the extent of maltreatment of women by men became public, the need for shelters and aid became apparent.

In dealing with issues of poverty, child welfare, health services and housing, feminists were following what appeared to be an old tradition. These issues are women's issues and have long been recognized as the areas that deserve a feminine touch, mainly because they deal with caring and social welfare. Women traditionally have been seen as the "civilizing" influence on society through their demands for the development of a state that would be responsible not only for its traditional functions of raising taxes, moving the mail and making war, but also for addressing social welfare issues.[1] Women throughout the history of this country, and elsewhere, have sought to humanize the cruelest and roughest aspects of the private market economy by recognizing that everything of value could not be provided through exchange on the market or through the private household, and that some services would have to be provided through collective action if they were to meet the needs of those other than the wealthy. So, if health care was to be universally available, it would need to be organized through the state. Similarly, if education was to be available to everyone, it would need to be publicly funded and publicly provided.

Feminist action on social policy that called for improved or new social services certainly followed this tradition. But there was a difference too because part of the feminist analysis of society was the recognition that social policy and programs themselves were a reflection of the gendered and hierarchical nature of society. This analysis emphasized not only the ways in which women were marginalized in the main approaches to social policy, but also the ways in which the state, in the interests of men and capital, was able to gain control over spheres that had traditionally been in women's domain. So, for example, the process of taking education and health care out of the home and placing them under male control in the public sphere, during the late nineteenth and early part of the twentieth centuries was frequently identified as one of the avenues through which women not only lost control over these issues, but also lost status in society.[2]

Despite male control of social policy, women continued their roles as the defenders and developers of what has become known as the "welfare state." Although this sometimes appears to be a contradiction in political focus, feminists have made the distinction between "more of the same" in the development and delivery of social services and how these might be designed to include and better serve women.[3] Whether social policy and social services were instruments of oppression or liberation depended on who was in control and who carried out the programs. When women demanded child care, they were not asking the state to raise their children, but to provide a public structure for child care with parents in control. The primacy of women's taking control over their own services was evident also in women's health clinics, set up for women by women, and in women's co-op housing, rape crisis centres and shelters for battered women.

The early days of the feminist renaissance was a time of optimism about the possibility that new social programs could be developed that would meet some of the needs of women. The late 1960s and 1970s was a period of expansion of the public sector and at least public rhetoric took the humane approach that seemed to recognize both the need for a redistribution of income to lessen inequalities and a need for the expansion of social programs, not only to help the most needy, but also the population in general. During this period new forms of services for women were initiated, and while getting recognition for any specific problem as well as wresting money from the state required amazonian efforts, new institutions were created, sometimes even under feminist and progressive terms of organization.[4] This is not to imply that the state under the control of the Liberal government of Pierre Elliot Trudeau was particularly sympathetic to feminism, but rather that it behaved pragmatically under extraordinary pressure from women for change. The Report of the Royal Commission on the Status of Women was too powerful to be ignored.[5] Women sensed this and were able to point to the government's own report as the basis for some change. Nothing occurred without a struggle, but change was under way and the rhetoric of liberalism was used by women to wrest even meagre resources for improving women's conditions.

But during the twenty-five years under review in this book, a dramatic reversal in approach to public policy and social service delivery occurred. By the mid-1980s social policy objectives did not emphasize the redistributive and universal features of programs. In fact, these features began to be eliminated from social programs. The major shift in policy was a result of the election in 1984 of a Progressive Conservative government with Brian Mulroney as Prime Minister. During the election campaign Mulroney's position on social policy did not seem to differ much from his primary opponent, John Turner. He claimed that the principle of universality in social programs was a "sacred trust" not to be tampered with, and, in what many Canadians considered to be a progressive position on employment, he promised "jobs, jobs, jobs."[6] He even, in a televised debate between the prime ministerial candidates during the election, promised a national child care program.

Not only did none of the promises materialize, but programs that seemed secure because of their popularity with the majority of Canadians began to fade over the ensuing decade. Canadians have been rather smug about the success of collective social programs, particularly when their provision in Canada is compared with the inadequacy of those of the U.S., our primary country for comparison. How, then, were these programs undermined? The erosion has taken place in a politically expedient way. The philosophy of providing medicare or pensions or communications and transportation systems was not a subject of political debate in parliament or during an election. The Tory government did not usually attack social programs head-on, rather, these social programs were changed by a thousand little cuts, or "social policy by stealth" as one policy analyst called it.[7] This is a process that uses technical changes to taxes and transfers to provinces to effect very large changes that simply could not pass public scrutiny, were they debated in Parliament as changes in social programs. They are not only obscure and difficult to understand, but exceedingly complicated to explain. As a result, the public, and particularly the media, simply has not paid attention to what was happening until the deed was done. These changes in social policy have been an integral part of the economic policy changes initiated by the Conservative government and cannot be separated from them.[8] They are related to an ideological shift to the right, a shift that substitutes the notion of collective responsibility with that of individualism and self-reliance. It is on these grounds that government withdrawal from programs has been legitimized. The ability to carry this shift in ideological objectives was also strengthened by the massive campaign of the Conservative government to identify the government debt as the most significant economic problem of the country, one which, it claimed, was fuelled by overspending on social programs.

The strategy has been to focus on the programs that serve specific minority groups first — social assistance, low-income housing and unemployment insurance. As a political strategy, whittling away at these programs, or even eliminating them altogether, as in the case with co-op housing, was effective because rather limited opposition was likely to be encountered, since these programs did not affect everyone. But the universal mainstream programs were not safe, and the gradual underfunding through budget cuts has just as effectively eroded pensions, health care and education. The deficiencies in these programs certainly has been felt by people, but the argument put forward by government and its business allies is that the best remedy to the problems in the delivery of social services is to increasingly privatize all or part of the programs.

Since 1984 women's groups have been on the defensive and have struggled as hard to maintain the provision of social services as they originally worked to get them. The sense of possibility that characterized the 1970s was replaced by pessimism. Proposals for new programs seemed futile, considering the extent to which existing programs were being decimated. Also, there is extreme skepticism about the motives of the state. It seems intent on pursuing a dynamic petrifaction of the system, producing a considerable flurry of activity that purports to be progressive, but that is designed to effect as little change as possible. The day-care proposal by the government is an excellent example of this principle: if the state will do it, it will do it badly.[9] To most day-care advocates, the National Day Care Program was a farce and would have actually provided no more child care spaces than would have occurred without it.

The documents in this section deal with social services that are traditionally seen as social welfare issues, or more specifically, the caring services. But women also recognized that the provision of other kinds of services have marginalized women and so have worked to see that these services also meet the distinct needs of women. Some of these services, such as those dealing with transportation, communication and unemployment insurance will be discussed in other chapters in these volumes.

Poverty and Income Support

The term "the feminization of poverty" was a new way of looking at poor women and also became a way of dramatizing the extent of poverty among women. That women are disproportionately represented among the poor is clear, although it is only relatively recently that this fact was discovered. The extent of poverty among women was "an unexpectedly significant finding in our investigation,"[10] according to the Royal Commission on the Status of Women. What was important about this was the discovery that it was not just a condition of the sick or the old, but was prevalent among women because they were women.

> The women of this country are particularly vulnerable to the hazards of being poor. The relationship between women and poverty is apparent in the average earnings of those who are employed, and is even more obvious when one considers the women who are not in a position to earn incomes of any sort.[11]

The usual assumptions about who would be poor simply did not apply to women — it could happen to anyone. Often it is believed that poor people come from a "culture of poverty," and that the conditions and conditioning of poverty are passed from parents to children. But women didn't have to be from poor families to become poor. In the 1970s in Toronto two-thirds of the mothers receiving social assistance grew up in two-parent families who were never poor.[12] Also, poverty was not just a condition of those who either could not or would not work for pay. While the majority of poor women did not have jobs, many of them, in fact in 1986 a full 37% of poor women, were working poor.[13]

Women have a good chance of experiencing poverty at some point in their lives, particularly if they have children or live to be old.[14] If they

Jerry Sevier Courtesy: *Chatelaine*

This cartoon is from the May 1973 issue of Chatelaine. *Plus ça change...*

are disabled or native, they are almost certain to be poor. Poverty in this respect is a relative condition also; it is one thing to be poor as a student with the probability of a future that is full and secure. It is something else altogether when one is disabled, unable to work and experiencing increased illness because of poverty. Joanne Doucette, the author of a brief on disabled women and the welfare system, provides a horrific example of how a simple procedure that is readily available to anyone who can afford dental aid is denied those receiving social assistance because it is not considered essential for them to live. Because an inexpensive dental treatment (a fluoride rinse) was not covered by social assistance payments, Joanne Doucette experienced a degeneration of her jaw that will require painful, life-threatening surgery that ultimately will cost the state much more than the original treatment. Joanne received only $3.50 more each month from social assistance than she had to pay for rent. As she said, "you either pay your rent or you eat adequately. You cannot do both." Of course, the health of disabled people deteriorates even further when they are poor.[15]

The state's role in keeping the poor in a state of poverty is a consistent theme of poverty groups, as Joanne Doucette's brief's title "Institutionalizing Permanent Poverty" suggests, and some groups, like End Legislated Poverty, in Vancouver, place an emphasis in their analysis of poverty on how the state and its institutions not only keep people poor, but actually make them poor. The state makes people poor when it institutes policies that accept high levels of unemployment as inevitable: if some people are not allowed to work, they certainly cannot provide for themselves. The state makes people poor when it permits employers to pay some workers less than a living wage. The state makes people poor when it perpetuates an under-valuation of some forms of labour, particularly the labour involved in caring for and raising children.

Social Assistance

Once people are poor, the institutions that have been developed to "help" almost guarantee that they remain poor. The inadequacy of social assistance benefits has consistently been a problem throughout the last twenty-five years. But particularly absurd have been the built-in disincentives to improve one's earning power while on social assistance. In Toronto in 1974 a group of poor mothers organized a "Mother Led Union" to try to change some of these most egregious features of the system.[16] They could never get out of poverty while the government took back 75 per cent of everything they earned at part-time jobs, over a certain minimum level. In 1974 women on social assistance were allowed to earn $24 a month plus $12 for each child under age 16. So, for example, a mother with two children could earn $48 a month, but after she reached this limit, the government would take back 75 per cent of any additional earnings.[17] The Mother Led Union wanted a modest change — that the government take back only half of their earnings! They also wanted to receive as much for their mothering work as foster mothers. In Ontario, when newborn children were placed in foster care the mothers received $85 a month, while mothers on social assistance received only $25.00.[18] The Mother Led Union demanded that motherwork be recognized as real work, which is why they formed a union. The fear of provoking thousands of mothers to strike and to leave their children in the offices of provincial legislators did bring some change, but the problem of poor women with children is chronic. As a *Toronto Star* article in 1989 pointed out, most single mothers in Canada are still poor.[19]

Family Allowance

The few other social programs that could help women escape poverty have been badly undermined since Brian Mulroney's government has been in power. The family allowance, or "baby bonus," has been more than a symbolic gesture of the cost of motherhood — it could make all the difference between coping and being hungry. The monthly $93.81 Debbie Hughes-Geoffrion received because she had three children provided food for her family for three weeks.[20] This program, which began in 1944, was the first universal social program to be instituted in Canada. This money was sent to mothers each month, regardless of their incomes. Eventually when it became a taxable benefit, it was assigned as income for tax purposes to the largest income earner in the family (usually fathers), so that if the "family income" was large, the highest income earner would be taxed. This was, in a small way, a redistribution of money within the family from males to females. To many women, even in families with relatively decent incomes, the family allowance was the only money they could call their own. It was a very important program that women across the country fought desperately to maintain, in what unfortunately has been a losing battle.[21] First, through a scheme called de-indexing, the value of the allowance diminished each year. But in 1992 the government decided to eliminate the family allowance altogether.[22] Brian Mulroney, when first elected, defined his government's goal of eliminating the universal delivery of social programs. In doing this, he raised the "problem" of rich people getting more than they deserved: "Are we making proper use of taxpayers' money by giving a bank president who makes $500,000 or $600,000 a year a baby bonus? Should that money not be more properly used to assist someone who desperately needs help?"[23] There is certainly something disingenuous about this example, since there are *no* female bank presidents in Canada. The concern about the rich getting more than they deserve also is not credible, since through changes in the tax system, the richest in Canada had $2,330 a year more in disposable income in 1991 than they did in 1984, while the tax burden for the working poor increased.[24]

Minimum Wage

One of the most important income measures that can make the difference between whether a woman lives in poverty is the minimum wage. More than any other single program, the minimum wage deals with those at the margins of poverty and determines what those margins will be. Since women are disproportionately found among minimum wage-earners, any change in the value of the minimum wage has a greater effect on women's earnings than on men's. Since 1975 the real minimum wage has decreased by between 20 and 30 per cent, depending on the province. The real minimum wage has decreased because for most of this period inflation rates have been high while minimum wage rates have risen only slightly. The minimum wage is now significantly below what is required to keep a family out of poverty: a single parent with one child working for the minimum wage will earn only 65 per cent of the poverty line. If that parent lives in British Columbia, her earnings will be only 56 per cent of the poverty line.[25] The minimum wage is now so low that even single people with no children working full-time, full-year at the minimum wage will live in poverty.

The problem of the eroding value of the minimum wage is compounded for women because in many provinces some types of work in which women predominate are governed by a lower minimum wage than other kinds of work. While the two-tiered minimum wage is usually justified because it applies to young people who, it is argued, would be unattractive as workers if employers were required to pay them the normal minimum wage, the lower minimum wage also applies to domestic cleaners, nannies and people who receive tips in restaurants. Women's groups have noted that raising the minimum wage would do much more for improving women's overall wage rates than the elaborate pay equity programs that have been initiated by some governments. Yet any attempts to restore the value of the minimum wage are vigorously resisted by business groups and their academic supporters. They tend to argue not only that businesses cannot afford a higher minimum wage, but also that the very groups it was designed to help would be at a disadvantage because if employers had to pay them more, they wouldn't hire them at all.[26]

Unless women are on social assistance, or are perceived as dependents of the state, their poverty goes unnoticed. Even the traditional appeal of many poverty groups is more likely to focus on "child poverty" and "family poverty" in a way that makes the poverty of women invisible. As Jean Swanson of End Legislated Poverty points out, for every poor child, there is a poor mother and by focusing only on poor children it is possible to ignore the fact that the very poverty of children arises in most cases because of the poverty of their mothers.

Welfare State

The solution to poverty is to eliminate the conditions that give rise to gross inequalities in our society. This was the idea of the "welfare state," but it is an idea that has degenerated from a belief that the state should be responsible for how well its citizens fare, to one that now sees welfare as state hand-outs to the unfortunate or the lazy.

The institutions of the welfare state are not only needed by the poor. Decent and universal medical care, pensions, inexpensive transportation and communication systems, affordable housing, work at reasonable wages and adequate child care are not services that are needed just by the poor (although they certainly do need them) but are needed by all in order to provide a decent way of life and to enable people to take care of themselves. Also, many women live in a state of near-poverty. For these women the provision of more generalized social programs in a universal way is the significant difference that keeps them from falling into the category of the truly poor.

Pensions

If one asks almost any young woman about the pension plan where she works, she will likely know little, if anything, about how it works; how much her employer pays; whether it is "vested" and she can take her full share if she leaves that job; or how much income she will have from it in old age. Thinking about pensions is an old person's task, and taking a job because it has a good pension scheme is about the last thing in many women's minds when they begin their work lives. But, we will all be old eventually (if we're lucky) and will have to live on whatever pension scheme we either were or were not a part of in our twenties and thirties. Many women, like Judith B. of Victoria, B.C., will reach their mid 40s doubtful of whether they will have enough money to cope, having just twenty years to make contributions to a pension scheme.[27] Her life-pattern was typical: when first married and while her children were small, she worked at jobs that either did not provide pensions or did not allow them to be transferred when workers moved. When she divorced in the early 1970s, she was not entitled to any portion of her husband's pension credits.

Most women who work are not covered by private pension schemes. But even if they are covered, they will not receive the same benefits as men because benefit levels for both public and private employment-based schemes are calculated according to contributions of employers and employees based on the level of earnings of the worker.[28] Since women, on average throughout the period covered by this book, earned between 60 and 66 per cent of the wages of men, their pension benefits are commensurably lower. The inequalities women face as workers are carried through in retirement.

The extent of women's poverty in old age has become a national disgrace. Of the elderly poor, over 70 per cent are women, and women's chances of being poor when old are very high. According to the chart listed in the document section of this book, about 45 per cent of women living alone who are over 65 are poor. Women's poverty in old age is directly related to the poor provision of pensions for them. While few women who worked for pay receive pensions, no women who spent their lives working in the home receive work-related pensions. These are the women most likely to spend the last years of their life in extreme poverty. The description by Mary S. of what it means to live on the government's old age pensions is grim indeed.[29] There is enough to live on, but that is all: "It's hating having to buy toilet tissue or soap or toothpaste, because you can't eat it."

All Canadians over 65 years of age receive the Old Age Security (OAS) pension. By the end of 1989 this was $337.04 a month.[30] Until the 1991 Budget, this pension was indexed so that when inflation rose, the value of the pension did not deteriorate. In the first budget of the Mulroney government in 1985, Finance Minister Michael Wilson tried to partially de-index this pension, which would have made its real value decline every year the inflation rate was above 3 per cent. However, strong opposition from seniors' groups prevented this. Over time, however, and after having successfully de-indexed the family allowance, the government had its way and OAS was partially de-indexed.

For old people who have no other income than the OAS, the federal government provides a Guaranteed Income Supplement (GIS). By the end of 1989 this was $400.53 a month for a single pensioner and $521.76 a month for a two-pensioner couple, if they qualified for the maximum amount. The two programs combined (OAS plus GIS) would not give a single person enough income to live above the poverty line. The "poverty gap" for a single person living in a city in 1989 was $3,393 a year.[31]

As can be seen from the recommendations proposed by the National Action Committee on the Status of Women (NAC), a variety of changes would need to be made to eradicate poverty for the elderly.[32] Among these was the call for a pension for homemakers, or more specifically a change to the Canadian and Quebec Pension Plans (CPP/QPP) to include women who did not work for pay. The CPP/QPP are run by governments as pension plans for workers that are financed by contributions from both employers and employees. The proposal to include "housewives" in these pensions became the subject of much discussion and debate as the result of the efforts of women like Louise Dulude of NAC, who felt strongly that women who worked in the home should be treated as workers, and that the people they work for (either the public, if they had children, or their husbands if they didn't have children) should contribute to the plans on their behalf. Many groups, such as trade unions, did not support this proposal, mainly because it called for men, rather than the state or employers, to pay for women's pensions. The unions argued that a better plan would be to increase the value of the OAS to at least the poverty level. Other women objected to the idea of a "homemakers'" pension because they believed it would exclude part-time homemakers and women who work full-time in the workplace, but have either no or inadequate pensions.[33]

In the early 1980s when the debate about homemakers' pensions was raging, the possibility that it might actually happen seemed real enough. As all social programs are now under attack, and the value of existing federal government pension schemes have been eroded, ways of eliminating the poverty of old women through pension schemes seem more remote than ever.

Living Spaces: Housing, Hostels, and Shelter

Finding safe and decent places for women to live has become a serious problem as more women are living independently from men. The social facts of women living longer, raising their children as single parents and living alone or with other women, in themselves are not problems or cause for concern. But they are often treated as "social problems" because these women are living in ways that do not conform to how our social institutions have been designed.[34] Our society has constructed cities, houses, schools and other institutions as though the very existence of individuals who live outside the nuclear family is an anomaly. Therefore, as women live longer, adequate housing for the aged becomes an issue; as more teenage women decide to keep their babies, they need special kinds of housing with special kinds of support; as more women leave abusive relationships, more shelters are needed; and as more women live alone or with each other or with their young children, they need places that are welcoming and safe. Housing is an issue of class, gender, age, sexual preference and race. As the documents in this section show, women are consistently discriminated against in housing when they do not live with men.[35] Adult-only buildings are still legal in some areas and the "preference" of landlords for "normal" tenants means that old women, lesbians, women with many children and women of colour have an even narrower selection of housing options than other women living without men. But most of all, housing is an issue of class. With money, housing is not a problem and distinct or different living arrangements can be bought, but without it, differences can only be accommodated through special planning and specific housing programs.

Creating safe places for women in desperate circumstances became a priority for many women's groups throughout the country in the 1970s. While some women were leaving abusive relationships, many more were remaining in them because of the overwhelming obstacles they encountered when trying to leave. The most serious obstacle was having no place to go. Publicity about the truly brutal conditions women endured because there were no alternatives when they were poor and had to feed, clothe and house children, became the impetus that finally prompted government agencies and charities to fund women's attempts to help each other. Women's hostels, like Nellie's in Toronto that opened in 1974 as a place for temporary refuge for battered women, were a first step for many women in redirecting their lives.[36] The hostels were almost always under-funded and did not provide permanent housing, but they did give battered women a place to go and get support in pursuing independent lives. The experience of women in the Cape Breton Transition House indicates the overwhelming need for a safe place for these women and their children.[37] But as the Northern Women's Centre noted,

Hinda Avery Courtesy: *Women and Environments*

Sitka, a women-initiated housing co-op, in Vancouver. It is owned and occupied by forty-two women.

simply having shelter and food was not the "be all and end all" in crisis situations.[38] What was important about transition houses, as the Cape Breton women emphasized, was being with women who had had similar experiences and being supported by a sympathetic staff.

Finding a permanent place to live has been a persistent problem that some women have tried to solve through non-profit co-op housing. Many women find homes in existing cooperatives, but some have tried to work together to create cooperatives specifically designed for women with their needs in mind. The first was the Joint Action Coop in Regina, which was incorporated in 1972 specifically to provide housing for single women.[39] The first specifically feminist co-op was the Constance Hamilton project in Toronto, which admitted its first residents in 1982. Although the idea of co-op housing has great appeal to women, the difficulties involved in actually building projects has meant that this route has not been the hope for solving women's housing crisis that some thought.[40] There are still fewer than twenty women's co-ops in Canada, and they provide few housing units for women: most are quite small and the average woman's co-op houses thirty people.[41] This will not improve over time either because in the 1992 Federal Budget, the Mulroney government eliminated the cooperative housing program altogether.[42]

More recently women's groups have tried to expand activity in the area of housing to look at other issues and housing needs for other groups. The desperate plight of beaten women or single, poor women with children often overshadowed the real need for a place to live for teenage girls and other single women. As a 1983 *Globe and Mail* article shows, traditional social services that are supposed to help the homeless simply are unequipped and unprepared to deal with homeless single women.[43] But other issues, such as sexual harassment by landlords have also begun to surface as issues to be talked about and circumstances to be changed.[44] Since housing is one of the most basic issues of life, the inability to find safe, decent, affordable housing has become a political issue of major proportions. As with many issues that women have identified as a "woman's issue," the more we know about women's circumstances, the more we know we will need to rely on collective and imaginative solutions to solve the problems. Many women's housing needs clearly will not be met by the normal, private housing market.

Care for Children

The demand for organized, universal, state-funded child care has probably involved the action of more women than any other single issue in the women's movement.[45] This is because most women, at one time or another, confront the very serious problem of having their children properly cared for while they are working outside the home.

Between the late 1960s and the present, the working conditions of women changed dramatically, yet social institutions have remained amazingly unresponsive to these changes.[46] As economic changes became more visible, the myth that women were "choosing" to work for pay was exposed. Women knew that if their families were to maintain a reasonable standard of living, they had to earn money. The fact of mothers working outside the home changed a great deal of what was considered "normal" about family life. Mom might not be around when the kids got home from school, and she might not even be around when the babies were very small. This raised all kinds of questions about who was responsible for the children. Was child care just a woman's problem? Was the mother, as the primary parent, a condition to be maintained for all time? Did society have any responsibility for seeing that children received proper care?

While many people believed that the shift of women's locus of work from inside to outside the home signalled the demise of the family and its most cherished institution (mothering), many others saw that it indicated new possibilities for a different kind of family, one that was based on shared parenting between mothers and fathers or one that extended the notion of what constituted the family altogether. The new day-care centres that sprang up in places like university campuses in the late 1960s and early 1970s made conscious efforts to explore new forms of raising children.[47] Children were not just to be taken care of, but rather day-care was to be a community experience organized around the developmental needs of the child. Rooted in the expansive notion of what early childhood education should be, was the idea of developing both a non-hierarchical family, one where shared parenting occurred, and a state that was enabling, but non-intrusive.

Mike Phillips Courtesy: *The Canadian Tribune*

*Demonstrations demanding provincial funding for day-care centres,
like this one at Queen's Park in Toronto, 1981, failed to achieve their
goal of universal child care.*

State funding for parent-controlled child care centres located within
the community was usually seen as preferable to developing child care
centres in the workplace. The concern of many women's groups was
that employers would gain even more control over women's lives if they
also had control over their children. It was feared that it would be
difficult for women to leave their jobs or go on strike if their children's
welfare would be implicated in any way. The location of day-care and
who should fund it, ideally, was the subject of much debate among

feminists. Some unions tried to find ways in which workplace day-care would be acceptable and specifically negotiated to provide day-care on the job. This usually meant that when child care was set up in the workplace, it was not organized or run by the employer, although the employer would be responsible for part or all of the costs, as in the case of the day-care centre at Simon Fraser University[48]

In some ways, the debates about day-care that took place in the early period of the feminist renaissance seem amazingly optimistic. The lack of progress in this is so striking that now the women's movement would undoubtedly welcome any new day-care centre, regardless of its location. According to NAC's *Review of the Situation of Women in Canada 1991*, the proportion of children with access to licensed child care (at 12 per cent of all children under 13 years of age) remained the same from 1977 to 1987. So despite all of the statistics gathered to show the tremendous need for the creation of more day-care spaces, all that had been done over this time was to maintain the status quo.[49]

Without a national child care scheme that would not only provide money but would also set standards for appropriate care, the establishment of child care centres remained a provincial responsibility. This resulted not only in very poor provision of child care, but extreme variability in accessibility across the country. So much depended on the political views of a provincial or municipal government. In Newfoundland, for example, the minister responsible for social services, Charles R. Brett, believed that working mothers contribute to juvenile delinquency, so he was against day-care. Unsurprisingly, Newfoundland has the lowest day-care availability in the nation.[50]

Throughout the country, those living in urban areas have greater access to child care than those who live in rural or remote areas. The work schedule of farm women often means that they are in the field throughout the day, for at least part of the year, but care for their children is virtually non-existent. Other workers need child care for unusual hours and the normal operating hours of day-care centres from eight or eight-thirty to five-thirty or six simply do not suit their needs. For example, women working in fish plants often work intensively for just a few months a year. In canneries in B.C., sometimes the workforce operates around the clock with two twelve-hour shifts. The child care needs of these workers are distinct. Also, as the brief from women on mother's allowance shows, women who do not have paid jobs in the workforce also need child care since they too must sometimes be away from their children.[51]

These special needs led to the demand for twenty-four-hour child care to be available free to all who needed it. Child care is seen by many as a logical extension of the provision of public education and health care, and as such, should be universally available.[52] Of course, the call for twenty-four-hour child care was roundly criticized by anti-feminists who used this demand as proof that women were abandoning their children to institutionalized care. The horror stories of neglected children and the high incidence of sickness in day-care centres were told to discourage the proliferation of child care spaces, not to convince governments of the need for more funding for increased spaces and better care.

The biggest news in the child care world was a non-event. Child care advocacy groups and the women's movement had long called for a national child care policy that would be affordable, government-supported and provide universally accessible child care for those parents who needed it. In the 1984 election Brian Mulroney promised the women of Canada that his government would create a national child care program. During his first term nothing materialized, but the Conservatives, again in the 1988 election, said they would institute the program soon after the election was over. But the national child care program that was long promised and much worked on didn't happen. The scheme that was ultimately unveiled by the federal government soon after the election was roundly criticized by all child care advocacy groups, but rather than changing the program to satisfy these objections, the government withdrew the program altogether. In order to give the illusion that something was being done to help in the care of the nation's children, instead of creating new spaces in child care centres, various types of changes to taxes were instituted. As the *Toronto Star* editorial shows, the only beneficiaries would be upper-income families who receive the most from tax breaks.[53]

Sometimes all of the issues of help for children are bound together, as in the case of providing services for teenage mothers at Jessie's in Toronto.[54] The services for children who have children were virtually non-existent until this centre, which is primarily a charity although partially funded by various levels of government, was established. The limited resources of the organization could provide some important forms of child care for both the mothers and their children, but until recently other even more significant forms of care remained absent. For example, sixteen- and seventeen-year-old mothers were not eligible for subsidized housing and as a result many would spend as much as two-thirds of their income on rent. This meant they were forced to live in unsuitable quarters such as basement rooms without plumbing or cooking facilities. The stress of inadequate housing for very young mothers is something that compounds an already difficult situation. While organizations like Jessie's have been able to relieve some of the stress, the people involved realized that until very basic living needs were met, the conditions under which these new babies were raised would not be good. When, in 1991, Jessie's built a new counselling centre with sixteen units of non-profit housing, its efforts were blocked by one of their neighbours. Fortunately, the courts ruled that the neighbour's thwarting actions were a "demonstration of sheer cussedness," and construction was allowed to continue.[55]

Jessie's is a non-profit charitable organization established in recognition of the large number of teenaged parents who were struggling to raise their children without adequate support.

Public policy is critical for providing support even for women who want to care for their children themselves. The issue of paid leave from work for birthing mothers and new fathers has not been resolved easily or well in this country. As chapter five will show, discrimination in social policy against pregnant women has not been considered a form of sex discrimination in this country until very recently. Women about to give birth had little assurance that they could return to their jobs, and they could count on an almost certain decline in income. Canada's leave and benefit provisions for birthing mothers provided through the Unemployment Insurance Act are not generous, in comparison with provisions made in other countries of the world. But even these meagre allowances were threatened as a result of a court case in which a man claimed that the federal government was practicing sex discrimination because it did not provide parental benefits for fathers under the Unemployment Insurance Act. While women's groups like NAC had long called for paid parental leave so that fathers could also participate in the caring for young children, they were alarmed at the possibility of the whole issue of paid leave for fathers being resolved through the reduction of the money and time available for birthing mothers.[56]

The inadequacy of state support has been the focus of much child care advocacy work. But for native people the focus, rather, has been on the intrusive and oppressive role of the state in maintaining practices that amount to trafficking in children. The federal government has empowered provincial governments to take native children from their homes and place them in foster (usually non-native) care in other communities. These removals are fully funded by the federal government at a cost of about $5,000 a year.[57] In contrast, according to the Assembly of First Nations' *Report of the National Inquiry Into First Nations Child Care*, between 1975 and 1989 there was no capital funding for provincial native child care centres. So while the state would fund whites to care for native children, it did not provide the necessary funding so that better care could occur in native communities. The process of removing native children from their communities began in the 1950s and, according to the brief of the Indian Homemakers' Association of B.C., this much-condemned practice not only has not ended but actually has increased since 1981.[58] While provincial governments have the power to remove children from any situation they believe is damaging to the child, the extent to which native children are removed is truly alarming. As the Indian Homemakers' brief shows, in B.C. native children comprise 3 or 4 per cent of all the province's children, yet they account for over half of all the children in the "care" of B.C.'s welfare authority.

Conclusion

The attempt to shift the focus of social services so that women's special needs could be "seen" was a project that could be considered a success for the organized feminist movement. However, this did not mean that gains that had been made early on could be sustained. Under the guise of deficit reduction and targeting only the very poorest, some of the programs that have been or were potentially most enabling for women, have been cut back or eliminated. Because even basic services for those desperately in need are now so inadequate, and in many cases are deteriorating even further, the ability to promote the idea of the worth of the collective provision of social services universally as a legitimate action of government has fallen into oblivion. Women's demands for themselves and their children are now interpreted as demands of a "special interest group." While women are told that governments would like to help the unfortunate more, the priorities are such that in tough economic times, it is "business confidence" that must be strengthened. For some unaccountable reason, business feels more confident when the poor receive less and when inequalities grow. The lesson we have learned during the past twenty-five years is that when times get tough, chivalry raises its ugly head — women and children first!

NOTES

1. See for example, Linda Kealey, ed. *A Not Unreasonable Claim: Women and Reform in Canada 1880s–1920s* (Toronto: The Women's Press, 1979).
2. See for example, Barbara Ehrenreich and Deirdre English, *For Her Own Good* (N.Y.: Doubleday, 1979).
3. Gillian Pascall, *Social Policy: A Feminist Analysis* (London: Tavistock, 1986), 25.
4. The types and organization of these institutions will be discussed in later sections.
5. Canada, *Report of the Royal Commission on the Status of Women in Canada* (Ottawa: Information Canada, 1970).
6. No government in Canada, unlike many other western governments in the post-war period, has ever been committed to full employment as a policy objective. [Ramesh Mishra, *The Welfare State in Capitalist Society* (Toronto: University of Toronto Press, 1990), 17.]
7. Gratton Gray, "Social Policy by Stealth," *Policy Options* 11, no. 2 (March 1990), 17-29.
8. These issues are more fully discussed in the chapter on Economic Policy and Issues in Volume II.
9. See also the analysis of the Employment Equity Act in the chapter on employment in Volume II.
10. Canada, *Report of the Royal Commission on the Status of Women in Canada* (Ottawa: Information Canada, 1970), 331.
11. Ibid.
12. National Council of Welfare, *Women and Poverty* (Ottawa: National Council of Welfare, 1979), 2.
13. Morley Gunderson and Leon Muszynski with Jennifer Keck, *Women and Labour Market Poverty* (Ottawa: Canadian Advisory Council on the Status of Women, 1990), 62.
14. "Women's poverty 'shocking,'" *Toronto Star*, 14 August 1990. See the table, "Portrait of women's poverty," reprinted in the documents section.
15. Joanne Doucette, "Disabled Women and the Social Welfare System: Institutionalizing Permanent Poverty," submission to the Social Assistance Review Committee, 24 November 1986. Permission to reprint denied.
16. Letter from Joan Clark, chairperson, Mother Led Union, to Women's Groups, 1 October 1974, reprinted in the documents section.
17. The conditions for retaining earnings actually deteriorated in some provinces so that by the end of the 1980s although women could earn up to $300 a month depending on the province, everything earned above this level was taxed back. This made the marginal tax rate of welfare recipients higher than that of the highest income earner in Canada. [Gunderson, Muszynski, Keck, *Women and Labour Market Poverty*, 191.]
18. "Angry mothers plan to abandon children on legislators' laps," *Globe and Mail*, 24 August 1974.
19. Leonard Shifrin, "Jobs alone can't help female poor," *Toronto Star*, 11 December 1989.
20. "Family allowance rally takes 'no cutbacks' message to Ottawa," *Feminist Action féministe* 1, no.3 (December 1985), reprinted in the documents section.
21. Madeleine Parent, "Family allowances are major issue," *Feminist Action féministe* 1, no. 3 (December 1984).
22. Geoffrey York, "Family allowances come to an end," *Globe and Mail*, 17 July 1992.
23. "PM changes stand on social programs," *Globe and Mail* 10 November 1984, 1, cited in Mishra, *The Welfare State in Capitalist Society*, 74.
24. Lawrence J. Nestman, "Family allowance: investment in Canada's kids," *Globe and Mail*, 27 April 1989. See also "National Economic Issues," Volume II.
25. These figures are based on 1985 data. [Gunderson, Muszynski, Keck, *Women and Labour Market Poverty*, 114.]
26. See for example, Walter Block, "Economic Intervention, Discrimination, and Unforeseen Consequences," in *Discrimination, Affirmative Action, and Equal Opportunities*, eds., W.E. Block and M.A. Walker (Vancouver: The Fraser Institute, 1982).
27. Memo submitted to the Federal Parliamentary Task Force on Pension Reform by the Status of Women Action Group, Victoria, B.C., June 1983, reprinted in the documents section.
28. "Pension Reform: A Women's Issue," Fact Sheet on Women and Pensions, Canadian Advisory Council on the Status of Women, 1982.

29. "Case Four," *Women and Poverty* (Ottawa: National Council of Welfare, 1979), 12, reprinted in the documents section.

30. Figures for the value of pension schemes are taken from the National Council of Welfare, *A Pension Primer* (Ottawa, 1989).

31. Ibid., 11.

32. National Action Committee on the Status of Women, *Pension Reform: What Women Want* (Toronto: NAC, 1983), reprinted in the documents section.

33. For an example of the debate, see Louise Delude, Marie Corbett, "Pensions for Housewives? A Debate," *Status of Women News* 7, no. 3 (June 1982).

34. Gay Alexander, "More Than Just a Roof Over Our Heads: Women & Housing," *Status of Women News* (December 1984), 9.

35. Women's Network Inc., (P.E.I.) "Submission to Special Committee on Legislative Proposals Hearings (Landlord-Tenant Act Rent Review Act)," 5 November 1986, reprinted in the documents section. See also, Vancouver Status of Women, *A Brief Proposing Changes in The Landlord and Tenant Act*, 27 August 1973.

36. Joanne Kates, "A shoulder to cry on," *Globe and Mail*, 7 December 1977, reprinted in the documents section.

37. Joan Bishop, "The Transition House Experience," Cape Breton Transition House, reprinted in the documents section.

38. "Women in Crisis Have a Place," *The Northern Woman Journal* 2, no. 3 (October 1975).

39. Gerda R. Wekerle, "Canadian Women's Housing Cooperatives: Case Studies in Physical and Social Innovation," in *Life spaces: Gender, Houseold, Employment*, ed. by Caroline Andrew and Beth Moore Milroy (Vancouver: University of British Columbia Press, 1988), 108.

40. Hinda Avery, "Sitka Housing Co-operative: Women House Themselves," *Women & Environment* (Winter 1989), reprinted in the documents section.

41. Wekerle, "Canadian Women's Housing Cooperative."

42. Alice de Wolff, "Review of the Situation of Women in Canada 1992" (Toronto: NAC, May 1992).

43. Regina Hickl-Szabo, "Housing Problems for Single Women," *Globe and Mail*, 22 December 1983, reprinted in the documents section.

44. "Test Case in the Making," *NAC Housing Newsletter* 2, no. 2 (Fall 1988), reprinted in the documents section.

45. Status of Women Action and Co-ordinating Council of B.C., "Our Brief on Day Care to All Members of the British Columbia Legislature and to All B.C. Members of Parliament in Ottawa," January 1972, reprinted in the documents section.

46. For a discussion of these changes, see the chapter on employment in Volume II.

47. "The Women's Liberation Campus Community Cooperative Daycare," background paper, Toronto, January 1971, reprinted in the documents section.

48. Janice Pentland-Smith, "Provisions for Women in B.C. Union Contracts," July 1977, copy at Vancouver Status of Women, reprinted in the documents section.

49. NAC, *Review of the Situation of Canadian Women*, February 1991, 7.

50. Martha Muzychka, "Day care in Newfoundland: Nine out of ten have no place to go," *Breaking the Silence* 6, no. 4 (June 1988), reprinted in the documents section.

51. Women on Mothers' Allowance, "Brief on Day Care," Toronto, 6 May 1974, reprinted in the documents section.

52. Canadian Advisory Council on the Status of Women, "Caring for our Children: Summary of the Brief Presented to the Special Committee on Child Care," 10 June 1986, reprinted in the documents section.

53. "Child care policy now a costly farce," *Toronto Star*, 3 May 1989, reprinted in the documents section.

54. "All about Jessie's," CWMA file *Jessie's Centre for Teenaged Mothers*, Toronto, reprinted in the documents section.

55. Joseph Hall, "Teen centre wins fight with bar next door," *Toronto Star*, 5 October 1991, reprinted in the documents section.

56. Marjorie Cohen, "Giving fathers an equal break," *Globe and Mail*, 29 February 1988, reprinted in the documents section.

57. NAC, *Review of the Situation of Canadian Women*, February 1991, 7.

58. Rose Charlie and Kathleen Jamieson, "Assimilation or Genocide? Native Children and the Child Welfare system in B.C.," Indian Homemakers' Association of B.C., 27 March 1986, reprinted in the documents section.

Documents: Chapter 4

Poverty and Income Support

Portrait of Women's Poverty
August 1990, Ottawa [1]

Portrait of Women's Poverty		
Women living alone or with no relatives	*Total*	*Poor*
Under age 65	1,008,000	335,000
65 and over	625,000	274,000
Women living in two-spouse families		
Wives under 65 with children under 18	2,981,000	285,000
Wives under 65, no children under 18	2,344,000	164,000
Wives 65 and over	601,000	34,000
Live-in adult daughters and other relatives	1,244,000	77,000
Single women with children under 18		
Never-married mothers	80,000	60,000
Divorced, separated and widowed mothers	287,000	148,000
Live-in adult daughters and other relatives	73,000	18,000
Other women	759,000	120,000
Total	10,002,000	1,515,000
1987 figures	*Source: National Council on Welfare*	

1. Table reprinted from David Vienneau, "Women's poverty 'shocking.'" *Toronto Star*, 14 August 1990.

Mother-Led Union
Toronto, 1974[2]

Dear Sisters,

The Mother-Led Union is a union of mothers, heads of mother-led families, raising children on family benefits, welfare, or inadequate wages from an outside job. The brief which accompanies this letter outlines our understanding of the problems we struggle with daily in our position as mothers.

In the last year and a half we have worked through acceptable legal channels to bring to the attention of "responsible" social agencies, the urgent necessity to alleviate these problems. We have been to City Hall to meet with the Social Services and Housing Committees of Metro Council. We have met with Social Services critic Eli Martell. We have sent numerous letters and briefs to all three levels of government and have received no positive response. In June, we held a conference for poor women and decided that we need a union to take action to press our demands, which are the following:

- 1) parity with foster parents
  A mother who raises her own child should at least receive as much as a foster parent.
- 2) greater earning capacity
  We demand a reduction in the recoupment figure from 75% to 50%.
- 3) day care
  We feel that women who work in the home are also "workers" and should be entitled to the same rights. We favour a drop-in day care organization where a mother might leave her child for awhile, whether she has to shop, go to the doctor, or just spend some time alone.

We have met informally with Glen Heagle, Minister of Income Security and have set up an October meeting with Rene Brunelle, Minister of Community and Social Services. During the coming months we will continue to write letters and talk with provincial government representatives.

However, we are now extending our efforts to organize as poor mothers for a possible — hopefully unnecessary — strike action. We are presently contacting agencies and organizations throughout Ontario to gather support on the issues raised in the brief.

We are requesting official endorsement in the form of a letter, addressed to Rene Brunelle, Minister of Community and Social Services

2. Joan Clark, CWMA file: Women's Action Group.

with copies to the M.L.U., 84 Augusta Ave. If you would like more information, please call us at 364-8456.

Thank you for your consideration,

Joan Clark, chairperson

"Family Allowance Rally Takes 'No Cutbacks' Message to Ottawa"
December 1985[3]

Two hundred angry women rallied on Parliament Hill Oct. 23 to give a message to Prime Minister Brian Mulroney: leave family allowances alone.

The protest, organized by NAC and coalitions from Ontario and Québec, was against the government's plan to reduce family allowances by cutting out the cost-of-living index for the first three per cent increase each year. According to the government, this move, combined with changes to the child tax credit, would mean the highest benefits will go to the families with the lowest incomes.

But Debbie Hughes-Geoffrion of the National Anti-Poverty Organization, and a member-at-large on the NAC executive, told a reporter: "I have three children and I receive $93.81 a month in baby bonus. For me, that $93 represents at least three weeks' groceries. You keep taking away from that, and at the end of five years, it'll be one week's groceries. I think it's the cruellest thing I've ever seen a government do, making people believe they're getting more when they're not. They'll be getting less."

Of the 211-member Tory caucus in the federal government, only three — all women — showed up at the rally. Organizer Lynn Kaye, NAC Southern Ontario representative asked: "Does this mean men in the Progressive Conservative party are not ready to listen to women and children who come to Parliament?" NAC vice-president Louise Dulude's question: "Are we going to remember in the next election?" was met with a resounding "Yes!" from protesters.

The rally did receive support from Opposition leader John Turner and NDP leader Ed Broadbent ...

"Family Allowances Come to an End"
July 1992[4]

Ottawa – Despite almost unanimous criticism from two dozen expert witnesses, a House of Commons committee has approved a bill to eliminate family allowances and create a new system of monthly payments for low-income families.

---

3. *Feminist Action féministe* 1, no. 3, (December 1985).
4. Geoffrey York, *Globe and Mail*, 17 July 1992.

The legislation, Bill C-80, was approved by the Conservative majority after less than an hour of debate yesterday. The bill will abolish one of the oldest social programs in Canada, a system of baby bonuses that has been paid to Canadian families since 1945.

"It was rammed right by us," Liberal MP David Walker said after the legislation was approved by a 4-3 vote yesterday.

Almost every witness at the committee's hearings had called for drastic changes to the bill, but the Tories refused to permit any amendments. "This has been a sham, a futile process," New Democrat MP Chris Axworthy said. "The government will do what it was going to do from the beginning, without paying any attention to the witnesses at all."

The legislation will allocate $500-million to provide bigger monthly payments for a carefully targeted group of low-income Canadians, beginning in January when the family allowances are abolished.

Critics say the program will create "the illusion of new wealth" for thousands of low-income Canadians in the months leading up to the federal election, which is expected next year. Most recipients will not realize that the bulk of the money is simply a repackaging of existing tax credits, the opponents say.

"Bill C-80 should be thrown in the garbage can," said Sam Snobelen, chairman of a coalition of British Columbia anti-poverty groups.

Even a federal advisory agency, the National Council of Welfare, called for several major amendments to the bill. The program will provide only an extra $500 a year for a selected number of low-income families, and this amount "won't make much of a dent in family poverty," council spokesman Steve Kerstetter told the committee.

The welfare council is supposed to give advice to the federal Health and Welfare Minister, but it was never consulted when the new program was developed, Mr. Kerstetter said.

The committee's chairman, Conservative MP Rene Soetens, said the critics are misunderstanding the bill. "This program is not designed to be the cure-all to every ill that exists in Canada," he said.

"It's a very narrow bill. The witnesses have suggested we've forgotten a whole bunch of people — those on welfare, those earning less than $3,700 a year. I guess it's a fair comment, but this bill wasn't designed to address that group of people."

The new monthly payments "won't change the life of an individual, but it's a step in the right direction," Mr. Soetens said.

Most witnesses, however, were scathing in their criticism of the bill. Social policy researcher Richard Shillington said the government has withdrawn $1.2-billion from child benefits over the past eight years. He said that the new program will be quickly eroded by inflation because it is not fully indexed to the cost of living.

"It's putting child benefits on an escalator that's going down," Mr. Shillington said. "Every once in a while, the government helps people up a step ... but it's leaving them on the escalator."

The government justified the elimination of family allowances by arguing that a wealthy bank president does not need the extra money. But millions of ordinary Canadians will be losing the monthly cheques, Mr. Shillington said. "We've succeeded in taking the family allowance away from bank presidents and bank tellers and clerks and the people who sweep the floor."

A Quebec women's group, the Network of Action and Information for Women, said the elimination of family allowances is "unfair and mean-minded." The federal government is attacking women and children who are "the most vulnerable" people in Canada, the group said.

"The government is afraid of adults who know how to defend themselves, but targets children and mothers who do not have the real means to defend their rights."

Judith B.
Victoria, June 1983[5]

I am a 45 year old single woman, having divorced some twelve years ago. I was a wife, mother, and homemaker for twelve years prior to that. As a single person prior to marriage I worked a period of six years for institutions offering minimal work related pensions that were not transferable and as a young, self-supporting individual, [I] found other uses for the money. Canada Pension, at that time, had not been instituted. As a homemaker from 1959-1971 I contributed nothing to Canada Pension and of course earned nothing to contribute to private plans. My husband, of course, was during that time and is still a full contributor. Upon our divorce there were no amendments in Albertan law, providing me with any pension credits. Immediately following my divorce in 1971 I invested my time and energy to university studies over a period of seven years, working in part-time jobs offering absolutely no pension benefits. I also had to rely on student loans to supplement my budget, therefore, accumulating long term debt. This I felt was a compromise to attaining self respect and autonomy as an individual, able to contribute to the community as a Social Worker. From graduation to the present, I have been contributing for five years to Canada Pension and work related pensions. However, having just moved to another province to improve my present quality of life, I find my work pension is not portable, therefore losing the contribution of my employer. My new employer does not begin deductions for a period of three months, therefore, I am losing more contributor time. At forty-five years of age, if I am fortunate enough to remain able and healthy I have twenty years of contribution time left ... I feel doubtful of how I'll cope in my old age. When I see the bag ladies on the streets of Victoria I cannot help but wonder what circumstances prevailed to dampen their incentive ...

5. From a memo submitted to the Federal Task Force on Pension Reform by the Status of Women Action Group, Victoria, B.C., June 1983. Copy at SWAG.

Low-Income Women Living Alone: Case Four
October 1979[6]

"If you're really interested," said 67-year-old Mary S., "I'll tell you what it's like being an old woman alone who's only got the government pension to live on ... It's wearing out your second-hand shoes going from one store to another trying to find the cheapest cuts of meat. It's hating having to buy toilet tissue or soap or toothpaste, because you can't eat it. It's picking the marked-down fruits and vegetables from the half-rotting stuff in the back of the stores that used to be given away to farmers to feed their animals. It's hunting the thrift shops and Salvation Army stores for half-decent clothes.

"Emergencies come up; grand-children have birthdays; clothes wear out; cleaning products run out; bus rates go up. How do we manage? We pay our rent and utilities and we eat less."

What Are the Solutions?
March 1983[7]

What Are the Solutions?

Everyone agrees that our pension system must be reformed. But a variety of opinions exist on what exactly should be changed, and to what degree.

We at the National Action Committee on the Status of Women (NAC) would like to see immediate action to help the poverty-stricken elderly — mostly women, AS WELL AS a remodelling of the system to ensure that future generations of Canadian women will enjoy a standard of living in retirement that reflects their contribution to this country.

In designing a better system for the future, we believe that two crucial factors must be kept in mind.

First is that women's participation in the labour market is an established and irrevocable fact of modern life. Women must be given equal opportunities, pay and benefits in the labour market. Pensions that are too low for male earners are inadequate for women too.

Second is that as far into the future as we can see, important numbers of women will still be working mainly in their homes. NAC's position on full-time child-rearing and homemaking is that it is neither desirable nor realistic to force all women to take paid jobs.

As much as possible, in our view, both men and women should have the choice between paid work or work for their families. In terms of pensions, this means recognizing the value of work done in the home.

NAC's goals for pension reform are:
- to eliminate poverty among the elderly
- to provide adequate replacement income to those who spend most of their lives in the labour market
- to equalize the pension entitlements of spouses

6. *Women and Poverty*, (Ottawa: National Council of Welfare, October 1979) 12.
7. *Pension Reform: What Women Want*, pamphlet, (Toronto: NAC, March 1983).

- to include the work of homemakers in the Canada/Québec Pension Plan on a fair basis
- to improve employer-sponsored pension plans.

A. Abolish Poverty in Old Age

Women over age 65, and particularly widows, are the poorest group of people in Canada.

NAC fully agrees with the following statement by the National Council of Welfare about them:

> After a lifetime spent taking care of their spouses and children, these women who had no opportunity to become financially self-sufficient are now abandoned by the generation that benefitted most from their work. It is a disgrace that a rich country like Canada is unwilling to take proper care of its old.

NAC RECOMMENDS: THAT THE GUARANTEED INCOME SUPPLEMENT FOR THE AGED POOR BE INCREASED IMMEDIATELY. THIS INCREASE SHOULD BE LARGE ENOUGH TO BRING THE FEDERAL GUARANTEED INCOME OF ALL SENIORS TO THE POVERTY LINE FOR LARGE CITIES AS ESTABLISHED BY STATISTICS CANADA ...

Immigrants who come to Canada after July 1977 are also denied access to adequate basic pensions. The new rule introduced at that time requires that new Canadians live here for 40 years — instead of the former ten — to qualify for a full Old Age Security pension and Supplement at age 65.

The change was made to allow immigrants to collect pensions from their home countries. The problem is that women are seldom entitled to such pensions from their countries of origin. Also, most Third World countries have no government pensions of any kind.

As a result, we are now creating a sub-class of poor female immigrant senior citizens in Canada.

NAC RECOMMENDS: THAT THE GOVERNMENT REINSTATE THE OLD RULE GIVING IMMIGRANTS FULL OLD AGE SECURITY PENSIONS AFTER TEN YEARS IN CANADA IMMEDIATELY BEFORE THE AGE OF 65;

or, at the very least,

THAT THE GOVERNMENT GUARANTEE THE EQUIVALENT OF A FULL OAS-GIS PENSION TO ALL LOW-INCOME SENIOR CITIZENS WHO HAVE BEEN IN CANADA FOR MORE THAN TEN YEARS ...

B. Give Adequate Replacement Income to Paid Workers

It is easy to demonstrate that our pension system is unable to generate benefits high enough to maintain our standard of living after the age of 65.

Adding up the benefits from the only two sure sources of income of retired workers,

- the OAS, which replaces 14% of the average industrial wage, and
- the C/QPP, replacing 25% of earnings of the average wage,

we get a total replacement rate of 39% on previous earnings, which is certainly too low to keep the same lifestyle after retirement ...

NAC RECOMMENDS: THAT THE CANADA AND QUÉBEC PENSION PLANS BE EXPANDED TO GIVE BENEFITS EQUAL TO 50% OF EARNINGS UP TO THE AVERAGE INDUSTRIAL WAGE ...

C. Treat Spouses Equally

Pension rights and retirement savings plans usually belong only to the spouse who earned the money used to pay for them. This is a flagrant denial of the equal contribution of the spouses within the marriage partnership ...

NAC RECOMMENDS: THAT THE SPLITTING OF CANADA/QUÉBEC PENSION PLAN CREDITS BETWEEN THE SPOUSES UPON DIVORCE BE MADE AUTOMATIC AND MANDATORY IN ALL CASES.

NAC ALSO RECOMMENDS: THAT IN ON-GOING MARRIAGES, CANADA/QUÉBEC PENSION PLAN CREDITS BE SPLIT AUTOMATICALLY BETWEEN THE SPOUSES WHEN THE YOUNGER OF THEM REACHES THE AGE OF 65 ...

Provincial family laws control the sharing (or lack thereof) of credits from employer pension plans and RRSPs between the spouses on divorce. At this time, British Columbia and Manitoba are the only provinces where these laws clearly give husbands and wives a right to an equal share.

NAC RECOMMENDS: THAT LAWS REQUIRING THE EQUAL SHARING OF EMPLOYER-SPONSORED PENSION PLAN CREDITS AND RRSPs BETWEEN THE SPOUSES ON DIVORCE BE ENACTED AS SOON AS POSSIBLE IN ALL JURISDICTIONS ...

D. Include Homemakers' Work in the Canada/Québec Pension Plan

If the C/QPP were expanded and pension credits were shared equally between the spouses, there are still many women who would not have adequate pensions at the age of 65. What is absolutely necessary to remedy this are special measures to account for the particular lifestyles and family responsibilities of women.

For women who spend most of their lives in the labour market, stopping only for a few years to take care of their young children, the obvious solution is the "child-care drop-out" provision in the Canada and Québec Pension Plans.

This measure, already in force in Québec, works by leaving out of a person's lifetime earnings — on which her or his pension entitlement is based — the years of low or zero income spent outside the labour market taking care of young children aged less than seven. The effect is to provide fully subsidized C/QPP coverage to "occasional homemakers" during that time.

NAC RECOMMENDS: THAT THE ONTARIO GOVERNMENT IMMEDIATELY WITH-DRAW ITS UNJUSTIFIED VETO OF THE "CHILD-CARE DROP-OUT" PROVISION IN THE CANADA PENSION PLAN. THE PERIOD COVERED BY THE DROP-OUT PROVISION SHOULD ALSO BE BROADENED TO INCLUDE THE ENTIRE MATER-NITY LEAVE PERIOD AS WELL AS THE PERIODS SPENT AT HOME CARING FOR VERY DISABLED FAMILY MEMBERS ...

But even with the "child-care drop-out" provision in both the Québec and Canada Pension Plans, most homemakers would still be without personal pension protection. This is because the "drop-out" measure is worth very little or nothing at all to women who did not spend a good part of their lives full-time in the paid labour force ...

NAC RECOMMENDS: THAT LONG-TERM HOMEMAKERS WITH CHILDREN AGED LESS THAN SEVEN OR VERY DISABLED FAMILY MEMBERS BE DIRECTLY IN-TEGRATED IN THE C/QPP ON THE BASIS OF A HYPOTHETICAL INCOME EQUAL TO ONE-HALF THE AVERAGE INDUSTRIAL WAGE (ABOUT $10,000). AS AT LEAST PART OF THE SERVICES THESE HOMEMAKERS RENDER BENEFITS ALL OF US, THIS PARTICIPATION IN THE C/QPP SHOULD BE FREE AND SUBSIDIZED BY ALL OTHER C/QPP PARTICIPANTS ...

NAC RECOMMENDS: THAT THEY ALSO BE DIRECTLY INTEGRATED IN THE C/QPP ON THE BASIS OF A HYPOTHETICAL INCOME EQUAL TO ONE-HALF THE AV-ERAGE WAGE, BUT WITH FULL CONTRIBUTIONS — EMPLOYER AND EMPLOYEE SHARES — PAYABLE BY THE ADULT(S) BENEFITING FROM THE HOMEMAKERS' SERVICES. THIS WOULD USUALLY, BUT NOT ALWAYS, BE THE HUSBAND.

Other NAC recommendations on homemakers include:

- THAT THE SYSTEM OF HOMEMAKER PARTICIPATION DESCRIBED ABOVE BE MANDATORY. NAC REJECTS VOLUNTARY PARTICIPATION BY HOME-MAKERS IN THE C/QPP BECAUSE IT WOULD MAINLY BENEFIT WELL-OFF WOMEN AND WOULD PUT WIVES IN THE SITUATION OF HAVING TO

BEG FROM THEIR HUSBANDS TO OBTAIN THE NECESSARY CONTRIBU-
TIONS.

- THAT PART-TIME WORKERS BE INTEGRATED IN THIS SYSTEM AS PART
  EARNERS AND PART HOMEMAKERS.

- THAT WHERE A CONTRIBUTION IS REQUIRED, LOW-INCOME FAMILIES
  BE GIVEN A SUBSIDY.

- THAT IF DIRECT INTEGRATION OF HOMEMAKERS IS INTRODUCED, BENE-
  FITS FOR SURVIVING SPOUSES OVER AGE 65 BE ABOLISHED. HOWEVER,
  A "GRANDMOTHER" CLAUSE SHOULD ALLOW PEOPLE AGED MORE THAN
  35 AT THE TIME THE NEW SYSTEM IS INTRODUCED TO CHOOSE TO RE-
  MAIN UNDER THE OLD RULES IF THEY ARE MORE ADVANTAGEOUS TO
  THEM ...

E. Improve Employer-Sponsored Pension Plans

Even if all the changes mentioned above were implemented, employer-
sponsored pension plans would still continue to play an important role
in our pension system. They would be needed by workers with special
needs (those wanting to take early retirement, for example), and by those
who want additional protection because their incomes are higher than
the average industrial wage.

Now, many employer-sponsored plans are so bad that it is practically
a waste of money to contribute to them. To improve them to the point
where they could play their role efficiently, NAC has made the following
recommendations:

1. THAT VESTING (MEANING THE ACQUISITION OF AN IRREVOCABLE
   RIGHT TO A PENSION) OCCUR AS SOON AS AN EMPLOYEE JOINS A PEN-
   SION   PLAN.

2. THAT VESTED BENEFITS AND PENSIONS BE FULLY PROTECTED
   AGAINST THE RAVAGES OF INFLATION.

3. THAT "JOINT AND LAST SURVIVOR" PENSIONS BE REQUIRED IN ALL
   EMPLOYER PENSION PLANS. THIS WORKS BY REDUCING THE RETIRE-
   MENT BENEFIT TO PAY FOR A WIDOW(ER)'S PENSION. THE SURVIVOR'S
   PENSION SHOULD BE PAID WHICHEVER SPOUSE DIES FIRST, AND IT
   SHOULD AMOUNT TO AT LEAST 80% OF THE ORIGINAL PENSION.
   SPOUSES SHOULD BE ABLE TO WAIVE THE SURVIVOR PENSION BUT
   ONLY UPON WRITTEN AGREEMENT BY BOTH OF THEM AFTER INDE-
   PENDENT LEGAL ADVICE.

4. THAT THE PRACTICE OF DISCONTINUING SURVIVORS' BENEFITS UPON
   REMARRIAGE BE ABOLISHED.

5.   AS MENTIONED EARLIER, THAT ALL EMPLOYER PENSION CREDITS AND RETIREMENT SAVINGS BE DIVIDED EQUALLY BETWEEN THE SPOUSES ON DIVORCE.

6.   THAT ANNUITIES UNDER MONEY PURCHASE PENSION PLANS AND RRSPs BE CALCULATED WITHOUT REGARD TO THE SEX OF THE ANNUITANT.

7.   THAT PENSION PLAN PARTICIPANTS BE SENT A DESCRIPTION OF THEIR PLANS AS WELL AS AN ANNUAL FINANCIAL STATEMENT GIVING THE INVESTMENT POLICY AND PERFORMANCE OF THE PENSION FUND ASSETS.

8.   THAT PENSION FUND MANAGERS, WHILE BEING URGED TO OBTAIN ADEQUATE AND SECURE RETURN ON INVESTMENTS, BE ENCOURAGED TO INVEST THEIR PLANS' FUNDS IN CANADA.

9.   THAT BOARDS AND COMMITTEES MANAGING PENSION FUNDS INCLUDE WORKERS, AND THAT WOMEN BE PROPORTIONALLY REPRESENTED ON THEM.

Conclusion

Women make a very important contribution to the economy of this country. They deserve equitable treatment under our retirement income system as well as a secure dignified old age. We, at the National Action Committee on the Status of Women, believe that the adoption of our recommendations would go a long way toward achieving these goals.

Living Spaces: Housing, Hostels and Shelter

"A Shoulder to Cry On"
December 1977[8]

Nellie's welcomes women from every social class. It is the only hostel in Toronto that will take almost any woman. Interval House and Women in Transition take women with children. Street Haven takes women with drug and alcohol problems. Stop 86 takes women aged 25 and under. For women over 30, according to a new Toronto study, facilities of this kind for women drop off dramatically.

Nellie's opened its doors in 1974 with 30 beds, thanks largely to the efforts of June Callwood and Vicky Trerise. Trerise was a law student who had worked in hostels and realized that women over 26 just were not being serviced in that way in Toronto, and that women over 26 do have crises. Callwood had been helping young people at Digger House, and she too grew to realize that older women had acute needs ...

On the front door is a poster of the pioneer Canadian agitator for women's rights, Nellie McClung. On it is a quote from Nellie: "Never retract, never retreat, never apologize. Get the thing done and let them

8. Joanne Kates, *Globe and Mail*, 7 December 1977.

howl." And inside, in the big warm kitchen, there is a coffee urn steaming. Somebody has just taken chocolate cakes out of the oven for lunch, and a huge pot of stock is bubbling on the stove. A pregnant young woman is boiling eggs for her breakfast. A black woman with her daughter hiding behind her skirt is at the door. The woman has been beaten by her husband, and Nellie's is her place to go.

A Nellie's staffer shows her to a room with clean sheets, and one for her daughter, and tells her when lunch will be served. She also gets a shoulder to cry on, support to let out some of her anger and frustration. If she wants it, there will be help contacting Legal Aid, the police to press charges, or the Children's Aid Society if what she needs is someone to take care of her daughter while she gets back on her feet. The average stay at Nellie's is 11 days in winter, seven in summer ...

Lorie is 67 and she's dying of cancer. She's here today because the police brought her in. She was sitting in the park, was raped, and had no place to go for a cry and a cup of tea and a warm bed. She gets mugged often. Nellie's gets a lot of street women, some of them as old as 70. Women who are basically transients, existing from hospital to boarding house to hostel. Sometimes they sleep in the Don Jail, for not having the money to pay the fines they get for sleeping in the park ...

The future of Nellie's is in serious doubt. The Nellie's house sits on the back yard of a YMCA which has been bought by a developer and is slated for demolition. On Nov. 1, Nellie's signed an agreement to buy the house from the developer, and CMHC promised to lend Nellie's the $70,000 purchase price plus $250,000 for renovations — if Nellie's can prove its ability to make the repayments. At first glance, $250,000 seems an enormous sum, hardly necessary. But the fly in the ointment is that the Nellie's house has no furnace, no sewage system, no hookup to water mains. Its physical plant is basically some lines running into the YMCA building, and when that goes some time this winter, Nellie's has to have a furnace and plumbing — in a big hurry.

Nellie's ability to make the CHMC payments is not yet assured. It gets a $13 per diem grant from Metro Social Services for every night spent by a woman in the house. That doesn't cover women who just come for food or companionship. It doesn't cover streetcar tickets, diapers, formulas for babies, taxi fares to the hospital. It covers one staff member on duty 24 hours a day in a house that sleeps 30. It is not unusual to have one woman slashing upstairs, somebody in labour in the living room, the cops at the door with a battered woman and somebody in trouble on the phone. And the Metro money provides enough for one staff member on duty in that situation. Nellie's has been running on a staff of seven. Each earns $195 a week for 40 hours of work and infinite Nellie's committee work.

The Transition House Experience
Cape Breton, Nova Scotia, 1986-1989[9]

… A Safe Shelter

Transition House advertises itself as a safe place for women and their children. When we asked the women what the best thing about Transition House was, twelve answered safety. Another fourteen also described the safety that Transition House offers as important for them.

> Safe. I was safe. I was never so safe in my entire life. And my children were safe too.

> The best was peace of mind. And not having the fear of what I was living with at home.

> I was safe. I felt safe. He couldn't get to me.

> It was a safe place and that was something we never had before.

One of the biggest fears that battered women have is losing their children. Often women have been told for years by their mates that if they leave they will lose their children. Many women valued Transition House because their children were safe there.

> In the beginning it wasn't for myself it was for the children. I wanted to make sure they were safe.

> My husband made threats. He found the school where the children were and went there. He was threatening to take the kids. Once they were inside Transition House I knew there was no way he could get at us.

One of the things that contributed to women's feeling of security was the fact that the location of Transition House is kept confidential. Many of the women interviewed had left their homes before and had been pursued by their mates. They appreciated the fact that going to Transition House left their parents and friends safe …

Transition House Staff

The two words that women use to describe Transition House staff are listen and understand. For battered women who have been isolated and emotionally undermined by their mates, the impact of being with women who listen is very strong.

9. Joan Bishop, CWMA file: Cape Breton Transition House.

Understanding — the feeling that you belong and that you finally found people who understood exactly what you felt. You would start a sentence and they could finish it for you. They understood.

I had to know I wasn't the only person in the world going through this. And if I was going to stay I needed help dealing with it. I didn't need more than Transition House. On the phone they had such a calming effect. I'd be so upset. By the time I hung up I felt "I'll make it through and if I can't there's some place to go."

Women singled out one staff person who herself had been a battered woman. They valued very highly her sharing of her own experience. The women also described the staff as caring and supportive.

You could feel the caring from them. You could feel that they cared. They tried to get it across to me that I wasn't the only one that felt this way. I wasn't alone.

I'd never thought people could care about anyone so much in my life as they've cared about me. To think that complete strangers could be so concerned...

Two women said that one of the best things about being at Transition House was being able to show emotion. They expressed relief at realizing that showing emotion and crying were natural releases.

A feature of Transition House that is particularly helpful for women in crisis is the fact that the staff are available around the clock.

I like the idea that no matter what time it was there was always somebody there. If you felt alone or scared or just wanted to talk you could do so. You can panic at 3 or 4 in the morning and they weren't going to mind if you went down and woke them up to talk.

I was really exhausted emotionally. I couldn't sleep. I came down at midnight or so and started talking to Bea ... we talked till 4 or 5 that morning.

They're there for you all the time, even at 3 or 4 in the morning if you want to talk. They always had time.

Two of the women interviewed had negative comments about their experience with Transition House staff. One woman who stayed at the house the first year it was open said she was extremely lonely and felt no one wanted to bother with her. One woman there in 1987 criticized one staff person for "acting shocked" at something one of the residents said ...

Other Women

For many women who go to Transition House one of the most powerful experiences is just being with other women who have similar experience. Twelve out of the 42 women interviewed mentioned the other women as one of the best things about Transition House. Over and over again women say that the other women at the house made them realize that they were not alone.

> There were people there who knew what you were going through and understood what was happening. The other women knew how you felt — most had the same problem. I felt good.

> I thought they would think I was crazy if I'd open up. But then I got comfortable and realized the others were going through the same thing.

> Seeing everyone else who had gone through it helped me realize that it wasn't just me. I had always thought it was. I also realized that it wasn't my fault.

> From the moment I walked in the door I felt I was not an outsider ... there's a general feeling of "hey, we're all in this together." I've never known anything like it.

> To know you're not alone. I was amazed to know others were going through the same thing.

To understand the impact of this feeling one must understand the tremendous feeling of isolation that battered women live with. Many have been told day after day that they are worthless ... that they cause the abuse. These women come to rely on their mates as authorities. Further, battering happens in a conspiracy of silence and secrecy partly fuelled by the reluctance of many professionals to get involved. The woman may have taken her injuries to a family doctor who carefully avoided asking about abuse. She may have talked with a parish priest who urged her to be more understanding (just one way of assigning the blame to the woman). Because the women are made to feel they cause the abuse and because they think they are the only ones to do so many are profoundly embarrassed or ashamed to acknowledge what they are going through.

> What made you feel good ... everyone was going through something. You weren't alone. You didn't have to feel embarrassed of having a black eye. If you're beaten you can't go out in public. You are very embarrassed to let strangers know.

I'd tell my story and they'd tell their stories. We were leaning on one another. At one point there were only three of us ... we became very close. We became good friends. When you got down there was somebody there to talk to you, to encourage you. They were very supportive. Some of their stories were worse than mine. We did carry on our friendships after Transition House for a time. I wasn't from around here ... to know you could make friendships — that was a real plus for Transition House.

Women and Housing
Charlottetown, P.E.I, November 1986[10]

These facts illustrate that Women's Network represents the views of a wide diversity of Island women. After hearing this tonight, all of us will be going home. Some of us will be going to a safe, secure house which falls within our budget. Others will return to modern apartments with brightly-lit corridors and security-locked doors. Some of us will return to our co-operative housing unit at Hensley Green or Princley.

But, there is a much greater proportion of people in Prince Edward Island who will be returning home tonight to conditions which contradict even minimum housing needs needs, that in this country, one would expect, were a basic human right ...

Discrimination

Larkin's study (Larkin, Irene, *Tenant Housing Study for Charlottetown and Area,* prepared for the Charlottetown Christian Council, 1985) shows that in spite of the new Charter of Human Rights, there is wide discrimination by landlords on the basis of age and sex. We have landlords who still do not accept children. Discrimination exists against single parents, 83% of whom are female. We have discrimination against the elderly, discrimination against the physically and mentally limited, discrimination against students, discrimination against those in need of social assistance. In essence, we have discrimination against the poor — the majority of whom are women.

The study further reports many cases of discrimination after move-in. Here we find intimidation, sexual harassment of women, failure of some landlords to maintain living units to meet even minimal Department of Health standards. There is the constant threat of eviction without just cause. Many cases were reported where the Office of the Rentalsman, the Landlord and Tenant Act and the Rent Review Act were completely ignored. Tenants in many cases did not know they had any rights at all as tenants.

10. Women's Network Inc., "Submission to Special Committee on Legislative Proposals Hearings (Landlord-Tenant Act Rent Review Act)" (Charlottetown, P.E.I.: Women's Network, Inc., 5 November 1986). From the files of the P.E.I. Status of Women.

Let me tell you a story—

One woman, a single parent named Susan, was so shaken by her experience with her last landlord that she felt ready to overlook anything in return for a little respect. "In the beginning, he was so friendly. The first time he came in to repair, he did not knock, but used his master key ... he did this three times." (*Do you think this happens often with male renters?*)

After eight months of trying unsuccessfully to heat the two-bedroom duplex, Susan gave notice. Although she put heavy plastic over the doors and windows and spent $200/month on fuel, the house was still freezing. Because she had a small child, she gave only two and a half weeks notice, but offered to pay rent for the remainder of the month.

"That was when the abuse really started. He threatened to come over and did. He abused me verbally and also accused me of damage which had been done before I moved in."

When Susan asked the landlord to leave, he threatened to throw her belongings out on the road if she wasn't out by the end of the month. (*Do you think he would have employed these tactics with a male tenant?*)
...

"Sitka Housing Co-operative: Women House Themselves" Vancouver, Winter 1989[11]

The Sitka spruce withstands winds better than other evergreens and is the first to grow closest to the water's brink, often on the edge of a forest. Sitka is also a reminder of a group of striking saw-mill women who milled the Sitka tree. The name Sitka is an appropriate choice for the Sitka Housing Co-operative, in Vancouver, British Columbia, which is owned and occupied by 42 women.

The Sitka co-op is a dream come true. Twenty women who realized they could never afford their own homes met in August, 1981 to start an all-women's co-op. Their task was not an easy one, and needed persistent lobbying. Linda Baker, their architect, had to fight Canada Mortgage and Housing Corporation (CMHC) through the entire design process because the standards set by the Corporation, the funder, were different from those of the women. After five years of concerted effort, Sitka Housing Co-operative was finally completed.

Sitka is striking in many ways. It is particularly attractive. It fits into and complements the surrounding neighbourhood. The buildings themselves are formed around an inner core, creating a circular courtyard which serves as communal space. Units are different from one another; they are individually designed, non-typical and non-repetitive. Sitka was built to support and reflect the concerns of its owner/occupants — children's needs were given top priority, "Environmental Suites" were included, communal spaces co-exist with private spaces. And most important, it demonstrates that women working together can overcome

11. Hinda Avery, *Women and Environment* (Winter 1989), 19.

obstacles and create housing for themselves and their children. The Sitka Housing Co-operative is a landmark: it is the first women-initiated housing project in British Columbia and the first major all-women's housing co-operative in B.C. designed for and by women. The architect involved herself in the community spirit of planning and, as a result, was able to meet the needs of the residents. Sitka serves as an example for future all-women's housing co-operatives. It has broken new ground, and, the women of Sitka are demonstrating what urban design, community development and planning are all about.

"Housing Problems Growing for Single Women" Toronto, December 1983[12]

The barefoot redhead sits slouched in a chair in the lobby of the Street Haven shelter for women.

It is mid-afternoon and she has dark, red circles under her eyes. She is 17 and five-months pregnant, has lost her job and can't return to her parents because of long-standing conflicts.

She will be moving on the next day to a home for unwed mothers, but for now she shares a room at Street Haven with a 56-year-old who has an obsession for cleaning, a 19-year-old prostitute and a 26-year-old transient from Nova Scotia who ran out of money on her way through Toronto.

The shelter sleeps 15, and when there is no room at any of the other six women's hostels in Metro a woman is sometimes allowed to sleep on a couch downstairs.

There's no charge for the housing. People who live in hostels can't collect welfare because that requires a permanent address. Hostels don't count as permanent homes; most ask residents not to stay longer than two weeks.

There is never an empty bed in the house, and nights when homeless women aren't turned away at the door are rare, says Street Haven director Peggy Ann Walpole.

A few blocks away at Peggy Ann Walpole House (named for the Street Haven director but run by Metropolitan Toronto), as many as 45 women have been squeezed into the 30-bed, single women's unit recently, says John Jagt, Metro's manager of hostel operations.

Women have always needed some shelter space, but the growing demand has taken planners across the country by surprise.

As winter sets in, staff at emergency shelters across Toronto are reporting they have enough room for destitute families and single men but are short of space for single women.

Social workers say the women's liberation movement accounts in part for the increase, giving many women the courage to leave abusive husbands in hopes of finding a better life.

---

12. Regina Hickl-Szabo, *Globe and Mail*, 22 December 1983, D12.

How many homeless men and women are roaming Toronto streets is the subject of much debate. But no one argues that the shortage of emergency shelter for single women is becoming acute.

A study based on research last summer [1983] in Toronto found there were 3,400 homeless people in hostels and signed up with housing registries and some social service agencies. Of those, about 500 were single women. (Neither figure includes the number of transients sleeping in makeshift shelters, cars, in malls or on doorsteps.)

Municipal figures show that only 202 of the 2,200 emergency shelter beds in Toronto are for single women. Another 207 are reserved for women with children. One Metro official involved in the study estimates there could be between 4,000 and 6,000 homeless people wandering around Metropolitan Toronto.

"There's not that there are many more street women today, it's just that they're more willing to come out and ask for help," Miss Walpole said ...

Karen Ciupka, program supervisor at Sistering, a new drop-in centre for homeless women, said at least 10 of the 35 women who take part in the program every day resort to prostitution to help them survive.

Richard Picherak, Metro's social services commissioner, has been asked to examine the need for more shelter space for single women, but those who have studied the problem say more emergency beds won't solve anything in the long run.

Social policy observers agree the problem is one of a shortage of affordable housing.

Apart from more low-income housing, Miss Walpole said, "we need money for more meaningful programs to teach some of these people life skills and to follow up some of them."

Metro bureaucrats and politicians acknowledge the housing need exists, but say that there's not much they can do without dollars from the federal or provincial governments and that providing emergency shelter is better than nothing.

"Substantial changes in the system are the responsibility of the upper levels of government," Metro's John Jagt said. "A lot more needs to be done for us to say we've got a totally humane city to live in."

"Test Case in the Making"
Fall 1988[13]

... In early October 1987, a black woman asked the superintendent in her apartment building to help her replace a broken light fixture. When the fixture had been replaced, the "super" pulled his penis out and said if she was grateful for his assistance she should "suck this." The woman refused and demanded he leave her apartment. He did not leave, and proceeded to verbally abuse her. The only way to get the harasser out was for the woman to leave her own place and to wait till he had gone.

13. Elizabeth Bateman, *NAC Housing Newsletter*, 2, no. 2, (Fall 1988).

Gone, but with access at any time because the superintendent had a key. Gone for the moment, but living in the same premises.

Of course the story does not stop here. This woman has experienced constant threat and harassment since this incident. Her car tires have been flattened regularly, her apartment has been entered even after the lock was changed (the chain was cut because of a plumbing "emergency" twenty minutes before she arrived home from work), her apartment has been intentionally flooded by workmen sent by the building management, and a workman sent to do repairs left her toilet blocked, white plaster footprints in every room including the bedroom, and damage to a glass table.

"Why stay?" you ask; because this brave woman decided to fight, to stand up for her and every woman's right to freedom from sexual harassment. This is her home not the exploitative domain of the landlord or superintendent! The property management company involved in this case is a notorious outfit of callous profiteers who run the largest density housing project in Canada. There are many immigrant and refugee families, single mothers and their children, and low income people who live in the project. Historically, the management has sided against the people in any dispute. The upkeep and safety in the buildings is questionable at best. Threats and intimidation are common practices by management and superintendents.

This is the backdrop to a potentially historic case on sexual harassment in housing. The woman went to her tenant association and got linked up with other tenant activists. Legal representation was secured and a letter sent to the property management company regarding the sexual harassment and property damages. The response from the managers was absolutely dismissive of possible sexual harassment (thus condoning and covering up for the perpetrator) and focused entirely on the woman's altering her lock in contravention of the Landlord and Tenant Act (thus condoning and covering up for the damages done to her property and person). The next stage in the battle for her rights brought the laying of a complaint of sexual harassment in accommodation at the Ontario Human Rights Commission. This case is currently in process. No other case of sexual harassment in accommodation has ever been brought to a Board of Inquiry in Ontario.

An informal security strategy is in place with women who live close by on call night or day. Another woman in the building has come forward to be a witness; she also experienced an assault from the superintendent in one of the buildings' elevators. Community awareness of this case is being developed and support is growing. The case will be made public after the investigative phase of the Human Rights Commission has begun. Despite this woman's courage and strength, her story illustrates the oppressive conditions that many women must overcome in their daily struggle for safe, affordable and decent housing. The pervasive racism and sexual exploitation of tenants by landlords and their agents must be exposed and challenged by all of us.

Care for Children

Day Care Is Our Highest Priority
Vancouver, January 1972[14]

Day care is our highest priority! The Status of Women Action and Co-ordinating Council of B.C. would like you to know that, of all the Recommendations of The Report of The Royal Commission on The Status of Women in Canada, we consider the Sections 115-120, concerning day care, to be the most imperative for immediate action. We request that you do all in your power to make this priority known, and to initiate the steps necessary for implementation.

Day care should be broadly defined to include a wide range of supplementary child care arrangements so that a family can choose an appropriate service which will enhance the family's ability to parent the child, and the child's opportunity to grow and develop ...

Cooperative Daycare Centre
Toronto, January 1971[15]

... The Centre operates on a cooperative basis and is increasingly bringing parents, volunteers and children into a social and communal experience with each other. Parents and interested individuals direct the Centre through bi-weekly meetings in which we discuss the policy of the Centre and our concern about, and ideas for the children, as well as the program and philosophy behind what we're doing. Parents are asked to contribute a half-day a week (or equivalent service in clean-up or organizing work) in staffing the Centre. We depend greatly upon thirty or forty volunteers, interested men and women who are students or working people with flexible hours, to make up the six staff persons on hand at all times. Since we are located close to the University where more than half the parents work or study, many mothers and fathers come at lunch time to play with and help feed the children.

The Centre's open and cooperative mode of operation makes it a rather unique approach in the present daycare world of Toronto, with parents and individuals involved in ways which the present provincial legislation dealing with daycare establishments, in its concern with professionalism, was not designed to comprehend or encourage.

We hope that we shall be able to expand our present operation, and, using the experience gained by the organization of the Centre, that we

14. Status of Women Action and Coordinating Council of B.C., "Our Brief on Day Care to all members of the British Columbia Legislature and to all B.C. Members of Parliament in Ottawa" (Vancouver, B.C.: Status of Women Action and Coordinating Council of B.C., 3 January 1972). From the files of the Vancouver Status of Women.
15. The Women's Liberation Campus Community Cooperative Daycare," background paper, CWMA file: The Women's Liberation Campus Community Toronto.

shall be able to assist other community groups and interested people in the city to organize similarly.

We have been encouraging parents to see our daycare centre as more than a drop-off baby-sitting service, and to become involved by thinking and talking about the problems and concerns we face in bringing up our children. The daycare centre is an extremely important base for learning about, and beginning to change, the attitudes of our society in raising children in the nuclear family, to giving and sharing according to one's needs, and being part of a cooperative group sharing responsibilities for each other's children, learning cooperation and finding friendship and help ...

To be more specific, one thing we stand for is free daycare: free in the sense that we feel it's the kind of service governments should provide so that women, as well as men, can participate fully in our society in any way they choose. It should not be a service limited only to those people who need or want to "work", as that term has traditionally been defined. Reading, making clay pots, conversation, travelling or struggling against social injustice, to mention only a few, should also qualify as legitimate reasons for the responsibility of children to be shared by society as well as by individuals.

There's another, related, thing we stand for that adds up to a whole new approach to family structure. The conventional family structure, with its emphasis on the dominant role of the father as a decision-maker for the group, is a weak and exploitive way to organize society. Too often, it produces frustrated fathers, unfulfilled mothers and stultified, unhappy children. Its strength as a social unit is constantly being successfully challenged by the pressures of a highly complex, profit-oriented society. Because the family chops people up into small groups, it turns them into bigger consumers — one television set is just as effective in groups of 15 to 25 as in groups of two or four — and makes them more vulnerable to exploitation.

We feel that a parent-controlled, cooperative daycare centre should be a community which, in a sense, becomes a family, with everyone in that community sharing responsibility for the children and the children relating freely as individuals to each other and to adults.

This idea of community-controlled daycare is not the one held by the Day Nurseries Branch of the Ontario Department of Social and Family Services. This body, which controls through its licensing powers all day nurseries in the province, has laid down approved guidelines for the "cooperative nursery school." Such a school, state its regulations, must have at least one full-time paid staff member possessing qualifications suitable to the Branch; a formalized committee structure for administration; and a commitment to running the enterprise "as efficiently as possible." Parents' chief concern, described in "What is a Cooperative Nursery School?" published by the Branch, "is with the hiring of well-qualified staff and setting up and maintaining a nursery school of good standard."

It's our view that matters of staff and standards should be decided by parents and not arbitrarily imposed by ill-informed governments. Providing the children are not being badly treated *in clearly demonstrable ways*, we see no reason why parents of pre-school children should not be free to select the kind of school and teachers they want, just as parents of school-age children are allowed to place their children in the school of *their* choice.

We also believe that daycare centres should be whole day operations, not half day luxuries that hamstring working mothers with worries about where to find lunches for their children. Such centres are perhaps useful in middle-class neighbourhoods where mothers want time for social or cultural activities, but half-days are not good for parents who either want or must have a career. By offering a full program first, rather than starting with half-day and working up, we hope that our Centre will provide valuable socializing experiences for its children, staff and volunteers, as well as serve the needs of 9 to 5 working people. Our aims can be easily summarized:

1. Programs that reflect the skills and values of our community for the benefit of the individual child.
2. No aim beyond the best and most sensitive care of our children.
3. Free child care of the highest quality for everyone who wants it.
4. No conflict of interest resulting from daycare centres at places of work—this makes the worker too vulnerable.
5. Our children. Our money. Our control.

Despite many problems, we feel our Centre has accomplished much in a very short time. It is providing men with an opportunity to learn about, and be responsible for, infants. The children are learning they can be sensitively cared for by adults other than their mothers and fathers. Mothers and fathers are learning the same thing. Through our Centre, a few more women have been able to fulfil themselves as individuals outside the home and family. Most important, the kids have created a community of their own ...

Maternity Parental Leave/Child Care
B.C., 1977[16]

Question 6. Does the employer provide day care facilities?

Only one employer, Simon Fraser Student Society, makes a provision for daycare in its collective agreement with SORWUC. Although the employer does not provide daycare — it is located at the University — the employer pays 50% of the employee's daycare costs. The VMREU

16. Janice Pentland-Smith, "Provisions for Women in B.C. Union Contracts" (July 1977) 16-20. Copy at Vancouver Status of Women.

does not provide day care but was instrumental in the past in setting up the City Hall daycare centre.

Provision of daycare has long been a demand of the women's movement but whether this should be provided by government or the private sector, in the community or at the workplace, is open for discussion. Some union representatives feel that the private sector will never accept that daycare could be their responsibility. There is, however, a growing demand that, where the government is the employer, daycare should be provided at the workplace.

Question 7. Is the employer attempting to provide child care in the future?

Five contracts contained provision for the employer and the employees to investigate the possibilities of providing day care either at the work place or in a community facility. These clauses stated that a committee should be established to investigate the feasibility ...

"Day Care in Newfoundland: Nine out of Ten Have No Place to Go"
1988[17]

Newfoundland has the lowest day care availability in Canada and the lowest provincial government contribution to day care services. The minister responsible for social services, Charles R. Brett, has publicly stated that he does not believe in day care; in fact, he believes mothers working outside the home contribute to juvenile delinquency.

Given this attitude by the minister responsible for day care, most day care advocates in the province hold out little hope for change in day care services here.

The Royal Commission on Employment and Unemployment in Newfoundland recommended day care services be increased since more women are working outside the home to support their families. The commission also found many women weren't going out to work because there is no day care available for their children.

Current Services

There are approximately 50,000 pre-school children (under five years old) in the province. Of these children, 15,000 have both parents (or the only one) working outside the home. In September 1987 there were 77 licensed day care centres with 1,401 full-time spaces for children older than two years. The majority (44) of the day care centres are located in the St. John's area, Newfoundland's largest urban centre.

According to the Department of Social Services, which licenses day care centres, there has been a 12 per cent increase in spaces available in the last six months. In 1986 there were 922 full-time spaces, while in March 1987 there were 1,253.

17. Martha Muzychka, *Breaking the Silence* 6, no. 4, (June 1988)) 23-24, 37. Copy at CWMA.

The government does not license any other model of child care. Private arrangements must be made with babysitters, friends or relatives for infant child care. An independent caregiver can look after up to four children in her own home without requiring a licence or following any of the regulations governing licensed day care centres.

As one day care worker described it, "No one knows what's being done with a lot of these children." The Newfoundland Advisory Council on the Status of Women says in many cases children in private care lack nutritious meals, stimulating play, outdoor activities and attention to development.

But as many women are discovering, the need for day care does not end when children go to school full time. Many children aged 6 to 12 need care after school. There are only two centres in the entire province which offer after-school care, and both are located in St. John's. If private babysitting arrangements cannot be made, these children stay home alone after school, waiting for their parents.

While the day care situation in St. John's is poor, in rural Newfoundland it is much worse. There are fewer licensed day care centres, and more private/family care arrangements. Many women must work shifts at the fish-processing plants during the short summer season, and so do not always work from nine to five. Many husbands and wives who work at plants together have chosen to work opposite shifts in the absence of adequate day care.

Workplace centres are slowly becoming a reality in Newfoundland, although the only three centres that exist are all in St. John's. Workplace day cares usually offer spaces to employees first, and then to the community at large. For example, Memorial University's Pre-school Centre offers subsidized rates and priority to MUN students ...

Although many parents would like to see their children cared for by trained day care workers, two things stand in the way of an increase in the number of trained personnel: the lack of legislative requirements for trained programs, and the poor wages of day care workers.

There are only two programs in the province designed to train day care workers, and again both are in St. John's ...

Day care workers do not earn much money, whether they are trained or not ... Most centres in Newfoundland pay their staff between $4.25 and $5 per hour, or about $9,000 to $10,000 per year. The national average is about $14,000 to $17,000 per year for unionized, trained workers. Morris's centre [Joanne Morris, Director of the Early Childhood Training Centre] pays between $6 and $7 per hour. (Most centres will not reveal how much they pay their workers.)

... some day care workers are reluctant to get training because they will not get better jobs or salaries as a result ... But there is a Catch-22 in increasing the salaries of day care workers. For most non-profit centres, it means raising the fees charged to parents ...

Single parents (either the working poor or those on social assistance) often find it difficult to pay for day care with only the one salary to cover all the costs of food, rent, and clothing. Subsidies are available through the Department of Social Services for those receiving social assistance but often the subsidy is not enough. For some people, staying at home on welfare makes more economic sense than working at a minimum wage job; at least, when they stay at home, they are sure of what is happening to their children ...

The Newfoundland Day Care Advocates Association has sponsored two conferences on day care in the last four years. The group is affiliated with the national Canadian Day Care Advocacy Association and, together, they lobby government, raise public awareness and collect information on day care services in Newfoundland and Canada.

The Newfoundland chapter has set its priorities for quality, affordable and accessible day care in Newfoundland. These are:

1) licensed care for children under two years; 2) after-school care for primary and elementary pupils to cover the period between school closing at 3 and parents' arrival at 5; 3) day care outside of the 9 to 5, Monday to Friday shifts, to include evening and weekend services for shift workers such as nurses or fish plant employees; 4) licensing other models of day care such as family homes for greater flexibility, availability and security in serving day care needs.

Women on Mother's Allowance: Brief on Daycare Toronto, May 1974[18]

As women on Mother's Allowance, our daycare needs are different from those of the working or two parent family. We're in a bind. We're raising our children without another person to help cope with the pressures that all parents and children face. We need some sort of relief so that we can go shopping, do volunteer work, take a part-time job to get some skills and experience, read, sew, take a walk alone, visit friends and do any one of the thousand things that round out a person's life. Our children need to be with other kids. *YET*, at this point, even *if* we can get space in a daycare programme, we can't afford the fees. The following statements will give you some idea of the situation we face:

> We want our kids to have some kind of nursery school programme — you know a sort of 'head start'. They also need to be with other kids in a group sometimes, not just playing in the street or alone in the apartment all day. The O.H.C. [Ontario Housing Corporation] will give us space and a bit of money to start playschools, but they won't pay for teachers or really good equipment. We need a teacher — I don't know what to do with 20 four-year-olds.

18. CWMA file: Childcare.

We really need a drop-in daycare centre. I have to take my children *everywhere* — even to go to a friend's to get my hair cut.

I live on the 14th floor of an apartment building. My two younger kids don't get as much time as they should outdoors because it takes me nearly an hour to get them both ready and take them downstairs to the playground. Then I have to stay with them while they play and one of them always has to go to the bathroom as soon as we get down there. If I had somewhere to take them in the morning, they could play without me and I could get some house-work or shopping done or just have some time to myself. I'd really like that.

Last spring I was offered a part-time job. I'm allowed to make an extra $48.00 a month for myself and my two children. I couldn't take the job because the money I'd earn wouldn't pay for the daycare I needed and I wasn't working enough hours to get a subsidy.

In the last six months I've become involved in a lot of committee and volunteer work and I really enjoy it. My main problem is finding someone to take care of my child. I don't get much out of meetings when I take her because she's like any two-year old — she hates being confined. There's no programme where I can afford to send her and you can't always ask friends to babysit.

Because we're single parents we have no one to turn to for relief from our kids or for sorting out their problems. If we had a supervised playschool we could have some time off and also have someone else to talk to who knows our kids. The staff would see them everyday and could help us when problems came up. When Brad started throwing tantrums I had no one to talk to except my neighbour next door — and she couldn't help much because she only saw him two or three hours a week.

We need more daycare. I'm back to school and my kids are subsidized at a good centre, but I had to wait four months to get them in. Every centre near me had a waiting list. Four months! I registered for my course in the nick of time!

I tried to put my kid in a daycare centre. I couldn't afford the fees so I tried to get subsidy. They told me I needed a letter from the Children's Aid or the Public Health Nurse saying that I was unfit to look after him before they would help. I'm not unfit! It's just that he needs other kids and I need some time away from him. I'd like to see Mr. Brunelle talk to a three-year-old all day long.

"Caring for Our Children"
Ottawa, June 1986[19]

...VI. RECOMMENDATIONS

In summary, the recommendations of the CACSW presented in this brief are:

The CACSW believes Canadians deserve a comprehensive, universal system of quality child care.

The CACSW believes that child care — like education and health — is an essential service which should be universally accessible. The CACSW believes that the federal government can and must take a major role in rectifying the current state of inadequate access to quality child care. Canadian children need to be assured of a reasonable standard of care no matter where they live, regardless of their family's circumstances.

The CACSW also recognizes the important contribution that stay-at-home parents make in the nurturing of children and realizes that 24-hour child care is stressful. Therefore, the Council recommends that child care services should be available to those parents who have no paid employment for a maximum of one day a week.

The CACSW believes that, in the long term, there should be a major restructuring of federal funding on child care to ensure its provision as a universal program comparable to education and health.

The CACSW has recommended that, in order to improve the availability of day care services in the short term, the federal government extend the range of child care costs eligible for cost sharing under the Canada Assistance Plan to include capital construction costs and start-up grants for all child care spaces in provincially approved agencies.

The CACSW would like to point out that until child care workers are paid wages commensurate with their responsibility, staff turnover will remain unnecessarily high and will negatively affect the quality of care. Therefore, we encourage the federal government to direct funds to the provinces and its own training programs for the establishment of courses which would lead to the certification of individual caregivers.

The CACSW believes that parental leave should be based on the principle that both women and men must have the opportunity to pursue labour force careers and family responsibilities at the same time.

The CACSW recommends that parental leave of 26 weeks in total, available to either or both parent(s), whether natural or adoptive, be paid at the full salary of the parent(s) taking the leave who is (are) eligible for benefits under the *Unemployment Insurance Act.*

The CACSW recommends that a fixed number of paid days be allotted as an employee's right in order to permit parents to stay at home during the illness of a child. The CACSW suggest that a paid leave

19. Canadian Advisory Council on the Status of Women. Brief presented to the Special Committee on Child Care, 10 June 1986.

package of ten days be examined — up to three days leave without a certificate and seven days with a medical certificate.

The CACSW urges the Special Committee to recognize the changes that have taken place in society, the family and the workforce, and challenges the Special Committee to take a leading role in giving the future citizens of our country the best possible start in life.

"Child Care Policy Now a Costly Farce"
May 1989[20]

Pleading poverty, the Progressive Conservatives in Ottawa abandoned child care yet again in last week's budget.

As a cost-cutting move, it's nothing less than a sham. Canadians have been sold a bill of goods on child care that — instead of saving money — has turned into a costly muddle.

Instead of targeting money to help working women raise children, the government is squandering it on the wealthy and on stay-at-home mothers who need help least.

It is the worst of all possible worlds: Instead of more federal money to pay for new, desperately needed day-care spaces, Canadians are getting $2.4 billion in child tax breaks from Ottawa.

The money is going out under the first phase of the government's original $6.4 billion national child care strategy, approved just before the election. Ironically, these costly tax breaks won't create a single new child care space.

Prime Minister Brian Mulroney pulled the plug on the second phase — $4 billion to create 200,000 new spaces — when he called last year's election, promising, that if re-elected, "We will press home a national child care program."

Last week, Mulroney broke that promise. Instead of reducing a pressing shortfall of more than one million day care spaces nationwide, the government is going ahead with these dubious tax breaks:

- It has increased child tax credits by $200 for parents *without* any child care bills to pay, mostly stay-at-home mothers;
- It has doubled the tax deductions for child care bills to $4,000 — even though deductions benefit wealthy taxpayers far more than the needy. The scheme is of no use at all to families who still can't find child care.

Last year, Mulroney boasted with "pride" that his program would double the number of spaces available and help more mothers "participate in the labour force." But his pride was clearly premature.

Now, stay-at-home mothers and wealthier women are getting generous help from Ottawa, while the working poor are being told there's not enough money to help them hang on to their jobs while raising children.

It's not sound — or fair — public policy.

---

20. Editorial, *Toronto Star*, 3 May 1989.

Mulroney campaigned in 1984, and again in 1988, on promises of "economic and social justice" for women through better child care. Yet his tax breaks only exacerbate economic and social injustice.

Instead of scrapping plans for new spaces, Mulroney should use the money from his misguided tax breaks to provide the day-care spaces he vowed to create last year. Anything else would be an insult to working women.

"All About Jessie's"
Toronto, 1983[21]

Purpose

Jessie's is a community resource centre designed to meet the needs of teenaged mothers and teenagers who become pregnant. The Ontario Medical Association estimates that every year in Ontario 20,000 teenagers become pregnant. Jessie's uses a comprehensive approach in order to meet the complex needs of this population. Many of the teenagers who decide to keep their babies rather than place them for adoption are lacking family support. This is especially true in a large metropolitan centre such as Toronto. The major problems identified among adolescent mothers are: isolation, low income, interruption of education, scarcity of affordable housing, and lack of child-care services. The major problems identified among babies of adolescent mothers are: low birth weight, lack of stimulation and chronic ill-health.

Achievements

Jessie's is the first holistic service for teenagers in Canada. In order to provide for the variety of needs of such a vulnerable population Jessie's has created some services which have never existed anywhere — the 24-hour Respite Care program, run jointly with Family Day Care Services, is an example; it allows mothers in stress to place their babies in private homes for periods of up to three weeks, the country's first "half-way house" for babies. The Toronto Board of Education has placed a teacher in Jessie's whose flexibility is unique: she can provide counselling, assessment, referral and formal teaching. Mount Sinai Hospital's Family Practice unit comes to Jessie's one day a week. The prenatal class for couples is unique; seven young couples enrolled in the first one, which was led by the nurse clinician placed in Jessie's fulltime by the Toronto Department of Public Health and a male social worker from Metro Toronto Children's Aid Society. Jessie's after-hours telephones are answered by a social worker from Community Information Centre. Volunteers contribute time and skills to the Swap Shop, the nursery, crafts classes and the reception desk.

---

21. CWMA file: Jessie's Centre for Teenaged Mothers.

Size

In its first year of operation, Jessie's provided services for some 200 teenagers. In 1983, Jessie's second year, indications are that more than double that number will have been seen. The nursery has cared for almost 150 babies. Clients are referred by school guidance staff, public health nurses, the children's aid societies, hostels, hospitals and distress centres all over Metro and extending from Hamilton to Oshawa ...

"Giving Fathers an Equal Break"
February, 1988[22]

The Federal Government is faced with a dilemma — how to extend parental benefits to men without adding many costs to the unemployment-insurance system.

The problem of men and parental leave has been around for a long time, but the recent case of John McInnis, a Kitchener, Ont., truck driver who was denied unemployment benefits to care for his motherless newborn daughter, has dramatized the absurdity of the law. Mr. McInnis's wife died, but because maternity benefits are paid only to mothers, he was forced to go on welfare to stay at home to care for his child.

What makes the case even more absurd is that adoptive parents may receive unemployment-insurance benefits to care for new children. What is more, they may decide whether these benefits will go to the mother or the father. So, while adoptive fathers can collect unemployment to care for children, biological fathers cannot, under any circumstances.

Clearly something needs to be done to clear up this anomaly and to recognize that fathers are involved parents who need public support to assume their parental responsibilities.

Employment and Immigration Minister Benoît Bouchard has indicated that he will move quickly to change unemployment-insurance regulations so widowed fathers and men with disabled spouses will receive maternity benefits. In the case of widowed fathers, this is straightforward and will incur no extra costs.

But there is mounting pressure for the Government to provide benefits for all fathers. This is when the issue gets messy. If the Government were prepared, in the name of sex equality, to extend full benefits to men, there would be no problem because those that already exist for birthing mothers would not be restricted.

However, this is not the solution anyone in government is talking about. The main issue is the cost: the Government has made it clear that, if any rights are going to be extended to men, it must be within the 15 weeks of benefits currently available to women.

Various schemes are being proposed as reasonable ways to provide access to men without increasing costs. The most common suggestion is that a certain portion of the 15 weeks' paid leave now given women

22. Marjorie Cohen, *Globe and Mail*, 29 February 1988.

would be designated as time necessary for a woman to cope with the physical effects of pregnancy and birth, and the remaining period would be available to either parent ...

However, not all women experience childbirth in exactly the same way. For some there are no problems, and they can resume work soon after birth; for others, however, the physical toll is serious.

The different kinds of work women perform also must be considered. Some jobs are very physically demanding. Women required to stand for long periods of time, to lift heavy objects or to work on assembly lines may be unable to resume their duties as quickly as those whose jobs are more flexible and allow for rest periods or different pacing.

The point is that trying to decide how much of the 15 weeks is necessary for the mother, rather than for the care of the child, will be an arbitrary decision that will be very hard on some women.

Sheila Copps, the Liberal member of Parliament for Hamilton East, intends to introduce a bill that would allow either parent to receive unemployment benefits to care for newborns. The onus would then be on the parents to decide how they want to share the leave and benefits. This sounds reasonable if you assume that decisions within families are always made in mutual respect and perfect harmony.

However, beatings, even of pregnant women, and mental harassment are certainly not unknown. The casual assumption that "families" will come to some reasonable solution in distributing maternity benefits is wishing away the fact that many women are in very precarious positions. How would the law treat family disputes over who should receive benefits?

A senior policy adviser in Mr. Bouchard's office, while careful not to commit the ministry to any specific position, indicated that women could be protected by requiring the mother to sign away her right to the benefit in favour of her spouse. That is, the father would not receive the benefit unless she said he could. This is in no way a protection, and would be an exception in law, which recognizes the fragility of any right that can be relinquished due to pressure.

It is likely that the Government will delay making substantial decisions in this matter by taking the easier route of allowing the issue to be fought out in the courts. But even Ottawa's intention to extend benefits to men with disabled spouses, as reasonable as this seems, could be a problem if not done carefully.

The important issue here is that whatever benefits a disabled woman is entitled to should not be denied when her spouse becomes eligible for benefits. That is, he should not be given her benefits (whether they are for disability, sickness or pregnancy) but should be given benefits in his own right. It would be inhumane to eliminate a disabled woman from unemployment benefits because her husband needed to care for their child.

Many women's and labour organizations have demanded parental benefits so fathers can be included. The National Action Committee on the Status of Women, for example, calls for 24 weeks of leave and benefits, that could be taken by either parent in addition to the 15 weeks already available to the mother. It also recommends eliminating the two-week waiting period when the mother receives no benefits at all. The total, then, would be 41 weeks of combined maternity and parental benefits for care of children.

Canada's maternity provisions are not generous by international standards. Sweden provides nine months of leave with benefits at 90 per cent of earnings, Denmark six months at 90 per cent, Italy five months at 80 per cent, Finland 11 months at 80 per cent and West Germany six months at full pay. Canadian benefit levels are absurdly low at only 60 per cent of insurable (not total) earnings.

The cost of this program is not high — it represents only 4 per cent of total unemployment-insurance benefits paid, and costs the Government nothing, as it is financed totally from employer and employee contributions.

Employers are certain to resist any attempts to provide extended parental benefits, if their contributions will increase. If the Government fears their wrath, it can pick up the tab. Canada could and should provide better conditions for parents.

Dividing the existing benefits presents the problem as a power struggle between equality rights of men and women. This is being reinforced by at least one male group, Fathers for Justice, which condemns women's groups that do not want to see women's access to maternity leave jeopardized. The odd thing about this approach is that it accepts the idea that increasing rights for men must necessarily reduce benefits for women.

This has never been an acceptable course, and certainly not one that women's groups have championed as they have tried to extend women's rights. International human-rights conventions (to which Canada subscribes) are adamant that equality provisions not be financed by reducing benefits already granted to one group.

This has been particularly important in equal-pay legislation. Women's groups have argued for, and won, acceptance of the principle that giving women equal wages cannot be at the expense of lower men's wages.

The same principle holds with maternity benefits. If men receive them, it cannot be at the expense of what women already have. This approach would be equality with a vengeance.

"Teen Centre Wins Fight With Bar Next Door"
Toronto, October 1991[23]

Calling his actions a "demonstration of sheer cussedness," a judge has ordered a Toronto bar owner to stop his repeated attempts to thwart the construction of a neighbouring centre for teenaged mothers.

23. Joseph Hall, *Toronto Star*, 5 October 1991.

Mr. Justice John O'Driscoll of the Ontario Court, General Division, yesterday ordered John Bottan to tear down the scaffolding he erected on his roof to block the completion of Jessie's Centre next door.

"The defendants (Bottan) have deliberately given everyone associated with the plaintiff (Jessie's) a difficult time. They denied service and, generally, were not amenable to common sense," O'Driscoll wrote.

"One ounce of reasonableness on the part of the defendant would have rendered unnecessary all these proceedings."

Specifically, O'Driscoll ordered Bottan to dismantle within 24 hours the rooftop scaffolding he erected to prevent completion of a wall on the new six-storey structure beside his Parliament St. bar, the Rear View Mirror.

The new building, which towers over Bottan's bar, combined a counselling centre with 16 units of non-profit housing.

Bottan, who has dumped garbage on the work site and pushed a worker off a ladder, ignored an August order from a city building inspector to take the scaffolding down.

Twice charged with assaulting people working on the building, Bottan was demanding $100,000 from Jessie's to allow workers on to his roof and to temporarily erect a swinging scaffold over the roof.

When the centre refused to pay that much for the violation of his "air rights," Bottan erected his own scaffold in June.

Since then, many of the mothers who had expected to move in to Jessie's apartments with their children starting Sept. 1, have had to find temporary shelter.

"We're so glad this is over, and we can get on with moving those people in," said Nancy Dodington, the centre's relocation co-ordinator.

"Assimilation or Genocide? Native Children and the Child Welfare System in B.C."
Vancouver, March 1986[24]

As President of the Indian Homemakers' Association of B.C., I thank this Committee for the opportunity to bring to the attention of the federal government and the Canadian people the urgent need to put a halt to the wholesale removal of Native children from their families and communities by the Ministry of Human Resources of this Province. This practice began in the 1950s when the federal government transferred responsibility for Indian child welfare to the provinces without any consultation with Native people. A major element of the system that is now established is that the province must apprehend Indian children before it has jurisdiction over them or can provide any services. As a result there are no preventative services and many apprehensions. Native

---

24. Rose Charlie and Kathleen Jamieson. From a paper presented by the Indian Homemakers' Association of B.C. to the Parliamentary Committee on Child Care. Copy at Vancouver Status of Women.

families then become enmeshed in a legal process from which they seldom emerge unscarred.

Ever since the Indian Homemakers' Association was incorporated in 1969 as a non profit society that would serve as a voice for Native women and their families in B.C., we have been deeply concerned with this issue. We have acted as advocates for parents and children trapped in a system which they do not understand and in which their interests are not protected. It is our experience that many apprehensions are without due cause and unwarranted: they occur as a result of cultural biases, discrimination or misunderstanding. Indeed many parents go to the Ministry of Human Resources (MHR) for help but they do not understand the rules, the concepts or the terminology and they may sign away their children into permanent care without knowing that they are doing so. We know about the despair of the families who have lost their children to this system and about the suffering of the children who are torn away from their families and put into foster homes or institutions. These are the children who grow up to fill penitentiaries and skid rows and to die violent deaths.

This Association has compiled many documents and made many presentations on this issue before national and international bodies over the past 15 years yet we see little progress being made. Indeed statistics for 1984-85 supplied to us by the Ministry of Human Resources and by the Department of Indian Affairs (DIA), though incomplete, show that the traffic in children of Native ancestry has not diminished and may in fact have increased since 1981. Although the Province has sometimes argued that to keep such statistics would contravene provincial human rights legislation it probably does do so in order to be reimbursed by the Department of Indian Affairs for the "in care" costs of some status Indian children.

In 1955 before jurisdiction for Native children was transferred to the province it was estimated that less than 1 per cent of all children in care of B.C.'s welfare authority were children of Indian ancestry. A comparison of 1981 and 1985 figures show the following situation today: For 1980-81 the MHR figure for all Native children described as status, non-status Indian and Métis was 2674 or 36.7 per cent of all children in care. Yet only 3 to 4 per cent of the children in this province are likely to be Native children. 1984-85 statistics provided to us by MHR indicate that MHR has identified 2208 out of the total number of 7158 children "in care" or 30.8 per cent as "Indian". But this figure does not include Métis or most non-status Indians as the 1981 figure does, and since the total number of people of Native ancestry is usually calculated to be between one half or equal to that of status Indians, then the total figure of all Native children "in care" in B.C. for 1984-85 is at least 46 per cent (30.8 + 15.4) of all children "in care" and likely very much higher.

The Department of Indian Affairs (DIA) transfers payments to the Province for the costs of only some of the status Indian children "in care." For 1984-85 that number was 917 children. For these children the Department of Indian Affairs paid the Province $12.9 million or approximately $14,000 per child for the year. None of this money can be claimed by the province, however, until the Indian children are actually apprehended. Since no monies can be transferred to the Province by DIA for preventative measures or for assessments this practice, in our view, clearly constitutes an inducement to the Province to first apprehend and ask questions later. A review of national statistics by Philip Hepworth in his 1980 book, "Foster Care and Adoption in Canada" showed that once Native children come into the care of the courts they are less likely than other children to be returned to the care of their parents. Although fewer Native children are adopted than other children, they remain in institutions or are shunted from one foster home to another instead of being returned to their families. The social costs are clearly very high. If we extrapolate from the financial cost of $14,000 per child that DIA transfers to the province, the total per annum cost for all Native children "in care" in this province is possibly around $50 million. We cannot believe that such expenditures have gone unremarked or that the whole system has unintended consequences. We believe that this system falls within the U.N. definition of genocide ...

We believe that the situation of Native children in B.C. is a national tragedy. We do not believe that it will go away by itself and we cannot wait for it to be resolved by Indian government. In any case the status Indian population is now being increased as a result of the 1985 amendments to the Indian Act by about one third. Many of these people will not have band membership or affiliation with any Indian tribal group. Moreover about one third of all status Indians in B.C. presently live off reserve and there are as well an unspecified number of other people of native ancestry who will not come under Indian government but who are also at risk. There is no simple solution and there can be no single solution. But piecemeal agreements with bands or tribal groups such as are being made in other provinces or tripartite arrangements with the province do not in our view provide sufficient protection for all Native children. As a partial remedy to this vast problem we urge that this Committee recommend the creation of federal umbrella legislation that will encompass the broad principles of the U.S. Indian Child Welfare Act of 1978 and adapt the specifics to the Canadian situation (see Appendix). It is important in so doing that the federal and provincial governments set aside the jurisdictional disputes that have prevented any progress from occurring in this area for so long ...

Chapter 5

Women, Law and the Justice System

Paula Bourne

Law and the justice system govern nearly every facet of Canadian women's lives. This is as true today as it was for our foremothers, and the efforts of the modern feminist movement to achieve legal equality represent a continuation of the long struggle begun in the last century by the first women's movement. This first wave of feminists achieved political, economic and social rights but the changes effected did little to improve the status of women's lives. Disillusioned with the lack of progress, women's groups in the 1960s demanded, and got, a Royal Commission on the Status of Women (RCSW) to "enquire into ... the status of women in Canada ... to ensure for women equal opportunities with men in all respects."[1] Committed to "a principle that permits no distinction in rights and freedoms between men and women,"[2] the Commission's Report listed 167 recommendations to facilitate women's economic independence and to promote their participation in public life.

The Report sparked the establishment of new organizations, like the National Action Committee on the Status of Women (NAC), which, along with older organizations such as the Federation of Women Teachers' Associations of Ontario (FWTAO), challenged the federal, provincial and territorial governments to implement the recommendations. But even after the adoption of many of them, women again found the results disappointing and the promised equality remained as elusive as ever. Gradually, it became clear to feminists in the late seventies that true equality was a more complex concept than equal treatment and opportunity. To bring about meaningful change in women's lives required a redefinition of the term and the development of new laws. This chapter examines equality rights as they have evolved over the last twenty years. Beginning with the Constitutional debate around the Charter of Rights and Freedoms, which focused attention on the meaning of equality, it

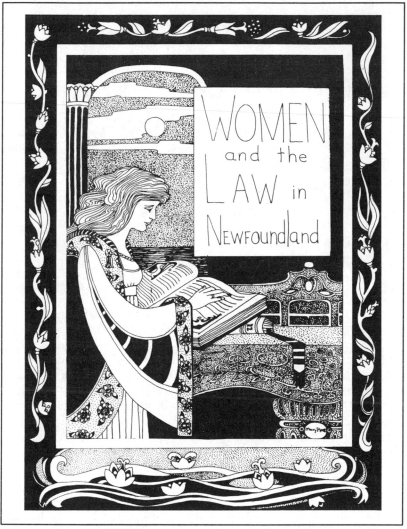

The cover for this 1972 feminist pamphlet is by artist Mary Pratt. The booklet was intended to make women more aware of their legal rights and of the laws that governed their daily lives.

goes on to discuss many of the legal issues confronted by feminists in the pre- and post-Charter years.

The Constitution

The Charter of Rights and Freedoms

"When Canada's constitution was to be repatriated, Canadian women rose up by the thousands and demanded the inclusion of strong equality provisions in the proposed Charter of Rights and Freedoms. Women did so in light of the realities they faced as second class citizens in the workplace, the home, the courts and the legislatures."[3] These realities reflected the inadequacy of existing legislation to address effectively women's inequalities. Although political outsiders to the male-dominated constitution-making process, the Canadian women's movement's role in this process illustrated both its vitality and its unity of purpose.

In her book, *The Taking of Twenty Eight: Women Challenge the Constitution*, Penney Kome documents the drama surrounding the political struggle waged by women to entrench meaningful equality rights within the *Charter of Rights and Freedoms*.[4] The first draft of the equality section of the Charter, section 15, tabled in the House of Commons in 1980 and drawn up without consulting women's groups, repeated, almost exactly, the language of the 1960 *Canadian Bill of Rights*, a piece of legislation that had never been interpreted to women's benefit. Once the draft was made public, Doris Anderson, president of the Canadian Advisory Committee on the Status of Women (CACSW), wrote Prime Minister Pierre Trudeau detailing objections to the proposed wording. At the same time, the CACSW alerted Canadian women through the mass distribution of explanatory flyers and asked women to sign and return the attached coupons demanding wording changes. Some 17,000 responses were received. Under duress, the government held hearings before a joint committee of the House of Commons and the Senate. Briefs presented by women's groups, including CACSW and NAC,[5] called for substantial changes to the wording of section 15. After agreeing to some changes, the government then moved to stifle further discussion by pressuring the CACSW to postpone its planned February 14, 1981 conference on the Constitution and the Charter. In protest at such unprecedented interference in a supposedly independent council, Doris Anderson resigned.

Charter activists responded by organizing an Ad Hoc Committee on the Constitution to stage an alternative conference on the same date as the cancelled one. Committee members recruited the support of feminist groups such as NAC, the Canadian Research Institute for the Advancement of Women and the National Association of Women and the Law as well as more traditional groups like the Canadian Federation of University Women and the Federation of Women Teachers' Associations of Ontario. Despite the short lead time and the lack of financial resources, meeting rooms were booked, billets found and food arranged for the 1,400 women who descended on Ottawa on February 14th.

Over the next two days women decided what further changes they wanted in the Charter and developed a vigorous lobbying campaign. Their efforts resulted in an equality clause that provided for equality under the law and equal benefit of the law — wording carefully crafted to facilitate consideration of a law's impact on women. Their efforts to include marital status, sexual orientation and political belief in the list of named grounds of discrimination, and to allow for open-ended protection from discrimination so that grounds other than those named could be covered did not, however, succeed. The final version of the Charter's section 15 reads:

15.(1)Every individual is equal before and under the law and has the right to equal protection and benefit of the law without discrimination and, in particular without discrimination based on race, national or ethnic origin, colour, religion, sex, age or mental or physical disability.

(2)Subsection (1) does not preclude any law, program or activity that has as its object the amelioration of conditions of disadvantaged individuals or groups including those that are disadvantaged because of race, national or ethnic origin, colour, religion, sex, age or mental or physical disability.

Perhaps the best known achievement of the February 14 conference and subsequent lobbying campaign was the guarantee of equality between the sexes as enshrined in section 28. This states:

28. Notwithstanding anything in this Charter, the rights and freedoms referred to in it are guaranteed equally to male and female persons.

The need for this additional equality protection derived from women's recognizable concerns with the wording of two other Charter sections. Section 1 subjects all Charter rights to "such reasonable limits prescribed by law as can be demonstrably justified in a free and democratic society" and women feared that, without section 28, the limits allowed in section 1 could be used to restrict women's right to equality. Section 28 is also intended to prevent the application of section 27, the multiculturalism clause, to undermine women's equality. This clause instructs that the Charter be interpreted in a manner consistent with the preservation and enhancement of the multicultural heritage of Canadians. Through the addition of section 28's guarantees, women sought "to ensure that cultural practices that discriminated on the basis of sex would not survive Charter review."[6]

The campaign took one further turn at the federal-provincial conference of First Ministers held on November 2, 1981. At this conference, the First Ministers, with the exception of Premier René Lévèsque of Quebec, agreed to a new clause, section 33, which would give any government the power to override the Charter rights, including the equality rights of sections 15 and 28. Once again women protested en masse and their lobby redoubled in strength. Although unsuccessful in having section 33 removed, the women claimed some victory when, on

November 24, 1981, the then Minister of Justice, Jean Chrétien, announced that the provincial and federal governments had agreed to remove the application of the override clause from section 28.

The Meech Lake Accord

Before the Charter's potential for extending true equality to all aspects of Canadian women's lives could be tested in the courts, however, feminists faced a major threat in the form of the Meech Lake Accord. Hastily patched together by the federal and provincial governments in June 1987, the Accord was heralded by its all-male framers as the 'deal' to bring Quebec back into the constitutional fold. While women's groups supported the "distinct society" clause, they objected vociferously to, once again, being excluded from the constitution-making process. In a classic case of déjà vu, the results of this exclusion were appallingly apparent.[7] Two of the Accord's clauses immediately became major focuses of concern. Clause 16 specifically exempted multicultural and native rights from the Accord's guarantees of linguistic duality and the distinct society. The lack of reference to women gave rise to well-founded fears that women's equality rights were at risk. A history of judicial interpretations disadvantaging women reinforced this concern, and the federal government's patronizing approach to demands that clause 16 be deleted or include women, mobilized feminist protests across the country. NAC, the Legal Education Action Fund (LEAF), the National Association of Women and the Law, and the Ad Hoc Committee on the Constitution joined with other groups to press for a satisfactory resolution. In addition to the problematic clause 16, women also wanted clause 7, the Accord's "opting out" provision, amended so as not to jeopardize future national shared-cost programs such as a national day-care program.

The ultimate demise of Meech Lake in June 1990 did little to assuage women's anger. If their concerns could be so easily dismissed, as they had been throughout this process, the same could happen in future constitution-making deals. Determined to avoid a repeat of previous scenarios, NAC and other feminist advocacy groups participated vocally and ardently in the 1991–1992 national unity conferences. They supported "distinct society" status for Quebec, native women's struggle for an assurance that the gender equality provisions of the Charter of Rights and Freedoms would apply to aboriginal self-government and they called for 50 per cent of the seats in a reformed senate.[8] Once more, however, August 1992 witnessed an all-male constitutional package, the Charlottetown Accord, presented to the Canadian public.

The Charlottetown Accord

The Charlottetown Accord engendered considerable debate among Canadian women's groups. The only unanimously endorsed provision was that giving Quebec distinct society status. The constitutional proposal

The Native Women's Association of Canada demanded that native
women's equality rights would be guaranteed under the Charlottetown
Accord.

for aboriginal self-government, although supported in principle, was
openly criticized by NAC and the Native Women's Association of
Canada (NWAC) for its failure to state explicitly that, under self-government, native women would continue to be protected by the Charter's
equality clauses. These groups claimed that the Accord's legal wording
would allow aboriginal governments to use the infamous section 33 of
the 1982 Constitutional package to override equality guarantees for
native women.[9] The Métis National Council of Women (MNCW), on
the other hand, disagreed with this interpretation and unequivocally
endorsed the proposal for aboriginal self-government.[10] The opposing
views held by MNCW and NWAC reflected, in part, the fact that Métis
women had been directly involved in drafting the legal language for
self-government while native women were the only major aboriginal
organization excluded from this process. In August 1992, the Federal
Court of Appeal ruled this exclusion discriminatory on the grounds that
none of the native groups invited to the constitutional talks, and financed
by the federal government, put the native women's position strongly
forward. Subsequently, NWAC sought a court order to block the national
referendum scheduled for October 26, 1992, on the new constitutional
agreement. Since the federal government violated native women's rights
by denying them a place at its constitutional talks with native groups,
NWAC argued, the constitutional agreement based on these talks was
illegal.[11]

While NWAC strove to have the referendum declared null and void, other Canadian women, individually and collectively, aligned themselves with both the "yes" and the "no" sides in the referendum campaign. Conflicting opinions focused on three areas of the constitutional agreement: the Canada Clause, social programs and the proposed new Senate. Foremost among the "no" supporters was NAC, led by its president, Judy Rebick. The Canada Clause, included in a preamble to the constitution, was viewed by NAC as setting up a hierarchy of rights that made some groups more equal than others. This clause required "Canadians and their governments" to be committed to the development of minority linguistic rights but only "Canadians" to be committed to the rights of women and other minority groups. Equally alarming to NAC was the clause's lack of any specific mention of the many groups protected by the Charter, including people with disabilities, lesbians and gays, the poor and the aged. Although agreeing that the Canada Clause was flawed and did little to improve the status of women, feminists like Audrey McLaughlin, leader of the federal New Democrats and Lynn McDonald, a former NAC president, claimed the clause did not make women's position worse. Along with other feminists, female politicians and trade unionists, they urged Canadian women to vote "yes" for the Charlottetown Accord to promote national unity. Rejection, they feared, could lead to Quebec's separation and the loss of aboriginal self-government.

The potential effect of the constitutional proposals on social programs also divided feminists. NAC opposed the inclusion of an "opting out" clause for new social programs, borrowed from the Meech Lake Accord, and further insisted that even existing programs, such as medicare, were threatened through a new provision restricting federal spending capacity. "Yes" supporters disagreed, stating that all national social programs, existing or future, depended less on constitutional wording than on government resources and the political will to implement them.[12]

Perhaps the constitutional issue that most angered NAC was the First Ministers' decision to drop the plan for proportional representation in the reformed Senate. This plan, designed to promote gender equality and minority representation in the Upper House, had been endorsed by both the national unity conferences preceding the Charlottetown Accord and the parliamentary Beaudoin-Dobbie Report on constitutional changes. The promises of provincial premiers from Ontario, Saskatchewan, British Columbia, Manitoba and Nova Scotia to implement measures ensuring 50 per cent female representation among their provinces' elected senators, did little to persuade the "no" forces to drop their opposition to the agreement. They wanted explicit constitutional guarantees of Senate gender equality for Canadian women who, they pointed out, make up 52 per cent of the population but had never been represented by more than 15 per cent of the seats in the federal Parliament. While sympathetic to the need to increase female representation, women supporters of the "yes" side disagreed over strategies for achieving this. Some opposed any scheme for female quotas, while others called for provincial discretion in appointing or electing an equal number of female senators once the constitutional deal was approved.

Despite the splits in feminist opinions during the referendum campaign, most agreed that the "no" side's concerns were legitimate. On balance, however, the "yes" supporters found the deal flawed yet acceptable. After ten years of constitutional wrangles, they wanted to bring Quebec back into the constitutional fold, provide for aboriginal self-government and then work towards redressing the problems identified by the "no" side. To the "no" side, the Accord's shortcomings were greater than the potential losses posed by its rejection. It reduced equality, undermined social programs and disappointed women's political aspirations. The overwhelming rejection of the deal by Canadians in the October 26, 1992 referendum was thus greeted by many Canadian women with relief, along with a pledge to continue the fight for a constitutional package that could be supported by all women, minority and aboriginal groups, and Quebec.

Equality Rights Interpretation

Although proclaimed on April 17, 1982, along with the repatriated Constitution, section 15 of the Charter did not come into effect until three years later. This moratorium, ostensibly designed to give provincial and federal governments time to review, alter and delete legislation in conflict with the equality provisions, allowed women, many of whom had been involved in the Charter campaign, "to plan for the day when they could take their unresolved equality claims to court, armed with the hard won guarantees of section 15 and 28".[13] Examples of such unresolved claims were plentiful, particularly those of women who had sought relief under the equality provisions of the Canadian Bill of Rights. Section 1(b) of this 1960 Bill guaranteed "equality before the law and protection of the law without discrimination because of ... sex," among other grounds. Despite its explicit equality guarantees, the identification of sex as a prohibited ground of discrimination and the requirement that all other federal laws be applied and interpreted to comply with it, the Bill had been a dismal failure for women.

Two key decisions handed down in the 1970s clearly illustrated that the Bill's equality protection provided no support for women. The first was the challenge by Jeannette Lavell and Yvonne Bedard to section 12(1)(b) of the Indian Act.[14] Under this section, Indian women who married non-Indians lost their status, while Indian men who married non-Indians did not lose their status but, in fact, conferred Indian status on their non-Indian wives.[15] As a result of this provision, upon marriage both Lavell and Bedard had forfeited membership in their bands and all the ensuing rights, including the right to own property and live on their reserves. At the Supreme Court of Canada, Lavell and Bedard alleged that the offending section of the Indian Act discriminated against them because of sex and violated their equality before the law as guaranteed under the Canadian Bill of Rights. In a now notorious 1973 decision, the Supreme Court of Canada ruled, in the *Lavell* case, that section 12(1)(b) of the Indian Act did not infringe section 1(b) of the Canadian Bill of Rights because the guarantee to "equality before the law" in the latter meant only equality in the administration and enforcement of law. The actual substance of the law could discriminate between men and women, as long as the law was applied by its administrators in an even-handed way.[16]

The second decision involved a challenge to the Unemployment Insurance Act.[17] As outlined in the document reprinted below, in 1978 Stella Bliss was denied regular unemployment insurance compensation (UIC) benefits because she was pregnant, despite the fact that she had paid the requisite number of contributions to qualify for them. Section 46 of the Unemployment Insurance Act stipulated that a pregnant woman could not claim regular benefits in the 15 weeks immediately surrounding the birth of her child. Bliss, who submitted her claim within the 15-week disentitlement period, also failed to qualify for UIC pregnancy benefits. This disqualification stemmed from the requirement that a women be employed "for 10 or more weeks of insurable employment in the twenty weeks that immediately preceded the thirtieth week before her expected date of confinement." Bliss had been unemployed at the time she became pregnant and, therefore, did not meet this requirement. Refused pregnancy benefits because she did not qualify and refused regular benefits because she was pregnant, Bliss took her case to the Supreme Court of Canada claiming sex discrimination contrary to the Canadian Bill of Rights. The Supreme Court's 1978 decision denied her claim stating that Bliss' right to equality *before* the law was not violated insofar as she was denied benefits not because she was a woman but because she was a "pregnant" woman. In a wondrous twist of logic, the judges ruled that pregnancy discrimination was not sex discrimination, since the distinction being made was not between male and female persons, but between pregnant and non-pregnant persons. The Court's view that pregnancy was a "voluntary" state and that since all women did not become pregnant, the distinction was not one based on sex, completely ignored the fact that only women become pregnant and that laws that discriminate against those who are pregnant discriminate against women.

The judgements in the *Lavell* and the *Bliss* cases illustrated not only the inadequacy of the Canadian Bill of Rights in terms of its equality protection but also the Court's narrow interpretation of equality language. Legal judgements such as these reconfirmed a growing concern among women's groups across the country that the notion of equality based on treating women the same as men and providing them with the same opportunities would not improve women's lives. In the early days of the revived movement, when women were implicitly or explicitly excluded from doing many things — for example, applying for jobs that could legally be advertised for men only — it had made sense to claim equal treatment for women. By the late seventies, women's organizations rejected this simple equality notion, replacing it with a broader definition that called for equality of results. To achieve this goal, feminists developed an approach to equality emphasizing the reality of women's lives and the importance of looking at the impact of legislation, policy and government action on women. They fought for and won Charter equality guarantees that provided for equality *under the law* and *equal benefit of the law*, thus addressing the Bill of Rights' shortcomings. But as their experience with that Bill had taught them, legal language is always open to interpretation and susceptible to judicial discretion. Therefore, in the equality rights discourse that preceded the Charter's enactment and continues today, feminist lawyers built upon the work of other feminists to argue cogently for the rejection of the traditional and dangerous method of determining inequality known as the "similarly situated test". According to this test of equality, those who are alike should be treated alike, while those who are different should be treated differently. Experience had shown that judicial discretion in identifying which characteristics constitute "alikes" had been used with extremely discriminatory results for women, as evidenced in the *Lavell* and *Bliss* cases, which, by defining Indian women as "alikes" and pregnant women as "alikes," had allowed the courts to conclude there was no discrimination because all Indian women and all pregnant women received the same treatment.

To facilitate a meaningful equality interpretation, feminist lawyers called for the court's adoption of a *substantive* and *purposive* model of equality — a model that seeks to accommodate differences and remedy disadvantages experienced by individuals and groups. A substantive model of equality does not permit women's equality claims to be dismissed just because women cannot prove that they are "similarly situated" to men. Its application requires the contextualization of women's lives and, as such, directs the courts to examine the discriminatory impact of laws and practices as they affect women disadvantaged by gender, race, sexual preference, physical disability, marital status, etc. At the same time, the substantive equality model validates the special treatment and affirmative action programs protected under section 15(2) of the Charter while rejecting claims by men for equal access to these programs. This equality model focuses on the inequality faced by disadvantaged groups and, although individual men may be disadvantaged by isolated legislative provisions, they are clearly not disadvantaged relative to women.[18]

Many women involved in developing and articulating the substantive equality model also became founding members of the Women's Legal Education and Action Fund (LEAF), a feminist advocacy group whose

Steve Roberts Courtesy: LEAF

In the late 1980s, the Women's Legal Education and Action Fund began celebrating the 1929 decision that made women persons by hosting Person's Day Breakfasts such as this one in Toronto, 1991

objective is to promote women's equality in the courts. Planning for LEAF began during the three-year interim period after the Charter's proclamation, and its official début on April 17, 1985, coincided with the date that section 15 came into force.[19] LEAF's founders and supporters recognize that equality as a reality requires both legal education and the taking-up of relevant cases in the courts. Funding is provided through donated legal services, charitable donations and a variety of fundraising activities. The federal government's Court Challenges program that helped fund Charter-based cases undertaken by disadvantaged groups also provided LEAF with some financial support until its cancellation in February 1992. Given the high cost of litigation, coupled with a lack of sufficient financial resources on the part of disadvantaged groups, the cancellation caused serious questioning of the government's commitment to equality.[20]

Equality Litigation under the Charter

The Rape Law

The first four years of equality litigation under the Charter of Rights brought mixed results. The vast majority of cases originated with persons or organizations whose main interest was *not* the promotion of equality for women or disadvantaged groups. A 1989 report showed that of 44 Charter cases on sex equality, 35 were initiated by men challenging the few laws and programs designed to alleviate the inequities women experienced.[21] One involved two accused rapists claiming that section 276 of the Criminal Code, which banned the introduction into a rape trial of evidence of a woman's sexual history with anyone other than the accused, violated their right to a fair trial under the Charter. In August 1991, the Supreme Court of Canada struck down section 276, also known as the "rape shield" law. Introduced in 1983, as part of a series of amendments relating to rape and sexual assault, this provision was intended to encourage women to report rape by reducing their well-founded fear of being "raped" again in court by lawyers prying into their personal lives. Although criticized at the time by women's groups for not being strong enough, the loss of this safeguard galvanized women into demanding a tough and innovative new law. Justice Minister Kim Campbell consulted with women's organizations from across Canada, including representatives from LEAF and NAC, giving women, for the first time, the opportunity to help create a law that affects them directly. The result — Bill C-49 — was initially applauded as "an important step forward in making sexual assault charges more responsive to the problem of sexual violence against women."[22] In a rare show of feminist solidarity, white women joined with black, visible minority, aboriginal, lesbian, and disabled women in calling for a clause in the preamble recognizing the special vulnerability of "doubly oppressed" women to sexual assault and their lack of accessibility to the justice system. The request was rejected. Opposition by well-known male civil rights activists and lawyers also resulted in amendments that further outraged women's groups. One amendment removed a reference to "intoxication" from a clause that would have prevented an accused person from saying consent was given when the complainant was "incapable of consenting by reason of intoxication or other condition." Another deleted the word "all" from the section requiring an accused to show that "all reasonable steps" had been taken to obtain consent. Despite the amendments, the bill, which was enacted on June 15, 1992, provides stringent legal guidelines and procedures to determine admissibility of past sexual history as evidence, and defines the concept of consent to sexual activity. This new definition restricts use of the controversial defence of mistaken belief that allowed accused rapists to argue that they honestly believed a woman had consented.

At the time of its passing, the 1983 sexual assault legislation, which included the "rape shield" provision, had been viewed by women's groups as representing a first step towards having legislation that adequately protected women and properly defined rape as a form of violence. By removing restrictions against charging a husband with the rape of his wife, and by replacing the old offences of "rape" and "indecent assault" with a three-tiered offence of sexual assault, along with a corresponding sentencing scheme and evidentiary rules, it was hoped that more women would report rapes and that their participation in the criminal justice system would be less painful and would result in higher conviction rates. Although concerned by the legislation's failure to define "sexual assault" (thus allowing for wide judicial discretion), its lack of sufficient protection to victims regarding questioning of their past sexual history and its inclusion of "honest belief" as a valid defence, women's groups agreed to support the amendments on the condition that the government implement a comprehensive monitoring program.[23]

As a 1987 report showed, women's concerns were well-founded.[24] The omission of a sexual assault definition, the report points out, has permitted wide judicial discretion and has led to frequently contradictory decisions. For example, one New Brunswick judge held that touching a woman's breast did not constitute sexual assault because breasts, unlike genitalia, are only secondary sexual characteristics, much like men's beards.[25] Yet another judge, in the Northwest Territories, decided that because breasts are sexualized by our society, such non-consensual touching should be punished as sexual assault.[26] The sexual assault legislation presents other problems beyond those associated with vagueness. While higher reporting rates with respect to some types of assault have occurred, there is no clear evidence of increased conviction rates. Indeed some feminist legal scholars argue that the "overall effect of the gender-neutral offence of sexual assault is to minimize and mask the very specific harm that women suffer from rape."[27] And, in many cases, the "rape shield" law did not prevent judges from exercising their discretion to allow the questioning of victims about their sexual history.[28] Meanwhile, severe limitations in the allocation of both time and money to the government monitoring program brought protests from women's groups [29] and, in the aftermath of the 1991 Supreme Court decision on the rape shield law, demands for a new sexual assault law.[30]

The Abortion Law

In addition to sexual assault, another area of criminal law that women continued to protest was that contained in section 251, which specified the conditions under which a woman could have a legal abortion. These conditions were that the abortion must be performed in a hospital, with the prior approval of the hospital's therapeutic abortion committee consisting of three physicians who had to unanimously agree that the woman's continued pregnancy "would or would be likely to endanger her life or health." The abortion law did not define what it meant by "health" and allowed individual hospitals to decide whether to provide abortions at all. Despite Dr. Henry Morgentaler's third acquittal by the Quebec Court of Appeal in 1976,[31] on the charge of performing illegal abortions, protests, lobbies and even a legal suit[32] failed to have abortion decriminalized. In 1983, Dr. Morgentaler opened clinics in Winnipeg and Toronto. Charged with breaking the law by the Metro Toronto Police, Morgentaler made Ontario legal history when he was acquitted by an Ontario Supreme Court jury in 1984. After the Ontario Court of

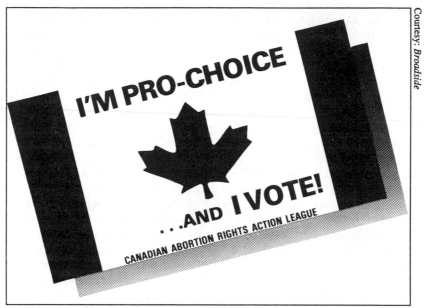

This CARAL postcard was one of many to be used to pressure the government to decriminalize abortion.

Appeal ordered a new trial, Morgentaler appealed the order to the Supreme Court of Canada. On January 28, 1988, the Court struck down the abortion law, declaring that it denied women's rights to life, liberty and security of the person, as guaranteed in section 7 of the Charter of Rights and Freedoms. The Court ruled 5-2 that the Criminal Code's requirements that abortion be performed in accredited hospitals with the approval of a committee of three doctors "clearly interferes with a woman's physical and bodily integrity," caused problems of access and delay, and imposed health risks on women. In her part of the written majority judgement, Madam Justice Bertha Wilson presented the most sensitive comments, acknowledging the reality of women's lives. Simply put, Wilson wrote that a decision to have an abortion was something men could never understand. "It is probably impossible," she stated, "for a man to respond, even imaginatively, to such a dilemma, not just because it is outside the realm of his personal experience, but because he can relate to it only by objectifying it, thereby eliminating the subjective elements of the female psyche, which are at the heart of the dilemma."[33]

Jubilant at the Court's decision, women's organizations determined that, after such a long and difficult struggle, abortion should never again be criminalized. Anti-abortion activists, however, immediately pressed for a new law. The summer of 1989 witnessed two cases that illustrated the precariousness of women's right to a now legal abortion. In the first, an Ontario judge granted an injunction to the former boyfriend of a

pregnant woman to prevent her from obtaining an abortion. Although
the injunction was quickly set aside on technical grounds, a second
similar case occurred soon after in Quebec. This time the injunction
obtained by Jean-Guy Tremblay to prevent his former girlfriend, Chan-
tale Daigle, from terminating her pregnancy was upheld in the Quebec
Court of Appeal before being quashed by a hastily convened Supreme
Court of Canada. While awaiting the high court's decision, 10,000
Montreal women rallied in Daigle's support. Daigle, 22 weeks pregnant,
fled to Boston for an abortion without knowing the Court's decision.
Eventually the Court did decide that fathers have no rights, on behalf of
the fetus or themselves, to prevent a woman from having an abortion.[34]

Partly in response to these cases, and the demands of anti-abortion
groups, the federal government introduced a new abortion bill on November 3, 1989. This bill was attacked by both anti-abortion and pro-
choice supporters, albeit for different reasons. The former found the bill
too liberal while the latter found its very existence an affront to women.
Both sides presented briefs to the Parliamentary Committee considering
the bill. On May 29, 1990, the House of Commons passed the bill with
a 9-vote margin. Members of Parliament were allowed a free vote but
Conservative cabinet ministers were required to vote in its favour. Subsequently, the bill died when it failed to receive the Senate's majority
support.[35]

Decriminalization alone, however, has not guaranteed women's access to abortion because of attempts by several provinces to erect local
barriers to abortion clinics after the 1989 Supreme Court decision. And,
as the results of a December 1992 survey conducted by the Canadian
Abortion Rights Action League (CARAL) showed, most hospital abortion services are concentrated in urban areas and are reduced or non-existent in many parts of the country, particularly in remote areas. Even
for women living in provinces that permit and pay the full cost for
abortions performed in clinics as well as hospitals, such as Ontario and
British Columbia, access depends on where they live. In Prince Edward
Island, no abortions have been performed since 1982 and an estimated
200 women leave the province annually to have abortions in Halifax.[36]
Clearly, as the authors of a recent study stress, the fact that Canada no
longer has an abortion law is not an unmitigated victory for women's
reproductive freedom so long as anti-abortion groups continue to oppose
women's right to choose in the guise of protecting the rights of the
fetus.[37]

The Andrews Case

Despite the legal frustrations and obstacles faced by Canadian women
over the last 25 years, there is cause for some optimism. The promise
of meaningful equality, as enshrined in section 15 of the Charter, has
yielded some important decisions. Most significant was the 1989 Supreme Court of Canada ruling in the *Andrews* case. Mr. Andrews, a

British lawyer, argued that the B.C. rule restricting the practice of law to Canadian citizens violated his equality rights under the Charter on the basis of his citizenship. While clearly this case did not involve facts relevant to LEAF's mandate, feminist lawyers quickly recognized its importance insofar as it would lead to the Supreme Court's first pronouncement on the interpretation of section 15. LEAF successfully sought intervenor status and used the opportunity to urge the court to adopt a purposive approach to equality and to reject the "similarly situated test." In a written submission, LEAF argued that "... this purpose of promoting the equality of the powerless, excluded and disadvantaged should animate interpretations of the guarantees of substantive equality in section 15." The Court decision in Andrews' favour accepted the basic concept that section 15 is designed to protect those groups who suffer social, political and legal disadvantage in our society. For LEAF and other equality-seeking groups, this historic decision signalled a new era for equality litigation. As one LEAF lawyer commented: "The language used in this decision ... provides a basis for differentiating true discrimination claims from those of advantaged groups such as men who have been using the sex equality provisions to challenge legislation that treats women differently." Moreover, the Court's focus on disadvantage when considering who may make a legitimate section 15 claim was lauded as providing an important test for legitimating future claims brought on the basis of marital, economic and sexual orientation status among others. And, at the same time, the Court's substantive equality interpretation was seen as having "... the potential to address the socially imposed disadvantages women experience around pregnancy, sexual assault, family relations and in areas such as employment."[38]

Workplace Equality

Soon after the *Andrews* decision, this promised potential was indeed realized when the Supreme Court ruled unanimously that pregnancy discrimination and sexual harassment constitute sex discrimination and violate sex equality guarantees provided in human rights legislation. The first case, *Brooks, Allen and Dixon* v. *Canada Safeway*, involved three pregnant Canada Safeway employees denied coverage under their employee health insurance plan during the 17-week period they were entitled to unemployment insurance maternity benefits. LEAF argued that pregnancy discrimination is sex discrimination and, therefore, in violation of both the Charter and human rights legislation. The Court agreed. "Pregnancy discrimination is a form of sex discrimination because of the basic biological fact that only women have the capacity to become pregnant," said Chief Justice Dickson.[39] In making this ruling, the "similarly situated" approach to equality used in the *Bliss* decision 10 years earlier was resoundingly rejected.

The second case, *Janzen and Govereau* v. *Platy Enterprises*, involved two waitresses who had been sexually harassed at the restaurant where they worked. Appearing for the appellants, LEAF drew upon existing feminist documentation[40] to argue that sexual harassment is a form of sex discrimination based upon the socially constructed ways in which men and women interact rather than biological differences between the sexes. Sexual harassment, LEAF told the Court, creates a discriminatory environment for women and is a significant barrier to their equality. The argument advanced by LEAF spelled out the power imbalance between men and women in the workplace, an imbalance recognized by the Court in its written decision:

> Perpetrators of sexual harassment and victims of the conduct may be either male or female. However, in the present sex stratified labour market, those with the power to harass sexually will pre-dominantly be male and those facing the greatest risk of harass-ment will tend to be female.[41]

The court ruled that the two waitresses had been sexually harassed. It concluded that sexual harassment constitutes sex discrimination and that employers are legally responsible for providing a work environment free from such harassing behaviour. As a result of these two decisions, all human rights legislation against sex discrimination in the workplace now encompasses protection from discrimination based on pregnancy and sexual harassment.

Through its rulings in the *Brooks, Allen, Dixon* and *Janzen and Govereau* cases, the Supreme Court acknowledged some aspects of the biological, social and economic realities of women's working lives. By telling women's stories and identifying their oppression, LEAF and its many supporters achieved two major victories for women's equality in the workplace. Other legal victories in women's employment rights, such as employment and pay equity, have also been realized over the last twenty years through the efforts of various women's groups and trade unions.[42]

Gender Bias in the Judicial System

Abortion and sexual assault are only two issues where the "politics of the body" have been played out in the legal arena. Others include pornography and prostitution.[43] The law's response to women's struggle to assert and gain control over their bodies is, in the opinion of feminist observers, sexist and biased. In an historic address delivered in February 1990 and entitled, "Will Women Judges Really Make a Difference?", Supreme Court of Canada Justice Bertha Wilson gave credibility and prominence to the problem of legal gender bias that years of feminist lobbying and scholarship had not been in a position to accomplish.[44] A recurring theme of her address was that true judicial neutrality can only be achieved when the law and the judicial system reflect female, as well as male, perspectives of the world. As confirmed by American studies,

Wilson noted, male judges adhere to traditional values and beliefs about the nature of men and women and their proper role in society. She concluded her remarks by calling for a government-sponsored task force on gender bias and the development of judicial educational programs. In doing so, Wilson echoed the earlier demands voiced by many participants at the Banff, Alberta May 22–24, 1986 conference on "The Socialization of Judges to Equality Issues"[45] and the conclusions reached in the Manitoba Association of Women and the Law 1988 report *Gender Equality in the Courts*.[46] The meaning of gender as a topic for study and education is, however, subject to considerable scrutiny by feminist theorists, activists and lawyers. They recognize that gender is not a unitary concept and to regard it as such poses the danger of reducing women to a unitary group, usually white, middle-class, heterosexual, thus suppressing race, class, disability and sexual identity.[47] To genuinely overcome legal gender bias, therefore, requires that all participants in the legal system — from police to judges — be educated as to the multiple subjectivities of women.

Given the overwhelming male dominance of the judiciary in particular, educational programs and courses for judges need to focus on issues concerning the oppression of women and reflect the reality of women's lives. As of 1990, there were 849 federally appointed judges in Canada, of whom only 73 — or 9 per cent — were women, while three women sat on the nine-member Supreme Court of Canada. Wilson, the first woman appointee to the Supreme Court in 1982, retired in 1991 and was replaced by a male judge. During her tenure, she sought to negate the judicial system's male bias by lending credence to women's reality. She championed the concept of the "reasonable female person" in a case involving a 22-year-old Manitoba woman who shot and killed her live-in partner. The woman had been severely beaten by this man on many occasions. On the night of the shooting he beat her and threatened her again. He handed her a loaded gun and said, "Either you kill me or I'll get you." As he turned to leave the room, she shot him. When the case reached the Supreme Court, Madam Justice Wilson ruled expert evidence about the "battered woman syndrome" as admissible. This evidence bolstered the defence's argument that the woman acted in self-defence because, under the circumstances, it was reasonable for her to believe that this was the only way to defend herself. Wilson, in a written decision acquitting the woman, stated: "If it strains credulity to imagine what the 'ordinary man' would do in the position of the battered spouse, it is probably because men do not typically find themselves in that situation. Some women do, however."[48]

The application of the "reasonable female person" concept as opposed to that of the "reasonable person", normally interpreted as male with a particular view of the world and experience of life different from that of women, nevertheless remains rare within our judicial system. And the persistent application of this male-defined "reasonable person" concept is particularly evident from results of a recently released study, *Hatred in the Heart,* which documents the cases of 44 Montreal men charged with killing their spouses between 1982 and 1986. According to the author, Ottawa lawyer Andrée Côté, Crown prosecutors help wife-killers get away with murder by agreeing to withdraw murder charges in exchange for guilty pleas on lesser offences such as manslaughter. Often the reason used to justify this policy is the Crown's acceptance of the accused's excuse that the victim provoked him, thus causing a "reasonable" (male) reaction. Judges, Côté wrote, agree to plea bargaining without allowing any opportunity to hear from the victim's relatives or friends who might tell a different story. Most of the victims, she noted, had left or were in the process of leaving abusive relationships. Of the 44 men charged, none was convicted of first-degree murder, eight were convicted of second-degree, 29 of manslaughter, two of lesser offences and five acquitted.[49]

Family Law

Marriage, Separation and Divorce

Family law, as it relates to marriage breakdown, is governed by both federal and provincial legislation. The federal Divorce Act covers the conditions for obtaining a divorce while provincial legislation outlines the rules for dividing family property and assets. Criteria for determining child custody, spousal maintenance and child support are contained in the Divorce Act and provincial family laws.

Despite 25 years of legislative measures to promote equality between husbands and wives, the prejudicial effects of male judicial bias remain evident. Although, theoretically, the 1968 and 1986 federal Divorce Acts[50] treat both sexes equally, the effects of divorce on women, especially those with custody of children, are frequently economically disastrous. The expectation that the various family law reform acts, passed in all provinces and the Northwest Territories during the 1970s and 1980s, would equalize the financial situation between divorced men and women has failed to materialize. Indeed, the idea that women are "just one step away from welfare" has never been so true nor so frighteningly possible, given that approximately 43 per cent of marriages end in divorce.[51] Consequently, while situations such as that experienced by Irene Murdoch, the Alberta farm wife who worked for 25 years alongside her husband on the family farm yet was denied any share in it upon the breakdown of her marriage, no longer occur,[52] economic equality for separated and divorced women remains a legal illusion.

The need for family law reform incorporating "the concept of equal partnership in marriage" was recommended in the 1970 *Report of the Royal Commission on the Status of Women in Canada.*[53] At the time of the Report's release, only the province of Quebec, through its Partnership of Acquests law, provided married women with the legal right to some share in family assets upon marriage dissolution. Although marriage contracts, designed to regulate marital relations during and upon dissolution of marriage, were advocated by some women's groups, their use was limited and their credibility shrouded in legal uncertainty. It took the national attention caused by the *Murdoch* case in the early 1970s, and the subsequent concerted demands of Canadian women, to goad all provincial legislatures into enacting new family laws. In theory these legal reforms promote equality of opportunity for men and women. Indeed legal rules have been made so gender-neutral that there are no longer "wives" and "husbands" in family law, only spouses. The legislation acknowledges the physical and emotional contribution of a spouse (usually the wife) involved in homemaking and child care as equal to the financial contribution of the other spouse (usually the husband). In accordance with this philosophy of equality between spouses, both are entitled to an equal share of family assets upon divorce.

Marital Property and Support

The assumption that "rule equality" would result in actual equality for women has yet to be proved. And legislative amendments[54] to provide for equal sharing of business assets, as well as such personal assets as the family home, car, etc., have done little to improve the economic plight of separated and divorced women. The fact is that "most couples have minimal amounts of property" to share.[55] Consequently, it is to the maintenance and child support provisions of family law that the majority of women turn for the "equality" promised them under the law. In keeping with the "rule equality" concept, maintenance awards mean that each spouse is expected to be self-supporting. The function of maintenance, enshrined in the 1986 federal Divorce Act and all provincial family law statutes, is rehabilitative. As stated in section 15 of the Divorce Act, spousal support orders should "promote the economic self-sufficiency of each spouse within a reasonable period." It is to be awarded according to the "needs" of one spouse and the "ability" of the other spouse to pay and is intended "to readjust the economic consequences flowing from the division of labour within a marriage."[56]

The effects of this insistence on spousal self-sufficiency, coupled with judicial ignorance of the economic reality that women and their custodial children face upon marriage breakdown, is well-documented. Recent government figures show that in the event of divorce, the woman grows poorer by 76 per cent and the man becomes richer by 42 per cent.[57] These figures reflect the fact that women are frequently denied maintenance and, where awards are made, they are usually small and for a limited time. Such decisions illustrate judges' failure to recognize women's lower earning capacity, limited employment opportunities and the burden of child care after separation. And, as a 1992 study shows, maintenance awards do not compensate women for their loss of earning potential arising from career interruptions for marital reasons.[58] This study found that labour force interruptions lasting as little as two years can have significant long-term costs, in lost earnings of $30,000 or more. Even more disturbing than unfair and inadequate financial settlements is the high default rate on maintenance and child-support payments. Despite special provincial efforts to enforce court orders, divorced men continue to evade their support obligations. In 1989, for example, only 32.5 per cent of Alberta men were complying and, in 1992, 75 per cent of the 91,650 support orders in Ontario were in arrears.[59] Yet, recent federal justice department statistics demonstrate that even if all court-ordered payments were made on time, two-thirds of divorced mothers and children households would remain impoverished. By contrast, only 16 per cent of their ex-husbands are below the poverty line after making court-ordered payments. Concern over the outrageously low level of child and spousal support and its concomitant undervaluing of women's work in, and the high cost of, child rearing has been shared by women's groups and feminist family lawyers for many years. In response, the federal government promised in 1990 to implement new, realistic standards for support orders, but, to date, discussion papers and federal-provincial consultations have failed to bring about the much-needed changes.[60]

Custody

In addition to the disproportionate economic impact of divorce on women, the application of "rule equality" in disputed custody decisions is a growing concern. Although in 85 per cent of cases custody is awarded to the mother with the consent of both spouses, where it is contested, men won custody at least 50 per cent of the time.[61] In such cases, judicial adherence to the rhetoric of equality and the application of assumptions relating to the ideology of motherhood operate to the detriment of women. Thus mothers who are forced to work outside the home because of inadequate child support and the law's insistence on spousal self-sufficiency are denied custody, while fathers' greater economic security and ability to provide mother-substitutes, in the form of parents, aunts or new wives, are viewed favourably by judges. Custody decisions that favour the parent offering a family set-up closely resembling the traditional nuclear family clearly illustrate how the ideology of motherhood and the ideology of equality disadvantage women. For lesbian mothers, the clash of these ideologies is particularly poignant as judges frequently reject their custody claims, citing lesbian lifestyles as deviant from stereotypical family lifestyles.[62]

Access to and Treatment by the Legal System

A major problem faced by women seeking custody and/or post-separation/divorce support is the high cost of litigation. Women's access to the legal system, whether seeking relief in civil or criminal courts, is thus circumscribed by their relatively low, compared to men's, income levels.

Provincial legal aid plans and community-based legal education clinics are seriously under-funded and, in most instances, provide only limited services. Initiatives like family courts, designed to assist women with family-related legal issues, have helped but, as one Vancouver observer notes, women remain disadvantaged even in these settings. Power imbalances in relationships are replayed in courts, resulting in unfair settlements especially for physically and emotionally battered women. Many appear without a lawyer because they work in low-paying jobs and do not qualify for legal aid yet cannot afford a lawyer of their own. When they are represented, it is often by inexperienced lawyers.[63]

Equitable and fair treatment requires a sensitivity to women's issues and realities. In addition to family law disputes, nowhere has this been more lacking than in rape trials.[64] Even under the 1983 "rape shield" law, judges could exercise their discretion as to whether a woman's past sexual history was relevant and admissible in court. Permitting such latitude flew in the face of considerable evidence of judicial insensitivity to sexual assault. And Crown prosecutors have not always protected women from inappropriate questioning, underscoring the fact that, in a rape trial, the woman is merely a witness; the prosecutor is not her lawyer, but, rather, the state's lawyer. The extent to which rape victims' treatment will improve under the 1992 rape law remains to be seen. This new law still allows the introduction, as evidence, of a woman's past sexual history, although judicial discretion is now replaced with specific guidelines for exercising this option. For "doubly oppressed" women — the disabled, aboriginals, visible minorities and lesbians — however, the 1992 legislation's power is most seriously limited by the government's refusal to include a preamble highlighting their particular vulnerability to sexual assault.[65]

The reality of the racist and sexist treatment experienced by "doubly oppressed" women came into sharp focus during the RCMP's Public Complaints Commission 1992 hearing into the case of an Inuit rape victim. Two years previously, Kitty Nowdluk-Reynolds had been choked, raped and beaten in Iqaluit in the Northwest Territories. The rapist confessed immediately. Kitty and her fiancé then moved to British Columbia in an attempt to put the whole incident behind her. When she failed to answer a subpoena to testify in court in Iqaluit, an RCMP officer arrested her. She was led away from her home in handcuffs. It took almost eight days to return to Iqaluit, in part because her RCMP escort overslept and they missed their flight. In all, Nowdluk-Reynolds spent time in five separate jails before arriving at her destination. There she faced the trauma of being transported to the court in the same vehicle as the man who had raped her. The attacker pleaded guilty and Kitty never testified. After the trial she was flown back to B.C. and dropped off on a highway to catch a bus home. At no time throughout this ordeal, as Kitty told the RCMP Commission, did the police explain their actions or inform her of her right to legal counsel. The Commission's report condemned Nowdluk-Reynold's "callous and insensitive treatment" but stopped short of upholding her complaint of racial discrimination.[66]

Human Rights

Employment

The lack of effective enforcement of anti-discrimination legislation led the Royal Commission on the Status of Women (RCSW) to recommend the establishment of federal, provincial and territorial Human Rights Commissions. At the time the Royal Commission's Report was released (1970), only four provinces — Nova Scotia, New Brunswick, Ontario and British Columbia — had human rights commissions. Over the intervening years, women's organizations fought to establish commissions in all the jurisdictions identified by the RCSW, lobbied to extend anti-discrimination provisions[67] and provided women with information about their human rights.[68]

Improvements in provincial and federal human rights legislation and procedures now give women wider access to the legal remedies covered under their anti-discrimination provisions. Sex and marital status are, for example, prohibited grounds for discrimination in all jurisdictions, and the 1989 Supreme Court's rulings in the *Brooks, Allen, Dixon* and *Janzen and Govereau* cases have extended human rights protection to include pregnancy and workplace sexual harassment in all jurisdictions.[69] These two cases represent examples of how women have successfully challenged discriminatory practices using human rights mechanisms to widen the definition of their rights. There are many others.[70] One main advantage for women is that complaints can be brought forward without the need for expensive lawyers and the costs incurred in adjudicating cases are borne by human rights commissions. On a less positive note, the backlog of cases faced by most commissions results in lengthy delays for complainants and the penalties and awards assessed are frequently low.[71]

Sexual Orientation

A more serious criticism, however, is the fact that, apart from Quebec, Ontario, Manitoba and the Yukon Territory, sexual orientation remains an excluded ground for discrimination in all human rights legislation. Efforts to amend the federal Human Rights Act to prohibit this form of discrimination continue to be stonewalled. A recommendation by the 1985 Parliamentary Committee on Equality Rights to include sexual orientation was ignored for seven years. Then, in December 1992, the federal government finally introduced legislation that would forbid discrimination on the basis of sexual orientation. The government action came in the wake of an October 1992 Federal Court of Canada ruling that the dismissal from the military of a lesbian woman violated her right to equality under the Charter of Rights and Freedoms. It was the impli-

Grapevine

Newsletter of the Lesbian Mothers' Defence Funds/Canada
Toronto, Calgary, Vancouver and Montreal

Spring 1983

B.C. lesbian grandmother wins custody

In November 1982, in a landmark decision, a 38 year old lesbian was awarded custody of her two-and-a-half year old granddaughter. This victory is a milestone for lesbians country-wide, as it is the first time custody has been awarded to a homosexual who is not one of the child's natural parents.

After having temporary custody for almost 18 months under an agreement of unspecified duration which was signed by both natural parents, Marge, the grandmother (not her real name), brought the issue up for review with her daughter and son-in-law.

Marge's daughter fully supported her mother's application for permanent custody. She evaluated the stable, loving home of Marge and her lover of ten years as the most suitable atmosphere for her child to grow in. The child's father, however, was determined to seek custody himself.

The presiding judge, Philip Collings, of the British Columbia Family Court, stated early in his decision: "If all considerations to the child's interests were equal [the child] should go to [the father]." As the trial unfolded, it became clear that awarding custody to Marge would best facilitate a happy, healthy life for her.

The first ruling made by Judge Collings was that since the father had consented to Marge's temporary custody of the child for 18 months, the court would view the case as a custody dispute rather than a general application for custody.

As the judge held the presumption that the best interest of the child require that she go to her natural father, it became Marge's and her lawyer Brenda Kaine's task to refute this. Marge's lesbianism was one of the first issues to be ruled on. Four cases

were cited: B vs B(Ontario); Case vs Case (Saskatchewan); K vs K (Alberta); and D vs D (Ontario). All these cases "are unanimous in judging that homosexuality is not a bar to a claim for custody, but is a factor to be considered with all the others. In other words, it is a question of fact rather than law, now far the particular homosexual relationship in question relates to the best interests of the particular child," explained Judge Collings. "At the least .... a homosexual relationship is a minus factor for a custody claimant," he said.

Evidence from the Family Court Counsellor and the case of B vs B which indicated the sexual preference of the custodial parent doesn't dictate the sexual identity of the child was then cited. Collings held that "common sense dictates that a child is brought up with a view to the norms of the society in which she resides. Homosexuality is not a norm of our society -- it is abnormal. If it were an accepted norm we wouldn't be arguing about it." Although he judged that living without a role model of a normal heterosexual relationship held dangers, he felt the evidence didn't map out for him "the nature or extent of the dangers." In conclusion he decided to assess Marge's lesbianism in relation to the five factors outlined in Section 24(1) of the BC Family Relations Act. This decision was a key ingredient in ensuring the fair appraisal of Marge's parenting ability.

The assessment was as follows:
Factor 1: The health and emotional well-being of the child including any special needs for care and treatment.
The child was healthy but mildly asthmatic. The judge found it hard to predict which claimant would contribute more to the child's emotional well-being in the future.
Factor 2: Where appropriate, the views of the child.
Was not appropriate in the case.
Factor 3: The love, affection and similar ties that exist between the child and other persons.
It was recognized that, while the child had ties

The Lesbian Mothers' Defence Fund was set up in March 1978 to provide a permanent resource for mothers who are fighting for child custody. We can offer:

- *Pre-legal advice and info on successful cases*
- *Referrals to sympathetic, expert lawyers*
- *Financial help in building a strong court case*
- *Personal and emotional support*

Grapevine *was the newsletter of the Lesbian Mothers' Defence Fund, set up in March 1978 to provide a permanent resource for mothers who were fighting for child custody.*

cation of this decision — that the Canadian Human Rights Act should include protection against discrimination based on sexual orientation — that forced the government's hand.[72] Celebration over the proposed amendment was, however, marred by the government's refusal to include a definition of marriage recognizing same-sex relationships.[73] The expectation that the heterosexual definition of marriage would be widened had been raised after an Ontario Human Rights Tribunal found, in August 1992, that the traditional definition of marital status, which excludes gays and lesbians from benefits such as pensions, health care or tax advantages, is a breach of the Charter of Rights and Freedoms. Right-wing opposition to the legalization of same-sex marriages clearly inhibited the government and, by March 1993, it appeared that the same opposition had doomed the proposed amendment which was then quietly dropped from the list of priorities for the legislative session.[74]

Women Prisoners

Women's organizations have long supported the uphill struggle against sexual orientation discrimination. Similarly, they have fought for improved human rights for women prisoners. In 1981, Women for Justice, a group of Ottawa women, filed a third-party complaint with the Canadian Human Rights Commission concerning the treatment of inmates at the Prison for Women in Kingston, Ontario — the one federal institution housing women. All women serving sentences of two years or more are sent to Kingston although male inmates have the option of being located in prisons closer to their homes. Separated from their families, women prisoners also have fewer options than men in rehabilitation, job retraining and work programs. Although the Commission made a preliminary finding of discrimination on December 14, 1981, and appointed a conciliator to reach a satisfactory settlement, it took another nine years before the federal government agreed to replace the Kingston prison with five small regional centres by 1994. Meanwhile, this antiquated prison, described in a 1990 federal task force report as "unfit for bears, much less women" has witnessed many suicides, particularly on the part of native women who, as evidenced by the document reprinted at the end of this chapter,[75] are shockingly over-represented in all prisons. Federal plans to build a long-promised healing lodge for aboriginal women were finally announced in May 1992.[76]

Conclusion

The last twenty years have witnessed many legal changes affecting Canadian women. While some have improved the status of women, it is clear that the law and the justice system still fail us in various aspects of our daily lives. This has led some feminist commentators to question the wisdom of investing work and hope in a legal system that reflects a mainly white, middle-class, able-bodied, heterosexual male bias.[77] These critics argue that women and other disadvantaged groups would be wiser to put their efforts into the democratic system through political means. Certainly, all feminists agree that full equality will only be realized when women share political power at all government levels and the fight for this goal will continue. But the fact that there is still much to be accomplished should not deflect attention from the gains made by feminists' individual and collective efforts. The broadening of the legal and judicial concept of equality from one based on identical treatment to one that encompasses equality of results is a major victory. And redefining equality forced the feminist movement to recognize that, although equality has commonality, it is not homogeneous because women's experience of inequality differs depending on their class, race, age, marital status, disability and sexual orientation. The challenge ahead is to press for changes in both the political and the legal arenas to enable all women to take their rightful place in Canadian society.

NOTES

1. *Report of the Royal Commission on the Status of Women in Canada* (Ottawa: Information Canada, 1970), ix.
2. Ibid.
3. Christie Jefferson, "The Promise of Equality," *Leaf Letter* no. 7 (Summer 1989), 1.
4. Penny Kome, *The Taking of Twenty Eight: Women Challenge the Constitution* (Toronto: Women's Educational Press, 1983).
5. Reprinted below is the NAC "Proposed Resolution Regarding the Constitution of Canada," based, in large part, on its brief to the 1980 Joint Senate-Commons Committee on the Constitution.
6. Gwen Brodsky and Shelagh Day, *Canadian Charter Equality Rights for Women: One Step Forward or Two Steps Back?* (Ottawa: Canadian Advisory Council on the Status of Women, 1989), 17.
7. See "Meech Lake Accord: Summary of Concerns, Implications and Positions," reprinted in the documents section.
8. Judy Rebick, Barbara Cameron and Sandra Delaronde, "Why we want half the Senate seats," *Globe and Mail*, 15 October 1991, A15; Michelle Landsberg, "Feminists have backed native women from the outset," *Toronto Star*, 31 March 1992, D5; Doris Anderson, "Don't leave men in suits in charge of national unity crisis," *Toronto Star*, 20 April 1992, A19.
9. Rudy Platiel, "Native women fear loss of rights," *Globe and Mail*, 13 July 1992, A5.
10. Sheila D. Genaille, "Métis women endorse agreement," *Globe and Mail*, 30 September 1992, A25.
11. Sean Fine, "Native women aim to block national referendum in court," *Globe and Mail*, 13 October 1992, A10.
12. Rosemary Speirs, "Women face split over 'no' vote," *Toronto Star*, 19 September 1992, C4.
13. Sherene Razack, *Canadian Feminism and the Law: The Women's Legal Education Fund and the Pursuit of Equality* (Toronto: Second Story Press, 1991), 36.
14. R.S.C. c. I-6. 1970.
15. See Chapter 2 and "The Jeanette Lavell and Yvonne Bedard Cases" reprinted in the documents section.
16. The same decision was handed down in the Bedard case. Clearly, while equality *before* the law was protected, equality *under* and equal *benefit* of the law was not, and, as long as all Indian women were treated in the same discriminatory way, there was no violation of the *Canadian Bill of Rights*.
17. Unemployment Insurance Act, S.C. 1970-71-72, c. 48, s.46, 1971.
18. For a detailed discussion of the substantive equality model see Brodsky and Day, *Canadian Charter Equality Rights for Women*, 187-98.
19. For a history of LEAF, see Razack, *Canadian Feminism and the Law*.
20. David Vienneau, "Budget cuts undermine legal group's fight for equality rights," *Toronto Star*, 2 March 1992, C1.
21. Brodsky and Day, *Canadian Charter Equality Rights for Women*, 49.
22. "New sexual assault legislation a step forward," *Leaf Lines* 4, no. 4 (January 1992). Excerpted in the documents section.
23. For one critique of the legislation see "A Brief to the Department of Justice, Criminal Law Amendments Division ... concerning the proposed amendments to the Criminal

Code regarding sexual offenses against the person and the protection of young persons,"
reprinted in the documents section.
24. Elizabeth A. Sheehy, *Personal Autonomy and the Criminal Law: Emerging Issues for Women* (Ottawa: Canadian Advisory Council on the Status of Women, 1987), 19-27.
25. Ibid., 20.
26. Ibid.
27. Ibid., 21
28. Christine Boyle and Susannah Worth Rowley, "Sexual Assault and Family Violence: Reflections on Bias," *Equality and Judicial Neutrality*, eds. Sheila L. Martin and Kathleen E. Mahoney, (Toronto: Carswell, 1987), 312-325; Nancy Pollack, "Rape Shield Law Struck Down: Big Loss of Little Protection," *Kinesis*, (September 1991), 3-4.
29. For an early critique see "Sexual Assault Monitoring — The Struggle Continues," *Action: A Bulletin from the National Action Committee on the Status of Women*, November 1986.
30. "Women's groups meet with Justice Minister," *Leaf Lines* 4, no. 4 (January 1992), 4.
31. See Chapter 2.
32. See CARAL Suit Against the Attorney General of Canada, 18 May 1983, reprinted in the documents section.
33. William Walker, "Court strikes down abortion law," *Toronto Star*, 29 January 1988, A4.
34. T. Bettel Dawson, ed., *Relating to Law: A Chronology of Women and Law in Canada* (Toronto: York University Captus Press, 1990), 103-104.
35. Geoffrey York, "Senators kill abortion bill with tied vote," *Globe and Mail*, 1 February 1991, A1, A6.
36. David Vienneau, "A woman's right, with no guarantees," *Toronto Star*, 27 January 1993, A17.
37. Janine Brodie, Shelley A.M. Gavigan and Jane Jenson, *The Politics of Abortion* (Toronto: University of Toronto Press, 1992).
38. All quotes from *Leaf Lines* 3, no. 2 (October 1989), 7. For a discussion of the *Andrews* case see "Ruling launches new era for equality litigation," *Leaf Letter* no. 7 (Summer 1989), 3; and Razack, *Canadian Feminism and the Law*, 100-107.
39. As quoted in *Leaf Lines* 3, no. 2 (October 1989), 8.
40. Examples of feminists pre-Charter work on the issue of sexual harassment include Constance Backhouse and Leah Cohen, *The Secret Oppression: Sexual Harassment of Working Women* (Toronto: Macmillan of Canada, 1978); and Susan Attenborough, "Sexual Harassment: An Issue for Unions," *Union Sisters: Women in the Labour Movement*, eds. Linda Briskin and Lynda Yanz (Toronto: The Women's Press, 1978), 136-43.
41. As quoted in *Leaf Lines* 3, no. 2 (October 1989), 8.
42. See Volume 2, Chapter 8 for a more complete discussion of legal issues pertaining to women in the workplace.
43. Discussed in Chapter 2.
44. Christine Schmitz, "S.C.C. Judge Supports Task Forces to Probe Gender Bias in Courts," *Relating to Law*, ed. T. Bettel Dawson, 108-10.
45. The proceedings for this conference are published in *Equality and Judicial Neutrality*, eds. Sheila L. Martin and Kathleen E. Mahoney.
46. *Gender Equality in the Courts* (Manitoba: Manitoba Association of Women and the Law, 1988).
47. Sherene Razack, "Using Law for Social Change: Historical Perspectives," *Queens Law Journal* 17, no. 1 (Spring 1992), 31-53.
48. Jeff Sallot, "Redefining Reasonable: Justice removes her blindfold," *Globe and Mail*, 14 December 1991, D3.
49. David Vienneau, "Crown deals called easy on wife killers," *Toronto Star*, 17 February 1992, A3.
50. The 1968 Act specified 15 grounds for divorce, the most commonly used being cruelty, adultery and separation for a period of three years. The 1986 Act adopted "marriage breakdown" as the sole ground for divorce and reduced the separation period to one year.
51. Martha Muzychka, *A Report on the Effectiveness of the Support Enforcement Agency in Newfoundland and Labrador* (St. John's: Provincial Advisory Council on the Status of Women, Newfoundland and Labrador, 1992), 1. According to Statistics Canada, in 1968 about 11,000 marriages ended in divorce and by 1987 that figure had risen to 90,000.
52. See "*Murdoch v. Murdoch*" reprinted in the documents section.
53. *Report of the Royal Commission on the Status of Women in Canada* (Ottawa: Information Canada, 1970), 246.

54. For a summary of the 1986 improvements to the Ontario legislation see "Family Law Reformed Again," excerpted in the documents section. The deficiencies in the 1978 legislation are illustrated in the document "Urgent Message to Ontario Women" also excerpted in the documents section.

55. Freda M. Steel, "Alimony and Maintenance Orders," *Equality and Judicial Neutrality*, eds. Martin and Mahoney, 164.

56. Ibid., 160.

57. Rhéal Séguin, "Quebec to pay child support," *Globe and Mail*, 14 April 1992, A7.

58. Richard Kerr, *An Economic Model to Assist in the Determination of Spousal Support* (Ottawa: Prepared for the Department of Justice and Status of Women Canada, 1992).

59. Sean Fine, "Men still escaping support payments despite stricter rules, more resources," *Globe and Mail*, 21 November 1989, A1, A18; "New family support plan," *Toronto Star*, 17 March 1992, A7.

60. *The Financial Consequences of Child Support Guidelines: Research Report* (Ottawa: Department of Justice. Report of the Federal/Provincial/Territorial Family Law Committee, 1992); Leonard Shiffrin, "How much is a child worth?" *Toronto Star*, 11 May 1992, A17; Michelle Landsberg, "Legal system out of order on spousal, child support," *Toronto Star*, 16 May 1992, G1.

61. *Gender Equality in the Courts*, v.

62. See "Help Lesbian Mother Win Custody," reprinted in the documents section.

63. Murray Dykeman, "Family court watcher claims men are getting away with a lot," *Vancouver Sun*, 7 April 1992, A3.

64. Nancy Pollack, "Rape Shield Law Struck Down: Big Loss of Little Protection," *Kinesis* (September 1991), 3-4.

65. For a discussion of the law's limitation with respect to disabled women see Shirley Masuda, "Ignored Again: The 'Rape Law' and women with disabilities," *The Womanist* 3, no. 2 (Fall 1992), 5.

66. "RCMP 'callous' to Inuk rape victim commission says," *Toronto Star*, 12 August 1992, A3.

67. One early example of such lobbying is the Victoria Voice of Women's brief, "Discrimination Against Women in the British Columbia Labour Force," presented to the B.C. Minister of Labour, December 1971. Copy at WERC.

68. See, for example, *Women and Law in New Brunswick* (Fredericton, NB: The Fredericton Women's Action Coalition, June 1973). Copy at WERC.

69. Prior to the decisions in these two cases, some jurisdictions had amended their human rights laws specifically to include protection from discrimination because of pregnancy or sexual harassment.

70. See, for example, "Human Rights Issues," reprinted in the documents section.

71. *Women and Legal Action: Precedents, Resources and Strategies for the Future* (Ottawa: Canadian Advisory Council on the Status of Women, 1984), 33-36.

72. Sean Fine, "Courts set seal on gay revolution," *Globe and Mail*, 24 November 1992, A1, A8.

73. Graham Fraser, "Bill protects gay and lesbian rights," *Globe and Mail*, 12 November 1992, A4.

74. Geoffrey York, "Human rights bill appears doomed," *Globe and Mail*, 18 March 1993, A5.

75. Claire Culhane, "Women and Prisons," *Resources for Feminist Research/ Documentation sur la recherche féministe* 14, no. 4. (December/January 1985/86), 32-33.

76. "Women's prison," *Globe and Mail*, 23 May 1992, A4.

77. Brodsky and Day, *Canadian Charter Equality Rights for Women*, 3.

Documents: Chapter 5

The Constitution

The Charter of Rights and Freedoms

"The Proposed Resolution Regarding the Constitution of Canada"
Toronto, November, 1980[1]

...

1. 'Equality before the law' — the wording proposed in the federal government's Charter of Rights, has been interpreted to mean only that laws, once passed, will be equally applied to all individuals in the category concerned — the law itself can treat women unequally, and that's acceptable. Thus the Supreme Court of Canada decided *against* Lavell and Bedard, two Indian women who lost their status on marriage to non-status men. If the wording as presently proposed is passed, there is no guarantee that Indian women will not continue to be denied equal rights with Indian men.

— NAC RECOMMENDS AMENDMENT SO THAT EQUALITY IN THE LAWS THEMSELVES, AS WELL AS ADMINISTRATION OF THE LAWS, IS PROVIDED;

— Further, we deplore the three-year moratorium on the Charter's application, and RECOMMEND THAT IT BE DELETED.

2. Entrenchment of rights means that the courts, and ultimately the Supreme Court of Canada, will decide on what rights Canadian women will enjoy. Yet it was the Supreme Court of Canada that decided

— women were not persons — the famous 1928 Persons' Case;

— that discrimination against Indian women in the Indian Act does not violate 'equality before the law';

1. National Action Committee on the Status of Women, Special NAC Memo, 1-2. Copy at WERC.

— that Stella Bliss was not discriminated against because she was a woman, but a pregnant person;

— and that, again in the Bliss case, there was no discrimination because not *all* pregnant women were denied benefits under the Unemployment Insurance Act.

— Can we reasonably expect that, without fair representation of women in the courts, including the Supreme Court of Canada, women's rights will be understood and protected?

— NAC RECOMMENDS AMENDMENT TO GUARANTEE THE APPOINTMENT OF A REPRESENTATIVE NUMBER OF WOMEN TO THE COURTS, INCLUDING THE SUPREME COURT OF CANADA.

3. The first clause in the Charter of Rights has a loophole (the so-called MackTruck clause) allowing for 'reasonable limits as are generally accepted in a free and democratic society with a parliamentary system of government.'

— NAC RECOMMENDS PREFERABLY DELETION OF THE LIMITING CLAUSE OR AT LEAST AMENDMENT TO SPECIFY WHAT RIGHTS CANNOT BE ABROGATED IN TIME OF WAR, OR REAL OR APPREHENDED INSURRECTION, NAMELY — THE RIGHT TO LIFE, LIBERTY AND SECURITY; NOT TO BE SUBJECTED TO CRUEL OR UNUSUAL TREATMENT OR PUNISHMENT; AND THE *RIGHT TO EQUALITY*.

4. Vague wording in the section on affirmative action makes us nervous — will we have to spend years in court proving that an affirmative action program for women does not constitute discrimination.

— NAC RECOMMENDS SPECIFYING WOMEN AS A DISADVANTAGED GROUP REQUIRING AFFIRMATIVE ACTION. BETTER STILL, THERE SHOULD BE A STATED OBJECTIVE OF ACHIEVING EQUALITY.

5. WE RECOMMEND AN AMENDMENT PROHIBITING DISCRIMINATION ON THE BASIS OF SEX EVEN IF NOT ALL MEMBERS OF A SEX ARE DISCRIMINATED AGAINST.

Remember the Stella Bliss case.

The Meech Lake Accord

"Summary of Concerns, Implications and Positions"
Ontario, 1988[2]

The Ad Hoc Committee has three principal concerns with the Meech Lake Accord:

(1)   the lack of consultation in this process of constitutional change;
(2)   the risk to women's equality rights;
(3)   the allowing of provinces to opt-out of national programs ...

Concern

1.   **Process**
-     The process has been, and continues to be, unacceptable in a democracy.
-     Canadians were not consulted before the Accord was signed in June 1987.
-     Canadians have been told by politicians that no change to the Accord is possible.
-     If no change is permitted, are public hearings "for show" only?

2.   **Individual and Equality Rights**
-     Clause 16 of the Accord specifically exempts multicultural and Native rights from being affected by the Accord's guarantees of linguistic duality and the distinct society. This gives an opening for judicial interpretation that *other* individual rights (of women, minorities, disabled, etc.) *are* affected by these provisions.

3.   **Opting-out**
-     The Accord allows provinces not to participate in national shared-cost programs "if the province carries on a program or initiative that is compatible with national objectives."
-     The vagueness raises concern that no national social programs, such as Medicare, can ever again be established — that Canadians in different parts of the country will not receive equal treatment ...

6.   **The Senate and the Supreme Court**
-     The Accord changes the method of appointments to the Senate and Supreme Court: from a federal prerogative to requiring the federal government to choose from lists submitted by the provinces.

2. Ad Hoc Committee of Women on the Constitution (Ontario), 1-3. Copy at WERC.

- This means provincial *government* control over two very important federal institutions, rather than representation of the *people of
the regions* at the national level.
- Women have to lobby 11 governments for more
women's appointments, instead of only 1 ...

8.   Native Peoples
- The pressing concerns of the Native peoples on self-determination, land claims, and individual equality rights are ignored ...

Implication and Position

1.   Process
- Public hearings should be taken seriously, given
credibility.
- Amendments are necessary now before the Accord is entrenched
in the Constitution.
- Amendments can be made without unravelling the
whole Accord and without losing Quebec's signature to the Constitution.

2.   Individual and Equality Rights
- Women's rights are put at risk by the Accord.
- One alternative is to add women's equality rights in the Charter
(Sections 15 and 28) to Clause 16 of the Accord.
- Another is to delete Clause 16 and add provision that Charter
rights prevail over the Accord.

3.   Opting-out
- Canadians want the same level of services no matter
which province they live in — they believe in fairness.
- Contributes to regional inequalities.
- The meanings of "national objectives," "initiatives" and "compat-
ible" need to be clarified
- No standards to meet these national objectives are
included (standards have been key to success of national pro-
grams such as Medicare).
- Alternative is to delete provision from Accord ...

6.   The Senate and the Supreme Court
- Gives control over federal legislative and judicial bodies
to provincial governments.
- The Accord provision is tantamount to giving the *federal* government the right to name MLAs in each *provincial* legislature, sufficient to block provincial legislation.
- Return to current practice and proceed with Senate
reform ...

8. **Native Peoples**
- Once again, Canada's aboriginal people (like women)
   are left out of negotiations on major changes to their country …

The Charlottetown Accord

"NAC Response to Federal Constitution Proposals"
Toronto, 25 October 1991[3]

NAC's starting point in considering the federal constitution proposals was the decision of our 1990 Annual General Meeting to adopt a framework for the Constitution that recognized that Canada is made up of different national communities, as well as regions and different ethnic and racial groups. Unlike the other provinces, Quebec and the aboriginal people consider themselves nations and ask for special rights and protection accorded to nations. NAC recognizes the right of self-determination for Quebec, aboriginal people and the rest of Canada, meaning that each of these nations within the Canadian state has the right to decide what it wants in a Constitution. We said that Canada is a voluntary association of these nations and that any constitutional change should be negotiated among them. NAC believes that this framework is the only one that will permit, whether Quebecois, aboriginal or living in the rest of Canada, the kind of constitution they want.

The people of Quebec want certain powers to protect their language, culture and political institutions. The people in the rest of Canada want a strong federal government that will protect equality rights and provide standards and universal access to social programs. Recognizing that Quebec is different and needs different powers than the other provinces is the only framework that can meet the needs of all people living within the Canadian state.

Aboriginal people want their inherent right to self-government recognized. They want Canada to recognize that the aboriginal people have always had the right to self-government but that this right has been denied to them for generations. Once the inherent right to self-government is recognized then negotiations can take place over how that right will exercised in specific circumstances. Aboriginal people want to be treated equally with Quebec. If Quebec is considered a "distinct society," so should aboriginal peoples.

At the AGM, NAC member groups decided that it was not enough to take a position on women's issues in the Constitution. To successfully address women's issues without being divided from our sisters in Quebec and our aboriginal sisters, it was necessary to take a position on self-determination. NAC will be consulting with aboriginal women's groups and women's groups in Quebec to further develop our position on these issues.

3. NAC Information Package. Copy at CWSE.

"What Women Want in the Constitution"
June, 1992[4]

Process

- a women's delegation organized by NAC seated with "
  voice at any First Ministers' Conference or future multi-lateral
  conference on the Constitution;

- a seat with voice and vote at the constitutional table for
  the Native Women's Association of Canada;

- a broad constitutional conference to ensure that the
  people in Canada have a real say on the constitution;

- no pan-Canadian referendum, because it will take place under
  undemocratic legislation with no spending limits and could pit
  one part of the country against another.

"Equality Rights For Aboriginal Women

- full protection of the equality rights of aboriginal
  women.

Canada Clause

- a Canada clause which contains a commitment to overcoming
  the inequality of women, eliminating racism, removing the barriers
  to the full participation of people with disabilities, eliminating
  discrimination against lesbians and gays and preserving the rights
  of national linguistic minorities.

Spending Power

- opting out of new social programmes with compensation only
  for Quebec; failing that, in any instance of a province opting
  out of cost-shared programmes there must be a constitutionally
  entrenched democratic process requiring public notice and a one-
  year delay during which time public hearings and votes of the
  provincial legislature concerned and the federal Parliament will
  be held.

Devolution of Powers

- no devolution of labour market training and culture to any provinces except Quebec.

---

4. NAC Pamphlet, distributed with *Feminist Action: News from the National Action Committee
on the Status of Women* 6, no. 2, (June 1992). Document in personal possession of Paula Bourne.

Senate

- a constitutional guarantee of equal representation for women in the Senate and of appropriate representation for other underrepresented groups.
- election to the Senate by proportional representation rather than the "first-past-the-post" system used to elect members of Parliament.

Equality Rights Interpretation

The Bill of Rights

"The Jeannette Lavell and Yvonne Bedard Cases" Ottawa, 1973[5]

History
Jeannette Lavell — married a non-Indian and thus her name was deleted from the Indian Register.

Ms. Yvonne Bedard — married a non-Indian — 2 children — separated — returned to Reservation to live in a house left to her by her mother.

Indian Council gave her special permission to reside on the Reserve in order to dispose of her property. Ms. Bedard, under that pressure, transferred the title of the house to her brother, but continued to live in the house. A year after she returned to the Reserve the Indian Council tried to have her and her children removed from the house and the Reserve.

Indian Councils
The Indian Councils, to justify their actions, used a part of the Indian Act, Section 12 (1) (b), which states:

> "The following persons are not entitled to be registered, namely, ... a woman who married a person who is not an Indian."

Action in the Lower Courts
Ms. Lavell took her case to the Ontario Supreme Court stating that it was in conflict with the *Canadian Bill of Rights* (Section 1) which states:

> "It is hereby recognized and declared that in Canada there have existed and shall continue to exist without discrimination by reason of race, national origin, colour, religion or sex, the following human rights and fundamental freedoms, ..."

5. Flyer prepared and distributed by Ad Hoc Committee for Women's Rights, Ottawa, Ontario, 5 September 1975. Document in private possession of Marjorie Cohen. Now at CWMA.

These rights include the enjoyment of property and equality before the law.

The Ontario Supreme Court rejected her case saying that there was no violation of the *Bill of Rights* "because the respondent on her marriage had equality in that status with all other Canadian married females."

Ms. Lavell then took her case to the Federal Appeal Court which agreed that there was discrimination by reason of sex and that this discrimination infringed upon the respondent's rights to equality with other Indians before the law.

The Indian Council, supported by other Indian groups appealed this decision to the Supreme Court.

Ms. Bedard took her case to the Ontario Supreme Court, which agreed that this clause of the *Indian Act* was invalid, quoting the Lavell case as precedence.

Action in the Supreme Court

As a result both cases came before the Supreme Court which in a 5-4 decision declared that section of the *Indian Act* was valid after all.

Judge Ritchie, in his decision, stated that:

> "equality before the law under the *Bill of Rights* means equality of treatment in the enforcement and application of the laws of Canada before the law enforcement authorities and the ordinary courts of the law" and that essentially the *Bill of Rights does not refer to the content of these laws.*

Judge Laskin disagreed with Judge Ritchie saying:

> "I am unable to appreciate upon what basis the command of the *Bill of Rights* that the laws of Canada shall operate without discrimination by reason of sex, can be ignored in the operation of the *Indian Act.*"

Further:

> "There was an intimation during the agreement of these appeals that the *Bill of Rights* is properly involved only to resolve a clash under its terms between two Federal statutes ... It is a spurious contention...because the *Bill of Rights* is itself the indicator to which any Canadian statute or any provisions thereof must yield unless Parliament has declared that the statute or particular provision is to operate notwithstanding the *Bill of Rights.*"

Problems this Supreme Court decision has created:

(1)   The *Bill of Rights* is no longer valid for all Canadians — i.e. Parliament has to reinstate it.

(2)   There now is no law guaranteeing protection of all women from sex discrimination

(3)   Indian women of Canada now are left with no alternative but to demand the repeal of the discriminatory sections in the Indian Act through an Act of Parliament.

Ad Hoc Committee for Women's Rights
Ottawa, Ontario
5 September 1973

On August 27, 1973, the Supreme Court of Canada, in a 5-4 decision, ruled in favour of the Appellants v. Jeanette Corbiere Lavell and Yvonne Bedard, the Indian women who were dismissed from their respective Reservations and deprived of their status as registered Indians upon marriage to men who were not themselves Registered Indians. Such deprivation is in accord with Section XII i B of the Indian Act   which states that an Indian woman who married a non-registered Indian or non-Indian loses her status as an Indian and is thereby not entitled to any of the benefits, including living on the Reserve, inheriting property on the Reserve, etc. After three years of court proceedings at ascending levels, the Supreme Court of Canada has ruled that the Canadian Bill of Rights cannot take precedence over an Act of Parliament simply because that Act is found to discriminate by reason of race, national origin, colour, religion or sex.

What to Do

I   *There is an* immediate need for women throughout Canada to add their moral and political support to this cause which already has rallied support from both non-status and status Indian women.

Will you:

1) sign either or both of the attached telegrams and forward them during the current emergency session of Parliament,

2) write the Minister of Indian Affairs concerning changes in the Indian Act to eliminate the discrimination against native women,

3) write your own member of Parliament to inform him/her of this situation and to urge his/her support for the necessary changes.

II   Women must continue to voice their demands for the amendment of all legislation which is discriminatory on the basis of sex, and urge the government to reassess the Bill of Rights as a means of legitimizing such action. One of the major implications of this decision by the Supreme Court is that the Canadian Bill of Rights is in fact impotent to protect the individual from discrimination within the law.

We urge you to sign these telegrams and to either send them forward yourselves or give us your names to add to the telegram being prepared here, which will be sent to the Government and Advisory Council on the Status of Women, on September 14, 1973.

Telegrams to be forwarded:

I.   AS CANADIANS AND AS WOMEN WE DEMAND:

1. AN IMMEDIATE ACT OF PARLIAMENT TO REPEAL SECTION XII i b OF THE INDIAN ACT

2. IMMEDIATE PRIORITY TO THE AMENDMENT OF ALL FEDERAL LEGIS-LATION IDENTIFIED BY THE ROYAL COMMISSION ON THE STATUS OF WOMEN AS DISCRIMINATORY ON THE BASIS OF SEX

3. THE INTRODUCTION OF A BILL TO AMEND THE CANADIAN BILL OF RIGHTS DURING THE CURRENT SESSION OF PARLIAMENT TO ENSURE ITS SUPREMACY OVER ALL FEDERAL LEGISLATION AS RESPECTS DIS-CRIMINATION BY REASON OF RACE, NATIONAL ORIGIN, COLOUR, RE-LIGION OR SEX.

Send to: Rt. Hon. Pierre Elliott Trudeau
           Prime Minister of Canada
           House of Commons, Ottawa.

           Robert Stanfield
           Leader of the Opposition
           House of Commons, Ottawa.

           David Lewis
           Leader, National Democratic Party
           House of Commons, Ottawa.

II.   WE, (name of group) STRONGLY URGE THAT YOU IMMEDIATELY CALL AN EMERGENCY MEETING OF THE ADVISORY COUNCIL ON THE STATUS OF WOMEN TO HEAR REPRESENTATIONS, INCLUDING THOSE FROM THE NON-STATUS NATIVE WOMEN, ON THE SERIOUS BREACH OF THE RIGHTS OF CANADIAN WOMEN AS NOW SHOWN IN THE INDIAN ACT RECENTLY CONFIRMED BY THE SUPREME COURT DECISION ON THE JEANETTE LAV-ELL AND YVONNE BEDARD CASES.

Stella Bliss
Ottawa 1984[6]

The *Unemployment Insurance Act* was passed to guarantee continuity of income to those who lose their jobs under certain circumstances. In 1976, a Vancouver working woman, Stella Bliss, found that the protections of this Act were not available to her when she was fired by her employer because she was pregnant. Her case, which resulted in a decision of the Supreme Court of Canada, provided yet another significant inspiration to the women's lobby for improved Charter of Rights guarantees against sex discrimination.

Shortly after the birth of her child in 1976, Bliss, unemployed because her employer had fired her, applied for unemployment insurance benefits. She was clearly capable of and available for work but was unable to find suitable employment. Given the length of time she had worked before being fired, she would have qualified for regular unemployment benefits. However, the Unemployment Insurance Commission disallowed her claim. They stated that Bliss, having been pregnant, could collect only pregnancy benefits provided for in the *Unemployment Insurance Act*, for which the qualifying period was longer than that required for ordinary benefits. Unfortunately, Bliss did not qualify for the longer period. She appealed the decision on the basis that the Commission's action, and the provisions of the *Unemployment Insurance Act* which allowed it, offended the guarantees of equality before the law in the *Canadian Bill of Rights*. As only women can become pregnant, she argued, provisions making it harder for pregnant people to get unemployment insurance deny equality to women. This argument was successful before the "umpire" in the appeal process under the *Unemployment Insurance Act*. However, the government appealed to the Federal Court of Appeal, and Bliss was unsuccessful there. She appealed to the Supreme Court of Canada.

The Supreme Court of Canada heard the case in 1978, and denied her appeal. The Court held that Bliss was refused benefits, not because she was a woman, but because she had been pregnant. The Court adopted the reasoning of the Federal Court of Appeal that, in the circumstances, the discrimination arose not because of law, but because of nature.

6. Canadian Advisory Council on the Status of Women, *Women and Legal Action: Precedents, Resources and Strategies for the Future*. (Ottawa: Canadian Advisory Council on the Status of Women, 1984), 20-21.

Equality Litigation under the Charter

The Rape Law

A Brief to the Department of Justice, Criminal Law Amendments Division — concerning the proposed amendments to the Criminal Code regarding "sexual offenses against the person and the protection of young persons."
Vancouver, September 1981[7]

Since the 1970's Canadian women's organizations have advocated legislative change with regard to the Criminal Code provisions covering rape and sexual assault. In the previous session of Parliament (December 1980), the government introduced Bill C-53 which proposed amendments to the Criminal Code regarding "sexual offenses against the person and the protection of young persons."

Two important improvements represented by the legislation are the reclassification of rape and indecent assault as *assault* offenses and the removal of spousal immunity.

However, there are serious flaws in the proposed amendments which require revision before reintroduction of the legislation. These flaws are obvious when the amendments are analyzed in terms of their consequences for rape victims and also in terms of their consequences for victims of wife battering.

Most notably, the proposed changes in the definition of assault would be particularly problematic for battered women. In addition, amending the Criminal Code provides an opportunity (not widely discussed to date) to include in the law necessary provisions with regard to sexual harassment. Regarding rape and sexual assault, our major concerns with the amendments are the lack of a definition of sexual assault as well as inconsistencies and inadequacies relating to consent, honest belief, credibility, the rule of recent complaint and questions as to sexual conduct. We also propose a scheme of graduated or incremental sentences for assault, assault causing bodily harm, sexual assault and aggravated sexual assault. Further, we propose changes to the proposed amendments regarding the sexual exploitation of young persons and provisions to cover women (i.e. adults as well as children) who are coerced into participating in pornography ...

Five of the major areas of recommendations...are outlined below...

(1)   Definition of Assault:

---

7. Legislative Review Committee, Women's Research Centre, Vancouver, B.C. Copy at the Vancouver Status of Women.

(A) Amendments proposed in Bill C-53 would change the definition of assault by including "lack of resistance" and "honest belief as to consent" (sub-sections 4 and 5 of Section 244). Including these provisions, which currently apply only to rape and indecent assault, imports previously unavailable defenses in charges of assault.

These changes have serious consequences which become obvious in considering wife battering cases. Under the proposed amendments, a man who has assaulted his wife could argue that his wife did not 'resist' or that he honestly believed she 'consented' and, therefore, the attack/beating was not truly an "assault." The woman's previous conduct would also become an issue: for example, the husband might argue that, when he had beaten his wife in the past, 'we made love afterwards'; or, if the woman had been beaten in the past without pressing charges against her husband, he might argue that her legal inaction led him to believe honestly that she 'consented' to the assaults.

There is no reason presented (for example in the Information Paper on Bill C–53) that warrants changing, in this way, the definition of assault as it appears at present in Section 244 of the Criminal Code and there are serious negative consequences to the proposed changes.

Furthermore, "honest belief" is a subjective standard; it is usual in criminal cases to apply objective standards. And, sub-section 3 of Section 244 defines standards for determining "consent" or resistance, rendering sub-sections 4 and 5 redundant.

Therefore, sub-sections (4) and (5) of Section 244 should be deleted.

(B) The standards for determining "consent" (sub-section 3 of 244) require two additions in order to cover situations many women face. First is the addition to (b) "threats or fear of application of force" of the words: "or threats or fear of the application of force to a third person." A battered woman, for example, may not "resist" assault by her husband for fear he will act on his threats to harm their child(ren) if she does resist. Second is the addition to (c) "fraud" of the words: "or fear of economic prejudice." This provision would cover those cases, for example, where a woman does not "resist" an assault by her employer for fear of losing her job or a promotion, et cetera.

(2)   Punishment for Assault:
Past experience indicates that discharge will continue to be the
frequent disposition for assault, especially in wife assault cases,
unless changes are made to the Criminal Code's provisions regarding "punishment for assault" — Sections 245, 245.1 and 245.2.
Therefore, we recommend the establishment of minimum sentences for assault conviction.
Furthermore, since assault should be regarded as no less serious
an offense than impaired driving offenses, punishment for assaults
should be increased with each offence, just as punishment for
driving offenses are incremental.

Finally, the lack of definition regarding "serious bodily harm" is
a critical flaw in the proposed Sections 245.1 and 245.2 that serves
to "flag" or draw attention to issues which defense counsel may
use to cast aspersions on complainants. For example, in the case
of a complainant who is a battered woman, this lack of definition
opens the way for the insinuation that she is a malingerer. Therefore, we recommend a scheme of incremental sentences and the
establishment of minimum sentences to resolve the most critical
problems with the proposed Section 245.

(3)   Definition of Sexual Assault and Punishment:
The absence of a definition of "sexual assault" and "aggravated
sexual assault" is a serious omission in Section 246.1 and 246.2
of the legislation. The Criminal Code is a *code* and as such is used
to define crimes. Therefore, definitions are essential.
In addition, the stated — and laudable intent of the proposed amendments to "de-stigmatize" rape and sexual assaults and to emphasize
the violent nature of such acts has been met, in part, by the transfer
of "sexual offenses" to the assault section of the Criminal Code (Part
VI) which covers "sexual offenses, public morals and disorderly
conduct."

Although it is necessary to emphasize the violent nature of such acts,
the sexual nature of such acts cannot be denied. It is unrealistic and
irresponsible to assume that the sexual aspect of rape and sexual
assaults is irrelevant to the victim and, therefore, should not be relevant under the law.

Therefore, we recommend a definition of sexual assault in such
terms as to make clear both the violent and sexual aspects of the
crime.

Furthermore, the definition we recommend includes provision for
cases of sexual harassment, the use of a weapon, and cases of

multiple offenders — gang rape. As in Section 245 regarding "punishment for assault," a system of graduated sentences is recommended.

"New Sexual Assault Legislation a Step Forward"
Toronto, January 1992[8]

"The proposed sexual assault legislation, introduced by Justice Minister Kim Campbell on December 12, is an important step forward in making sexual assault law more responsive to the problem of sexual violence against women," said Helena Orton, LEAF Litigation Director.

LEAF was one of a number of women's organizations which met with Ms Campbell and Department of Justice staff to urge a major review of sexual assault laws. "It is clear that Justice Minister Campbell listened to the input from women's organizations," said Ms Orton. "There is a recognition that women have constitutional rights at stake, as well as the accused."

The proposed amendments to the Criminal Code (1) define the notion of consent to sexual activity, and (2) provide guidelines and procedures in determining admissibility of past sexual history as evidence.

Consent

The proposed legislation defines consent as "the voluntary agreement of the complainant to engage in the sexual activity in question." As well, it outlines specific situations which do not constitute consent by the complainant, such as when there is incapacity to consent due to intoxication, when agreement to sexual activity is extracted by someone in a position of authority, when initial agreement to sexual activity is revoked.

"The definition of consent will help deal with some of the stereotypes and myths about women's sexuality which have traditionally infused the laws of sexual assault," said Ms Orton, on first reading of the Bill. "It makes clear that no means no."

The legislation leaves open the defence of honest belief in consent but requires that the accused has taken reasonable steps to ascertain consent. Similarly the law makes clear that wilful blindness, self-induced intoxication or recklessness cannot be used to excuse a failure to recognize that a woman was not consenting.

"These are important equality-promoting developments," said Ms Orton.

Past Sexual History

The Bill says that past sexual history of the complainant with the accused or any other person cannot be used at trial to suggest that the complainant is more likely to have consented to the activity or is less worthy of belief.

8. *LEAF Lines* 4, no. 4 (January 1992), 1, 4.

In addition, evidence that the complainant has engaged in other sexual activity will not be allowed unless the judge determines, according to a legal test which balances relevance, fairness and other considerations, that the advantages of admitting the evidence outweigh the disadvantages.

Helena Orton said, "Significantly, the Bill recognizes that sexual history evidence is inherently prejudicial and that judges need guidance for considering whether to admit this evidence."

"By further defining consent, the legislation should minimize the circumstances in which past sexual history evidence could be considered relevant," said Ms Orton.

The Bill sets out procedures which must be followed for admissibility of sexual history evidence.

"LEAF will be examining the Bill in detail over the next month," said Helena Orton. "While there are clearly areas in which we would like to see improvement, such as recognition in the preamble that sexual assault victimization is not gender or race neutral, we are nevertheless greatly encouraged by the equality promoting steps that we see."

Women's Groups Meet with Justice Minister

After the rape shield law was struck down, LEAF and other women's groups sought meetings with the Department of Justice staff to discuss the need for a new law which would not only take account of the fair trial rights of those accused of sexual assault, but would take account of the Charter guarantees to the women and children of Canada who are, as a group, the victims of sexual assault.

Women's organizations met with Justice Minister Kim Campbell to urge her to consider the issue fully. "We made the point that more consultation was necessary to ensure that the new law meets the needs of all women survivors of sexual assault who want to use the courts, including women of colour, women with disabilities, aboriginal women, immigrant women and domestic workers who are particular targets for sexual assault," said LEAF Executive Director Christie Jefferson.

The Abortion Law

CARAL Suit against the Attorney General of Canada
Toronto, 18 May 1983[9]

BETWEEN:

> NORMA SCARBOROUGH in her individual capacity
> and NORMA SCARBOROUGH as representative of a class of persons
> referred to by the Style of cause of "Canadian Abortion Rights

---

9. CWMA file: CARAL. The legal suit was dropped by CARAL when Dr. Henry Morgentaler launched his appeal to the Supreme Court of Canada.

Action League" or "Association Canadienne Pour Le Droit a L'Avortement".

Plaintiffs

-and-

The Attorney General of Canada

Defendant

STATEMENT OF CLAIM

1. The Plaintiff Norma Scarborough, of the City of Toronto is a taxpayer to the Canadian government and president of the Canadian Abortion Rights Action League or Association Canadienne Pour Le Droit a L'Avortement (hereinafter referred to as CARAL or ACDA).

2. The Plaintiff CARAL or ACDA was originally established in 1974 as the Canadian Association For Repeal of the Abortion Law. As a national organization whose head office is situated in the City of Toronto CARAL or ACDA was formed to ensure that no woman in Canada was denied access to a medically safe and legal abortion. CARAL and ACDA is composed of men and women who work on a full-time and volunteer basis, and is the only national organization whose primary purpose is the repeal of s. 251 of the *Criminal Code*.

3. The primary goal of CARAL or ACDA is the decriminalization of abortion by its removal from the *Criminal Code*, so that the decision whether or not to have an abortion is left to any Canadian woman on the basis of her conscience and consultation with her physician and whomever she chooses.

4 ...

5. Under the present *Criminal Code* Section 251(1) and (2) prohibits abortion with one exception. Pursuant to section 251(4) an abortion may be performed by a "qualified medical practitioner" only upon the issuance of a certificate of a "therapeutic abortion committee."

6. "Qualified medical practitioners" of an "accredited or approved hospital" are therefore prohibited from performing abortions which do not comply with section 251(4) of the *Criminal Code*. À *fortiori* women are denied the fundamental right to choose whether or not to have a medically safe and legal abortion. The Plaintiffs state that they and their affiliated organizations are prohibited from advising pregnant women

how to obtain medically safe abortions which do not comply with section 251(4) of the *Criminal Code*. To do so would subject them to the risk of criminal conviction for counselling or as party to an offence under section 21 or 22 and 251 of the *Criminal Code*.

7. CARAL or ACDA represents women who at various times are pregnant and want to seek a medically safe abortion but who cannot, practically speaking, subject the legislation to judicial review because the progress of a pregnancy does not await the inevitable lengthy lapse of time involved in court proceedings leading to a final judgement. CARAL or ACDA further represents women who may become pregnant and may wish an abortion.

8. CARAL or ACDA represents women who at various times are pregnant and want to seek a medically safe abortion which does not comply with section 251(4) of the *Criminal Code*, but are prevented from doing so because they risk criminal liability under section 251(2).

9. The Plaintiffs as taxpayers object to the permitting of publicly funded hospitals to deny pregnant women the right to exercise their freedom of choice to have a medically safe abortion.

10. The Plaintiffs further state that many women are denied the right to have a legal abortion because a number of hospitals are unable or unwilling to comply with the requirements in respect of therapeutic abortions in section 251(4) of the *Criminal Code*.

11. The Plaintiffs further say that they have exhausted all legitimate and practical means in respect of the repeal of the prohibition against abortion in *Criminal Code* section 251.

12 ...

13. On all occasions the actions of the Plaintiffs to induce public officials to change the abortion provisions in section 251 of the *Criminal Code of Canada*, R.S.C. 1970, C. C-34 by judicial proceedings or by legislative amendment have been uniformly unsuccessful.

14. To date the issue of whether section 251 of the *Criminal Code of Canada* violates the guarantees entrenched in the *Canadian Charter of Rights and Freedoms* has not been determined. When the aforementioned Bill dealing with the abortion provisions in section 251 of the *Criminal Code* was enacted the *Canadian Charter of Rights and Freedoms* had not been proclaimed.

15. The Plaintiffs further state that the substantive and procedural requirements in section 251(4) of the *Criminal Code* deny pregnant women their rights in law and the right to privacy of their person, both of which are guaranteed by the *Canadian Charter of Rights and Freedoms*.

16. The provisions in section 251(4) of the *Criminal Code* unduly distinguish abortion from all other medical procedures by the introduction of criteria which are irrelevant to health care and criminality and thereby reduce the quality of the health care available to women.

17. The prohibition against freedom of choice in respect of abortion in section 251 of the *Criminal Code* and the exemptions are inconsistent with the provisions of the *Canadian Charter of Rights and Freedoms*.

18. The Plaintiffs therefore seek:
    (a) A declaration that section 251 of the *Criminal Code of Canada* is inconsistent with the *Canadian Charter of Rights and Freedoms* and is therefore of no force and effect;

    (b) Costs as between a solicitor and his own client;

    (c) Such further and other relief as this Honourable Court deems appropriate and just.

The Plaintiff proposes that this action be tried at the City of Toronto, in the Municipality of Metropolitan Toronto, in the Judicial District of York.

DELIVERED at Toronto, this 18th day of May, 1983.

MORRIS MANNING, Q.C.
390 Bay Street
Suite 2900
Toronto, Ontario
M5H 2Y2
Solicitor for the Plaintiffs

Gender Bias in the Judicial System

Comments from the Bench
Ottawa, 1984[10]

On August 25, 1977, the case of a 21-year-old man who was accused of unlawfully confining an 18-year-old woman came to trial in Provincial Court in Vancouver. His Honour Judge Albert Bewley presided over the trial. The accused allegedly went to a house with a knife in his hand, broke down a door, ripped the telephone off the wall, and forcibly seized the woman. Prior to this incident he had been convicted of a similar offence and he was still on probation when these events occurred. The trial judge found the accused guilty of the offence and sentenced him to prison for six months.

During the trial, Judge Bewley made the following comments about the young woman and her friends:

> There is a girl here, or a couple of girls, young nubile females, who've been around a little bit, eh? They've travelled from Ontario to here, they're a free floating type of female, young for their age, very nubile, very attractive, surely, but I suppose, basically I have to look at it this way, still impressionable, still stupid…you know, women don't get much brains before they're thirty anyway, Mr. Rhodes, but at the age of eighteen or so, they make some stupid mistakes, mostly because we males who know better, lead them into it.

> Mr. Rhodes, look, I understand the picture perfectly. We've got some silly, stupid seventeen, eighteen year old girls, they're on their own from back in Ontario. They meet up with him and I guess they all think they're swingers or some damn thing. He's got a macho personality obviously and he comes in, he's going to talk to this girl, he's going to get her to talk to him one way or another, he had a knife in his hand and he's going to show her, you know, and she's willing to go along with him. I found him technically guilty of unlawful confinement, you know, but I'm not too sympathetic towards these stupid girls. There's no big deal, right? It isn't as if he held up a — as in the other case, where, he may have held up an innocent driver, getting away from something or threatened a Policeman with a knife or something. He's demonstrating his manhood to a little girl eighteen years of age who's probably half inclined to think he's a man by showing a knife, so big deal, eh?

10. Canadian Advisory Council on the Status of Women, *Women and Legal Action,* 40-42.

So I could give him five years but I don't think under the circumstances of this case, I'd be entitled to give him five years because
as we clearly have said before, he got mixed up with a silly, little
bunch of girls who mean well, they got scared because he was
proving himself a macho man, was going to haul one of them out
and talk to her even if she got scared and ran into the bedroom, so
we've got a bunch of clucking females running around and they're
all so scared that they have to call the Police.

The Crown appealed the sentence given the accused. The Court of
Appeal said that the sentence was far too lenient and imposed a sentence
of one year determinate and two years less one day indeterminate.

Judge Bewley's comments may well have passed unnoticed were it
not for the fact that the transcript of the trial came to the attention of
some British Columbia women's groups. After reading the transcript of
the trial which was prepared for the appeal, the British Columbia Federation of Women, the Service, Office and Retail Workers' Union of
Canada, and the Vancouver Status of Women filed a complaint with the
Chief Judge of the Provincial Court of British Columbia concerning the
sexist comments made by Judge Bewley and requested his dismissal.
The complaint was investigated and an inquiry into the allegations was
held by the Judicial Council of British Columbia.

Lynn Smith, a Vancouver lawyer, was retained as counsel by the three
women's groups. They sought standing in order to introduce evidence,
cross-examine witnesses, and make submissions to the inquiry on behalf
of the young women victims. Counsel to the Judicial Council was A.
McEachern, who became Chief Justice of British Columbia in 1979.
Judge Bewley was also represented by counsel, Mary Southin. Standing
was denied to the three women's groups, and this decision was upheld
in the court of appeal.

The complaint against Judge Bewley was dismissed and he remained
a judge. The inquiry held that there was not sufficient evidence in his
remarks of bias against women in general. Certain expressions were
found to be off colour and in bad taste. An observation made by Judge
Bewley that even if the accused had stabbed the woman it would not be
any loss to society was found to be improper. The inquiry expressed its
disappointment at the inability of an experienced judge to express himself with more care.

"NWT Gender Bias Review: Hope or Appeasement"
October 1991[11]

When a British Columbia judge said that a three year old girl had
contributed to her own victimization because she was provocative,
women's groups across Canada were outraged. Women's groups in the

11. Jodi Whyte, *Feminist Action: News From the National Action Committee on the Status of
Women* 6, no. 1B (October 1991), 10. Copy at CWSE.

Northwest Territories (NWT) joined their southern sisters in condemning such misinformed and abusive statements. But then NWT women have been fighting such statements for a long time.

Take for instance the judge who felt that a man had cause to kick and beat his partner because she refused to change a t-shirt he did not like. Or the judge who said that a 12 year old girl did not suffer psychologically from a multiple rape because she was mentally disabled. Then there was the most well publicized case of a judge who said in an interview that sexual assault in the north cannot be compared with those in the south because, unlike "southern co-eds", most northern women are drunk at that time. (This judge was cleared of any wrongdoing by a female judge appointed from the Alberta Court).

These not so isolated incidents must be added to northern courts' blatant disregard for the safety and dignity of northern, (primarily aboriginal) women. Courts arrive the morning of the trial, and often fail to even talk with the victims.

For some time now women in the NWT have been calling for a commission to investigate the gender bias of the courts. After much stalling Michael Ballantyne, Minister of Justice, has asked women to settle for a review to be conducted by Yellowknife lawyer Katherine Peterson.

While women are not satisfied at the refusal to set up a full commission, most are pleased with the appointment of Ms. Peterson. As past-president of the NWT Advisory Council on the Status of Women, a committed feminist, a long time northern resident, and a respected member of the legal community, Ms. Peterson is known to be nobody's pawn.

Most importantly, her review is shaping up to be a bit of a mini-commission in that it will both consult with the legal community and travel to the communities to hold public meetings (and private ones on request).

Many expect that Ms. Peterson's recommendations will be both pragmatic and compassionate and that they will strike a balance between what can realistically be accomplished and what commands immediate change. With few organized women's groups, thousands of miles and many languages to cross in order to communicate or participate in direct action, and a government that began the process reluctantly, many women remain sceptical that the recommendations will be implemented.

Perhaps the brightest light at the end of this procedure is the fact that there is an election in the NWT and more women than ever before are seeking office. This is where the hope lies for the women who are now meeting with Ms. Peterson.

Family Law Reform

Marriage, Separation and Divorce

"Marriage by Contract: A Radical Alternative"
Saskatoon, June 1973[12]

... Marriage by contract is an attempt to "equalize" the partners' relationship. It allows the couple to assume responsibility for the decisions involved in separating, recognizing their desire not to involve lawyers as "hired guns," and their choice not to leave such critical decisions to a judge whom neither of them know personally, nor to precedents with which they have not been involved.

The preambles to individual contracts present the underlying philosophy and values of the partners. For example:

I,_____ and I,_____ hereby declare our love and allegiance and enter into this contract to symbolically and legally commit ourselves one to the other.

We consider this contract to be equivalent to marriage. We have written it to suit our needs and to represent our particular values and we do not consider the State nor the Church to have the right to govern the terms of our relationship nor the terms of any future separation. We enter this contract in order to safeguard ourselves, our present children and our future children as best we can from the pain caused by antiquated laws governing the rights and obligations of the husband, wife and children during and after a marriage. We enter into this contract because we love one another and wish to spend the rest of our lives together.

Recognizing that at some future point it is possible that some aspects of this Agreement may come before the Courts for determination we wish to make it known that this contract is not merely an attempt to by-pass the law, but rather an attempt to make our relationship as explicit as possible and so to facilitate justice to all parties concerned.

Loving one another and desiring to spend the rest of our lives together we have agreed to live together in the same house as husband and wife and share all income, all debts and all property.

Another contract states:
> We believe in equality of all men and women.
> We believe marriage is a partnership of equals.
> We believe in the concept of communal property between husband and wife.
> Marriage itself is the supreme consideration.
> Outside sources of money are not consideration.

12. Nola Symor, *Saskatoon Women's Liberation Newsletter* (June 1973), 2. Copy at CWMA.

We believe that both partners share equal responsibility for raising children.

We reject the traditional role of woman as a housekeeper and man as the sole provider. Talents and enjoyment of individual roles are more important.

We also believe that marriage, while binding two people together, also allows both partners the luxury of many individual freedoms. One partner should never become wholly dependent on the other.

Based on these assumptions then, the contracts spell out the rights and obligations of the partners, regarding areas such as: property debts and income, child care, contraception, custody in case of separation, careers, conflict mechanisms, and termination procedures....

The New Divorce Act
Thunder Bay, 1986[13]

... The most notable change is the elimination of fault oriented divorce, at least partially. There are now three grounds for an application for a divorce: the first is living separate and apart for 12 months; the second is adultery; and the third is physical and mental cruelty. The Federal officials are hoping that since litigation on the fault grounds (adultery and cruelty) is so costly, emotionally messy, and would probably take more than a year to get through the Courts anyway, that the one year separation is going to be a serious alternative.

Secondly, the new *Divorce Act* attempts to move toward mediation rather than litigation as the forum for resolving disputes concerning the marriage breakdown. At this time mediation is not mandatory but must be suggested by the lawyers acting for either spouse. If at a later date standards have been established for mediation services across the country then it is possible that mediation would become mandatory.

The new *Divorce Act* also contains a provision allowing the two spouses to make a joint application for divorce when the grounds are living separate and apart. Another improvement is the elimination of the necessity of a trial in uncontested divorces. Therefore if there are no contentious legal issues in the divorce and both parties want the divorce, then neither will have to attend at Court in order to obtain the divorce.

The New Act also shortens the time it will take to obtain a divorce. In the past in areas outside of Toronto where the Supreme Court did not sit regularly, there was often a significant waiting period for a trial date. Once the hearing had been held, there was a further 90 day waiting period before the divorce was final. Now, an uncontested application for a divorce can proceed speedily since the parties will not have to wait for a trial date and the order is final 30 days after it has been signed by a Judge....

13. Lynn Beak, "Family Law Reformed Again," *The Northern Woman Journal* 10, no. 2 (November 1986). Copy at CWMA.

Marital Property and Support

Murdoch v. Murdoch
2 October 1973[14]

Some Background Notes on the Law

(1)   the law generally recognizes two kinds of ownership. A person has legal ownership when title to the property is held in that person's name (car registration, deed, etc.) A person can have beneficial ownership when title is not in his or her name if the person who does have title is really holding it for the benefit of the other.

(2)   In many situations involving husband and wife, the husband alone will be the registered (legal) owner of the property — the matrimonial home, for example. If the wife wants to assert a claim on this property, she must show that she is the beneficial owner — that her husband is really holding the title on her behalf. There are, basically, two ways of showing this.

(3)   Where the wife contributes part or all of the purchase price of the property, but title is placed in her husband's name, there may be a presumption that the husband holds part or all on a *resulting trust* in her favour. He is holding that part as her trustee and not for his own benefit. The size of the part may depend upon the size of her contribution. As this is just a presumption, however, the husband could rebut it by showing that they intended a different arrangement.

(4)   Where the wife has made no financial contribution, she must establish that there was a *common intention* on the part of the spouses that she benefit from the purchase of the property. This intention must have existed before or at the time the property was acquired. She could prove the intention by showing an express agreement, or by evidence of facts from which the intention might be inferred.

(5)   There are many questions arising from these principles. What if a wife doesn't contribute to the down payment or mortgage, but uses her salary for household expenses, leaving her husband's salary free for the house purchase? What if she doesn't contribute to the purchase price, but pays for renovations and repairs later? What if her contribution is not financial, but of labour (building the house, clearing land)? What if the spouses don't think of beneficial own-

14. "Supreme Court of Canada: summary prepared by Mary Eberts." Document in the personal possession of Marjorie Cohen.

ership at all when they buy their house, and the question arises only after years of marriage?

The Case of Irene Murdoch: Facts

(1)   The Murdochs were married in 1943 and separated in 1968.

(2)   From 1943 to 1947, they worked together on several ranches, receiving as a couple $100.00 per month and room and board. Mrs. Murdoch did the cooking for work crews and assisted her husband.

(3)   In 1947, Mr. Murdoch and Mrs. Murdoch's father bought a guest ranch, each paying $3,000; some of Mr. Murdoch's share may have come from the couple's saved earnings. While in the guest ranch business, Mr. Murdoch worked at another job for five months each year, leaving his wife to accompany guests on pack trips and hikes and do other chores in the business.

(4)   In 1952, Mr. Murdoch paid $4,000.00 advance rent for some grazing land in the form of a loan to the owner, Mr. Sturrock. Mrs. Murdoch had been given this money by her mother. It came from the proceeds of her father's life insurance. Mr. Murdoch claimed that he regarded this as a loan from his mother-in-law; and showed that he had repaid part of it to her; his wife said it was her own money.

(5)   In 1956, Mr. Murdoch bought "the Ward property" for $4,500; part of the price came from the proceeds of sale of the guest ranch, part from Mrs. Murdoch's bank account (more of her father's insurance money). In 1958, this property was sold for $8,000.00.

(6)   In 1958, Mr. Murdoch bought three quarter sections of land for $25,000.00. The down payment of $6,200 and over $3,000 worth of farm machinery was paid for with the proceeds of the sale of the Ward property, and the repayment of the Sturrock loan. The balance was paid on instalments.

(7)   All through this time, and right up to their separation Mr. Murdoch continued to be away at his other job for five months each year, leaving his wife to perform his work in his absence. When asked the type of work this involved, Mrs. Murdoch told the trial court:

Haying, raking, swathing, moving, driving trucks, tractors and teams, quietening horses, taking cattle back and forth to the reserve, dehorning, vaccinating, branding, anything that was to be done.

(8)   Mrs. Murdoch also purchased all their household appliances and furniture, except their stove.

Mrs. Murdoch Goes to Court

(1)   After their separation in 1968, Mrs. Murdoch brought two actions against her husband. The first was for judicial separation, alimony, custody of their son, and possession of the family home. The second was for a half-interest in the ranch land, because she claimed that she and her husband were partners in the ranch business and he therefore held the land on her behalf. In her first action, she was granted a judicial separation and $200 per month maintenance; her second action was dismissed.

(2)   She then appealed to the Appellate Division of the Alberta Supreme Court, and her appeal was dismissed.

(3)   She then appealed to the Supreme Court of Canada. In the Supreme Court she did not argue that she and her husband were partners, but claimed that he held the land on a resulting trust for her because she had contributed to its acquisition.

The Judgment of the Supreme Court of Canada

(1)   Put quite simply, the Court had to decide whether Mrs. Murdoch had established enough of a contribution to the purchase of the ranch to entitle her to an interest in it, and what had been the intention of the spouses regarding ownership of the land (as Mr. Murdoch held legal title).

(2)   The majority of the Court found that she had not established a financial contribution to acquisition of the land. The trial judge had not dealt with her financial contribution, as Mr. Justice Laskin pointed out in his dissent, and an appeal court cannot make its own inquiry into the facts. Normally it accepts the trial judge's finding of facts; however, it can look at the transcript of evidence put in at the original trial.

(3)   Nor did the majority find that Mrs. Murdoch's labour was a contribution to the purchase; it appeared satisfied with the trial judge's conclusion that she had made only the normal contribution of an ordinary rancher's wife.

(4)   Finally, the majority decided that there was no common intention that the wife would have any beneficial interest in the land. Here

again, the findings of the trial judge and evidence of the original trial were accepted.

(5)   As a result, the majority of the Supreme Court dismissed Mrs. Murdoch's appeal.

(6)   Mr. Justice Laskin dissented from the majority judgment. He found a modest direct financial contribution by Mrs. Murdoch, by tracing the course of her original earnings as a hired hand through the various transactions. He also found [an] "extraordinary" contribution of physical labour.

(7)   Mr. Justice Laskin would have recognized her claim to an interest in the ranch. Instead of doing so on the basis of the resulting trust, which is discussed above in the notes, and which depends on evidence of the intention of the spouses, Mr. Justice Laskin would support his decision on the basis of a *constructive trust*. This does not depend on the intention of the spouses. Rather, it is a method used by law to prevent one person from being *unjustly enriched* from the labour or property of another.

"Urgent Message to Ontario Women"
Thunder Bay, February 1978[15]

The undersigned, acting as individuals, believe that the Family Law Reform Bill (Bill 59) will have disastrous consequences for women if it is adopted in its present form.

The government of Ontario has stated its intention of passing this Bill within the next few weeks so that it would be law by March 31st, 1978.

We strongly urge you to join us in attempting to stop this Bill in its present form. The Bill should be amended as follows:

1)   To broaden the assets to be shared on separation or divorce (called "family assets" in the Bill) to include pension rights, savings and investments acquired during the marriage. This change would do much toward recognizing the equal contribution of the wife to the marriage partnership. (Section 3)

2)   To guarantee widows a share of the matrimonial assets upon the death of their husbands. As the Bill abolishes dower rights without providing for sharing of the marital assets upon death, it would make widows worse off than they are at present. The law should ensure that women whose marriages continue until death get at least the same rights to their husbands' property as women whose marriages have broken down.

15. *The Northern Woman Journal* 4, no. 2 (February 1978), 11.

3)   To change the Bill's *retroactive* presumption that a wife who received property from her husband is holding it in trust for him (in other words, he is still the real owner). Whenever a spouse transfers or buys property in the name of the other, the transaction should be considered to be one of gift. This would affirm women's rights over property they have received from their husbands and would bring the law into line with most people's beliefs and practices. (Section 11)

The Bill will apply to all Ontario spouses who do not opt out of it through a *joint* contract. As the above indicates, the authors of the Bill did not recognize the equality of the spouses during the marriage and have not given adequate consideration to the effects this legislation would have on continuing marriages.

ACTION: (Most effective before February 28, 1978) (DO IT NOW)

1)   Communicate with your Provincial Member of Parliament immediately, stressing that the Bill in its present form is not acceptable to you and why. All M.P.P.s can be reached at the Parliament Buildings, Queen's Park, Toronto.

2)   If your M.P.P. is in one of the opposition parties, request that the party drop its support of this Bill.

3)   Also write to the Premier (Hon. William Davis, same address).

4)   Use all possible avenues (including your local media) to get similar immediate action by other women.

Louise B. Dulude
Lawyer and Research Officer
Advisory Council on the Status of Women

Charlotte M. England
Past President
Council of Women of Ottawa and Area

Margaret J. Mason
Lawyer and Member of the Steering Committee of the National Association of Women and the Law

Trudy Wiltshire
Past President

Provincial Council of Women of Ontario and Member of the Ontario Status of Women Council

"Family Law Reformed Again"
Thunder Bay, Ontario, August 1986[16]

Family Property (Married Couples Only)

The most significant changes have occurred in the area of division of family property for legally married couples. Now a spouse can apply for a division of property not only on separation but also within six months after the death of their spouse. This means that the surviving spouse has to choose within six months whether she wishes to take what her spouse has left her under the will (or the rules of intestacy if there is no will) or to apply for division of family property. It will be necessary for the surviving spouse to see a lawyer soon after the death of her spouse to determine how she wants to proceed.

The other major change is in the definition of family assets; these now include virtually *all* assets acquired by either spouse during the marriage. This means that pension funds, family farms, businesses and private bank accounts are now included in the items to be divided as well as household belongings, vehicles, campers, etc. Exclusions are limited to assets owned by each spouse before the marriage (except the matrimonial home), gifts, inheritances, insurance policy proceeds, damage awards and subsequent property traceable to one of these exclusions.

The family property (minus debts and liabilities) owned by each spouse is then totalled and the spouse who has the higher value must compensate the spouse with the lower value so that the value of assets held by each will be equal. Some limited reasons are stated for allowing exclusions to the complete equalization of family property.

Division of Assets Before Separation

An interesting provision, included for the first time, allows a legally married spouse to apply to the court for division of family property even though the spouses are still living together *if* the applying spouse can demonstrate that her husband will squander, waste or deplete the assets. This section may be useful for a woman married to a chronic gambler or alcoholic who wishes to preserve her share of the family assets but to remain with her husband ...

"Spousal Support (Married Couple)

A legally married spouse who wishes to sue for support for herself (not the children) must now commence the application within two years after separation, or else she will be required to obtain a judge's consent to allow her application to proceed.

16. Lynn Beak, *The Northern Woman Journal* 10, no. 1 (August 1986), 10, 14.

Furthermore, spousal support is being seen by the courts only as a backup to division of property and only for the purpose of helping the applying spouse to get back on his or her feet. The primary obligation for spouses is to support themselves, and therefore the courts have been giving support awards for shorter periods of time. Of course, if someone is disabled or otherwise unable to consider entering or re-entering the workforce, the judges have the choice to award spousal support for a longer period of time.

Spousal Support (Common Law Couples)

For couples in a common law relationship spousal support is the only benefit provided by the FLA. If two people have been living together for more than three years (reduced from 5 years), or if a child was born to the couple, then either spouse can apply for spousal support within two years of separation.

The same considerations as discussed in the previous section on amount and duration of the support award apply here except that the concept of "family property" does not apply to common law couples.

However, if a woman has contributed to the acquiring of an asset registered in a man's name (or vice versa) then she should speak to a lawyer since other laws may assist her to recover her investment ...

"Top Court Considers Touchy Issue of Alimony"
Ottawa, 2 April 1992[17]

The Supreme Court of Canada is tackling the touchy question of how long alimony should be paid.

Seven judges — five men and two women — yesterday reserved their decision on whether a man must pay alimony to a woman from whom he has been divorced for 12 years and separated from for 19.

Andrzej Moge of Winnipeg says his ex-wife has had more than enough time to become financially self-sufficient and he should not have to pay her $150 a month.

But Zofia Moge says she remains "economically disadvantaged" by the marriage because she had primary responsibility for raising their three children and that left her dependent on her ex-husband for financial support ...

The Moges were married in Poland in 1957, moved to Winnipeg and had three children before their 1973 separation. He was a welder and she stayed at home during the day but worked six hours every night as a janitor.

They divorced in 1980. Andrzej Moge's monthly child and spousal support payments were increased to $200 in 1987. Two years later he went to court and had the payments terminated.

Zofia Moge successfully appealed to the Manitoba Court of Appeal, which in 1990 awarded her spousal support of $150 a month. It ruled

17. David Vienneau, *Toronto Star*, 2 April 1992, A17.

she remained economically disadvantaged as a result of her role as care-giver in a traditional marriage.

Andrzej Moge, who has remarried and bought another house, appealed to the high court, asking how long he had to continue paying support.

The children are now adults and don't live with either parent.

"The issue is, should Mr. Moge be required to continue to support her?" his lawyer, Patrick Johnston, told the court.

Johnston said Zofia Moge probably would have been economically disadvantaged even if she had never married. He said she had only a Grade 7 education and since her separation had done nothing to improve her lot in life.

For example, he said, she continues to work only 20 hours a week as a janitor.

"She had no career before her marriage and she had no career after her marriage other than as a cleaning person," Johnston said.

His comments did not receive much sympathy from the court.

Mr. Justice Peter Cory said Zofia Moge raised three children and "in some miraculous way" put them through university.

"It's not really much fun working from 5 p.m. to 11 p.m. as a janitor to supplement the family income," Cory scolded.

He noted Zofia Moge had unsuccessfully applied for 38 jobs after the last of her children moved out. She speaks little English and is somewhat physically disabled.

Custody

"Help Lesbian Mother Win Custody"
Toronto, 1979[18]

Gayle's Story

I married George on May 30, 1970. Things were fine until I found out I was pregnant with Sean when Lisa was 4 months old. That's when George started to beat me. He'd come home drunk with one or two of his work buddies. The humiliation I felt as he verbally and/or physically assaulted me was unbelievable. The day I came home from hospital after my hysterectomy, he was drunk again and threw me down the stairs. I had to go back to hospital and they refused to release me until I assured them that I would leave George immediately.

It was after leaving George that I became aware of my lesbian feelings. I had a very close relationship with Marilyn, an old high school buddy. When we broke up in November 1978, she went to George and told him we had been lovers. He then filed for divorce on the grounds that I was a lesbian. He also applied for custody of the children for the

18. Gayle Bezaire Defence Committee flyer, CWMA file: Lesbian Mothers.

same reason and added that I abused the children and exposed them to "perverts."

In January, 1979, after a month's battle before a homophobic Catholic male judge, I was granted custody of Lisa and Sean. All the evidence was positive about me being a good parent, even though court evidence proved I was involved with the Gay Activist League (London), The Lesbian Collective (London), and the Lesbian Organization of Toronto/Three of Cups.

But I was given only conditional custody. The judge wanted to allow the father reasonable access and to approve of anyone I lived with and where I lived. Unfortunately, he did not grant me the $3,500 that George was in arrears for child support. So I moved to Toronto to work and I accepted an offer from a friend, later to become my lover, to stay with her and her child and share expenses.

On Easter vacation, Lisa and Sean spent the weekend with their father and returned extremely hyper. Lisa had bruises down her back and behind and they told me they didn't want to visit their father again. It seems George left them alone with his girlfriend who spanked them and punished them.

On April 19, 1979 we returned to court as ordered and Sean was directed to undergo psychological testing. Every test showed that he wished to remain with me and that he didn't have a very good relationship with his father who rarely spent any time with him. Even so, when the judge learned I was living in a lesbian relationship he decided to reverse his decision. He did this even though all the evidence went in my favour; my parenting abilities, the strong, healthy relationship that I share with my kids and the fact that the kids' evidence showed that they desperately wanted to stay with me.

Since then, I have been working to raise the $3,500 that I need to appeal the court decision. As soon as I can raise the money, I can go to court and get my children back. Time is essential. The longer that George has the kids, the less likely the court is to remove them from him.

Because my legal expenses already total $5,000, I desperately need the support of other people. If the courts can take my kids away from me because I'm gay, then we are all in trouble.

The Rights of Mothers Are Under Siege
Toronto, 1989[19]

Custody used to be something most of us took for granted. Although as a women's issue it has been around since the turn of the century, custody has not been viewed as a contemporary feminist cause for the simple reason that mothers' rights have not been perceived as being in jeopardy. It is assumed the struggle for women's rights and two decades of legal reforms have raised the consciousness of the judiciary at least to the

19. Susan Crean, "In the Name of the Fathers: Joint Custody and the Anti-Feminist Backlash," *This Magazine* 22, no. 4 (February 1989), 19-25.

point where women are not being brutally deprived of children they want and are fully capable of rearing. In the past year, though, evidence has been accumulating that all is not well, that the rights of mothers are under siege, and women who are perfectly good mothers — outstanding, even — can and have lost custody of their children for no other reason than that their former husbands have persuaded a court they could do the job just as well. Often men have more resources at their disposal to make their case, including replacement "mothers" to care for the children.

In one recent instance, a young doctor who proposed to hire a housekeeper to care for his daughter was awarded custody on the grounds the mother had to make a similar arrangement because she was working full time too. This despite the fact that the child had been living with her mother for two years, and custody was claimed by the father only after the mother made a request for increased child support. In another case, a father whose evidence was considered unreliable by the court was awarded custody of his two teenage sons even though the judge noted he "only really became a father to the boys after the separation." Their mother was in an excellent position to take them; she had a job with regular hours which she had had for years, and she was used to raising them on her own. But the judge felt were she given custody, the father would lose interest in the children entirely. The mother, he said, "is sufficiently strong in her own right to handle the situation. Even though she does not have custody of the children, she will continue to be a mother to the children."

Access to and Treatment by the Legal System

"Poor Women and the Legal System"
Prince Edward Island, 1986[20]

... The family Legal Aid program is supposed to provide services in family law matters such as separation, divorce, custody and child protection. The limited staff available means that, in reality, only "emergency" family cases can be addressed ...

For women who seek the services of the legal system and are unable to pay, there are few avenues open to them. Barely able to support themselves, they cannot afford the costs of hiring a private lawyer and must remain in limbo. To have the peace of mind of having their relationship issues settled will take many years of saving the fee. Alternatively they can borrow money and spend many years repaying loans.

One questions the claim that, in this country, all people enjoy equality before the law. In the words of one woman I interviewed who had been

---

20. Joan Murray, *Common Ground* 5, no. 4 (September 1986), 6-7. Copy at CWMA.

unable to get satisfaction through the Legal Aid system, "Now I'm fighting for custody and paying my own lawyer with money I should be using for food, clothing, furniture. I'm below the poverty line and can little afford to pay this fee".

The length of time it takes for legal procedures to be completed is a big concern of many women. A woman who has made the break from an intolerable situation feels very vulnerable. She's coping with the trauma of a shattered relationship, children who are upset and often unable to understand what's going on and the uncertainties of her financial future. The longer the delay in getting legal issues settled, the more threatened she will feel.

The Canadian Bar Association-National Legal Aid Liaison Committee Study, published in January 1985, has recommendations to improve the system, e.g., clarifying and increasing eligibility for accessing the service. The Committee sees the need to expand the coverage of Legal Aid to include workers' rights, UIC, Immigration and Welfare appeals, housing and pension rights cases, none of which are covered in P.E.I. now. A strong plea is made that public legal education and advice be available for all members of society. Some provinces have legal aid systems administered not by a government department but by separate corporations. These are run by boards of directors made up of representatives of community, government and legal professions. These and other recommendations in this report, if implemented, could greatly improve the accessibility to legal aid for all who need it ...

Rape Victim Sues Police
Toronto, 1991[21]

TORONTO — Metro Toronto's police commission was denied leave yesterday to appeal a ruling that allows a rape victim to sue police for failing to warn women that a serial rapist was operating in their immediate area.

Three judges of the Ontario Court of Appeal took only a few moments to rule that the case should go directly to trial.

The victim, described in court documents as Jane Doe, is suing police for $600,000.

Mary Cornish, the lawyer for the woman, told the court that the victim has been trying to get the matter to trial for four years. "That doesn't make the court system very accessible when an appeal can be dragged on that long," she added.

Christie Jefferson, executive director of the Women's Legal Education and Action Fund, said the ruling finally gives the woman a chance to question why police failed to warn residents in the area near Church and Wellesley Streets in Toronto, the stalking ground of convicted rapist Paul Callow.

21. Rudy Platiel, "Toronto police fail to block suit," *Globe and Mail* 5 February 1992, A6.

"What happens now is that we go through a phase called discoveries, where we finally get access to police records which we have not been allowed to as long as this has been going on," Ms. Jefferson said.

"Now we can determine exactly what went on; whether it was a policy decision; by whom, how broad, based on what assumptions. We can also get access to records as to what exactly happened in the investigation because there are a lot of questions that we have around the negligence side of this case," she said.

Ms. Jefferson said the victims were all white women living alone in second- or third-floor balcony apartments in walkup buildings that had easy access.

The suit alleges that police failed to warn residents because of a "stereotypical" belief that it would cause hysteria among women in the area and because it might cause the rapist to flee and strike elsewhere.

It alleges that by using woman "as bait" and failing to put enough resources into the investigation and the protection of women in the area, the police acted discriminatorily, contrary to the Charter of Rights and Freedoms.

Human Rights

Employment

Human Rights Issues
Victoria, 1978[22]

Consent Order in Sex Discrimination Case

Marilyn Toms was referred by Canada Manpower, Nanaimo, to a summer job as a landscaper with Van Deleur Contracting Limited. She alleged that when she phoned the employer, she was told "I do not hire girls." Canada Manpower referred two other women to the job, also both of whom, when contacted by the Human Rights Branch, stated that they were told by Van Deleur Contracting Limited that they would not be hired because they were female.

Marilyn Toms succeeded in obtaining other work for the summer as a waitress.

Efforts by the Human Rights Branch to settle Ms. Toms' complaint against Van Deleur Contracting Limited were not successful and the Minister of Labour referred the case to a Board of Inquiry. Prior to the date of the Hearing, a Settlement Agreement was achieved which became a Consent Order of the Board of Inquiry. By Consent, the Board Ordered:

22. British Columbia of Ministry of Labour, Human Rights Branch, Kathleen Ruff, Director. From the files of Victoria Status of Women.

1)   "That Van Deleur Contracting Limited shall offer its employment opportunities to all persons in a manner consistent with the letter and spirit of the Human Rights Code of British Columbia and in particular, shall select persons for employment on the basis of ability to perform.

2)   That Van Deleur Contracting Limited shall forthwith pay to the complainant, Marilyn Toms, the sum of $150."

$50,000 Settlement in Equal Pay Case

In February 1978 six women signed a complaint form alleging discrimination in pay on the basis of sex. The women were employed as "cleaning assistants," a position held only by women. The women alleged that they performed substantially similar work as "cleaners," a position filled only by men. Two of the men in the cleaner position were required at times to wash floors and bale garbage, duties the women did not do. However, neither did the other men in the cleaner position do these duties, yet [they] received the higher rate of pay.

A Human Rights Officer was appointed to investigate the complaint and as part of his investigation, spent two nights in a row observing the functions of the cleaners and the cleaning assistants. The Officer's investigation indicated that the complaint was valid and a settlement was reached with the company whereby:

1)   The company gave a written commitment to adhere to the provisions of the Human Rights Code.

2)   All 19 women in the cleaning assistant position were given equal pay with the male employees and received $48,000 in backpay.

3)   In addition, three female employees who had left their job were sought out and given the $2,000 backpay to which they were entitled. It was not possible to track down a fourth female employee ...

Sexual Orientation

"Bill 7: Real Protection for Lesbians?"
July, 1987[23]

... As a lesbian working in the office of the MPP who introduced the amendment Bill 7, to Ontario's Human Rights Code, I was privy to a unique view of the lobbying that occurred beforehand. Across Ontario, there were equal numbers of proponents and opponents. Since my boss, Evelyn Gigantes (NDP, Ottawa Centre) introduced Bill 7, her support

23. Cindy Moriarty, *Breaking the Silence* 5, no. 4 (July 1987), 4-6. Copy at CWMA.

was guaranteed. Those supporting the Bill wisely chose to direct their lobbying efforts elsewhere. The opponents, however, were another story. Our office was inundated with calls and mail voicing fear, hate, distortion and, every once in a while, hostile civility.

Opponents saw homosexuality, at best, as unnatural; at worst, as the root of all evil, responsible for the destruction of society, and as the leading cause of child molestation. Among this homophobic insanity one thing was abundantly clear: people thought the bill concerned gays; they gave little thought to lesbians.

Over the years I have learned, personally and politically, all about lesbian invisibility, but it has never been so clear to me as during the lobbying process. As a feminist, I've been speaking and educating and rabble-rousing for years. I've dealt with all sorts of confrontations and attacks for my beliefs. As my life has changed, I have gained the "privilege" of dealing with issues on a quasi-intellectual level. Reaction to the Bill eroded my intellectual armour and everything was brought down to gut-level emotions. I was exposed daily to raw hate and fear that bordered on panic. The ugliness and distortion often made it impossible to comprehend the limits of human intolerance.

No knowledge, intellectual understanding or analysis hits home like knowledge of the heart. For me that knowledge came with identifying myself as a lesbian. But the big deal wasn't lesbians. Lesbians are women, and women have never been a big deal (except to other women). Men were the big deal. Gay men. Depraved men assaulting young boys. Assaulting young girls and women has never been a big deal.

The lobby against the amendment was closely connected to the anti-feminist movement. In the Ontario Legislature, Evelyn Gigantes said:

> The sexual pecking order is intimately linked to the economic pecking order of our society. Any man who declares that he is not a full-blooded man of whatever macho notion is, simply, a traitor to the most important system. It is the ultimate act of treason to the system. The system is one which connects the notion of men's "ownership" rights and role in the family structure, with the rights and privileges of owners in the economy...women don't rate as traitors. They can be rebels against authority, but not traitors because it's not their system.
>
> ... There are 125 elected representatives in the Ontario Legislature; 10 are women. If the sexual numbers and the social powers were reversed I believe the clauses of section 18 relating to sexual orientation might not even be necessary. ... It is the maleness of economic and social domination of our society that is threatened by this reform, not the womanness or the childness, but the maleness that so profits by its domination through being male.[24]

24. *Hansard*, 25 November 1986

From R.E.A.L. Women to religious and business coalitions, the opposition stormed Queen's Park, but like all storms their protest blew over and the skies cleared with the passing of the Bill.

Does the new legislation mean protection for gays and lesbians under the Human Rights Code? I believe the legislation has provided us with a battle-ground and not necessarily a victory. The onus remains on us to complain against discrimination to the Human Rights Commission.

While the Bill provides a signal to employers, service deliverers and legislators, it does not solve an age-old problem. Rather, it provides a starting point for discussion and reform.

It brings the issue out of the closet, but a lesbian has to be pretty much "out" to lodge a complaint with the Human Rights Commission. The woman whose personal security is threatened unless she keeps her lifestyle private, will not be able to walk into her office and ask that her lover be covered under the pension plan. Landlords and employers can always find other avenues of discrimination and other reasons for dismissal or eviction. The law does not protect us against exile and family outrage. Often, we will be on trial and we will still have to prove our "innocence."

EGALE (Equality for Gays and Lesbians Everywhere) is a national lobbying group based in Ottawa that co-ordinated a tremendous campaign around Bill 7 and is continuing its efforts on the federal level. Debbie Hughes of EGALE expressed qualified optimism. She sees Bill 7 as helpful, but is not convinced it will change much without federal legislation. "You have to be out to use Bill 7 and in order to be out you have to be very vulnerable."

Ironically, Hughes says homophobic hysteria might ultimately work in our favour. She explains that legislators who might not normally have voted in favour of the Bill did so in reaction to the hatred and viciousness expressed by the opposition. The more hysterical and vindictive those lobbying against the Bill became, the more apparent it was to the fence sitters where logic lay.

As to what impact will Bill 7 have on the Charter of Rights? Speculators wonder about past provincial cases and the implications of Bill 7 before the federal courts. Federal government policy says that "sexual orientation is irrelevant to whether one can perform a job or use a service or facility." Further, "sexual orientation is not grounds for denial of security clearance, or basis for discrimination within federal jurisdiction."[25]

Discrimination continues in employment practices, particularly within the RCMP and armed services. Federal policy may not be law, but I would wager it's one of the few federal government policies that can be so gallantly ignored by its own ministries.

As the new legislation takes hold we can hope to gain true equality and a sense of freedom in the lives we lead. While the nature of the law

25. *Toward Equality Report*, 4 March 1986

will be muddy for some time, the passing of the Bill clearly signals an acknowledgement of and disagreement with homophobia.

The phones in my office are still ringing. A woman calls, outraged, trying to instill some "sense" into my head and warning me of the dangers of homosexuality. "Would you want one of those people teaching your kids?" "Would you want one of those in your home?" "You bet!!!"

CALL TO ACTION: To support EGALE, you can donate your time or money (or both). Write or phone your MP and encourage her/him to support an amendment to the constitution that would prohibit discrimination on the basis of sexual orientation. Call or write the Minister of Justice and the opposition critics to voice your support for the amendment.
For more information:

EGALE
P.O. Box 2891, Station D
Ottawa, Ontario
K1P 5W9

The Canadian Human Rights Act and Sexual Orientation Toronto/Ottawa, March/June 1991[26]

The Ontario Institute for Studies in Education
252 Bloor Street West, Toronto, Ontario M5S 1V6
Centre for Women's Studies in Education

March 4, 1991

Ms. Kim Campbell
Minister of Justice and Attorney
General of Canada
House of Commons
Ottawa, Ontario
K1J 0A6

Dear Minister of Justice Campbell:

On behalf of the Centre for Women's Studies in Education of the Ontario Institute for Studies in Education, I am writing to urge you finally to take the action promised by a spokesperson for the Justice Department of the Progressive Conservative government of Canada over four years ago, namely to "take whatever measures are necessary to prohibit discrimination based on sexual orientation in all areas of Federal jurisdic-

26. Ruth Roach Pierson, letter. Copy at CWSE. Kim Campbell declined permission to reprint her response.

tion." As members of the feminist educational community of Canada, we of the OISE Centre for Women's Studies in Education find it deplorable that your office has not acted more speedily and responsibly on this commitment. We, therefore, exhort you to introduce without further delay an amendment to the federal Human Rights Act that will incorporate "sexual orientation" within its anti-discrimination provisions. Social justice requires that you take this action immediately in order to begin the process of dismantling institutionalized heterosexism in Canada.

Yours sincerely,
Ruth Roach Pierson
Professor and Head
Centre for Women's Studies in Education

Women Prisoners

"Women and Prisons"
Vancouver, 1985[27]

To have the courage to face up to the shocking overrepresentation of native women in the prison population of this country, to realize that they are the most disadvantaged minority in Canadian society and that this situation results directly in their being incarcerated in outrageous numbers, to carry this outrage into the entire women prison scene is to do more than just compile statistics, express shock and dismay, or declare solidarity with our sisters in prison. It is to map out strategies that attack — yes, attack — the problem, here and now.

Although there may not be a jail, prison, or penitentiary in every city and town in this country, there is a police lockup in every area where people are picked up, where they can be held up to 24 hours without being charged. If charged, they must be brought before a magistrate within 24 hours. At least, that is what the law says. Several years ago, a self-appointed concerned Citizens Committee of two women in a small Vancouver Island town announced their intention to monitor the local lockup to make sure that young native Indian girls and boys (in particular) were not being held indefinitely for such "crimes" as running away from home or alcoholism. When brought to trial, these young people, in most instances without adequate legal assistance, and not understanding their charges, would plead guilty. Thus would begin a life long trip down the prison tube.

A few examples: in Saskatchewan at the Pine Grove Correctional Centre for Women, 87.2 percent of all admissions in 1970-71 were of native women who made up only six percent of the total provincial population that year. At the Women's Prison at The Pas, Manitoba in 1971, 91.2 percent of the admissions were of native women who made up approxi-

27. Claire Culhane, *Resources for Feminist Research/documentation sur la recherche féministe* 14, no. 4 (December/January 1985/86), 32-33.

mately six percent of that province's population. In B.C. where native women constitute approximately two and a half percent of the population, 28 percent of all female admissions to prison were of native women.

More telling perhaps than statistics is the comment of a first time visitor to the Portage Women's Jail in Manitoba, who asked: "Don't white girls get into trouble?" Yes, of course white girls get into trouble too, ones who come from low income situations, many of them single mothers. From a Canadian Association of Elizabeth Fry Societies' National Survey concerning female prisoners in provincial and territorial institutions in May of 1982,

> ...most serious offenses are theft under $200, impaired driving, breach of probation, public mischief, failure to appear, forgery, bail skipping, conspiracy, arson — the majority of fraud charges being related to cheques or credit cards — and for such 'crimes' we find that in 1982, 65 percent of those charged were serving sentences from 1-6 months, 27 percent were serving 6-24 months, and only 8 percent (58 women in 1982) were serving Federal sentences.

By now the question must surely pose itself — why do we need a 4 billion dollar criminal justice system to incarcerate 2,536 women (part of the 27,000 people who are doing time on any given day in this country)? The figure of $62,872, the cost to maintain a woman in the Federal system, takes on macabre proportions when we realize that not even a fraction of that amount is ever available for the same woman to keep her family together, for job training, or for much needed medical care. It is essential that we recognize the class position of women who are doubly exploited — as a part of the 95 percent prison population who are socially and economically deprived, women offenders suffer additional deprivation because of their personal disadvantaged position in relation to the work force and because of their responsibility for child rearing. ...

The struggle to improve the lot of women prisoners can only be realistically addressed within the scope of abolishing the prison system altogether. About 80 percent of those detained are not violent, not dangerous, and could be better consigned to paying fines, adjusted to income, or making restitution for damage committed — assuming that we were living in a civilized society where people could count on being gainfully employed. But this is not the case. As it is, prisoners are held hostage to the economy. Fifteen percent of violent prisoners, unable immediately to cope with readjustment to society for whatever physical and psychological problems, or for lack of training and skills, require community support which is certainly not forthcoming while sitting in a cell. The five percent balance (of which only 1.1 percent are officially rated as violent along the lines of a Clifford Olson) might indeed have to be detained for life, in which case we would require only one, not 250 prisons. It could conceivably be administered in a humane fashion to the advantage of the keepers as well as the kept.

Any investigation into the nature of crimes committed by women in Canada, including their personal case histories, clearly reveals the striking relevance of their economic, cultural, and social position in society. Non-violent civil disobedience actions at prison gates would be a useful means of exposing a prison system which has so much to conceal.

"I dreamed I visited the Prison for Women, and no one was home."

"Prisons Deny Human Dignity, Self-Respect"
Halifax, March 1988[28]

I am writing to you today from the Prison for Women in Kingston, Ontario.... Today is the wedding day of my eldest daughter. Here in prison in Kingston, I will not see or hear or feel or touch a single moment or breath of her day of commitment and celebration. Like many other women, my attachment to my first born child is especially profound. Despite the passing of 23 years, the event of her birth remains clearly etched in my own soul as a birth of glorious joy.

She knows of my feelings. But I am in Kingston, a thousand and hundreds of miles from her wedding feast in Antigonish, Nova Scotia.

Gentle public, lawful readers, this is, oh, so very sad, I can honestly say I was once much like you. I tended my family's needs. I cooked most loving meals and more dutifully washed the clothes and tended the home, assisted on the family farm and worked for wages.

A dear partner and I lived lives of external productivity, fuelling our energy and fantasies with the soul poison of alcohol often disguised in glittering shards of crystal goblets. Our pleasure grew to be a problem and the problem unfolded and in turn engulfed us in addiction.

Maybe it was absolute despair and self-loathing: we were kindred spirits — both Gemini — sometimes lovers, always friends, but in May 1985, I shot and killed this man.

The RCMP charged me with second degree murder. The Crown Attorney prosecuted the case. The jury disregarded alcoholism as a mitigating factor and found me guilty as charged. The judge was obligated by Canadian law to sentence me to life in prison. I may be considered for parole after serving ten years ... I arrived at the Prison for Women in the fall of 1985. I had few, if any, preconceived notions of what prison was or should be, beyond stereotyped images from B movies and a generalized idea that I was being punished on my way to rehabilitation as a safe individual. The fact that I was female seemed rather irrelevant to the whole procedure (in my eyes). How totally wrong and ignorant I was on all these counts!

I was sent to Kingston because I was a woman. The province of Nova Scotia, indeed the entire Maritime region, has no facility for female

28. Jo-ann Mayhew, *Pandora* 3, no. 2 (March 1988), 17. Copy at WERC.

offenders sentenced to prison for two years or more. My deportation was predetermined ...

The fact is, I write in Ontario while my daughter marries in Nova Scotia. The fact is, my best friend is agonizingly attempting to be allowed to serve her sentence in British Columbia, close to a husband recovering from a major cardiac arrest. Her request for a humanitarian transfer on compassionate grounds is being denied. The fact is, Native women from the Prairie Provinces are most commonly singled out, earmarked, for transfer to Kingston because they are native.

Both federal and provincial governments claim that there are not enough funds available to incarcerate women in their home provinces. The fact is, it is costing you, the tax-payer, between $60–70,000 per year for each female prisoner housed in Kingston, away from family and community, in a living situation of combined cages and recycled army barracks with only a superficial semblance of programming.

I was confused, disoriented and distressed upon my arrival at this prison. I was allowed to go to the Psychiatric Treatment Centre. This is a quasi-medical unit located at Kingston Prison (KP), one of the oldest prisons in Canada and now dedicated to handling protective custody inmates, frequently men who have demonstrated severe attitude problems toward women. Women have been allotted five cells in what is best described as a setting for a Gothic horror movie. This represents a recent compromise between a proposed psychiatric hospital complex and nothing.

After several winter months in such surroundings, I was pleased to return to the Prison for Women. I was given work as a cleaner and permitted to brush up the typing and word-processing skills with which I had previously been acquainted.

My own single interest was in receiving help/treatment for alcoholism. I attended AA meetings and was dismayed to find them cancelled if their scheduling conflicted with bingo or a dance. I would not ignore the seriousness of my addiction and found the passive acceptance of so little programming in this area very hard to understand. The administration took time to explain that their function was to incarcerate not rehabilitate — apparently efforts (?) in that direction had proved unsuccessful.

However I inadvertently learned that male prisoners in this same area of Ontario were being offered an extensive substance abuse rehabilitation program called "Brentwood" while serving their sentences. With the self-serving determination quite characteristic of the alcoholic, I attempted to propose a similar program be offered to women at the Prison for Women ... My personal observation confirmed that about 80% of the women at P4W had been affected by substance abuse. Similar grim statistics also revealed that 60% or more of this prison's population had been victims of incest, rape or battering.

With renewed purpose, I pursued the "Brentwood" concept until, through a wonderfully inadvertent meeting, I was introduced to members of Women In Sobriety. This is a relatively new women's self-help concept basically dedicated to promoting what I call active sobriety.

It took many months to have this positive program introduced into this prison. The entire project was almost abandoned for "lack of available funds." The visiting moderators had asked for a bi-monthly fee of $65 to cover their travelling costs from Ottawa to Kingston and back.

Keeping in mind the $60,000 cost per year and the magnitude of the substance abuse problem, this "lack of funding" would be ludicrous if not so tragic in human terms ...

Chapter 6

Women, Culture and Communications

Philinda Masters

The period from 1970–1993 saw the proliferation of cultural production in Canada, inspired by a newly articulated feminist ideology. This chapter will look at the ways cultural institutions have, or have not, taken up the challenge of feminist artists to examine systemic bias. It will discuss the new forms of performance art and culture devised by women to counter the influence of the dominant white heterosexual male culture. It will look at forms of communication, such as feminist presses and newspapers, which emerged during the seventies and eighties to report "news about women that's not in the dailies," as one feminist newspaper put it.[1] Finally, it will explore some of the debates that have engaged feminist cultural workers and activists, as feminist theory and practice evolved and expanded over this period.

Institutional Representation

The 1970 Report of the Royal Commission on the Status of Women devotes a short chapter to women and culture and deals with the representation of women in the arts at the end of a section on women in the Canadian economy. None of the Report's 167 recommendations, however, specifically addresses the concerns raised.[2] Nevertheless, the two decades following the Report saw a proliferation of reports, surveys, briefs to other royal commissions and recommendations on women in the arts, communications and Canadian cultural life.

A main preoccupation of these documents and of the task forces on women in the arts was the poor representation, participation and the subsequent sense of profound alienation of women in mainstream Canadian culture. Unquestionably, one of the first concerns many women expressed when first coming to consciousness about the status of women was the appalling representation — what amounted to sexist images — of women in the media. One Toronto consciousness-raising (CR) group in the early 1970s, for example, eschewing the traditional "confessional" model of CR, chose instead to form an action group to fight sexist images of women in advertising. These concerns later led to the formation of a number of media-monitoring groups, including the Coalition for Fair and Responsible Media (1977), the Women's Coalition Against Sexist Advertising (1983), and MediaWatch (1981), a national organization first formed as a subcommittee of the National Action Committee on the Status of Women, with a mandate of monitoring what was originally known as "sex-role stereotyping" in the media and lobbying governments and other regulatory bodies to effect change.

The Canadian Radio-television and Telecommunications Commission (CRTC), which regulates the broadcast media in this country, first began its scrutiny of sexism in radio and television programming when the then Minister of Communications, the Hon. Jeanne Sauvé, called for a task force on sex-role stereotyping. The task force first met in October 1979 and its report, "Images of Women," was released in 1982. The committee heard submissions from the Canadian Association of Broadcasters, representatives from the advertising industry, the CBC, CRTC and members of the public.[3] Not surprisingly, it found women vastly underrepresented both as purveyors and as subjects of news, sports and other programming (including drama and commercials) in comparison to men, and it found also that stereotyped images of women ran the gamut from infantilizing to degrading:

> Women in general, and women as homemakers in particular, are characterized as subservient to and/or dependent on men. Men tell them what to do and their instructions seem to be gratefully accepted. In general, women are shown serving men and boys, but boys and men are rarely shown to serve women other than by opening doors or holding chairs, stereotypic evidence of women's apparent weakness or dependency. Women are often portrayed in isolation from each other or engaged in petty competition.[4]

The task force proposed recommendations and urged the various bodies involved to "self-regulate" rather than have legislative change forced upon them. As is well-documented in other areas, self-regulation rarely, if ever, works effectively — a result clearly demonstrated by subsequent reports of the CRTC in its ongoing monitoring of the problem. The follow-up "Report on Industry Self-Regulation," published in 1986 shows again and again (though it intentionally offers no analysis), in tables and reports from industry committees set up for the purpose, that the pace of change is glacial.[5] A report by MediaWatch published around the same time found that not only are the images of women in the media misogynist, but also that despite research and lobbying over the years, very little progress had been made.[6]

A curious finding of yet another follow-up to the 1982 report was that the greatest imbalance in the representation of women vis-à-vis men was in the age bracket 35-64.[7] As women enter the years of greatest potential productivity, apart from the childbearing of earlier years, the mainstream consciousness appears to lose interest, and women's adult years are ignored. Once they reach grandmother status, they are again admitted to the picture (although as the report stresses, very few women *or* men over 65 are represented). Another not-so-curious finding was expressed by one group submitting to the CRTC task force hearings:

> If today's advertisements were the only indication of the modern woman's life-style it would appear that we are all white, middle class, models, housewives, and sex objects. This is fully supported not only by documentation, but by even the skimpiest viewing of television or an hour's worth of radio.[8]

In an environment where the CBC once fired an announcer for having a Scottish accent,[9] the broadcast media had an even longer way to go in representing women of colour and covering their stories in the news.

The CBC itself, simultaneously with the CRTC task force, produced a major study on the images of women on television.[10] Published in 1982, the report set out to describe the presence, role and images of women on prime time English language CBC television programs and, not shying away from analysis, attempted to identify major social issues involved with the stereotypical portrayal of women, and how these affect the perceptions of the television-viewing Canadian public. It went a step further than other reports, too, in suggesting that exposure to traditional television content reinforces, and in some cases creates, negative sex-role attitudes. The cumulative effect of limited portrayals of women is to institutionalize these attitudes, and thereby contribute to the systemic discrimination against women. The report further contends that adding positive portrayals of women on television could go a long way toward improving the status of women in general.

> Given that TV is a social force of some significance, and that control of its content is possible, it has a responsibility in terms of social development. The practical question is what goal to pursue: to reflect the status quo of the society, to portray a more rigidly sex-linked set of roles than presently exist in society, or to portray a more diversified set of options.[11]

One recommendation of the report was that the CBC would be able to exercise more control over the content of its drama programs, and thereby positively influence the portrayal of women, by maintaining its practice of producing shows in-house, and not subcontracting them or buying them from freelance producers and directors. Unfortunately, the CBC did not heed this recommendation, although it remains to be seen whether independent producers are more, or less, sexist than the CBC.

Not only were the portrayals of women in the media at issue, but also the conditions of women working within the major Canadian cultural institutions. In 1978, women at the National Film Board (NFB) produced a report on discriminatory employment practices at the NFB.[12] The report found that women were at a disadvantage in terms of pay and promotions, were ghettoized in certain less technical jobs and were not supported in their efforts at change by their male colleagues. But it was not until 1986, after the Employment Equity Act had been proclaimed federally, that the NFB adopted an employment equity program.[13]

A concern with access, numbers and fairness, as opposed to image, was reflected in a number of other reports and studies conducted throughout the 1980s. In 1987, for example, women from the broadcast industry and the women's movement met at a national conference to review the state of Canadian broadcasting, with a view to formulating policy to be included in a new broadcasting act. The conference was attended by feminist activists and media workers, advertising executives, politicians and communications policy analysts. In a report summarizing the conference proceedings, "Adjusting the Image," the authors suggested that the debate had "moved from important but narrow concepts of sex-role stereotyping and sexist language to issues of dignity, equality and freedom of expression for half our population."[14]

At the beginning of the decade, in 1981, the Applebaum-Hébert Commission[15] heard briefs from many women's groups relating to federal cultural policy. "The underrepresentation of women in Canada's cultural life," states a brief from the National Action Committee on the Status of Women (NAC), "and the uneven distribution of women within the arts constitute a hidden, but nonetheless insidious, form of censorship... a consequence of a complex system of discrimination."[16] For example, Sasha McInnes-Hayman's report on the Ontario Arts Council found that women were underrepresented as both grant recipients and as jurors (by about 3:1, men to women), and that the amount of money awarded to women artists closely corresponded to the proportion of female jurors who adjudicated the applications.[17]

And in an independent study, Montreal poet Sharon H. Nelson noted that women poets did not have fair and equal access to funding or to publication: although the League of Canadian Poets' membership at the time was about one-third female, women represented only about 7 per cent of the entries in poetry anthologies. "Women writers," says Nelson, "suffer the eternal conundrum: their work goes unpublished or unnoticed or unreviewed and when no-one has heard of it we are told that 'good' writers succeed in any case and that the rest of us do not have a high enough profile for inclusion in anthologies, or for jobs, or for awards."[18]

Winnipeg artist Sharron Zenith Corne was appalled when in 1975 she learned that the Winnipeg Art Gallery was planning to use a $10,000 International Women's Year federal grant to mount a show to explore the ways women have been portrayed and perceived in nineteenth- and twentieth-century art. Realizing that this necessarily meant art by men, and that the show would therefore celebrate stereotypical images of women, Zenith Corne formed a committee and approached the gallery. Eventually, after much resistance, the director agreed to let the women mount their own parallel show. He did not offer any financial or resource support, though he did offer the admonition that the art chosen must be "of suitable quality" and that it must not violate acceptable community standards. Happily, the show opened to great critical acclaim and, ironically, the original show was considered by local journalists to be pale and vulgar by comparison.[19]

The director's fear that "community standards" might be violated by feminist art was to some extent realized (though his expectation that the public would only attend a "moderate" show was not): one selection was a sculpture by Vancouver artist Phyllis Green, of wood and crochetwork, called "The Boob Tree." It is unlikely that such playful treatment would be found, much less appreciated, in a retrospective of traditional men's art.

It is not surprising that a recurring concern expressed in many briefs to the Applebert hearings was that women's art has never been taken seriously, or has not been viewed, as one submission put it, "as examples of aesthetic achievement of a high order."[20] This lack of understanding or appreciation for women's cultural endeavours translates directly into lack of funding and lack of visibility for women cultural producers. In any national policy for the arts, the NAC brief contended, special recognition must be given to the renaissance of women in the arts. "Their work is more experimental, on the one hand, and more polemic on the other, a combination that is threatening to established art critics and art institutions which have no system of norms for judging the quality of such work."[21]

Feminist Cultural Production

In the two decades since the Royal Commission on the Status of Women report, there was a burgeoning of women's art and culture, both in new forms and in re-visioning of old forms. In a phrase common in the early seventies, it was a culture specifically "by, for and about women" — that is, it was not by men, for men and about men, or worse, by men, for men and about women. It sprang from a newfound sense of women's identity (or varied identities), and was invariably woman-centred and often feminist-inspired.

A 1985 show, at a Toronto alternative gallery, of graphic arts in the women's movement built on the holdings of the Canadian Women's Movement Archives to showcase the posters, T-shirts, buttons, flyers and other paraphernalia used to publicize and illustrate events and themes in the Ontario women's movement from 1970 to 1986. Unlike many art exhibits, this show, called Graphic Feminism, underlined the connection between art and activism, and portrayed the selections as part of a movement for social change.

> The women's movement has exposed the misrepresentation of women not only in history but in other areas as well, including popular and "high" art culture. We have learned that as long as we do not develop and produce our own cultural images we will be subjected to someone else's messages and someone else's perspective of how we should think, feel and be. The past and present monopoly of culture depends on our silence. Feminists working in all aspects of culture are refuting the traditional myths that constrain women.[22]

While many women were engaged in the struggle to open up mainstream cultural institutions to women, others (often in fact the same women) were involved in producing and promoting new forms that could "rewrite" the cultural terrain, and give women cultural workers a forum for new, and often unpopular or at least unfamiliar, views.

As the catalogue for "Graphic Feminism" suggests, the concept of culture was being redefined, the old practices transformed and the boundaries between "low" arts (like crafts or design) and "high" art blurred. The modernist tradition of separating art from life, by displacing or disguising content, was being replaced with an emphasis on recognizable subject matter related to familiar contexts, and the conscious communication of a feminist/post-modern ideology.[23]

In the early days, feminist cultural endeavours often involved the reclaiming and sometimes reshaping of the past. A 1974 production by the feminist Redlight Theatre, *What Glorious Times They Had,* was a play about women's struggle for the vote at the turn of the century. It incorporated a version of Winnipeg feminist Nellie McClung's Mock Parliament, where the women were in charge and the government of the day ridiculed.[24] Redlight's enormously popular play toured Canada during International Women's Year, despite the lack of reviews in the mainstream press — one Toronto newspaper excused its lack of coverage by saying the play was a "revival."[25]

In an effort to reclaim and promote women's work in film, a number of groups emerged in the mid-1970s. In Vancouver, Women in Focus, a feminist film collective, was started in 1974 to provide alternative images of women. As founder Marion Barling said, "I wanted to see a women's aesthetic established: see a women's sensibility represented, understand what it is and what work comes out of it when you view the world through it. My general vision was to literally put women in focus." In the first four years of existence, Women in Focus managed to make

The Women and Film International Festival toured Canada in 1973.
The catalogue's cover logo was a familiar sight to many feminists.

available for distribution over 50 films, on topics ranging from images
of women in the media, to alcoholism, to transition houses.[26] A Toronto
group, Innervisions/ARC, began to catalogue existing women's film and
video and to survey the types of work produced, both in mainstream and
alternative or feminist film. It began as an educational tool, and became
more expansive each year.

Also in 1974, the National Film Board's Studio D, the English-lan-
guage women's studio, was established. It emerged without fanfare,
simply an announcement of the "Challenge for Change" series under the
direction of Kathleen Shannon (later Executive Producer of Studio D)
and Anne-Claire Poirier. Its repertoire of films on women, mainly docu-
mentaries in keeping with the general feminist goal of reclaiming
women's history and promoting women's visibility, grew very quickly
and today, less than 20 years later, boasts many of the NFB's most
popular, and often award-winning, films. Among them are Anne-Claire
Poirier's film about rape, *A Scream from Silence* (1980), Bonnie Sherr

Klein and Anne Henderson's *Not a Love Story: A Film About Pornography* (1981), Terri Nash's film on the anti-nuclear movement, *If You Love This Planet* (1983), Margaret Wescott and Gloria Demers' *Behind the Veil: Nuns* (1985), Dorothy Todd Hénaut's documentary on three Québec women writers, *Firewords* (1987), and Dionne Brand and Ginny Stikeman's film on black women community activists, *Sisters in the Struggle* (1991).

Although the NFB Studio D has been prolific over the years in producing films, and has in fact been criticized for holding somewhat of a monopoly in the field and for not fully representing the interests of Canadian women,[27] there have also been many women making films and videos independently. In the 1970s, films such as Sylvia Spring's *Madeleine Is* (1972), Joyce Wieland's *The Far Shore* (1974), Patricia Gruben's *The Central Character* (1977) and Kay Armatage's *Speak Body* (1979) were among the varied offerings of feminist filmmakers. But it was not until the 1980s that feminist film and video production began to gain momentum. Perhaps coincident with the efforts of the women at Studio D, feminists were engaged in the production of everything from experimental video art to full-length drama, involving filmic techniques from cinéma-vérité to post-modern deconstruction of the traditional narrative.[28]

Throughout the eighties, film festivals abounded, giving space and encouragement for the creating, and more importantly the screening, of feminist films. The Canadian Images Festival and the Grierson Documentary Seminar, while not specifically women's events, nevertheless indicated the influence of women and feminism in Canadian filmmaking. At the Grierson festival in 1985, for example, viewers could see Peg Campbell's *Street Kids* (Vancouver), Tahani Rached's *Haiti: Québec* (Montreal), Brenda Longfellow's *Breaking Out* (Toronto) and the Women and Video Exploration (WAVE) production of *Our Two Cents Worth* (Halifax).[29] At mainstream festivals, like the Toronto Festival of Festivals and the Vancouver Film Festival, many Canadian women's films have been shown (in Toronto, largely thanks to festival programmer Kay Armatage). Past films have included features, like Janis Cole and Holly Dale's *P4W: Prison for Women* (1981), Sandy Wilson's *My American Cousin* (1985) and Patricia Rozema's *I've Heard the Mermaids Singing* (1987), or shorts like Midi Onadera's *Ten Cents a Dance/Parallax* (1985). At Colour Positive, an international anti-racism festival in Toronto, one could see, for example, Jennifer Hodge's *Home Feeling: Struggle for a Community* (1983) and at the many feminist multi-media festivals, like those sponsored by the Women's Media Alliance (1984) or FemFest '85 in Toronto, feminist films were screened, such as Janis Lundman's *Matinale,* Marusia Bociurkiw's *75 Terrific Looks at Advertising* and Nancy Nichol's *Mini Skools Pay Mini Wages.* Given the difficulties in obtaining financing for feminist film and video production, and the serious and sometimes overwhelming obstacle to film distribution in this country, it is heartening to know just how many films have been made, though unfortunate that most people will rarely, if ever, see them. Without the festivals and retrospectives, much of what is produced in Canada would be lost forever.

Judging from the "calendar of events" pages in various feminist newspapers during the 1970s and 1980s (*Kinesis* in Vancouver, *Broadside* in Toronto, *Pandora* in Halifax, for example), women across the country were constantly engaged in a cultural movement of revolutionary proportions. Not only were the festivals, exhibitions, events and performances from all the different art forms impressive in their sheer numbers, but also in their explicitly feminist premises. Women didn't just make movies, or paint pictures, or write plays, or choreograph dance pieces, they did so with a very clear message: they intended to replace old forms with new and break down stereotyped views of women's experiences. Not content to remain isolated artists, in one-woman shows, they organized arts festivals and conferences,[30] formed production companies[31] and joined together to establish "women's buildings," which housed anything from the local women's bookstore, to meeting rooms for consciousness-raising groups, to art galleries and theatre space.

Although women in the arts communities in the 1970s were a little more likely to be swayed by the argument that "art doesn't have a sex," by the 1980s they were responding heartily with "but artists do!" The line between activism and art was now considered to be either very fine, or non-existent. Two Nova Scotia women, for example, drew on their experiences in their black communities to expose racism and sexism through their art. Photographer Donna James was interested in exposing the racist notion of black women as "exotic" in an exhibition of her work that juxtaposed the texts of "companion-wanted" ads — where many white men advertise specifically for black women — with photographs of "ordinary" black women in the context of their own communities.[32] And Delvina Bernard, singer and songwriter for the Halifax *a cappella* quartet, *Four the Moment,* felt compelled to write songs about her own life because most song lyrics did not address the concerns of black women, particularly Canadian black women.[33]

Feminist artists everywhere wrote and sang out of their own experiences in, and understandings of, the women's movement. They often got their start, in fact, performing for feminist gatherings — women's centre fundraisers, coffee houses, rallies and benefits. Women like Winnipeg's Heather Bishop, who sang songs clearly articulated from a lesbian and socialist feminist perspective, and Vancouver's Ferron, whose songs reflected a vibrant women's counterculture. Rita MacNeil sang of life as a transplanted Cape Bretoner, a woman raising children on her own, and Lillian Allen, DUB poet and songwriter, was eloquent testament to the activism of black and immigrant communities in Canada. Her 1987 album, "Revolutionary Tea Party," included "I Fight Back," a song

Lin McInnes Courtesy: *Broadside*

Dub poet Lillian Allen performs at the Second Annual Women's Music and Cultural Festival in Winnipeg in 1985.

about anger at racism. Lorraine Segato, lead singer for The Parachute Club, wrote and performed the popular, feminist "Rise Up!"

Another project in the feminist cultural revolution was the seven-woman rock group, Mama Quilla II, whose members were dedicated to providing "alternative rock music" without the sexism of traditional male bands.[34] They appealed not only to women music lovers, but also to feminist activists. Their lyrics were political and their promotional material humorously iconoclastic: one Mama Quilla II poster was a spoof on the 1950s Tupperware party phenomenon that advertised the plastic containers as useful for all sorts of terrorist activities.

With respect to the visual arts, traditional gallery showings of works by established women artists, like painter Joyce Wieland or sculptor Maryon Kantaroff, began to give way during the 1970s and 1980s to multi-media performance/art installations, and art began to show up in unconventional venues. Daria Stermac's poster series, "When We Dead Awaken: Decoding Patriarchy," (1985) was first shown on billboards at the busy downtown Toronto intersection of Queen Street and Spadina Avenue and was then on display at the Toronto Women's Bookstore (where the posters were also for sale). The series explored topics that in the past were not considered proper subjects of art: the dictates of fashion, including the mutilation and distortion of women's bodies, bondage as entertainment for men and the destructive cult of youth and its effect on women.[35]

Vancouver's Persimmon Blackbridge and Sheila Gilhooly mounted a sculpture/text installation called "Still Sane," a look at psychiatric

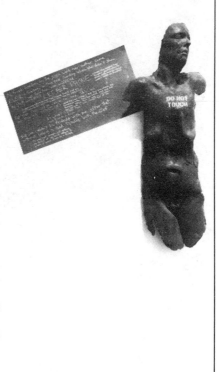

Kiku Hawkes Courtesy: *Broadside*

"My friend Rose Ann on the psych ward, her mother came every Sunday, so this one Sunday when she didn't show up, Rose Ann was worried. The staff wouldn't let her phone 'cause she needed her shrink's permission for phone calls and her shrink wasn't there on Sundays. So she was sitting on her bed crying. And I had my arm around her, comforting her. She was my friend. But then the nurse came in and saw us and started yelling about how she was afraid that this was where our friendship would lead and did Rose Ann know I was a lesbian and how could I take advantage of her.

It wasn't like that. And Rose Ann knew it too. But she couldn't be friends with me after that without being in bad trouble with the staff. It was hard enough just getting by. None of us could afford to make it worse. Even for a friend.

The Royal Hospital: Rose Ann"

A work from "Still Sane," a sculpture/text installation on the topic of psychiatric abuse of lesbians, by Persimmon Blackbridge and Sheila Gilhooly. (Vancouver: Press Gang Publishers, 1985). Reprinted with permission of the authors and publisher.

oppression of lesbian sexuality. The show was part of a 1985 art exhibition, combining painting, photography, sculpture, drawings and text, all by lesbian artists with a view to promoting lesbian visibility, if not a lesbian aesthetic. Another exhibition, called "Sight Specific: Lesbians and Representation" (1987), combined the "plastic" arts with video. It included works of painter Lynne Fernie (the co-director with Aerlynn Weisman of the 1992 lesbian docudrama *Forbidden Love*), photographer Cyndra MacDowall, filmmaker Marg Moores and artist Grace Channer. The offerings explored the connection between artistic and lesbian identity, through lesbian relationships, personal stories, lesbian pulp fiction and sexual politics.[36] As part of the annual Desh Pardesh cultural festival of the South Asian community, 1993 saw an exhibition curated by Sharon Fernandez, called In-Sight. It included the art of 14 South Asian women in the diaspora, with works by local artists Smita Dayal, Sur

The Clichettes as She Devils in a performance at the Factory Theatre, Toronto, 1985. Left to right: Janice Hladki, Joanna Householder, and Louise Garfield.

Mehat and Sharona Plakidas, among others. "This Show comes out of Desh," Fernandez said, "and out of my own feelings of isolation as a South Asian artist working in this community."[37]

Theatre was also undergoing a major shift. From the early historical productions of Redlight Theatre, through the more "traditional" feminist fare of, for example, Nightwood Theatre's production of Cynthia Grant's *Pope Joan*[38] or their adaptation of Sharon Riis's book *The True Story of Ida Johnson*,[39] to the performance art installations, such as The Clichettes, the 5-Minute Feminist Cabarets or FemFests, which showcased new and established artists and performers, feminist theatre producers were bent on breaking the boundaries of conventional theatrical forms. It was a movement in keeping with a broader context of activism; as one feminist theatre critic-cum-producer wrote, "the synchronous flowering of feminist culture has been drawn forth by a cultural/political/historical process, antithetical to patriarchal culture, which has acted as a catalyst for social change."[40]

Out of this tradition of performance activism came a number of increasingly well-known feminist performers, all of whom contributed to the festival/cabaret scene: singer Holly Cole, comedian Sandra Shamas, actor and playwright Anne Marie MacDonald and director/actor Diana Braithwaite. MacDonald was first seen by feminists in a skit at Toronto's FemFest '85 with Beverley Cooper called *Clue in the Fast Lane,* in which the two played Nancy Drew and her boyfriend Ned. She went on to act in Patricia Rozema's film *I've Heard the Mermaids Singing* and to write plays, including *Goodnight Desdemona (Good Morning Juliet),* which was a feminist take on Shakespeare. Diana Braithwaite started performing on the festival/cabaret circuit, and went on to become artistic director of a black community theatre company, Imani Theatre Ensemble (formerly Pelican Players) and to produce her play *Do Not Adjust Your Sets,* directed by Ahdri Zhina Mandiela.[41] For all these women, and many others, art was a medium for social change. Their role as artists was to translate feminist ideology into a cultural language, and to entertain. Women were less and less entertained by a male version of "fun," or informed and enriched by a male version of "art," the expression of male cultural ideology.

The contradictions between patriarchal culture and the impetus for social change were a common thread throughout all feminist cultural projects. In 1984 a right-wing, Christian fundamentalist, anti-feminist group, the R.E.A.L. Women (for Real, Equal, Active, for Life) emerged. Within a year, Nightwood Theatre had responded with their production of *Ladies Against Women,* an evening's entertainment that doubled as a "consciousness-lowering" session, for which graduation certificates were handed out that were only "valid when signed by your husband."[42] In a somewhat more serious, though not humourless, vein, another theatre troupe was formed as a spin-off from Nightwood called The Company of Sirens, which, through skits and take-offs on popular culture, explored topics such as wife assault, sexual harassment, employment equity and lesbian sexuality. The Company operated along thoroughly collective lines, and from the beginning was committed to what it originally called a multicultural perspective: the majority of its performers were black, Asian and Native women, and an anti-racist agenda was always an implicit part of its work of deconstructing white patriarchal culture.

Feminist Presses and Periodicals

Feminist activists in the early 1970s were concerned with communicating their message of equality through the printed word, as well as through the performing arts. If the mainstream press was not interested in getting the message out, as was usually the case, small but energetic groups across the country were, both in alternative presses open to new debates and in publishing houses started specifically to address the needs of women. In 1972, one of the first Canadian feminist books, *Women Unite!,* was published by The Women's Press (then the Canadian Women's Educational Press). In the book's frontispiece, members of the fledgling press wrote, "The Canadian Women's Educational Press is a group of women working together because of our concern for the appalling absence of available material written by or about Canadian women."[43] The book, an anthology of Canadian writing on women's liberation past and present, was in fact prepared in 1971 for a small leftist press that ultimately was unable to come up with the funds to publish the manuscript. After sending it to mainstream publishers who demanded the right to make changes, the editors formed their own press and published it themselves. Simultaneously in Montreal, women's studies professor Margret Andersen compiled an anthology of women's essays and poetry, called *Mother Was Not a Person*, referring to the 1929 court case in which women were declared "persons" in Canada for the first time.[44] It was published jointly by two small alternative Montreal presses, Content Publishing and Black Rose Books, and sold over 6,000 copies — a bestseller by Canadian standards.

Shortly after, in 1974, the House of Anansi — another small, mainly literary, press in Toronto — published an anthology edited by Eve Zaremba called *Privilege of Sex* that chronicled the writing of Canadian women in the past century. One of its gems was an unedited version of writing by English nineteenth-century traveller and essayist Anna Jameson. In previous editions of her work, Jameson's (male) editors had generally excised passages that they considered unnecessarily "pontificating," — passages which, as it happened, mainly concerned the nature and position of Victorian women. The title of the anthology is in fact a quote from Jameson, written in 1839:

> Where she is idle and useless by privilege of sex, a divinity and an idol, a victim or a toy, is not her position quite as lamentable, as false, as injurious to herself and all social progress, as where she is the drudge, slave and possession of the man?[45]

By 1975, International Women's Year, the number of books on women published by feminist and alternative presses had grown to such an extent that it was becoming difficult for any student of feminism to keep up. Not only were more books being published, but new presses were emerging to meet the needs of an increasing public interest. Some presses, like Press Gang in Vancouver, started as alternative presses staffed by men and women that were then "taken over" by the women. Press Gang was in fact a print shop, producing flyers and pamphlets for progressive and leftist organizations, which eventually expanded to include a feminist publishing operation.

In the mid-1980s, a number of presses were established in response to more specific (or perhaps more broadly defined) goals of feminism. Sister Vision Press emerged to publish the work of black women and women of colour and to make it available to the general Canadian public. As their promotional flyer states, "We are dedicated to providing a forum for the writings and other artistic work of Black women, Asian women, Caribbean women, women of First Nations, and all others who define themselves as Women of Colour."[46] In 1989, Charlottetown's Ragweed Press created a second imprint, gynergy books, specifically to address the needs of lesbian-feminist writers and readers. Its mandate was to create space for the voice of women and to portray women's lives "without the language of sexism, racism or homophobia."[47]

Feminist presses were (and are) closely connected to an activist women's movement, and accountable to its ever-expanding sense of feminist identity. What started in the early 1970s as a movement to give voice to the supposedly undifferentiated category "women" (the early presses were almost exclusively run by and for white socialist-feminist, women's liberationists) has become a movement to empower many women with varied identities and from varied cultures. The Women's Press itself underwent a period of intense debate and struggle, forcing changes to policy and structure, and has emerged as a feminist press that strives to be inclusive and representative of race and class differences.

The question of "voice" has always been a crucial one for feminist activists working in a variety of cultural fields. Where women have generally met with serious resistance and obstacles in communicating (be it lack of access to existing facilities, lack of funding, or just lack of "interest" on the part of the mainstream), feminists have had to form alternate means of creating visibility and establishing networks for information dissemination.

First and foremost in providing a means of communication across the country have been the many newsletters, newspapers, magazines and quarterly journals produced by feminists since the early 1970s. Perhaps because print is the easiest and cheapest of the media to operate and control, periodicals have always been a mainstay of the women's movement.

The early newsletters of women's centres were usually cranked out on Gestetners, without much regard for aesthetic appeal, and sent to a limited number of readers, although *Images* (started in 1972 by a Nelson, B.C. collective) showed the deft touch of a graphic artist and was printed in red ink, and the Toronto *Women's Place Newsletter* (1972-76) had a circulation of 3,000 in its heyday (a large circulation, even by today's standards in feminist publishing). More ambitious projects, the feminist tabloid newspapers, began to emerge early in the decade in a number of Canadian cities: *Velvet Fist*, Toronto, 1970; *Kinesis*, Vancouver, 1971; *The Other Woman*, Toronto, 1972; the *Northern Woman Journal*, Thunder Bay, Ont., 1973; and *The Optimst*, Whitehorse, Yukon, 1974. The newspapers were both regional in their appeal and national in their scope, serving both to inform their local women's movement of events and trends in the immediate vicinity, and to provide a forum for feminist debates and issues taking place across the country.

By the end of the decade more, and perhaps more sophisticated, publications emerged. While maintaining the local/national appeal, these periodicals often had a more specific focus, and were less in the nature of in-house movement publications and more like reviews or special interest magazines. *Fireweed*, a feminist quarterly of politics and culture, started in 1978; *Healthsharing* magazine, a women's health publication, started in 1979; *Broadside*, a feminist newsmagazine (in the cheaper tabloid format), also started in 1979; *La Vie en rose*, a Montreal glossy feminist magazine that quickly gained a vast Québécoise readership, started in 1980; the *Manitoba Women's Newspaper*, a well-designed tabloid, started in 1979 and in the mid-1980s was transformed into the four-colour, wide-appeal magazine, *Herizons*.[48] By the end of the 1980s, other magazines, such as *Diva: A Quarterly of South Asian Women* (Toronto), *Aquelarre: Latin American Women's Magazine* (Vancouver), *Our Lives* (Toronto) and *Tiger Lily* (Stratford, Ont.), began publishing to address the needs, often ignored or sidelined by other publications, of women of colour in Canada.[49]

Although circulation figures for feminist publications in Canada have rarely surpassed the 2,500 mark, and as a long-time feminist publisher wrote in 1982, "There is still a large population of women in Canada who have never seen *Broadside*, read a Women's Press book or heard of *Kinesis*,"[50] the feminist press has always intentionally directed its content to the already converted, or at least engaged. Without its press, the women's movement in Canada would have suffered a lack of continuity, a lack of cohesion. In 1981 in the United States, an FBI document, leaked to participants of a feminist print media conference, suggested that without its feminist publications, presses and bookstores, the U.S. women's movement could not survive.[51] Similarly in Canada, the movement has required an active press for the interchange of information, and as a tool for inventing and reinventing itself. Although most, if not all, Canadian feminist periodicals depend in part on subsidies in the form of government grants, the governments in question have always been uncomfortable with the potential of the feminist periodicals to inspire and promote change.

In the mid-1980s, with the advent of a Conservative government, the Secretary of State Women's Program (probably the biggest financial supporter of feminist publications) was required to establish "eligibility criteria" that forbade women's groups from advocating any particular stand on abortion (read pro-choice), or promoting any particular lifestyle (read lesbian).[52] By 1990, the federal budget under the leadership of Finance Minister Michael Wilson had cut all operational support to the nationally funded feminist periodicals. It was generally felt that the cuts sounded the death knell for feminist magazines and newspapers in Canada, but according to a 1991 survey, there were almost as many periodicals then as there had been in 1986 (44 as opposed to 46). While some fold, others pop up, though not with the assumed jack-in-the-box regularity: longevity and stability appear to be more common characteristics of the feminist press than is generally expected. Of the current periodicals, at least one-third are well into their second, and some entering their third, decade.[53]

The existence of the periodicals themselves has spawned a support network of communications within the movement. Within two or three years of the first feminist newsletter, a feminist print media conference was held, in Saskatoon in December 1974, to be followed the next year by a conference in Winnipeg (March 1975), and others in Ottawa (June 1980), Montreal (June 1985) and Toronto (May 1986). These conferences brought together practitioners and activists involved in feminist periodical publishing to share information and skills and to provide a sense of common interest and endeavour in an otherwise widely dispersed, and diverse, movement in Canada.[54] To minimize the effects of distance, and to circulate news of interest to feminists that was not picked up by other wire services in existence, plans were developed at the first two conferences to create a Feminist News Service. Another attempt to create a line of communication was "Network Nellie," a long-distance phone tree to be activated at any point on the string and spread out to connect with women across the country. Despite enthusiasm, both these attempts at networking were short-lived, owing mainly to lack of funds.

Two other offshoots of the work of feminist publishers have contributed to the disseminating, and in both cases, preserving of information within the women's movement. The first is the Canadian Women's Movement Archives (CWMA), now housed at the Université d'Ottawa Morisset Library, which began life in the filing cabinets of *The Other Woman* newspaper in the early 1970s, and was carefully fostered over the years by one of the paper's editors, Pat Leslie. Leslie, along with later CWMA collective members, spent much time exhorting feminists not to throw away anything, but instead to send it to the archives, a task that has undoubtedly paid off.[55] The second is the ambitious task, this time a joint effort of feminist researchers and librarians, of publishing an in-depth subject/author index of feminist newspapers and magazines, starting in 1972 and continuing to the present. Much information on the Canadian women's movement would have been lost without such a tool to provide access to the materials available (often available, interestingly, because of the CWMA). *The Canadian Feminist Periodical Index* was published in 1991 and the collective plans to publish future volumes as the time-consuming work of indexing is completed.[56]

Feminist presses and periodicals provided a method of communicating the events and debates of the movement and of reflecting its strength and diversity. They did not exist in a cultural or political vacuum.

Debates in the Cultural Terrain

As in other areas of feminist activism, cultural pursuits were not disengaged from the major debates of the period. In the early years, when the concept of "sexism" was barely understood by the general public, feminists battled against the pervasiveness of sexist language, in the face of ridicule, hostility and resistance. That the so-called universal "he" did not in fact include women was a point hard won, a point that is apparently still being contested. In the late 1970s, the Ontario Status of Women Council circulated an article on sexist language that had first appeared in the U.S. magazine *Redbook*. In 1984, it was obviously considered timely by a Toronto community college, which reprinted the article in its newsletter.[57] Also in the mid-80s, a feminist newspaper editorial criticized the adolescent male language used by men in Canada's House of Commons which, it suggested, served to make the substance of women's contribution to Parliament invisible.[58] Unlike the early days, when it was thought sexist language was unconscious, it was obvious that it had become purposive — an attempt not only to intimidate, but also to silence, women. By 1993, after two decades of struggle, nothing much appears to have changed. A pamphlet on sexist language published by the Ontario Women's Directorate[59] became the focus of attack. In its introduction, the pamphlet takes issue with our national anthem, specifically the phrase "in all thy sons command," which, it points out, excludes girls and women from any sense of belonging as Canadians. The publication generated a flurry of calls to the Directorate and attacks during an open-line radio show calling the pamphlet creators "idiots" and "bimbos,"[60] demonstrating once again the familiar ridicule, hostility and resistance.

On another front, in the 1970s feminists across the country were concerned with the pervasive violence against women in society. At first, women set up rape crisis centres and shelters to begin to address the needs of victims of violence. By 1977, women were becoming involved as well in the fight against representations of misogyny, or of pornographic imagery. Groups known as Women Against Violence Against Women (WAVAW) began to form in many major cities, following on the heels of two U.S. groups. In Los Angeles, women banded together to challenge the misogyny of the recording industry as expressed on its album covers, and in New York City another WAVAW group challenged the porn and strip theatres of 42nd Street. In Toronto, a group organized to promote one of the first annual "Take Back the Night" marches found itself spontaneously demonstrating in front of a "snuff" movie theatre on Yonge Street. (Snuff movies allegedly involve the killing of real women on screen for the delectation of male viewers.)[61] By the mid-1980s, feminists were becoming more concerned with the real harm of pornography, which they considered led to (and involved) actual violence against women, not just its representation. The growing strength of the call to halt pornography was met with a returning cry of censorship. Although many (mostly male) critics of the anti-pornography movement were vociferous in championing "freedom of speech" (interpreted as the right to produce pornography), there was an increasing number of feminists, many of them cultural workers, who also took an anti-censorship line. They feared that giving the state the right to regulate cultural production (of which pornographic magazines were a part) would rebound on the very groups that were attempting to effect social change through their art, while leaving the pornographers alone.

Their fears were not unsubstantiated. In 1985, as part of a feminist arts festival, a group of artists called the Woomers mounted an installation in the windows of Toronto's Pages Bookstore. The display was called "I'm a Girl" and featured various artifacts of women's lives, including a sanitary pad sprayed with red paint. The police officers who subsequently laid charges of obscenity against the store's owner deemed the display disgusting.[62] In 1986, as part of a community art project to use billboards and other community spaces in Toronto for political/cultural messages, artist and filmmaker Lynne Fernie planned to display the message "Lesbians Fly Air Canada: Private Desires, Public Sins" on a pixel board at the intersection of Church Street and Wellesley Street (a predominantly gay neighbourhood). Air Canada was not pleased, and Fernie's message became "Lesbians Fly Canada.... "

More recently, in 1992, owners of the gay bookstore, Glad Day, were charged with carrying "obscene" material, namely the U.S. lesbian erotic magazine *Bad Attitude* that allegedly offended ill-defined "community standards." Arguing that community standards find male heterosexual hard-core porn "acceptable," and that 45,000 copies of Madonna's book, *Sex*, had cleared Canada's customs, one trial witness contended that "*Bad Attitude's* material was less violent and more consensual."[63] As one anti-censorship advocate warned during the trial, "If we don't win, we can expect a lot more repression."[64] In another form of censorship, an annual Vancouver women's arts festival, "Women in View," prompted vociferous criticism from a B.C. right-wing magazine for its lesbian content. The editors of the magazine, *BC Report*, called on government and corporate sponsors to stop funding art they considered "morally offensive and even blasphemous."[65] The festival lost about $10,000 in sponsorship after the 1992 attack, though supporters rallied and the show goes on.

One of the consequences of the pornography/censorship debate was that in framing the discussion in the context of censorship and freedom of speech, the original concern of feminists about the violence against women in pornography and media imagery was lost in the shuffle. A similar process occurred in the late-1980s struggle of Women's Press to institute anti-racist policies and practices. As a result of difficult discussions over the treatment of a manuscript, members of the press were made to see how their policies and structures had been endemically racist. When attempts were made to formulate an anti-racist politics, as some members wrote in a public statement at the time, "it quickly became apparent that the women of the Press were deeply divided on understandings of, and perspectives on, anti-racism." The statement continued:

In view of our recognition of endemic racism in the society in which we live, and our acknowledgement of our involvement in those social forces, we declare our intention to form alliances against racist oppression, to take a public stand regarding our alliances and to fight racism wherever it exists, in ourselves, in our organizations and in our publishing houses.[66]

However, when the ensuing debate was taken up by the mainstream media, and indeed by many white writers across Canada, it was transformed once again into one of censorship and freedom of speech. The issue of racism, like violence against women, was lost in the shuffle. As novelist and journalist M. Nourbese Philip wrote a year later (in an article called "The Disappearing Debate"), "Racism was the issue that detonated the explosion at Women's Press; to the exclusion of any other, censorship became the issue that has monopolized the media's attention. ... The quantum leap from racism to censorship is neither random nor unexpected, since the issue of censorship is central to the dominant cultures of liberal democracies like Canada."[67] In particular, it was in the matter of appropriation of cultural experience, or writing in the voice of the Other, that cries of censorship were heard the loudest: in a set of Anti-Racist Guidelines published in the fall of 1988, Women's Press sought to inform the public of their new publishing policies. Manuscripts they would not accept included those where "the protagonist's experience in the world, by virtue of race or ethnicity, is substantially removed from that of the writer," and where "a writer appropriates the form and substance of a culture which is oppressed by her own." Many white writers reportedly felt they should continue to be able to write "from the imagination," in any voice they chose, ignoring the racist implications of such a choice. The fact that the Guidelines also stated that the Press would not accept manuscripts in which "white, middle-class women's experience is characterized as normal, and the perspective of Women of Colour is presented as unusual or exotic," apparently went unnoticed.

The publishing of the Anti-Racist Guidelines came after many months of painful discussion on the issue of racism in the Canadian feminist press. As M. Nourbese Philip wrote, "if every white writer were, voluntarily or otherwise, to decide not to write from the point of view of African, Asian or Native women, this would in no way ensure access to publication by these latter women."[68] While the issue of appropriation was important, it was inclusiveness that was the central concern to Women's Press and to those women whose voice had been denied. Access to publishing was seen as an essential element of anti-racist work, and while establishing women of colour presses like Sister Vision Press or journals such as *Tiger Lily* and *Diva* was one solution, much more remained to be done to change the colour, or white dominance, of other feminist publishing concerns, and indeed the cultural life of Canada as a whole.

Conclusion

It could be said that in all areas of cultural life for women in Canada, much remains to be done. In many cases, things have even seemed to stand still. Where women started out in the 1970s protesting and challenging the main cultural institutions, like the CBC and CRTC, women in the 1990s are still at it. One advocacy group, Toronto Women in Film and Television, has submitted a brief to the *current* round of CRTC hearings, recommending a special television channel for women. "We have a right to see ourselves reflected in our broadcasting system," said one activist, echoing the words of her 1970s sisters.[69] In the area of censorship, the police still lay charges, which the courts then uphold. In the case of the lesbian magazine *Bad Attitude*, a February 1993 court judgement found the magazine "obscene" but gave the bookstore owners absolute discharges, a truly ambivalent ruling that will do nothing to prevent other obscenity charges, perhaps even ones directed at the same magazine.[70] However, in surveying the achievements of the past 20 to 25 years, there is no question that feminist artists, performers and communicators have immeasurably enriched the Canadian "cultural mould," as the Royal Commission on the Status of Women put it in 1970. Without all those hours put in by feminist cultural workers on the stages, behind the cameras and at the light tables across the country, "culture" might still be considered the preserve of the privileged, white, heterosexual, Canadian male.

NOTES

1. Vancouver's feminist newspaper, *Kinesis*.
2. Canada, *Report of the Royal Commission on the Status of Women* (Ottawa: Information Canada, 1970).
3. Canada, *Images of Women: Report of the Task Force on Sex-Role Stereotyping in the Broadcast Media* (Ottawa: Supply and Services, 1982).
4. Ibid., 5.
5. Canada, *Sex-Role Stereotyping in the Broadcast Media: A Report on Industry Self-Regulation* (Ottawa: CRTC Information Services, 1986).
6. Ana Wiggins, *Sex-role Stereotyping: A Content Analysis of Radio and Television Programs and Advertisements* (Vancouver: MediaWatch, 1985).
7. Canada, *The Portrayal of Gender in Canadian Broadcasting: Summary Report, 1984-1988* (Ottawa: CRTC/Erin Research, 1990), 8.
8. Submission to the task force by the Feminist Party of Canada, "Images of Women," 11.
9. Gordon Donaldson was let go from the CBC in the 1960s for not sounding "Canadian" enough.
10. George Spears, Nancy Torrance and Kasia Seydegart, *The Presence, Role and Images of Women in Prime Time on the English Network of the CBC, Pts. 1 and 2.* (Ottawa: Office of the Coordinator, Portrayal of Women, CBC, April 1982).
11. Ibid., 15.
12. Claire Brassard, Terri Nash, Micheline St-Arnaud and Marie-Pierre Tremblay, *Women at the National Film Board: An Equal Opportunity Study* (Montréal: National Film Board of Canada, 1978).
13. 15 December 1986. The Employment Equity Act followed on the *Report of the Royal Commission on Equality in Employment* (Ottawa: Supply and Services, 1984). It was in

the so-called Abella Report that Judge Rosalie Abella coined the phrase "employment equity."

14. *Adjusting the Image: Women and Canadian Broadcasting.* Conference proceedings, Ottawa, 20-22 March 1987. The conference was sponsored by MediaWatch, the Canadian Coalition Against Media Pornography, and the National Action Committee on the Status of Women.

15. The Federal Cultural Policy Review Committee, named for its chairmen, Louis Applebaum and Jacques Hébert. It was often referred to as the "Applebert" Commission.

16. Thelma McCormack, Lynn McDonald and Diana Mason, National Action Committee on the Status of Women, "Canadian Cultural Development with Equity for Women." Brief to the Federal Cultural Policy Review Committee, Ottawa, 4 June 1981, 1.

17. Sasha McInnes-Hayman, Kalene Nix and Julie Guard, *Women and the Ontario Arts Council: A Study* (London, Ont.: September 1981).

18. Sharon H. Nelson, "No Poetic Licence for Women," *Broadside*, 3, no. 2 (November 1981), 17-18. See also *Fireweed*, Winter 1982. For an exploration of women and theatre, see Rina Fraticelli's report to the Canadian Advisory Committee on the Status of Women in Theatre, Ottawa, 1982. An abbreviated version of the report is published in *Fuse*, September 1982.

19. Sharron Zenith Corne, "The Politics of Pioneering Art Feminism on the Prairies," *Branching Out* 5, no. 2 (1978), 7-10. See also Noelle Boughton, "Sharron Corne: From Solitary Artist to Radical Feminist," *Canadian Woman Studies* 3, no. 3 (Spring 1982), 61-63.

20. National Action Committee on the Status of Women brief to the Applebaum-Hébert Commission, 12.

21. Ibid., 6.

22. Carla Murray, *Graphic Feminism.* Catalog for the Graphic Feminism show at A Space Gallery, Toronto, 14-31 May 1986.

23. Ibid. [n.p.]

24. "What Glorious Times They Had" first played at Toronto's Bathurst Street United Church on 8 May 1974. Redlight's artistic directors were Francine Volker, Marcella Lustig and Diane Grant.

25. See Diane Grant, "Nellie McClung and the Redlight Theatre," *This Magazine* 8, nos. 5/6 (January/February 1975), 16-19.

26. See Gael McCool's interview [untitled] with Women in Focus members, *Women's éducation des femmes* 6, no. 2 (Spring 1988).

27. See Barbara Halpern Martineau, "Independent Images," *Broadside* 2, no. 6 (April 1981), reporting on the 4th annual Canadian Images Film Festival in Peterborough, Ontario.

28. See Kass Banning, "From Didactics to Desire: Building Women's Film Culture," in *Work in Progress: Building Feminist Culture*, Rhea Tregebov, ed. (Toronto: Women's Press, 1987), 149-176.

29. Grierson Documentary Seminar, Brockville, Ontario, November 1985. See Suzanne Pope, "Grierson Documentary Festival," *Broadside* 7, no. 3 (December 1985/January 1986), 12.

30. One such conference was "Women and Words" held in Vancouver in July 1983 and attended by 700 Canadian women working in various forms of cultural production involving words. An offshoot of this conference was the annual summer school for women writers, West Words. See the conference proceedings, *In the Feminine: Women and Words/les femmes et les mots*, Ann Dybikowski et al., eds. (Edmonton: Longspoon Press, 1983).

31. One Toronto production company, Womynly Way, brought hundreds of performers to the attention of avid audiences for many years during the 1980s. It also formed coalitions with other groups to sponsor concerts, such as the 1985 co-production with Dakota Ojibway Productions of "Spirit of Turtle Island — Native Women in Concert."

32. Lani Maestro, "Photographs by Donna James Challenge Our Ways of Seeing," *Pandora* 4, no. 2 (December 1988), 10.

33. Faith Nolan, "Nova Scotian Cultural Activist Delvina Bernard," *Our Lives* (March/April 1987).

34. Mama Quilla II, promotional flyer, CWMA files, n.d.

35. Randi Spires, "Atrocity Acknowledged," *Broadside* 6, no. 7 (May 1985), 11.

36. Ingrid MacDonald, "Sight Spectacular," *Broadside* 8, no. 6 (April 1987), 11.

37. Deirdre Hanna, "Diverse Artists Offer In-Sight at Desh Pardesh group show," *Now Magazine*, 25-31 March 1993, 71.

38. Amanda Hale, "Review of 'Pope Joan,'" *Broadside* 6, no. 1 (October 1984), 11-12.

39. Kari Reynolds, "Review of 'The True Story of Ida Johnson,'" *Broadside* 1, no. 2 (November 1979), 16.

40. Rhea Tregebov, ed., *Work in Progress: Building Feminist Culture* (Toronto: Women's Press, 1987). See Amanda Hale, "A Dialectical Drama of Facts and Fictions on the Feminist Fringe," 77-99.

41. For a retrospective of Canadian feminist theatre in the 1980s, see Kate Lushington, "Feminist Theatre: The Changing Body of Women's Work," *Broadside* 10, no. 5 (August/September 1989), 20-21.

42. Amanda Hale, "Femmes Against Feminists," *Broadside* 6, no. 8 (June 1985), 12.

43. *Women Unite!* (Toronto: Canadian Women's Educational Press, 1972), frontispiece. The full title was *Up from the Kitchen, Up from the Bedroom, Up from Under, Women Unite!*

44. Margret Andersen, ed. *Mother Was Not a Person* (Montreal: Content/ Black Rose Books, 1972).

45. Anna Jameson, *Winter Studies and Summer Rambles* (New York: Wiley and Putnam, 1839). Quoted in *Privilege of Sex,* Eve Zaremba, ed. (Toronto: House of Anansi, 1974).

46. See Philinda Masters, "A Word from the Press: A Brief Survey of Feminist Publishing," *Resources for Feminist Research* 20, nos. 1 & 2 (Spring/Summer 1991), 31.

47. Ibid., 29.

48. "Feminist Print Media Conference, 1980." Conference Proceedings, Ottawa, 27-29 June 1980 (mimeographed). Of the papers started in the early 1970s, only *Velvet Fist* and *The Other Woman* have since folded, in 1971 and 1977 respectively. Of those started later in the decade, only *Healthsharing* and *Herizons* (which took a three-year break in publishing) are still in existence.

49. See Philinda Masters, "A Word from the Press," Appendix 3, for a list of currently existing periodicals.

50. Margie Wolfe, "Working with Words: Feminist Publishing in Canada," in *Still Ain't Satisfied: Canadian Feminism Today*, Maureen Fitzgerald, Connie Guberman and Margie Wolfe, eds. (Toronto: Women's Press, 1982), 268.

51. See Marge Dumond, "Feminism in the US: Publish or Perish," *Broadside* 3, no. 2 (November 1981), 7. Dumond, then on the editorial staff of *Time* in Washington, DC, was a participant at the conference.

52. See Becki Ross, "Heterosexuals Only Need Apply: The Secretary of State's Regulation of Lesbian Existence," *Resources for Feminist Research* 17, no. 3 (September 1988), 35-38.

53. See Philinda Masters, "A Word from the Press," 27.

54. For reports on the conferences, see *The Other Woman* 3, no. 4 (Spring 1975), 2; Susan Bazilli, "Feminist Print Media Conference report," *Resources for Feminist Research* 9, no. 3 (November 1980), 14-15; and Ingrid MacDonald, "Power of Our Press," *Broadside* 6, no. 9 (July 1985), 3.

55. See Pat Leslie, "Don't Throw Your Movement Past Out With the Trash," *Kinesis*, August 1980, 19; Eve Zaremba, "CWMA: Collective Collections," *Broadside* 6, no. 5 (March 1985), 4-5.

56. Canadian Women's Indexing Group, "Canadian Feminist Periodical Index, 1972-1985" (Toronto: OISE Press, 1991). See also Philinda Masters and Gillian Michell, "Access to Information: The Canadian Feminist Periodical Index and the Canadian Feminist Thesaurus," *Resources for Feminist Research* 20, nos. 1 & 2 (Spring/Summer 1991), 13-14; also Deborah Green and Jeanne Guillaume, "Canadian Women's Studies: Toward a New Periodical Index," *Canadian Library Journal*, June 1988, 175-178.

57. Alma Graham. "Words That Make Women Disappear." *Redbook*, 1977. Reprinted in the George Brown College Affirmative Action Advisory Committee Newsletter, no. 8 (January 1984).

58. Broadside editorial. "You've Come a Long Way, Baby?" *Broadside* 6, no. 9 (July 1985), 2.

59. Ontario Women's Directorate. *Words that Count Women In,* 1993.

60. Alanna Mitchell, "Infuriated Callers Attack Non-Sexist Language Guide," *The Globe and Mail*, 8 January 1993, A5.

61. As far as we know, snuff movies did not actually kill women actors, but the promotional hype was very successful, and obviously touched a nerve in consumers and critics alike.

62. Letter printed in *Resources for Feminist Research* 14, no. 4 (December/January 1985/86), 32. Special issue on Women and the Criminal Justice System.

63. Val Ross, "Glad Day Case Tests Community Standards: Lesbian Magazine Subject to Charges," *The Globe and Mail*, 17 December 1992, C1.

64. Liz Czach, "The Thousand Cuts," *Xtra!* (Toronto Lesbian and Gay Newspaper), no. 213 (25 December 1992), 9.

65. Chris Dafoe, "Women in View Expands Horizons," *The Globe and Mail*, 29 January 1993, C2.

66. Statement of the Popular Front of the Bus Caucus, Women's Press, May 1988. Printed in *Broadside* 9, no. 8 (June 1988), 5.

67. M. Nourbese Philip, "The Disappearing Debate," in her book *Frontiers: Essays and Writings on Racism and Culture* (Stratford, Ont.: Mercury Press, 1992), 269-86; first published in *This Magazine*, 1989.

68. M. Nourbese Philip, "Gut Issues in Babylon," in *Frontiers*, 217.

69. Christopher Harris, "Film Group Advocates TV Channel for Women," *The Globe and Mail*, 11 March 1993, C5; and "TV by and for women," front page blurb, A1.

70. "Lesbian Magazine Ruled Obscene," *The Globe and Mail*, 19 February 1993, C1.

Documents: Chapter 6

Institutional Representation

Canada: Report of the Royal Commission on the Status of Women
Ottawa, 1970[1]

Woman is often presented as a sex object, defined as a superficial creature who thinks only of her appearance, who sees herself mainly in terms of whether she is attractive to men. She conforms to the beauty and youth standards which men are said to want of her. In a study prepared for the Commission, it was found that over 89 per cent of the women pictured in Canadian newspapers and magazines are less than 35 years of age. As presented by the advertiser, women are hardly ever associated with intelligence, sincerity, culture, originality or talent. Instead, they are depicted as being young, elegant and beautiful. "The mass media must in some way be encouraged to change their emphasis ..."

"Women and the CBC"
1982-83[2]

Two studies recently released by the Canadian Broadcasting Corporation have confirmed that women are under-represented and frequently portrayed in a stereotypical manner in prime time television.

In response to statements from women's groups at the October, 1978 Canadian Radio and Television Commission hearings, the CBC commissioned PEAC Developments to collect solid data on the role, image, and presence of women in its television programming. Using similar methodology, separate studies were set up for the English and French networks.

There were two parts to the studies: content analysis to document the presence and role of males and females in television programming; viewer perception using members of the general public, CBC staffers, and feminists to measure how the portrayal of women on television is perceived.

During the spring of 1981, three weeks of prime time programming were analyzed under three codings: drama/comedy, variety, and information. This amounted to 86-1/2 hours or 125 shows on the English and about 50 hours on the French. About 2/3 of the programs were CBC produced with the remainder mainly from the United States.

1. Canada, *Report of the Royal Commission on the Status of Women in Canada* (Ottawa: Information Canada, 1970), 15, s. 50.
2. Jennifer Grange, *Spirale* 1, no. 4/2, (1982-83), 10-11.

In the drama/comedy category, male characters outnumbered females by almost 2-1. While a larger proportion of the women in the shows were depicted as working outside the home than is true of "real life" this was offset by the fact that overall there were few women. The majority were played "in role," i.e. in positions traditionally occupied by women. In keeping with this trend they tended to lack positions of authority or tended to be viewed only as nurturing figures or involved in love relationships.

The bright light here was that the Canadian-produced shows conformed less to this pattern than the imported programs.

Women and men fulfilled the same roles on variety shows — singers, dancers, whatever — when they managed to make it onto the screen. Here men were seen about four times as often as women. Pointed out in the French network study was the fact that no women host game shows.

Perhaps the most disturbing statistics came from the information section. Here male reporters made 12 appearances for every one by a female. Voice-overs on film clips were usually done by men. Worst of all, when experts were consulted, the experts were almost always men.

Since the report was completed, Barbara Frum and Mary Lou Findlay have been named co-anchors of "The Journal," but this is small comfort when their talents, at least in the first few months, have often been overlooked.

The second part of the studies examined viewer reactions to sex role portrayals on television.

At four centres across the country, feminists, CBC personnel, and members of the general public were shown 16 film segments depicting men and women in several roles. On first viewing, subjects were asked to judge the appeal of the character. After a second viewing, subjects were asked to indicate whether the character's behaviour was suitable to her or his sex. In addition, subjects answered a questionnaire on sex role attitudes and took part in discussion on sex role portrayal on television.

While there are many dimensions to appeal, sex role seemed to be a major determining factor. The three groups usually agreed on appeal, although the degree varied amongst the group. The feminists tended to express progressive attitudes, with the CBC employees in the middle, and the general public holding more traditional views.

Overall, subjects felt that television, although it affects social values, is lagging behind reality in the range of roles it provides for women.

"Portrayal of Women in Programming"
November 1985[3]

Policy

To follow through on the commitments made in February 1979 ... the CBC issued an official policy respecting the portrayal of women in programming. The policy, which came into effect on December 10, 1979, reads as follows:

"The CBC accepts as part of its mandate the need to reflect in its programming the role of women in Canadian society and to examine its social and political consequences. The CBC believes that its programming should also contribute to the understanding of issues affecting women.

"In applying this policy, CBC programming must:

- Avoid the use of demeaning sexual stereotypes and sexist language.
- Reflect women and their interests in the reporting and discussion of current events.
- Recognize the full participation of women in Canadian society.
- Seek women's opinions on the full range of public issues."

In 1980, the CBC issued a complementary policy on stereotypes in programming. A summary of the policy follows:

Stereotypes are generalizations, drawn from perceptions that certain qualities and characteristics are commonly shared by certain groupings in society. Ill-advised use of stereotypes tends to reinforce prejudices, and constitutes an assault on the dignity of the individual.

Those responsible for program content should be alert to the cumulative power of the electronic media to shape tastes and to contribute to the definition of individual and social ideals, and, therefore, should refrain from indiscriminate portrayal of detrimental stereotypes.

Common sense, good judgment and good taste should be part of the basic discipline of all production and on-air broadcasters who should not only present people as individuals, but also challenge stereotypes when these may be introduced uncritically by other participants.

Stereotyping in CBC programming is acceptable only when it is essential to the realization of a program's purpose.

"The Thirty Per Cent Solution: Sexism as a Fine Art"
January 1984[4]

In 1978 Ottawa artist Jane Martin was the first to brave the opprobrium of the art world by tallying up figures on the number of Canada Council grants awarded to women in the visual arts, comparing that to the

---

3. CBC, Office of the Portrayal of Women, November 1985. Copy at CWMA.
4. Susan Crean, *This Magazine* 17, no. 6 (January 1984), 26-27, 30.

number of women present on the juries. What was truly startling about Martin's findings was the underrepresentation of women. In the eight years surveyed there were a total of 229 jurors of whom twenty-eight were women, twenty of them artists. (Some of the twenty did serve on more than one committee.) Women never formed a majority and in several instances no women were present at all. When that happened the success rate of female applicants took a nose-dive to the bottom of the graph.

More recently Sasha McInnes Hayman discovered the same 'direct, dramatic and irrefutable' correlation between the success rate of women applying for writing grants and the presence of women on juries. Here too the percentages hover between twenty and thirty (slightly better than the visual arts) and seeing that these figures have remained consistent over time, some, like Montréal poet Sharon Nelson, speculate that a *de facto* quota against women is in operation.

Nelson conducted her own extensive study of women in the writing profession for Status of Women Canada, which was published in *Fireweed* (Winter 1982) and in which she documents the inner workings of a self-perpetuating system of exclusion which keeps most women writers on the edge of Canadian literary life. This is the picture that emerges from the statistics. Supposing you are a woman and manage to eke out enough money to keep body and soul together while you write. Supposing you complete your manuscript. You will then have a one-in-four chance of getting it published compared to any man and after that a one-in-four chance of seeing it reviewed in a magazine. Your chances of getting newspaper coverage are even lower (80 per cent of that space is allotted to reviews of books written by men), and should you decide to apply for a teaching position in a creative writing department or a writer-in-residency at a university to help finance your next book, you are looking at a field that in 1980/81 hired women 20-29 per cent of the time.

While Nelson was researching her report, Rina Fraticelli was doing the same thing on theatre. Fraticelli's study was published in a shortened version in *Fuse* (September 1982) and also surveyed Canada Council grants to women and the employment patterns of Canadian theatre companies. Women, she found, receive 33 per cent of Canada Council individual grants in theatre and 30 per cent of the money. From there it goes straight downhill. The 104 theatres she studied produced 1,156 plays between 1978 and 1981 of which 10 per cent were written by women, 13 per cent were directed by women and only about 12 of the companies were under the artistic direction of a woman.

If aspiring theatre artists who also happen to be women successfully break into the profession, guess what? It is most likely to be in the area of children's theatre and least likely to be at Stratford or the Manitoba Theatre Centre or any of the super-eighteen companies which gobble up 57 per cent of the Canada Council's available funds. Not only do our premier theatres have the worst record of hiring women directors, play-wrights and artistic directors, they are also the least friendly to Canadian playwriting, period, and produce Canadian plays half as often as the national average (which is to say a mean 26 per cent). Whenever a serious commercial risk is perceived, be it Canadian or female, the dinosaurs split.

"Adjusting the Image: Women and Canadian Broadcasting" Ottawa 1987[5]

"Adjusting the Image" was a national conference concerning women and Canadian broadcasting. Over 250 delegates representing women's organizations, broadcasters, advertisers, government, and cultural agencies met together for two days to learn from each other and to work toward achieving equality for women in the broadcast media.

This report documents not only an historic national conference at which women brought together the key players in Canadian broadcasting to meet with representatives of the Canadian women's movement, but also a time in the history of Canadian broadcasting when women have recognized that their presence, their perspective, and their accurate portrayal in the mass media is not only an issue of fairness and equality but a critical antidote to global confusion.

The debate has moved from important but narrow concepts of sex-role stereotyping and sexist language to issues of dignity, equality, and freedom of expression for half our population. We are insisting that women's voices must be heard in the board rooms and in the news rooms. We are claiming equal status in our portrayal, fair representation of our views on matters of national and global importance, and programming which meets our needs and interests. And we are finding we have allies in broadcasting, advertising, and government who are prepared to champion our cause.

We are discussing powerful remedies: employment equity, the *Canadian Charter of Rights and Freedoms*, and a new *Broadcasting Act* which will entrench equality for women.

The major events that have addressed the status of women in broadcasting are summarized in Part II: Background. These events highlight progress made, but at the same time give stark testimony to how much farther we still have to go. Part III: Industry Perspective sets out the comments made by the spokespeople at the Conference for the private broadcasting industry, the advertising industry and the CBC. In Part IV: Dialogue the visions are articulated, key questions asked, and information exchanged. Part V: Recommendations contains legislative solutions as well as recommendations for specific remedial action to be taken by government and women's organizations. Part VI: Celebration describes the first annual MediaWatch Awards for the positive portrayal of

5. Samantha Sanderson and Rose Potvin, Report of a National Conference on Canadian Broadcasting Policy, 20-22 March 1987, Ottawa. Copy at WERC.

women. And in Part VII: Postscript are documented key events subsequent to the Conference — events that demonstrate positive response by government and industry to women's concerns and provide a focus for ongoing advocacy. For equality and dignity for women in broadcasting to become the reality envisioned at the Conference, women must ensure that:

- Canadian broadcasting policy, expressed in a new *Broadcasting Act*, makes equality for women (and other disadvantaged groups) — in portrayal, presence, and access to the means of communication — an unequivocal principle of the organization, operation, and programming of the broadcasting system;
- employment equity requirements are imposed on all broadcasters with meaningful enforcement mechanisms, clearly set out in a new *Broadcasting Act*;
- boards and commissions of cultural and communications agencies, particularly the CBC, National Film Board, and Telefilm, reflect the composition of the population which is 50% female;
- the CBC assumes leadership in offering programming that is balanced in relation to the needs and interests of the Canadian population and is a model for the new principle of equality in Canadian broadcasting;
- the CBC seeks out and supports a range of programming sources so that productions by Canadian women and men are aired in fair proportion to their presence in the population;
- guidelines on sex-role stereotyping for broadcasters are acceptable to Canadian women;
- there is meaningful assessment of broadcaster performance and enforcement of sex-role stereotyping guidelines by the CRTC without undue reliance on public complaint;
- there is effective education of the public on sex-role stereotyping standards for broadcasters and complaint mechanisms, through such means as public service announcements;
- there are non-industry based complaint-handling mechanisms;
- there is generous government financial support for public broadcasting and effective financial incentives for Canadian programming;
- there is effective regulation to ensure private broadcasters contribute to Canadian culture;
- the CRTC is committed to achieving the goals of the *Broadcasting Act*.

In the next few months women will have an opportunity to assess the performance of the government, CRTC, and public and private broadcasters on many of the above points. We must pay close attention to the wording of new broadcasting legislation and revised guidelines on sex-role stereotyping, as well as monitor CBC actions to improve the status of women in employment and programming and CRTC plans to assess broadcaster performance. Over the next few years, we will be watching to see how these measures affect what we see on television and hear on radio.

"Women in Exhibition:
The Politics of Pioneering Art Feminism on the Prairies"
Winnipeg, 1978[6]

During February 1975, a trip to the library of the public art gallery catapulted me from a previously sheltered existence into a series of public confrontations and a commitment to feminism which would drastically alter the course of my life. Reading the gallery newsletter I came across the following announcement by the women's auxiliary of the gallery of their project for International Women's Year:

> "In December, 1975, we will hang an exhibition demonstrating the Changing Role of Women Through Art ... Through the paintings and prints and sculpture of 19C and 20C Canada, we will explore the ways women have been portrayed and perceived. While many galleries outside our province are participating in IWY by planning exhibitions of work of women artists, we feel our treatment, including the work of both female and male artists, is both original and stimulating."

As I read it, my excitement turned first to discomfort and then to anger. The gallery was going to use a $10,000 grant from the meagre coffers of IWY to celebrate men's stereotyped images of women. As almost no women artists were recognized before 1960, this would be a predominately male exhibition. The visual arts field is well documented as a male bastion where women's art has always been trivialized and rejected. Studies show that psychological and economic barriers still keep women artists from participating significantly in the art world. Any exhibit which would focus on men's work about women rather than on work *by* women would only reinforce the status quo.

I had avoided risks and confrontations all my life but now I felt compelled to do something. Group organization, political manoeuvres or attempts at changing society were quite beyond my experience. My energies had been devoted to child care and housekeeping, then to completing a Fine Arts degree. It seemed obvious, however, that a support group should be recruited to meet with the gallery and correct the negative approach of their exhibition.

The response of women artists — from whom I anticipated unanimous support — was the beginning of my turbulent education. Refusals

6. Sharron Zenith Corne, Winnipeg Committee for Women Artists, *Branching Out* 5, no. 2 (1978), 7-10.

to support this "obvious" cause varied from, "I'm for people's liberation because men have a difficult time too," to, "Because the gallery may be including me in an exhibition soon, it would be impolite to criticize them." Eight women were interested enough to appear at my studio for a meeting in March. They were professional artists, university art teachers and people involved in the visual arts field. Naively, I assumed that once I had a group behind me, the gallery would hear our criticisms and gratefully reply, "Thank you for telling us. We will mend our ways." The group too, underestimated the complexity of the problem and the depth of the gallery's resistance to change.

Our first meeting at the gallery was with a staff member acting as adviser for the women's auxiliary project. Our ideas were barely heard, much less welcomed. She explained that a historical perspective was necessary because the public required this moderate approach. While agreeing that any retrospect of 19thC and 20thC works would constitute a predominantly male exhibition she felt that women artists would feel insulted by the segregation of their work. She boasted that their project was designed to give work to 100 volunteers, as well as extend beyond the gallery's walls to affect women who would not normally come to the gallery.

The implication seemed to be that only people from this illustrious institution could really know about art or for that matter, feminism. She prodded us to join their project. To take part in an exhibition whose goals conflicted with those of International Women's Year would only validate their misconception. We refused and began to make other plans.

Our number was now down to four. Few women could devote the time or energy required for our efforts. The responsibilities of jobs, studio work and families were more than enough. Also, to publicly contradict an institution which has such control over your recognition and success demands enormous sacrifice. The gallery wondered about our diminishing numbers but, in view of these obstacles, we were surprised we still had a group at all.

It seemed that perhaps the endorsement of a recognized women's group would add status to our side in our confrontations with the gallery. My naivete again led me to believe that upon contact these women's groups would immediately sympathize with our plight and rush in. From the first delegate we hoped for at least a letter of support — this was refused. A call to a second group brought an indifferent reaction. Eventually we did find individuals and groups to endorse our protest. Whether or not they affected our status in the gallery's eyes became immaterial. What was important was the psychological effect on our somewhat demoralized group.

Feeling more confident, we attempted to meet with the gallery director. He felt our complaints were not really his responsibility but that of the women's auxiliary, so we met the executive of that group in the gallery's board room, complete with chandeliers and luxurious carpets.

Our suggestion of an exhibition of women's work was again rejected. We were challenged to organize our own exhibition in a small gallery or shopping mall. We explained that a lesser setting would immediately give us an unequal footing. "Why don't you ask the gallery for space here?" they suggested. The idea seemed bizarre, but at this time everything did. We went to see the gallery director. He agreed!

Then came the if's. A large gallery space would be available to us in late November if we could assume complete responsibility for co-ordinating, curating, financing, and publicizing the events. The 100 volunteers on the other project had the use of a paid adviser, office assistance and other valuable aids from the gallery, and we hoped to share these resources. However, our request for assistance was refused by the gallery because "this could best be handled by your group. This is really a matter of time rather than potential expense to your group." Our "group" foolhardily agreed to all these stipulations, which put so little value on our time.

We thought the worst was over, but new issues continued to arise. The gallery director wished to exercise controls. A letter from him stated that "the two concerns I have are that the material be of suitable quality and that it be deemed acceptable within general social standards." He insisted on having veto power on the jurors or the works. He went on to insist that at least one juror be a "prominent community personality." One of his suggestions was the Minister of Public Works.

We were able to find a prominent community personality who had enough faith in our discretion to contribute his name to the jury, while allowing us a free hand.

The first step on our agenda was an application for a federal grant. We decided on a juried exhibition in order to provide the opportunity to as many women as possible to exhibit in a prestigious public gallery. Our title was "Woman as Viewer," based on John Berger's book *Ways of Seeing*. We wished to celebrate women's view of herself and her world, an aspect of life which has been constantly overlooked in mainstream art. Our two major criteria were quality and feminist content. The latter was an important but elusive objective as little information was available on contemporary women's art, let alone feminist work. Our submission was sent off by the May 15th deadline to await a July 1st decision from Ottawa.

By the first week in August we had heard nothing. In mid-August, when all hope had been abandoned, a cheque arrived for $9500. We had lost 6 weeks on an already tight schedule, had a deficit of $8500, and were down to a staff of three. The other project with its 100 volunteers had begun organizing approximately 6 months earlier, with more than ample funds. With trepidation we decided to proceed.

My commitment to the feminist show was an enormous personal breakthrough for me. I had always succumbed to society's dictum that women's energies should be channelled into domesticity. Not only was I now undertaking a public risk, it was one which could easily fail.

Desperate for more funds, two of us made a brief foray into the corporate world. This brought some enlightening experiences, but no rewards. We then looked to the civic and provincial governments, suspecting that they had not contributed to IWY. We were right. Even though our schedule was running late, we continued to write more briefs and attend more meetings to procure funds.

At one finance meeting, we sat around a conference table attempting to describe our aims to an intimidating and unsympathetic group of men. The first question we were asked was what our profits would be. Fortunately, we had already learned what an invaluable help personal contacts are and had armed ourselves with two skilled advisors who knew this committee well. We finished our submission and retreated to the hallway to await their verdict. We were soon informed that we had been awarded $1000. We were thrilled. But the Grey Cup football float had received $11,000. Upon hearing this, our adviser became enraged. She charged back into the committee room and came back with $2500.

It was not until October that we received enough money to reasonably fund our project. Given the obstacles, some gallery personnel felt we could never complete the show. However, we found the basic organization of the exhibition was simple and pleasurable compared to years of housework. Our lack of experience in large galleries often gave us an advantage. We had, instead, experience in managing a home and children while attending classes which has taught us to juggle many taxing jobs. We brought a creativity to our approach which years of gallery experience can dull.

The group which we expected to most appreciate our efforts was the artist community. About three weeks before the show opened, I received a call from a representative of a national artists' association, reprimanding us for not paying rental fees to our artists. We did not disagree with this new concept; nor did we have the required $2500. It seems they had not adequately communicated their policies to the artist community and most artists in our province did not belong to the group or fully understand these policies. We attempted to meet with the women in the Association to clarify some of the misunderstandings but they refused. One wrote me a scathing letter from her studio, accusing me of exploiting women artists. Ironically, at this point I was working 16 hours a day, 7 days a week and had long abandoned all my studio work. This association with its all male executive proceeded to mount a national attack on us, including denouncements on CBC radio, and the promise of boycotts and pickets to close the show. The attack was curtailed by the intervention of a sympathetic government agency which covered the rental fees.

Miraculously we would be ready for opening night. Our catalogue delivery was more precarious. At the last minute, the original printer refused it when he realized it included a male nude. Luckily we found another printer who was able to meet our deadline.

Opening night brought an enormous turnout, in spite of a mail strike. We had received good media coverage prior to the opening; response after the opening was overwhelming. The public did not seem to want a moderate approach after all. The show appealed to more people and a wider spectrum than we had ever anticipated. The *Winnipeg Free Press*, gave it a full page. One of its critics, Katie Fitzrandolph, wrote:

> ....the gallery through no fault of its own has a winner on its hands. "Woman as Viewer," the protest show occupying two of its galleries is funny, witty, topical, and provocative. The gallery must be acutely embarrassed that its first real hit since moving ... was organized by an ad hoc outside committee with no previous experience. The exhibition it was organized to protest, "Images of Women" is pale and sometimes vulgar by comparison with "Viewer." "Viewer" has proven that Winnipeg will visit the gallery in large numbers if offered a challenging and stimulating show. The gallery should swallow its pride and give thanks that such a show has arrived."

Feminist Cultural Production

"Graphic Feminism"
Ontario, 1970-86[7]

It was an 18" x 24", black ink on melancholy beige cover stock. The type was crooked Letraset. The graphic was so nondescript I can't now remember it. But the poster was easily my favourite piece in the show.

Reading like last week's feminist top 40 — prostitution, rape, radical lesbianism, socialism and women, imperialism and women's work — it advertised a 1972 discussion series at U of T.

My first reaction: incredulity at the realization that we're still talking about those same issues 14 years later and that in 1972 I was in grade 7 and had never even heard of feminism. Yet there it was, looking remarkably similar to the movement I know today.

An exhibition of graphic art from the Ontario women's movement, 1970–1986, Graphic Feminism is a project of the Canadian Women's Movement Archives. Magazines, posters, books, leaflets, T-shirts, buttons, postcards and a token album cover document the issues and aesthetics of this most recent feminist era. The collection gives us an opportunity to assess where the movement has come from and how it has changed. It's also a gentle reminder that you can't hurry a revolution.

The U of T series concluded with a discussion on "The Limits of Feminism." Of course I've no idea what those women actually talked about, but I found myself admiring them for having even broached the

---

7. Mary Louise Adams, *Broadside* 7, no. 8 (June 1986), 15.

topic at a time when the movement was smaller and less institutionalized than it is now. It's a recurring discussion in a changing context.

Approaching the rest of the posters in the show with the benefits of hindsight one gets a sense of the limitations we've actually managed to exceed and of the ones we're just now recognizing. In confronting them we expand and transform the definition of feminism. Where the early posters speak solely and specifically of women's liberation, or of issues that are explicitly women's, later pieces illustrate a broader range of concerns, some of which only recently have been defined as feminist.

Certainly a similar show a decade ago would not have included Stephanie Martin's 1984 poster for Colour Positive, an anti-racist film festival, or Barbara Klunder's poster from the same year, "Fighting for a Union at Eaton's."

The series of posters from International Women's Day events in Toronto makes the point blatantly clear. In the late 70s they called for "Women's Liberation." Period. The list of endorsers was recognizably feminist. In the early 80s, IWD posters demanded solidarity with women's struggles around the world. The list of endorsers diversified. In 1986 the headlining slogan was "Women Say No to Racism from Toronto to South Africa." Again the endorsements changed.

Similarly the presentation and tone of our messages has evolved dramatically. A 1977 poster by Deena Rasky shows a photo of three women obviously angry, white on black extra-bold type, "Women Against Violence Against Women." There's no mistaking the intent of the piece. A 1973 poster, "Strike While the Iron is Hot" by C. Watson for Wages for Housework has the same sense of militancy. Both designers seem to have been more concerned with advertising the ideology than the organization.

Recent posters are more subtle, are more focused on events — rallies, concerns, benefits — and groups than on ideology, though ideology still has its place. They are also more sophisticated, artistically and technically. Feminism has grown more comfortable and more self-assured of its position in society. "Professionalism" is no longer feared as a sign of the patriarchy. As a result the women's community now has its own cadre of skilled graphic artists producing quality work. Indeed Graphic Feminism highlighted the work of a handful of artists over and over: Gail Geltner, Liz Martin, Joss Maclennan, Susan Sturman and Wendy Wortsman among others.

But existing alongside the glossy, four colour posters and book jackets are the far more prevalent and familiar photocopied flyers and leaflets. As Carla Murray writes in the program book, their role in spreading the feminist message has been critical, photocopiers now being more accessible than even the Gestetners of the recent past (and where were the examples of work done on Gestetners?).

In displaying "16 years of women's issues," Graphic Feminism, which runs at A Space (204 Spadina Avenue, Toronto) until May 31, is

commendable. In amassing an impressive assortment of feminist paraphernalia (which Pat Jeffries has done a wonderful job of displaying)
the curators have given testament to the fact that this is a truly grassroots
movement, with all the limitations and possibilities that term evokes.
They have given present day feminist activists a historical context for
our work.

But as a document of the Ontario Women's Movement the show is
inadequate. The small number of contributions from outside Toronto
does little to illuminate the issues or concerns of women in the rest of
the province. As valid but isolated examples they pale beside the slick
four-colour artwork around them. A tour of the exhibition could do much
to inspire more submissions for a sequel. As someone wrote in the guest
book, "Can we have more?"

"Nellie McClung and the Redlight Theatre"
Toronto, 1975[8]

Redlight Theatre began on January 7, 1974 in Toronto. It was formed
to produce plays by and about women and to develop the skills and
talents of women playwrights, administrators and technicians.

We called it Redlight because every actress has played enough
whores and harlots in her career to make it appropriate.

It is perhaps because we have played so many whores with hearts of
gold that we want to produce plays written by women. So many male
playwrights leave women out altogether or write about harpies, shrews
and neurotic mothers. We want to portray women as people whose
existence in a play is not determined by their relationship — sexual or
otherwise — to the men and whose concerns are wider than their feelings
about the men in their life.

We intend to both improvise plays and use published scripts. During
our first season, we presented *Entrances,* a play created by Marcella
Lustig and Francine Volker and *Ex-Miss Copper Queen on a Set of Pills,*
plus *The Gloaming, O My Darling*, two one-act plays by Megan Terry.

Because the history of women is not taught in the schools, we want
to dramatize specific women's contributions to society. We plan a series
called *Biographies of Lost Women* which we hope to play for school-
children and their teachers as well as for the general public. The first in
the series is a play called *What Glorious Times They Had* which is about
Nellie McClung and the campaign for votes for women.

What Glorious Times They Had was written by me and the members
of the original cast and was first performed on May 8, 1974 at the
Bathurst Street United Church and was subsequently revised and re-
mounted at the Enoch Turner Schoolhouse on October 16, 1974.

Set in Winnipeg from 1912 to January 27, 1916, when the vote was
won, the play uses six actors — four women and two men — and one
musician. It features songs of the era — temperance songs like "Going

8. Diane Grant, *This Magazine* 8, nos. 5 and 6 (January-February 1975), 16-18.

Dry" and tender ballads like "Heaven Will Protect the Working Girl" and "I Must Go Home Tonight."

It was improvised from researched material. I drew up a scenario of chronological events and we worked scene by scene, improvising and writing.

It began as an idea for a play about the life of Nellie McClung. I had become interested in Nellie McClung after the Canadian government issued an 8¢ stamp in 1973 which commemorated the 100th anniversary of her birth. I had not been taught about her in school and knew only that she had been a staunch member of the Women's Christian Temperance Union. I then discovered that she had also written many novels, including one of the first Canadian best sellers, *Sowing Seeds in Danny*, that she had been elected to the Alberta Legislative Assembly in 1921, had been a representative to the League of Nations, and had been instrumental in the fight to have women declared "persons" and therefore eligible for the Senate.

I soon realized that the dramatization of so full a life would require a cast of thousands. Any one of the events of her life would have been theatrically interesting but I finally decided on a play about her role in the enfranchisement of women in Manitoba.

The women of Manitoba were the first to win the vote and were immeasurably helped by Nellie McClung's wit, oratory and energetic campaigning. Secondly, there were many other independent, active women who were involved in the movement and who have been buried in old newspapers. They, along with Nellie, became our central characters.

Three were journalists — E. Cora Hind, Frances Beynon and Lillian Beynon Thomas. E. Cora Hind could predict the annual wheat crop almost to the bushel — a skill for which she became world famous. She taught herself to type and ran the typing bureau in Winnipeg. After twenty years of waiting, she was hired by the *Winnipeg Free Press* and eventually became its Agricultural Editor. An eccentric, she bicycled, flagged down trains and wore pants to ride through the wheat fields.

Frances Beynon was the Women's Page Editor of the *Grain Growers Guide*, an influential prairie newspaper. She used her columns to fight for legal reforms and suffrage. She reported all the activities of the Political Equality League, the suffrage organization, told people where to write for suffrage petitions and carried on long debates with correspondents. She was not always popular. In 1913, one Saskatchewan farmer wrote:

> If you don't stop advocating women suffrage in your paper, you can cancel my subscription. My wife gets the *Guide* and reads your articles to me at the supper table, and it makes things very unpleasant in my house.

A pacifist, Ms Beynon apparently was forced to leave the paper in 1919. She emigrated to the United States. Unfortunately, we have not been able to find out more about her.

Even less is known about her sister, Lillian Beynon Thomas, a journalist for the *Manitoba Free Press*. She also used her columns for campaigning. She was known as a brilliant speaker and organizer and was the first president of the Political Equality League. Like Frances, she also opposed the war and she and her husband left Canada for New York.

All these women were reformers rather than revolutionaries and operated within the system. The Political Equality League sent petition forms and speakers throughout the province, printed suffrage literature and lobbied for support. It used persuasion as a weapon and rejected militancy.

Canadian to a woman, they resented foreign influence. Mrs. Thomas stated:

> We resented very keenly the fact that some English women came out and tried to stampede us into taking violent methods ... We did not need anything like that.

Their methods and spirit are most clearly illustrated in their use of the Mock Parliaments, a political burlesque. This entertainment which was presented by the Political Equality League on January 28, 1914 in Winnipeg, created one of the turning points in the battle for enfranchisement.

This Mock or Women's Parliament simply reversed the existing situation. Women had the vote and the men were voteless. Women held the power and the men were powerless.

The idea was not new. The Equal Suffrage Club had performed a Women's Parliament in 1896 and Lillian Beynon Thomas had heard about one presented by the Women's University Club in Vancouver.

However, Mrs. Thomas and the P.E.L. saw its possibilities and made it a part of a brilliant campaign plan. They first decided to send a delegation of women to the Legislative Assembly on January 27, 1914. The delegation would ask for the vote and the premier, they felt sure, would refuse it. (Sir Rodmond Roblin, the Premier of the province, had been in power for 14 years and was an adamant anti-suffragist). They planned to present their play the following night. They would satirize the events of the day before and the climax of the parliament would be a humble delegation of men, pleading for the vote. Furthermore, they asked Nellie McClung to portray Sir Rodmond. She accepted with delight.

In *The Stream Runs Fast*, the second volume of her autobiography, she describes her feelings while listening to Roblin's reply to the delegation:

> What would be the fate of our play if Sir Rodmond were wise enough to give us a favourable reply? ... I sat there in nervous

panic, but I need not have feared. The orator of the old school ran true. He was at his foamy best, and full of the eloquence which Anatole France once described as 'that which glides but never penetrates'. I did not want to forget his exact phrases, but I knew I must not write a word, so I just sat there with every fibre of my brain stretched to absorb his diction and the exact tones of his voice.

The P.E.L. rented the Walker Theatre for the performance. The Walker, a handsome legitimate theatre brought in only the best — *Uncle Tom's Cabin, Ben Hur*, Mrs. Shumann-Heink, and George Arliss in *Disraeli*. By January 28th, the Women's Parliament was sold out.

The evening began with songs by the Assiniboine Quartet and a London import called "How They Won The Vote." They were well received but the Mock Parliament was the hit of the show. Nellie McClung portrayed Sir Rodmond with such gusto and accuracy that she brought down the house.

Even the Conservative newspaper, the Winnipeg *Telegram*, was impressed and reported that "Mrs. McClung's reply was the choicest bit of sarcasm ever heard locally ..."

The performance achieved its purpose:

> to make the attitude of government ridiculous and set the whole province laughing at the old conception of chivalry, when it takes the form of hat lifting, giving up seats in street cars, opening doors and picking up handkerchiefs, pretending that this can ever be a substitute for common, old fashioned justice.

The League made money and the movement gained respectability.

These scenes took a while to write. The Delegation to Premier Roblin was well recorded so that the delegation scene required only editing and shaping. The Mock Parliament, on the other hand, presented a number of difficulties, the first one being, of course, that no copy of it exists. It was not found in Mrs. McClung's papers or the Manitoba archives and the University Women's Club of Vancouver has not preserved its version.

The newspaper accounts of the event offered some clues, although much of the humour seemed to revolve around local issues and local politicians, and no longer was funny. We knew that Miss Kenneth Haig had said that she was "keen on men" and that the delegation's slogan was "We have the brains. Why not let us vote?" Parts of Nellie's speech were recorded and posed another problem. The style of the speech was dated and obviously the humour of it would have to lie more in the playing than in the writing.

The most interesting problem though, was not in writing the actual words but in determining the nature of the play. We knew it was a burlesque but did not know exactly what we were burlesquing.

At first we satirized male politicians by adopting male prejudices about women and male attitudes. We took the point of view that men (i.e. women) operated best in the kitchen and were too hysterical to vote. We spoke in low, pompous voices, twirled imaginary moustaches and felt very uncomfortable.

Finally, we realized that we — and the P.E.L. before us — were not satirizing men but a system of government which was attempting to preserve a situation based on myths and preconceptions about the *roles* of men and women. The description of the mace used in the play helped us to arrive at the correct attitude: "It was decorated with yellow and purple ribbons and several bouquets of flowers." We became delicate, sensitive creatures — mothers all — who were absolutely determined to maintain the status quo. The point was power. Those who had it were determined to keep it, and to denigrate the qualities of those who lacked it. So *men* in power denigrate women and their qualities. And women in power — in an inverted image of the same society — would denigrate *men* and *their* qualities.

"Women in Focus"
Spring 1988[9]

Gael McCool: Why did you start Women in Focus?

Marion Barling: Essentially, I wanted to provide alternative images of women. In 1974 I was working on my MA at the University of British Columbia in Theatre and Film and I was very much at odds to know where to find images that reflected my own life as I knew it. There were no materials available. You were lucky to see one woman in a hundred artists whose work was even represented in any collection. There were no tapes available on women artists, there were no books that represented women's contribution to the arts.

I wanted to see a women's aesthetic established: see a women's sensibility represented, understand what it is and what work comes out of it when you view the world through it. My general vision was to literally put women in focus.

In many ways the arts were the last to come to terms with sexism. There was a denial of sex as an issue in how the world was viewed, presented and controlled. In those days you were not a woman artist, you were an artist. Artists were not male or female. The fact that it was considered offensive or verboten to think of oneself as a woman artist says a lot.

There were new areas of aesthetic as well as social concern opening up for women and we had a huge amount of energy but no skills bank or financial resources to draw upon.

I wanted to start a film and video production centre, so I got a group of women together and applied for funding. There were basically only two sources to draw upon: the Secretary of State Women's Program, and the Canada Council.

---

9. Gael McCool, Interview with members of Women in Focus, a Vancouver feminist film centre, in *Women's Éducation des femmes* 6, no. 2 (Spring 1988), 17, 19.

The Secretary of State funds social issues not art, and the mandate of the Canada Council is to fund art not social issues. Eventually however we did receive a small amount of project funding and started working on production.

Gael: What type of productions were initially encouraged by WIF?

Sue Donaldson: At that point, in the first flush of the women's movement, there was a lot of work in issue-oriented productions. It was called deconstruction and it had to do with breaking down media images of women into their component parts and pointing out the sexism. We were beginning to look at the things going on around us, what they meant to women, how women were being portrayed, and how we felt about that. There were close to 50 productions between 1974 and 1978 about these issues. Pornography, media images of women, alcoholism, transition houses, etc., were incorporated by women artists into their own background and experience and translated into their artwork. A lot of these were poorly produced technically, but they were very important in establishing a groundwork of personal and political art ...

Gael: What needs to be done to ensure the survival of WIF?

Sharon Costello: It is essential that there are organizations, to foster, develop and support the talent of women in the arts. Mainstream cultural organizations do not, financially or any other way. There is still a stigma against feminist resource centres in terms of funding and access to funds. It is a question of political priorities. There is a real need for women to acquire financial knowledge and to take a financial part, because no matter what kind of organization you have if you don't have knowledge of how to access funds you will fail ...

Gael: Has WIF successfully fulfilled your original vision?

Marion: It has gone much farther than my original vision. We need a place where women can express their creativity, think things through, develop and produce their work. We need something to assist women and men in finding and expressing a feminist aesthetic. We need at least a decade and a volume of work to regard, to go back and reflect upon, to find out what goes on in women's heads when they are free, or at least conscious, of the dominant ideology. Then we can go on to the next step. Then we will know what it is to have a feminist aesthetic.

innervisions/ARC
Toronto, September 1975[10]

Dear People;

Since May 1975, we have been working on a film and video catalogue of films and tapes by/for/about women that are available within the Toronto area. The catalogue includes 800 titles, of which we have screened and annotated about 200. Included are also articles on various topics that directly and indirectly involve media, a section on care of tapes and film, courses available in schools in the Toronto area, how to

10. Innervisions/ARC, open letter, September 1975. Copy at WERC.

set up a film forum, basic instructions on projection, and some topics researched with a view to the use of media in educating and communicating the particular topic.

The purpose of this catalogue is to stimulate the use of film and video as a grass roots communication tool. We expect this to be done by showing community groups, schools, etc. what films are available, by giving a subjective view of their uses, by showing the kinds of information that producers feel we want, and by encouraging the production of information from within the groups who need and want it, when the existing material is unsuitable. I have included a copy of the editorial to the catalogue for more background information.

The catalogue is now at the printers and will be ready for distribution the end of September.

We are now planning the next catalogue which will update and expand this edition; we will include more distribution companies, more independent and student filmmakers and videographers, more articles and will include more of Canada.

We will also be organizing film showings on a regular basis, so that student and independent filmmakers, who do not normally have the opportunity, will be able to show their 8mm and 16mm films in a public situation. We hope these film showings will become a forum for discussion of media and for exchange of experimental ideas. They will provide opportunity for people who are not in the more professional areas of film to meet and talk with each other. We feel that this will not only encourage new filmmakers to produce, but will encourage a constructive criticism of media: that which is so much of our life, but which is not often discussed critically. It is possible that these showings will become more practical workshops if people want to form production groups.

We are interested in your comments, advice and suggestions. We are in the process of applying for financial assistance and would appreciate a letter of support if you feel our endeavours are worthwhile ... And more practically, if you could be of assistance to us in terms of space and/or equipment, we would be more than happy to hear from you, and to perhaps arrange a meeting.

innervisions/ARC
Toronto, September 1975[11]

In 1974, women in several cities across Canada developed a touring/media/workshop, based on the needs and consciousness of women in their particular areas. In Ontario, working from Toronto, was the Women and Film Touring Media Bus. Working on the media bus, which included three feature films, several shorts, and many, many documentary and educational films, and many, many video tapes of the same nature, plus equipment for showing these and for workshops, not only in media, but

---

11. innervisions/ARC, flyer, September 1975. Copy at WERC.

in health, law and dance, we learned a great deal about the accessibility of media.

We did have some background knowledge required to make our research relatively easy, but to the uninitiated community group, perhaps wishing to use film for the first time, it would be very difficult to find all films on a given topic, to screen them, and to choose the most suitable. We had to take what we could find, that is, we had to rely on the opinions of others, or just accept something that was less suitable because we did not have time for a thorough search. It seemed then, and has been proven to us through working on the catalogue that there is very little information that is up to date on, for example, laws that pertain to women, or to new sensibilities that women have developed towards their bodies and towards learning about their bodies. Tapes were more up to date than films, obviously due to their expense and their accessibility; unfortunately most tapes are not kept for any length of time, and are not supported by the same kinds of structures that surround film. It was from this experience that Innervisions/ARC (for Access Resource Catalogue) was developed.

We were all involved with film and video and were interested in expanding and exploring their uses. The next step was logical: set up a communications centre that would include a production unit, a newsletter, a catalogue, a video exchange, and community animation — workshops, screenings, forums, etc. ... First we developed the questionnaires, one for community groups, one for distributors, and one for producers. These were to determine the nature of the particular organization, who uses their services, whether and how they use media, if they could use media to promote their activities, what sort of information they offered, etc. Then we found that there were an incredible number of community organizations, more than we could mail our questionnaires to at this time. We also discovered that film distribution companies are not listed in the yellow pages, so we began by asking the companies that we knew about for other ones, checking advertisements, the Women's Yellow Pages, looking in the phone book under Film, Cine, and talking to people who might know.

The amount of films available is incredible; we have about 900 titles, which is not complete and of which we were able to screen 200, but we have found of those screened that most are out of date, that most do not represent a viable life style, that most do not speak to anything of particular importance, that most are the result of some desire of some company or system, that most do not relate to where people are or would like to work to be. We would really like to screen all films and tapes and give the complete picture, but it seems that we do have an idea of what it is. However, we have included all film titles that are related to the world of women, not only as we see it but as film has seen it to be. To decide this was not particularly easy and in a sense we are perpetuating the situation by determining that the films included in the catalogue be only those that are about/for/by women, thereby excluding worlds and worlds of good films and tapes that are of interest to women: "History Through Art," "Living Off the Land," "Only One Earth: the Stockholm Conference," or "How the Thunderbird Lost His Courage." Perhaps the catalogue will be eventually a catalogue of films that deals in creative ways with the realities and possibilities of living on this earth.

So, all this means that we have included topics from child care through discovery of one's self to how to colour your hair. In this way the catalogue has become a survey, showing the types of films produced for women, showing what filmmakers and producers, and therefore what society thinks of us. It shows attitudes not only to women but to humanity as a whole. Most maintained the status quo; there are very few films that either deal with possibilities or deal with reality. They are mostly theories and projections; theories of why things are the way they are, and projections of already formulated theories that have remained static in that projection. Inclusion in the catalogue of films that maintain the situation or attitudes is not meant to support them, but to point to holes in the information that we require. We might recommend some of these films only to show an example of existing attitudes and to perhaps give background information for discussion or awareness raising. Many films are extremely humorous in this context...

The catalogue is not finished. It is the basis from which to reach out further. We would like to include films and video tapes by independent people, students, all of whom we didn't have time to contact for this edition. We would like to screen more films and tapes. We would like to start a regular film screening where people could bring their own films and tapes and meet with other people who are doing film and video as well as alternative cinema in the home grown sense, have workshops for not only use of equipment, but for expanded possibilities of the use of the media and for better use of media.

"Nova Scotian Cultural Activist Delvina Bernard"
March/April 1987[12]

On singing in Nova Scotia Delvina [Bernard] says, — you have to dig your heels in because as singers we are cultural bearers, we have to be aware of not only our lives but the lives of people in our community. Four the Moment has allowed me the opportunity to sit and talk with so many Black women from different communities, the church sisters and just older women who tell me their experiences. Our songs have to contain the musical elements and some of the lyrics are written by community poet George Elliot Clarke, and I write songs about what happens in my own life, like when I was unemployed I wrote *U.I. Line*. When a friend of mine, poet Sylvia Hamilton, wrote a screenplay about Black Nova Scotian women, I was inspired to write my feelings about

12. Faith Nolan, *Our Lives* (March/April 1987), 3.

my mother and sisters and I wrote, *I love you woman — Black Mothers, Black Daughters.* That's how songs come about naturally.

When I think about Black women's concerns and issues in Nova Scotia the bulk of the literature I've read and music I've heard comes from the U.S. because that is where most of it is published. There are very few books and music published by Black women in Nova Scotia ...

Black women in Nova Scotia have always excelled in formal education and community organization, for every qualified Black man there are probably ten qualified Black women, yet it seems like a Black man is dug up even if he's not as qualified to head the organization.

As a woman, I'm at a stage of realizing this, as I think are other Black women. We need to get together to validate our thoughts to each other and ourselves. We need to connect with Black women everywhere. Black women here who are political are contained within the church structure as is most of our community. We have to start working outside of this as well to deal with the legislators and educators because that affects the conditions under which we live as Black women ...

"Mama Quilla Who??"
Toronto, 1981-2[13]

Mama Quilla II is a seven-woman rock band which performs its irresistibly danceable music with no-nonsense, dynamic style. Add to this a vision of the world from a woman's perspective, and you have the unique ensemble that is Mama Quilla II.

The rock music business has long been one of the toughest male bastions to crack. Women have found it difficult, if not impossible, to enter that particular world on their own terms. "It killed Janis Joplin, but it won't kill us," says Linda Robitaille, Mama Quilla II saxophonist. The band's survival strength comes from its members' collective determination to be who they are, to break through stereotypes and define an alternative rock music without violence and sexism. What seems like a contradiction in terms results in some very fresh, energetic and vital music; in performance the group projects its enjoyment of sharing a musical process together, an enjoyment which, judging from enthusiastic audiences, is infectious.

"Mama Quilla" is the name of a Peruvian moon goddess: Mama Quilla I (of which MQ II members Linda Jain, Linda Robitaille and Jacqui Snedker are alumnae) was a band formed in the early 1970s by Sara Ellen Dunlop, a major independent figure on the Toronto music scene who died of cancer in 1975. Mama Quilla II was named in memory of this woman who did much to further women's involvement in the local music scene, forming her own record label and encouraging other women musicians.

13. The Mama Quilla Collective, promotional flyer. Copy at CWMA.

Femmes Against Feminists
June 1985[14]

Nightwood Theatre's production of *Ladies Against Women* had a full house rolling in the aisles on opening night in Toronto. They also had us up on our feet doing Consciousness Lowering exercises, led by Candy Cotton, LAW's version of Jane Fonda. Candy, the genotype cheerleader, led us in exercises guaranteed to "Get rid of excess cranial bulk." She refreshed our memories on how to combine weak feminine body language with such phrases as, "Sir, could you lift that? It's too heavy for me."

Ladies Against Women, An Evening of Consciousness Lowering, was presented by Nightwood in association with Womanly Way Productions. The show was written and performed by the Plutonium Players of San Francisco. The group consists of Jain Angeles, Selma Vincent, Gail Ann Williams, and Jeff Thompson of the men's auxiliary.

Mrs. T. Bill Banks, alias Selma Vincent, appeared on stage with her master charge card on her hat, briefed us on LAW, and told us why the ladies felt we needed them in Toronto. She surmised that we had all been ESTed, Rolfed, Polarized, in short thoroughly liberated, and were now unable to leave the Annex. Mrs. Banks was joined by Candy Cotton (Jain Angeles) and Mrs. Virginia Cholesterol (Gail Ann Williams) — *real* name, Mrs. *Chester* Cholesterol — for the reading of the LAW Manifesto. The Ladies led us in such rousing slogans as Support BRA not ERA; Make America A Man Again, Invade A-Broad; I'm No Queer, I Have a Baby Every Year; and Lady Nancy's special chant, China Today, Curtains Tomorrow.

Mrs. Cholesterol expressed a special interest in the right of the unconceived. "Sperms are people too," she said. "We must save them from those dreadful rubber concentration camps. We must abolish penal colonies." She also called for abolition of menstruation, masturbation and other forms of mass murder. Mrs. T. Bill Banks expressed a preference for suffering over suffrage. And Virginia Cholesterol agreed that if God had wanted ladies off their pedestals he would not have made them shorter than their husbands.

Fred Shrapnel of the men's auxiliary made an appearance as a representative of NAGO, the National Association of Grenade Owners. He advocated the carrying of grenades for hunting, fishing and self-defence. And Colonel Beauregard Bullrun Lee of the Lt. Calley Academy for Boys lectured the male members of the audience on how to stop being wimps, how to "put the bounce back in your balls," and become "real men, rough as burlap."

The Lady of the Year award was presented to Phyllis LeShaft who thanked her father, minister, husband and four sons for allowing her to

---

14. Amanda Hale, *Broadside* 6, no. 8 (June 1985), 12.

appear. She expounded on the dangers of a gender-free society — "Nothing should be free!"

We were treated to a fashion show of endangered accessories such as the leopardskin hat, the snakeskin purse, the baby harp seal fur stole, and of course a large South African diamond to complete the international ensemble. Strains of "Born Free" provided antithetical background music.

We were urged to "Adopt a Missile," with the promises of a special Foster Missile Kit, and a choice of which country your missile is based in and which country it is aimed at.

Then it was time for "Cooking with Cholesterol." Virginia gave us tips on Sweet and Sour Fruitloops, and demonstrated Twinkies from Scratch, on an ironing board. Virginia, who believes that "originality is a sin," recommended making Twinkies from such wholesale products as supermarket pound cake and Coolwhip. The recipe was dedicated to President Reagan, that great believer in white sugar, white flour, and white power.

The Ladies are big on bake sales, and set them up whenever and wherever possible, on the street. They showed slides of their summer vacation in Texas where they set up a bake table outside the Republican convention headquarters. Their opinion is that, "Reagan should get a life term — he deserves it." Plutonium Players, which was formed in 1977 and springs from a tradition of satirical street theatre, led a campaign in 1980 — Reagan for Shah — and the Ladies Against Women movement is sprouting "street action chapters" all over the USA.

The Ladies keep their show up to date with topical and local references. Mrs. T. Bill Banks read some letters she had received: one from 'Bitter in Bitberg' complaining about the Senate's cut in defence spending; one from 'Hassled at the Hague' (the Pope didn't know there were dykes in Holland); and a special letter from 'Mistrusting the Mrs. in Mississauga.' This gentleman was a CBC reject who suspected his wife of cavorting on the U of T campus. The Ladies' advice was to install in his loved one an intra-uterine detector and cervical cop, obtainable from the Federal Bureau of Infidelity.

Virginia Cholesterol, far from a one issue lady, called for abolition of the environment, to be replaced with features which would make it easier to take care of. Take Lake Ontario for instance, she said. No wonder it's polluted with all that loose grit on the shore. Mrs. Cholesterol recommends carpeting all beaches, then ladies can spend their vacations walking their vacuum cleaners along the shore. Sport Vacuuming, she calls it. "Who says nature abhors a vacuum?"

Mrs. T. Bill Banks bemoaned her fate as a member of a special minority group — filthy rich landlords. She doesn't mind renting to poor people as long as they have enough pride to pay her ridiculous rents.

Candy Cotton, the gum chewing cheerleader, kept order during question period by insisting that members of the audience raise their hands before speaking. But when asked what advice the Ladies could offer to lesbians, Candy dropped her pom-poms in horror and hid behind Mrs. Cholesterol, who denied all knowledge of the word. Mrs. Banks, a more experienced woman, said she thought it was too late for lesbians. But she urged the real ladies to keep the boys in blue diapers and the girls in pink, to avoid that lavender area.

On the dot of ten, Mrs. Banks decided to wrap up the evening so that all the unescorted ladies in the audience could hurry home to their husbands. After a closing benediction for the Right, Right, Right Reverend Gerry Fallout, who warned us against feeding the starving millions at the expense of God's chosen few, we were issued with pink graduation cards as members of LAW Consciousness Lowering. "Your cards will be valid when signed by your husbands," we were told.

Unfortunately the Ladies were only in Toronto for a week. There's a whole continent of women out there who need their consciousness lowered. The ladies have their work cut out.

Feminist Presses and Periodicals

Feminist News Service!!
1975[15]

The *Feminist News Service* exists to publish news and news-related material by, for and about Canadian women from a feminist viewpoint. News and information concerning Canadian women can be submitted by an interested woman or women's group for consideration. The service will provide monthly news packets to all individuals or groups that subscribe. Included in the packets, at frequent intervals will be relevant graphics and photos by Canadian women.

FNS started in December 1974. Since that time the news service has become national. At present, we have offices right across Canada. Each province (except for the Atlantic provinces and the territories) has a provincial office. To submit information (be you a woman or part of a woman's group) send your copy into the regional office in your area. The *FNS* will be putting out both French and English Packets. If you wish, you may write to us or receive information in either French or English.

The *Feminist News Service* will carry only information written by Canadian women.

The *Feminist News Service* is completely run and owned by Canadian women.

The *Feminist News Service* needs your support. Donations are greatly appreciated. A receipt will be sent to you for any donation over $5.00.

If *you* have information that you think should be reaching Canadian women send your information to the office in your region.

15. Feminist News Service, subscription form, 1975. Copy at CWMA.

Feminist News Service
Toronto, 12 September 1975[16]

Linda O'Neil
31 McClary Avenue
London, Ontario
Dear Linda:

I must apologize for the long delay in replying to your letter received on August 10th. However, I had been on holiday for a month and am just getting back into things again.

The *Feminist News Service*, as you probably know, operates along the same lines as *Canadian Press*. There are 24 members of FNS (all independently run by women) and 7 representatives soliciting news and subscriptions across the country (all 7 of whom belong to one of the member organizations). I am one of them and I also work for *The Other Woman*, a 3–1/2 year-old feminist newspaper (bi-monthly) which is distributed nationally. Both can be full-time jobs, however, I am doing both jobs part-time after my full-time job!

I want to thank you for your interest and please do send us whatever you would like; we welcome it. You should also know, however, that it is not a magazine as you mentioned but a *newspacket*. *The Other Woman* is more of a magazine although in newspaper format. Yes, free-lance stuff (whether in French or English) from Africa would, again, be more than welcome. This is one area that we need to have more information although it would be more appropriate for *The Other Woman* than for FNS because one of our first-year policies is to not consider anything not about women actually living in Canada, the scarcity of which is one of the major reasons for our own news service.

As a journalist, you could receive the $7.00 individual fee but could not use it in your writing as it is copyrighted and newspapers themselves pay a much larger fee in proportion to their circulation. I am sending you a sample from May (though there have been a July and an August issue since).

Hope we will hear from you again re contributions etc.

Sincerely,
Pat Leslie

"Network Nellie"
2 March 1975[17]

PRESS RELEASE: "NETWORK NELLIE"

(FNS) For the first time, on February 28, March 1 and 2, in Thunder Bay, Ontario, 47 women's and native women's centres from across Canada met to discuss the possibility of forming a federation for communication and mutual support.

16. Letter of 12 September, 1975, Toronto. Copy at CWMA.
17. Feminist News Service Press Release, 2 March 1975. Copy at CWMA.

Agreement was reached on the formation of a grassroots communication network which will operate nationally and regionally. This will enable rapid communication concerning pressing issues which relate to women and women's centres such as the common problem of women's centres closing due to lack of funds. The network will lessen the sense of isolation felt by centres.

On March 7, the eve of International Women's Day, St. John's, Newfoundland will start a message which will be relayed across the country to test the communication system.

Resolutions were also passed in support of regional cultural affiliations, the Feminist News Service and the Clearing House for Feminist Media.

Debates in the Cultural Terrain

Words That Make Women Disappear
Toronto, January, 1984[18]

The Ontario Status of Women Council thinks language is important. Sex stereotyping is deeply engrained in our day-to-day language. And while there are those who scoff and make poor jokes about "personhole covers," the OSWC views the misuse of language as a major obstacle in the attainment of total equality for women. If, as children grow older, they hear only of policemen then they learn to think of police officers in male terms. Society assigns roles to its members through language — we are what people say we are! All of us must develop a greater awareness of the implications of sexist language in all forms of communication.

What is sexist language? It's language that excludes women or gives unequal treatment to women and men. It's language that tells a woman she is two things. She is a man and she is not a man. If a woman is swept off a ship into the water, the cry is "Man overboard!" If she is killed by a hit-and-run driver, the charge is "manslaughter." But if she encounters visible or invisible signs that say "Man Wanted" or "Men Only" [under Ontario human rights, visible signs give her the legal right to complain] she knows that the exclusion does not apply to plants or animals or inanimate objects but to female human beings ... If all human beings are consistently referred to as "men," then a woman is automatically denied equal status.

And in employment practices, only in recent years has an effort been made to eliminate sexist labels from job titles. Newspapers now have changed their job listings from the segregated "Help Wanted — Male" and "Help Wanted — Female" to a single, nonsegregated list.

18. Alma Graham, *Redbook Magazine* (March 1977), reprinted with permission by Affirmative Action Advisory Committee, George Brown College of Applied Arts and Technology, *Newsletter* no. 8 (January 1984). Copy at WERC.

Yet gender-free job titles can make a difference. When the Los Angeles City Council approved a plan to abolish the titles of "policeman" and "policewoman", replacing them with the classification police officer, women on the force became eligible for promotions to ranks for which they had been ineligible in the past ...

"[M]an" is one of the most overworked nouns in the English language. It is used to mean a person, worker, member, agent, candidate, representative, voter, even astronaut. Consider the legislator. He is a man of the people. To prove that he's the best man for the job, he takes his case to the man in the street. He is champion of the working man. He speaks up for the little man. He remembers the forgotten man. And he believes in the principle "One man, one vote."

If we agree to stop overworking the word "man," what other words are we going to use in its place? The cardinal rule is simple: Be inclusive. When referring to the human species, we can say people, human beings or men and women. For "mankind" we can substitute humankind, humanity or the human race ... "Pre-historic men" can become pre-historic human beings; "man's conquest of space" can be the human conquest of space.

Where job titles are concerned, the major rule is: Be specific. Name the occupation by the work performed, not by the gender of the worker. "Mailmen," "firemen," and "cameramen" are mail carriers, fire fighters, and camera operators. A "workman" is a worker, a "newsman" is a reporter, a "foreman" is a supervisor and a "watchman" is a guard.

Whether a male or a female does the job shouldn't affect its title. Instead of saying "steward" and "stewardess," we should use the inclusive term flight attendant; and instead of saying "maid" or "janitor," we can specify whether we want a house or office cleaner or a building superintendent or custodian.

But the pronoun is the real problem. How do we avoid referring to the unknown singular subject as "he"? Our language needs a common pronoun but none of the various ones suggested has yet shown signs of gaining acceptance. The likeliest candidate is already in the language, at least on the level of informal speech. This is the quasi-singular "they," as in "Everybody will wear what they want to wear." Often you can reword a sentence to avoid singular pronouns altogether. Thus, instead of saying, "If the student practices this exercise, he can learn it," you can say, "If students practice this exercise, they can learn it." Finally, once we have included both females and males in our language, we should remember to treat them equally. Instead of saying: "Henry Harris is an up-and-coming lawyer and his wife Ann is a striking brunette," we might say either: "The Harrises are an attractive couple. Henry is a handsome blond and Ann is a striking brunette," or "The Harrises are highly respected in their fields. Ann is an accomplished musician and Henry is an up-and-coming lawyer."

Equal treatment also should be accorded women of achievement. Consider a headline that appeared a few years ago: "Writer's Wife Becomes Mayor." This "wife" had been the first woman ever elected to the local City Council but even when she became mayor she remained a "writer's wife."

In 1976 the *New York Times* updated its Manual of Style and Usage, cautioning writers that "in referring to women we should avoid words or phrases that seem to imply that the *Times* speaks with a purely masculine voice." But despite this resolve a front page story that same year, reporting on a study of retirement income, cited statistics on a "married retiree and his wife" — without any indication that some married retirees might have husbands!

Wife. Ladies. Girls. A man's property. Someone fragile and polite. An innocent. Not only has a woman been defined as something less than a lady and something more than a girl; she has been called fickle and foolish, silly and superficial and, above all, weak. In our language the qualities of the adult — strength, courage, will, wisdom and self-reliance — have been given exclusively to the male.

Now increasing numbers of women are showing a new pride in their adulthood. They do not like to be called "honey" or "dear" by male grocers or bank tellers who hardly know them. They do not like to be called an "old maid" if they're single or a "housewife" if they're not. They are not "girls," "gals," "wives," "ladies" or "the fair sex." They are women — and beginning to be happy about the fact.

"You've Come a Long Way, Baby?"
Toronto, July 1985[19]

Canadian women learned a few things about the extent to which sexist values are entrenched in the country's central institutions. Twice during the recent session in Parliament a female Member was silenced, neutralized and negated by sexist language. First, it was Justice Minister John Crosbie who barked "Quiet down, baby" to Sheila Copps (Hamilton East). Then he muttered something about "titmice" in the Commons. During the session the next day, Finance Minister Michael Wilson called out to Copps, "Get out of here, baby" after she had asked one or two too many questions.

These attempts to reduce the status of a Member of Parliament, this attack on a woman *qua* woman, bring a few points into sharp focus. To begin with, these types of barbs are extremely effective in making the substance of criticism in Parliament almost invisible. At this point, Canadians remember that a female member of Parliament was referred to as "baby," but the precise question Copps was asking has fallen by the wayside. (For those who want to know, she was asking Wilson about old-age pensions.) Using this kind of language works to eclipse content.

19. Editorial, *Broadside* 6, no. 9 (July 1985), 2.

Second, there seemed to be no outrage recorded on the part of Mr. Wilson's party for this verbal abuse, but uproarious applause instead. What does Flora MacDonald really think of all this? Or Pat Carney? Or any of the other female Progressive Conservatives who, because these episodes are met with approval, become vulnerable to similar abuse?

Third, there does not seem to be an epithet we can counterpose to "baby" for female Members of Parliament to hurl at male Members. "Turkey," "scoundrel" and "scum" (Hansard is full of such puerile records directed at men by men) do not silence men in the same way "baby" silences a woman. Mr. Wilson explained that he used the word because he had become frustrated with Ms. Copps, that he had lost "respect" for her. In fact, he used the word because men use language to undermine the respect, or dignity, of women: Women should be seen and not heard.

And the use of such words is not considered against parliamentary protocol, according to the Speaker of the House, John Bosley. Canadian women should be profoundly insulted by this. Sexist language has to be made unparliamentary if the governing body expects to maintain a modicum of respect from the female population. Bosley's apology that the word is "offensive," but not necessarily "unparliamentary," misses the point that these words, sexist words, are directed at a specific segment of the population. When Wilson and Crosbie baited Copps in that way, they were baiting every single woman in the country. Perhaps they never had any "respect" in the first place.

"The Politics of Censorship"
Toronto, 1985[20]

The following is an excerpt from a letter sent to one of the editors of this issue from Lynn King, a lawyer working on the case identified in the letter.

"Once again, artists in Toronto are being persecuted by unjust laws which apparently are on the books to help women. This time a feminist art display has been seized by the police and the owner and manager of the bookstore in which the display was exhibited have been charged with exhibiting a disgusting object. This is a very serious charge and will need a lot of preparation. The display was part of a feminist art program known as "Fem Fest" and was put on by three young women artists called the "Woomers." The name of the display was "I'm a Girl" and it was meant to trace the life of a woman from being a baby on into adulthood. The window contained, among other things,

- a baby bed
- white bead purses
- two birth control packages

20. Lynn King, *Resources for Feminist Research/Documentation sur la recherche féministe* 14, no. 4 (December/January 1985/86), 32.

- male condoms
- a Barbie doll
- an empty Pampers diaper box
- a plaster cast of a penis
- make-up products
- a plastic toy machine gun
- tampons
- white gloves
- comic books
- and several Kotex pads covered with red paint

The male police officers who ultimately, as I have always said, are in charge of laying charges and putting people through long, torturous, and expensive trials thought the display was "disgusting." What they thought particularly disgusting were the Kotex pads. So did the male editorial writers of the *Globe and Mail*. None of the women that I have spoken to since the charge think that Kotex pads with or without paint are the least bit disgusting; they use them or like products every month. But this is the dilemma we are constantly in when proposing laws which will be enforced (until we have a huge shift in power) and interpreted by male police officers, male crown attorneys, and male judges. My feeling is that you can tinker with the law until you are blue in the face and the result will be, and always has been, the same."

"Women's Press Anti-Racist Guidelines"
Toronto, December 1988–January 1989[21]

Women's Press is entering a new phase of its development. We are a socialist-feminist publishing house which has been an integral part of the development of Canadian feminism since 1972. Like many Canadian feminist organizations, we have been defined and run by white, middle-class women. As a publishing house that has always been political, we have applied our understanding of sexism and class when evaluating manuscripts. We are now focusing on our responsibility to ensure that our feminism is also anti-racist. We are working to make Women's Press a racially integrated publishing house which is anti-racist in all aspects of its work.

This means that our publishing policy has changed. We are looking for manuscripts that we did not seek out before. We look forward to working with writers who, in the past, may not have experienced Women's Press as a suitable publishing house. And we are applying our anti-racist policy to all manuscripts that are submitted to us.

These guidelines are meant to assist writers in making a judgement about whether we are an appropriate publishing house for their work, and to assist us in assessing manuscript submissions. These guidelines

21. *Broadside* 10, no. 3 (December 1988/January 1989), 4.

are Women's Press now, the best contribution we can make to Canadian feminism in the 1980s.

Women's Press has published books which promote and develop feminism in Canada through social criticism, imaginative writing and children's books. This will continue.

But, we are now committed to publishing a wider range of women to reflect the diversity of all women's experience. Our expanded list of titles includes writing by and from the perspectives of Black women, Native women, Women of Colour and women whose first language is not English. We continue to welcome the writing of white women in Canada, particularly work that challenges the popular literary representation of Canada and the world as white and middle class. We welcome writing that challenges racism. We want to be truly a women's press.

We will publish analytic feminist writing which incorporates race and class into its analysis. We will publish fiction and non-fiction work by Women of Colour on issues determined by their concerns. We want to publish manuscripts which acknowledge or highlight differences between women. We want material which contributes to understanding how anti-racist work can be done, and how racism functions within Canada and within the feminist movement. We also want to publish manuscripts with an international focus.

We are aware of indicators which signal that a manuscript is not suitable for us. We want writers to know what our current thinking is so that they can determine whether our priorities coincide with theirs.

We will avoid publishing manuscripts which contain imagery that perpetuates the hierarchy black = bad, white = good.

We will avoid publishing manuscripts which adopt stereotypes — the use of oversimplifications and generalizations about a particular group of people.

We will avoid publishing manuscripts which use terminology that reinforces stereotypes and words which are indelibly associated with prejudiced usage.

We will avoid publishing fiction manuscripts in which the protagonist's experience in the world, by virtue of race or ethnicity, is substantially removed from that of the writer.

We will avoid tourist's or traveller's point of view writing which does not recognize the limitations of the perspective within the writing itself.

We will avoid publishing manuscripts in which a writer appropriates the form and substance of a culture which is oppressed by her own.

We will avoid publishing manuscripts in which white, middle-class women's perspective is characterized as normal, and the perspective of Women of Colour is presented as unusual or exotic.

We will avoid publishing a manuscript whose analysis includes women of colour as a supplement to a text, rather than incorporating Women of Colour into the overall content and structure.

Permissions

Every effort has been made to trace the ownership of all copyrighted documents and illustrations reprinted or reproduced in this book. We regret any errors and will be pleased to make any necessary corrections in future editions.

Grateful acknowledgement is made to the following people for permission to reprint their documents:

MARY LOUISE ADAMS, "Graphic Feminism."
ANGLES, "Self insemination."
HINDA AVERY, "Sitka Housing Co-operative: Women House Themselves."
GWYNNE BASEN, "Experiments on women and children."
ELIZABETH BATEMAN, "Test Case in the Making."
GERT BEADLE, "Being a Woman at Sixty." Reprinted by permission of *Northern Woman Journal*.
LYNN BEAK, "Family Law Reformed Again." Reprinted by permission of *Northern Woman Journal*.
MARY E. BILLY, A Letter to Jake Epp.
JOAN BISHOP, "The Transition House Experience."
ROSEMARY BROWN, "Running a Feminist Campaign."
CANADIAN ADVISORY COUNCIL ON THE STATUS OF WOMEN, "Women and Legal Action."
BARRY CRAIG, "Women's march may back call for Rights Probe." Reprinted by permission of *Globe and Mail*.
SUSAN CREAN, "In the Name of the Fathers: Joint Custody and the Anti-Feminist Backlash"; "The Thirty Per Cent Solution: Sexism as a Fine Art."
CLAIRE CULHANE, "Women and Prisons."
RAVIDA DIN & MUTRIBA DIN, "Sisters in the Movement."
DISABLED WOMEN'S NETWORK (TORONTO), "DAWN Toronto Fact Sheet on Reproductive Rights"; "DAWN Toronto Fact Sheet on Violence"; "An Open letter from the Disabled Women's Network."
SUSAN DUSEL, "The Regina Immigrant Women's Centre: Primary Health Care Project."
RUTH DWORIN, "My Horror Story." The author would like to clarify that for the past 18 years, she has not needed birth control, as her partners are no longer male.
MARY EBERTS, "A Summary of *Murdoch* v. *Murdoch*."
JOHN FERGUSON, "Debate Historic Benchmark for Women." Reprinted by permission of Southam News.
barbara findlay, "Racism: Learning to Change."
SUE FINDLAY, "Canadian Advisory Council on the Status of Women: Contradictions and Conflicts."
JO-ANNE GOTTFRIEDSON, BC Native Women's Society *Newsletter* excerpt.
AMANDA HALE, "Femmes Against Feminists."
JOSEPH HALL, "Teen centre wins fight with bar next door." Reprinted with permission — The Toronto Star Syndicate.
BARBARA HERRINGER, "For the Sounds of Our Bodies" from *Telling It*. Reprinted by permission of Press Gang Publishers.
REGINA HICKL-SZABO, "Housing problems growing for single women." Reprinted by permission of the *Globe and Mail*.
MEG HOGARTH, "MediaWatch: Some Success Stories."
JOAN HOLMES, "Heterosexual and Feminist."
GENE JAMIESON, "Farming No Picnic."
JESSIE'S, "All About Jessie's."

JOANNE KATES, "A shoulder to cry on."

LYNN KING, "The politics of censorship." Reprinted by permission of *Resources for Feminist Research.*

EMMA KIVISILD, "Women Challenge CKVU." Reprinted by permission of *Kinesis.*

BONNIE SHERR KLEIN, "We Are Who You Are: Feminism and Disability." Reprinted by permission of *Ms. Magazine,* ©1992.

EUNICE LAVELL, "Women Study Class."

NOREEN LAVOIE, "What's in a Name." Reprinted by permission of *Northern Woman Journal.*

CHRISTINA LEE, "Consultation Meeting with the Federal Ministers."

MYRT LENTON, "Rural Ramblings."

PAT LESLIE, Letter to Linda O'Neil; "Feminist News Service!!"

LYNN MCDONALD, "The State of Federal Funding."

BARBARA MACKENZIE, *History of the Native Women's Association of the NWT.* Reprinted by permission of the Native Women's Association of the N.W.T.

PHILINDA MASTERS, "Feminism's Psychic Imperative — an Editorial"; "You've Come a Long Way, Baby? — an Editorial."

CINDY MORIARTY, "Real Protection for Lesbians?"

JOAN MURRAY, "Poor Women and the Legal System."

MARTHA MUZYCHKA, "Day care in Newfoundland: Nine out of ten have no place to go."

NATIONAL ACTION COMMITTEE ON THE STATUS OF WOMEN, "The Proposed Resolution Regarding the Constitution of Canada"; "NAC Response to Federal Constitution Proposals"; "What Women Want in the Constitution"; "Family allowance rally takes 'no cutbacks' message to Ottawa"; "Pension Reform: What Women Want."

NATIONAL ASSOCIATION OF WOMEN AND THE LAW, "Getting Started"

NORTHERN WOMAN JOURNAL, "Regional Reports: Thunder Bay Anishinabequek"; "Urgent Message to the Women of Ontario."

DOROTHY O'CONNELL, "Income Makes All the Difference."

THE OTHER WOMAN, Anonymous article, "Women's Liberation and Lesbians."

YVETTE PERRAULT, Letter to The B.C. Federation of Women — Lesbian Rights Sub-Committee.

ANNE PIERRE, "Into a Wood."

RUDY PLATIEL, "Toronto police fail to block suit." Reprinted by permission of the *Globe and Mail.*

CINDY PLAYER, "Government Funding of Battered Women's Shelters."

ROSE POTVIN & SAMANTHA SANDERSON, "Adjusting the Image: Women and Canadian Broadcasting."

JUDITH RAMIREZ, "Immigrant Women's Action Group"; "Domestic Workers Organize!"

JUDY REBICK, "Women Leading the Way."

THE RED RAG, "Women Troubles?"

JOAN RIGGS, "The June Callwood phenomenon."

NORMA SCARBOROUGH, material from suit against the Attorney General, filed along with Canadian Abortion Rights Action League (CARAL).

WENDY STEVENS, "Anorexia Nervosa." Reprinted by permission of *Northern Woman Journal.*

SUNERA THOBANI, "Making a Commitment to Inclusion."

LYNN TYLER, "Coming Together."

MAXINE TYNES, "Being," from *Woman Talking Woman.* Reprinted by permission of Pottersfield Press.

ALICE VAN WART, "Abortion: A Woman's Right."

THE VANCOUVER SUN, "Media Watch demonstrators form protest at CKVU studios." Reprinted by permission.

DAVID VIENNEAU, "Top court considers touchy issue of alimony." Reprinted with permission — The Toronto Star Syndicate.

JODI WHYTE, "NWT Gender Bias Review: Hope or Appeasement."

WOMEN'S LEGAL EDUCATION AND ACTION FUND (LEAF), "New sexual assault legislation a step forward"; "Women's groups meet with Justice Minister."

THE WOMEN'S LIBERATION CAMPUS COMMUNITY COOPERATIVE DAYCARE CENTRE, background paper.

WOMEN'S PRESS, "Women's Press Anti-Racist Guidelines."
WOMEN'S SELF-HELP NETWORK, excerpts from *Working Collectively*, Ptarmigan Press. Reprinted by permission of North Island Women's Services Society.
ELLEN WOODSWORTH, "The Adventures of Cora, the Bookmobile."
ELLEN WOODSWORTH AND JUDITH QUINLAN, "How to Start a Political Rap Group."
CAROLÄNN WRIGHT, "It's not just about burning crosses."
GEOFFREY YORK, "Family allowances come to an end." Reprinted by permission of the *Globe and Mail.*

Index